T0350228

INFORMATION STUDIES AND THE QUEST FOR TRANSDISCIPLINARITY

Unity through Diversity

World Scientific Series in Information Studies
(ISSN: 1793-7876)

Series Editor: Mark Burgin *(University of California, Los Angeles, USA)*

International Advisory Board:

Søren Brier *(Copenhagen Business School, Copenhagen, Denmark)*
Tony Bryant *(Leeds Metropolitan University, Leeds, United Kingdom)*
Gordana Dodig-Crnkovic *(Mälardalen University, Eskilstuna, Sweden)*
Wolfgang Hofkirchner *(ICT&S Center, University of Salzburg, Salzburg, Austria)*
William R King *(University of Pittsburgh, Pittsburgh, USA)*

World Scientific Series in Information Studies — **Vol. 9**

INFORMATION STUDIES AND THE QUEST FOR TRANSDISCIPLINARITY

Unity through Diversity

Editors

Mark Burgin

University of California, Los Angeles, USA

Wolfgang Hofkirchner

Vienna University of Technology, Austria

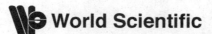 **World Scientific**

NEW JERSEY · LONDON · SINGAPORE · BEIJING · SHANGHAI · HONG KONG · TAIPEI · CHENNAI · TOKYO

Published by

World Scientific Publishing Co. Pte. Ltd.

5 Toh Tuck Link, Singapore 596224

USA office: 27 Warren Street, Suite 401-402, Hackensack, NJ 07601

UK office: 57 Shelton Street, Covent Garden, London WC2H 9HE

Library of Congress Cataloging-in-Publication Data
Names: Burgin, M. S. (Mark Semenovich), editor. | Hofkirchner, Wolfgang, 1953–   editor. |
    International Society for Information Studies. Summit (2015 : Vienna, Austria)
Title: Information studies and the quest for transdisciplinarity : unity through diversity / edited by:
    Mark Burgin (UCLA), Wolfgang Hofkirchner (Vienna University of Technology, Austria).
Description: [Hackensack], New Jersey : World Scientific, 2016. | Series: World Scientific series
    in information studies ; volume 9 | Second volume of a two-volume edition based
    on the Summit of the International Society for Information Studies on
    "The Information Society at the Crossroads : Response and Responsibility
    of the Sciences of Information" held in Vienna in June 2015.
Identifiers: LCCN 2016045893 | ISBN 9789813108998 (hbk : alk. paper)
Subjects: LCSH: Information society. | Information society--Social aspects. |
    Technological innovations--Social aspects.
Classification: LCC HM851 .I5345 2017 | DDC 303.48/33--dc23
LC record available at https://lccn.loc.gov/2016045893

British Library Cataloguing-in-Publication Data
A catalogue record for this book is available from the British Library.

Desk Editors: V. Vishnu Mohan/Tan Rok Ting

Typeset by Stallion Press
Email: enquiries@stallionpress.com

Printed in Singapore

About the Editors

Mark Burgin from UCLA has Ph.D. in Mathematics and is Doctor of Science in Logic and Philosophy. He is doing research, has publications, and taught courses in various areas of mathematics, artificial intelligence, information sciences, system theory, computer science, epistemology, logic, psychology, social sciences, and methodology of science publishing more than 500 papers and 21 books. He originated such theories as the general theory of information, theory of named sets, mathematical theory of schemas, theory of oracles, hyperprobability theory, system theory of time, theory of non-Diophantine arithmetics and neoclassical analysis (in mathematics) and made essential contributions to such fields as foundations of mathematics, theory of algorithms and computation, theory of knowledge, theory of intellectual activity, and complexity studies. Mark Burgin was the first to discover non-Diophantine arithmetics, the first to axiomatize and build mathematical foundations for negative probability used in physics, finance and economics, and the first to explicitly overcome the barrier posed by the Church–Turing thesis.

Wolfgang Hofkirchner is Professor for Technology Assessment at the Faculty of Informatics of the Vienna University of Technology. He works on ICTs and Society, Science of Information, and Complexity (see his book *Emergent Information — A Unified Theory of Information Framework*). He is member of the *International Academy of Systems and Cybernetic Sciences* (IASCYS), President of the *Bertalanffy Center for the Study of Systems Science*, Past President of the *International Society for Information Studies*.

Contents

vii

Chapter 1

Introduction: Omnipresence of Information as the Incentive for Transdisciplinarity

Mark Burgin[*,§] and Wolfgang Hofkirchner[†,‡,¶]

*University of California, Los Angeles
520 Portola Plaza, Los Angeles, CA 90095, USA
†Vienna University of Technology
Institute of Design and Technology Assessment
Argentinierstraße 6, 1040 Vienna, Austria
‡Bertalanffy Center for the Study of Systems Science
Paulanergasse 13, 1040 Vienna, Austria
§mburgin@math.ucla.edu
¶wolfgang.hofkirchner@bcsss.org

According to literary sources [cf. Bernstein, 2015], the term transdisciplinarity was introduced in 1970 at the seminar on interdisciplinarity in universities, which took place at the University of Nice and was jointly sponsored by the Organization of Economic Cooperation and Development and the French Ministry of Education, as well as in the Doctoral dissertation of Mahan [1970]. Three presenters, the eminent Swiss psychologist Jean Piaget, the French mathematician André Lichnerowicz and the Austrian astrophysicist Erich Jantsch, used the term *transdisciplinarity* although only Piaget is generally credited with coining this term. They all published their first works on this topic in the same book [Jantsch, 1972; Lichnerowicz, 1972; Piaget, 1972].

After the dormant period, which lasted almost two decades, the research on transdisciplinarity was revitalized becoming more and more popular [cf., for example, Nicolescu, 2002, 2012; Max-Neef, 2005; Choi and Pak, 2006; Hadorn *et al.,* 2006; Clark and Button, 2011; Evans, 2015].

There are many definitions and interpretations of the concept *trans-disciplinarity*. To further develop our understanding of this concept, as well as to augment the main approach to information studies presented in this book, we analyze the concept *transdisciplinarity* in the context of the concept *discipline* and related terms such as *monodisciplinarity* (*intradisciplinarity*), *multi-disciplinarity* (*pluridisciplinarity*), *crossdisciplinarity*, and *interdisciplinarity*.

A *discipline* corresponds to an academic field of research and education that is unified by a system of epistemological and methodological principles leading to scientific knowledge and theories about an object of study that enable to improve solutions for societal practice and usually has its journals and academic departments.

Monodisciplinary or *intradisciplinary research* goes inside one discipline. For instance, distributions are studied in the theory of distributions and electrons are studied in quantum physics.

Multidisciplinary or *pluridisciplinary research* includes several separate disciplines, e.g., when researchers from different disciplines work together on a common problem, but from their own disciplinary perspectives. However, contemporary science is built hierarchically, i.e., some disciplines include several other disciplines. For instance, physics includes classical mechanics, quantum mechanics, electrodynamics, relativity theory, quantum field theory, mathematical physics, physics of fluids, chromodynamics, thermodynamics and several other disciplines. That is why research that involves, for example, relativity theory and quantum field theory is multidisciplinary, crossdisciplinary or interdisciplinary with respect to these disciplines but it is intradisciplinary with respect to physics.

Crossdisciplinary research is based on utilization of knowledge from several disciplines aimed at solving a problem or researching a topic at the intersection of multiple disciplines, e.g., when biologists, chemists and mathematicians collaborate to find how to cure some disease.

Interdisciplinary research involves interaction and coordination between several disciplines aimed at the development of knowledge in these disciplines, e.g., when researchers collaborate transferring knowledge from one discipline to another and/or transforming knowledge of one discipline under the influence of another discipline.

Transdisciplinary research encompasses problems from different disciplines but goes on a higher level than each of thesedisciplines goes. In other words, transdisciplinarity treats problems that are at once between the disciplines, across the different disciplines, and beyond any of the individual disciplines involved. It is aimed at understanding of broad spheres of the world directed at the unity of knowledge. Examples of transdisciplinary areas are system theory, complexity theory and mathematics.

Some authors [cf., for example, Nicolescu, 2012] assume that transdisciplinary research goes between, across and beyond all disciplines. However, this interpretation looks too broad because the case of transdisciplinarity boils down to philosophy only, which, of course, is the all-embracing example. We suggest to apply the term transdisciplinarity whenever research reaches a meta-level that goes beyond the levels of the participating disciplines and those disciplines are not mere parts of just another discipline (as in the case of intradisciplinary research) but retain their relative autonomy in a dialectical relationship with the meta-level science. For example, the study of cooperation that takes an evolutionary systems stance comprises the stage of cooperation of viruses, of great apes, of humans and social groups (as contributions in the volume at hand show) — it transcends disciplines like life sciences or social sciences and makes at the same time those disciplines not a subdiscipline of systems theory.

Transdisciplinarity is necessary when the considered sphere of reality cannot be reduced to and thus, studied by a single discipline. This is the exact situation with information because information is in everything. It has become the foremost concept in biology, physics, economics, engineering, philosophy, decision-making, methodology of science, artificial intelligence, computer science, etc. Naturally, in different domains, information appeared in different forms and shapes, which depend on the context and environment. This situation with relativity of information was resolved in [Burgin, 1997; 2010] based on the parametric definition of information and later discussed in [Logan, 2011] demonstrating that many existing definitions of information are at odds at one another.

Due to such a diversity of information forms and shapes, researchers have built many specialized information theories trying to reflect important aspect of information. The most recognized of these theories are: statistical information theories of Shannon and Fisher, semantic information theory, algorithmic information theory, pragmatic information theory and dynamic information theory.

Multiplicity of forms and manifestations of information even caused an opinion that it would be impossible to find or elaborate a unified all-encompassing definition of information and build a comprehensive theory of information reflecting various approaches in this area [Capurro *et al.,* 1999; Capuro and Hjorland, 2003].

In spite of this pessimistic attitude, researchers with better intuition and deeper insight believed that it is not only necessary but also possible to build a unified theory of information [Hofkirchner, 1999, 2010, 2013]. This standpoint was validated by creation of the general theory of information, which suggests a way for a synthesized understanding of information phenomena and information processes unifying all diverse theoretical approaches and developing mathematical tools for investigation of information processes in all spheres of reality — in nature, society, human organisms and technical systems [Burgin, 2010].

However, that does not mean that specialized information theories are not necessary. History of science and mathematics persuasively demonstrates that creation of general theories did not make their particular theories superfluous. For instance, the theory of abelian groups is an important mathematical field although it is a subtheory of the theory of groups, while the theory of groups is an important mathematical field although it is a subtheory of the theory of universal algebras, which in turn is a subfield of algebra as a whole. Therefore, it is necessary to continue research in specialized information theories and develop theories of biological information, of economical information, of medical information and so on.

That is why transdisciplinarity was one of the main directions at the Summit of the International Society for Information Studies on "The Information Society at the Crossroads — Response and Responsibility of the Sciences of Information" in Vienna in June 2015. The organizers called to focus, among others, *"on the foundations of the sciences of information*: how can we improve the *concepts* we use for the study of information at all levels, from natural information processes to the information society and information technology, such that they open new vistas that allow for improved applications" [Call for Participation].

This book contains results and ideas of the selected Summit speakers and other leading experts in the area of information studies dealing with foundations of information processes. Although the editors do not agree with some of these ideas and statements, they believe that it is necessary to provide a possibility for a free exchange of information and constructive discussion of different ideas and approaches in science is vital to its advancement. Violation of this ethical principle hinders the development of science.

In addition to contributions that discuss the role of transdisciplinarity in the field of information, the volume also includes contributions to transdisciplinary theories of information processes and structures, as well as particular applications of information methodologies in the transdisciplinary context.

All contributions are divided into three groups comprising three parts of the book: (1) theory of information, (2) philosophy of information, and (3) applications of information. Inside each group, the authors are ordered alphabetically.

References

Apostel, L., Berger, G., Briggs, A., and Michaud, G. (Eds.) (1972) *L'interdisciplinarité — Problèmes d'enseignement et de recherché dans les universités*, Centre pour la Recherche et l'Innovation dans l'Enseignement, Organisation de Coopération et de Développement Économique, Paris.

Bernstein, J. H. (2015) Transdisciplinarity: A review of its origins, development, and current issues, *Journal of Research Practice*, 11(1), Article R1. Retrieved from http://jrp.icaap.org/index.php/jrp/article/view/510/412.

Burgin, M. (1997) *Fundamental Structures of Knowledge and Information*, Academy for Information Sciences, Kiev (in Russian).

Burgin, M. (2010) *Theory of Information: Fundamentality, Diversity and Unification*, World Scientific, New York/London/Singapore.

Call for Participation (2015) http://summit.is4is.org/calls/call-for-participation.

Capurro, R., Fleissner, P., and Hofkirchner, W. (1999) Is a unified theory of information feasible? in *The Quest for a Unified Theory of Information, Proceedings of the 2nd International Conference on the Foundations of Information Science*, pp. 9-30.

Capuro, R., and Hjorland, B. (2003) The concept of information, *Annual Review of Information Science and Technology*, 37(8), 343-411.

Choi, B. C. K., and Pak, A. W. P. (2006) Multidisciplinarity, interdisciplinarity, and transdisciplinarity in health research, services, education, and policy: 1. Definitions, objectives, and evidence of effectiveness, *Clinical Investigative Medicine*, 29(6), 351-364.

Clark, B., and Button, C. (2011) Sustainability transdisciplinary education model: Interface of arts, science, and community, *International Journal of Sustainability in Higher Education*, 12(1), 41-54.

Evans, T. L. (2015) Transdisciplinary collaborations for sustainability education: Institutional and intragroup challenges and opportunities, *Policy Futures in Education*, 15(1), 70-97.

Hadorn, G. H., Bradley, D., Pohl, C., Rist, S., and Wiesmann, U. (2006). Implications of transdisciplinarity for sustainability research. *Ecological Economics*, 60, 119-128.

Hofkirchner, W. (1999) Towards a unified theory of information: The merging of second-order cybernetics and semiotics into a single and comprehensive information science, in *15e Congrès International de Cybernétique*, Namur, pp. 175-180.

Hofkirchner, W. (2010) How to achieve a unified theory of information, *tripleC*, 7(2), 357-368.

Hofkirchner, W. (2013) *Emergent Information*, World Scientific, New York/London/Singapore.

Jantsch, E. (1972) Vers l'interdisciplinarité et la transdisciplinarité dans l'enseignement et l'innovation", in *L'interdisciplinarité — Problèmes d'enseignement et de recherché dans les universités,* Centre pour la Recherche et l'Innovation dans l'Enseignement, Organisation de Coopération et de Développement Économique, Paris, pp. 97-121.

Kessel, F., and Rosenfield, P. L. (2008) Toward transdisciplinary research: Historical and contemporary perspectives, *American Journal of Preventive Medicine*, 35(2S), 225-234.

Lawrence, R. J., and Després, C. (2004) Futures of transdisciplinarity, *Futures*, 36(4), 397-405.

Leavy, P. (2011) *Essentials of Transdisciplinary Research: Using Problem-Centered Methodologies,* Left Coast, Walnut Creek, CA.

Lichnerowicz, A. (1972) Mathématique et transdisciplinarité, in *L'interdisciplinarité – Problèmes d'enseignement et de Recherché dans les universités*, Centre pour la Recherche et l'Innovation dans l'Enseignement, Organisation de Coopération et de Développement Économique, Paris, pp. 122-126.

Logan, R. K. (2011) What is information? Why it is realistic and what is its relationship to materiality, meaning and organization, *Information*, 2.

Mahan, L. L. (1970) *Toward transdisciplinary inquiry in the humane sciences*. PhD Dissertation, International University, San Diego, CA.

Max-Neef, M. A. (2005) Foundations of transdisciplinarity. *Ecological Economics*, 53, 5-16.

Nicolescu, B. (2002) *Manifesto of Transdisciplinarity*, K. C. Voss, (Trans.), State University of New York Press, Albany, NY.

Nicolescu, B. (2012) Transdisciplinarity: The hidden third, between the subject and the object, *Human and Social Studies*, 1(2), 13-28.

Piaget, J. (1972) The epistemology of interdisciplinary relationships, in *L'interdisciplinarité — Problèmes d'enseignement et de recherche dans les universités*, Centre pour la Recherche et l'Innovation dans l'Enseignement, Organisation de Coopération et de Développement Économique, Paris, pp. 127-139.

Plsek, P. E., and Greenhalgh, T. (2001) Complexity science: The challenge of complexity in health care, *BMJ*, 323, 625-628.

Part I

Theory of Information

Chapter 2

How to Produce a Transdisciplinary Information Concept for a Universal Theory of Information[a]

Søren Brier

Department of International Business Communication
Copenhagen Business School, Frederiksberg, Denmark
sb.ibc@cbs.dk

If we want to define a universal concept of information, we have to cover not only objective statistical information, but also subjective experiential and meaningful cognition as well as intersubjective meaningful communication in nature, technology, and society. In that case the main problem is to decide which transdisciplinary philosophy of knowledge framework the concept of information should be based on and integrated in. All the ontological attempts to create objective concepts of information result in concepts that cannot encompass meaning and experience of embodied living and social systems. There is no conclusive evidence that proofs that the core of reality across nature, culture, life and mind is purely either statistical or of a computational nature. Therefore the core of the information concept should not only be based on pure logical or mathematical rationality. We need to include interpretation, signification and meaning construction in our transdisciplinary framework for informa-tion as a basic aspect of reality alongside the physical, chemical and molecular biological. It is difficult to produce a pure quantitative statement independently of a qualitative analysis based on some sort of relation to

[a]This book chapter is an integration of several earlier papers: Brier [2013a]: How to define an information concept for a universal theory of information, Proceedings of the 1st International Conference on Philosophy of Information by International Society for Information Science, 19-21 Nov. 2013 at International Center for Philosophy of Information Xi'an Jiaotong University, China,. pp. 277-299. A more developed version was published as Brier [2015a]. Finding an Information Concept Suited for a Universal Theory of Information. *Progress in Biophysics & Molecular Biology*, 119(3), 622-633 as well as Brier [2015c] Cybersemiotics and the reasoning powers of the universe: philosophy of information in a semiotic-systemic transdisciplinary approach, *Green Letters, Studies in Ecocriticism.* 19(3), 2015, pp. 280-292.

the human condition as a semiotic animal. But this direction of research leads us out of the world of technology into the world of the living. To follow the transdisciplinary ambition in much information science and philosophy leading to cognitive science we need to include a phenomenological and hermeneutical ground in order to encompass a theory of interpretative meaning and signification to achieve a transdisciplinary theory of knowing and communication. This is also true if we start in cybernetics and system theory that also have transdisciplinary aspirations for instance in Bateson's ecological concept of information as a difference that makes a difference and in Luhmann's triple autopoietic communication based system theory, where information is always a part of a message. Charles Sanders Peirce's pragmaticist semiotics differs from other paradigms in that it integrates logic and information in interpretative semiotics. I therefore suggest alternatively building information theories based on semiotics from the basic relations of embodied living systems meaningful cognition and communication. I agree with Peircean biosemiotics that all transdisciplinary information concepts in order to work across the natural, technical, social and humanistic sciences must be defined as a part of real relational meaningful sign-processes manifesting as tokens. Thus Peirce's information theory is empirically based in a realistic worldview, which through modern biosemiotics includes all living systems.

Keywords: Transdisciplinary information; Peirce's information concept; cybernetics; systems and semiotic; Luhmann's communication theory; realistic worldview; phenomenology; hermeneutics.

1. Introduction

After many years of research we have had to realize that the attempts to create objective concepts of information were good for technology [Brillouin, 1962] and the first steps of development of AI, robotics and machine translation. But this foundation has not been deep and broad enough to enable us to develop theories and technologies that could include the experiential aspect of informing, which seems to be essential for the production of meaningful cognition and communication in the social setting of culture [Brier, 2015b] and therefore language interactions at machine/man interface for instance with computers, AI and robots. So far there is no conclusive evidence to make us believe that the core of reality across nature, culture, life and mind is purely logic, mathematical or algorithmic. Penrose has argued very convincingly that human embodied reasoning cannot be captured by a formal system in Penrose [1989, 1994].

The statistical concept of Shannon [1949] is the most famous objective concept that was essential for spawning the modern development of information science and informatics. It was a technical invention based on a mathematical concept of entropy, but never intended to encompass meaning. But Wiener [1963] combined the statistical concept of information with Boltzmann's thermodynamically entropy concept and defined information as neg-entropy. Wiener then saw the statistical information's entropy as a representation for mind and the thermodynamically entropy as representing matter [Brier, 1992]. So he thought he had solved the mind matter problem through his and Schrödinger's [1944] definition of information as neg-entropy. Most famous is Schrödinger's [1944] idea of developing this further on in to a theory of what life is. The idea was developed further into an evolutionary and ecological framework by Gregory Bateson [1972, 1979, 1987] resulting in an ecological cybernetic concept of mind as self-organized differences making differences for cybernetically conceptualized minds [Brier, 2008b]. But this concept does not really encompass meaning in the hermeneutic understanding and phenomenological experience of embodied living and social systems [Brier, 2008a, 2010, 2011a].

There are several efforts in the development of a universal, also called general or unified, theory of information [Burgin, 2010, 2011; Hofkirchner, 2009, 2013; Markov *et al.*, 1993, 2006]. In this chapter, a different approach based on cybersemiotics is suggested.

My main point is that we do not from the present material, energetic or informational ontologies worldview have any idea of how life, feeling, awareness and qualia could emerge from that foundation. Ever since Russell and Whitehead's attempt in *Principia Mathematica* to make a unified mathematical language for all sciences and logical positivism failed [Carnap, 1967; Cartwright *et al.*, 1996] the still more dominating transdisciplinary theory of signification and communication in nature, humans, machines, and animals, is the information-processing paradigm of cognitive science [Gardner, 1985] used in computer informatics and psychology [Lindsay and Norman, 1977; Fodor, 2000] and in library and information science [Vickery and Vickery, 2004]. It is also found integrated with system theory and cybernetics as well as a general renewal of the materialistic evolutionary worldview [e.g., Stonier, 1990, 1992, 1997] and now developed into a pan-informational and pan-computational paradigm for al processes in nature, culture, society and technology [Dodig-Crnkovic, 2010; Dodig-Crnkovic, and Müller. 2013 Davies and Gregersen, 2009]. It is Wheeler [1994] who has formulated the most radical theory of regarding the whole physical world as basically made of information, with matter, energy, as only secondary aspect of foundational reality. It has been developed further and today the strongest paradigm attempting unification is now the info-computational paradigm based on mathematic developed by Gregory Chaitin [2006, 2007]. The paradigm is only in its early beginning and is looking for a concept of natural computing [Dodig-Crnkovic, 2012] going beyond the Turing concept of computing. They want to go from a foundation in the machine into a foundation in the world of nature, culture and integrating them all with an info-computation concept stronger than the statistical information concept, on which cognitive science was started. This paradigm is in its early development stage [Rozenberg *et al.*, 2012]. But still it does not encompass the experiential feeling mind and the meaning orienting aspect of intersubjective communication [Brier, 2014d].

In developed forms of general system theory the organizing power of neg-entropy is combined with the principle of emergence and is used as explaining how life and consciousness arose from matter through self-organization as a theoretical explanation of how matter became alive through emergence [Stonier, 1990, 1992, 1997; Jantsch, 1980]. Gregory Bateson [1972, 1979] developed a non-technical and more wide-ranging concept of cybernetic information in a cognitive and an ecological direction based on Wiener's cybernetic view of information as negentropy. He defined information as "a difference that makes a difference" for a cybernetic mind. He attempted to link information and meaning in an ecological cybernetic mind. Here are the basic criteria for the cybernetic informational mind: (1) The system shall operate with and upon differences. (2) The system shall consist of closed loops or networks of pathways along which differences and transforms of differences shall be transmitted. (What is transmitted on a neuron is not an impulse; it is news of a difference). (3) Many events within the system shall be energized by the responding part rather than by impact from the triggering part. (4) The system shall show self-correctiveness in the form of negative feedback in the direction of homeostasis and/or in the direction of runaway. Self-correctiveness (negative feedback) implies trial and error.

The strength in Bateson's work was that he developed a non-technical concept of information and attempted to link information and meaning in an ecological cybernetic mind-framework including the whole biosphere, as well as culture and social systems. Through a functionalistic concept of cybernetic mind, Bateson further develops the idea of the biosphere as the ultimate cybernetic mind and thus finding "the pattern that connects." This view was later supported by Lovelock's [1972, 2000, 2009] vision of the whole biosphere as one self-regulation system, which he called Gaia after the classical Greek god for Earth and the great mother of all. In this ultimate cybernetic vision of self-regulating systems, there is no theory of the role of experiential mind. The informational aspect of reality has continued to be more and more recognized in physics [von Baeyer, 2004], but still without producing a theory of how experiential life emerged. It is to the credit of Barbieri's work that he has attempted to develop the information theory into a new theory of codes to explain the emergence of experiential life. I have in [Brier, 2015b] discussed why I do not think it is sufficient yet. Thus I do not find any of the approaches building on objective pan-computational and/or pan-informational metaphysics or paradigms are able to explain and model human meaningful social communication and information exchange in nature and machines at the same time.

As Nagel [2012], I see no way of developing a theory, which can lead to a theory encompassing the living, experiencing body and its consciousness' integration with communicational networks such as natural and artificial languages in humans [Brier, 2010] if we start in mathematics and physics in the form of the present idea of objective conception of information bits and thermodynamically defined energy.

Therefore I find it unavoidable that we must start in a way that includes the "experiential life world" not so much of Husserl and Merleau-Ponty, than of the phaneroscophy of Peirce [Ransdell, 1989]. Even Gregory Bateson's [1972, 1979] definition of information as a difference that makes a difference for at cybernetic mind lacks a basic theory of experiential consciousness and emotions or what the phenomenologists call the "life world." As Schrödinger wrote:

> The scientific world-picture vouchsafes a very complete understanding of all that happens — it makes it just a little too understandable. It allows you to imagine the total display as that of a mechanical clockwork which, for all that science knows, could go on just the same as it does, without there being consciousness, will, endeavor, pain and delight and responsibility connected with it — though they actually are. And the reason for this disconcerting situation is just this: that for the purpose of constructing the picture of the external world, we have used the greatly simplifying device of cutting our own personality out, removing it; hence it is gone, it has evaporated, it is ostensibly not needed. [Schrödinger, 1948, page 96]

Meaning is a way of making 'sense' of things for the individual in the world perceived. It is a non-mathematical existential feeling aspect of life for living systems, enhanced by language, writings and culture for humans. In animals it is connected to survival, procreation and pleasure. In humans it develops an existential value also. Gadamer [1992] in hermeneutics sees human being as foundationally interpreting beings. In groups with embodied language communication we produce culture that for instance can make it a mortal sin to commit suicide or an act of heroism for which you go straight to heaven. One way to create meaning is by narrations, telling stories, which is also becoming a more and more important tool for companies and organizations to coordinate the behavior of its employees. By interpretation others and our surroundings, we make a story about our own self, our organization or our company, what we are doing here and what the meaning of life is [Brier, 2008a] and we also develop the idea of scientific truth.

My conclusion is therefore that a broader foundation is needed in order to encompass the basis for information and communication in living systems. Therefore my argument is that in order to follow the transdisciplinary ambition in much information science and philosophy leading to cognitive science we need to include a phenomenological, hermeneutical and semiotic grounding order to integrate a theory of interpretative meaning and signification with a theory of objective information, which has a physical grounding. This is also true if we start in cybernetics and system theory that also have transdisciplinary aspirations for instance Luhmann's triple autopoietic communication based system theory [Luhmann, 1995].

Thus it comes down to the problem of how we can establish an alternative transdisciplinary model of the sciences and the humanities to the logical positivist reductionism on one hand and to postmodernist relativist constructivism on the other in the form of a transdisciplinary concept of Wissenschaft? (I prefer the German conception to the English, as the English has a tendency to be interpreted only as natural sciences and the quantitative part of the social sciences, where the German concept — like the Danish — include all of social science and the humanities.) Starting with the situated living body as agent in meaning-making processes cultural history is to be considered as integrated into the evolutionary process propelled by man's biological existence, with its range of perceptions, experiences, desires and imaginations. The aware body and its meaning-making processes is a complex multidimensional object of research that necessitates trans-disciplinary theoretical approaches including biological sciences, biosemiotics and biocybernetics, cognition and communication sciences, phenomenology, hermeneutics, philosophy of science and philosophical theology [Harney, 2015; Davies and Gregersen, 2009; Brier, 2015a, b].

Many analytical philosophers of science might argue that meaning and experience are not central notions while truth, objectivity, scientific method, observation, theory, etc., are [Carnap, 1967; Bar-Hillel and Carnap, 1953; Bar-Hillel, 1964]. In the view of many researchers this is seen as due to a lack of accept of phenomenology and hermeneutics [e.g., Plamen *et al.*, 2015; Brier, 2010]. Husserl's early phenomenology had a problem with getting out to the outer world [Harney, 2015], where Peirce develops his pragmaticism as a way to unite empirical research, meaning and experience [Ransdell, 1989]. His phaneroscopy makes it clear that his ontology is not only materialistic science using only mechanistic explanatory models but does also include meaning through embodied interaction through experiential living bodies and thereby the social as well as the subjective forms of cognition, meaning and interpretation [Brier, 2015a, b].

Thereby Peirce goes further than Popper's [1978] view of the three worlds. Communication is not only a world of "objective knowledge," but is intersubjective meaningful information. Here Peirce coincides with Luhmann's autopoietic system theory [Luhmann, 1995] that sees the social as communication and these communications as symbolic generalized systems of autopoietic nature each with its own code. Peirce's idea of 'the world' is much bigger than what natural science considers being 'the world' [Brier, 2014a, b]. He does not make the quantitative scientific model of the world to be all of reality in that the real also includes Firstness and Thirdness exemplified by the combination of true probabilities in the form of would-bes and habits or regularities. Thus he produces a realist process ontology integrated by the dynamic triadic sign [Deely, 1990, 2001].

2. Where to Start the Development of an Information Concept?

C. S. Peirce showed that the starting point for the concept of information must be not only mathematical and logical but also phenomenological. Still it should stay within a realistic — but not mechanistic — worldview connected to an empiricist and fallibilist view of knowledge if it has to connect to the results of the natural and technical sciences within the information area. In a philosophy of science we have great problems in inserting the subjective first person experiential aspect of reality in our view of information. But philosophy — and that goes for information philosophy too — aims primarily at developing the kind of knowledge that gives unity and system to the whole body of human, social and natural sciences. This is done through a critical examination of the grounds of our convictions, prejudices, and beliefs and the methods we use in the sciences, which we think could benefit by being further developed on a Peircean pragmaticist framework [Brier, 2012].

Thus I find Peirce's[b] attempts to broadening the view by working towards showing that logic is semiotic — meaning that formal logic is only one aspect of logic — very promising. Peirce [1931-1958/1994, 1992; Peirce Edition Project, 1998, 1982-2009] and Smolin [2014] argue against the idea of transcendental universal law as the eternal foundation for the emergence of the universe. Instead they believe in a process view encompassing the idea that laws develop with the unfoldment of the universe and manifest on different levels, which is pretty close to Prigogine's [1980, 1996; Prigogine and Stengers, 1984] view. The tendency to take habit is what Peirce calls these regularities behind a process universe developing through evolution from a potential state of Firstness or even emptiness before that [Brier, 2014a, b]. This change is in my view an important opening towards the value of the more narrative approaches in the human sciences, which are based on experience and meaning. It also means that we do not start with matter, energy or information, but with possibilities and the tendency to take habits. This idea of emptiness as a lack that draws a process is also important in Terrence Deacon's main argument for a new view of morphodynamics in his latest book Incomplete *Nature* [Deacon, 2011].

Living organisms can be described from a natural scientific as well as a phenomenological-hermeneutical humanistic type of knowledge system. Organisms' genes and physiology, as well as their experiences, learning capability and social role, have causal influence on their behavior. Thus, the general study of embodied life falls between the traditional organizations of subject areas grouped in Snow's two cultures of quantitative science and qualitative humanities [Snow, 1959]. A

---

[b] I uphold the tradition of referring to Peirce's work with the following abbreviations: CP for Collected Papers (see Peirce [1931-1958]. *Collected Papers*); EP for *Essential Peirce* (see Houser, Nathan and Kloesel (eds.) (1992). *The Essential Peirce. Selected Philosophical Writings*, Volume 1 (1867-1893) and Peirce Edition Project (ed.)(1998). *The Essential Peirce. Selected, Philosophical Writings*, Volume 2 (1893-1913)); W for Writings (see Peirce Edition Project (1982-2009) *Writings of Charles S. Peirce: A Chronological Edition*, Volume 1-8 (1857-1892). NEM vol. pages: Carolyn Eisele (ed.), (1976), *The New Elements of Mathematics by Charles S. Peirce*); MS for unpublished manuscripts that are now often publish on websites like for instance Arisbe.

central problem is that this 'two cultures' view lacks a common epistemological and ontological framework, unless you are into hard dualism. The two cultures view was based on a knowledge organization founded before evolutionary theory was trans-disciplinarily, accepted. But we expect to explain life from physic and chemistry and consciousness from life [Brier, 2015b]. But how can biology be an experiential as well as an empirical Wissenschaft when animals have no human language games to convey their first person experience, but only instinctual sign games? Actually in the light of behaviorism and ethology, and even in much cognitive science today, it has been fashionable to deny animals any experiential capability that can have any causal effect on their behavior for many years. One reason for that is that the concept of experience and meaning does not exist in the vocabulary of the theoretical framework of natural sciences. This is a fact which Lorenz [1970-1971] had to recognize when he worked hard over a period of 30 years to establish a theoretical framework for ethology [Brier, 2011b]. The development of biosemiotics over the last 50 years [Favareau, 2010; Hoffmeyer 1996, 1998, 2008a, b; Hoffmeyer and Emmeche, 1991] is an attempt productively to solve this transdisciplinary problem.

3. Building Blocks of a Transdisciplinary Framework

At the moment this is mainly done by combining the transdisciplinary frameworks of system science and cybernetics with Peircean semiotics and Jacob von Uexküll's work on functional cycles and Umwelt [Kull *et al.*, 2009]. Practically, biosemiotics has had to make its own international scientific association with yearly conferences, and create its own journal *biosemiotics* [Brier and Joslyn, 2013] and book-series [Brier, 2008b] with Springer. The contemporary challenge of biosemiotics is now to develop new empirical methods and a new transdisciplinary framework for its interdisciplinary work in a better understanding of non-human organisms and human cultural phenomena. Such a new theoretical framework and experimental methods hold a promise, in particular, for medicine that needs to integrate biomedicine with psychosomatics and social medicine (for instance in dealing with placebo effects in a productive way [Brier, 2014d].

Biosemiotics usually wants to see itself as a complementary view to the molecular paradigm, not taking over its role as dominating understanding and socially accepted explanations of the living. But what then is the theoretical platform for such an endeavor if we do not accept logical empiricism and the reductionist and 'dataistic' unity of a science view (for instance in its modern pan-informational cognitive science form [Chaitin, 2006, 2007]), and if we do not want to end up in a radical constructivist postmodernism giving up the realistic foundation for empirical work and truth as an ideal for Wissenschaft [Brier and Joslyn, 2013]? If interdisciplinarity is going to compete with the long disciplinary traditions, and stop being 'a jack of all trades, but master of none', it has to develop deep interdisciplinary theoretical frameworks that make it possible for us to go beyond the pan-informational philosophy or what, these days, is also called the info-computational paradigm.

It is my view that C.S. Peirce — by at the same time contributing to the development of modern logic and science within semiotics as well as inventing a transdisciplinary semiotics that embraced phenomenology — also tried to heal the split between science and phenomenology. Thus logic and rationality is an aspect of the pragmatic semiotics of cognition and communication of all living being. I therefore find it necessary to add a biosemiotics to transdisciplinarity if we want to encompass living nature as well as the machine and the human experiential mind a transdisciplinary theory of signification, cognition, and communication. We need to be able to include perception, signification and meaning construction from the start on as a basic aspect of reality alongside the physical, biological and social. A semantic probability information theory like Bar-Hillel and Carnap's [1953] and Bar-Hillel [1964] is not enough, because it imagines a formal language consisting of all sentences that might be true in a given possible universe [see Bar-Hillel, 1964, p. 224] as the basis for its probability models. This is problematic since Chomsky [1957] has pointed out, natural language has the intrinsic capacity to generate an infinite number of well-formed sentences and, that no natural language has a finite determinable number of sentences that could serve as a basis for determining all true sentences or any reliable kind of probability models.

Thus information in the theory I want to develop is not 'objective', but relativized in relation to the sender's as well as the receiver's knowledge. This makes it difficult to operationalize the idea of probability in reality if not on some kind of Bayesian foundation. This makes it difficult to produce a quantitative statement that is more reliable than a qualitative analysis based on some sort of relation to the human condition. We seem to have to combine both. The alternative to start in mathematics and physics is to build information theories from the basic context of human meaningful communication. This is what Machlup's [1983] famous analysis of information promotes. Beginning from a traditional humanistic viewpoint, Machlup suggests that only people can send and receive information all other uses of the word information are metaphors no matter if we go up in the social realm of institutions or down into biology, chemistry, physics and computer science [Brier, 2013c].

But then what about other living systems are they not communicating? In *Knowledge and the Flow of Information* Dretske [1981] defines information as the content of new, true, meaningful, and understandable knowledge produced in cognition and communication. Gibberish and sentences uttered or written in a foreign language that we have not mastered fail to convey information; furthermore, telling a person something s/he knows already does not count either as real information in this theory, nor do false statements. An informative message for Dretske must convey new and comprehensive knowledge. But most of cognition and communication is not formed in natural language, but is embodied signs of which humans are not always conscious aware and animals never are. With the growing acceptance of living systems as sentient beings [Thompson, 2007] we need to include them in a general theory of information that as an experiential and interpretational aspect based on the living body and here semiotics seem to be the obvious choice.

4. Why add Semiotic to Information Theory?

Semiotics is the doctrine and science of signs and their use. It is thus a more comprehensive system than language itself and can therefore be used to understand language in relation to other forms of communication and interpretation, such as nonverbal forms. One can trace the development of semiotics starting with its origins in the classical Greek period (from medical symptomatology), through subsequent developments during the Middle Ages [Deely, 2001], and up to John Locke's introduction of the term in the seventeenth century. But contemporary semiotics has its foundations in the nineteenth century with Charles Sanders Peirce (1839-1914) and Ferdinand de Saussure's (1857-1913) semiology. They were working independently of each other, developed different conceptions of the sign. Where Saussure's semiology has been integrated in the development of linguistics and analysis of cultural products, including computers, the development of semiotics as a broad field that includes nonverbal as well as paralinguistic signs is nevertheless mostly based on Peirce's framework, which is therefore adopted here.

What Charles Sanders Peirce attempted was to change our worldview in order to encompass the world of science and logic with the world of meaning and communication through a triadic evolutionary pragmaticist theory of semiotics. This new but unfinished approach has attracted a multitude of researchers to make a consistent interpretation of his scattered work. See for instance Apel [1981], Boler [1963], Brent [1998] Colapietro [1989], Corrington [1993], Deledalle [2000], Esposito [1980], Fisch [1986], Hookway [1992], Liszka [1996], Menand [2001], Savan [1987-1988] and Short [2007].

Semiotics is a transdisciplinary doctrine that studies how signs in general — including codes, media, and language, plus the sign systems used in parallel with language — work to produce interpretation and meaning in human and nonhuman living systems such as pre-linguistic communication systems. In the founding semiotic tradition of Peirce, a sign is anything that stands for something or somebody in some respect or context. To explain further; a sign is a medium of perception and communication of a form in a triadic (three-way) relation. The representamen (the phenomenon acting as sign vehicle) refers (passively) to its object, which determines it, and to its interpretant, which it determines, without being itself affected. The interpretant is the interpretation in the form of a more developed sign in the interpreting and receiving mind or quasi mind. The representamen could be, for example, a moving hand that refers to an object for an interpretant; the interpretation in a person's mind materializes as the more developed sign "waving," which is a cultural convention and therefore a symbol [Peirce, 1931-1958/1994].[c] All kinds of alphabets are composed of signs. Signs are mostly imbedded in a sign system based on codes, after the manner of alphabets of natural and artificial languages or of ritualized animal behaviors, where fixed action patterns, such as feeding the young in gulls, take on a sign character when used in the mating game.

Ever since Eco [1976] formulated the problem of the "semiotic threshold" in trying to keep semiotics within the cultural sciences Peircean semiotics has developed further into the realm of biology, crossing threshold after threshold into the sciences. Although semiotics emerged in efforts to scientifically investigate how signs function in culture, the twentieth century witnessed efforts to extend semiotic theory into the non-cultural realm, primarily in relation to living systems and computers. Because Peirce's semiotics is the only one that deals systematically with non-intentional signs of the body and of nature at large, it has become the main source for semiotic theories of the

---

[c] It is important to be aware of that Peirce's semiotic and pragmaticist paradigm of science is neither a monist or a dualist world view — and thus somewhat different from the received worldview of present science — but is a triadic, Synechist, Tychist and Agapist philosophy, which is built on phenomenology and mathematics and view logic as semiotic. See Houser, Nathan and Kloesel (eds.) (1992) and Peirce Edition Project (ed.) (1998) or Brier (2008). Thus Peirce's sign is a triadic unending semiotic process connected to a network of other types of ongoing semiosis (the semiotic web). All objects of perceptions are sign processes and only some of those are things. Signs are as real as matter. See also Deely (2001), who declared Peirce to be the first true post-modern in that he broke with the Cartesian dualist tradition that dominated (and still dominates a lot of) modern philosophy, philosophy of science and much thinking in the sciences in the area of brain science and cognitive research.

similarities and differences among signs of inorganic nature, signs of living systems [biosemiotics; see Favareau, 2010; Kull *et al.*, 2009], signs of machines [especially computer semiotics; see Andersen, 1997], and the cultural and linguistic signs of humans living together in a society that emphasizes the search for information and knowledge [Brier, 2009]. Resulting developments have then been deployed to change the scope of semiotics from strictly cultural communication to a biosemiotics that encompasses the cognition and communication of all living systems from the inside of cells to the entire biosphere, and a cybersemiotics that in addition includes a theory of information.

Peirce integrated his semiotics with a pure mathematical analysis of phenomenology through which he coined three 'new' basic categories: Firstness, Secondness and Thirdness [Esposito, 1980]. He furthermore viewed logic, aesthetics and ethics as basic normative sciences necessarily connected with the metaphysics developed for any philosophy of cognition and communication. Peirce writes:

> Philosophy has three grand divisions. The first is Phenomenology, which simply contemplates the Universal Phenomenon and discerns its ubiquitous elements, Firstness, Secondness, and Thirdness, together perhaps with other series of categories. The second grand division is Normative Science, which investigates the universal and necessary laws of the relation of Phenomena to Ends, that is, perhaps, to Truth, Right, and Beauty. The third grand division is Metaphysics, which endeavors to comprehend the Reality of Phenomena. Now Reality is an affair of Thirdness as Thirdness, that is, in its mediation between Secondness and Firstness... [CP 5.121]

The normative sciences are those sciences driven by questions of value and purpose. Since facts do not simply speak for themselves, this means that researchers in these fields must be aware of the part (not necessarily negative) that their own values and purposes play in identifying the apparent drivers of phenomena. Logic is about how inference ought to be made. This, in turn, will tend to dictate what counts as scientific progress. As Peirce points out this is inevitably, in fact, a question of metaphysics. Peirce's own view is that the 'logic' of the normative sciences is semiotic: i.e. science grows because it is in the nature of signs to grow.

This led him to develop the highly original view on logic that its core is the study of the essential nature of signs. Logic is semiotic. His triadic categorical theory was connected to a dynamic triadic semiotic web viewed as the dynamics of objective mind. This philosophical view sets him clearly apart from logical positivism and dialectical materialism, even though his three categories in many ways were close to Hegel's process logic dialectics of thesis, anti-thesis and synthesis and their further development in dialectical materialism. The important difference is Peirce's concept of Secondness as brute specifics not immediately or completely explainable by law, like the grain of sand in our mouth when eating at the beach. Law cannot exhaustively explain why this specific grain of sand was to be here at that spot in that time.

We can see Peirce's semiotic pragmaticism as the synthesis of the phenomenological objective idealism of Hegel and Marx-Engels and Lenin's dialectical materialism through his theory of semiosis, because Peirce is neither an idealist nor a materialist. Peirce's pragmaticism combines his theory of logic-as-semiotic with an evolutionary theory of forms. He thereby creates a philosophy different from Hegel's, and improving considerably on Schelling's [1809/1989], who was an important influence on his philosophy. Peirce's ontological foundation is semiotic rather than either spiritual or informational in that information is seen as an aspect of semiosis.

Stjernfelt [2014] in his book *Natural Propositions* points out that one of the most important lessons to take from Peirce's semiotics is its vast reorientation of the whole domain of sensation, perception, logic, reasoning, thought, language, images etc. towards the chain of reasoning as its uniting primitive phenomenon. The point of Peirce's semiotic philosophy of pragmaticism is that this development of reasoning may be formally described independently of the materials in which it may be implemented. This view implies that propositions are not primarily entities of language, nor do they presuppose any conscious 'propositional stance'. Rather, reasoning capacity is developed through evolution in nature. The evolution of consciousness and language should rather be seen as scaffolding, serving and increasing reasoning, which is one the most important overall selecting factors during evolution, Stjernfelt [2014] argues. Thus, language, images, perception etc. should be re-conceptualized for the roles they may play in the chain of propositions that construct the reasoning processes. Here is a quote that makes it clear how Peirce sees semio-logical processes permeating all levels of living systems:

> The cognition of a rule is not necessarily conscious, but is of the nature of a habit, acquired or congenital. The cognition of a case is of the general nature of a sensation; that is to say, it is something which comes up into present consciousness. The cognition of a result is of the nature of a decision to act in a particular way on a given occasion. [CP 2.711].

Ontologically this means that evolution is neither completely random nor completely mechanical, but is a development of the reasoning powers of the universe. This is a move away from the reductionist pure physicalism into a broader philosophical framework that can encompass a transdisciplinary view of *Wissenschaft* man and universe.

It is well-known that we do not see data [Popper, 1959, p. 76]. We see things, forms, classes, and behavior. The concepts of our languages form our sense experiences and cognitions and what we consider meaningful and can perceive. On this basis, Bateson's [1972] definition of information 'as a difference that makes a difference' is still valid. Information is what one receives in reply to a question of living. I agree with Bateson [1972], Maturana [1988a, b], and Peirce that we must start our understanding of information with the process of knowing. Bateson's definition of information as a difference that makes a difference is very fruitful. His problem is that he nearly makes every cybernetic system a communicator and a knower, be it a homeostatic machine, an organism or an ecosystem or organization. The main achievement of Maturana and Varela's [1980, 1986] theory of autopoiesis is that they have conceptualized the basic limit of living and knowing, namely the auto-poietic system, and shown that there is a basic connection between living and knowing! In Maturana's vision the autopoietic system is closed in its structure-dependent organization.

Once autopoietic reproduction begins, natural selection becomes possible, and survival knowledge — in the form of structural couplings' readiness to act in an orderly way on certain disturbances from the environment — begins to emerge and grow. These autopoietic structures that are connected to the ability to produce their own macromolecules create 'semantic closure'. Solutions to survival problems are kept as kinds of reaction potentials within the organism, some of them as molecular structures in the DNA-RNA-protein-synthesis processes. This is why Konrad Lorenz, in his development of ethology, was very keen on viewing instinct as the connection between motivation and fixed action patterns. This enables the system to perpetuate its autopoiesis from one instant to the next through generations of self-production as a full-bodied individual, and self-reproduction through the 'digital coding' in the DNA that is transferred and mixed in mating [Brier, 2008a]. Jesper Hoffmeyer and Claus Emmeche [1991] called these two forms of 'memory' (in DNA-RNA and in the flesh) code-duality. The analogue code is the actual living body as phenotype, and the digital code is the genotype of the genome. These two codes then interchange over time. One can say that discreteness and continuity are two irreducible complementary modes of thinking and also of existence. Thus autopoiesis and biosemiotics can fruitfully be integrated as autopoiesis gives a dynamic embodiment to semiotic interaction.

It is Peirce's view of the sign as a real and dynamical developing relational and reasoning process that makes him argue that there is nothing in thought or in sensation, which was not first in signs. Peirce's probably most famous definition of his new conception of signs is this:

> A sign, or Representamen, is a First which stands in such a genuine triadic relation to a Second, called its Object, as to be capable of determining a Third, called its Interpretant, to assume the same triadic relation to its Object in which it stands itself to the same Object. The triadic relation is genuine, that is its three members are bound together by it in a way that does not consist in any complexus of dyadic relations. That is the reason the Interpretant, or Third, cannot stand in a mere dyadic relation to the Object, but must stand in such a relation to it as the Representamen itself does. Nor can the triadic relation in which the third stands be merely similar to that in which the First stands, for this would make the relation of the Third to the First a degenerate Secondness merely. [C.P. 2-274].

This non-reducible triadic process relation — that is not primarily driven by any human subject's consciousness and therefore opens a foundation for a biosemiotics — is foundational to Peirce's pragmaticist philosophy. The Sign as an irreducible triad is a syllogism — although not of the familiar type found in Barbara (e.g. major premise: all men are mortal; minor premise: Socrates is a man; conclusion: Socrates is mortal). The major premise is the Representamen relation; the minor premise is the Object relation and the conclusion is the Interpretant. In other words, the major premise presents us with a sign, a piece of information about the world; the minor premise stands in the background of our thought as something that is in the world and which can arise on the basis of the major premise; the conclusion is akin to Bateson's formulation that only a 'difference that makes a difference', can become information. When it does and we need to use it again — we create a sign and therefore an awareness of the possible significance of the sign, so that our Interpretant will not only be a new thought, but will also result in a difference in our thinking (and behaving) more generally. We can see how this growth of the sign is important in science as well as art.

This is a dynamic transformative process. It's not just a mechanical conveyor belt because the information is acted upon and 'thought about' (interpreted) from input sensation to result. It is this conception of semiosis that makes inter- and transdisciplinarity possible. The best way to explain cosmogony and evolution is as a dynamic interaction between the three categories or universes as Peirce also calls them [Colapietro, 1989]. None of the categories can be reduced to the other, but cosmogonically viewed they are derived from each other.

Since Firstness is a state of absolute possibility and radical indeterminacy, it is an absolute permissibility with no cause outside itself. From here Secondness emerges as one of many possibilities as difference, other, individuality, limit, force and will. Thirdness is the mediating habit-taking aspect of evolution that contributes to the creation of an emergent order theoretically attempted modeled by Hegel's dialectical evolution and the dialectical materialism of Frederick Engels' [1968] *Dialectics of Nature* as well. But in contrast to Engels, Peirce's categories also have a phenomenological aspect and in contrast to Hegel his secondness assures a realistic aspect.

Thus if we start from the level of life 'knowledge' exists only as embodied in the inherent structural dynamics of the autopoietic entity. This would then, over a long time, result in the precise tri-nucleotide 'codes' which are used in DNA in all present organisms to determine specific amino acids to be produced by the ribosomes. But how exactly this is supposed to happen as a mechanical process, we do not know or can explain. But the general idea in Peircean biosemiotics is that, starting from random noise, the autopoietic functions of the cell make it possible to filtrate selectively for useful functionality. As such, researchers often say that this process gradually built knowledge of the world into the DNA sequence. But it cannot exist as knowledge *per se*. It only works if placed within a living cell with a full synthesis apparatus and a lot of other functional cycles and organelles surrounded by membranes.

The experiential agency that we have been talking about so far as missing from traditional biological science is a distinct domain, of a self-referential autonomous state, which other regularities govern, and which cannot be reduced by the laws of the dual domains. A difference cannot become knowledge before it has been interpreted to be sufficiently meaningful and important that an observer/knower attaches a sign to it. *Then* it will make a difference. We have thousands of aspects of our reality, which we have not called anything and which therefore cannot easily be communicated or thought constructively about. Thus, what are transferred are sign-vehicles, not information. Signs have to be interpreted, and it has to happen on at least three levels. On the most basic level we have the basic coordination between the bodies as a dance of black boxes to allow for meaningful exchange. This goes on at the next level of instinctual sign plays of drive and emotionally based communication about meaningful things in life like mating, hunting, dominating, food seeking, territory etc. Based on these two levels a field of meaning is created, which, eventually, the socio-communicative system can modulate to conscious linguistic meaning.

5. Biosemiotics and Its Controversies

Sebeok (1920-2001) extended semiotics to cover all animal species-specific communication systems and their signifying behaviors under the term zoösemiotics [Sebeok, 1965, 1972]. Later Sebeok concluded that zoösemiotics rests on a more comprehensive biosemiotics [Sebeok and Umiker-Sebeok, 1992]. This global conception of semiotics equates life with sign interpretation and mediation, so that semiotics encompasses all living systems, including plants [Krampen, 1981], bacteria, and cells in the human body [called endosemiotics by Uexküll, Geigges, and Herrmann, 1993]. Although biosemiotics has been pursued since the early 1960s, it remains controversial in much of the sciences as well as the humanities, because many linguistic and cultural semioticians see it as requiring an illegitimate broadening of the concept of code and sign from culture to nature [Brier, 2013c, 2014c, d].

A code is a set of transformation rules that convert messages from one form of representation to another. Obvious examples can be found in Morse code and cryptography. Broadly speaking, code thus includes everything of a more systematic nature (rules) that source and receiver must know a priori about a sign for it to correlate processes and structures between two different areas. This is because codes, in contrast to universal laws, work only in specific contexts, and interpretation is based on more or less conventional rules, whether cultural or (by extension) biological. Hoffmeyer and Emmeche [1991] are known for suggesting that species could be understood as code-dual systems shifting between a digital and an analog code (genotype and phenotype). Hoffmeyer wrote some of the most important modern syntheses of biosemiotics [Hoffmeyer, 1996, 2008a].

DNA is an example of a biological code. In the protein production system, which includes the genome in a cell nucleus, the RNA molecules going in and out of the nucleus, and the ribosomes outside the nucleus membrane triplet base pairs in the DNA have been translated to a messenger RNA molecule, which is then read by the ribosome as a code for amino acids to string together in a specific sequence to make a specific protein. The context is that all the parts have to be brought together in a proper space, temperature, and acidity combined with the right enzymes for the code to work. Therefore this only happens inside cells in a way that produces useful three-dimensional protein forms.

An important difference between living and technical systems (such as the computer) is that only living systems develop their own code-based signs. Internally, there is no semiosis in a computer that is not put there intentionally by humans. Sebeok writes of the genetic code, as well as metabolic, neural, and verbal codes. Living systems are self-organized not only on the basis of natural laws but also using codes developed in the course of evolution. In an overall code, there may also exist sub-codes grouped in a hierarchy. To view something as encoded is to interpret it as sign-ment [Sebeok, 1992].

I agree with biosemiotics [Kull *et al.*, 2009, Hoffmeyer, 1996, 2008a, Favareau, 2010] that signs are real relational processes manifesting as tokens connecting all living beings with each other and with the environment.

A symbol is a conventionally and arbitrarily defined sign, usually seen as created in language and culture. In common languages, it can be a word, but gestures, objects such as flags and presidents, and specific events such as a soccer match can be symbols (for example, of national pride). Some biosemioticians — like me — claim that the concept of symbol extends beyond cultures, because some animals have signs that are 'shifters'. That is, the meaning of these signs changes with situations; for instance, the head tossing of the herring gull occurs both as a precoitally display and when the female is begging for food. Such a transdisciplinary broadening of the concept of a symbol is a challenge for linguists and semioticians working only with human language and culture.

To see how this challenge is dealt with in Peircean biosemiotics consider seven different examples of signs such as that a sign stands for something for somebody:
(1) as the word black stands for a certain range of color, but also has come to stand for an emotional state;
(2) as the flag stands for the nation;
(3) as a reddening of face and neck un-intentionally can indicate nervousness;
(4) as red spots on the skin can be a symptom for German measles;
(5) as the wagging of a dog's tail can be a sign of friendliness for both dogs and humans;
(6) as pheromones can signal heat to the other gender of the species;
(7) as the hormone oxytocin from the pituitary can cause cells in lactating glands of the breast to release the milk.

Linguistic and cultural semioticians in the tradition of Saussure would usually not accept examples (3) to (7) as genuine signs, because they are not self-consciously intentional human acts. But those working in the tradition of Peirce also accept non-conscious un-intentional signs in humans (3) and between animals (5) and (6), as well as between animals and humans (5), non-intentional signs (4), and signs between organs and cells in the body (7) Oxytocin has many other communicative functions in the body, so this function is situation specific.

On this basis biosemiotics allows a concept of an "immunological self" and names the combined coding between the immune, the nervous, and the hormone systems as the "biological self".

6. Triadic, Evolutionary, Realist Pragmaticist Semiotics

The modern mechanistic ontology of science leaves us — as Jacques Monod [1972] already concluded in his analysis of a mechanical molecular biology — as *Gypsies on the border of the universe*. Peirce agrees with Monod that the mechanical view is insufficient as philosophical transdisciplinary ontology and epistemology even in an evolutionary setting. From a cybersemiotic perspective combining a cybernetic informational perspective with a semiotic one [Brier, 2008a] the bit (or basic difference) of information science becomes a sign only when it makes a difference for someone. Thus Gregory Bateson is seen as a precursor for second-order cybernetics [Bateson, 1972, 1979] as well as for biosemiotics [Hoffmeyer, 2008b]. For Peirce, a sign is something standing for something else for someone in a context.

Information bits are at most pre- or quasi-signs, and, insofar as they are involved with codes, they function only like keys in a lock. Information bits in a computer do not depend for their functioning on living systems with final causation to interpret them. They function simply on the basis of formal causation, as interactions dependent on differences and patterns. But, when people see information bits as encoding for language in a word-processing program, then the bits become signs for them.

Peirce's pragmaticist semiotics [Peirce, 1931-1958/1994] therefore seems to be a good place to start looking for a modern transdisciplinary framework for information, cognition and communication sciences, as it has its foundation in a combination of a phenomenological and pure mathematics [Ransdell, 1989; Parker, 1998]! Peirce writes that:

> Phenomenology, which does not depend on any other positive science, nevertheless must, if it is to be probably grounded, be made to depend upon the Conditional or Hypothetical science of Pure Mathematics, whose only aim is to discover not how things are but how they might be supposed to be, if not on our universe, then in some other. [CP 5.40].

It is Peirce's view that logic requires that any valid study of the whole cosmic process must be thus grounded in phenomenology, and not in any special science such as physics.

We see that Peirce does not start with objective quantifiable facts collected by statistical models to create patterns or mathematical models for us to unravel cognition and communication. No, he starts in phenomenology, pure mathematics, ethics aesthetics and logic as foundation for any perception of meaning.

This view is further combined with a process realistic view based on a triadic categorical philosophy attempting to use mathematics as the foundations for its metaphysics, but in a time-irreversible non-deterministic metaphysics, where he has spontaneity and continuity between mind and matter (synechism) as a basic ontological assumption. Peirce suggestion that man can be seen as a symbol growing and the world as a big argument combines very nice with Bateson's idea of that what connects those two and all living being to each other (Bateson's "pattern that connects") is the process of sign-(in)formation. Thus information is attached to signification and sign communication. According to Peirce:

> Phenomenology ascertains and studies the kinds of elements universally present in the phenomenon; meaning by the phenomenon, whatever is present at any time to the mind in any way. [CP 2.186].

In recent times Evan Thompson [2007] defines phenomenology broadly as 'any systematic project of investigating and describing experience' [Thompson, 2007, p. 474] and point to the deep connection between life and experiential mind just similar to the continuity (Synechism) that is so central for Peirce's philosophy. To Peirce emotions are basic unites of experiential reality (intuitions) and does not carry meaning in themselves as such. "Meaning" must somehow be constructed by the receiver from the information gathered by the interpretation of signs, within certain frames that reality imposes on us for survival and procreation (the situation).

With Peirce I suggest measuring the amount of information that symbols acquire through their individual and cultural history of use; or what Peirce calls the "growth of symbols". As mentioned this can be seen as a semiotic interpretation and development of Gregory Bateson's cybernetic definition of information as a difference that makes a difference and Niklas Luhmann's triple autopoietic theory of social-communication systems, which he attempt to connect to Husserl's phenomenology [Luhmann, 1995]. Thus Peirce adds a phenomenological grounding to these cybernetic views that have no theoretical concept for the experiential world that Husserl for instance was trying to model.

Thus I do find the requirements of meaningfulness and truthfulness for semantic information proposed by Floridi [2011] highly necessary, but will add with Pierce that also deceptive statements need to have some aspect of truth in them and with biosemiotic I want to enlarge its scope to all living systems. To sum up then semiosis is an informational process and since mechanical interactions — as they are defined in classical physics — are driven only by kinetic force, rather than information, they are theoretically understood as non-semiotic. It means that we need to integrate information in semiosis as well as matter/energy if we want a universal concept of information [Brier, 2008a, 2011a; Davies and Gregersen, 2009].

We thus have to embrace what Peirce called *cenoscopic science* or, to use Smith's [1998] modern phrase, *intentional sciences* [further discussed in Brier, 2010]. This means that we need to integratively reflect our phenomenological point of departure for knowledge-creation in the sciences. If our transdisciplinary efforts do not do so, but base themselves on physicalism or informationalism, it is going to be difficult to make any real progress in the understanding of the relation between human consciousness, nature, computation, and cultural meaning simply because no theory of consciousness of qualities and meaning can be built from that foundation [Brier, 2012].

In *Chance and Necessity* Jacques Monod [1972] highlighted the apparent epistemological contradiction between the teleonomy of living organisms and the principle of objectivity in science based on the ontological assumption of the natural sciences that there are no intentions or meaning in inanimate nature. Consciousness is not only a product of culture but also a product of the natural evolution of living bodies. Furthermore, we should not view culture as part of a reality outside nature (dualism), but as a special developed part of nature in a broadened naturalism [Brier, 2012; Fink, 2006].

But the big difference between computers and humans is this embodied field of meaning in which human communication operates. Computers can only provide pragmatic meaning within a system like chess, for instance, if that meaning is modeled in the computer's own memory. This is why the type of un-personalized, un-embodied logical and mathematical reasoning that has been the foundation of the mechanical paradigm of classical science cannot be the sole support of a transdisciplinary foundation for rationality. The paradox is that the sciences think this domain of conscious sense experiences, meaning, and rationality emerges later in evolution than energy, matter, and information, but we have also shown that it is the prerequisite for the intersubjective knowing process from which the whole idea of science springs.

Like the Danish philosopher Fink [2006], I object to the use of the term "nature" to mean only what the physic-chemical sciences can describe. What we can measure intersubjectively is a part of the reality we call nature. Thus the meaning of a sign, a word, or a sentence has some kind of existence more or less independent of the individual human being. The natural sciences see humans primarily as connected to all other entities and processes in the world by being made of the same "stuff". But inspired by Aristotle Peirce also claims that *forms* exists as well as tendencies or "would-bes".

This means that the sign we perceive are only tokens and they are a product of types or forms, which are thirds, as they provide all the regularity in the world and in our mind. But they are not transcendental eternal idea like Plato's, and not forms in the things as Aristotle suggested, but evolutionary forms developing through evolution of the world and out knowledge. With Peirce I see no reason to assume that physics has a special privilege to explain what the universal "stuff" is. I agree with biosemiotics [Kull *et al.*, 2009] that signs are real relational processes, which connect all living beings with each other and with the environment. With Peirce, I prefer the concept of hylé to characterize the basic "stuff" the world is made of as it — in contrast to the modern physical concept of matter — does not carry the indication of matter being completely inert and dead. This concept was fundamental to Aristotle's philosophy but has been moved, in Peirce's semiotic philosophy, into an evolutionary process-oriented paradigm and further developed along semiotic lines.

My suggestion for finding a transdisciplinary commensurable framework for all Wissenschaft is to start in the middle, with our daily lived semiotic, social, and linguistic practice. This is very much the core of Peirce pragmaticism. Near the end of 1896 Peirce accepted "the possible or would bes" as real, because when we say that a knife is sharp, we do not only mean now; we also mean that it would be sharp tomorrow if we tried to cut with it. Peirce thereby rejected the nominalist view that the possible is merely what we do not know not to be true. This acceptance of real possibilities puts Peirce in the Aristotelian wing of the realist camp as a three-category realist, no longer regarding the potential as what the actual makes it to be, and now distinguishing the generality of firsts from the generality of thirds. So, as late as1905 Peirce integrated semiotics and pragmatism in the realist view that the communicative and semiotic mind, in combination with a concept of information is that which binds all four worlds together. This semiotic view integrates the sciences' view of reality as well as the cybernetic, informational and systems views of reality into a single model, which I call Cyber-semiotics, in an attempt to avoid the inner inconsistencies described earlier.

As a consequence of the widely shared perspective that human beings are embodied, feeling, knowing, and culturally formed beings participating in semiosis and language processes, our analysis so far points to the fact that they can be seen as living simultaneously in at least four different worlds. One way to describe and classify these worlds — as much as possible in accordance with the currently present received view of the many sciences mentioned — is:

1. The physico-chemical part of the natural world that also constitutes the pure material-energetic aspect of our body.
2. Our embodiedness as the source of life, which we share with other living species. It is a product of ecology and evolution; but also formed by cultural practices.
3. Our world of feeling, will, drives, affects, and thoughts, manifested as mind, consciousness, and self-consciousness. We think it is partly produced by our embodied nervous system and formed by culture most strongly through our childhood. We do not so far have managed to reduce this experiential world to brain physiology. The felt self is not the same as the physiological model we call "our brain"[McGinn, 2000; Brier, 2013b].
4. The cultural world of language, meaning, power, and technology, such as the informational machines we call computers. Language, pragmatically viewed, connects our perception with our thinking, communication, and acting in the social world.

These 4 types of knowledge, which are often considered incommensurable, are seen as having their origin in our primary semiotic intersubjective life world processing of observing and interpreting within social communication and action of which language is a part.

Cybersemiotics is built on the idea of Peircean evolutionary, pragmaticist semiotics as well as his phaneroscopy,[d] his three basic categories, his sign typology, and his synechism, tychism, and agapism. As it is well-known then Aristotle listed ten categories and Kant twelve as minimum for establishing reliable cognition. Peirce reduces this to three basic simple categories and therefore calls them, first, second, and

---

[d] Peirce's name for his brand of phenomenology.

third, or Firstness, Secondness, and Thirdness. They are defined from a phenomenological stance, so Firstness is, among other things, the category of feeling, but also spontaneity. By this basic term Peirce means an instance of that kind of consciousness, which involves no analysis, comparison as it does not consists in whole or in part of any act by which one stretch of consciousness is distinguished from another. Thus it has its own positive quality:

> A feeling, then, is not an event, a happening, a coming to pass, . . . a feeling is a state, which is in its entirety in every moment of time as long as it endures. [CP1.306].

Firstness, as the category of feeling in this sense, is the category of the pre-reflexive. Getting completely absorbed in the enjoyment of a piece of music, so much that you are forgetting anything else (including reflecting) at the same time, is close to experiencing one or more firsts.

When some sort of resistance emerges forcing us to re reflection we enter the realm of Secondness, as there is now a difference between me and the experience. This is the category of the actual existent and the category of the other recognized as other. Secondness it is like the knock on the door, the no of another person (free will), the cut of a knife in the finger, the bruising of you toe on something you did not see and the unexpected car collision. It is an object to a subject. Seconds are unique existences, unique in space and time like each grain of sand on a beach or, specific observations as recorded in a laboratory (data) are seconds. The brute thereness might lead us to think of Secondness as the category of the "most real." But it is crucial to understand Peirce that he considers this to be an inadequate analysis.

Reality, he held, is more than a matter of discrete events occurring at given points in space-time. It is also a matter of the more or less stable relations between events. *Thirdness* is the category of relatedness, of law and regularity, of habit, of continuity that binds together for instance the Symphony structure that makes an overall pattern to the music we listened to, where the single notes and sound are Secondness. It is the Thirdness of the cords and harmonies that bind them together on one level and the melody line on another. Peirce writes:

Now Reality is an affair of Thirdness as Thirdness, that is, in its mediation between Secondness and Firstness... [CP 5.121].

Thirdness is also the mediating habit-taking aspect of evolution that contributes to the creation of an emergent order.

7. Peirce's Concept of Information

Peirce's concept of information generalizes Shannon's [1949] to the degree that triadic sign relations generalize dyadic cause-effect notions of information transmission. But Peircean information is substantially different inasmuch as it makes sense only in a context of prior uncertainty, the 'irritation of doubt' that drives inquiry, and its measure is based on the power of signs in a given sign relation to reduce the uncertainty of an interpreter about an object. In that view, signs bear information on account of their place in a specified sign relation, and it is a matter of secondary concern whether the sign is a picture, proposition, term, or something else entirely, like the state of a computer system. In what sense and to what degree might this 'information' be measured? Thus from a Peircean semiotic view scientific terms can hold a great deal of implicit information as well as the explicit information that scientists are working with at a given time. Therefore the information to be quantified is not that of what a given term will come to mean to us in some distant future, but rather that of what it means to us now or what we now conceive to be its practical bearing in general on conduct.

According to Peirce percepts are not, in themselves, objects of experience. Though the percept makes knowledge possible, it offers no information, as it does not contain any Thirdness in its immediateness, but is Secondness in its physical clash with the perceptual organ. But experience, understood as the knowing process imposed upon us in the course of living, is 'perfused' with Thirdness. Thirdness takes the form of generality and continuity within a fallible account of percepts. 'Meaning' must somehow be constructed by the receiver from the information produced by the interpretation of signs, within certain frames that reality imposes on us for survival. Peirce writes:

At any moment, we are in possession of certain information, that is, of cognitions which have been logically derived by induction and hypothesis from previous cognitions which are less general, less distinct, and of which we have a less lively consciousness. [CP 5.311, 1868].

Thus Peirce develops an information theory that starts with a physical event hitting the perceptual organs — i.e., Secondness — but he does not construct a probability-based theory of information as Shannon [1949] or Wiener [1963] do.

Thus Peirce defines his concept of information directly from his semiotics and its most important species of signs, namely, the symbol. For Peirce, plants and animals are constrained mainly, or nearly so, to iconic and indexical sign use. Instead of the probability-based theory of information as developed by Shannon and by Wiener, Peirce develops a theory of human knowledge based on a kind of logical quantities within a field of dynamic meaning in that he introduces a new way of calculating the value of information conveyed by new propositions as a logical area composed of the informational breadth and depth of the symbol. He writes:

> In a paper ... I endeavored to show that the three conceptions of reference to a ground, reference to a correlate, and references to an interpretant, are those of which logic must principally make use. I there also introduced the term "symbol," to include both concept and word. Logic treats of the reference of symbols in general to their objects. A symbol, in its reference to its object, has a triple reference: First, Its direct reference to its object, or the real things which it represents; Second, Its reference to its ground through its object, or the common characters of those objects; Third, Its reference to its interpretant through its object, or all the facts known about its object. What are thus referred to, so far as they are known, are: First, The informed breadth of the symbol; Second, The informed depth of the symbol; Third, The sum of synthetical propositions in which the symbol is subject or predicate, or the information concerning the symbol. By breadth and depth, without an adjective, I shall hereafter mean the informed breadth and depth. It is plain that the breadth and depth of a symbol, so far as they are not essential, measure the information concerning it, that is, the synthetical propositions of which it is subject or predicate. This follows directly from the definitions of breadth, depth, and information. ...we term the information the area, and write — Breadth X Depth = Area. [CP 2.418-419, 1868].

Thus symbols have extension, since they denote classes of objects, and intension, as the objects they denote must have certain characters in common. Peirce furthermore suggests measuring the amount of information that symbols acquire through their individual and cultural history of use. This idea is connected to what Peirce calls the 'growth of symbols' [Nöth, 2012]. The meaning of a symbol grows and develops through the years it is used in a culture. This growth is also augmented by the combination of terms in propositions as they then interact and change each other's meaning. Peirce writes:

> No proposition is supposed to leave its terms as it finds them...; and there are three objects of symbols the connotative, denotative, informative; it follows that there will be three kinds of propositions. [W 1:277].

When an adjective precedes a noun, the logical content of the noun is modified by the adjective. If the noun, 'information' is modified by the adjective 'physical', then the logical content of the abstract concept of information is modified by what the author understands the term 'physical' to mean. Thus, propositions are a further source of the growth of symbols and, in the sciences; synthetic propositions are a source of the acquisition of new knowledge. Although Peirce's information theory is built on meaningful signs, he still has an information theory based in realism. One needs to have empirical reference in order to produce real information. Peirce writes:

> If there be anything that conveys information and yet has absolutely no relation nor reference to anything with which the person to whom it conveys the information has, when he comprehends that information, the slightest acquaintance, direct or indirect — and a very strange sort of information that would be — the vehicle of that sort of information is not, in this volume, called a Sign. [CP 2.231].

In other words, analytical statements lack informativity. The more synthetic a proposition is (i.e., the greater the empirical reference that it has), the more informative it is. Quantity is a measure of the extension of a symbol. It refers to the fact that different symbols 'may denote more or fewer possible things; in this regard they are said to have extension.' [W 1:187]. Thus, the extension of the symbol fish is larger than the one of shark since fish is applicable to more animals than shark. Quality, on the other hand, is dependent on the intension of a symbol, which is the number of characters attributed to a term. That is a logical quantity. This is a quantity very different from the probability theory underlying Shannon's [1949] and Wiener's [1963] objective information theories. In this sense, informational implication takes into account all available knowledge and not only the defining characters from which lexical definitions are made up. Peirce is saying that information is a process in which the symbol of shark, for instance, as a concept with a content that I know, is constantly undergoing development. When I see a documentary showing me many different species of sharks, that I did not know before, like reef sharks, then my symbol of sharks grows, because I have added information to my conception of the species shark by increasing the quantities of extension or intension of the symbol connected to it, which now include hammerheads within their scope. Peirce writes:

> An ordinary proposition ingeniously contrives to convey novel information through signs whose significance depends entirely on the interpreter's familiarity with them; and this it does by means of a 'predicate,' i.e., a term explicitly indefinite in breadth, and defining its breadth by means of 'Subjects,' or terms whose breadths are somewhat definite, but whose informative depth (i.e., all the depth except an essential superficies) is indefinite, while conversely the depth of the Subjects is in a measure defined by the Predicate. [CP 4.543, 1905].

So it is not the lexical definition of 'shark' that carries the information, but all the other things I know about sharks' behavior, size, colors, way of movement, prey, and how many of them we catch each day and eat in shark fin soup. Peirce underlines that 'the information of a term is the measure of its superfluous comprehension' [W 1:467], which is all the extraneous world knowledge I have about sharks, including if I have been bitten by one and where that was. In other words, information is all the knowledge 'outside' the lexical definitions! As Peirce holds a fallibilist view of science combined with a pragmaticist and realistic view of knowledge, he must conclude:

> The cognitions which ... reach us ... are of two kinds, the true and the untrue, or cognitions whose objects are real and those whose objects are unreal. And what do we mean by the real? ... The real, then, is that which, sooner or later, information and reasoning would finally result in, and which is therefore independent of the vagaries of me and you. [CP 5.311, 1868].

Peirce produces a new transdisciplinary theory of information, connected to his semiotic theory of cognition and communication, which differs substantially from the usual conceptions. Peirce's theory combines the concepts of meaning and information within a framework of pragmatic realism established on a semiotic understanding of cognition and communication. Peirce's theory can be modernized by combining it with Luhmann's [1990, 1995] communicative systems theory, which introduces autopoiesis at the level of biology, psychology, and social communication [Brier, 2008a, 2011a; Luhmann, 1990]. Luhmann and Peirce both share the idea of form as the essential component in communication. Peirce writes:

> [...] a Sign may be defined as a Medium for the communication of a Form. [...]. As a medium, the Sign is essentially in a triadic relation, to its Object which determines it, and to its Interpretant which it determines. [...]. That which is communicated from the Object through the Sign to the Interpretant is a Form; that is to say, it is nothing like an existent, but is a power, is the fact that something would happen under certain conditions. [MS 793:1-3].

In Peirce's dynamic process semiotics, a form is something that is embodied in an object as a habit. Thus, form acts as a constraining factor on interpretative behavior or what he calls a real possibility in the form of a 'would-be'. The form is embodied in the object as a sort of disposition to act [Nöth, 2012]. This is, by the way, probably also a better way of understanding the formal causal power of genes, not as deterministic and mechanical, but as dispositions to act in certain ways under certain environmental conditions. Laws are not absolute and mechanical but developing forms in the continuum of mind and matter and our ever developing fallibilist knowledge, of which symbols are an essential feature. As physicist Lee Smolin writes:

> The Cosmological questions such as Why these laws? and Why the initial conditions? cannot be answered by a method that takes the laws and initial conditions as input. [Smolin, 2014, p. 250].

Since mechanical determinism cannot explain the novelty of evolution and the emergence of the laws of nature, Peirce was aware that we needed an alternative ontology to the mechanistic one. Laws are not absolute and mechanical but developing forms in the continuum of mind and matter and our ever developing fallibilist knowledge of which symbols is an essential feature:

> Once you have embraced the principle of continuity no kind of explanation of things will satisfy you except that they grew. The infallibilist naturally thinks that everything always was substantially as it is now. Laws at any rate being absolute could not grow. They either always were, or they sprang instantaneously into being by a sudden fiat like the drill of a company of soldiers. This makes the laws

of nature absolutely blind and inexplicable. Their why and wherefore can't be asked. This absolutely blocks the road of inquiry. The fallibilist won't do this. He asks may these forces of nature not be somehow amenable to reason? May they not have naturally grown up? After all, there is no reason to think they are absolute. If all things are continuous, the universe must be undergoing a continuous growth from non-existence to existence. There is no difficulty in conceiving existence as a matter of degree. The reality of things consists in their persistent forcing themselves upon our recognition. If a thing has no such persistence, it is a mere dream. Reality, then, is persistence, is regularity. [CP 1.175].

But to think that laws are eternal and universal is what modern classical physics used to do and therefore Smolin's work here is quite revolutionary, and he is quite aware that the thought was foundational to Peirce's cosmogony and quotes him several places in the book.

One of the alternatives to mechanicism is to take the objective reality of irreversible time seriously, as Prigogine [1980, 1996; Prigogine and Stengers, 1984] and Peirce did, and now this is also accepted by Smolin. From here it is possible to start with some of kind of non-mechanical objective chance as ontologically foundational. Peirce did that long before Prigogine and called it Tychism.

Peirce holds that signs grow in information through the development of their interpretants [CP 3.608, 1908]. This binds up information with the interpretations of signs as an ongoing personal and social process. Human communication involves a very complex interpretation by the "receiver". As mentioned a percept enters through our senses and clashes with our mind. A percept is the result of our interaction with what seems exterior to consciousness. Regarding percepts, Peirce writes:

The direct percept [...] has no generality; [...] it appears under a physical guise [...] it does not appear as psychical. The psychical, then, is not contained in the percept. [CP 1.253].

According to Peirce's three categories the process of the percept is a pure 'Second': a clash between two different phenomena. Thus, it includes Firstness, but not Thirdness, as there is no interpretation of any kind of regularity or meaning yet. Thus, to Peirce, Thirdness in perception emerges with the construction of perceptual fact or the interpretative function in cognition, which is the intellect's fallible production of meaning through a generalization operated upon the percept and most often based on experience of a series of percepts and concepts. This knowledge process of making sense of the immediate perceptual situation beyond logical deduction is what Peirce calls abduction. This perceptual judgment constitutes an irresistible hypothesis for consciousness with regards to making sense through interpretation, a bit in the same way as we make gestalts. As mentioned according to Peirce percepts are not, in themselves, objects of experience. Though the percept makes knowledge possible, it offers no information, as it does not contain any Thirdness in its immediateness, but is Secondness in it physical clash with the perceptual organ. But experience, understood as the knowing process imposed upon us in the course of living, is "perfused" with Thirdness. Thirdness takes the form of generality and continuity within a fallible account of percepts. "Meaning" must somehow be constructed by the receiver from the information produced by the interpretation of signs, within certain frames that reality imposes on us for survival. Peirce writes:

> At any moment, we are in possession of certain information, that is, of cognitions which have been logically derived by induction and hypothesis[e] from previous cognitions which are less general, less distinct, and of which we have a less lively consciousness. [CP 5.311]

Thus Peirce develops an information theory that starts with a physical event hitting the perceptual organs. Peirce then develops a theory based on the logical quantities of extension and intension associated with the concept of symbol that is so vital for his semiotics. Thus Peirce defines his concept of information directly from his semiotics and its most important species of sign, namely, the symbol;which is the kind of sign that is complete enough to convey information. It is a proposition. A verbal proposition is a symbol, and pieces of it (such as words) are traditionally also called "symbols." It conveys information by combining an indexical sign with an iconic one. It is the combination of those two functions, with the symbolic function, that enables the sign to convey information about its object to its interpretant.

Peirce is aware of the fact that the amount of information transferred in communication is dependent on the knowledge horizon of the receiver or, rather, interpreter. He writes "If you inform me of any truth, and I

---

[e] Hypothesis is the early term for what he later called abduction.

know it already, there is no information" [MS 463:13, 1903]. Thus information has to be able to combine with what you already know. "Actual information extends the knowledge horizon of the interpreter. Information is the measure of how much a symbol involves more or less real knowledge" [W 1:187]. Thus 'objective' does not means 'interpreter-independent'! Peirce writes:

> I do not call the knowledge that a person known to be a woman is an adult, nor the knowledge that a corpse is not a woman, by the name 'information,' because the word 'woman' means a living adult human being having female sexuality. Knowledge that is not informational may be termed 'verbal.' [MS 664:20, 1910].

Precisely here is where "analyticity" comes in: Peirce is saying that the concept of adult is contained in Woman: thus, to say "A woman is an adult" is to make an analytic statement. Thus information is a process in which the symbol of shark, for instance, as a concept with a content that I know, is constantly undergoing development. When I see a documentary showing me many different species of sharks, that I did not know before, like hammerheads, then my symbol of sharks grows, because I have added information to my conception of the species shark by increasing the quantities of extension or intension of the symbol connected to it, which now include hammerheads within their scope.

Information increases when the breadth is increased, when we learn that a known form actually applies to an object that we didn't already know it applied to. Information also increases when depth is increased, when the form applied to a known object is specified or determined more fully than it was before. A sign must have some breadth and depth in order to represent a fact. Breadth is extrinsic because it refers to the object, which is necessarily other than the sign and related to it indexically. Depth is intrinsic because it refers to the form of the sign itself, which is related iconically to the object and to the interpretant determined by the sign. In the logic of relations, the predicate of a proposition provides any depth it has, by signifying the recognizable form which is shared by object and sign, and conveyed to the interpretant by the act of recognition or the event of interpretation. The subject of the proposition denotes its object, and thus the indexical relation provides the proposition with its breadth. Peirce sums up:

What we call a "fact" is something having the structure of a proposition, but supposed to be an element of the very universe itself. The purpose of every sign is to express "fact," and by being joined with other signs, to approach as nearly as possible to determining an interpretant which would be the perfect Truth, the absolute Truth, and as such (at least, we may use this language) would be the very Universe. [EP 2:304].

It is not the lexical definition of "shark" that carries the information, but all the other things I know about sharks' behavior, size, colors, way of movement, prey, and how many thousands of them we catch each day and eat in shark fin soup. Peirce underlines that "the information of a term is the measure of its superfluous comprehension" [W 1:467], which is all the extraneous world knowledge I have about sharks, including if I have been bitten by one. In other words, information is all the knowledge "outside" the lexical definitions! Indeed, Johansen [1993, p. 148] has suggested that "One way to define information is this: the set of characters which can be predicated of a symbol minus the characters contained in its verbal definition."

But, what if one of my students includes something undetermined living underwater looking like a fish and which might possibly be a whale in her symbol or conceptualization of fish — is there then no information? Peirce would conclude that, in this case, we are dealing with the possible, who he considers to be real but having to do with propensities rather than certainties: "that is possible which, in a certain state of information, is not known to be false" [CP 3.442, 1896]. Moreover, "the Possible, in its primary meaning, is that which may be true for aught we know, that whose falsity we do not know" [CP 3.374, 1885]. As Peirce holds a fallibilist view of science combined with a pragmaticist and realistic view of knowledge, he must conclude:

"The cognitions which ... reach us ... are of two kinds, the true and the untrue, or cognitions whose objects are real and those whose objects are unreal. And what do we mean by the real? ... The real, then, is that which, sooner or later, information and reasoning would finally result in, and which is therefore independent of the vagaries of me and you." [CP 5.311, 1868].

Thus Peirce produces a new transdisciplinary theory of information connected to his semiotic theory of cognition and communication, which differs substantially from the usual conceptions. Nöth explains:

> In modern linguistics, the intensions of words are described in the form of semantic features, whereas their extension is studied in a reference semantic framework. For Peirce, however, extension and intension cannot be separated from each other since the extension or denotation of a symbol "is created by its connotation" (W1: 287), that is, through the predicates attributed to a subject term. We can only determine the referent (denotatum or extension) of a word if we know its meaning (intension or connotation) and vice versa: we must know the referent if we want to specify its semantic features ... [Nöth, 2012, p. 139].

Thus, Peirce's theory combines the concepts of meaning and information within a framework of pragmatic realism established on a semiotic understanding of cognition and communication. Peirce's theory can be modernized by combining it with Luhmann's communicative systems theory, which introduces autopoiesis at the level of biology, psychology, and social communication [Brier, 2008a, b, 2013a]. Luhmann and Peirce both share the idea of form as the essential component in communication.

In Peirce's dynamic process semiotics, a form is something that is embodied in an object as a habit. Thus, form acts as a constraining factor on interpretative behavior or what he calls a real possibility in the form of a 'would-be'. Thus the form is embodied in the object as a sort of disposition to act [Nöth, 2012].

8. Conclusion

When scientific methods are applied to information, cognition, and communication, we are only left with codes, grammar, phonetics, programs, formal language, copy machines, adaptors, but then the analysis of meaningful relations is lost amidst all the formal technicalities. Contrary to reductionist loss of meaning Cybersemiotics, following in the footsteps of Peirce, whose semiotics allows us theoretically to distinguish between the information the sender intended to be in the sign, the (possible) information in the sign itself and the information the interpreter gets out of the sign, instead of meaning that the information is the same in all three.. The knowledge in the sign must be interpreted for a full semiosis to happen and for the receiver in order to acquire the information imparted by his or her interlocutor. As such, it is central to any conception of knowledge and information. As Peirce writes then signs have the "active power to establish connections between different objects, especially between objects in different Universes" [CP 6.455; 1908].

We must accept that experience and meaning are just as real as matter. This does not mean that what physicists call the "world" or "reality" as such is imbued with meaning. It means that their concept of "world" and "reality" is unable to reflexively encompass the embodied psychological and social foundation of knowledge. Thus their idea of reality does not take our full measure as conscious, linguistic and social creatures. It lacks an embodied phenomenological foundation in the understanding of Wissenschaft.

From a semiotic viewpoint, we can see man as a parasite of symbols [Nöth, 2012], because we use them to create our perceived selves as self-conscious, cultural communicative beings. Peirce points out that self-reproduction and self-replication are not only characteristics of organisms and chromosomes, but also of symbols. Signs replicate through and in their tokens. Replicas of symbols in their acoustic or written form are indeed dead things (phenomena of Secondness), but symbols as genuine Thirdness live on as self-replicative beings

It is within that wider reality of life connecting subjects in language and social actions to nature and technology that information is created. "Meaning" in the form of the Thirdness of taking habit must somehow be constructed by the receiver from the information gathered by the interpretation of signs, within certain frames that reality imposes on us for survival and procreation. Thus, in the Cybersemiotic transdisciplinary frame for interdisciplinarity the sign process is viewed as transcending the division between nature and culture, between the natural sciences, the life sciences, the social sciences, and the humanities and between phenomena that are exterior and those that are interior to human consciousness.

We have moved from a mechanical idea of the *Cosmos* to a system theoretical self-organized evolutionary super-system: *The self-organizing Universe* [Jantsch, 1980]. Though the combination of thermodynamics and the info-computational paradigms attempts to naturalize information computations to an *Infos* as imagined by Chaitin [2007] and Wheeler [1994], now through Peirce and Cybersemiotics we have started to move towards a *Semios*, that through a physio-semiotic cosmogony [Deely, 1990] is encompassing and integrating the former understandings of matter and information in to the cybersemiotic view of a *Cybersemios*.

References

Andersen, P. B. (1997). *A Theory of Computer Semiotics: Semiotic Approaches to Construction and Assessment of Computer Systems.* Cambridge University Press, Cambridge.

Apel, K.-O. (1981). *Charles S. Peirce: From Pragmatism to Pragmaticism*, trans. J. M. Krois. University of Massachusetts Press, Amherst, MA.

von Baeyer, C. (2004). *Information: The New Language of Science.* Harvard University Press, Cambridge, MA.

Bar-Hillel, Y. (1964). *Language and Information.* Addison-Wesley, Reading, MA.

Bar-Hillel, Y. and Carnap, R. (1953). *Communication Theory*, ed. W. Jackson, "Semantic Information." Butterworth, London, pp. 503–512.

Bateson, G. (1972). *Steps to an Ecology of Mind: Collected Essays in Anthropology, Psychiatry, Evolution and Epistemology.* Paladin, St. Albans, UK.

Bateson, G. (1979). *Mind and Nature: A Necessary Unity* (*Advances in Systems Theory, Complexity, and the Human Sciences*). Hampton Press, New York.

Bateson, G. and Bateson, M. C. (1987). *Angels Fear: Towards and Epistemology of the Sacred.* Bantam Books, Toronto.

Boler, J. F. (1963). *Charles Peirce and Scholastic Realism: A Study of Peirce's Relation to John Duns Scotus.* University of Washington Press, Seattle.

Brent, J. L. (1998). *Charles Sanders Peirce: A Life,* rev. ed. Indiana University Press, Bloomington, IN.

Brier, S. (1992). Information and consciousness: a critique of the mechanistic foundation of the concept of information, *Cybernetics & Human Knowing, 1*(2/3), pp. 71–94. (http://www.imprint.co.uk/C&HK/vol1/v1-23sbr.htm).

Brier, S. (2003). The cybersemiotic model of communication: an evolutionary view on the threshold between semiosis and informational exchange, *tripleC, 1*(1), pp. 71–94.

Brier, S. (2008a). *Cybersemiotics: Why Information is Not Enough.* Toronto University Press, Toronto.

Brier, S. (2008b). *A Legacy for Living Systems: Gregory Bateson as a Precursor for Bio-semiotic Thinking, Biosemiotics 2,* ed. Hoffmeyer, J., Chapter 12 "Bateson and

Peirce on the Pattern that Connects and the Sacred." Springer Verlag, London, pp. 229–255.

Brier, S. (2009). Cybersemiotic pragmaticism and constructivism, *Constructivist Foundations, 5*(1), pp. 19–38.

Brier, S. (2010). Cybersemiotics: Entropic information, evolution and meaning: A world view beyond entropy and information, *Entropy (An electronic journal), 12*(8), pp. 1902–1920. (http://www.mdpi.com/1099-4300/12/8/1902).

Brier, S. (2011a). *Information and Computation*, eds. Dodig-Crnkovic, G. and Burgin, M., Chapter 1 "Cybersemiotics and the Question of Knowledge." World Scientific Publishing Co., Singapore, pp. 11-47.

Brier, S. (2011b). *Semiotics Continues to Astonish: the Intellectual Heritage of Thomas Albert Sebeok*, eds. Deely, J., Kull, K. and Petrilli, S., Chapter 4 "Ethology and the Sebeokian way from Zoosemiotics to Cyber(bio)semiotics." Mouton de Gruyter, Paris, pp. 41–84.

Brier, S. (2012). "Peircean philosophy of science and modern transdisciplinary understanding of Wissenschaft" to Professor Roland's Posner's 70 years festschrift," *Sign Culture/Zeichen Kultur*, ed. Hess-Lüttich, E. W. B, Verlag Königshausen & Neumann GmbH, Würzburg, Germany, pp. 85–105.

Brier, S. (2013a). *Origins of Mind* (Springer series in Biosemiotics), ed. Swan, L., "Cybersemiotics: a new foundation for Transdisciplinary Theory of Consciousness, Cognition, Meaning and Communication." Springer, New York.

Brier, S. (2013b). Cybersemiotics: a new foundation for transdisciplinary theory of information, cognition, meaningful communication and the interaction between nature and culture, *Integral Review: A Transdisciplinary and Transcultural Journal, 9*(2),   pp. 220–263.

Brier, S. (2013c). *Fundamental Notions of Information, Communication and Knowledge: Its Effects on Scientific Research and Inter-Disciplinarity*, ed. Ibekwe-San Juan, F. and Dousa, T., "Transdisciplinary View of Information Theory Seen from a Cybersemiotics Point of View." Springer, New York, pp. 23–49

Brier, S. (2014a). *Charles Sanders Peirce in His Own Words: 100 Years of Semiotics, Communication and Cognition*, ed. Thellefsen, T. L. and Sørensen, B., Chapter 32 "Pure Zero." Walter de Gruyter, Berlin, pp. 207–212.

Brier, S. (2014b). *Death and Anti-Death, Volume 12: One Hundred Years After Charles S. Peirce (1839-1914)*, ed. Tandy, C., Chapter 2 "The Riddle of the Sphinx answered: On How C. S. Peirce's Transdisciplinary Semiotic Philosophy of Knowing Links Science, Spirituality and Knowing." Ria University Press, Ann Arbor, MI, pp. 47–130.

Brier, S. (2014c). *Ethics, Science, Technology, and Engineering: A Global Resource, Vol. 4*, 2nd edn., ed. Holbrook, J. B., "Nature and Machine." Macmillan Reference, Farmington Hills, MI, pp. 127–130.

Brier, S. (2014d). Phenomenological computation? *Constructivist Foundations, 9*(2), p. 15. (http://www.univie.ac.at/constructivism/journal/articles/9/2/234.brier.pdf).

Brier, S. (2015a). Finding an information concept suited for a universal theory of information. *Progress in Biophysics & Molecular Biology, 119*(3), pp. 622–633.

Brier, S. (2015b). Can biosemiotics be a "science" if its purpose is to be a bridge between the natural, social and human sciences? *Progress in Biophysics & Molecular Biology, 119*(3), pp. 576–587.

Brier, S. (2015c). Cybersemiotics and the reasoning powers of the universe: philosophy of information in a semiotic-systemic transdisciplinary approach, *Green Letters, Stu-dies in Ecocriticism, 19*(3), pp. 280–292.
http://www.tandfonline.com/doi/full/10.1080/ 14688417.2015.1070684.

Brier, S. and Joslyn, C. (2013). What does it take to produce interpretation? Informational, Peircean, and code-semiotic views on biosemiotics, *Biosemiotics, 6*(1), pp. 143–159.

Burgin, M. (2010) *Theory of Information: Fundamentality, Diversity and Unification,* World Scientific Publishing Co Pte Ltd, New York, NY, London, UK, Singapore.

Burgin, M. (2011) Information: concept clarification and theoretical representation. *tripleC, 9*, pp. 347–357.

Cantwell Smith, B. (1998). God, approximately, retrieved March 16, 2010 from: http://www.ageofsignificance.org/people/bcsmith/print/smith-godapprox4.pdf.

Carnap, R. (1967). *The Logical Structure of the World & Pseudoproblems in Philosophy.* University of California Press, Berkeley, CA.

Cartwright, N., Cat, J., Fleck, L. and Uebel, T. (1996). *Otto Neurath: Philosophy Between Science and Politics.* Cambridge University Press, Cambridge, UK.

Chaitin, G. (2006). Epistemology as information theory: from Leibniz to Ω, *Collapse 1,* pp. 27–51

Chaitin, G. (2007). *Information, Cognition—The Nexus and The Liminal,* ed. G. Dodig-Crnkovic, S. Stuart, "Epistemology as Information Theory, in Computation." Cambridge Scholars Publishing. Cambridge, UK, pp. 2–18.

Chomsky, N. (1957). *Syntactic Structures.* Mouton, The Hague.

Colapietro, V. (1989) *Peirce's Approach to the Self: A Semiotic Perspective on Human Subjectivity.* SUNY Press, Albany, NY.

Corrington, R. (1993). *An Introduction in C. S. Peirce: Philosopher, Semiotician, and Ecstatic Naturalist.* Rowman & Littlefield, Lanham, MD.

Davies, P. and Gregersen, N. H. (eds.) (2009). *Information and the Nature of Reality: From Physics to Metaphysics.* Cambridge University Press, Cambridge, UK.

Deacon, T. (2011). *Incomplete Nature: How Mind Emerged from Matter.* W.W. Norton & Company, New York.

Deely, J. (1990). *Basics of Semiotics.* Indiana University Press, Bloomington, IN.

Deely, J. (2001). *Four Ages of Understanding: The First Postmodern Survey of Philosophy from Ancient Times to the Turn of the Twenty-First Century.* University of Toronto Press, Toronto.

Deledalle, G. (2000). *Charles Peirce's Philosophy of Signs: Essays in Comparative Semiotics.* Indiana University Press, Bloomington, IN.

Dodig-Crnkovic, G. (2010). The cybersemiotics and info-computationalist research program as platforms for knowledge production in organisms and machines, *Entropy, 12*, pp. 878—901.

Dódig-Crnkovic, G. and Müller, V. (2013). *Information and Computation* (Series in Information Studies), eds. Dodig-Crnkovic, G. and Burgin, M., "A Dialogue Concerning Two World Systems: Info-Computational vs. Mechanistic." World Scientific Publishing Co, Singapore, pp. 149–184.

Dretske, F., I. (1981). *Knowledge and the Flow of Information.* The MIT Press, Cambridge, MA.

Eco, U. (1976). *A Theory of Semiotics.* Indiana University Press, Bloomington, IN.

Engels, F. (1968). *Dialectics of Nature*, trans. J. B. S. Haldane, 1939. International Publishers Co., New York. (written 1873–1886; translated 1939)

Esposito, J. L. (1980). *Evolutionary Metaphysics*: *The Development of Peirce's Theory of the Categories.* Ohio University Press, Athens, OH.

Favareau, D. (Ed.) (2010). *Essential Readings in Biosemiotics*: *Anthology and Commentary.* Springer, New York.

Fisch, M. H. (1986) *Peirce, Semeiotic, and Pragmatism*, eds. Ketner, K. L. and Kloesel, C. Indiana University Press, Bloomington, IN.

Fink, H. (2006). Three sorts of naturalism, *European Journal of Philosophy, 14*(2), pp. 202–221.

Floridi, L. (2011). *The Philosophy of Information.* Oxford University Press, Oxford.

Fodor, J. (2000). *The Mind Doesn't Work That Way*: *The Scope and Limits of Computational Psychology.* The MIT Press, Cambridge, MA.

Gardner, H. (1985). *The Mind's New Science: A History of the Cognitive Revolution.* Basic Books, New York.

Harney, M. (2015). Naturalizing phenomenology—a philosophical imperative, *Progress in Biophysics & Molecular Biology, 119*(3), pp. 205–734.

Hoffmeyer, J. (1996). *Signs of Meaning in the Universe*, trans. Haveland, B. J., Indiana University Press, Bloomington, IN.

Hoffmeyer, J. (1998). *Interdigitations. Essays for Irmengard Rauch.* Gerald, F. C., W. H., and Zhang, L. eds. "On the Origin of Intentional Systems". Peter Lang Publishing, New York.

Hoffmeyer, J. (2008a). *Biosemiotics: An Examination into the Signs of Life and the Life of Signs.* University of Scranton Press, Scranton, PA.

Hoffmeyer, J. (ed.) (2008b). *A Legacy for Living Systems*: *Gregory Bateson as a Precursor for Biosemiotic Thinking*, Biosemiotics 2. Springer-Verlag, London.

Hoffmeyer, J. and Emmeche, C. (1991). *On Semiotic Modeling*, eds. Anderson, M. and Merrell, F., "Code-Duality and the Semiotics of Nature," Mouton de Gruyter, New York, pp. 117–166.

Hofkirchner, W. (2009). How to achieve a unified theory of information. *tripleC, 7*, pp. 357-368.

Hofkirchner, W. (2013). *Emergent Information*, World Scientific, New York/London/ Singapore.

Hookway, C. (1992). *Peirce*. Routledge, London.

Jantsch, E. (1980). *The Self-Organizing Universe: Scientific and Human Implications of the Emerging Paradigm of Evolution*. Pergamon Press, New York.

Kull, K., Deacon, T., Emmeche, C., Hoffmeyer, J. and Stjernfelt, F. (2009). Theses on biosemiotics: prolegomena to a theoretical biology, *Biological Theory*, *4*(2), pp. 167–173.

Lindsay, P. and Norman, D. A. (1977). *Human Information Processing: An Introduction to Psychology*, 2nd edn. Academic Press, New York.

Liszka, J. J. (1996). *A General Introduction to the Semeiotic of Charles Sanders Peirce*. Indiana University Press, Bloomington, IN.

Lorenz, K. (1970-71). *Studies in Animal and Human Behaviour I and II*. Harvard University Press, Cambridge, MA.

Lovelock, J. E., (1972). Gaia as seen through the atmosphere. *Atmospheric Environment*, *6*(8), pp. 579–580.

Lovelock, J. E. (2000). *Gaia: A New Look at Life on Earth*. Oxford University Press, Oxford, UK.

Lovelock, J. (2009). *The Vanishing Face of Gaia: A Final Warning*. Basic Books, New York.

Luhmann, N. (1990). *Essays on Self-Reference*. Colombia University Press, New York.

Luhmann, N. (1995). *Social Systems*. Stanford University Press, Standford, CA.

Machlup, F. (1983). *The Study of Information: Interdisciplinary Messages*, eds. Machlup, F. and Mansfield, U., "Semantic Quirks in Studies of Information." John Wiley & Sons, New York, pp. 641–671.

Markov, K., Ivanova, K., and Mitov, I. (1993). Basic Structure of the General Information Theory. *International Journal "Information Theories & Applications"*, *14*(1), pp. 5-19.

Maturana, H. R. (1988a). Ontology of observing: the biological foundation of self-consciousness and the physical domain of existence. (Retrieved May 20, 2016 from: http://ada.evergreen.edu/~arunc/texts/cybernetics/oo/old/oo.pdf)

Maturana, H. (1988b). Reality: the search for objectivity, or the quest for a compelling argument, *The Irish Journal of Psychology*, *9*(1), pp. 25–82.

Maturana, H. and Varela, F. (1980). *Autopoiesis and Cognition: The Realization of the Living*. Reidel, London.

Maturana, H. and Varela, F. (1986). *Tree of Knowledge: Biological Roots of Human Understanding*. Shambhala Publishers, London.

Mcginn, C. (2000). *The Mysterious Flame: Conscious Minds in a Material World*. Basic Books, New York.

Menand, L. (2001). *The Metaphysical Club: A Story of Ideas in America*. Farrar, Strauss and Giroux, New York.

Monod, J. (1972). *Chance and Necessity: An Essay on the Natural Philosophy of Modern Biology*. Vintage Books, New York.

Murphey, M. G. (1961). *The Development of Peirce's Philosophy*. Harvard University Press, Cambridge, MA.

Nagel, T. (2012). *Mind and Cosmos: Why the Materialist neo-Darwinian Conception of Nature is Almost Certainly False*. Oxford University Press, Oxford.

Nöth, W. (2012). Charles S. Peirce's theory of information: a theory of the growth of symbols and of knowledge, *Cybernetics and Human Knowing, 19*(1-2), pp. 137–161.

Parker, K. A (1998). *The Continuity of Peirce's Thought*. Vanderbilt University Press, Nashville, TN.

Peirce, C. S. (1982-2014). *The Writings of Charles S. Peirce: A Chronological Edition*. Volumes 1–6 and 8, eds. Peirce Edition Project, Indiana University Press, Bloomington, IN (cited in text as W vol:page).

Peirce, C. S. (1992/*1867-1893*). *The Essential Peirce. Selected Philosophical Writings,* Volume 1 (1867-1893), eds. Houser, N. & Christian K., Indiana University Press, Bloomington, IN.

Peirce, C. S. (1994). *The Collected Papers of Charles Sanders Peirce*, cd version, ed. J. Deely reproducing Vols. I-VI, eds. Hartshorne, C. and Weiss, P., Harvard University Press, Cambridge, MA, 1931-1935; Vols. VII-VIII, ed. Burks, A. W., Harvard University Press, Cambridge, MA, 1958. Intelex, Carlottesville, VA. (cited in text as CP vol. and paragraph)

Peirce, C. S. (1998). *The Essential Peirce. Selected Philosophical Writings, Vol. 2*, eds. The Peirce Edition Project, Indiana University Press, Bloomington, IN.

Penrose, R. (1989). *The Emperor's New Mind*. Oxford University Press, Oxford, UK.

Penrose, R. (1994). *Shadows of the Mind*. Oxford University Press, Oxford, UK.

Popper, K. R. (1959). *The Logic of Scientific Discovery*. Routledge, London. https://archive.org/details/PopperLogicScientificDiscovery (retrieved May 20, 2016)

Popper, K. (1978). Tanner Lecture on Human Values, Delivered at The University of Michigan April 7, 1978. Retreived January 29, 2016 from, http://tannerlectures.utah. edu/_documents/a-to-z/p/popper80.pdf

Prigogine, I. (1980). *From Being to Becoming*. W.H. Freeman, San Francisco

Prigogine, I. (1996). *The End of Certainty: Time, Chaos, and the New Laws of Nature*. The Free Press, New York.

Prigogine, I. and Stengers, I. (1984). *Order Out of Chaos: Man's New Dialogue with Nature*. Bantam Books, New York.

Ransdell, J. (1989). Peirce est-il un phénoménologue? *Ètudes Phénoménologiques, 9-10*, pp. 51-75. (unpublished original English version retrieved May 20, 2016 from: http://www.cspeirce.com/menu/library/aboutcsp/ransdell/phenom.htm).

Raposa, M. (1989). *Peirce's Philosophy of Religion* (Peirce Studies No. 5). Indiana University Press, Bloomington, IN.

Rozenberg, G., Back, T. and Kok, J. (eds). (2012). *Handbook of Natural Computing.* Springer-Verlag, Berlin.

Savan, D. (1987-1988). *An Introduction to C. S. Peirce's System of Semeiotic.* Toronto Semiotic Circle, Toronto.

Schelling, F. W. J. (1989/1809). *Philosophical Inquiries into the Nature of Human Freedom.* Open Court, La Salle, IL.

Schrödinger, E. (2012/1944). *What is Life? With Mind and Matter and Autobiographical Sketches* (Canto Classics). Cambridge University Press, Cambridge, UK.

Schrödinger, E. (1948). *"Nature and the Greeks"* and *"Science and Humanism,"* Shearman lectures, Delivered at University College, London (*Canto Classics*). Cambridge University Press, London

Sebeok, T. A. (1965). Zoosemiotics: A new key to linguistics, *The Review*, 7, pp. 27-33.

Sebeok, T. A. (1972). *Perspectives in Zoosemiotics.* Mouton, The Hague.

Sebeok, T. A. and Danesi, M. (2000). *The Forms of Meaning: Modeling Systems Theory and Semiotic Analysis.* Walter de Gruyter, The Hague.

Sebeok, T. A. and Umiker-Sebeok, J. (1992). *Biosemiotics: The Semiotic Web 1991* (Approaches to Semiotics). Mouton De Gruyter, Berlin.

Shannon, C. (1949). *A Mathematical Theory of Communication*, Shannon C. and Weaver, W., "A Mathematical Theory of Communication." University of Illinois Press, Urbana, IL, pp. 29–125.

Short, T. L. (2007). *Peirce's Theory of Signs.* Cambridge University Press, Cambridge, UK.

Smolin, L. (2014). *Time Reborn: From the Crisis of Physics to the Future of the Universe.* Allan Lane, London.

Snow, C. P. (1959). *The Two Cultures.* Cambridge University Press, London.

Stjernfelt, F. (2014). *Natural Propositions: The Account of Peirce's Doctrine of Decisigns.* Decent Press, Boston, MA.

Stonier, T. (1990). *Information and the Internal Structure of the Universe: An Exploration into Information Physics.* Springer-Verlag, London.

Stonier, T. (1992). *Beyond Information: The Natural History of Intelligence.* Springer-Verlag, London.

Stonier, T. (1997). *Information and Meaning: An Evolutionary Perspective.* Springer-Verlag, London.

Thompson, E. (2007). *Mind in Life: Biology, Phenomenology, and the Sciences of Mind.* Harvard University Press (Belknap), Cambridge, MA.

von Uexküll, T. Geigges, W. and Herrmann, J. M. (1993). Endosemiosis. *Semiotica* 96(1-2), pp. 5-52.

Wheeler, J. A. (1994). *At Home in the Universe.* American Institute of Physics, New York.

Whitehead, A. N. (1978). *Process and Reality: An Essay in Cosmology*. The Free Press, New York.

Wiener, N. (1963). *Cybernetics*: *Or, Control and Communication in the Animal and the Machine*. The MIT Press, Cambridge, MA.

Chapter 3

Inaccessible Information and the Mathematical Theory of Oracles

Mark Burgin

University of California, Los Angeles
405 Hilgard Ave. Los Angeles, CA 90095, USA
mburgin@math.ucla.edu

People always need more information than they have. They can get some of this information by themselves but a good deal of information remains inaccessible. This situation, which always existed in human civilization, brought forth Oracles. The idea of an Oracle reflected interactions between systems, such as people and states, with less information and systems with more indispensable information. In the 20th century, it was proved that some information is intrinsically inaccessible and then the concept of an Oracle naturally came to computer science becoming popular in the realm of algorithms and computations. At first, Turing machines with an Oracle were introduced and studied. Later inductive Turing machines with Oracles, limit Turing machines with Oracles and evolutionary Turing machines with Oracles were established and explored. Here we create a theoretical background for the concept of an Oracle. In the first part of this work, we contemplate Oracles in human culture. In the second part, we contemplate Oracles in computer science and mathematics. In the third part, the variety of Oracles is analyzed and classified. In the fourth part, we develop a mathematical theory of Oracles, where the concepts of an Oracle and its brands are formalized and studied in the mathematical framework.

Keywords: Information; oracle; theory; science; mathematics; accessible information; relative computability; complexity; algorithm; Turing machine; inductive Turing machine; reduction; simplification; information supply.

> *… success could be attributed*
> *to following correct oracles.*
>
> Jeremy Black "The Power of Knowledge"

1. Introduction

People always need more information than they have. It was and it is possible to obtain some part of required information by observation, experimentation, and learning from experience, written sources or from other people but still some, often vital, information remained inaccessible. Therefore, people decided to get information from gods and other supernatural sources. They called a transmitter of information from a supernatural source by the name *Oracle*. In their history, people considered such oracles as people with special gifts, people connected to the Divine, e.g., prophets, "magic" expressions, e.g., names of the God, and "magic" procedures. Oracles played an important role in ancient cultures and this feature was reflected in several recently published books dealing with oracles (cf., for example, Curnow, 2004; Wood, 2004; Morgan, 2007; Stoneman, 2011).

The word *oracle* is derived from the Latin verb *ōrāre*, which means "to speak" or "to utter" and by the book, refers to the system that transmits such otherwise inaccessible information. In modern practice, the name *Oracle* is applied either to a prophet inspired by spiritual sources, or to a particular prophesy coming from mystical vicinity.

In contrast to this, ancient Greeks understood the Oracle as a medium or agency through which divine forces communicated with mortals (Hager, 2010). Usually, a medium was either the priest or priestess uttering the prediction or the site where predictions were delivered or the oracular utterances themselves. The key meaning of the word *oracle* is "the response of a god to a question asked of him by a worshipper." The word also denoted the shrine where responses were obtained, as well as the congregation of priests who administered an oracular shrine.

For instance, the most popular Oracle of Greek antiquity was Pythia, the acting priestess to Apollo at Delphi, who gave cryptic forecasts and guidance to both city-states and individuals. Delphi was an important ancient Greek religious site consecrated to the Greek god Apollo and located on Mt. Parnassus near the Gulf of Corinth. The temple priestesses who delivered prophesy and recommendations were called *Pythia* and treated as the mouthpiece of the utterances of the Greek deity Apollo (Fontenrose, 1978). The site originated in the late Bronze Age (1500-1100 B.C.E.) but took on its religious significance from around 800 B.C.E. (Burkert, 1985).

There were also other important Oracles in ancient Greece such as the oracle of Dione and Zeus at Dodona in Epirus where priests forecasted in a similar manner (Flower, 2008). Consultations with an Oracle were complicated rituals. This is how Pausanias, who lived in the second century, described the procedures at the oracle of Trophonios, who was a man swallowed up by the earth and transformed into an Oracular Daimon (Spirit) (Pausanias, 1918; Eliade, 1968).

When a man came to the oracle of Trophonios, at first, he had to stay in a special building consecrated to Agathos Daimon and Agathe Tyche (the Good Daimon and Good Fortune) for a prescribed number of days. While living there he followed certain rules of purity, which included, in particular, prohibition of warm baths. The person sacrificed to Trophonios and his children, as well as to deities Apollo, Kronos, Zeus, Hera and Demeter getting meat from the sacrifices. At each of the sacrifices, a diviner inspected the entrails from the sacrifice foretelling to the man intending to descend whether Trophonios would receive him kindly and graciously. The last sacrifice was on the night on which the man had to go down, and it was especially important. After this, two boys called Hermai and aged about thirteen, brought the man to the river Herkyna and there anointed him with olive oil and washed him. After this, the priests brought the man to springs of water where he had to drink the water called Lethe to achieve forgetfulness of all that he has hitherto thought of and the water of Mnemosyne, which gives him remembrance of what he sees when he has gone down to Trophonios. Then he had to pray to a statue, which is said to be the work of Daidalos and which the priests reveal to none save those who intend to go down to Trophonios. All this done, the man approached the oracle and went down to visit Trophonios, wearing a linen *chiton* girdled with ribbons, and shod with the native boots of the country.

The oracle of Asclepius at Epidaurus functioned in a very different manner. There the priests performed the healings of the sick attributing to the place and the divine powers that resided there but denying influence of local natural events (Hager, 2010).

A different kind of oracles was the Sibylline Oracles, which were a collection of prophetic declarations written in Greek hexameters ascribed to the Sibyl, who were uttering divine revelations in a possessed state. At first, Sibylla was a lone female Oracle usually related to ancient Rome and Cumae in ancient Italy. Later many different sibyls appeared in various localities. For instance, Marcus Terentius Varro wrote about ten sibyls who resided in Persia, Libya, Delphi, Cumae in Italy, Erythrae, Samos, Cumae in Aeolia, Marpessa, Ankara, and Tiburtis. Sibyls articulated their predictions not on being consulted, like other oracles, but spontaneously, in ecstatic exclamations.

Although Sybils were associated with ancient Rome, the legendary Sibyls actually originated in Greek Asia Minor. According to Pausanias (1918), the Sibyl Herophile lived so long ago that she was able to forecast the Trojan War.

Thus, Sybils were Oracles and their utterings were also called Oracles. The original Sibylline Oracles were securely-protected scrolls written by prophetic priestesses called Sibylls in the Etruscan and early Roman periods as far back as the 6th Century B.C.E. (Gottheil and Krauss, 1906) Sibylline Oracles were kept in the temple of Jupiter Capitolinus being consulted in situations when the senate had to make critical decisions. The scrolls were destroyed, partially in a fire in 83 B.C.E., and finally burned by order of the Roman General Flavius Stilicho (365-408 C.E.).

History of the human civilization shows that there were also Oracles in other cultures.

In ancient Egypt, there were different Oracles. The earliest evidence for oracular consultation in Egypt is several enigmatic imperial inscriptions of the mid-18th Pharaonic Dynasty (*c.* 1543–1292 B.C.E.), which contain accounts of Hatshepsut and Thutmose III telling that

Amun communicated his will through the medium of his portable barque (Moore, 2012).

Much later Pausanias, who lived in the second century, also wrote about an Egyptian sibyl (Pausanias, 1918; Eliade, 1968).

In ancient India, an Oracle was called Akashwani or Ashareeravani (a person without body or unseen), as well as Asariri (Tamil), literally meaning "voice from the sky." It was believed that Oracles transmitted messages of gods. Ancient Indian epics Mahabharata and Ramayana describe different Oracles. Besides, Oracles, such as the Copper Oracle (Tamrapothi) and Silver Oracle (Rupapothi) of Shri Achyutanda Das, exist in India even now.

In China, people used oracle bones as far back as the Shang Dynasty (1600–1046 B.C.E.). Another kind of Oracles is hexagrams from I Ching (the Book of Changes), which allegedly originated prior to the Shang Dynasty. A hexagram (*guà*) is a figure composed of six stacked horizontal lines, which may be broken or unbroken. There are 64 hexagrams. Each of them has a name (*guàmíng*), a short hexagram statement (*tuàn*) and six line statements (*yáocí*), which have been used to determine the results of divination. I Ching is used even now for the same purpose.

Oracles have played and continue to play an important role in Tibet, where they are referred to the spirit that enters men or women called *kuten* (the *physical basis* in English) acting as media between people and the spiritual sphere. For instance, the Dalai Lama, who lives in exile in northern India, consults several Oracles.

At the same time, it is necessary to remark that some authors were skeptical describing Greek and other Oracles (cf., for example, de Fontenelle, 1687/1753).

The goal of this chapter is not only to provide a brief exposition of the history of Oracles in human culture in general but above all to show how Oracles came to computer science and mathematics, analyze these processes and develop a mathematical theory of Oracles.

Thus, the chapter is organized as follows. In the second section of this work, the history and applications of Oracles in computer science and technology, as well as theoretical and computational mathematics is expounded and examined. Although many researchers in these areas believe there are only Turing Oracles that provide values of recursively incomputable functions, actually many other Oracles have been used and are used in computer science, computer technology and computational mathematics.

In the third section, we provide a methodological analysis of the concept of an Oracle constructing various classifications of Oracles and illustrating them by examples from human history, computer science and mathematics.

In the fourth section, we build a mathematical theory of Oracles in formal setting obtaining diverse properties of Oracles represented by mathematical structures. To make the text more comprehensible for the reader, we give informal interpretations and explanations of the used mathematical constructions and formulas.

The last section contains conclusions.

2. Oracles in computer science and mathematics

When science and mathematics started their successful advancement, it looked so that given appropriate time, all information would be accessible and all problems would be solved. This conviction was vividly expressed in the motto of the great mathematician David Hilbert (1862-1943) who said: "Wir müssen wissen, wir werden wissen", what in English meant, "If we must know, we will know." However, in the 20th century, mathematicians rigorously proved existence of inaccessible information.

At first, Gödel demonstrated (the first Incompleteness Theorem) that standard mathematical tools do not allow finding information about truthfulness of formulas in many mathematical systems such as the formal arithmetic (Gödel, 1931). Another result of Gödel (the second Incompleteness Theorem) explicated inaccessibility of information about consistency of the majority of mathematical systems using ordinary mathematical means. One more important result about inaccessible information was the proof of impossibility to determine using regular mathematical reasoning the, so-called, Halting Problem whether an arbitrary member of the most popular class of algorithms — Turing machine — gives the result or not (Turing, 1936). Later, researchers developed more powerful than Turing machines tools of computation. They allowed solving the Halting Problem for Turing machines, finding information about truthfulness of formulas in the formal arithmetic and some other problems unsolvable by the old technique but at the same time, new kinds of problems were discovered, which were unsolvable even by the new methods (Burgin, 2005a, b, 2010).

Naturally, this situation brought forth Oracles. One of the forefathers of computer science Alan Turing was the first to introduce the concept of Oracle into theoretical computer science (the theory of algorithms and computation) and thus, into mathematics as theoretical computer science is fundamentally based on mathematics (Turing, 1939). He invented abstract automata, which he called o-machines. It is necessary to remark that in his publications, Turing made only an obscure remark about o-machines, which are now called Oracle Turing machines (Turing, 1939):

"Let us suppose we are supplied with some unspecified means of solving number-theoretic problems; a kind of oracle as it were. . . . this oracle . . . cannot be a machine. With the help of the oracle we could form a new kind of machine (call them o-machines), having as one of its fundamental processes that of solving a given number-theoretic problem."

It was Post (1944, 1948), who formalized, considerably expanded and developed relative computability. Besides, independently of Turing, Post defined finite combinatory processes (Post, 1936), which closely resembled Turing machines but did not give a construction similar to the universal Turing machine. Another Post's achievement was introduction of the concept of production systems (Post, 1943), which gave algorithms for generating sets rather than computing a function and became very popular in expert systems for representation of procedural knowledge (Pospelov, 1990; Giarratano and Riley, 1998). Unfortunately, results of Post were underestimated at that time.

Some researchers think that Oracles in Oracle Turing machines are logical black boxes for carrying out incomputable tasks (Cleland, 2001). However, according to the Turing's conception, an Oracle is a system, e.g., a device, black box, person, whatsoever, that contains knowledge about the values of some, incomputable, function $f(n)$. If a Turing machine T has an Oracle for such a function $f(n)$, than T has an operation of supplying the Oracle with an arbitrary number n and receiving from the Oracle the value $f(n)$. In such a way, the Turing machine T can "compute" an incomputable function.

Computer scientists have used Oracle Turing machines for building a sophisticated theory of relative algorithms and computation (cf., for example, Rogers, 1987). In this theory, levels of incomputability are constructed and problems are classified according to these levels (Shoenfield, 1959). One more area of research in the theory of relative computations studies algorithmic reducibility of one set to another one constructing computationally equivalent classes of sets.

Soare (2015) even argues that actually relative computations are in the center and form the main content of theoretical computer science. He argues that "the notion of an oracle machine and relative computability is the single most important in the subject" due to the following reasons:

(1) All conventional Turing machines can be easily simulated by Oracle Turing machines and the latter is scarcely more complicated to explain.

(2) Most of the objects considered in computability theory and applications to algebra, model theory, geometry, analysis, complexity and other fields are incomputable not computable and relative computability unifies and explains them.

(3) Many if not most computing processes in the real world are online or interactive processes, better modeled by Oracle Turing machines than by conventional Turing machines.

It is interesting that there are other models of computation, which are more constructive but have the same abilities as Turing machines with arbitrary Oracles. For instance, general inductive Turing machines have the same computing power as Oracle Turing machines, that is, they can compute any function for finite words and decide any formal language with a finite alphabet (Burgin, 2005a, b).

A *general inductive Turing machine* is an abstract automaton that has hardware, software and infware as any computer.

The *infware* of a computer is the system of all data that can be processed by the computer. The *infware* of inductive Turing machines, as in the case of the majority of other abstract automata, such as finite automata or Turing machines, consists of words in some alphabet.

The *hardware* of an inductive Turing machine *M* consists of three abstract devices:

- the *control device A*, which is a finite automaton and controls the performance of *M*;
- the *processor* or *operating device H*, e.g., one or several *heads* of a conventional Turing machine;
- the *memory E*, e.g., the *tape* or tapes of a conventional Turing machine.

The memory *E* of the simplest inductive Turing machine consists of three linear tapes, and the operating device consists of three heads, each of which is the same as the head of a Turing machine and works with the corresponding tapes. Such machines are called *simple inductive Turing machines* (Burgin, 2005).

The *control device A* is a finite automaton. It controls and regulates processes and parameters of the machine *M*: the state of the whole machine *M*, the processing of information by *H*, and the storage of information in the memory *E*.

The *memory E* of a general inductive Turing machine is divided into different but as a rule, uniform cells. It is structured by a system of relations that organize memory as a well-structured system and provide connections or ties between cells. In particular, *input* registers, the *working* memory, and *output* registers of *M* are discerned. Connections between cells form an additional structure *K* of *E*. Each cell can contain a symbol from an alphabet of the language of the machine *M* or it can be empty. In what follows, we consider inductive Turing machine with a structured memory. Note that adding additional structure to a linear tape, it is possible to build many (even an infinite number of) tapes of different dimensions.

Another model, which has the computing power of Oracle Turing machines, is an advice-taking Turing machine (Balcazar *et al.*, 1988; Schöning, 1988).

An *advice-taking Turing machine* is a Turing machine enhanced with a tape where the values of the advice function are stored $f(x)$ and with the possibility to access the tape with the advice in constant time and read from it the value of its advice function $f(x)$ also in constant time.

In essence, the construction of an advice-taking Turing machine coincides with the contemporary formalization of an Oracle Turing machine (Homer and Selman, 2011; Soare, 2015).

However, in the theory of relative computability and complexity, only a special class of advice function have been used. In this context, an *advice function f(x)* is a function, the values of which depend only on the length of x and are written on a special tape of a Turing machine.

Advice functions provide external information to the machines, just as Oracles are doing. Thus, an advice function is an Oracle of a special type and the tape with the values of the advice function is also some kind of an Oracle. However, the information provided by an Oracle may depend on the actual input, whereas the information provided by such a restricted advice function used in advice-taking Turing machines does not because only the length of the input matters (Balcazar *et al.*, 1988; Schöning, 1988). Consequently, advice-taking Turing machines such a restricted advice function are equivalent only to a subclass of all Oracle Turing machines.

The feature that the value of the advice $f(x)$ can be obtained by the machine in constant time (while $f(x)$ can be an intractable or even undecidable function) essentially increases the power and efficiency of an advice-taking Turing machine in comparison with a conventional Turing machine. For instance, an advice-taking Turing machine can calculate in polynomial time many functions that a regular Turing machine cannot (including some intractable ones).

Advice-taking Turing machines are important in complexity theory because definitions and results are often based on special Turing machines that can determine information from the Oracle in constant time.

The theory of relative computability, Oracle Turing machines and advice-taking Turing machines provide a good mathematical framework for many cases of database or online computing just as conventional Turing machines provide one for offline computing processes, such as batch processing (Soare, 2015). This reflects the situation that Oracle Turing machines and advice-taking Turing machines acquire higher computing power from outer sources, such as an Oracle, although in the theoretical model these sources may be attached to the abstract automaton.

In contrast to this, inductive Turing machines achieve higher computing power due to their inner organization (structure), which is also described and assembled in a constructive way, i.e., this structure is built by an automaton (Burgin, 2005).

Computational Oracles (in the sense of Turing and in a more general sense) have been also used in other mathematical models of automata and computations such as inductive Turing machines with Oracles, limit Turing machines with Oracles (Burgin, 2005) and evolutionary Turing machines with Oracles (Burgin and Eberbach, 2009).

At the same time, computational theory and practice extended the concept of an Oracle in computer science making it closer to the historical understanding of Oracles. For instance, in Burgin (2005a), it is explained that a supercomputer can play the role of an Oracle for an average computer due to the fact that the computing power of the supercomputer can be much higher than that of the average computer. Information that both the supercomputer and the average computer have is computable. However, after one-hour work, for example, the supercomputer can provide information such that the average computer will need ten years to work out.

A database can also play the role of an Oracle for an individual or computer, especially, when this database contains data that come from a random source and thus, are incomputable (Burgin, 2005a; Soare, 2015).

In mathematics, the first introduction of Oracles essentially different from Turing Oracles happened in the area of matroids, which are abstract combinatorial structures used for describing linear dependencies between vectors in a vector space or the spanning trees of a graph. Namely, a matroid oracle is a subroutine through which an algorithm may access a matroid. As matroids are finite structures, information provided by matroid oracles is recursively computable, while information provided by Turing machine oracles is not recursively computable. Matroid oracles appeared in the earliest algorithmic work on matroids (Edmonds, 1965a; 1971).

There are optimization algorithms that utilize Oracle (Vondrak, 2008). However, these Oracles are different from Oracles in Turing machines. For instance, the value oracle model provides access to the values $w_i(S)$ of the utility functions w_i through a black box called the value Oracle. Each utility function $w_i : 2^{[m]} \to \boldsymbol{R}^+$ assigns the value $w_i(S)$ for a given set S of possible choices from the set m. However, in contrast to functions values of which are provided by Turing Oracles, utility functions are recursively computable only these computations can be too complicated and it becomes more efficient to use Oracles.

More general Oracles are employed in submodular optimization where oracles provide access to the submodular function and sometimes, to the list of constraints. Submodular optimization has applications combinatorial auctions, in which, n players compete for m items with different values for different players. Similar to matroid Oracles, optimization Oracles also provide information about recursively computable functions. The role of optimization Oracles is not to make more functions computable but to make computations more efficient and extend the scope of tractable problems when they provide information about solutions of intractable problems.

In addition to abstract Oracles in computer science and software (algorithmic) Oracles in computational mathematics, hardware Oracles have been studied and built in computer technology. For instance, the Oracle based computing paradigm called DIME network architecture that has been successfully used to implement self-managing distributed systems (Burgin and Mikkilineni, 2014; Burgin *et al.*, 2015; Mikkilineni *et al.*, 2012). A DIME network is represented by a grid automaton with such nodes as DIME units, servers, routers, etc. Each DIME unit is modeled by a basic automaton A with an Oracle O. The automaton A models the DIME basic processors P_i, while the Oracle O models the DIME agent DA. The Oracle O in a DIME unit knows the intent of the algorithm (along with the context, constraints, communi-cations and control of the algorithm) the basic automaton A is executing under its influence and has the visibility of available resources and the needs of the automaton A as it executes its function. In addition, the Oracle also has the knowledge about alternate courses of action available to facilitate the evolution of the computation to achieve its intent.

All considered cases demonstrate explicit utilization of Oracles in computer science and mathematics. However, there was also implicit exploitation of Oracles in these disciplines. Namely, the whole idea of reduction in computer science as well as related subrecursive hierarchies are based on specific Oracles.

Indeed, computer scientists construct subrecursive hierarchies utilizing different kinds of reduction (Basu, 1970; Zemke, 1975). A problem P (a set A or a function f) is reduced to a problem Q (a set A or a function g) if it is possible to solve the problem P (recognize the set A or compute the function f) allowing access to solutions of the problem Q (values of the indication function of the set A or values of the function g) as an oracle. In this case, the function f is called *computable relative to the function g*. If computation of the function f includes access to the values of the indication function of the set A, then f is called *computable in A*.

Examples of reducibility relation between the sets are "being polynomial time computable in" and "being (Kalmar) elementary in."

Each reducibility relation ρ in a set of problems (sets or functions) induces the corresponding equivalence relation in the same set. Namely, two problems (sets or functions) are ρ-equivalent if the first problem (set or function) is ρ-reducible to the second one and the second one is ρ-reducible to the first one. Classes of ρ-equivalent problems (sets or functions) are called the *degrees* of the reducibility relation ρ and form a hierarchy used to define degrees of unsolvability and complexity classes.

There are various kinds of reducibility relations in computer science (Post, 1943; Ladner *et al.*, 1975; Rogers, 1987):

✧ A *Turing reduction* of a problem (set or function) A to a problem (set or function) B is utilization of an oracle for B in solving (deciding or computing) A with a Turing machine.

✧ A *polynomial-time Turing reduction* of a problem (set or function) A to a problem (set or function) B is utilization of an oracle for B in solving (deciding, accepting or computing) A with a Turing machine T working in polynomial time, i.e., there is a polynomial $p(x)$ such that $x \in A$ if and only if T computes (accepts) x with B as its Oracle within $p(x)$ steps.

✧ A *log-space Turing reduction* of a problem (set or function) A to a problem (set or function) B is utilization of an oracle for *B* in solving (deciding or computing) *A* with a Turing machine working with log-space.

✧ A *many-to-one reduction* of a set *A* to a set *B* implies that there is a computable function *f* and an element *n* is in *A* if and only if *f*(*n*) is in *B*, i.e., *B* is a potential Oracle for *A* and *f* is the Oracle *access function*.

✧ A *one-to-one reduction* of a set *A* to a set *B* implies that there is a computable one-to-one function *f* and an element *n* is in *A* if and only if *f*(*n*) is in *B*, i.e., *B* is a potential Oracle for *A* and *f* is the Oracle *access function*.

✧ A *polynomial-time many-to-one reduction* of a set *A* to a set *B* implies that an element *n* is in *A* if and only if *f*(*n*) is in *B*, with the access function *f* computed in polynomial time, i.e., *B* is a potential Oracle for *A* accessible in polynomial time.

✧ A *truth table reduction* of a set *A* to a set *B* restricts utilization of the Oracle in such a way that all of its oracle queries are presented at the same time, together with a Boolean function (a truth table) which, when given the answers to the queries, will produce the final answer of the problem.

✧ A *positive reduction* of a set *A* to a set *B* is a truth-table reduction of *A* to *B* in a way that it is possible to compute for every *x* a formula consisting of atoms of the form *B*(0), *B*(1),... combined by logical operations & and ∨.

✧ A *disjunctive reduction* of a set *A* to a set *B* is a truth-table reduction of *A* to *B* in a way that it is possible to compute for every *x* a formula consisting of atoms of the form *B*(0), *B*(1),... combined by the logical operation ∨.

✧ A *conjunctive reduction* of a set *A* to a set *B* is a truth-table reduction of *A* to *B* in a way that it is possible to compute for every *x* a formula consisting of atoms of the form *B*(0), *B*(1),... combined by the logical operation &.

✧ An *arithmetical reduction* of a set *A* to a set *B* is performed by a formula of Peano arithmetic with *B* as a parameter, which plays the role of an Oracle.

✧ A *hyperarithmetical reduction* of a set A to a set B is performed by recognition (decision) of the set A using the α-iterated Turing jump of B for a recursive ordinal α as the Oracle access function.

Each type of reducibility utilizes a specific type of Oracles. These types are defined by three parameters, which describe:

1. what Oracles are doing
2. how Oracles function
3. how the access to the Oracle is organized (functions)

3. Diversity of Oracles: A methodological analysis

To analyze the variety of Oracles, we treat an Oracle M as a system with definite properties with respect to another system T, which can be a human being or an artificial information processing system such as a computer, cell phone, smart phone or computer network. As the Athenian historian Thucyclides (*c.* 460-400 B.C.E.) pointed out, there were "oracles of various kinds" (cf. Black, 2014). In two previous sections, we saw that an Oracle could be:

- a person, e.g., Pythia in ancient Greece or druids in ancient Wales
- a site, e.g., the ancient Oracles of Zeus were areas where priests unraveled the wind rustling through the trees
- special objects for divination, e.g., Urim and Thummim in ancient Israel or oracle bones in ancient China
- a collection of written utterances, e.g., the Sibylline Oracles
- an utterance that contains some unknown information, e.g., prediction of future events
- a person without a body in India
- a spirit in Tibet
- a set in computer science
- a program in computational mathematics
- an algorithm in applied mathematics
- a function in computer science

In this context, it is possible to discern various types and sorts of Oracles. We organize these types and sorts in several classifications starting with the functional typology. Traditionally, it is assumed that the function of Oracles has been providing necessary information to other systems. However, here we assume that Oracles are characterized as systems with more information or with better information than other systems have but due to this advantage, Oracles can perform various functions. This brings us to the following classification.

Functional classification of Oracles:

1. An *informative Oracle M* for *T* is a system that provides some necessary information for *T*.

2. A *performing Oracle M* for *T* is a system operation of which improves functioning of *T*.

3. A *service Oracle M* for *T* is a system that provides services for *T* that cannot be done by *T*.

The functional classification of Oracles describes functions or roles of Oracles.

Let us consider some examples.

Example 3.1. Pythia in ancient Greece and druids in ancient Wales were informative Oracles.

Example 3.2. Oracles in Turing machines are informative Oracles (cf., for example, Rogers, 1987).

Example 3.3. Oracles in the distributed intelligent managed element (DIME) network architecture are performing Oracles (Burgin and Mikkilineni, 2014). For instance, a DIME Oracle can control functioning of DIME basic computers.

Example 3.4. Some (but not all) inductive Turing machines can work as service Oracles for Turing machines executing different tasks more efficiently than Turing machines (Burgin, 2005). The reason for higher computing power is the higher level of modeling mental activity achieved by inductive Turing machines in comparison with Turing machines. While a Turing machine formalizes the work of an accountant or a human computer, an inductive Turing machine formalizes the work of a scientist or mathematician.

Example 3.5. The Oracle of Asclepius at Epidaurus (Hager, 2010), where the sick were treated, was a service Oracle.

Example 3.6. When Oracles from ancient Greece gave advice, they played the role of a service Oracle.

There are different types of Oracles in each class of the functional classification.

Temporal classification of informative Oracles:

1. A *one-time Oracle M* for a system *T* informs *T* only about one unknown event.

2. A *temporary Oracle M* for a system *T* informs *T* about unknown events in some time interval.

3. A *permanent Oracle M* for *T* informs *T* about arbitrary events.

Time-oriented classification of informative Oracles:

1. A *retrospective Oracle M* for a system *T* informs *T* about events in the past unknown to *T*.

2. A *present-time Oracle M* for a system *T* informs *T* about current events unknown to *T*.

3. A *prospective Oracle M* for *T* informs *T* about future events.

Let us consider some examples.

Example 3.7. It is possible to find an interesting example of a one-time Oracle in the following story. A Rothschild's agent brought to Nathan Mayer Rothschild, a top banker of England in the 19th century, information about the coalition victory at the Battle of Waterloo before anybody else in England was able to get this information (Ferguson, 1999). Rothschild used this information to speculate on the stock exchange and make a vast fortune. Thus, his agent became a one-time Oracle to Rothschild. This agent was also a retrospective Oracle because he brought information about the past.

Example 3.8. Oracles in ancient Greece and Rome were usually prospective Oracles as people who came to Oracles wanted to know about the future.

Example 3.9. Contemporary TV and the Internet usually play the role of a present-time Oracle when they inform people in America what is happening in Europe or in Asia.

Note that it is possible to split each class in the considered classifications into several subclasses. For instance, prospective Oracles contain the following subclasses:

     – Oracles that predict future

     – Oracles that outline possible consequences of some actions

     – Oracles that suggest possible (or necessary) actions

The next classification imparts what is known about the Oracle.

Organizational classification of Oracles:

1.   A *black-box Oracle M* is a system for which it is not described where its results come from.

2.   A *descriptive Oracle M* is a system for which it is described where its results come from but it is not specified how it gets its results.

3.   A *constructive Oracle M* for *T* is a system functioning of which is described in detail.

Let us consider some examples.

Example 3.10. Turing Oracles are black-box Oracles (Turing, 1939).

Example 3.11. Oracles in advice-taking Turing machines, i.e., tapes with values of some function, are descriptive Oracles.

Example 3.12. Oracles in the Distributed Intelligent Managed Elements are constructive Oracles (Burgin and Mikkilineni, 2014).

There are three levels of constructive Oracles:

1.   Functioning of the Oracle is described in the form of an algorithm.

2.   Functioning of the Oracle is portrayed in the form of a program for an automaton.

3.   Functioning of the Oracle is specified in the form of an automaton.

Let us consider some examples.

Example 3.13. The value oracle from optimization algorithms described in the previous section is a constructive Oracle, functioning of which is described in the form of an algorithm (Vondrak, 2008).

Example 3.14. The value oracle from optimization algorithms described in the previous section is a constructive Oracle, functioning of which can be also described in the form of a computer program (Vondrak, 2008).

Example 3.15. Oracles in the Distributed Intelligent Managed Elements are constructive Oracles, functioning of which is specified in the form of an automaton (Burgin and Mikkilineni, 2014).

Operational classification of Oracles:

1.   A *simplification Oracle M* for *T* is a system that solves some problems more efficiently (with less complexity) than *T*.

2.   An *augmentation Oracle M* for *T* is a system such that there are problems intractable for *T* but tractable for *M*.

3. An *extension Oracle M* for *T* is a system such that there are problems unsolvable for *T* but solvable for *M*.

The operational classification of Oracles describes what Oracles are doing.

Let us consider some examples.

Example 3.16. Different (but not all) Turing machines can serve as extension Oracles for finite automata. Note that that some Turing machines compute functions computable by finite automata and thus, they cannot be extension Oracles for these automata.

Example 3.17. Different (but not all) nondeterministic Turing machines can serve as simplification Oracles for deterministic Turing machines.

Example 3.18. Different (but not all) inductive Turing machines can work as extension Oracles for Turing machines (Burgin, 2005).

Example 3.19. Oracles in Turing machines are extension Oracles for Turing machines (Rogers, 1987).

Note that the operational classification of Oracles is orthogonal to the functional classification of Oracles. It means that each class of one classification is naturally divided into subclasses corresponding to the other classification. For instance, informative Oracles can be augmentation, extension or simplification Oracles.

Representational classification of Oracles:

1. A *functional Oracle F* for *T* is a function that can give information such that *T* does not have.

2. An *algorithmic Oracle M* for *T* is an algorithm such that there are problems intractable for *T* but tractable for *M*.

3. An *automaton Oracle M* for *T* is an automaton such that there are problems unsolvable for *T* but solvable for *M*.

The representational classification of Oracles elucidates in what form Oracles exist.

Let us consider some examples.

Example 3.20. Advice functions from advice-taking Turing machines described in the previous section are functional Oracles (Balcazar *et al.*, 1988; Schöning, 1988).

Example 3.21. The value oracle from optimization algorithms described in the previous section is an algorithmic Oracle (Vondrak, 2008).

Example 3.22. Oracles in the Distributed Intelligent Managed Elements (DIMEs), which are basic building blocks of a new network paradigm called the DIME network architecture described in the previous section, are automaton Oracles (Burgin and Mikkilineni, 2014; Burgin *et al.*, 2015; Mikkilineni *et al.*, 2012).

Domain types of Oracles:

1.   A *function-oriented Oracle* for a system $\mathbf{F} = \langle F, A \rangle$ of a set of functions F and a set of construction operations A is a function F that cannot be constructed using functions from F and construction operations from A.

2.   An *algorithmic-oriented Oracle* M for a system $\mathbf{A} = \langle B, A \rangle$ of a set of algorithms B and a set of construction operations A such that there are problems intractable (undecidable) for T but tractable (decidable) for M.

3.   An *automaton-oriented Oracle* M for an automaton T is a system (e.g., an automaton) such that there are problems unsolvable for T but solvable for M.

The domain classification of Oracles clarifies in what domain Oracles function.

Let us consider some examples.

Example 3.23. Oracles in Turing machines are automaton-oriented Oracles (Rogers, 1987).

Example 3.24. Oracles in the Distributed Intelligent Managed Elements are automaton-oriented Oracles (Burgin and Mikkilineni, 2014; Burgin *et al.*, 2015; Mikkilineni *et al.*, 2012).

Example 3.25. The value oracle from optimization algorithms described in the previous section is an algorithmic-oriented Oracle (Vondrak, 2008).

Example 3.26. Matroid oracles described in the previous section are algorithmic-oriented Oracles (Korte and Schrader, 1981).

Example 3.27. Regressive functions used in (Dekker and Ellentuck, 1974) to relativize the notion of a recursive function are function-oriented Oracles.

Different specific types of Oracles were introduced before. In computer science and theory of algorithms, automata and computation, two types of Oracles have been considered: function Oracles (Burgin, 2005) and set Oracles (Rogers, 1987).

A *function Oracle* is a system (a device, black box, person, whatso-ever) that contains knowledge about the values of some function $f(n)$.

Often, oracles are considered not for functions but for sets.

A *set Oracle* is a system (a device, black box, person, etc.) that contains knowledge about membership in some set X.

Usually, function Oracles and set Oracles are used in computations and complexity theory providing the base for relative computations and hierarchies of degrees (Basu, 1970; Post, 1948; Rogers, 1987; Shoenfield, 1959; Soare, 2015).

In combinatorial optimization, two types of Oracles are used (Vondrak, 2008):

- A *value Oracle* answers the questions of the following type:
  What is the value of $w_i(S)$ of the utility function w_i?
- A *demand Oracle* answers the questions of the following type:

Given an assignment of prices to items $p: [m] \rightarrow \mathbf{R}$, which set S maximizes $w_i(S) - \Sigma_{j \in S} \, p_j$?

There is also an assortment of *matroid Oracles*, which are classified by the type of information they provide (cf., for example, Korte and Schrader, 1981):

• An *independence Oracle* takes as its input a set of matroid elements, and returns as output a Boolean value, which is equal to 1 if the given set is independent and equal to 0 otherwise.

• A *rank Oracle* takes as its input a set of matroid elements, and returns as its output a numerical value, the rank of the given set.

• A *basis Oracle* takes as its input a set of matroid elements, and returns as output a Boolean value, which is equal to 1 if the given set is a basis and equal to 0 otherwise.

• A *circuit Oracle* takes as its input a set of matroid elements, and returns as output a Boolean value, which is equal to 1 if the given set is a circuit and equal to 0 otherwise.

• Three types of *closure Oracle* have been used: the Oracle of the first type tests if a given element belongs to the closure of a given set, the Oracle of the second type returns the closure of the set, and the Oracle of the third type tests whether a given set is closed.

•   A *spanning Oracle* takes as its input a set of matroid elements, and returns as output a Boolean value, which is equal to 1 if the given set is spanning (i.e., it contains a basis and has the same rank as the whole matroid) and equal to 0 otherwise.

•   A *girth Oracle* takes as its input a set of matroid elements, and returns as its output a numerical value, the size of the smallest circuit within that set (or ∞ if the given set is independent).

•   A *port Oracle* for a fixed element of the matroid takes as its input a set of matroid elements, and returns as output a Boolean value, which is equal to 1 if the given set contains a circuit that includes x and equal to 0 otherwise.

Algorithms on graphs use (cf., for example, (Hermelin *et al.*, 2011; Thorup, 2004)):*compact oracles*

- *distance oracles*
- $(1 + \varepsilon)$-*distance oracles*
- *dynamic distance oracles*
- *approximate distance oracles*
- *dynamic vertex-color distance oracles*

The concept of an Oracle is associated with the following structures, which facilitate formalization of this concept in the following section. We have two types of Oracles: one-way and two-way Oracles.

A *one-way Oracle O* has the structure

$$\text{System } R \xleftarrow{\quad \text{impact} \quad} \text{Oracle } O$$

This structure is called a *fundamental triad* or a *named set* (Burgin, 2011; 2012). For instance, this structure exists when an Oracle provides information to R without requests from R.

A *two-way Oracle O* has the structure

$$\text{System } R \xrightleftharpoons{\quad \text{impact} \quad} \text{Oracle } O$$

This structure is called a *bidirectional fundamental triad* or a *bidirectional named set*. For instance, this structure exists when an

Oracle provides information to R when R requests it. In such a way, Oracles in Turing machines with oracles work (Soare, 2015). Although any bidirectional named set is a composition of ordinary named sets, it is a fundamental structure such as a set, a category, a fuzzy set or a multiset.

4. A mathematical theory of Oracles

It is possible to formalize the concept of an Oracle in general and its specializations considered in the previous section, in particular. As the main functions of traditional Oracles are connected to information, in what follows we consider only information processing systems as Oracles assuming that in the formalized shape they have a mathematical representation, for example, in the form of abstract automata, functions or computing machines. The goal is to provide a sound mathematical background for construction and exploration of Oracles, their properties and functioning. In our study, we do not limit ourselves by conventional types of automata (computing machines), such as Turing machines or contemporary computers, but understand an information processing system as a system that given certain information (in the form of data or knowledge) as input, occasionally produces some information (also in the form of data or knowledge) as its output (e.g., as an answer to the given question). For instance, an Oracle receives a question as its input, processes it and gives an answer to this question as its output. This is how the majority of traditional Oracles worked. Note that even the best Oracles were not able to answer to all questions. Therefore, this example shows how traditional oracles are included in our schema and why our model is applicable to all known examples of Oracles. The next stages of the mathematical theory of Oracles are concerned with the quality of answers (such as relevance, efficiency, exactness or generality), as well as with the methods of achieving the results (e.g., giving answers or producing outputs). Here we describe only a part of the first stage of the theory. Other issues of the mathematical theory of Oracles are presented elsewhere.

Besides, we study here only operational types of Oracles, which comprise simplification Oracles, augmentation Oracles and extension

Oracles. Simplification Oracles includes five subtypes: total simplification Oracles, strong partial simplification Oracles, covering simplification Oracles, partial covering simplification Oracles and partial simplification Oracles.

Definition 4.1. A system M is a *total simplification Oracle* (TSO) for a system T in a domain D if the following condition is satisfied

$$\forall x \in D \ (T(x)! \ \& \ M(x)! \ \& \ (M(x) = T(x)) \ \& \ (c(M(x)) \prec c(T(x)))))$$

Here:

$c: A \times D \to L$ is a computational complexity measure;

$\prec$ is a partial order in the set of computational complexity measures (cf., Burgin, 2005; Arora and Barak, 2009);

the expression $A(x)!$ means that the system $A \in \{M, T\}$ gives the result given the input x or in other words, A solves the problem enclosed in x and we say that A is definable for x;

the condition $\forall x \in D \ (M(x)!)$ means that the system M is total in the domain D, i.e., M gives the result (an output) for any input x from the domain D.

For instance, when x is a question, $A(x)!$ means that A gives an answer to the question x, while $\neg A(x)!$ means that A does not give an answer to the question x. $\forall x \in D \ (A(x)!)$ means that A gives an answer to all questions of some kind (e.g., in some area) D.

Note that the relation $c(M(x)) \prec c(T(x))$ may mean simply $c(M(x)) < c(T(x))$ or $c(M(x)) \leq c(T(x))$. On the other hand, the relation $c(M(x)) \prec c(T(x))$ may also mean $k \cdot c(M(x)) \leq c(T(x))$ for some constant k or $c(M(x))^n \leq c(T(x))$ for some number n or $2^{c(M(x))} \leq c(T(x))$.

Informally, a system M is a total simplification Oracle for a system T in a domain D if both systems are defined for all input data from the domain D, for these data they solve the same problem and give the same results when their inputs are the same, but the system M is doing this in a (much) simpler way than the system T.

For instance, if the computational complexity measure c is time complexity and a Turing machine M computes the function $sq(n) = n^2$; twice as fast as a Turing machine T computes the function, then the machine M is a total simplification Oracle for the machine T in a domain N.

Note that it is possible to treat a static complexity measure (Burgin, 2005), e.g., the length of the program or of a system description, as a computational complexity measure that is the same (constant) for all inputs.

Example 4.1. Homer and Selman (2011) study computability using a computational model in which a subroutine for one problem in order to efficiently solve another problem. Naturally, the assisting subroutine plays the role of a simplification Oracle for the main program.

Searching for simpler solutions of a problem, it is reasonable to achieve simplification for an essential number (set) of input data. Thus, to define partial simplification Oracles, we introduce the property of being a sufficiently big (essential) subset of a given set. In the formal notation, we denote this property by the expression (predicate) $b_D(C)$ means the statement that the set C is sufficiently big (essential) in D. This property has many different realizations and forms as the following examples demonstrate.

Example 4.2. When D is infinite, the statement $b_D(C)$ is true for a subset C of D, if the C is also infinite.

Example 4.3. In the set N of all natural numbers, cofinite subsets are sufficiently big (essential), where a subset of N is cofinite when it contains almost all natural numbers, i.e., all natural numbers except a finite number of them.

Example 4.4. Let us consider a set D and an element a from D. Then for $C \subseteq D$, we define that the predicate $b_D(C)$ is valid when $a \in C$.

Example 4.5. Let us consider a set D and a subset X of D. Then for $C \subseteq D$, we define that the predicate $b_D(C)$ is valid when $X \subseteq C$.

Definition 4.2. A system M is a *partial simplification Oracle* (PSO) for a system T in a domain D if the following condition is satisfied

$$\exists C \subseteq D \, (b_D(C)) \, \& \, \forall x \in C \, (T(x)! \, \& \, M(x)! \, \& \, (M(x) = T(x)) \, \& \, (c(M(x)) \prec c(T(x)))\,)$$

Informally, a system M is a partial simplification Oracle for a system T in a domain D if there is a sufficiently big subset C of the domain D, both systems are defined for all input data from the domain C, for these data they solve the same problem and give the same results when their inputs are the same, but the system M is doing this in a (much) simpler way than the system T.

Note that any total simplification Oracle for T is also a partial simplification Oracle for T.

Definition 4.2 implies the following results.

Lemma 4.1. *A system M is a partial simplification Oracle for a system T in a domain D if and only if it is a total simplification Oracle in some sufficiently big subset of D for the system T.*

In particular, if any set is a sufficiently big subset of itself, which is a very natural condition, then any total simplification Oracle in a domain D is a partial simplification Oracle in the same domain.

Lemma 4.1 implies the following result.

Lemma 4.2. *If a system M is a total simplification Oracle for a system T in a domain D, then it is a partial simplification Oracle in any superset H of D for the system T such that D is a sufficiently big subset of H.*

For instance, when cofinite subsets are sufficiently big in the set N of all natural numbers and a system M is a total simplification Oracle in a domain $D \subseteq N$ for a system T, then M is a partial simplification Oracle for the system T in any set of natural numbers $H \supseteq D$.

Lemma 4.3. *If a system M is a total simplification Oracle for a system T in domains D and A, then it is a total simplification Oracle for the system T in the domain $A \cup D$.*

Let us assume that (**Condition I**) if a set C is a sufficiently big subset of D, i.e., $b_D(C)$ is true and $C \subseteq H \subseteq D$, then C is sufficiently big in H, i.e., $b_D(C)$ implies $b_H(C)$.

Lemma 4.4. *If $C \subseteq H \subseteq D$, a system M is a partial simplification Oracle for a system T in the domain D and a total simplification Oracle for the system T in the domain C, then it is a partial simplification Oracle for the system T in the domain H.*

Indeed, by Condition I, the set C is sufficiently big in the set H and by Lemma 4.2, M is a partial simplification Oracle for the system T in the domain H.

Let us assume validity of **Condition II**:
$$b_D(C)) \text{ and } b_A(B)) \text{ imply } b_{D \cup A}(B \cup C))$$

Lemma 4.5. *If a system M is a partial simplification Oracle for a system T in domains D and A, then it is a partial simplification Oracle for the system T in the domain $A \cup D$.*

Proof. Let us assume that a system M is a partial simplification Oracle for a system T in a domain D and in a domain A. Then by Definition 4.2, we have

$$\exists C \subseteq D \ (b_D(C)) \ \& \ \forall x \in C \ (T(x)! \ \& \ M(x)! \ \& \ (M(x) = T(x)) \ \& \ (c(M(x)) \prec c(T(x))))$$

and

$$\exists B \subseteq A \ (b_A(B)) \ \& \ \forall x \in B \ (A(x)! \ \& \ T(x)! \ \& \ (A(x) = T(x)) \ \& \ (c(T(x)) \prec c(A(x))))$$

By Lemma 4.1, M is a total simplification Oracle for the system T in the domain C and in the domain B. By Lemma 4.3, M is a total simplification Oracle for the system T in the domain $B \cup C$. By Condition II, the set $C \cup B$ is sufficiently big in the set $A \cup D$. Therefore, by Lemma 4.1, M is a partial simplification Oracle for the system T in the domain $A \cup D$.

The lemma is proved.

Definition 4.3. A system M is a *strong partial simplification Oracle* (SPSO) for a system T in a domain D if the following condition is satisfied

$$\exists C \subseteq D \ (\ b_D(C)) \ \& \ \forall x \in C \ \forall z \in D \ (\ T(z)! \ \& \ M(z)! \ \& \ (M(z) = T(z)) \ \& \ (c(M(x)) \prec c(T(x))))$$

Informally, a system M is a strong partial simplification Oracle for a system T in a domain D if both systems are defined for all input data from the domain D, there is a sufficiently big subset C of the domain D, for these data they solve the same problem and give the same results when their inputs are the same, but the system M is doing this in a (much) simpler way than the system T.

Definitions imply the following results.

Lemma 4.6. (a) *Any strong partial simplification Oracle for T in a domain D is also a partial simplification Oracle for T in the domain D.*
(b) *Any total simplification Oracle for T in a domain D is also a strong partial simplification Oracle for T in the domain D.*

Lemma 4.7. *If Condition II is satisfied and a system M is a strong partial simplification Oracle for a system T in domains D and A, then it is a strong partial simplification Oracle for the system T in the domain A $\cup D$.*

Proof. The proof is similar to the proof of Lemma 4.5.

Lemma 4.8. *If a system M is a total simplification Oracle for a system T in a domain D, then it is a partial simplification Oracle in any superset H of D for the system T such that D is a sufficiently big subset of H such that*

$$\forall z \in H \ (T(z)! \ \& \ M(z)! \ \& \ (M(z) = T(z)))$$

Theorem 4.1. *If a system M is a total simplification Oracle for a system T in a domain D and the system T is a total simplification Oracle for a system A in the domain D, then the system M is a total simplification Oracle for the system A in the domain D.*

Proof. Let us assume that a system M is a total simplification Oracle in a domain D for a system T and the system T is a total simplification Oracle in the domain D for a system A. Then by Definition 4.1, we have

$$\forall x \in D \ (T(x)! \ \& \ M(x)! \ \& \ (M(x) = T(x)) \ \& \ (c(M(x)) \prec c(T(x))))$$

and

$$\forall x \in D \ (A(x)! \ \& \ T(x)! \ \& \ (A(x) = T(x)) \ \& \ (c(T(x)) \prec c(A(x))))$$

As $\prec$ is a partial order in the set of computational complexity measures, we have

$$\forall x \in D \ (\ c(M(x)) \prec c(A(x)))$$

and consequently,

$$\forall x \in D \ (A(x)! \ \& \ M(x)! \ \& \ T(x)! \ \& \ (A(x) = M(x) = T(x)) \ \& \ (c(M(x)) \prec c(A(x))))$$

This predicate implies

$$\forall x \in D \ (A(x)! \ \& \ M(x)! \ \& \ (A(x) = M(x)) \ \& \ (c(M(x)) \prec c(A(x))))$$

It means that the system M is a total simplification Oracle for the system A in the domain D.

The theorem is proved.

Theorem 4.1 means that the relation "to be a total simplification Oracle" is transitive.

Besides, if a system M is a total simplification Oracle for the system T in the domain D, then the system T cannot be a total simplification Oracle for the system M in the domain D when the relation $\prec$ is a strict partial order where a strict partial order on a set X is a antireflexive and transitive relation.

Thus, Theorem 4.1 implies the following result.

Corollary 4.1. *If the relation $\prec$ is a strict partial order, then the relation "to be a total simplification Oracle" also is a strict partial order.*

Remark 4.1. For partial simplification Oracles, Theorem 4.1 is not always true as the following example demonstrates.

Example 4.6. Let Odd $= \{1,3,\ldots\}$ be the set of all odd numbers and Et $= \{8,16,32,\ldots\}$ be the set of all natural numbers divisible by 8. Assume the statement $b_N(C)$ is true for a subset C of N, if the C is infinite. Thus, both sets Odd and Et are sufficiently big in N.

Now let us take three Turing machines M, T and A such that: (1) the machine M is defined only in the set Odd where it computes the function $e(n) = n^2$; (2) the machine A is defined only in the set Et where it computes the same function $e(n) = n^2$; (3) the machine T is defined in the whole set N where it also computes the same function $e(n) = n^2$; (4) for numbers where both machines M and T are defined, M computes twice as fast as T, and (5) for numbers where both machines A and T are defined, T computes twice as fast as A.

Taking time complexity as the computational complexity measure c, we see that the machine M is a partial simplification Oracle in a domain Odd for the machine T and the machine T is a partial simplification Oracle in the domain Et for the machine A. However, the machine M is not a partial simplification Oracle in the domain D for the machine A because the domains where they are defined do not intersect.

Remark 4.2. For partial simplification Oracles, Corollary 4.1 is not always true as the following example demonstrates because it is possible that a system Q is a partial simplification Oracle for a system T in the domain D and at the same time, T is a partial simplification Oracle for the system Q in the domain D.

For instance, let us assume that the statement $b_N(C)$ is true for a subset C of N, if the C is also infinite and take two automata Q and T that compute the same function $f(n)$, e.g., $f(n) = 2^n$. However, Q computes faster the values of f for odd numbers n, while T computes faster the values of f for even numbers n. Then the system Q is a partial simplification Oracle for the system T in the domain N and at the same time, T is a partial simplification Oracle for the system Q in the domain N.

However, under additional conditions, Theorem 4.1 and Corollary 4.1 become valid for partial simplification oracles. Namely, let us consider the following
Condition III:
$$\forall E, C \subseteq D \ (b_D(C) \ \& \ b_D(E)) \Rightarrow b_D(C \cap E)$$

i.e., intersection of two sufficiently big in D subsets is a sufficiently big subset of D

Theorem 4.2. *If the function $b_D(C)$ satisfies Condition III a domain D, then a (strong) partial simplification Oracle M for a system T in the domain D, which is a (strong) partial simplification Oracle for a system A in the domain D, is a (strong) partial simplification Oracle for a system A in the domain D.*

Proof. Let us assume that a system M is a partial simplification Oracle for a system T in a domain D and the system T is a partial simplification Oracle for a system A in a domain D. Then by Definition 4.2, we have
$$\exists C \subseteq D \ (b_D(C)) \ \& \ \forall x \in C \ (T(x)! \ \& \ M(x)! \ \& \ (M(x) = T(x)) \ \& \ (c(M(x)) \prec c(T(x))))$$

and

$$\exists B \subseteq D \ (b_D(B)) \ \& \ \forall x \in B \ (A(x)! \ \& \ T(x)! \ \& \ (A(x) = T(x)) \ \& \ (c(T(x)) \prec c(A(x))))$$

These predicates imply the following predicate

$$\forall x \in (B \cap C) \ (A(x)! \ \& \ T(x)! \ \& \ M(x)! \ \& \ (M(x) = T(x) = A(x)) \ \&$$
$$(c(M(x)) \prec c(T(x))) \ \& \ (c(T(x)) \prec c(A(x)))) \qquad (4.1)$$

As $\prec$ is a partial order, i.e., it is transitive, in the set of computational complexity measures, properties of classical logic and formula (4.1) imply the following predicate

$$\forall x \in B \cap C \ (A(x)! \ \& \ M(x)! \ \& \ (M(x) = A(x)) \ \& \ (c(M(x)) \prec c(A(x))))$$

By Condition III, the statement $b_D(B \cap C)$ is true, and we have

$$\exists X \subseteq D \ (b_D(X)) \ \& \ \forall x \in X \ (T(x)! \ \& \ M(x)! \ \& \ (M(x) = T(x)) \ \& \ (c(M(x))$$
$$\prec c(T(x))))$$

It means that the system M is a partial simplification Oracle in the domain D for the system A.

Similar reasoning gives us validity of conditions for strong partial simplification Oracle in the domain D. Namely, we have

$$\forall x \in B \cap C \ \forall z \in D \ (\ T(z)! \ \& \ M(z)! \ \& \ (M(z) = T(z)) \ \& \ (c(M(x)) \prec c(T(x))))$$

and

$$\exists X \subseteq D \ (\ b_D(X)) \ \& \ \forall x \in X \ \forall z \in D \ (\ T(z)! \ \& \ M(z)! \ \& \ (M(z) = T(z)) \ \&$$
$$(c(M(x)) \prec c(T(x))))$$

These conditions mean that the system M is a strong partial simplification Oracle for the system A in the domain D.

The theorem is proved.

Corollary 4.2. *If the system of sufficiently big in a domain D subsets is a filter, then a (strong) partial simplification Oracle M in the domain D for a system T, which is a (strong) partial simplification Oracle in the domain D for a system A, is a (strong) partial simplification Oracle in the domain D for the system A.*

Indeed, any filter satisfies Condition III (Kuratowski and Mostowski, 1967).

Corollary 4.3. *If the system of sufficiently big in a domain D subsets is a set ideal, then a (strong) partial simplification Oracle M in the domain D for a system T, which is a (strong) partial simplification Oracle in the domain D for a system A, is a (strong) partial simplification Oracle in the domain D for the system A.*

Indeed, any set ideal satisfies Condition III (Kuratowski and Mostowski, 1967).

Corollary 4.4. *If the system of sufficiently big in a domain D subsets is a set algebra, then a (strong) partial simplification Oracle M for a system T in the domain D, which is a (strong) partial simplification Oracle for a system A in the domain D, is a (strong) partial simplification Oracle for the system A in the domain D.*

Indeed, any set algebra satisfies Condition III (Kolmogorov and Fomin, 1999).

Theorem 4.3. *If the relation $\prec$ is a strict partial order and the system of sufficiently big in a domain D subsets satisfies Condition III, then the relation "to be a partial simplification Oracle" also is a strict partial order.*

Proof. We remind that a strict partial order in a set X is an asymmetric antireflexive transitive binary relation Q on X.

By Theorem 4.2, the relation "to be a partial simplification Oracle" is transitive.

As $\prec$ is a strict partial order, any system T cannot be a partial simplification Oracle for itself, that is, the relation "to be a partial simplification Oracle" is antireflexive.

To prove asymmetry, we assume that a system M is a partial simplification Oracle for a system T in a domain D and the system T is a partial simplification Oracle for the system M in a domain D. Then by Definition 4.2, we have

$$\exists C \subseteq D \ (b_D(C)) \ \& \ \forall x \in C \ (T(x)! \ \& \ M(x)! \ \& \ (M(x) = T(x)) \ \& \ (c(M(x)) \prec c(T(x))))$$

and

$$\exists B \subseteq D \ (b_D(B)) \ \& \ \forall x \in B \ (M(x)! \ \& \ T(x)! \ \& \ (M(x) = T(x)) \ \& \ (c(T(x)) \prec c(M(x))))$$

These conditions imply the following condition

$$\forall x \in B \cap C \ (T(x)! \ \& \ M(x)! \ \& \ (M(x) = T(x)) \ \& \ (c(M(x)) \prec c(T(x))) \ \& \ (c(T(x)) \prec c(M(x)))) \tag{4.2}$$

As $\prec$ is a strict partial order, formula (4.2) cannot be true demonstrating that our assumption also was not true. It means that the relation "to be a partial simplification Oracle" is asymmetric.

The theorem is proved.

Definitions imply the following result.

Theorem 4.4. *If $E \subseteq D$ and a system M is a total simplification Oracle for a system A in the domain D, then the system M is a total simplification Oracle for the system A in the domain E.*

Remark 4.2. For partial simplification oracles, Theorem 4.4 is not always true.

Let us take the set N of all natural numbers as the domain D, the domain $C = \{101,102,103,...\}$ and the domain $E = \{1,2,3,...,100\}$.

Assume the statement $b_N(X)$ is true for a subset X of N, if the X is infinite. Thus, the set C is sufficiently big in N and $E \subseteq N$.

Now let us take two Turing machines M and T such that: (1) the machine M computes the function $f(n) = n^{25}$; (2) the machine T also computes the same function $f(n) = n^{25}$; (3) for numbers larger than 100, M computes twice as fast as T, and (4) for numbers less than 100, T computes twice as fast as A.

Taking time complexity as the computational complexity measure c, we see that the machine M is a partial simplification Oracle for the machine T in the domain N but not in the domain E although, $E \subseteq N$.

However, under additional conditions, a weaker counterpart of Theorem 4.3 becomes valid for partial simplification oracles.

Theorem 4.5. *If the system of sufficiently big in a domain D subsets satisfies Conditions I and III, $E \subseteq D$, $b_D(E)$ is true and M is a partial simplification Oracle for a system T in the domain D, then the system M is a total simplification Oracle for the system T in some sufficiently big subset H of the set E.*

Proof. Let us assume that a system M is a partial simplification Oracle for a system T in a domain D. Then by Lemma 4.1, the system M is a total simplification Oracle for the system T in some sufficiently big subset K of D. By Condition III, the intersection $E \cap K$ is a sufficiently big subset of D, i.e., the statement $b_D(E \cap K)$ is true. By Condition I, the intersection $E \cap K$ is a sufficiently big subset of E, i.e., the statement $b_E(E \cap K)$ is true. By Theorem 4.4, the system M is a total simplification Oracle for the system T in the intersection $E \cap K$, which we can take as the set H.

The theorem is proved.

Lemma 4.1 and Theorem 4.5 imply the following result.

Corollary 4.5. *If the system of sufficiently big in D subsets satisfies Conditions I and III, $E \subseteq D$, the predicate $b_D(E)$ is true and M is a partial simplification Oracle for a system T in the domain D, then the system M is a partial simplification Oracle for the system T in the set E.*

Indeed, by Theorem 4.5 the system M is a total simplification Oracle for the system T in a sufficiently big subset H of the set E. Then by Lemma 4.1, the system M is a partial simplification Oracle for the system T in the domain E.

Corollary 4.6. *If the system of sufficiently big in a domain D subsets is a filter that satisfies Condition I, $E \subseteq D$, the predicate $b_D(E)$ is true and M is a partial simplification Oracle in the domain D for a system T, then the system M is a partial simplification Oracle for the system T in the set E.*

Indeed, any filter satisfies Condition III (Kuratowski and Mostowski, 1967).

Corollary 4.7. *If the system of sufficiently big in a domain D subsets is a set ideal that satisfies Condition I, $E \subseteq D$, the predicate $b_D(E)$ is true and M is a partial simplification Oracle in the domain D for a system T, then the system M is, a partial simplification Oracle for the system T in the set E.*

Indeed, any set ideal satisfies Condition III (Kuratowski and Mostowski, 1967).

Corollary 4.8. *If the system of sufficiently big in a domain D subsets is a set algebra that satisfies Condition I, $E \subseteq D$, the predicate $b_D(E)$ is true and M is a partial simplification Oracle in the domain D for a system T, then the system M is a partial simplification Oracle in some sufficiently big subset H of the set E for the system T.*

Indeed, any set algebra satisfies Condition III (Kolmogorov and Fomin, 1999).

Condition IV. If $C \subseteq H \subseteq D$, while $b_H(C)$ and $b_D(H)$ are true, then $b_D(C)$ is true.

Theorem 4.4. *If $H \subseteq D$, the predicate $b_D(H)$ is true and a total in D system M is a partial simplification Oracle for a system T in the domain H, then the system M is a partial simplification Oracle for the system T in the domain D.*

Proof. If the system M is a partial simplification Oracle for a system T in the domain H, then by Lemma 4.1, M is a total simplification Oracle for a system T in some sufficiently big subset C of H, i.e., the predicate $b_H(C)$ is true. Then by Condition IV, the predicate $b_D(C)$ is also true. Consequently, by Lemma 4.1, the system M is a partial simplification Oracle for the system T in the domain D.

The theorem is proved.

Definition 4.4. A system M is a *covering simplification Oracle* for a system T in a domain D if the following condition is satisfied

$\forall x \in D \ (T(x)! \rightarrow (M(x)! \ \& \ (M(x) = T(x))) \ \& \ (c(M(x)) \prec c(T(x)))))$

Informally, a system M is a covering simplification Oracle for a system T in a domain D if the system M is defined where the system T is defined in the domain D solving the same problem and giving the same results when their inputs are the same, but the system M is doing this in a (much) simpler way than the system T.

Definitions imply the following results.

Lemma 4.9. (a) *Any total simplification Oracle M for a system T in a domain D is a covering simplification Oracle for the system T in the same domain.*

(b) *Any covering simplification Oracle M in a domain D for a system T, which is total in a domain D, i.e., defined for all inputs from D, is a total simplification Oracle for the system T in the same domain.*

Many properties of covering simplification Oracles are similar to properties of total simplification Oracles.

Theorem 4.6. *If a system M is a covering simplification Oracle for a system T in a domain D and the system T is a covering simplification Oracle for a system A in the domain D, then the system M is a covering simplification Oracle for the system A in the domain D.*

Proof. Let us assume that a system M is a covering simplification Oracle in a domain D for a system T and the system T is a covering simplification Oracle in the domain D for a system A. Then by Definition 4.4, we have

$$\forall x \in D \ (T(x)! \rightarrow (M(x)! \ \& \ (M(x) = T(x))) \ \& \ (c(M(x)) \prec c(T(x)))))$$

and

$$\forall x \in D \ (A(x)! \rightarrow (T(x)! \ \& \ (A(x) = T(x))) \ \& \ (c(T(x)) \prec c(A(x)))))$$

As $\prec$ is a partial order in the set of computational complexity measures, we have

$$\forall x \in D \ (\ c(M(x)) \prec c(A(x)))$$

Besides, predicates

$$A(x)! \rightarrow (T(x)!$$

and

$$T(x)! \rightarrow (M(x)!$$

imply the predicate

$$A(x)! \rightarrow (M(x)!$$

In addition, equalities

$$A(x) = (T(x)$$

and

$$T(x) = (M(x)$$

imply the equality

$$A(x) = (M(x)$$

Consequently, we have

$$\forall x \in D \; (A(x)! \; \to \; (M(x)! \; \& \; (A(x) = M(x))) \; \& \; (c(M(x)) < c(A(x)))))$$

It means that the system M is a covering simplification Oracle for the system A in the domain D.

The theorem is proved.

Theorem 4.6 means that the relation "to be a covering simplification Oracle" is transitive.

Definition 4.5. A system M is a *partial covering simplification Oracle* for a system T in a domain D if the following condition is satisfied

$$\exists C \subseteq D \; (b_D(C)) \; \& \; \forall x \in C \; (T(x)! \; \to \; (M(x)! \; \& \; (M(x) = T(x))) \; \& $$
$$(c(M(x)) < c(T(x)))) \;)$$

Informally, a system M is a partial covering simplification Oracle for a system T in a domain D if there is a sufficiently big subset C of the domain D such that the system M is defined where the system T is defined in the domain C solving the same problem and giving the same results when their inputs are the same, but the system M is doing this in a (much) simpler way than the system T.

Lemma 4.10. *If a system M is a covering simplification Oracle for a system T in a domain D, then it is a partial covering simplification Oracle in any superset H of D for the system T if D is a sufficiently big subset of H and $\forall x \in H \; (T(x)! \; \to \; (M(x)! \; \& \; (M(x) = T(x)))$*

Lemma 4.11. (a) *Any partial simplification Oracle M for a system T in a domain D is a partial covering simplification Oracle for the system T in the same domain.*

(b) *Any partial covering simplification Oracle M in a domain D for a system T, which is total in the domain D is a partial simplification Oracle for the system T in the same domain.*

(c) *Any covering simplification Oracle M in a domain D for a system T is a partial covering simplification Oracle for the system T in the same domain.*

However, not any partial covering simplification Oracle M in a domain D for a system T is a covering simplification Oracle for the system T in the same domain.

Lemma 4.12. *A system M is a partial covering simplification Oracle in a domain D for a system T if and only if it is a covering simplification Oracle in some sufficiently big subset of D for a system T.*

The following result shows how to extend the domain of an Oracle.

Lemma 4.13. *If a system M is a covering simplification Oracle for a system T in domains D and A, then it is a covering simplification Oracle for the system T in the domain $A \cup D$.*

The following result shows that it is possible not only to extend the domain of an Oracle but also to restrict this domain.

Lemma 4.14. *If Condition I is satisfied, $C \subseteq H \subseteq D$, a system M is a partial covering simplification Oracle for a system T in the domain D and a covering simplification Oracle for the system T in the domain C, then it is a partial covering simplification Oracle for the system T in the domain H.*

Stronger conditions than those that define partial covering simplification Oracles bring us to strong partial covering simplification Oracles.

Definition 4.6. A system M is a *strong partial covering simplification Oracle* for a system T in a domain D if the following condition is satisfied

$$\exists C \subseteq D \, (b_D(C)) \, \& \, \forall x \in C \, \forall z \in D \, (\, T(z)! \rightarrow (M(z)! \, \& \, (M(z) = T(z))) \, \& \, (c(M(x)) \prec c(T(x)))))$$

Note that any strong partial covering simplification Oracle for T is also a partial covering simplification Oracle for T.

Remark 3.1. For partial covering and strong partial covering simplification Oracles, Theorem 4.6 is not always true. However, under additional conditions, Theorem 4.6 becomes valid for partial covering and strong partial covering simplification oracles.

Theorem 4.7. *If the function $b_D(C)$ satisfies Condition III for a domain D, then a (strong) partial covering simplification Oracle M for a system T in the domain D, which is a (strong) partial covering simplification Oracle for a system A in the domain Đ, is a (strong) partial covering simplification Oracle for a system A in the domain D.*

Proof. The proof is similar to the proof of Theorem 4.2.

Corollary 4.9. *If the system of sufficiently big in a domain D subsets is a filter, then a (strong) partial covering simplification Oracle M in the domain D for a system T, which is a (strong) partial covering simplification Oracle in the domain D for a system A, is a (strong) partial covering simplification Oracle in the domain D for the system A.*

Corollary 4.10. *If the system of sufficiently big in a domain D subsets is a set ideal, then a (strong) partial covering simplification Oracle M in the domain D for a system T, which is a (strong) partial covering simplification Oracle in the domain D for a system A, is a (strong) partial covering simplification Oracle in the domain D for the system A.*

Corollary 4.11. *If the system of sufficiently big in a domain D subsets is a set algebra, then a (strong) partial covering simplification Oracle M for a system T in the domain D, which is a (strong) partial covering simplification Oracle for a system A in the domain D, is a (strong) partial covering simplification Oracle for the system A in the domain D.*

Similar to total simplification Oracles, covering simplification Oracles preserve their characteristic in transition from a set to its subset.

Theorem 4.8. *If $E \subseteq D$ and the system M is a covering simplification Oracle for a system T in the domain D, then the system M is a covering simplification Oracle for the system T in the domain E.*

Proof. Let us assume that a system M is a covering simplification Oracle in a domain D for a system T. Then by Definition 4.4, we have

$$\forall x \in D \ (T(x)! \rightarrow (M(x)! \ \& \ (M(x) = T(x))) \ \& \ (c(M(x)) \prec c(T(x))))$$

This formula implies

$$\forall x \in E \ (T(x)! \rightarrow (M(x)! \ \& \ (M(x) = T(x))) \ \& \ (c(M(x)) \prec c(T(x))))$$

It means that the system M is a covering simplification Oracle in the domain D for the system T.

The theorem is proved.

There are also other types of simplification Oracles. Here we consider one more of these types.

Let us assume $C \subseteq D$.

Definition 4.7. A system M is a *simplification Oracle* (PSO) for a system *T from the domain C to the domain D* if the following two conditions are satisfied

$$\forall x \in D \ (T(x)! \ \& \ M(x)! \ \& \ (M(x) = T(x)) \ \& \ \forall u \in D \backslash C \ (c(M(u)) \prec c(T(u))))$$

and

$$\forall z \in C \ ((c(M(z)) \preccurlyeq c(T(z))))$$

Here the relation $(c(M(z)) \preccurlyeq c(T(z)))$ means that the complexity $c(M(z))$ is less than or equal to the complexity $c(T(z))$.

Informally, a system M is a simplification Oracle for a system T from the domain C to the domain D if for all inputs from D, M and T are defined and give the same results when their inputs are the same, the complexity of solving by M is not worse than the complexity of solving by T for all inputs from C, but the system M is processing data in a (much) simpler way than the system T for all inputs from D that do not belong to C.

Lemma 4.15. *Any simplification Oracle for T from the domain C to the domain D is a partial simplification Oracle for T if the predicate $b_D(D \backslash C)$ is true.*

Lemma 4.16. *Any simplification Oracle for T from the domain C to the domain D is a total simplification Oracle for T in the domain $D \backslash C$.*

Lemma 4.17. *If a system M is a covering simplification Oracle for a system T from the domain C to the domain D and from the domain C to the domain A, then it is a covering simplification Oracle for the system T from the domain C to the domain $A \cup D$.*

Theorem 4.9. *If $C \subseteq H \subseteq D$, a system A is a simplification Oracle for a system T from the domain C to the domain H, and a system M is a simplification Oracle for a system A from the domain H to the domain D, then the system M is a simplification Oracle for the system T from the domain C to the domain D.*

Proof. Let us assume that a system M is a simplification Oracle for a system A from the domain H to the domain D and the system A is a simplification Oracle for a system T from the domain C to the domain H. Then by Definition 4.7, we have the following conditions

$$\forall x \in D\ (A(x)!\ \&\ M(x)!\ \&\ (M(x) = A(x))\ \&\ \forall u \in D \backslash H\ (c(M(u)) \prec c(A(u))))$$

$$\forall z \in H\ ((c(M(z)) \preccurlyeq c(A(z))))$$

$$\forall x \in D\ (T(x)!\ \&\ A(x)!\ \&\ (A(x) = T(x))\ \&\ \forall u \in H \backslash C\ (c(A(u)) \prec c(T(u))))$$

and

$$\forall z \in C\ ((c(A(z)) \preccurlyeq c(T(z))))$$

As $\preccurlyeq$ is a partial order in the set of computational complexity measures, we have

$$\forall x \in C\ (c(M(x)) \preccurlyeq c(T(x)))$$

As $\prec$ is a partial order in the set of computational complexity measures and $D \backslash C = (D \backslash H) \cup (H \backslash C)$, we have

$$\forall x \in D \backslash C\ (c(M(x)) \prec c(T(x)))$$

In addition, equalities

$$M(x) = A(x)$$

and

$$A(x) = T(x)$$

imply the equality

$$M(x) = T(x)$$

Consequently, we have

$$\forall x \in D\ (T(x)!\ \&\ M(x)!\ \&\ (M(x) = T(x))\ \&\ \forall u \in D \backslash C\ (c(M(u)) \prec c(T(u))))$$

and

$$\forall z \in C\ (c(M(z)) \preccurlyeq c(T(z)))$$

It means that the system M is a simplification Oracle for the system T from the domain C to the domain D.

The theorem is proved.

Defining simplification oracles, we employed an arbitrary complexity function c. This allows us to consider specific simplification Oracles for some important complexity functions, such as time complexity, space complexity and operational complexity.

Definition 4.8. A simplification Oracle M is called:

(a) A *temporal Oracle* if c is time complexity;

(b) A *space Oracle* if c is space complexity;

(c) An *operational Oracle* if c is operational complexity.

Note that for Turing machines, time complexity and operational complexity (which counts the number of performed operations) coincide. Consequently, Turing machines as operational oracles are also temporal oracles and vice versa.

It is interesting that a temporal Oracle M for a person A, like oracles from the Greek mythology, can predict future events for A being able to compute these events faster than A comes to them.

Example 4.7. It is proved in (Burgin, 1999) that inductive Turing machines with structured memory can serve as temporal (simplification) Oracles for conventional Turing machines.

However, not to make this text too long, these and other specific simplification Oracles are studied elsewhere.

Now let us consider augmentation Oracles, which make results achievable not only theoretically (in the ideal situation) but also practically (in real-life situations).

Definition 4.9. A system M is an *augmentation Oracle* in a domain D for a system T if the following condition is satisfied.

$$\exists z \in D \ \forall x \in D \ (T(x)!! \rightarrow ((M(x)!! \ \& \ (M(x) = T(x)))) \ \& \ \neg(T(z)!!) \ \& \ M(z)!! \ \& \ (M(z) = T(z)))$$

Here the expression $A(x)!!$ means that processing of the input x by the system $A \in \{M, T\}$ is tractable.

Thus informally, Definition 4.9 states that everything that is tractable for the system T is also tractable for the system M and in this case, both systems give the same result but there is, at least, one problem (one input) that is tractable for the system M but is not tractable for the system T.

Note that tractability $A(x)!!$ implies definability $A(x)!$, i.e., if processing of the input x is tractable for A, then A gives the result (is defined) for the input x.

In computer science, tractability is defined using time complexity. The standard definition of tractability is (cf., Garey and Johnson, 1979):

A problem is *tractable* if there is a polynomial-time algorithm, which solves this problem.

Examples of tractable problems:
- – Searching an ordered list
- – Sorting a list
- – Multiplication of integers
- – Finding a minimum spanning tree in a graph

Note that for intractable problems, the lower bound of time complexity is usually exponential.

The idea that polynomial time deterministic algorithms form the correct class to represent feasible computation and tractable problems was suggested by Cobham (1964) and Edmonds (1965). One of the main reasons for the development of this approach was theoretical advantages of the class of all polynomials *P*. Namely, the growth of polynomials is relatively slow in comparison, for example, with exponential functions. In addition, the class of all polynomials *P* is closed under composition, addition, subtraction, and multiplication. These features make possible subroutine calls, i.e., a polynomial-time algorithm (machine or program) making subroutine calls to polynomial-time subroutines yields an overall polynomial-time procedure. It is also workable to use polynomially bounded reduction without violation of tractability. All this supports the claim that the class *P* gives a reasonable resource bound, which is now

widely accepted in computer science as an asymptotic boundary for tractability.

Example 4.8. According to contemporary understanding, nondeterministic Turing machines can serve as augmentation Oracles for deterministic Turing machines.

Example 4.9. It is proved in Baker *et al.* (1975) that nondeterministic Turing machines with Oracles of a definite type can serve as augmentation Oracles for deterministic Turing machines with Oracles of the same type.

It is also possible to formulate the famous "**P** = **NP** ?" problem in terms of augmentation Oracles:

Find if there are deterministic Turing machines for which some nondeterministic Turing machine that can serve as an augmentation Oracle in the case of conventional tractability of algorithmic problems.

If it is possible to find such deterministic Turing machines, then

$$\mathbf{P} \neq \mathbf{NP}$$

If it is impossible to find such deterministic Turing machines, then

$$\mathbf{P} = \mathbf{NP}$$

Here we consider tractability of dynamic systems, such as algorithms or automata, and not of problems. However, it is possible to express tractability of systems (e.g., algorithms) as tractability of problems. Namely, we have the following definitions.

Let us take a problem P and consider tractability of P as existence of a system, e.g., an automaton or algorithm, from a given class **K**, e.g., from the class of polynomial-time algorithms (automata), that solves the problem P.

Definition 4.10. (a) Processing an input x by the system A is *tractable* if it is tractable as a problem.

(b) Processing any input from a domain D by the system A is *tractable* if it is tractable as a problem.

In this case, the input is considered as a problem.

Remark 4.3. In many cases, it is possible express augmentation using simplification reducing in such a way the concept of an augmentation Oracle to the concept of an simplification Oracle.

It is necessary to understand that here we do not confine tractability to polynomial time complexity but assume that tractability is a relative property that can be, for example, defined axiomatically in the context of the axiomatic theory of algorithms (Burgin, 2010).

Theorem 4.10. If a system M is an augmentation Oracle for a system T in a domain D and the system T is an augmentation Oracle for a system A in the domain D, then the system M is an augmentation Oracle for the system A in the domain D.

Proof. Let us assume that a system M is an augmentation Oracle for a system T in a domain D and the system T is an augmentation Oracle for a system A in the domain D. Then by Definition 4.10, we have

$$\exists z \in D \ \forall x \in D \ (\ T(x)!! \to M(x)!! \ \& \ \neg(T(z)!!) \ \& \ M(z)!! \ ) \qquad (4.3)$$

and

$$\exists y \in D \ \forall x \in D \ (\ A(x)!! \to T(x)!! \ \& \ \neg(A(y)!!) \ \& \ T(y)!! \ )$$

Because implication is transitive, we have

$$\forall x \in D \ (\ A(x)!! \to M(x)!! \ )$$

i.e., what is tractable for A is also tractable for M.

At the same time, processing the input z from the formula (4.3) is tractable for M but it is not tractable for A because it is not tractable for T. Consequently, the system M is an augmentation Oracle for the system A in the domain D.

The theorem is proved.

Theorem 4.10 means that the relation "to be an augmentation Oracle" is transitive.

Definition 4.11. A system M is an *essential augmentation Oracle* for a system T in a domain D if the following condition is satisfied

$$\exists C \subseteq D \ (b_D(C)) \ \& \ \forall z \in C \ \forall x \in D \ (\ T(x)!! \rightarrow (M(x)!! \ \& \ (M(x) = T(x)))) \ \&$$
$$\neg(T(z)!!) \ \& \ M(z)!! \ \& \ (M(z) = T(z)))$$

Informally, a system M is an essential augmentation Oracle for a system T in a domain D if the system M is defined where the system T is defined in the domain D solving the same problem and giving the same results when their inputs are the same, but there is a sufficiently big subset C of the set D such that all problems (inputs) from C are tractable for the system M but are not tractable for the system T.

Note that any essential augmentation Oracle is an augmentation Oracle.

Remark 4.3. In some cases, simplification Oracles are also augmentation Oracles.

Theorem 4.11. *If the function $b_D(C)$ satisfies Condition III a domain D, a system M is an essential augmentation Oracle for a system T in the domain D and T is an essential augmentation Oracle for a system A in the domain D, then M is an essential augmentation Oracle for the system A in the domain D.*

Proof. Let us assume that a system M is an essential augmentation Oracle for a system T in a domain D and the system T is an essential augmentation Oracle for a system A in the domain D. Then by Definition 4.11, we have

$$\exists C \subseteq D \ (b_D(C)) \ \& \ \forall z \in C \ \forall x \in D \ (\ T(x)!! \rightarrow (M(x)!! \ \& \ (M(x)$$
$$= T(x)))) \ \& \ \neg(T(z)!!) \ \& \ M(z)!! \ \& \ (M(z) = T(z)))$$

and

$$\exists E \subseteq D \ (b_D(E)) \ \& \ \forall z \in E \ \forall x \in D \ (\ A(x)!! \to (T(x)!! \ \& \ (A(x) = T(x)))) \ \&$$
$$\neg(A(z)!!) \ \& \ T(z)!! \ \& \ (A(z) = T(z)))$$

Because implication is transitive, we have
$$\forall x \in D \ (A(x)!! \to M(x)!!),$$
i.e., what is tractable for A is also tractable for M.

By Condition III, the predicate $b_D(B \cap C)$ is true as the predicate $b_D(E)$ and $b_D(E)$ are true.

In addition, equalities

$$M(x) = T(x)$$

and

$$A(x) = T(x)$$

imply the equality

$$M(x) = A(x)$$

Consequently, we have

$$\exists E \subseteq D \ (\ b_D(E)) \ \& \ \forall z \in E \ \forall x \in D \ (\ A(x)!! \to (M(x)!! \ \& \ (A(x)$$
$$= M(x)))) \& \neg(A(z)!!) \ \& \ M(z)!! \ \& \ (M(z) = T(z)))$$

It means that the system M is an essential augmentation Oracle for the system A in the domain D.

The theorem is proved.

Definition 4.12. A system M is a *complete augmentation Oracle* for a system T in a domain D if the following condition is satisfied

$$\exists z \in D \forall x \in D \ (T(x)! \ \& \ M(x)! \ \& \ T(x) = M(x) \ \& \ (T(x)!! \to M(x)!!)$$
$$\& \neg(T(z)!!) \ \& \ M(z)!! \ )$$

Informally, a system M is an complete augmentation Oracle for a system T in a domain D if both systems M and T are defined in D solving the same problems and giving the same results when their inputs are the same, all problems (inputs) from C are tractable for the system T are also tractable for the system M but there is a problem (input) in D that is tractable for the system M but is not tractable for the system T.

Theorem 4.12. *If a system M is a complete augmentation Oracle for a system T in the domain D and T is a complete augmentation Oracle for a* *system A in the domain D, then M is a complete augmentation Oracle for the system A in the domain D.*

Proof. The proof is similar to the proof of Theorem 4.11.

Definitions imply the following result.

Theorem 4.13. *A system M is a complete augmentation Oracle for a system T in a domain D in which T is not totally tractable if and only if both systems M and T are total in D and M is an augmentation Oracle for a system T in the domain D.*

This result and some others show relations between different types of Oracles.

Definition 4.13. A system *M* is a *total augmentation Oracle* for a system *T* in a domain *D* if the following condition is satisfied

$$\forall x \in D \ (\neg T(x)!! \ \& \ M(x)!!)$$

Informally, a system *M* is a total augmentation Oracle for a system *T* in a domain *D* if all problems (inputs) from *D* are tractable for the system *M* but are not tractable for the system *T*. In this case, we are not interested what is going on outside *D*.

Some properties of total augmentation Oracles are similar to the properties of total simplification Oracles, while other properties are different.

Definitions 4.9 and 4.13 imply the following result.

Theorem 4.14. *A system M is an augmentation Oracle for a system T in a domain D if and only if it is a total augmentation Oracle for the system T in some subset of D.*

Definitions 4.11 and 4.13 imply the following result.

Theorem 4.15. *A system M is an essential augmentation Oracle for a system T in a domain D if and only if it is a total augmentation Oracle for the system T in some sufficiently big subset of D.*

The property "to be a total augmentation Oracle" is hereditary with respect to subsets.

Theorem 4.16. *If $E \subseteq D$ and a system M is a total augmentation Oracle in the domain D for a system A, then the system M is a total augmentation Oracle in the domain E for a system A.*

This property is similar to the properties of total simplification Oracles.

Definitions imply the following results.

Lemma 4.18. *If a system M is a complete or total augmentation Oracle for a system T in a domain D, then it is an augmentation Oracle in D.*

Lemma 4.19. *If a system M is a total augmentation Oracle for a system T in all domains D_i ($i \in I$), then it is an augmentation Oracle in the domain $\bigcup_{i \in I} D_i$.*

Indeed, if the condition

$$\forall x \in D_i \; (\neg T(x)!! \;\&\; M(x)!!)$$

is satisfied for all $i \in I$, then the condition

$$\forall x \in \bigcup_{i \in I} D_i (\neg T(x)!! \;\&\; M(x)!!)$$

is also satisfied.

Now we can find a criterion for essential augmentation Oracles.

Theorem 4.17. *A system M is an essential augmentation Oracle for a system T in a domain D where T is not totally tractable if and only if there is a sufficiently big subset C of the domain D such that for any subset E of the domain D, if $E \cap C \neq \varnothing$, then M is an augmentation Oracle for the system T in the domain $E \cap C$.*

Proof. *Necessity.* Let us assume that a system M is an essential augmentation Oracle for a system T in a domain D and $E \subseteq D$. Then by Theorem 4.15, M is a total augmentation Oracle for a system T in the

domain D. By Theorem 4.16, if $E \cap C \neq \varnothing$, then M is a total augmentation Oracle for the system T in a domain $E \cap C$. Thus, by Lemma 4.18, if $E \cap C \neq \varnothing$, then M is an augmentation Oracle for the system T in a domain $E \cap C$.

Sufficiency. Let us assume that there is a sufficiently big subset C of the domain D such that for any subset E of the domain D, if $E \cap C \neq \varnothing$, then a system M is an augmentation Oracle for the system T in the domain $E \cap C$. Taking an arbitrary element x from the set C, we see that M is an augmentation Oracle for the system T in the domain $\{x\}$. By Theorem 4.14, the system is a total augmentation Oracle for the system T in the domain $\{x\}$. Consequently, by Lemma 4.19, the system M is a total augmentation Oracle for a system T in a domain C. Then by Theorem 4.15, the system M is an essential augmentation Oracle for a system T in a domain D.

The theorem is proved.

Theorem 4.15 implies the following result.

Theorem 4.18. *If a system M is a total augmentation Oracle for a system T in a domain D, then it is a essential augmentation Oracle in any superset H of D for the system T such that D is a sufficiently big subset of H.*

We know that according to Theorem 4.1, the relation "to be a total simplification Oracle" is transitive. In contrast to this, total augmentation oracles have, in some sense, the opposite property as the following results demonstrate.

Theorem 4.20. *If a system M is a total augmentation Oracle for a system T in a domain D, then there are no augmentation oracles in the domain D for M.*

Indeed, to have an augmentation Oracle in the domain D, the system M has to be intractable at least, at one point from D, but by Definition 4.13, there is no such a point in D.

Because any total augmentation Oracle is an essential augmentation Oracle and any essential augmentation Oracle is an augmentation Oracle, we have the following results.

Corollary 4.12. *If a system M is a total augmentation Oracle in the domain D for a system T, then there are no essential augmentation oracles in the domain D for M.*

Corollary 4.13. *If a system M is a total augmentation Oracle in the domain D for a system T, then there are no total augmentation oracles in the domain D for M.*

However, some systems have many different total augmentation oracles, essential augmentation oracles and augmentation oracles.

Now let us study extension Oracles, which solve problems unsolvable for others, e.g., provide information inaccessible to others.

Definition 4.14. A system M is an *extension Oracle* in a domain D for a system T if the following condition is satisfied

$$\exists z \in D \ \forall x \in D \ (\ (T(x)! \ \rightarrow \ (M(x)! \ \& \ (M(x) = T(x)))) \ \& \ \neg(T(z)!) \ \& \ M(z)!)$$

Thus informally, Definition 4.14 points out that everything that is solvable for the system T is also solvable for the system M (the Oracle) and in this case, both systems give the same result (the same solution) but there is, at least, one problem (one input) that is solvable for the system M (for the Oracle) but is not solvable for the system T.

Example 4.10. It is proved in (Burgin, 1983, 2001) that inductive Turing machines can serve as extension Oracles for conventional Turing machines.

Usually, undefinability, e.g., incomputability, implies intractability. This gives us the following result.

Lemma 4.20. *Any extension Oracle in a domain D for a system T is also an augmentation Oracle in a domain D for a system T.*

Theorem 4.21. *If a system M is an extension Oracle in a domain D for a system T and the system T is an extension Oracle in a domain D for a system A, then the system M is an extension Oracle in a domain D for the system A.*

Proof. The proof is similar to the proof of Theorem 4.10.

Theorem 4.21 means that the relation "to be an extension Oracle" is transitive.

Definition 4.15. A system M is an *essential extension Oracle* in a domain D for a system T if the following condition is satisfied

$$\exists C \subseteq D \, (\, b_D(C)) \, \& \, \forall z \in C \, \forall x \in D \, (\, (T(x)! \, \to \, (M(x)! \, \& \, (M(x) = T(x)))) \, \& \, \neg(T(z)!) \, \& \, M(z)! \,)$$

Informally, a system M is an essential extension Oracle for a system T in a domain D if the system M is defined where the system T is defined in the domain D solving the same problem and giving the same results (the same solutions) when their inputs are the same, but there is a sufficiently big subset C of the set D such that all problems (inputs) from C are solvable for the system M but are not solvable for the system T.

Theorem 4.22. *If the system of sufficiently big in D subsets satisfies Condition III, then an essential extension Oracle M in the domain D for a system T, which is an essential extension Oracle in the domain D for a system A, is an essential extension Oracle in the domain D for the system A.*

Proof. The proof is similar to the proof of Theorem 4.2.

Corollary 4.14. *If the system of sufficiently big in a domain D subsets is a filter, then an essential extension augmentation Oracle M in the domain D for a system T, which is an essential augmentation Oracle in the domain D for a system A, is an essential augmentation Oracle in the domain D for the system A.*

Corollary 4.15. *If the system of sufficiently big in a domain D subsets is a set ideal, then an essential extension Oracle M in the domain D for a system T, which is an essential extension Oracle in the domain D for a system A, is an essential extension Oracle in the domain D for the system A.*

Corollary 4.16. *If the system of sufficiently big in a domain D subsets is a set algebra, then an essential extension augmentation Oracle M in the domain D for a system T, which is an essential extension augmentation Oracle in the domain D for a system A, is an essential extension Oracle in the domain D for the system A.*

Definition 4.16. A system M is a *total extension Oracle* in a domain D for a system T if the following condition is satisfied

$$\exists z \in D \; \forall x \in D \; (M(x)! \; \& \; (T(x)! \; \rightarrow \; (M(x) = T(x))) \; \& \; \neg(T(z)!))$$

Informally, a system M is a total extension Oracle for a system T in a domain D if all problems (inputs) from D are solvable for the system M but are not solvable for the system T. In this case, we are not interested what is going on outside D.

Properties of total extension augmentation oracles are similar to properties of total augmentation oracles as the following results demonstrate.

Theorem 4.23. *If a system M is a total extension augmentation Oracle in the domain D for a system T, then there are no extension oracles in the domain D for M.*

Proof. The proof is similar to the proof of Theorem 4.20.

Because any total extension Oracle is an essential extension Oracle and any essential extension Oracle is an extension Oracle, we have the following results.

Corollary 4.17. *If a system M is a total extension Oracle in the domain D for a system T, then there are no essential extension oracles in the domain D for M.*

Corollary 4.18. *If a system M is a total extension Oracle in the domain D for a system T, then there are no total extension oracles in the domain D for M.*

1.5. Conclusion

Here we formalized the concept of an Oracle in general and its manifestations, in particular. We treat Oracles information processing systems because the main functions of traditional Oracles provided important information to people. In this context, it is possible to use abstract automata and computing machines for mathematical representation and modeling of informative Oracles. The developed approach allows establishment of reliable mathematical foundations for exploration of Oracles, their properties and functioning. However, we do not limit the research by utilization of only conventional types of automata (computing machines), such as Turing machines or contemporary computers. The basic object of the theory is an information processing system, which is interpreted as a system that given certain information (in the form of data or knowledge) as its input, occasionally produces some information (also in the form of data or knowledge) as its output (answer or solution). For instance, an Oracle receives a question as its input and gives an answer to this question as its output. This is how the majority of traditional Oracles worked. Note that even the best Oracles were not able to answer to all questions. Therefore, this example shows how traditional oracles are included in the suggested schema of informative Oracles and why the developed model is applicable to all known examples of informative Oracles. Performing and service Oracles are studied elsewhere.

Presented here theory is only the first step in the direction of theoretical modeling and exploration of Oracles. It opens perspectives for further studies of Oracles. In particular, obtained results bring us to the following problems.

Problem 1. Study operations with Oracles.

It is possible to compare Oracles by their results. `

Problem 2. Study power of Oracles.

Comparison of Oracles produces their hierarchies.

Problem 3. Study hierarchies of Oracles.

Here is one more problem.

Problem 4. Is it possible to build a universal Oracle?

We studied here Oracles for one system. It is possible to call them *personal Oracles*. At the same time, it is necessary to understand that in this context, a system that has an Oracle or that is an Oracle can be not only one person or one automaton, but also an organization, a community or a network, e.g., a computer network such as the Internet.

However, it would be also interesting (**Problem 5**) to study Oracles for classes of systems.

Considering Oracles in classes of automata or machines, it is possible to use the axiomatic theory of algorithms, automata and computation developed in (Burgin, 2010). This brings us to the following problem.

Problem 6. Study Oracles in an axiomatic setting.

For the majority of people, Oracles functioned in society, e.g., in ancient Greece. Thus, we have:

Problem 7. Study Oracles in a social setting.

Discussing Oracles that provide incomputable information, such as Turing Oracles, it is noteworthy to analyze processes in computer science related to the term *computable*. For a long time, *computable* was a generic term denoting what was possible to do using algorithms. However, the situation changed when the theory of algorithms emerged. "Starting from 1936, Church and Kleene used the term *recursive* to stand for *computable* even though Turing and Gödel later objected. Kleene later introduced the term *recursive function theory* for the subject although Gödel disagreed ..." (Soare, 2015). Although some computer scientists continued to use the term *computable* (cf., for example, Davis, 1958), only in the second half of the last decade of the 20th century, the term *computable* had again become prevalent instead of the term *recursive*. Some researchers used both terms at the same time (cf., for example, Cutland, 1980). It is interesting that in the 21st century, computer scientists came to the synthesis of both terms by introducing the term *recursively computable* (Burgin, 2005). As a result, the terminology in computer science has been developing in line with the dialectics of ancient Greeks and Georg Wilhelm Friedrich Hegel.

References

Arora, S. and Barak, B. (2009) *Computational Complexity: A Modern Approach*, Cambridge, UK.

Baker, T., Gill, J., and Solovey, R. (1975) Relativizations of the $P =?$ NP question, *SIAM Journal of Computing*, v. 4, pp. 431–442.

Balcazar, J.L., Diaz, J., and Gabarro, J. (1988) *Structural Complexity*, Springer-Verlag, Berlin/Heidelberg/New York.

Basu, S. (1970) On the structure of subrecursive degrees, *Journal of Computer and System Sciences*, v. 4, No. 5, 452–464.

Black, J. (2014) *The Power of Knowledge: How Information and Technology Made the Modern World,* Yale University Press, New Haven/London.

Burkert, W. (1985) *Greek Religion*, Harvard University Press, Boston.

Burgin, M. (1983) Inductive turing machines, *Notices of the Academy of Sciences of the USSR*, v. 270, No. 6, pp. 1289–1293 (translated from Russian, v. 27, No. 3).

Burgin, M. (1999) Super-recursive algorithms as a tool for high performance computing, *Proceedings of the High Performance Computing Symposium*, San Diego, pp. 224–228.

Burgin, M. (2001) How we know what technology can do, *Communications of the ACM*, v. 44, No. 11, pp. 82–88.

Burgin, M. (2005a) *Super-Recursive Algorithms*, New York, Springer.

Burgin, M. (2005b) Superrecursive hierarchies of algorithmic problems, in *Proceedings of the 2005 International Conference on Foundations of Computer Science*, CSREA Press, Las Vegas, pp. 31–37.

Burgin, M. (2010) Measuring Power of Algorithms, Computer Programs, and Information Automata, Nova Science Publishers, New York.

Burgin, M. (2011) *Theory of Named Sets*, Nova Science Publishers, New York.

Burgin, M. (2012) *Structural Reality*, Nova Science Publishers, New York.

Burgin, M. and Eberbach, E. (2009) On foundations of evolutionary computation: an evolutionary automata approach, in Hongwei Mo (Ed.), *Handbook of Research on Artificial Immune Systems and Natural Computing: Applying Complex Adaptive Technologies*, IGI Global, Hershey, Pennsylvania, pp. 342–360.

Burgin, M. and Eberbach, E. (2012) Evolutionary automata: Expressiveness and convergence of evolutionary computation, *Computer Journal*, v. 55, No. 9 pp. 1023–1029.

Burgin, M. and Mikkilineni, R. (2014) Semantic network organization based on distributed intelligent managed elements, in *Proceeding of the 6th International Conference on Advances in Future Internet*, Lisbon, Portugal, pp. 16–20.

Burgin M., Mikkilineni M. and Morana G. (2015) From personal computers to personal computing networks: a new paradigm for computation, in *Proceeding of Future Computing 2015, The Seventh International Conference on Future Computational Technologies and Applications*, pp. 24–30.

Cleland, C.E. (2001) Recipes, algorithms, and programs, *Minds and Machines*, v. 11, pp. 219–237.

Cobham, A. (1964) The intrinsic computational difficulty of functions, in *Proceedings of the 1964 International Congress on Logic, Methodology and Philosophy of Science*, Amsterdam, pp. 24–30.

Curnow, T. (2004) *The Oracles of the Ancient World: A Comprehensive Guide*, Duckworth, London.

Cutland, N. (1980) *Computability: An Introduction to Recursive Function Theory*, Cambridge University Press, Cambridge.

Davis, M. (1958) *Computability & Unsolvability*, McGraw-Hill, New York.

De Fontenelle, B. I. B. (1753) *The History of Oracles, in Two Dissertations*, R. Urie, Glasgow (Original French publication in 1687).

Dekker, J. C. E. and Ellentuck, E. (1974) Recursion relative to regressive functions, *Annals of Mathematical Logic*, v. 6, No. 3–4, pp. 231–257.

Edmonds, J. (1965) Paths, trees, and flowers, *Canadian Journal of Mathematics*, v. 17, No. 3, pp. 449–467.

Edmonds, J. (1965a) Minimum partition of a matroid into independent subsets, *Journal of Research of the National Bureau of Standards*, v. 69B, pp. 67–72.

Edmonds, J. (1971) Matroids and the greedy algorithm, *Mathematical Programming*, v. 1, pp. 127–136.

Eliade, M. (1968) From *Primitives to Zen: A Thematic Sourcebook of the History of Religions*, Collins, London.

Ferguson, N. (1999) *The House of Rothschild, v. 1: Money's Prophets, 1798–1848*, Penguin, New York.

Flower, M. A. (2008) *The Seer in Ancient Greece*, University of California Press, Berkeley.

Fontenrose, J. (1978) *The Delphic Oracle: Its Responses and Operations*, University of California Press, Berkeley.

Garey, M. R. and Johnson, D. S. (1979) *Computers and Intractability: A Guide to the Theory of NP-Completeness*, W. H. Freeman.

Gödel, K. (1931) Über formal unentscheidbare Sätze der Principia Mathematics und verwandter System I, *Monatshefte für Mathematic und Physik*, v. 38, pp. 173–198.

Gottheil, R. and Krauss, S. (1906) *Sibyl, Jewish Encyclopedia*, Funk and Wagnalls, New York.

Hager, G. (2010) *Oracle, Encyclopedia Mythica* (http://www.pantheon.org/articles/o/oracle.html).

Hermelin, D., Levy, A., Weimann, O. and Yuster, R. (2011) Distance oracles for vertex-labeled graphs, in *ICALP*, pp. 490–501.

Homer, S. and Selman, A.L. (2011) Relative computability, in *Computability and Complexity Theory*, Texts in Computer Science, Springer, pp. 145–179.

Kolmogorov, A.N. and Fomin, S.V. (1999) *Elements of the Theory of Functions and Functional Analysis*, Dover Publications, New York.

Korte, B. and Schrader, R. (1981) A survey on oracle techniques, in *Proceedings of the 10th Symposium Mathematical Foundations of Computer Science*, Štrbské Pleso, Czechoslovakia, Lecture Notes in Computer Science, v. 118, Springer, Berlin, pp. 61–77.

Kuratowski, K. and Mostowski, A. (1967) *Set Theory*, North-Holland, Amsterdam

Ladner, R. E., Lynch, N.A. and Selman, A.L. (1975) A comparison of polynomial time reducibilities, *Theoretical Computer Science*, v. 1, No. 2, pp. 103–123.

Mikkilineni, R., Comparini, A. and Morana, G. (2012) The Turing O-machine and the DIME network architecture: Injecting the architectural resiliency into distributed computing, in *Turing-100. The Alan Turing Centenary*, (Ed.) Andrei Voronkov, *EasyChair Proceedings in Computing*, v. 10, pp. 239–251.

Mikkilineni, R., Morana, G. and Burgin, M. (2015) Oracles in software networks: A new scientific and technological approach to designing self-managing distributed computing processes, in *Proceedings of the 2015 European Conference on Software Architecture Workshops*, Dubrovnik/Cavtat, Croatia, 2015, ACM, pp. 11:1–11:8.

Moore, T. (2012) Oracles, Pharaonic Egypt, *The Encyclopedia of Ancient History* (http://onlinelibrary.wiley.com/doi/10.1002/9781444338386.wbeah15311/full).

Morgan, C. (2007) *Athletes and Oracles: The Transformation of Olympia and Delphi in the Eighth Century BC*, Cambridge University Press, Cambridge.

Pausanias Description of Greece (1977) Harvard University Press, Boston.

Post, E. L. (1943) Formal reductions of the general combinatorial decision problem, *American Journal of Mathematics*, v. 65, pp. 197–215.

Post, E. L. (1944) Recursively enumerable sets of positive integers and their decision problems, *Bulletin of the American Mathematical Society*, v. 50, pp. 284–316.

Post, E. L. (1948) Degrees of recursive unsolvability, Preliminary report, *Bulletin of the American Mathematical Society*, v. 54, pp. 641–642.

Rogers, H. (1987) Theory of Recursive Functions and Effective Computability, MIT Press, Cambridge, MA.

Schöning, U. (1988) Complexity theory and interaction, in *The Universal Turing Machine — A Half-Century Survey*, Oxford University Press, Oxford, pp. 561–580.

Shapiro, S. (1983) Remarks on the development of computability, *History and Philosophy of Logic*, v. 4, pp. 203–220.

Shoenfield, J. R. (1959) On degrees of unsolvability, *Annals of Mathematics*, v. 69, pp. 644–653.

Soare, R. I. (1999) The history and concept of computability, in *Handbook of Computability Theory*, North-Holland, Amsterdam, pp. 3–36.

Soare, R. I. (2015) Turing Oracle machines, online computing, and three displacements in computability theory, *Annals of Pure and Applied Logic*, v. 160, pp. 368–399.

Stoneman, R. (2011) *The Ancient Oracles: Making the Gods Speak*, Yale University Press, New Haven, CT.

Thorup, M. (2004) Compact oracles for reachability and approximate distances in planar digraphs, *Journal of ACM*, v. 51, pp. 993–1024.

Turing, A. (1936) On computable numbers with an application to the entscheidungs-problem, in *Proceedings of London Mathematical Society* (2), v. 42, pp. 230–265.

Turing, A. M. (1939) Systems of logic defined by ordinals, *Proceedings of London Mathematical Society* (2), v. 45, pp. 161–228.

Vondrak, J. (2008) Optimal approximation for the submodular welfare problem in the value oracle model, in *Proceedings of the 40th Annual ACM Symposium on Theory of Computing (STOC'08)*, pp. 67–74.

Wood, M. (2004) *The Road to Delphi: The Life and Afterlife of Oracles*, Chatto.

Zemke, F. P. (1975) *Well-Regulated Systems of Notation and the Subrecursive Hierarchy Equivalence Property*, Claremont Graduate School, Claremont, CA.

Chapter 4

Emergence of Symbolic Information by the Ritualisation Transition

Rainer Feistel

Leibniz Institute for Baltic Sea Research
Warnemünde D-18119, Germany
rainer.feistel@io-warnemuende.de

Physically, information carriers are encountered in two occurrences, either in native form as physical structures, or in arbitrarily coded, symbolic form such as signal systems or sequences of signs. The symbolic form may rigorously be associated with the existence of life. In contrast, structural information may be present in various physical processes or structures independent of life. The self-organised emergence of symbolic information from structural information may be called *ritualisation*. A century ago, Julian Huxley had introduced this term in behavioural biology. Subsequently, this evolutionary key process of the emergence of animal and social communication was studied in depth by Konrad Lorenz, Günter Tembrock and other ethologists. Ritualisation exhibits typical features of kinetic phase transitions of the 2nd kind. From a more general viewpoint, the origin of life, the appearance of human languages and the emergence of human social categories such as money can also be understood as ritualisation transitions. Occurring at some stage of evolutionary history, these transitions have in common that after the crossover, arbitrary symbols are issued and recognised by information-processing devices, by *transmitters* and *receivers* in the sense of Shannon's information theory. In this paper, general properties of the ritualisation transition and the related code symmetry are described. These properties are demonstrated by tutorial examples of very different such transitions in natural, social and technical evolution, reviewed from the perspective of the emergence of symbolic information and its structural historicity.

Keywords: Information; ritualisation; symbols; code; kinetic phase transition; Goldstone modes; origin of life; insect communication;

sexual selection; kissing; laughter; yawning; tears; spoken language; written language; alphabet; numerals; measurement; computer; money.

In the beginning was the Word

John 1:1

Jn allen Sprachen des Ursprungs tȯnen noch Reſte dieſer Naturtȯne; nur freilich ſind ſie nicht die Hauptfȧden der menſchlichen Sprache. [1]

Johann Gottfried von Herder, 1772

1. Introduction

The development of a proper science of information still poses a fundamental challenge [Hofkirchner, 1999, 2009]. In a broad sense, the term *information* may be understood as "a capability (potential) to change (transform)" in any way a system that is considered as a "*receiver*, *receptor* or *recipient* of this information" [Burgin, 2010, 2011]. In the context of physics, interaction between two systems typically includes the mutual exchange of energy. *Information* is a special property of one of such systems, then regarded as the *carrier*, which via the interaction process may causally and lastingly change the state of the other system, termed the *receiver* of the information. In this chapter, we shall in particular consider forms of information whose receivers belong to the realm of life [Ebeling and Feistel, 1994, 2015; Feistel and Ebeling, 2011], be those living or technical systems. Numerous information and communication systems are known from the natural and social evolution history; in the following, a selection of very different such systems is reviewed, contrasting their mutually different and common properties along the transition where information as a new, irreducible quality emerged from its precursory, more elementary properties.

From a physical perspective, it is useful to distinguish between *str-uctural* and *symbolic information* [Feistel and Ebeling, 2011; Ebeling and Feistel, 2015], or, synonymously, between *bound* and *free information*

---

[1] In all aboriginal languages, vestiges of these sounds of nature are still to be heard; though, to be sure, they are not the principal fibres of human speech. English translation by Alexander Gode [von Herder, 1772].

[Ebeling and Feistel, 1994], respectively. The monument of Ludwig Boltzmann at the Central Cemetery in Vienna, Fig. 1, may demonstrate the distinct natures of these two kinds of information. Symbolic information is what relies on a convention between the transmitter, in this example the creator of the monument, and the receiver, namely the visitor at the grave. Symbolic information is carried by the letters, numerals and special signs engraved; the meaning of the equation at the top is symbolic information as well as the names and numbers displayed. This information is easily understood by any physicist of our days, and at least partially by anybody who can read Latin letters and Arabic numerals. The symbols cannot be decoded by individuals who do not know the social and historical context, such as aliens who may be visiting us and see Boltzmann's grave as the first thing they encounter on our planet, similar to today's scientists when they try to predict the phenotypical traits induced by an unknown genetic sequence. Structural information, on the contrary, is not based on conventions. Colour, shape, isotopic or chemical composition of the marble can be studied by scientists regardless of their cultural background, and even algae or molds may analyse the content of available useful nutrients.

Symbolic information is exclusively associated with the existence of life [Feistel and Ebeling, 2011], while structural information may be attributed to any physical processes or structures, and may often be quantified in terms of physical entropy [Schrödinger, 1944; Brillouin, 1953; Klimonovich, 1991]. An extreme example for the latter is a black hole; all its structural information is claimed to be its entropy, given by the surface area of the event horizon [Bekenstein, 1973; Hawking, 2001; Carlip, 2011; Wikipedia, 2016], plus perhaps its spin or charge. Structural information defined by entropy is conserved in reversible processes. The self-organised emergence of symbolic information from structural information exhibits typical features of kinetic phase transitions of the 2nd kind, see Section 2, and is referred to as a *ritualisation* transition [Feistel, 1990], a term originally coined by Huxley [Huxley, 1914, 1966] in behavioural biology. In this article, *ritualisation* is understood quite generally as a universal qualitative transition from elementary structural to the emergent symbolic information properties of signals or coded sequences of letters in the

Fig. 1. Monument of Ludwig Boltzmann at the Wiener Zentralfriedhof. While the shape and the composition of the marble represents structural information, the symbolic information carried by the engraved letters and numbers relies on conventions between writer and reader. Photo taken in October 2010.

course of evolution processes. Ritualisation had been defined previously as

- "the gradual change of a useful action into a symbol and then into a ritual; or in other words, the change by which the same act which first subserved a definite purpose directly comes later to subserve it only indirectly (symbolically) and then not at all" [Huxley, 1914],
- a process by which behavioural or physical forms, or both, that had originally developed to serve certain different purposes for

the species' survival, turned into symbols that serve the communication within a population [Lorenz, 1970],

- the modification of an animal behavioural pattern to a pure symbolic activity [Eibl-Eibesfeldt, 1970],
- the development of signal-activity from use-activity [Tembrock, 1977], or as
- the self-organised emergence of systems capable of processing symbolic information [Feistel and Ebeling, 2011].

From the general perspective of the physics of self-organisation and evolution, the origin of life, the appearance of human language or the establishment of emergent social categories such as private property or money can also be understood as ritualisation transitions [Feistel, 1990; Feistel and Ebeling, 2011; Ebeling and Feistel, 2015]. All these transitions have in common that as their results, arbitrary conventional symbols are issued and recognised by information-processing devices. These "transmitters" and "receivers" in the sense of Shannon's communication theory [Shannon, 1948] had developed during an evolutionary process along with the actual sets of symbols and coding rules such as "grammars" [Ebeling and Feistel, 1982; Jiménez-Montaño *et al.*, 2004]. The combination of sender, transmitted symbols and receiver ultimately replaces a related original non-symbolic causal chain, see Fig. 2.

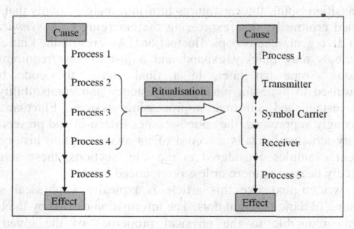

Fig. 2. By ritualisation, in the course of evolution, a certain part of an original causal chain becomes substituted by symbolic information-processing steps.

While the symbols descend gradually from the structural nature of the original process, they become liberated during the ritualisation crossover and turn into free conventions. As a simple technical example, when two persons communicated via telephone in the past, a microphone generated electric currents proportional to the sound amplitude. The currents were conducted through copper wires and eventually transformed back to sound by a magnetic coil. Today's mobile phones convert the sound to packets of data bits, send them through wireless and other links to a receiver which converts the digital symbols back to sound amplitudes. Here, the way the sound is encoded in symbols (bits) is irrelevant to the talking persons; it is a mere technical convention, a 'protocol' that is implemented mutually consistently at transmitter and receiver. As a rule, any particular protocol is a result of a historical process whose traces may still be discernible in the protocol's structural details.

Typically, three evolution stages of a ritualisation transition are observed [Feistel, 1990; Feistel and Ebeling, 2011]. In an initial phase, the original structure is only slowly variable in order to not degrade the system's essential functionality. Successively, affected structures reduce to some rudimentary "caricatures" of themselves, or "icons" or "pictograms", which represent the minimum complexity indispensable for maintaining the actual function [Klix, 1980]. Irrelevant modes or redundant partial structures are no longer subject to restrictions or restoring forces, and related fluctuations may increase substantially. At the transition point, the caricatures turn into mere symbols that may be modified arbitrarily, thus expressing the emerging *code symmetry*, and permit divergent, macroscopic fluctuations. As a result, the kind and pool of symbols may quickly expand and adjust to new requirements or functions. Somewhat later, in a final phase, the code becomes standardised to maintain intrinsic consistency and compatibility of the newly established information-processing system. Fluctuations are increasingly suppressed, the code becomes frozen-in and preserves in its arbitrary structural details a record of its own evolution history. In the different examples considered in the later sections, these stages will repeatedly be seen in more or less pronounced form.

A written text like this article is typically a physical structure consisting of dark and light dots. The information carried by the text is in no way reducible to the physical properties of the given spatial distribution of dye or brightness; in this sense, symbolic information is an emergent property.[2] However, written text appeared historically as a result of the evolution of human language from more primitive signal systems used by animals, and those in turn from elementary physical and chemical processes. A hierarchy of ritualisation transitions, see Fig. 3, marks the points where qualitatively new forms of symbolic information came up, mostly based on the results of the previous transition, each of those characterised by a related new code symmetry. General aspects of code symmetry will be considered in the following section.

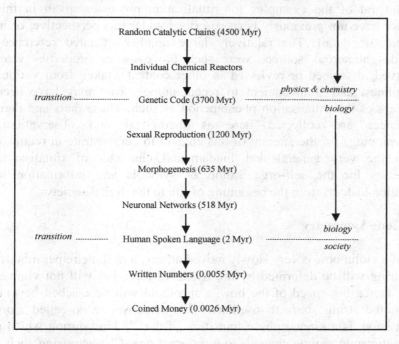

Fig. 3. Schematic hierarchy of ritualisation transitions during the evolution from pre-biological chemistry to the human society. Estimated times when those events happened in history are given in million years (Myr) before present (modified from [Ebeling and Feistel, 1992; Feistel and Ebeling, 2011]).

---

[2] An *emergent property* may be understood as a property "that is novel and robust relative to some natural comparison class" [Butterfield, 2012]. The term "*emergence* is broadly used to assign certain properties to features we observe in nature that have certain dependence on more basic phenomena (and/or elements), but are in some way independent from them and ultimately cannot be reduced to those other basic interactions between the basic elements" [Fuentes, 2014]. *Emergence* expresses the empirical fact that "the whole is more than the sum of its parts" [Feistel, 1991; Feistel and Ebeling, 2011; Ebeling, 2016].

In Section 3, some examples for information and ritualisation at the molecular level are presented, beginning with the origin of life. Section 4 continues with examples taken from the behaviour of animals, and Section 5 considers human verbal and non-verbal communication from the perspective of ritualisation. Section 6 completes this review with an example from the technical world of information processing, emphasising again the close analogies between all the processes observed at the rather different levels of organisation and complexity.

Several of the examples for ritualisation processes given in this chapter have not previously been described under this perspective, or in comparable detail. The relatively large number of cited references includes numerous sources were such processes or properties were observed, described or reviewed in other contexts, taken from various disciplines, and from ancient to recent authors who may have been unaware of the ritualisation phenomenon as such. These facts and their references are collected here as theoretical and observational underpinnings for the attempt of this chapter to demonstrate in requisite depth the very general and fundamental character of ritualisation processes for the self-organisation of symbols and information in evolution history, from the beginning of life to the digital society.

2. Code Symmetry

When a violin bow is very slowly moved at, say, a millimetre per minute, the string will be deformed by the frictional force but will not vibrate. With increasing speed of the bow, a threshold will be reached beyond which the string starts to oscillate. This crossover, a so-called *Hopf bifurcation*, is a kinetic phase transition of the 2nd kind during which a given dynamic regime changes to a different one. Characterising such a transition, the two regimes possess different symmetries but are indistinguishable from one another at the transition point. In the case of the violin, the state of the string at rest is the same at any point of time while, in contrast, the state of the vibrating string repeats only after each full oscillation period. In other words, the continuous time symmetry of the first state is broken in favour of a periodic time symmetry of the second. At the threshold, the stationary and the periodic regimes coincide, i.e., oscillations appear with zero amplitude. This phase transition is accompanied by strongly enhanced, 'critical' fluctuations

[Feistel and Ebeling, 1978, 1989, 2011]. To some extent, the magic of a violin concert results from these fluctuations at the onset of a tone.

A similar scenario is observed at the *ritualisation transition* which happens in the course of an evolutionary process. The initial physical state possesses structural information and may show certain symmetries. Beyond the threshold, symbols exist that carry symbolic information in addition to their structural information. Symbolic information is emergent and cannot be reduced to the structural information of the symbols, consequently, it is a mere convention which particular symbol is in use to represent a certain meaning. If everybody understood under the word "green" the colour of the sky and under "blue" the colour of leaves, all communication would work quite the same as vice versa. This invariance is the new fundamental code symmetry of symbolic information; symbols may be substituted by physically different symbols without affecting the meaning of the message. This invariance is in striking contrast to structural information, where a different physical structure always implies different information, intimately involved with one another. Immediately at the threshold, the nascent symbolic information is still identical with the structural information, but large fluctuations may occur which increasingly liberate the first from the latter. Ritualisation has the character of a kinetic phase transition of the 2nd kind. Elsewhere [Feistel and Ebeling, 2011], various properties are discussed in more detail which distinguish structural from symbolic information.

The code symmetry has several important and general implications which elucidate the reasons for the self-organised emergence of symbolic information, repeatedly and in various forms, in natural evolution history. Symbols may alternatively appear as sequences, such as in languages, or as communication signals, such as neuronal transmitter substances or human gestures. Here are some of those key features.

(i)   Discrete symbols are robust against small perturbations, i.e., symbols may be replaced by similar imitations. In simple information-processing systems, the receiver may be a dynamical system to which an incoming symbol appears as an imposed boundary or initial condition. Then, the system will approach an associated attractor state which physically represents the meaning of the symbol. Often, the *attraction basin,* i.e., the set of conditions leading to the same attractor, is a compact set, and slightly modified symbols within that basin will cause the same attractor to be reached. As an example, written letters are recognised as being equal even if their symbols are displayed in different fonts, sizes or colours; they may be irregularly hand-written, distorted, damaged or partially obscured. Reading a symbol can refresh it this way, permitting largely *lossless copies* to be produced if the refreshment happens within the physical lifetime of the symbol(s). Multiplying cells and organisms, but also computer memories implement the refreshment technique for safe long-term data storage.

(ii)   Robustness against small symbol perturbations permits *dialects* to evolve which increasingly use modified symbols that are similar in the sense that upon reading, they produce the same results as their originals. In turn, this process permits gradual deformation of the attraction basin, or even spawning of new basins, that is, *drift and diversification* of symbols, as shown later in Section 5.4, Fig. 7, for the evolution of numerals. "If signals are under selection for efficient transmission between signaler and receiver, then populations inhabiting environments that differ in their effect on signal transmission or detection are expected to evolve different signals — a process known as 'sensory drive'" [Endler, 1993].

(iii)   Symbolic information is *conventional.* A system of symbols may be replaced by a completely different set of symbols if this transformation is simultaneously applied to the message, the transmitter and the receiver. On a Chinese tablet computer, Chinese letters, their Latin transcription and the related binary machine code are permanently exchanged by one another while a tablet is used. Genetic DNA[3] or RNA[4] bases, together with their complementary strains, represent

---

[3] DNA: Deoxyribonucleic acid, a chain of a cyclic sugar molecules (nucleotides) that stores the genetic information, see [Crick, 1968].
[4] RNA: Ribonucleic acid, a chain of a cyclic sugar molecules (nucleotides), see [Lehman, 2010].

the same information. Symbolic information is invariant against such arbitrary symbol transformations.

(iv)   The replacement of a symbol by a physically different one, either with the same or with a different meaning, is energetically practically neutral. Any forces driving a modified message back to some fictitious distinguished "equilibrium message" are virtually absent. Physically formulated, so-called *Goldstone modes* [Obukhov, 1990; Pruessner, 2012] with vanishing Lyapunov exponents appear at the ritualisation threshold and permit exceptionally large fluctuations. Thermodynamically, particular messages appear as alternative "microstates" that populate a "Boltzmann shell" of an information processing system. In fact the famous Boltzmann formula, Fig. 1, for the thermal entropy, $S = k \log W$, of an equilibrium system with W microstates equals Shannon's formula for the information capacity if converted to the unit "bit".

(v)   As a result of the coincidence of structural and symbolic information immediately at the ritualisation transition point, in the Goldstone modes the structural information of the symbols keep a *trace of the evolution history* of the symbolic information system, until this trace may gradually be eroded by fluctuations and neutral drift. The physical form of symbols expresses and reveals their *historicity*.

(vi)   Looking at symbols from the symbolic side, the code symmetry *impedes conclusions* to be drawn from the meaning of the information on the physical properties of symbols. Running a computer program does not permit to decide whether the memory bits are stored by, say, charging electrical capacitors or swapping magnetic fields. Introspection of our mind while thinking does not offer any clues on which transmitter substances may be released between synapses, or on the nature of nerve pulse propagation.

(vii)   Looking at symbols from the structural side, the code symmetry *impedes conclusions* to be drawn from the structure of the symbols on the meaning of the symbolic message. This means, *symbolic information is an emergent property*. The same message may be expressed by different symbols, tokens or languages; a sequence of symbols may be reversibly compressed or redundantly inflated without affecting the meaning of the message. In order to produce a cup of coffee, a single on/off bit may be sent to a coffee machine, or a long instruction may be given to an unexperienced cook to prepare an equivalent result. The same mathematical problem may be solved by very different program codes whose mutual equivalence remains elusive without knowledge about the receiver, namely the rules how to compile and execute the code and to convert the message back into structural information.

(viii)   Added redundancy, such as partial repetition or embedded grammatical rules combined with orthographic vocabularies, leaves the meaning of symbolic information immediately unaffected but allows additional information-protection tools to evolve for *error-detection* and *-correction* of random perturbations. During later stages after the ritualisation, such tools partially counteract the neutral drift of symbols and constrict the set of available Goldstone modes. About half of written English text represents syntactic redundancy [Shannon, 1948].

Code symmetry, or coding invariance, is a key property of symbolic information that is found to be established along with any of the full ritualisation transitions reviewed in the subsequent chapters.

3. Molecular Ritualisation

Ritualisation was first described for animal populations and later generalised to certain forms of social behaviour of humans, but in fact this transition process is also highly relevant already at the molecular level for the understanding of how life emerged.

3.1. *Origin of Life*

Hypothetical scenarios for the origin of life on Earth have often focused on very special aspects of that process, such as spatial compartmentation [Oparin, 1924; Fox and Dose, 1972; Eigen, 2013], inorganic formation of certain organic molecules [Miller, 1955; Miller and Orgel, 1974], or replication properties of sophisticated catalytic feedback loops [Eigen and Schuster, 1977; Wächtershäuser, 1990]. Eigen [Eigen, 1971] emphasized the validity of Darwin's selection principles already at the molecular level; self-replicating chemical reaction systems with the highest selective value (i.e., reproduction rate) are expected to dominate in putative pre-biological populations. Symbolic information permits fast and (almost) loss-free copying and is superior to random mechanical division of growing droplets containing complex catalytic networks that represent structural information. It is manifest to associate with the origin of life the ritualisation transition by which the molecular symbolic information carriers emerged which characterise each living being to the present day in the form of the genetic apparatus.

Even a most simplified conceptual model of the very first ritualisation process, namely the origin of life, appeared to be fairly complicated [Feistel *et al.*, 1980; Ebeling and Feistel, 1982, 1994, 2015; Feistel, 1990; Feistel and Ebeling, 2011]. Starting from under-occupied random catalytic networks in an energy-rich "primordial soup" similar to the one that exists in the vicinity of hydrothermal vents [Wogan, 2015], and the spontaneous formation of spatial compartments in pores or droplets, the model includes ten hypothetical successive qualitative steps to logically provide the basis for the actual ritualisation process [Ebeling and Feistel, 1982]. At this initial stage of the crossover, self-reproducing protocells are assumed to consist of a few catalysts supporting key reaction steps (similar to recent proteins), and related chain molecules whose folded RNA copies [Shelke and Piccirilli, 2014] formed the building blocks which assembled the catalysts in the specific order. Subsequently, the symmetry of this system became broken in such a way that some of the identical chain molecules specialised to provide those RNA copies (similar to recent *transfer RNA, t-RNA*) while the others dictated the sequence in which the related blocks were to be mounted (similar to recent *messenger RNA, m-RNA*). In the latter group, keeping repeated copies of the entire RNA pieces became redundant and the production efficiency increased by replacing the full copy by a shorter identifier, a "codon". This first phase of the ritualisation transition ended with codons that had lost their direct chemical relation to the building blocks they represent, that is, their symbolic information had separated from the structural one. Rather, their mutual link turned into an arbitrary convention embodied by the t-RNA molecule, the codon became an arbitrary symbol [Crick, 1968], and the m-RNA molecules became symbolic information carriers for the instructions on how to mount a catalyst step by step from standardised building blocks.

As a result of the separation of the physical form of a symbol from its meaning, that is, as a result of the fundamental coding symmetry of symbolic information, in the second phase of the ritualisation process the symbols in use may randomly drift and diversify. To some extent, this process can be reconstructed from the symmetries of the modern genetic code [Crick, 1968; Ebeling and Feistel, 1982; Jiménez-Montaño, 1994, 2009, 2012; Jiménez-Montaño *et al.*, 1994, 1996; Jiménez-Montaño and He, 2009; Tlusty, 2010; Feistel and Ebeling, 2011]. Crick's [Crick, 1966] "wobble hypothesis" suggests that initially there was a large number of different codons representing the same building block (the recent amino acid), and that this redundancy, or "degeneracy", was successively reduced by differentiation of t-RNA types and more accurate distinction of the related codons. Because physically the arbitrary symbols possess structural information themselves, symbolic information systems always keep a trace of their own evolution history. The recent genetic code and the physico-chemical structures of the t-RNA molecules provide such traces [Jiménez-Montaño, 1994, 2012; Eigen and Winkler-Oswatitsch, 1981].

In a final phase of the ritualisation transition, mechanisms evolve which freeze, protect and repair the code. This is reflected by the fact that the modern genetic code is rather universal between regions and species, in contrast to, say, human spoken languages which diversified regionally [Axelsen and Manrubia, 2014] after the modern humans spread over the continents several 10,000 years ago. The freezing is visible from the universal genetic code table which specifies only 20 amino acids by means of 64 different symbols (triplets). It seems likely that immediately after the ritualisation also various "dialects" of the genetic code had evolved but only one of them has ultimately survived through all the selection processes and extinction events in evolution history.

The existence of a genome and the genetic code divides living organisms from unenlivened matter [Yockey, 2000, 2005]. The origin of information processes is intimately associated with the evolution of life [Eigen, 1994, 2013; Ayres, 1994, 2003]. Rigorously formulated, *there is no life without symbolic information processing, and there is no symbolic information without life* [Feistel and Ebeling, 2011]. Here, technology is understood as an "honorary living thing" [Dawkins, 1996], as a part of the human culture that belongs to the realm of life [Donald, 2008]. Once the beginning of life is associated with the point of emergence of symbolic information, this definition implies that *Darwinian evolution necessitates symbolic information processing*. The Bible quotation at the beginning may be read as "life began with the emergence of symbolic information by a molecular ritualisation transition", and this first "Word" was the very root of all later symbolic information systems that now exist in our world, including the Bible.

3.2. *Morphogenesis and Neuronal Networks*

With increasing multiplication speed of protozoons, their metabolism resulted in local depletion of available nutrients and accumulation of possibly toxic waste chemicals. Detecting the "taste" of surrounding water, i.e., its structural information, and actively responding to it, similar to the diurnal vertical migration of recent phytoplankton [Wasmund and Siegel, 2008], was certainly of selective advantage already at the early stages of life. By ritualisation, substances released by one organism, such as by-products, and recognized by another, may develop into signals for active communication. Haeckel's [Haeckel, 1874] hypothesis for morphogenesis originating from cell colonies is consistent with this approach. The substances that control the differentiation of genetically identical cells into different tissues [Turing, 1952; Gierer and Meinhardt, 1972], termed *morphogenes*, ultimately become conventional signals that act within a body apart from the environmental chemistry.

Of the few morphogenes discovered so far, the amino acid GABA[5] was found to control the growth of nerve cells in mice [Chen and

---

[5] GABA: γ-Aminobutyric acid, https://en.wikipedia.org/wiki/Gamma-Aminobutyric_acid.

Kriegstein, 2015] and to act as a transmitter in the communication between neurons. The emergence of morphogenes and of neuronal transmitters can be understood as ritualisation transitions [Feistel, 1990; Feistel and Ebeling, 2011]; they are derived from use-activities of the cell metabolism and developed to signals specified by conventions between the cells of an organism. Typically, the kind of molecule acts as a (discrete) symbol whose concentration may be continuously variable, in contrast to symbols in a sequence that are either present or not. Chemically similar molecules may act as "dialects", as we know from various drugs that pretend to be the body's own.

The evolution of neurons from ordinary tissue cells is a ritualisation [Feistel, 1990; Feistel and Ebeling, 2011] that permits neurons to diversify and modify for information processing in the brain by signals and network structures that exist completely separate from the external physical and chemical conditions and from the vital tasks the original tissues had to serve.

4. Ethological Ritualisation

Recent living individuals, in particular animals, are typically equipped with mechanical, chemical, optical and/or acoustical sensors. They exchange energy and matter with their environment, they may actively move to feed, to catch prey or to escape predators. Movements, sounds or metabolic waste of one individual can be recognized by another individual. This perception may affect the behaviour of the latter, which in turn has an influence on the chance of survival or multiplication of the first. Such elemental use-activities and their interaction effects are relevant in the course of Darwin's natural and sexual selection and may become amplified or suppressed during the evolution process. This way, the originally unintended communication effect of an activity may develop into a proper signal activity if it turns out to be more beneficial for selection than the original use-activity. This kind of positive feedback loop was frequently encountered in behavioural biology and was termed *ritualisation,* initially only in this context [Huxley, 1914, 1966; Lorenz, 1963; Simpson, 1976; Tembrock, 1977; Osche, 1979, 1983; Klix, 1980]. Some examples are briefly discussed in this section.

4.1. *Insect Communication*

Vibrational communication is widespread in insect social and ecological interactions [Cocroft and Rodriguez, 2005]. For example, male mosquitos locate flying females by detecting the sound of their wings [Johnson and Ritchie, 2015]. The sound is produced by a use-activity, namely flying, and represents a structural information that the males are able to extract from their physical environment. To constitute a signal activity that produces symbolic information, the females would need to attract males by the same sound independent of flying, which has not been observed, however. This example illustrates a situation without (or before) ritualisation.

The situation is different, for instance, in red mason bees [Conrad and Ayasse, 2015]. For mating success, male bees produce thoracic vibrations of a definite frequency. This frequency varies regionally, e.g., between British and German populations. Females evidently prefer mating with males from their own region. Those vibrations constitute a signal activity whose existence of local dialects indicates neutral drift of the symbol in use between sender and receiver. The appearance of such neutral drift or diversification is typically a result of the coding invariance of the symbolic information transmitted. This example suggests that a ritualisation transition had occurred in the past, even though the original use-activity that had required vibration remains elusive.

Several insect taxa respond to tactile stress by internally releasing stress hormones. If the hormone level exceeds a critical threshold, the individual may change certain properties, such as its behaviour or its colour. If the behavioural change includes intensified active motion, the stress becomes amplified by a positive feedback loop and may trigger a nucleation process and an avalanche-like front that quickly propagates across an entire insect population, similar to a phase transition of the 1st kind. Such phenomena have been investigated in great detail for swarming locusts [Uvarov, 1955; Tanaka, 2005; Ma *et al.*, 2015; Feistel and Feistel, 2015; Ariel and Ayali, 2015] which had repeatedly devastated human agriculture since ancient times. The crossover from solitary to swarming behaviour is caused by critical population densities as a result of rapid multiplication (due to, e.g., abundant feeding grounds) or shrinking territories (due to, e.g., seasonal or climatic changes) such as desiccating grass lands.

Swarming in honey bees is also triggered by excessive tactile stress. It developed into a symbolic communication activity, the so-called waggle dance [von Frisch, 1967; Lochmann, 2012], by which bees returning from excursions inform other bees symbolically about the distance and direction to food sources. The transition from swarming to communication by means of body contacts may be understood as a ritualisation transition; the existence of subspecies dialects [Rinderer and Beaman, 1995; Johnson *et al.*, 2002; Nieh, 2011] supports the assumption that the bee dance elements are arbitrary symbols that are subject to coding invariance of the message conveyed.

4.2. *Sexual Ritualisation*

By Darwinian evolution, structural information of the brightness conditions around diving penguins is phylogenetically extracted and stored as symbolic information in their genes, to be expressed in turn ontogenetically as structural information in the form of their feather "suit". The white belly seen from below against the surface light, and the black back in front of the deep-water darkness serve as optimized camouflage with respect to the penguin's prey such as small fish, and to its predators such as orca whales [Simpson, 1976; Culik, 2002]. In contrast, many other birds present flamboyant plumage colours [Dale *et al.*, 2015] that are assumed to result from sexual selection. Darwin [Darwin, 1859] wrote that he could "see no good reason to doubt that female birds, by selecting during thousands of generations the most melodious or beautiful males, according to their standard of beauty, might produce a marked effect". Most bird colours emerged from the use-activity of depositing metabolic waste such as melanin in feathers [Reichholf, 2011; Li *et al.*, 2014].

Selective pressure with respect to largely invariable environmental conditions produces analogous traits such as the similar colours of virtually all penguin taxa found on several distant continents. In contrast, selective pressure with respect to the capricious taste of potential mating partners is subject to arbitrary convention in the form of "their standards of beauty" and will likely result in traits that may strongly differ from place to place and from species to species. Such traits act as signals for sexual attractiveness that promise successful multiplication.

Numerous examples for the ritualisation of acoustical, optical or olfactory sex signals in plants, animals or humans are described in the ethological literature [Lorenz, 1963; Koenig, 1970; Tembrock, 1977; Osche, 1983]. Human use-activities such as walking, talking or dressing developed to sex symbols and diversified, often becoming entirely separate from their original intent or purpose. Presenting or veiling certain human body parts [Eibl-Eibesfeldt, 1970; Koenig, 1970; Wickler, 1970; Reichholf, 2011], for example, may be commonplace in one culture but may be recognized as a sex symbol in another, depending on the historical, religious or environmental context. An extreme example is the traditional garment in Afghanistan in contrast to the naked Indians at Tierra del Fuego at the time when the Spanish missionaries arrived. Human sex symbols may vary as traditions and fashion dictates [Darwin, 1871; Vieser and Schautz, 2016], as is typical for the code symmetry after ritualisation transitions.

5. Human Ritualisation

Ritualisation phenomena similar to those presented in the previous section were subsequently also described for the human society [Huxley, 1966; Koenig, 1970; Wickler, 1970; Osche, 1983; Grammer and Eibl-Eibesfeldt, 1990; Feistel, 1990; Feistel and Ebeling, 2011; Wunn *et al.*, 2015; Ebeling and Feistel, 2015]. Some prominent examples will briefly be considered in this section, even though various aspects of those are still highly speculative and deserve more thorough future investigations.

5.1. *Kissing, Laughter, Yawning, Tears*

When important social events or decisions are upcoming, humans meet personally even if discomfort of traveling large distances must be tolerated, such as gathering at marriages, funerals, scientific or political conferences. An important reason for preferring meetings to letters or phone calls is non-verbal communication behaviour among humans such as "reading faces", a fact that severely impedes automated translation [Rifkin, 2014, p. 131]. Humans use a wealth of gestures for this purpose, in particular muscle activities of the head such as lifting the eyebrow or the corner of the mouth, shaking the head or turning the eyes. Many of these symbolic actions are easily understood between people of different languages or cultures and may be assumed to have their roots in the common early human history [Eibl-Eibesfeldt, 1970]. Some, such as those we share with apes, are likely even older. These findings, commonly known as the "universality hypothesis", were already described by Darwin [Darwin, 1872].

Within a social group, humans naturally watch the activities of their fellows. Similar to the ritualisation process in animals, an observed activity may influence the activity of the observer, and this change may in turn be recognised by the former individual. By this positive feedback, certain activities become systematically accompanied by social interaction and may eventually turn into mere signals. From the distant past, fossils may hardly exist that could definitely prove the correctness of such hypothetical ritualisation processes, but in some cases the evolution of skull bones or episodes in the development of infants may to some extent support related theoretical models. Even though explanations for the origin of various gestures or facial movements remain somewhat speculative and controversial, some plausible familiar examples may illustrate here possible transitions from use-activities to signal-activities in the evolution history of humankind.

According to the most likely hypothesis, *kissing* derived from oral feeding, both in the sexual context as well as in mother-infant relations [Bilz, 1943; Wickler, 1969; Eibl-Eibesfeldt, 1970; Osche, 1983]. With the exception of some primitive peoples, modern humans actually feed each other orally only in special situations such as amorous plays. Kissing without feeding is also observed in adult chimpanzees. The original use-activity of presenting food, often performed by animals, has turned into a human signal-activity where the original feeding has changed to various social forms such as symbolic kisses between politicians which originate from Easter kisses in the Orthodox Catholic Church and the Roman *osculum*, the kiss of peace [Illich, 1998]. In the first Roman century, early Christians greeted each other as their virtual family members by kissing cheeks [Rifkin, 2014]. Other Roman kisses were the friendly *basium* and the erotic *suavium* [Vieser and Schautz, 2016]. In the course of evolution, kissing activities have diversified from mouth-to-mouth to symbolically kissing hands, cheeks or feet [Eibl-Eibesfeldt, 1970], mostly incompatible with the original aim of feeding, which indicates a complete ritualisation crossover. It is an open question whether or not the symbolic bright red colour of human lips is a result of co-evolution of kissing. A print of red lips at some object is usually understood as a symbol for a kiss. While it is unknown whether the word "kiss" may also have its ancient origin in feeding activities, see Section 5.2, the Sanskrit words for it, *busa* and *kus*, are so similar to their modern German counterparts that a deep common root may be suspected [Vieser and Schautz, 2016].

Neither the sound produced by *laughter* nor the reason for exposing teeth are entirely clear [McDougall, 1903; Eibl-Eibesfeldt, 1967, 1970; Grammer and Eibl-Eibesfeldt, 1990; Titze and Eschenröder, 2007; Ross *et al.*, 2009]. The latter may derive from taking meals together in a social group, or may result from a reversal of the aggressive symbolic bite that many apes and other animals show to threaten others [Wunn *et al.*, 2015]. Another hypothetical origin may be the friendly mutual hair care by teeth as observed in ape groups [Eibl-Eibesfeldt, 1970, p197]. In any case, the use-activity of biting seems to be the most likely root. Laughter as a social interaction is restricted to great apes and humans; it may be contagious in a group when the laughter of one person provokes laughter from others as a positive feedback [Camazine *et al.*, 2003], instinctively and almost irresistibly. From the ritualisation aspect, we note that laughter is a signal-activity that has strongly separated from its original use-activity so that the latter is hardly discernable anymore. It has diversified in various forms from silent smiling to convulsive laughter, and it may express emotions from happiness to sarcasm. While laughter is believed to also have close relations to the health state of single individuals [Titze and Eschenröder, 2007; Navarro *et al.*, 2016], its role as a social interaction symbol appears much more relevant.

Yawning is similarly contagious as laughter and is, as such, a signal-activity [Darwin, 1872; Heusner, 1946]. The related original use-activity remains elusive, but there is a well-known relation to the stretching of face muscles, joints and tendons [Fraser, 1989]. One may speculate that this stretching follows after heavy chewing, and that finishing a meal became a signal that synchronised the sleep phase of a group, which in turn may have offered selective advantages. During human evolution, extraoral food preparation reduced masticatory demands [Daegling, 2012; Zink and Lieberman, 2016] and possibly also the need for yawning as a use-activity. Yawning is known of many vertebrata, including fish and birds, and most mammals, such as cats, lions and apes, often as involuntary mimicry. As a signal, yawning is sometimes also recognised across species [Campbell and de Waal, 2014]. Yawning of unborn babies and non-contagious yawning of pre-school children [Anderson and Meno, 2003] suggests that yawning may still be an individual use-activity as well, or at least an ontogenetic percussion of a previous use-activity in past evolution stages. The related ritualisation transition appears incomplete and is perhaps still ongoing.

Properly functioning eyesight was certainly crucial for the survival of early humans and their animal ancestors; maintaining it was under high selective pressure. This importance is reflected in the acute hurt we feel when our eyeball is mechanically or chemically affected. To clean it, a disinfecting liquid is released to flush the ocular surface: *tears*. The salinity of typically 9 g/kg [Craig *et al.*, 1995] is similar to that of brackish water in the Baltic Sea and results from the osmotic production of the liquid. When strong emotions such as pain suddenly occur, additional tear fluid is rapidly secreted; the stronger the emotion, the more liquid, apparently prophylactically, even if the reason for the emotion may not be a hurt of the eye. If the nasolacrimal duct cannot drain as much liquid as produced, overflowing liquid becomes visible and may be recognised by nearby humans as a signal for true, overwhelming emotions [Lutz, 2001]. Although described already by Darwin [Darwin, 1872], theories explaining emotional tears are still controversial, and rigorous scientific studies are scarce [Messmer, 2009; Hasson, 2009]. Weeping is a rare human universal that is shared with no other creature [Lutz, 2001]. Tears may be contagious when they indicate extreme feelings of happiness, sadness, compassion or pride. Only good actors are able to purposefully produce tears, in contrast to most other humans. Especially children and women are often well aware of the effect their tears as signals impose on others, such as during quarrels. Shedding tears may have played a role as a subtle psychological protection behaviour against the superior physical force of male adults. "Tears are a kind of language, a primary, and often primal, form of communication" [Lutz, 2001]. From the perspective of ritualisation, human tears still represent a use-activity (*reflex* or irritant tears, e.g., when cutting onions) but may also act as a signal-activity (*psychic* or emotional tears, e.g., when mourning). The latter activity is not reduced to a simplified symbol and has not drifted or diversified; therefore this ritualisation transition is in an initial and incomplete stage. However, *basal* tears (which continuously lubricate the eyeball), reflex tears and psychic tears differ in composition and are produced by different glands [Lutz, 2001], indicating that emotional tears already represent a signal-activity that is physiologically separate from the use-activity related to other tears.

5.2. *Spoken Language*

Already a century before Darwin's book on the "Descent of Man" [Darwin, 1871] appeared, von Herder [von Herder, 1772] had argued that humans evolved from animals, and that it is language that distinguishes the one from the other. In the course of this process, "the voice of nature turns into an arbitrarily penciled symbol", a fact which "does not lead to a divine but — quite on the contrary — to an animal origin" [von Herder, 1772]. In the beginning of humankind "was the Word", but it was the human word rather than a divine one. The *infant hypothesis* of the origin of spoken language [Jonas and Jonas, 1975; Berger, 2008; Falk, 2009; Fitch, 2010; Feistel and Ebeling, 2011] that is briefly presented here is consistent with the way we learn to speak during our infancy [Janson, 2006] but is in contrast to the *adult hypothesis* [Tomasello, 2010: Gillespie-Lynch *et al.*, 2013] which assumes that collaboration and division of labour among adults was the primary driving force for the development of human oral communication, starting from ritualised animal signals such as gestures or sounds [Darwin, 1871].

When early humanoids began their new way of life in the African savannah, they learned to efficiently walk and run upright on two legs and to use their liberated hands for other purposes than walking. About 1–2 Myr ago, they lost their fur and developed pigments to protect their naked skin against sunburn [Rogers *et al.*, 2004; Jablonski, 2006, 2012; Rantala, 2007]. To be carried along by their mothers, babies of apes are hanging in the fur, see Fig. 4. In contrast, the baby of a naked, sweaty, upright-walking human must be carried in its mother's arms [Reichholf, 2004; Sutou, 2012], although the infantile Moro reflex to cling to its mother is still present in human newborns [Bronisch, 1979].

If a baby is put away and its mother is out of reach, an acoustic signal of the baby may call her for caretaking. About 1.8 Myr ago, in contrast to chimpanzees and other mammals, humans developed the ability of willfully controlling their airflow of breathing, a physiological prerequisite for fluent speech, singing and laughter [Provine, 2000; Levithin, 2007; Ross *et al.*, 2009; Fitch, 2010]. As it appears from retrospect, human babies crying for their mothers had selective advantages over their silent siblings.

From the first days on after birth, babies can suckle and drink. For these use-activities, the neuronal and mechanical control of lips, tongue, jaw and throat is well advanced, in contrast to many other skills. By those tools, babies are able to modulate the airflow of crying and to start babbling. Parents tend to repeat and to imitate that sound, and after some time, babies start to repeat and to imitate the parent's sound. If those signals are correlated with convenient or unpleasant situations for the baby, it will learn to indicate or to recognise such situations by the signal, i.e., to transmit or to receive a symbolic message. The first oral communication happens between babies and their mothers, amplified by a feedback loop [Gopnik *et al.*, 2000; Held *et al.*, 2011]. It is plausible that the phylogenetic origin of the spoken language was similar; crying babies could also babble, and developed a symbolic acoustic information exchange with the mother with respect to the baby's needs.

Fig. 4. Orangutan baby hanging in its mother's fur. Photo taken on 20 July 2013, Darwineum Rostock.

The diversification of available acoustic symbols was facilitated by various kinetic phase transitions that appear between the dynamical regimes of the physical vocal production system, so that small changes in the airflow may generate different and easily distinguishable sounds [Herzel *et al.*, 1994; Fitch *et al.*, 2002; Tokuda *et al.*, 2007] without relevant differences in energetic costs. On the receptor side, the spectral analysis of complex sound patterns by mammals had evolved already during the Jurassic [Luo *et al.*, 2011; Todd and Lee, 2015]. The ability to generate sound in a controlled manner is not lost when a child grows older; kids may use it also to communicate with other children, and later among adults. Adults in turn can use the oral signal system, once available physiologically, to coordinate social activities. Warning sounds are probably among the earliest nuclei of acoustic communication within a group. We instinctively produce them in cases of sudden hurt ("ouch"), disgust ("ugh") or surprise ("oops"); these "words" are incompletely ritualised and beyond regular vocabularies and grammars [von Herder, 1772; Berger, 2008; Jackendoff, 2002]. The hypothesis that human speech as a signal-activity is phylogenetically derived from feeding as a use-activity is well supported by physiological evidence [MacNeilage, 2008; Fitch, 2010]. Human spoken language is estimated to have evolved between 2 and 1.75 Myr ago [Janson, 2006; Berger, 2008; Morgan *et al.*, 2015]. The existence of various modern languages and dialects [Everett *et al.*, 2015] and their observed ongoing evolution and modification are typical indicators for a completed ritualisation transition. "A struggle for life is constantly going on amongst the words and grammatical forms in each language" [Muller, 1870].

As a consequence of the coding symmetry, it is a characteristic feature of symbolic information that some structural information "fossils" of the ritualisation transition are preserved in the physical structure of symbols over a characteristic relaxation time, that is, symbols keep a trace of their own evolution history. The virtual paradox whether our spoken words are conventionally defined or of onomatopoetic origin [Plato, 1857; Ebeling and Feistel, 1982; Fitch, 2010] represents such a trace, see von Herder's quotation at the beginning.

5.3. *Written Language*

Infants instinctively learn to speak but not to write. In contrast to spoken language that may have developed 1–2 million years ago, the earliest evidence of written language is the Sumerian's cuneiform writing which dates back as late as about 6000 years [Janson, 2006], when early seafarers spread their cultural and genetic seed across the Mediterranean [Lawler, 2010]. In contrast to religious and magical reasons sometimes discussed, the most convincing argument for writing is the existence of private property in a developed state [Rifkin, 2014], for registering cattle and other commodities, fixing the tax to be paid to the sovereign, taking notes of oral contracts and agreements, safely carrying such information over large distances and storing it away from one year to the next [Klix, 1980; Wimmer, 2004; Janson, 2006]. Likely, objects such as cows or huts had to be specified and counted. Similar to the onomatopoetic origin of many spoken words, many first "written words" were just pictograms of the objects they represented. Such a method is robust, does not require teaching or dictionaries, and can easily be understood by people of different tongues which certainly belonged to large ancient empires. Those pictograms were already simplified caricatures, symbols of real objects, but they were not completely arbitrary.

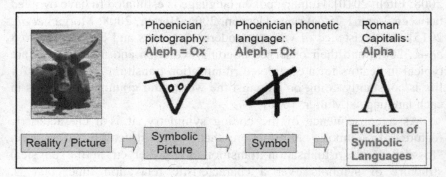

Fig. 5. Ritualisation transition of a real-world picture, such as an ox, to an abstract phonetic letter, such as an A, in the course of social evolution [Klix, 1980; Ebeling and Feistel, 1982; Logan, 1986].

The arbitrariness of written symbols came with the ritualisation transition caused by social evolution, the need for new and more abstract words, the flexibility of written language required to document, say, the personal and family history of an emperor, his glorious victories in wars, or the many titles and crowns carried by him. An instructive example is that of the Phoenician ox, Fig. 5. It shows how through the use in history the visual representation of an object gradually transformed into an abstract symbol which is now arbitrarily associated with an acoustic pattern. In the text of this article, the original relation between the letter A and an ox has completely disappeared.

Similar to other ritualisation transitions, the decoupling of the symbolic picture from the object it represented went along with neutral drift and diversification of the stock of symbols. Hardly any other example shows this process as obviously as the key to the secrets of the Mayan writing [Coe, 1999], where graphical and logical flexibility and diversification of symbols turned out to be an expression of stylistic elegance of those writers. Figure 6 shows the origin of the first four letters of the modern Latin alphabet. The objects listed in Fig. 6 are of very practical nature, related to the daily life rather than to religious or magic ceremonies. This information on the evolution history can be gained from the physical details of our modern symbolic alphabet.

The advanced Phoenician alphabet came up about 1050 BCE[6] [Duren, 2013], soon after the collapse of the Mycenean civilization. Excavated in 2005 near Jerusalem, a complete list of these letters was found carved in the "Zayit Stone", dated about 950 BCE [Tappy *et al.*, 2006]. The symbols and their standard sequence were conserved (while subject to some neutral drift, extension and differentiation) through many centuries; the Minoans passed it to the Greeks who in turn brought it to the Etruscans [Ifrah, 1991]. Romans learned it from their Etruscan neighbours and distributed it all over Europe, such as by Latin, Greek or Cyrillic letters. From there, it took another 2000 years for the Latin alphabet to develop into a universal global communication tool, mainly as a result of the unrivaled technical progress made by the Europeans and their descendants after the industrial revolution.

Sign	Name	Meaning	Greek	Latin
⟀	aleph	ox	A: alpha	A
⊴	beth	house	B: beta	B
⅂	gamel	camel	Γ: gamma	C, G
◁	daleth	door	Δ: delta	D

Fig. 6. First letters of the Phoenician alphabet, their original names and meanings [Luckenbill, 1919; Klix, 1980; Khalaf, 1996]. Note that even the modern word "alphabet" keeps a trace of this history.

---

[6] BCE: Before Common Era, https://en.wikipedia.org/wiki/Common_Era.

Starting already before 3000 BCE, cuneiform symbols had evolved from pictograms in a very similar way, such as the Assyrian cuneiform sign SAG[7] that arose from a schematic drawing of a human head [Borger and Ellermeier, 1981].

Implied by the code symmetry of symbolic information, the structural information of natural languages offers detailed preserved records on the evolution of human societies [Ebeling and Feistel, 1982, 1992; Feistel, 1990]. Comparative language analyses provide insight in the progress of natural sciences, historical events and ethnographic relations [Cavalli-Sforza, 2001; Janson, 2006; Gray and Atkinson, 2003; Hamel, 2007; Lindsey and Brown, 2008; Dunn *et al.*, 2011; Atkinson, 2011; Pagel *et al.*, 2013]. Similar to other evolution processes, new human languages may emerge by dynamic instabilities [Atkinson *et al.*, 2008] and survive by competition [Muller, 1870; Hull, 2010], while inferior languages become extinct [Haarmann, 2002; Janson, 2006] and never return [Darwin, 1871].

5.4. *Numerals*

Some tentative conclusions on the origin of numerals can be drawn from structural information of written language. The word "calculation" is derived from the Latin "calculus" for pebble stones once used to count, and has common linguistic roots with calcium or chalk [Dantzig, 1930; Ifrah, 1991]. The English words "tell", "teller" and "tally" for counting are related to the German words "Zahl" (number), "Tal" (valley) and "Delle" (indention), and refer historically to scratches [Taschner, 2013]. Similarly, "score" has that double meaning. Up to about thirty of such scratches, in groups of five, were found on 25–30 kyr old wolf spikes [Klix, 1980; Coolidge and Overmann, 2012]. This kind of book-keeping by one-by-one mapping of the elements of different sets, such as scratches or fingers, existed long before abstract number systems were invented [Ifrah, 1991]. The words used to describe numbers were often borrowed from body parts because sign language is assumed to be the predecessor of the spoken language with respect to numerals. Just like the letters in Fig. 6, in many languages, the pronunciation of numerals is still amazingly similar to the original Sanskrit words (sunya, eka, dvi, tri,

---

[7] Cuneiform sign SAG: https://en.wiktionary.org/wiki/File:Cuneiform_sign_SAG.svg.

catur, panca, sas, sapta, asta, nava) and preserves a trace to their roots [Ifrah, 1991].

Ifrah [Ifrah, 1991, p. 40] describes the evolution of numerals in terms of the typical three phases of the ritualisation transition. In a precursory phase, numbers are confined in the human's mind to multiple objects that can be recognised at a single glimpse. The imagination of numbers is bound to the observed reality and is not separable from the nature of the object immediately present [Lévy-Bruhl, 1928]. At this stage, numbers still represent structural information. In the second phase the actual ritualisation occurs. Numerals are basically names for body parts used for counting, they increasingly lose their original meaning when representing amounts of certain items, this way turning into half-concrete and half-abstract constructions. Numerals show the tendency to gradually separate from their original meaning to be applicable to arbitrary objects [Lévy-Bruhl, 1928], i.e., as symbolic information. In a final phase, the words used for counting developed to abstract numerals, to true symbols that may be freely modified and are then well distinguished from their original concrete objects [Dantzig, 1930].

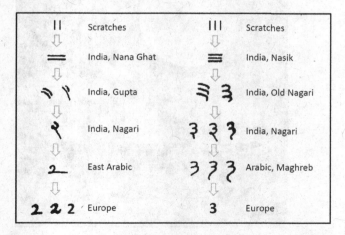

Fig. 7. Ritualisation and neutral drift of the "Arabic" numeral symbols 2 and 3, starting from the original physical structures. Schematic modified from Ifrah [Ifrah, 1991]; branches leading to other descendant Asian numerals omitted.

The written symbols for numerals underwent a ritualisation process similar to that of letters of the alphabet shown in Fig. 5. Adapted from Ifrah [Ifrah, 1991, p. 541, 542], two examples are displayed in Fig. 7 for the transition from physical structures to simplified pictograms and then to abstract numerals, finally losing their links to the original scratches (or fingers). In India, the 1, 4 and 6 are found in the Ashoka inscriptions (3rd century BCE); the 2, 4, 6, 7 and 9 appear in the Nana Ghat inscriptions about a century later; and the 2, 3, 4, 5, 6, 7 and 9 in the Nasik caves of the 1st or 2nd century CE[8] — all in forms that have considerable resemblance to today's [Encyclopedia Britannica, 2015].

Fig. 8. Definition of historical British units of distance and time by artefacts exposed at the Royal Observatory at Greenwich, London. Counting multiples and fractions of conventional measurement units provides symbolic information in the form of numerical measurement results, extracted by comparison from the structural information of the measurand. Similar to Fig. 1, the distances embodied physically represent structural information associated with the symbolic text information such as "BRITISH YARD". Photo taken in September 2013.

---

[8] CE: Common Era, https://en.wikipedia.org/wiki/Common_Era.

A tally stick or body parts may be handy for small numbers but are inconvenient for larger ones, and practically useless for, say, counting the days of a multi-year calendar. The modern method of writing numbers is a solution to a truly challenging problem; its development took a long time of about 3000 years between the first number symbols and the key inventions of zero and the position system [Klix, 1980], one of the most fundamental achievements of humankind [Feller, 2011]. The method permits a convenient representation of very large numbers because the length of the sequence of numerals grows only logarithmically with the value it describes. The invention of the zero symbol by the Babylonians about 2300 years ago was a complicated process that may have taken several centuries to reach maturity [Ifrah, 1991]. There is no natural object that may represent zero, and ritualisation could not happen in this special case. A dot or circle was used in India to indicate a "missing figure", termed "sunya" for void, translated to Arabic as "sifr", from which later the Italian words "zefiro" and "zero" were derived, and in turn "sifra", "chiffre", "cipher" or "Ziffer" elsewhere in Europe. Other position systems are that of the Mayas who independently invented a zero symbol, but in a less sophisticated form and much later [Cooke, 1997], and that of knotted strings, surprisingly used on both sides of the ocean, in Asia and America [Ifrah, 1991].

Counting is a very root of natural sciences. "Measurement implies comparison of quantities or counting of entities" [VIM, 2012], such as counting multiples or fractions of the historical artefacts defined at the Greenwich Royal Observatory (Fig. 8) as the standard units "yard" and "hour" of distance and time, respectively, that were in use prior to the International System of Units (SI). Ignoring here the fundamental difficulties encountered in quantum mechanics [Duwell, 2003], measurement means extracting symbolic information (in the form of numerical values) from structural information (in the form of physical states) by comparison [Maxwell, 1888; Einstein, 1969; Feller, 2011]. For the comparability of measurement results, i.e., for a uniform convention of this symbolic information, the length standard was set in force by the Weights and Measures Act of the British Parliament on July 30, 1855 [Maxwell, 1888]. However, symbolic information resulting from measurements may also take other than numerical forms [White, 2011]. While the particular representation of the resulting symbolic information may vary with the nomenclature, reference systems, units, numerals and number systems used, the meaning remains invariant against such formal transformations of the symbols. The invariance of physical quantities with respect to transformations of their arbitrary mathematical representations is a key element of theoretical physics.

5.5. *Money*

Among animals, claims for territories, nests, mates or food are usually implemented by physical force and fight. When of selective advantage in the course of evolution, such fights may be reduced by ritualisation to symbolic fights or just symbols such as the "aggressive" colours of coral fishes [Lorenz, 1963, 1970]. In the human social evolution, animal claims developed to personal property and symbols thereof, such as written contracts or documents expressing the warranty given by a social authority such as a king or a state. Property is a human convention [Hume, 1751], and "property and law are born and must die together" [Bentham, 1843]. Likely, the wish for documenting ownership was a significant driving force for the evolution of written language and numerals. A special kind of property is money, and its transformation to a symbol of property can also be understood as a ritualisation process [Feistel, 1990; Feistel and Ebeling, 2011].

Fig. 9. Earliest known coin with an inscription. "I am the sign of Phanes" is written on the back of the elk. Probably from Ephesos, Greece, about 600 BCE. Coin made from 14.22 grams of electrum, a naturally occurring alloy of half gold and half silver. Photo taken at the Staatliche Münzsammlung München, May 2013.

Exchange of property between two owners is primarily a mental process of the participants rather than a physical process affecting the items of the deal; if appropriate, the objects are symbolically handed over from the one to the other. Direct binary exchange of useful things may be difficult when the two have very different values to their owners, or are available at different times or locations [Schumpeter, 2008; Smith, 2013]. In such cases, a widely accepted, durable and preferably countable intermediate exchange good is temporarily used to confirm the barter, commonly known as money. "Money is the commodity which functions as a measure of value. Therefore, gold is money. The elementary expression of the relative value of a single commodity, such as linen, in terms of the commodity, such as gold, that plays the part of money, is the price form of that commodity" [Marx, 1951]. Metrologically formulated, the market price appears as a measurement result for the exchange value, obtained by comparison and expressed as a multiple of the currency as the measurement unit, see section 5.4. However, as a mental rather than a physical process in this context, comparison is affected by emergent social influences such as fashion or vanity, and can be reduced to physical comparison only if the exchanged commodities are of the same kind, such as two loaves of bread compared to one. Today, the gold price is "not a measure of any intrinsic value of the metal but, rather, a measure of the paranoia and fear" [Rifkin, 2014, p260]. As an emergent property, the unit of money cannot be reduced to the physical units of the SI. "Tauschwerte der Waren ... [können] nicht eine geometrische, physikalische, chemische oder sonstige natürliche Eigenschaft der Waren sein."[9] [Marx, 1951].

The ox was among the first standard "money units" to express exchange values [Ifrah, 1991]. The Latin word "pecunia" (money, wealth) derived from "pecus" (cattle). Around 280–242 BCE, copper bars "Aes Signatum" heavier than 1 kg with an engraved cow represented the value of one Roman "As" and were used as the first "coins" in the Roman economy [Overbeck and Klose, 1986]. Later, the Romans took over the more practical and already advanced coin system of the Greek towns in southern Italy. The first such coins are known from Ephesos, Milet and Phokaia in Asia Minor, likely at about 630 BCE. Nuggets of a natural gold-silver alloy, "ἤλεκτρον" (electrum, or green

---

[9] Exchange values of commodities ... cannot be either a geometrical, a physical, a chemical, or any other natural property of commodities.

gold), were first marked with simple carves and later with more complex patterns [de Callataÿ, 2013]. It is assumed that those coins were first used for regular payments to soldiers by the Lydian king, and only subsequently exploited for more convenient trade. The first such coin with an inscription is probably that from Ephesos at about 600 BCE (Fig. 9).

Early coins represented their values in the form of precious metals they consisted of. When the coins are circulating from hand to hand, they are gradually losing mass. This matters much less if the material value of the coin is small and can easily be replaced from time to time, while it still carries the symbol for the mass of gold it is worth. If there is an authority which grants the equivalence between symbolic money and a certain amount of gold or a similar valuable commodity, fiat money as a legal tender has a number of advantages over commodity money [Greco, 2001]. Already Plato[10] had suggested that money should be an arbitrary symbol rather than a metallic coin as proposed by Aristotle. The related ritualisation transition constituted a dramatic revolution in the human society [de Callataÿ, 2013], as Sophokles' King Creon lamented already in 442 BCE [Sophokles, 1964, p. 15].

Fig. 10. The British 10 £ banknote is a symbolic paper coupon for the exchange value of 10 pounds sterling silver (alloy of 92.5 % silver and 7.5 % copper), as declared on the note by the emitter: "Bank of Scotland plc promises to pay the Bearer on demand ten pounds sterling at its registered office, Edinburgh".

---

[10] Joan Bardina Studies Center. Chapter 5: Aristotle against Plato. http://chalaux.org/epdduk05.htm.

The possibility of lossless copies is a fundamental feature of symbolic information associated with its code symmetry. The latter permits modifications of the structural information of the symbols without affecting the symbolic information they convey. A new banknote (different serial numbers permitted) and various of its physically deteriorated instances belong to the same equivalence class and represent, by definition, exactly the same symbol and in turn the same value. Refreshment cycles and error-correcting processes permit virgin copies to be made from a slightly aged original as long as the latter is not beyond the "attraction basin".

The disestablished use-value of the money units during evolution indicates a ritualisation transition; the original exchange of values is replaced by an exchange of symbols for those values, see Fig. 10. Those symbols are arbitrary, they can be diversified, they are subject to coding invariance (improved paper notes may replace obsolete versions; damaged or dirty notes can be exchanged for fresh ones). The shape and structure of symbolic money preserves information on its evolution history. For example, the name "Pound" of the British currency is borrowed from the unit of the metal weight it stands for. The word "Dollar" printed on US notes is derived from "Thaler", such as the coins minted in the German towns of Brunswick and Luneburg in 1799. Those coins in turn received their name from the shorthand of "Joachims*thaler* Guldengroschen", a popular currency once emitted in Sankt Joachimsthal, Bohemia, in 1520. Here, "Gulden" again refers to the original gold, and "Groschen", English "groat", likely to the double cross "crossus" often found on Middle-Age silver coins.

Marx and Schumpeter described typical features of the ritualisation transition of money. „Vor ihrer Geldwerdung besitzen Gold, Silber, Kupfer bereits … Maßstäbe in ihren Metallgewichten, so daß z.B. ein Pfund als Maßeinheit dient. … Bei aller metallischer Zirkulation bilden daher die vorgefundenen Namen des Gewichtsmaßstabs auch die ursprünglichen Namen des Geldmaßstabs oder Maßstabs der Preise. … Die Geldnamen der Metallgewichte trennen sich nach und nach von ihren ursprünglichen Gewichtsnamen aus verschiedenen Gründen. … Wenn der Geldumlauf selbst den Realgehalt vom Nominalgehalt der Münze scheidet, ihr Metalldasein von ihrem funktionellen Dasein, so enthält er die Möglichkeit latent, das Metallgeld in seiner Münzfunktion durch Marken aus andrem Material oder Symbole zu ersetzen. … Das

Münzdasein des Goldes scheidet sich [schließlich] völlig von seiner Wertsubstanz. Relativ wertlose Dinge, Papierzettel, können also an seiner statt als Münze funktionieren. In den metallischen Geldmarken ist der rein symbolische Charakter noch einigermaßen versteckt. Im Papiergeld tritt er augenscheinlich hervor"[11] [Marx, 1951, pp102,107, 135,136]. "Nicht nur weisen Münzbezeichungen und Münzbilder öfters auf Warenbedeutungen hin, ... nicht nur ersetzt die Münze oft nachweisbar ein in früherer Zeit am gleichen Ort verwendetes Warengeld, sondern es ist sogar die Wandlung des Warengeldes in die Münze Schritt für Schritt nachweisbar"[12] [Schumpeter, 2008, p23].

6. Technical Ritualisation

In the history of human economy and technology, the advantages of symbolic information processing over manipulation of structural information resulted in various ritualisation transitions, based on the information processing capabilities of the human brain that had evolved biologically before. However, human decisions and inventions made the implementation of symbolic processing steps in established physical process chains often to happen abruptly and discontinuously in comparison to the slow and rather smooth changes that went on earlier at the molecular or biological level as described in the previous sections, see Fig. 3.

Computers are machines capable of automatically performing extended and complicated manipulation tasks in a fast and reliable manner. Early machines of this kind were analog computers such as the Greek Antikythera mechanism [Carman et al., 2012], likely invented between 200 and 100 BCE, mechanical clocks of the Middle Ages, or

---

[11] By their metallic weights, gold, silver, copper had already scales before their becoming money, such that, e.g., a pound serves as a measurement unit. Thus in each metallic circulation, the names of the related weight scale constitute the original names of the money scale or the scale of prices. For several reasons, the money names of the metal weights gradually separate from their original weight names. When the turn-over of money divides the real content from the nominal content of a coin, its metal existence from its functional existence, the latent possibility is implied that the metal money of the coin function may be substituted by tags of a different material or by symbols. The coin existence of gold [eventually] separates completely from its value substance. Relatively worthless things, chits of paper, can function as a coin in its place. In the metallic money tags the purely symbolic character is somewhat hidden. In paper money that character is obvious.

[12] Not only that names and appearances of coins often indicate a meaning of a commodity, not only that often the coin verifiably replaced commodity money used at the same place at earlier times; even the transition of commodity money to the coin is detectable step by step.

automatic looms and music instruments in the 19th century. Mechanical cash registers (tills) and cipher machines such as the German ENIGMA were in regular use in the 20th century. With the increasing availability of electricity and electrical devices, mechanical switches in such computers became replaced by electrical gates such as relays, vacuum tubes or transistors. Analog computers are dynamical systems whose initial and boundary conditions were often imposed in the form of mechanical levers or wheels, or electrical switches or plugs, powered by wound-up springs, lifted weights or electricity. The resulting phase trajectory of the system, such as the changing positions of the clock's hands, or its final attractor state in particular, such as a calculation result, represent the purpose of the machine for humans.

Punched cards, such as the one shown in Fig. 11, like those introduced by Hollerith in 1890 for the US census, are a paradigm for the ritualisation transition from analog to digital computers. Upon reading the card, the holes at various positions in the stiff paper can be detected by mechanical feelers or electric contacts, so that the card represents an array of mechanical or electrical switches whose actual settings specify the intended transition step from the current computer state to the next. From this perspective, the punched card provides structural information that is fed into a physical dynamical system, and the holes appear as reduced and extremely simplified "caricatures" of the original switches mounted at previous machine generations.

On the other hand, the holes in each column of the card represent a symbol for a numeral, a letter or a special sign, as defined by the EBCDIC[13] specification. This way, each card encodes a written line of 80 characters, for example of the ALGOL or FORTRAN programming languages, or of numerical values in certain formats. These languages represent symbolic information, such as mathematical algorithms, in the form of software, which — along with the further technical evolution — gradually separated from the hardware representation given by the punched card. Modern computers may internally use ASCII[14] or ANSI[15] code tables that still resemble EBCDIC but are not fully mutually consistent. Typing in some text via keyboard or touchscreen does not require knowledge of the internal coding rule. Binary representations of

---

[13]EBCDIC: Extended Binary Coded Decimal Interchange Code, https://en.wikipedia.org/wiki/ EBCDIC.
[14]ASCII: American Standard Code for Information Interchange, https://en.wikipedia.org/wiki/ASCII.
[15] ANSI: American National Standards Institute, https://en.wikipedia.org/wiki/Windows_codepage.

symbols on different hardware may vary, such as storing either the least ("LSB") or the most significant bit ("MSB") first in a byte. Algorithms can be written and executed in certain languages almost regardless of hardware details of the enormous variety of computers in worldwide use today. From the viewpoint of ritualisation, the relation between hardware and software, respectively, is similar to the relation between structural and symbolic information.

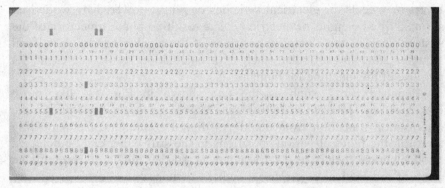

Fig. 11. Punched cards in the standardised "IBM format" with 80 columns and 12 rows were the routine input medium for many mainframe computers from the 1950s to the 1970s. While the holes act as rudimentary switches used in the past, each column represents a symbol in a line of code of programming languages to be used in the future.

Punched cards may mark the point of the ritualisation transition of computers in the course of technological evolution, from mere structural information of electrical circuits before the crossover to symbolic information processing after it. Modern code specifications still keep a historical trace of the arrangements of switches used before the transition. Programming languages convey the symbolic information and possess the code symmetry of being implemented and executed on machines with largely arbitrary structural information of their hardware. On the Internet, a "data packet is structured independently from the equipment, allowing the packet to be processed through different systems and networks, including copper wires, fiber-optic wires, routers, local area networks, wide area networks etc." [Rifkin, 2014, p. 219]. Various new programming languages developed, and still develop, as a result of the freedom of coding.

The emergence of digital computers spawned a wealth of subsequent digitalization processes, similar to the various molecular ritualisation processes that occurred after the emergence of the genetic code, and the behavioural ritualisations after the evolutionary appearance of neuronal networks. Famous examples are the production methods of books that evolved from hand-written copies via the printing press to modern eBooks, the rise and fall of the music industry from shellac records via CDs to Internet streaming, or the manufacturing of commodities from handicraft over industrial mass production to digital 3D-printing. The economic and social changes that have been and will be brought about by digitalisation are often described as the 3rd Industrial Revolution [Rifkin, 2014].

7. Conclusion

Despite their complexity and vulnerability, symbolic information systems proved superior to their structural forerunners at various stages in the natural history from molecular evolution to modern economy. The selective advantages of symbolic information arise from the code symmetry and certain related properties, such as fast and largely loss-free copying. Ritualisation, as a kinetic phase transition of the 2nd kind, is a self-organised phenomenon that resulted in the emergence of conventional symbols and their code symmetry in numerous incarnations of widely varying nature, maturity and significance. Genetic, neuronal and numerical information processing are particularly dramatic examples with far-reaching evolutionary consequences. Spoken words, written letters and numbers are fundamental elements that characterise the human society.

Symbolic information systems appeared exclusively during the evolution of life, provided that technical devices are understood as "honorary living things". Similarly exclusively, ritualisation may be the universal transition process by which symbolic information emerged from structural information. Accordingly, very different symbolic information system have universal properties in common which find their roots in the properties of the ritualisation transition, in particular, in the code symmetry which fundamentally distinguishes symbolic from native information. In turn, the physical carriers of symbols possess structural information apart from their symbolic meaning; these physical structures are percussions of the symbols' evolution history. The way emergent symbolic information, the "soul", became liberated from its original physical nature, the "body", may offer an evolutionary approach to a future unified theory of information.

Acknowledgements

In shorter form, this chapter was presented at the ISIS Summit Vienna 2015 — The Information Society at the Crossroads: Emergent systems, information and society, Vienna, 3–7 June 2015. The author is indebted to Wolfgang Hofkirchner for the kind invitation to this conference, and to Mark Burgin for valuable suggestions.

References

Anderson, J. R. and Meno, P. (2003). Psychological influences on yawning in children. Curr. Psychol. Lett., 2(11), 29 July 2003, http://www.baillement.com/replication/anderson-children.html.

Ariel, G. and Ayali, A. (2015). Locust collective motion and its modeling. PLoS Comput. Biol., 11, e1004522, pp. 1-25, doi:10.1371/journal.pcbi.1004522.

Atkinson, Q. D. (2011). Phonemic diversity supports a serial founder effect model of language expansion from Africa. Science, 332, pp. 346-349.

Atkinson, Q. D., Meade, A., Venditti, C., Greenhill, S. J. and Pagel, M. (2008). Languages evolve in punctuational bursts. Science, 319, p. 588.

Avery, J. (2003) *Information Theory and Evolution* (World Scientific, Singapore).

Axelsen, J. B. and Manrubia, S. (2014). River density and landscape roughness are universal determinants of linguistic diversity. Proc. R. Soc. B, 281, 20133029, http://dx.doi.org/10.1098/rspb.2013.3029.

Ayres, R. U. (1994) *Information, Entropy, and Progress — A New Evolutionary Paradigm* (AIP Press, Woodbury).

Bekenstein, J. D. (1973). Black holes and entropy. Phys. Rev. D, 7, 2333–2346.

Bentham, J. (1843) *Principles of the Civil Code. Part 1: Objects of the Civil Law*, https://www.laits.utexas.edu/poltheory/bentham/pcc/pcc.pa01.c08.html, retrieved 27 Nov 2015.

Berger, R. (2008) *Warum der Mensch spricht* (Eichborn, Frankfurt am Main).

Bilz, R. (1943) *Lebensgesetze der Liebe* (S. Hirzel, Leipzig).

Borger, R. and Ellermeier, F. (1981) *Assyrisch-babylonische Zeichenliste* (Verlag Butzon & Bercker Kevelaer, Neukirchner Verlag, Neukirchen-Vluyn).

Brillouin, L. (1953). Negentropy principle. J. Appl. Phys., 24, pp. 930-939.

Bronisch, F. W. (1979) *Die Reflexe* (Georg Thieme Verlag, Stuttgart).

Burgin, M. (2010) *Theory of Information: Fundamentality, Diversity and Unification* (World Scientific, Singapore).

Burgin, M. (2011). Information: concept clarification and theoretical representation. tripleC, 9, pp. 347-357.

Butterfield, J. (2012). Laws, causation and dynamics at different levels. Interface Focus, 2, pp. 101–114.

Camazine, S., Deneubourg, J.-L., Franks, N. R., Sneyd, J., Theraulaz, G. and Bonabeau, E. (2003) *Self-organization in Biological Systems* (Princeton University Press, Princeton).

Campbell, M. W. and de Waal, F.B.M. (2014). Chimpanzees empathize with group mates and humans, but not with baboons or unfamiliar chimpanzees. Proc. Roy. Soc. B, 281, 20140013.

Carlip, S. (2011). Effective conformal descriptions of black hole entropy. Entropy, 13, pp. 1355-1379, doi:10.3390/e13071355.

Carman, C. C., Thorndyke, A. and Evans, J. (2012). On the pin-and-slot device of the antikythera mechanism, with a new application to the superior planets. J. Hist. Astron., 43, pp. 93–116.

Cavalli-Sforza, L. L. (2001) *Gene, Völker und Sprachen* (dtv, München). Italian original (1996) *Geni, populi e lingue* (Adelphi Edizioni, Milano).

Chen, J. and Kriegstein, A. R. (2015). A GABAergic projection from the zona incerta to cortex promotes cortical neuron development. Science, 350, pp. 554-558.

Cocroft, R. B. and Rodriguez, R. L. (2005). The behavioral ecology of insect vibrational communication. BioScience, 55, pp. 323-334.

Coe, M. D. (1999) *Breaking the Maya Code* (Thames & Hudson, New York).

Conrad, T. and Ayasse, M. (2015). The role of vibrations in population divergence in the red mason bee. *Osmia bicornis*. Curr. Biol., 25, pp. 1–4.

Cooke, R. (1997) *The Native Peoples of Central America during Precolumbian and Colonial Times*, ed. Coates, A. G., "Central America. A Natural and Cultural History" (Yale University Press, New Haven and London), pp. 137-176.

Coolidge, F. L. and Overmann, K. A. (2012). Numerosity, abstraction, and the emergence of symbolic thinking. Curr. Anthropol., 53, pp. 204-225, http://www.jstor.org/stable/10.1086/664818.

Craig, J. P., Simmons, P. A., Patel, S. and Tomlinson, A. (1995). Refractive index and osmolality of human tears. Optom. Vision Sci., 72, pp. 718-724.

Crick, F. H. C. (1966). Codon-anticodon pairing: the wobble hypothesis. J. Mol. Biol., 19, pp. 548-555.

Crick, F. H. C. (1968). The origin of the genetic code. J. Mol. Biol., 38, pp. 367-379.

Culik, B. (2002) *Pinguine — Spezialisten fürs Kalte* (BLV Verlagsgesellschaft, München).

Daegling, D. J. (2012). The human mandible and the origins of speech. J. Anthrop., 2012, Article ID 201502, 14 pp., http://dx.doi.org/10.1155/2012/201502.

Dale, J., Dey, C. J., Delhey, K., Kempenaers, B. and Valcu, M. (2015). The effects of life history and sexual selection on male and female plumage colouration. Nature, 527, pp. 367-370.

Dantzig, T. (1930) *Number, the Language of Science* (Macmillan Company, London), http://blngcc.files.wordpress.com/2008/11/tobias-dantzig-number_the-language -of-science.pdf.

Darwin, C. (1859) *The Origin of Species by Means of Natural Selection or the Preservation of Favored Races in the Struggle for Life*, Reprinted (1911) from the Sixth London Edition, with Additions and Corrections (Hurst and Company Publishers, New York).

Darwin, C. R. (1871) *Descent of Man, and Selection in Relation to Sex* (John Murray, London).

Darwin, C. (1872) *The Expression of the Emotions in Man and Animals* (John Murray, London).

Dawkins, R. (1996) *The Blind Watchmaker* (W.W. Norton & Co., New York).

de Callataÿ, F. (2013) White gold: An enigmatic start to greek coinage. Amer. Numism. Soc., 2, pp. 7-17, https://www.academia.edu/3740426/White_Gold_An_ Enigmatic_Start_to_Greek_Coinage.

Donald, M. (2008) *Triumph des Bewusstseins* (Klett-Cotta, Stuttgart), American original (2001) *A Mind so Rare: The Evolution of Human Consciousness* (W.W. Norton & Co., New York).

Dunn, M., Greenhill, S .J., Levinson, S. C. and Gray, R. D. (2011) Evolved structure of language shows lineage-specific trends in word-order universals. Nature, 473, pp. 79–82.

Duren, S. R. (2013) *The History of "Proto-Writing", Indus Script, and the Minoan Writing Systems* (CreateSpace Independent Publishing Platform, Amazon Distribution, Leipzig).

Duwell, A. (2003) Quantum information does not exist. Stud. Hist. Phil. Sci. Part B: Stud. Hist. Phil. Mod. Phys., 34, pp. 479–499.

Ebeling, W. (2016) Ist Evolution vom Einfachen zum Komplexen gerichtet? Über Werte und Emergenz. Sitzungsberichte der Leibniz-Sozietät der Wissenschaften zu Berlin, 125/126, pp. 69-80.

Ebeling, W. and Feistel, R. (1982) *Physik der Selbstorganisation und Evolution* (Akademie-Verlag, Berlin).

Ebeling, W. and Feistel, R. (1992) Theory of selforganization: the role of entropy, information and value. J. Nonequil. Thermodyn., 17, pp. 303–332.

Ebeling, W. and Feistel, R. (1994) *Chaos und Kosmos: Prinzipien der Evolution* (Spektrum Akademischer Verlag, Heidelberg).

Ebeling, W. and Feistel, R. (2015) *Selforganization of Symbols and Information*, eds. Nicolis, G. and Basios, V., "Chaos, Information Processing and Paradoxical Games. The Legacy of John S Nicolis" (World Scientific, Singapore) pp. 141-184.

Eibl-Eibesfeldt, I. (1967) *Grundriß der vergleichenden Verhaltensforschung* (Piper, München).

Eibl-Eibesfeldt, I. (1970) *Liebe und Haß* (Piper, München).

Eigen, M. (1971) The selforganisation of matter and the evolution of biological macromolecules. Naturwiss., 58, pp. 465-523.

Eigen, M. (1994) The origin of genetic information. Orig. Life Evol. Biosph., 24, pp. 241-262.

Eigen, M. (2013) *From Strange Simplicity to Complex Familiarity* (Oxford University Press, Oxford).

Eigen, M. and Schuster, P. (1977) The hypercycle: a principle of natural self-organization. Part A: emergence of the hypercycle. Naturwiss., 64, pp. 541-565.

Eigen, M. and Winkler-Oswatitsch, R. (1981). Transfer-RNA, an early gene? Naturwiss., 68, pp. 282-292.

Einstein, A. (1969) *Grundzüge der Relativitätstheorie* (Akademie-Verlag, Berlin), (Pergamon Press, Oxford), (Vieweg & Sohn, Braunschweig).

Encyclopedia Britannica (2015) *Numerals and Numeral Systems: The Hindu-Arabic System,* http://www.britannica.com/topic/Nana-Ghat-inscriptions.

Endler, J. A. (1993) Some general comments on the evolution and design of animal communication systems. Phil. Trans. Biol. Sci., 340, pp. 215–255.

Everett, C., Blasi, D. E. and Roberts, S. A. (2015) Climate, vocal folds, and tonal languages: Connecting the physiological and geographic dots. PNAS, 112, pp. 1322-1327.

Falk, D. (2009) *Finding our Tongues. Mothers, Infants and the Origins of Language* (Basic Books, New York).

Feistel, R. (1990) *Ritualisation und die Selbstorganisation der Information,* eds. Niedersen, U. and Pohlmann, L. „Selbstorganisation und Determination" (Duncker & Humblot, Berlin) pp. 83-98.

Feistel, R. (1991) *Models of Selforganization in Complex Systems MOSES,* eds. Ebeling, W., Peschel, M. and Weidlich, W., "On the Value Concept in Economy" (Akademie-Verlag, Berlin) pp. 37-44. DOI: 10.13140/RG.2.1.4759.7609.

Feistel, R. and Ebeling, W. (1978) Deterministic and stochastic theory of sustained oscillations in autocatalytic reaction systems. Physica A, 93, pp. 114-137.

Feistel, R. and Ebeling, W. (1989) *Evolution of Complex Systems: Selforganisation, Entropy and Development* (Deutscher Verlag der Wissenschaften, Berlin; Kluwer Academic Publishers, Dordrecht/Boston/London).

Feistel, R. and Ebeling, W. (2011) *Physics of Self-organization and Evolution* (Wiley-VCH, Weinheim).

Feistel, R. and Feistel, S. (2015) *Locust Phase Transitions,* https://doi.org/10.13140/RG.2.1.1954.3203.

Feistel, R., Romanovsky, Yu. M. and Vasiliev, V. A. (1980). Evolution of Eigen's Hypercycles Existing in Coacervates. Biofizika, 25, pp. 882-887 (in Russian).

Feller, U. (2011) The International System of Units—a case for reconsideration. Accred. Qual. Assur., 16, pp. 143–153.

Fitch, W. T. (2010) *The Evolution of Language* (Cambridge University Press, Cambridge).

Fitch, W. T., Neubauer, J. and Herzel, H. (2002) Calls out of chaos: the adaptive significance of nonlinear phenomena in mammalian vocal production. Animal Behav., 63, pp. 407–418.

Fox, S. W. and Dose, K. (1972) *Molecular Evolution and the Origin of Life* (Freeman, San Francisco).

Fraser, A. F. (1989) Pandiculation: the comparative phenomenon of systematic stretching. Appl. Animal Behav. Sci, 23, pp. 263-268.

Fuentes, M. A. (2014) Complexity and the emergence of physical properties. Entropy, 16, pp. 4489-4496, doi:10.3390/e16084489.

Gierer, A. and Meinhardt, H. (1972). A theory of biological pattern formation. Kybernetik, 12, pp. 30-39.

Gillespie-Lynch, K. Greenfield, P. M., Feng, Y., Savage-Rumbaugh, S. and Lyn, H. (2013) A cross-species study of gesture and its role in symbolic development: implications for the gestural theory of language evolution. Front. Psychol., 06 June 2013, doi: 10.3389/fpsyg.2013.00160, http://www.frontiersin.org/Com parative_Psychology/10.3389/fpsyg.2013.00160/full.

Gopnik, A., Meltzoff, A. and Kuhl, P. (2000) *Forschergeist in Windeln* (Ariston, München). American original (1999) *The Scientist in the Crib* (William Morris, New York).

Grammer, K. and Eibl-Eibesfeldt, I. (1990) *The Ritualisation of Laughter*, ed. Koch, W.A., 'Natürlichkeit der Sprache und der Kultur, Acta Colloquii (Brockmeyer, Bochum), pp. 192-214.

Gray, R. D. and Atkinson, Q. D. (2003) Language-tree divergence times support the Anatolian theory of Indo-European origin. Nature, 426, pp. 435-439.

Greco, T. H. (2001) *Money: Understanding and Creating Alternatives to Legal Tender* (Chelsea Green, White River Junction).

Haarmann, H. (2002) *Lexikon der untergegangenen Sprachen* (C.H. Beck, München).

Haeckel, E. (1874). Die Gastrea-Theorie, die phylogenetische Classification des Tierreichs und die Homologie der Keimblätter. Jena. Z. Naturwiss., 8, pp. 1-55.

Hamel, E. (2007) *Das Werden der Völker in Europa* (Tenea, Bristol, Berlin).

Hasson, O. (2009) Emotional tears as biological signals. Evol. Psychol., 7, pp. 363-370.

Hawking, S. (2001) *Das Universum in der Nußschale* (Hoffmann und Campe, Hamburg). English original (2001) *The Universe in a Nutshell* (Bantam Books, New York).

Held, R., Ostrovsky, Y., deGelder, B., Gandhi, T., Ganesh, S., Mathur, U. and Sinha, P. (2011) The newly sighted fail to match seen with felt. Nature Neurosci., 14, pp. 551–553.

Herzel, H., Berry, D., Titze, I. R. and Saleh, M. (1994) Analysis of vocal disorders with methods from nonlinear dynamics. J. Speech Hearing Res,, 37, pp. 1008-1019.

Heusner, A. P. (1946) Yawning and associated phenomena. Physiol. Rev., 25, pp. 156-168.

Hofkirchner, W. (ed., 1999) *The Quest for a Unified Theory of Information* (Gordon and Breach, Amsterdam).

Hofkirchner, W. (2009) How to achieve a unified theory of information. tripleC, 7, pp. 357-368.

Hull, D. L. (2010) *Science and Language*, eds. Jahn, I. and Wessel, A., "For a Philosophy of Biology" (Kleine, München), pp. 35-36.

Hume, D. (1751) *An Enquiry Concerning the Principles of Morals* (Printed for A. Millar, London), http://www.davidhume.org/texts/epm.html, retrieved 27 Nov 2015.

Huxley, Sir J. (1914) The courtship-habits of the great crested grebe (*Podiceps cristatus*); with an addition to the theory of sexual selection. Proc. Zool. Soc. Lond., 1914, pp. 491-562.

Huxley, J. (1966) The ritualization of behaviour in animals and man. Phil. Trans. Royal Soc. 251, pp. 249-269.

Ifrah, G. (1991) *Universalgeschichte der Zahlen* (Campus-Verlag, Fankfurt/Main). French original (1981) *Histoire Universelle des Chiffres* (Editions Seghers, Paris).

Illich, I. (1998) *The Cultivation of Conspiracy* (Culture-and-Peace-Prize speech, Bremen, Germany, 14 March 1998), http://www.davidtinapple.com/illich/1998_Illich-Conspiracy.PDF.

Jablonski, N.G. (2006) *Skin: A Natural History* (University of California Press, Los Angeles).

Jablonski, N. G. (2012) Human skin pigmentation as an example of adaptive evolution. Proc. Amer. Phil. Soc., 156, pp. 45-57, http://www.amphilsoc.org/sites/default/files/Jablonski1561.pdf.

Jackendoff, R. (2002) *Foundations of Language (Brain, Meaning, Grammar, Evolution)* (Oxford University Press, Oxford).

Janson, T. (2006) *Eine kurze Geschichte der Sprachen* (Elsevier, München). English original (2002) *A Short History of Languages* (Oxford University Press, Oxford).

Jiménez-Montaño, M. A. (1994) On the syntactic structure and redundancy distribution of the genetic code. BioSystems, 32, pp.14-23.

Jiménez-Montaño, M. A. (2009) The fourfold way of the genetic code. BioSystems, 98, pp. 105-114.

Jiménez-Montaño, M. A. (2012) A markov information source for the syntactic characterization of amino acid substitutions in protein evolution. Symm. Cult. Sci., 23, pp. 225-448.

Jiménez-Montaño, M. A., de la Mora-Basanez, C. R. and Pöschel, T. (1994) *On the Hypercube Structure of the Genetic Code*, eds. Lim H. A. and Cantor, C. A.,

"Proc. Bioinformatics and Genome Research" (World Scientific, 1994) pp. 445-485, http://arxiv.org/abs/cond-mat/0204044.

Jiménez-Montaño, M. A., de la Mora-Basanez, C. R. and Pöschel, T. (1996) The hypercube structure of the genetic code explains conservative and non-conservative aminoacid substitutions in vivo and in vitro. BioSystems, 39, pp. 117-125.

Jiménez-Montaño, M. A., Feistel, R. and Diez-Martínez, O. (2004) On the information hidden in signals and macromolecules: I. Symbolic time-series analysis. Nonlin. Dyn. Psychol. Life Sci., 8, pp. 445-478.

Jiménez-Montaño, M. A. and He, M. (2009) *Irreplaceable Amino Acids and Reduced Alphabets in Short-term and Directed Protein Evolution*, eds. Mandoiu, I., Narasimhan, G. and Zhang, Y. "Bioinformatics Research and Applications" (Springer-Verlag, Berlin) pp. 297–309.

Johnson, B. J. and Ritchie, S. A. (2015) The Siren's song: exploitation of female flight tones to passively capture male *Aedes aegypti* (Diptera: Culicidae). J. Med. Entomol., 2015, pp. 1-4, doi: 10.1093/jme/tjv165.

Johnson, R. N., Oldroyd, B. P., Barron, A. B. and Crozier, R. H. (2002) Genetic control of the honey bee (*Apis mellifera*) dance language: segregating dance forms in a backcrossed colony. Amer. Gen. Assoc., 93, pp. 170–173.

Jonas, A. D. and Jonas, D. F. (1975) Gender differences in mental functions: a clue to the origin of language. Curr. Anthropol., 16, pp. 626-630.

Khalaf, S. G. (1996) *Table of the Phoenician Alphabet*, http://phoenicia.org/tblalpha.html.

Klimonovich, Yu. L. (1991) *Turbulent Motion, the Structure of Chaos* (Kluwer Academic Publishers, Dordrecht).

Klix, F. (1980) *Erwachendes Denken. Eine Entwicklungsgeschichte der menschlichen Intelligenz* (Deutscher Verlag der Wissenschaften, Berlin).

Koenig, O. (1970) *Kultur und Verhaltensforschung* (Deutscher Taschenbuch-Verlag, München).

Lawler, A. (2010) Tracking the Med's Stone Age Sailors. Science, 330, pp. 1472-1473.

Lehman, N. (2010) RNA in evolution. Wiley Interdisc. Rev. RNA, 1, pp. 202-213, DOI: 10.1002/wrna.37.

Levithin, D. J. (2007) *This is Your Brain on Music* (PLUME, New York).

Lévy-Bruhl, L. (1928) *Les fonctions mentales dans les sociétés inférieures* (Les Presses universitaires de France, Paris). English edition (1926) *How Natives Think* (Allen & Unwin, London).

Li, Q., Clarke, J. A., Gao, K.-Q., Zhou, C.-F., Meng, Q., Li, D., D'Alba, L. and Shawkey, M. D. (2014) Melanosome evolution indicates a key physiological shift within feathered dinosaurs. Nature, 507, pp. 350–353.

Lindsey, D. T. and Brown, A. M. (2008) World Color Survey color naming reveals universal motifs and their within-language diversity. PNAS, 106, pp. 19785–19790.

Lochmann, D. (2012) *Information und der Entropie-Irrtum* (Shaker Verlag, Aachen).

Logan, R. K. (1986) *The Alphabet Effect* (William Morrow and Company, New York).

Lorenz, K. (1963) *Das sogenannte Böse* (Borotha-Schoeler, Wien).

Lorenz, K. (1970) Foreword to [Koenig, 1970].

Luckenbill, D. D. (1919) Possible Babylonian Contributions to the So-Called Phoenician Alphabet. Am. J. Semitic Language Literat., 36, pp. 27-39, http://www.jstor.org/stable/528221.

Luo, Z.-X., Ruf, I., Schultz, J. A. and Martin, T. (2011) Fossil evidence on evolution of inner ear cochlea in Jurassic mammals. Proc. R. Soc. B, 278, pp. 28-34.

Lutz, T. (2001) *Crying: A Natural and Cultural History of Tears* (W. W. Norton & Company, New York).

Ma, Z., Guo, X., Lei, H., Li, T., Hao, S. and Kang, L. (2015) Octopamine and tyramine respectively regulate attractive and repulsive behavior in locust phase changes. Sci. Rept. 5:8036, DOI: 10.1038/srep08036.

MacNeilage, P. F. (2008) *The Origin of Speech* (Oxford University Press, Oxford).

Marx, K. (1951) *Das Kapital. Kritik der politischen Oekonomie,* Erster Band (Dietz, Berlin). Original of 1867, (Otto Meißner, Hamburg).

Maxwell, J. C. (1888) *Theory of Heat* (Longmans, Green and Co., London and New York).

McDougall, W. (1903) The Theory of Laughter. Nature, 67, pp. 318-319.

Messmer, E. M. (2009) Emotionale Tränen (emotional tears). Ophthalmologe, 106, pp. 593-602.

Miller, S. L. (1955) Production of some organic compounds under possible primitive Earth conditions. J. Am. Chem. Soc., 77, pp. 2351-2361.

Miller, S. L. and Orgel, L. E. (1974) *The Origins of Life on Earth* (Prentice Hall, Englewood Cliffs).

Morgan, T. J. H., Uomini, N. T., Rendell, L. E., Chouinard-Thuly, L., Street, S. E., Lewis, H. M. Cross, C. P., Evans, C., Kearney, R., de la Torre, I., Whiten, A. and Laland, K. N. (2015) Experimental evidence for the co-evolution of hominin tool-making teaching and language. Nature Communications, 6, #6029.

Muller, M. (1870). Darwinism tested by the Science of Language. Translated from the German of Professor August Schleicher. Nature, 1, 256-259.

Navarro, J., del Moral, R., Cuesta-Alvaro, P., Lahoz-Beltra, R. and Marijuán, P. C. (2016). The entropy of laughter: discriminative power of laughter's entropy in the diagnosis of depression. Entropy, 18, 36, doi:10.3390/e18010036.

Nieh, J. C. (2011) The evolution of honey bee communication: learning from asian species. Formos. Entomol., 31, pp. 1-14.

Obukhov, S. P. (1990) Self-organized criticality: Goldstone modes and their interactions. Phys. Rev. Lett., 65, pp. 1395-1398.

Oparin, A. I. (1924) *Origin of Life* (Moskovski Rabochi, Moscow) (in Russian).

Osche, G. (1979) Zur Evolution optischer Signale bei Blütenpflanzen. Biologie in unserer Zeit, 9, pp. 161-170, DOI: 10.1002/biuz.19790090604.

Osche, G. (1983) *Zur Evolution optischer Signale bei Pflanze, Tier und Mensch* (Ernst-Haeckel-Vorlesung, Friedrich-Schiller-Universität, Jena).

Overbeck, B. and Klose, D. O. A. (1986) *Antike im Münzbild* (Staatliche Münzsammlung München, Stadt Oberkochen).

Pagel, M., Atkinson, Q. D., Calude, A. S. and Meade, A. (2013) Ultraconserved words point to deep language ancestry across Eurasia. PNAS, 110, pp. 8471-8476.

Plato (1857) *Kratylos,* German translation by Friedrich E.D. Schleiermacher, Platons Werke, 2. Band (Georg Reimer, Berlin), http://www.opera-platonis.de/Kratylos.pdf.

Provine, R. (2000) *Laughter: A Scientific Investigation* (Penguin Books, New York).

Pruessner, G. (2012) *Self-organised Criticality* (Cambridge University Press, Cambridge).

Rantala, M. J. (2007) Evolution of nakedness in *Homo sapiens*. J. Zool., 273, pp. 1-7.

Reichholf, J. H. (2004) *Das Rätsel der Menschwerdung* (dtv, München).

Reichholf, J. H. (2011) *Der Ursprung der Schönheit* (C.H. Beck, München).

Rifkin, J. (2014) *The Zero Marginal Cost Society: The Internet of Things, the Collaborative Commons, and the Eclipse of Capitalism* (Palgrave Macmillan, New York).

Rinderer, T. E. and Beaman, L. D. (1995) Genetic control of honey bee dance language dialect. Theor. Appl. Gen., 91, pp. 727-732.

Rogers, A. R., Iltis, D. and Wooding, S. (2004) Genetic variation at the MC1R locus and the time since loss of human body hair. Curr. Anthropol., 45, pp. 105-108.

Ross, M. D., Owren, M. J. and Zimmermann, E. (2009) Reconstructing the evolution of laughter in great apes and humans. Curr. Biol., 19, pp. 1106-1111.

Schrödinger, E. (1944) *What is Life — the Physical Aspect of the Living Cell* (Cambridge University Press, Cambridge).

Schumpeter, J. A. (2008) *Das Wesen des Geldes: Aus dem Nachlaß herausgegeben und mit einer Einführung versehen* (Vandenhoeck & Ruprecht, Göttingen).

Shannon, C. E. (1948) A mathematical theory of communication. Bell Syst. Techn. J., 27, pp. 379-423, 623-656.

Shelke, S. A. and Piccirilli, J. A. (2014) Origins of life: RNA made in its own mirror image. Nature, 515, pp. 347–348.

Simpson, G. G. (1976) *Penguins — Past and Present, Here and There* (Yale University Press, Yale and London).

Smith, A. (2013) *Der Wohlstand der Nationen* (dtv, München). English original (1789) *An Inquiry into the Nature and Causes of the Wealth of Nations* (Methuen & Co., London).

Sophokles (1964) *Antigone* (Philipp Reclam jun., Leipzig).

Sutou, S. (2012) Hairless mutation: a driving force of humanization from a human–ape common ancestor by enforcing upright walking while holding a baby with both hands. Genes to Cells, 17, pp. 264–272, DOI: 10.1111/j.1365-2443.2012. 01592.x.

Tanaka, S. (2005) Hormonal control of phase polyphenism in locusts. formos. Entomol., 25, pp. 131-143.

Tappy, R. E., McCarter, P. K., Lundberg, M. J. and Zuckerman, B. (2006) An Abecedary of the Mid-Tenth Century B.C.E. from the Judaean Shephelah. Bull. Amer. Sch. Orient. Res., 344, pp. 5-46.

Taschner, R. (2013) *Die Zahl die aus der Kälte kam* (Carl Hanser Verlag, München).

Tembrock, G. (1977) *Grundlagen des Tierverhaltens* (Akademie-Verlag, Berlin).

Titze, M. and Eschenröder, C. T. (2007) *Therapeutischer Humor* (Fischer, Frankfurt/Main).

Tlusty, T. (2010) A colorful origin for the genetic code: Information theory, statistical mechanics and the emergence of molecular codes. Physics Life Rev., 7, pp. 362-376.

Todd, N. P. M. and Lee, C. S. (2015) The sensory-motor theory of rhythm and beat induction 20 years on: a new synthesis and future perspectives. Front. Hum. Neurosci., 9, Article 444, doi: 10.3389/fnhum.2015.00444.

Tokuda, I. T., Horáček, J., Švec, J. G. and Herzel, H. (2007) Comparison of biomechanical modeling of register transitions and voice instabilities with excised larynx experiments. J. Acoust. Soc. Amer., 122, pp. 519-531.

Tomasello, M. (2010) *Origins of Human Communication* (The MIT Press, Cambridge, London).

Turing, A. M. (1952) The chemical basis of morphogenesis. Phil. Trans. Roy. Soc. Lond. B, 237, pp. 37-72.

Uvarov, B. P. (1955) *The aridity factor in the ecology of locusts and grasshoppers of the Old World* (Unesco Report NS/AZ/204, Paris), http://unesdoc.unesco.org/ images/0014/001486/148632eb.pdf.

Vieser, M. and Schautz, I. (2016) *Für immer und jetzt. Wie man hier und anderswo die Liebe feiert* (Antje Kunstmann, München).

VIM (2012) *International Vocabulary of Metrology — Basic and General Concepts and Associated Terms (VIM)*, 3rd edition, JCGM 200:2012, http://www.bipm.org/en/ publications/guides/vim.html.

von Frisch, K. (1967) *The Dance Language and Orientation of Bees* (Harvard University Press, Cambridge).

von Herder, J. G. (1772) *Abhandlung über den Ursprung der Sprache, welche den von der Königl. Academie der Wissenschaften für das Jahr 1770 gesezten Preis erhalten hat* (Christian Friedrich Voß, Berlin), http://www.deutschestextarchiv. de/book/show/herder_abhandlung_1772. English translation: Gode, A. (1966) *Essay on the Origin of Language. In: Two Essays On the Origin of Language, Jean-Jacques Rousseau and Johann Gottfried Herder* (The University of Chicago Press, Chicago and London) pp. 85-166.

Wächtershäuser, G. (1990) Evolution of the first metabolic cycles. PNAS, 87, pp. 200-204.

Wasmund, N. and Siegel, H. (2008) *Phytoplankton*, eds. Feistel, R., Nausch, G. and Wasmund, N. "State and Evolution of the Baltic Sea, 1952 – 2005" (Wiley, Hoboken, NJ), pp. 441-482.

White, R. (2011) The meaning of measurement in metrology. Accred. Qual. Assur., 16, pp. 31-41.

Wickler, W. (1969) *Sind wir Sünder?* (Droemer & Knaur, München).

Wickler, W. (1970) *Stammesgeschichte und Ritualisierung* (Piper-Verlag, München).

Wikipedia (2016) *Black hole information paradox* Page last modified on 28 January 2016, at 05:10. https://en.wikipedia.org/wiki/Black_hole_information_paradox.

Wimmer, S. (2004) *Die Hieroglyphen — Schrift und Schrifttum*, eds. Schulz, R. and Seidel, M., "Ägypten. Die Welt der Pharaonen" (Könemann in der Tandem Verlag, Königswinter) pp. 343-356.

Wogan, T. (2015) How Earth's earliest life overcame a genetic paradox. Science, 26 January 2015, DOI: 10.1126/science.aaa6397.

Wunn, I., Urban, P. and Klein, C. (2015) *Götter - Gene - Genesis: Die Biologie der Religionsentstehung* (Springer Spektrum, Berlin, Heidelberg).

Yockey, H. P. (2000) Origin of life on earth and Shannon's theory of communication. J. Comput. Chem., 24, pp. 105-123.

Yockey, H. P. (2005) *Information theory, evolution and the origin of life* (Cambridge University Press, Cambridge).

Zink, K. D. and Lieberman, D. E. (2016) Impact of meat and Lower Palaeolithic food processing techniques on chewing in humans. Nature, 531, pp. 500-503.

Chapter 5

The Law of "Information Conversion and Intelligence Creation"

Yixin Zhong

School of Computing Beijing
University of Posts and Telecommunications
Beijing 100876, China
zyx@bupt.edu.cn

All intelligent information systems in general and human information system in particular should possess such functions as information acquisition, transfer, processing and information conversion to knowledge and further to intelligence for problem solving so that they can well successfully interact with their environment for living. Furthermore, all these functions must also be integrated into a process of "information conversion and intelligence creation". In this chapter, we present the law that governs the entirety of these processes. In addition, we briefly explain the methodology, models, concepts, theories and principles that support this law.

Keywords: Methodology of information ecology; subject-object interaction; comprehensive information; information conversion; intelligence creation.

1. Introduction: Methodology Issue in Information Studies

Because the methodology of "reductionism (divide and conquer)" has widely been applied to information studies in the past, the information discipline has been broken up into a number of mutually isolated sub-disciplines, i.e., information theory research, knowledge theory research, and intelligence theory research. These sub-disciplines have been further divided: information theory research into syntactic, semantics, and pragmatics, with the latter two ignored [Shannon, 1948]; knowledge theory research into two fields (knowledge engineering [Feigenbaum *et al*., 1977] and knowledge discovery [Fayad, 1996]); and intelligence theory research into three fields (artificial neural networks [McCulloch and Pitts, 1943; Rumelhart, 1986; Hopfield, 1982], physical symbol systems [Turing, 1950; Newell, 1980; Simon, 1981; Nilsson, 1982], and sensor-motor systems [Brooks, 1990; Brooks, 1991]). This can roughly be conceptualized in Fig.1.

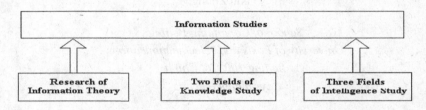

Fig. 1 "Divide and Conquer" and Information Studies

As can be seen in Fig.1, within the information studies discipline, there are no links among the fields of information theory research, knowledge theory research, and intelligence theory research. In reality, however, information, knowledge, and intelligence do form a sort of an ecological process via the interactions between the human subject and environment. This contradiction between the theoretical study and reality is caused by the methodology of reductionism featured as "divide and conquer".

To eliminate the contradiction between the theoretical study and reality, it is crucial to consider a new and more proper methodology for information studies, which should be able to reflect the links connecting information, knowledge, and intelligence so that a unified theory covering the entire information process can be established.

2. New Model, New Methodology, and New Results for Information Studies

The most influential model for information studies used so far has been the one established by Shannon in 1948 that basically includes source for information generation, channel for information transmission, and sink for information receiving, associated with coding and decoding [Shannon, 1948]. The model's major weakness is that its applicability is limited to statistical communication and, as a result, it loses the generalities of the information process, both in the depth and the width of the studies. Many researchers have already discussed this deficiency (cf., for example, [Burgin, 2010]).

The information process that exists within the interaction between the human subject and the object in the environment is the most meaningful to humans and is thus, the right scope of information studies. It is an ecological system able to make information grow into knowledge, and then into intelligence. The model for information studies can then be formulated as is shown in Fig. 2 [Zhong, 1988].

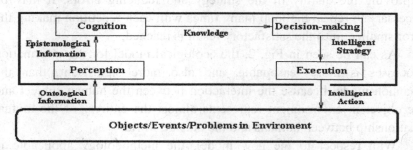

Fig. 2 Ecological Model of Information process within subject-object interaction

The lower part in Fig. 2 represents the object/event/problem that exists in the environment, and exerts influence on the human subject and thus should be carefully dealt with by humans. The upper part in Fig. 2 stands for the human subject who possesses the typical functions of perception (for information): cognition for knowledge; and producing, based on information and knowledge, decision making for strategy-creation, and execution for applying an action to the object according to the strategy.

Specifically, the ecological process of information that exists in the interaction between the human subject and the object in the model includes the following elements and functions.

(1) Ontological Information (OI for short) is presented by object in environment.

(2) Epistemological Information (EI) is conversed from OI via perception.

(3) Knowledge (K) is conversed from EI via cognition.

(4) Intelligent strategy (IS) is conversed from K and EI via decision-making.

(5) Intelligent action (IA) is conversed from IS to deal with the object.

(6) If there is an error between the state resulting from the above action and the preset goal, the error should serve as new ontological information and should be fed back into the input of the upper part of the model.

The loop (1)–(6) would be repeated in the process of optimization for improving the quality of the strategy and reducing errors. It may be necessary to repeat the loop many times with each repetition making the error smaller, until the satisfactory result is reached.

As can be seen in Fig. 2, the ecological model for the information processes is more reasonable, and also more significant, than the Shannon model because the interaction between the human subject and the object in environment represents almost the entirety of the mutual relationship between humans and the outside world.

With respect to the new model, the methodology applicable in information studies can be termed "ecology-ism". The 'ecology-ism' methodology reflects the following views: the view of the information, but not the view of the matter; the view of the system, but not the view of the individuality; the view of ecology, but not the view of statics; and the view of the interaction between the subject and the object, but not the view of the isolation between them.

Clearly, "ecology-ism", the methodology applicable in the information discipline, is radically different from "reductionism", which is methodology suitable for classical physics.

Having applied the methodology of "ecology-ism" in information studies, a series of new results have thus been achieved (see Fig. 3 below): a group of new concepts (ontological information and epistemological information; knowledge; and Intelligence); new theories (comprehensive information theory; the theory of knowledge ecology, and the theory of mechanism simulation of intelligence), and new principles (the three information conversions: 1#, 2#, and 3#). All of these results have been integrated into information science in a way that the above contradiction disappeared.

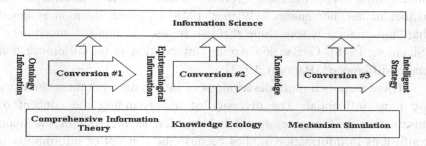

Fig. 3 New Methodology and New Results in Information Science Studies

Most interestingly, *the Law of "Information Conversion and Intelligence Creation" emerged from the ecological process of information carried on within the interaction between the human subject and the object in environment* (see Fig. 3 again).

In the following sections, all of the results, including the concepts, the theories and the principles supporting this law, will be explained. Due to the limitations of the space, the explanations will be in brief. Detailed information can be found in the works [Zhong, 1988, 2000, 2007, 2013, 2014].

3. Concept Reformation Based on Ecology-ism

The concepts concerning ontological information, epistemological information, knowledge, and intelligence constitute an ecological chain in information studies as we can see in Fig. 3.

3.1. *Concepts related to information*

Information is the most fundamental, yet also the most confusing, concept in information studies. It is therefore necessary to clarify the concepts and definitions of information based on "ecology-ism."

3.1.1. *Existing understandings for information*

In the literature, there have been different understandings of the term 'information'. For instance, Norbert Wiener wrote, "information is neither matter, nor energy" [Wiener, 1948]. Claude Shannon assumed that "information is something that can be used to remove uncertainty" [Shannon, 1948]. G. Bateson wrote, "information is the difference that makes difference" [Bateson, 1972].

There are much more descriptions of information but these three are the most influential. The diversity of understanding the concept of information in literature should be regarded as the root of the main confusions in information studies because the concept of information is really the foundation of the discipline.

3.1.2. *Definitions of information*

As we can see in Fig. 2 and Fig. 3, there exist two kinds of information (and not one) in reality: one is ontological information and the other is epistemological information. The former is the one produced by the object in the environment and is before the subject's percept. The latter is the product from the subject's percept of the former.

Definition 3.1.1 Ontological Information (Object Information)
The ontological information presented by any object is defined as "the states, in which the object may stay, and the pattern, with which the states vary" (or as the "states-pattern") [Zhong, 1988].

Ontological information is so named because this kind of information is determined uniquely by the object itself and has nothing to do with the subject.

Definition 3.1.2 Epistemological Information (Perceived Information) Epistemological information that a subject possesses about any object is defined as the form, the meaning, and the utility of the "states-pattern" that the subject perceives from the ontological information of the object. In epistemological information, the form is named 'syntactic information'; the meaning, 'semantic information'; and the utility, 'pragmatic information [Zhong, 1988].'

Note that the triad "the syntactic information, the semantic information, and the pragmatic information" is named *comprehensive information* [Zhong, 1988].

Different from the ontological information, epistemological information is determined not only by object, but also by the subject. It is clear that only by possessing the so-defined comprehensive information can a subject have the complete information about the object.

It is reasonable to accept that (1) "the states at which an object may stay and the pattern with which the states vary, presented by an object" are "*neither matter nor energy.*" (2) "The states at which an object may stay and the pattern with which the states vary, presented by an object" are also "*something that can be used to remove uncertainty*" in communication, and (3) "the states at which an object may stay and the pattern with which the states vary, presented by an object" are just "*the difference that makes difference.*" This is because how an object is different from others is exactly its "states at which the object may stay and the pattern with which the states vary".

The analyses above indicate that *the definition of ontological information given in 3.1.1 and the definition of epistemological information given in 3.1.2 can serve as the universal definitions of information*, with the ability to unify the statements given by Wiener, Shannon, Bateson, and others.

3.2. *Resolving the confused concepts: "data" and "information"*

Having explained the definitions of information above, it is now possible and necessary to clarify some concepts such as 'data' and 'information' that have been puzzled over by many researchers in the discipline for quite some time and have been obstacles to achieving progress in information studies.

It is well known that voice, text, graph, picture, and video are different kinds of analog signals. They respectively carry analog information and are thus called analog carriers for information. Similarly, data is also a kind of carrier of information. Different from analog carriers, however, data, particularly binary digital data, has the special feature of "discrete in time domain and quantum in value domain." Thus, there are many advantages to data in signal/information processing and transmission in information systems.

Thanks to the advancement of digital technology, analog carriers/signals of information can easily be digitized into the digital form via discretizing, quantizing and coding technology. As a consequence, all kinds of carriers of information have been digitized into digital form, the same form as digital data. Therefore, all kinds of carriers of information have the same term, "data". In other words, different from situations in the past, the term "data" today refers to all kinds of carriers of information.

Referring back to the definitions of epistemological/comprehensive information given above, it should be noted that data, as a general term representing digital audio, digital text, digital graph, digital video, and the real data, is just the syntactic (formal) component of epistemological/comprehensive information. Above all, *the general term 'data' is not a concept independent from that of information, but instead is a part of the concept of information, i.e., syntactic information.* This is to say, when people say "data", it should be understood as "syntactic information".

There is another confusing concept. *When people talk about the term "information," they often really mean "semantic information"* because semantic information is what concerns people the most. *However, the information that people find in the literature of science and technology is only the "information in the Shannon sense".* Therefore, whether the term "information" should be understood as "information in the Shannon sense, i.e., syntactic information", or should be understood as "semantic information," sometimes there is no way to know. This kind of chaos we can see very frequently both in oral and written forms of discussion. This has been the most serious obstacle in making progress in information studies.

According to the definitions of information stated in section 3.1.2, the confused concepts of "data" and "information" may in most cases be described as that shown in Table 1.

Table 1. The Confusing Concepts of "Data" and "Information"

Confused Items	What People Say	What It may really Mean
Item 1	Data	Syntactic Information
Item 2	Information	Semantic Information

Because we did not have the concepts of "syntactic information" and "semantic information" in the past, when one says "data", he may really mean "syntactic information" and when one says "information", he may really mean "semantic information," thus leading to great difficulties in information studies.

3.3. *Concept of knowledge based on ecology-ism*

According to the new methodology then, knowledge grows from epistemological information and can grow further into intelligence. Therefore, knowledge plays the important role of bridge, linking information on one hand and intelligence on the other. This we can clearly see in the ecological model of the information process in Fig. 2.

There are not many discussions about the definition of knowledge in scientific literature, even in the literatures concerning 'knowledge engineering' and 'knowledge discovery'. Therefore, it is wise to develop an understanding of the definition of knowledge.

Definition 3.3.1 Knowledge

Knowledge that human subjects possess about a class of objects is defined as the "states that the objects may stay and the law with which the states vary," including their form, meaning, and utility_that human subjects have refined from a large amount of epistemological information samples in the class [Zhong, 2000].

It is easy to see that the definition of knowledge is very directly related to that of epistemological information. Comparing the definition of epistemological information in 3.1.2 and that of knowledge, the difference between the two lies in that there is the word "pattern" connected to epistemological information while the word "law" is connected to knowledge.

More specifically, information concerns specific phenomenon that tells "what it is" while knowledge is concerned with the essence of the phenomena and able to explain "why it is so". It is important to note that the essence must come from the phenomena.

3.4. *Concept of intelligence based on ecology-ism*

Intelligence is the central concept in information studies. In practice, the purpose of seeking information in most cases is to produce knowledge and intelligence that is needed for solving complex problems people face.

However, there is confusing between intelligence and wisdom in literature.

To the author's understanding, wisdom is a power much stronger than that of intelligence and can only be possessed by humans, not by machines. Generally speaking, *human wisdom could have two abilities*: (1) the *ability to properly find and define problems, and* (2) the *ability to understand and solve the problems defined.* The former sets up a framework for problem solving and needs abstract factors to support it, such as clear objectives, sufficient knowledge, intuition ability, imagination ability, inspiration ability and aesthetical feelings; thus it can properly be regarded as *implicit intelligence.* The latter solves problems within the framework given by the implicit intelligence and needs some kinds of operational abilities for producing certain amount of information, knowledge and strategy for problem solving. Hence, it can be termed *explicit intelligence.* Obviously, implicit intelligence would be difficult, if not impossible, to simulate technically, whereas with explicit intelligence, to do so is possible.

The artificial intelligence that we are talking about here is the discipline that understands and simulates the explicit intelligence of human wisdom, instead of the implicit intelligence.

Definition 3.4.1 Intelligence

Intelligence, or more precisely explicit intelligence, is defined as the ability to understand problems, and to produce appropriate strategy for solving problems under the framework given beforehand [Zhong, 2007].

Obviously, in order to produce the intelligence (intelligent strategy) needed for problem solving, one needs the necessary information, knowledge, goals, and the mechanism for conversing information to knowledge and to intelligence under the guidance of the goal.

4. Theories Reestablishment in the Line of Ecology-ism

As is clearly seen in Fig. 3, the Law of Information Conversion and Intelligence Creation is collectively supported by the theory of comprehensive information, the theory of knowledge, and the theory of intelligence. All the three categories of theory need to be reestablished.

4.1. *The theory of information*

The Shannon theory titled 'The Mathematical Theory of Communication' [Shannon, 1948] was the first theory of information in the world. It was established in 1948 to meeting the needs of communication research and has made great contributions to the development of communication technology and engineering.

4.1.1. *Limitations of Shannon theory of information rooted from old methodology*

With the employment of the methodology of 'Divide-and-Conquer,' the Shannon theory of information has at least two limitations that prevent it from being applied successfully in the fields beyond statistical communication.

The first limitation is that it is unable to deal with the content and value factors of information and only the formal factors of information have been considered. Its second limitation is that it is unable to handle non-probabilistic information and only probabilistic information is taken into account.

These limitations are major obstacles for the basic requirements of the 'ecology-ism' information methodology. The Shannon theory, without the content and value factors, cannot support the studies of the ecological information system, the intelligent systems in particular.

4.1.2. *Establishment of comprehensive theory of information*

For overcoming the limitations aforementioned, the 'Comprehensive Theory of Information' was established in 1984 and summarized in the book "Principles of Information Sciences" published in 1988 and reprinted in the years of 1996, 2002, 2005, and 2013 [Zhong, 1988].

The form, content, and value factors of the information, which are respectively termed syntactic information, semantic information, and pragmatic information, are taken into account in the new theory. The describing parameters that are adopted are "certainty" for syntactic information, "logic truth" for semantic information, and "utility" for pragmatic information. They are respectively denoted by the vectors C, T, and U.

Typically, for any given variable $X' = (x_1, x_2, \ldots x_n)$, the comprehensive information will then be described by the matrix of parameters:

$$
\begin{matrix}
x_1 & x_2 & \ldots & x_n \\
c_1 & c_2 & \ldots & c_n \\
t_1 & t_2 & \ldots & t_n \\
u_1 & u_2 & \ldots & u_n
\end{matrix}
\tag{4.1.1}
$$

Where in (4.1.1) $\{x\}$ represents the set of states at which the object may stay, $\{c\}$, $\{t\}$, and $\{u\}$ represent the features of the pattern with which the states vary. Note that parameter certainty c may be either the probability p if x is a random variable, or membership μ if x is a fuzzy variable. Parameters t and u are memberships because the logic truth and utility here are fuzzy in nature.

Based on the representations for the information shown in the matrix (4,1,1), the measurements for the syntactic, the semantic, and the pragmatic information can be established by using probability theory and fuzzy set theory [Zadeh, 1965]. For more details, please see the reference [Zhong, 1988].

Consequently, syntactic, semantic, and pragmatic information, either probabilistic or non-probabilistic, are uniformly defined, described and measured. It is not difficult to prove that the Shannon theory of information is indeed a kind of statistically syntactic information theory, a special case of the comprehensive theory of information when $c_i = p_i$ with t_i and u_i are ignored for all i in eq. (4.1.1).

4.2. *The theory of knowledge*

There have been two recent research studies in the field of knowledge. One was the so-called Knowledge Engineering established by Feigenbaum [Feigenbaum *et al.*, 1997] in the 1970s to deal with expert systems. The other was the Data Mining and Knowledge Discovery research started in the 1990s to extract knowledge from certain databases [Fayat *et al.*, 1996] . Unfortunately, there have been no links between these two researches.

4.2.1. *Limitations of the knowledge research rooted from the old methodology*

Due to the prevalence of the methodology of 'Divide-and-Conquer', there has been so far no systematic and unified theory of knowledge exists.

As one can see, the research of Knowledge Engineering is concerned with the needs of certain expert system designs whereas the research of Knowledge Discovery deals with a few specific databases.

Little effort has been made in basic research for a general theory of knowledge. What is the definition of knowledge? What is the relationship between knowledge and information and knowledge and intelligence? There are no solutions for such fundamental questions. As a result, the current status of knowledge theory cannot provide with effective support to the law of information conversion and intelligence creation.

4.2.2. *Discovery of ecological features for knowledge*

To improve the situation of the research in knowledge theory stated above, we made efforts in the study of knowledge theory during the 1990s. A paper titled 'A Framework of Knowledge Theory' was published in the Journal of China Engineering Science in the year 2000 [Zhong, 2000].

In addition to the discussions on the basic definition of knowledge, the classifications of knowledge, and the measurements for the classes of knowledge, a new scientific issue, the ecological process of knowledge, was reported in the paper. The new discoveries on two categories of the ecological chain of knowledge were described.

The first discovery is the internal ecological chain of knowledge: empirical knowledge (which is in the under-matured state) grows to be regular knowledge (in the normal-matured state) and then grows further to be commonsense knowledge (in the over-matured state) via certain operations respectively. As we will show in next section, the internal chain in the knowledge ecology provides the solid foundation for integrating the three contemporary schools of the artificial intelligence research.

The second discovery is the external ecological chain of knowledge: epistemological information can grow to become knowledge and further grow to become intelligence. The most valuable, and also most interesting, thing for this discovery is that the external ecological chain of knowledge reveals the secret of the mechanism of the intelligence growth.

The two discoveries do demonstrate that the results of the knowledge ecology theory did provide essential contributions to the study of intelligence theory. Without such contributions from knowledge theory research, the mechanism of intelligence growth and the unification of the three AI theories would be impossible.

4.3. *The theory of artificial intelligence*

There have been three major schools of artificial intelligence research in literate. One is the artificial neural network research based on the structural simulation of the human brain [McCulloch and Pitts, 1943; Rumelhart, 1986; Hopfield, 1982] initiated in 1943, and termed the "structural approach, or approach 1, to AI". The second is the physical symbol system research based on the functional simulation of human brain [Turing, 1950; Newell, 1980; Simon, 1981; Nilsson, 1982] initiated in 1956, and termed the "functional approach, or approach 2 to AI". The third school is the sensor-motor system research based on the behavioral simulation of intelligent beings [Brooks, 1990; Brooks, 1991] initiated roughly in 1990, and termed "behavioral approach, or approach 3, to AI".

4.3.1. *Limitations of artificial intelligence research rooted from old methodology*

Again, due to the employment of the methodology of 'Divide-and-Conquer', all the three schools have been isolated from each other and unable to merge into an integrative theory of artificial intelligence research.

Many researchers are not satisfied with the situation of mutual isolation in AI. Recently, attentions have been paid to the establishment of a unified theory of artificial intelligence [Russell & Norvig, 1995; Nilsson, 1998]. However, the progress for the unification of AI has been far from a success.

4.3.2. *Discovery and establishment of mechanism for intelligence creation*

As is mentioned above, the root cause for the isolation among the three schools of artificial intelligence research is due to the fact that all the three research schools employed the methodology of 'Divide-and-Conquer', that is, dividing the intelligent system in three respects: structure, function, and behavior, with no understanding of the mutual links among the three.

Recalling the external chain of knowledge ecology, it is clearly indicated that the mechanism of intelligence growth is the "information–knowledge-intelligence conversion". More precisely, it is the series of conversion — (*a*) from ontological information to epistemological information, (*b*) from epistemological information to knowledge, and (*c*) from epistemological information and knowledge to intelligence.

In consequence, the new approach to intelligence simulation, based on the mechanism of intelligence growth, that is the information-knowledge-intelligence conversion, has been successfully established [Zhong, 2007], and termed the "mechanism approach, or approach 4, to AI".

4.3.3. *Unification of AI approaches within mechanism approach*

Using the mechanism approach to AI, we achieve another result important to the artificial intelligence theory.

That is, we now have four approaches to AI research. Approach 1 is the artificial neural network based on structure simulation and empirical knowledge. Approach 2 is the physical symbol system based on function simulation and regular knowledge. Approach 3 is the sensor-motor system based on behavior simulation and commonsense knowledge. Approach 4 is the universal intelligent system based on mechanism simulation and universal knowledge. In turn, approaches 1, 2, and 3 are the harmonious components of the Approach 4 according to the internal chain of knowledge ecology. This leads to a unified theory of artificial intelligence as we can see in Table 2 [Zhong, 2013].

Table 2. Unification of the Approaches to AI

Approach 4	Information	Knowledge	Strategy	Examples
Mode A of Approach 4	Information	Empirical	Empirical	Approach 1
Mode B of Approach 4	Information	Regular	Regular	Approach 2
Mode C of Approach 4	Information	Commonsense	Commonsense	Approach 3
Mode D of Approach 4	Information	Innate	Innate	

As we can see in Table 2, approach 1, the artificial neural network, is the example of mode A of approach 4 with empirical knowledge; approach 2, the physical symbol system, is the example of mode B of approach 4 with regular knowledge; and approach 3, the sensor-motor system, is the example of mode C of approach 4 with commonsense knowledge.

In other words, approach 4, the mechanism approach to AI, is the universal approach that harmoniously unifies the previous three approaches to AI. This result ends the separated relationship among the three AI approaches completely.

5. Principles Exploration: The Information Conversions

Having the three classes of the fundamental concepts and the three categories of basic theories as the mainstays of the law, what we have to do next is to find the conversion principles for effectively linking the comprehensive information theory, the knowledge theory, and the intelligence theory, and for eventually implementing the entirety of the law.

5.1. *First conversion: from ontological information to epistemological information*

It is clear by looking back to the ecological model for information studies in Fig. 2 that the first class of the information conversion should be the one that is able to converse ontological information to epistemological information, or equivalent comprehensive information.

It is particularly important to explain the principle of the first class of information conversion because some people do not know how epistemological information can really be conversed from ontological information.

The principle of the first information conversion can be shown in Fig. 4 [Zhong, 2013; Zhong, 2014].

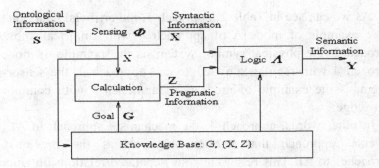

Fig. 4 Principle of First Information Conversion

As we can see in Fig. 4, syntactic information X can be acquired directly from ontological information S by using the sensing system. This can be expressed as a map function in mathematics:

$$\Phi: S \rightarrow X \qquad (5.1.1)$$

Pragmatic information Z can then be produced as the correlation calculated between X (the syntactic information achieved already) and G (the subject's goal).

$$Z = \text{Cor}\ (X,\ G) \qquad (5.1.2)$$

Finally, semantic information Y can be determined by the mapping into the space of semantic information from the joint of syntactic information X and pragmatic information Z:

$$Y = \lambda\{X,\ Z\} \qquad (5.1.3)$$

This process of (5.1.3) can also be explained in Fig. 5 in which X is given in the domain of syntactic information and Z is given in the domain of pragmatic information and then the corresponding scope of Y can be uniquely defined in the space of semantic information by the joining of X and Z. The symbol λ in (5.1.3) is an operator of mapping and naming.

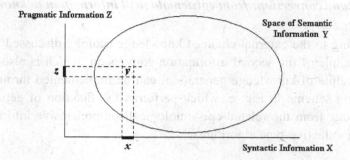

Fig. 5 Semantic information Defining

As consequence, the ontological information S at the input of Fig. 4 has been conversed into the three components of the comprehensive information — syntactic information X, semantic information Y, and pragmatic information Z— at the output in Fig. 4.

It is very interesting to note that the first class of information conversion expressed in Figs. 4, 5 and Eq. (5.1.3) clearly reveals the definition, the meaning, and the generative approach of semantic information. Y can serve as the representative of X and Z. This is why people are concerned with semantic information the most.

This result is also of high significance because there have been difficulties around the concept of semantic information. Because of this confusion, very few people have been able to say exactly what semantic information is in the past.

It is worth pointing out that syntactic information, typically the Shannon information, can meet the needs of communication calculations while semantic information, as the legal representative of both syntactic and pragmatic information, can support the needs of content processing and meaning inference in such areas as computing and intelligence studies.

Therefore, the epistemological/comprehensive information theory, the trinity of syntactic, semantic, and pragmatic theory of information, can legally serve as the integrative theory of information, forming the foundation of knowledge and intelligence.

5.2. *Second conversion: from epistemological information to knowledge*

According to the external chain of knowledge ecology discussed above, the principle of the second information conversion, which is also called the principle of knowledge generation, can be implemented through the following scheme in Fig. 6, which performs the function of generating knowledge from the related epistemological/comprehensive information through inductive-type algorithms.

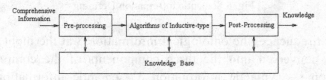

Fig. 6 Principle of Second Information Conversion

As we can see in Fig. 6, the input of the scheme is the epistemological/comprehensive information whereas the output of the scheme is the knowledge newly produced. This is a typical process of learning, learning knowledge from the comprehensive information.

The learning operation that will be performed in the scheme of the second information conversion is the inductive-type algorithm. This is understandable because information is a kind of phenomenon in nature whereas knowledge is essence in nature and because essence can only be abstracted from phenomena via induction. As the inductive-type algorithm, it may have many forms such as standard mathematical inductive algorithms, statistical inductive algorithms, analogical algorithms, associative algorithms, and so on.

The knowledge base, a fundamental element of the scheme (at the bottom of Fig. 6), supports the unit of inductive-type algorithms by giving 'the scope of the knowledge interested' and 'the knowledge already had' so that the unit of inductive-type algorithm works properly. At the same time, the knowledge base also supports the units of pre-processing and post-processing.

It is worth pointing out here that the quality of the results derived from the inductive-type algorithm depends on the quality and scale of the sample set used for the induction. Generally, the better the quality and the larger the scale of the sample set, the better quality the results. Furthermore, the interesting phenomenon of 'emergence' exists in the inductive process and expresses the turning point beyond which the high quality of the results will come true.

As it is well known, inductive algorithms cannot always provide the guarantee with the right results. Therefore, the evaluation process of the inductive results is necessary. If the results are valid under certain criteria, they are regarded as new knowledge and are fed into the knowledge base. Otherwise, the results will be fed back to the inductive process for reprocessing. These functions are performed via the unit of post-processing.

On the other hand, the unit of pre-processing is arranged for monitoring whether the scope of the epistemological information at the input of the scheme is correlative to the goal of the system learning: feeding in if the information is correlative one and filtering out others. This kind of function can well be performed and easily be implemented by utilizing the technique of correlation calculation.

5.3. *Third conversion: from knowledge to intelligent strategy*

The function of the third information conversion is to produce the intelligent strategy so that the subject can intelligently interact with the stimulus that is given by the object in the real world via the ontological information.

The intelligent strategy can be produced on the basis of (1) the epistemological information, which is the subject's reflection of the ontological information, (2) the subject's goal, preset for problem solving, and (3) the knowledge already possessed, representing the subject's understanding toward the entire problem.

The strategy is called intelligent because the execution of it should be able to achieve the double win — on one hand, the result of the interaction should reach the subject's goal (the subject's requirements), and on the other hand, the result of interaction should maintain the knowledge constraints (the object's requirements).

To meet all the criteria described above, the principle of the third information conversion could be implemented by the scheme shown in Fig. 7.

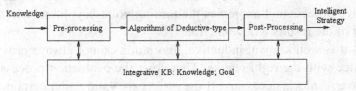

Fig. 7 The third Class of Information Conversion

As we can see in Fig. 7, different from the situation in the second information conversion, the major algorithm performed in the third information conversion is the deductive type. The function of the deduction is to converse the knowledge, as well as the epistemological information, to the intelligent strategy under the guidance of the subject's goal.

In any case, the evaluation for the quality of the intelligent strategy produced is necessary. If it meets the criteria of the double win described above, the intelligent strategy can be accepted and transmitted to the next unit for conversing into the intelligent action to be executed. Otherwise, it will be returned back to the deduction unit for reproduction.

Up to now, the major process of information ecology within the framework of interaction between subject and object expressed in Fig. 2, also stated as the loop (1)-(5) in section 2, has been explained. The final function denoted by (6) in the loop, i.e., error fed back to the input of the model, new knowledge learnt, optimized strategy developed and optimized action executed, will be performed without new difficulties.

In other words, the new views, the new methodology, the new model, the new concepts, the new theories, and the new principles presented in the paper have been completed and the law of information conversion and intelligence creation has been proved.

6. Summaries and Conclusions

Referring back to the ecological model of information studies shown in Figs. 2 and 3, and comparing it with the other information studies known already, one can see that a number of new results have been presented in this paper:

(1) New scientific views on information are proposed and emphasized, including the view on information, the view on the system, the view on ecology, and the view on the interaction between the subject and the object.

(2) New methodology applicable to information studies, the "ecology-ism", instead of "reductionism", are refined based on the new scientific views.

(3) A new model for information studies, as the embodiment of the new scientific views and the new methodology, is presented as expressed in Fig. 2.

(4) New concepts needed in information studies have been derived including ontological and epistemological/comprehensive information, knowledge ecology, and the mechanism of intelligence creation.

(5) The new concept of comprehensive information, specifically the concept of semantic information, is created, which is different from, and much more significant than, the concept of information in the Shannon information theory.

(6) The new theories in information studies are established, including the comprehensive information theory, the theory of knowledge ecology, and especially the intelligence theory of mechanism simulation that successfully unified the three schools of AI.

(7) New principles of information conversion in information studies are discovered, i.e., the conversion of ontological information to comprehensive one, the conversion of comprehensive information to knowledge, and the conversion of knowledge to intelligence.

(8) The law of information conversion and intelligence creation emerges from the interaction between the human subject and the object, which is the integration of all the results above.

(9) The great role that the law of information conversion and intelligence creation plays in problem solving within the framework of information studies that can be explained in Fig. 8.

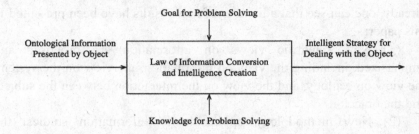

Fig. 8 General Model for problem Solving in information studies

As is shown in Fig. 8, whenever a subject is facing an object of any kind, in principle, he will receive the ontological information presented by the object, in reality, as input. By applying the law of information conversion and intelligence creation, supported by the right knowledge and guided by his clever goal, he will be able to achieve the intelligent strategy to solve the problem with the 'double win' criterion.

The law of information conversion and intelligence creation clearly reveals the secret of how the intelligent strategy can successfully be created for humans when the subject faces the stimulus from the object in the outside world. This result is really meaningful for the understanding of human intelligence. The law of information conversion and intelligence creation also gives inspiration to how intelligent strategy can successfully be created for machines. This is also meaningful for understanding information science and universal artificial intelligence.

More significantly, if combining the laws of information conversion and intelligence creation in information science with the law of energy conversion and conservation in physics, human kind will greatly benefit from both laws: the latter tells how to observe the sustainability of nature and society while the former tells how to solve problems to improve living standards and maintain sustainability in nature and society. They are complementary, and also fundamental, laws.

Acknowledgment

The author would like to express his sincerest gratitude to the China National Natural Science Foundations for giving great support to the author's research. It would have been impossible for the author to achieve these results without this support. At the same time, the author would like to sincerely thank the reviewers, Dr. Mark Burgin in particular, for their valuable comments and advice. The author's gratitude also goes to Ms. Elyse Weingarten for her language editing.

References

Bateson, G. (1072). *Steps towards an Ecology of Mind*, Jason Aronson Inc.

Brooks, R. A. (1990). *Elephant cannot Play Chess*, Autonomous Robot. No. 6, pp. 3-15.

Brooks, R. A. (1991). *Intelligence without Representation*, Artificial Intelligence, 47: pp. 139-159.

Burgin, M. (2010). *Theory of Information: Fundamentality, Diversity and Unification*, World Scientific, New York/London/Singapore

Fayad, U. *et al.* (1996). *Advances in Knowledge Discovery and Data Mining*, MIT Press.

Feigenbaum, A., *et al.* (1997). *The Art of Artificial Intelligence: Themes and Case studies in Knowledge Engineering*, IJCAI 5, pp. 1014-1029.

Hopfield, J. J. (1982). *Neural Networks and Physical Systems with Emergent Collective Computational Abilities*, Proc. Nat. Acad. Sci., No. 79, pp. 2554-2558.

McCulloch, W. C. and Pitts, W. A. (1943). *A Logic Calculus of the Ideas Immanent in Nervous Activity.* Bull. Math. Biophys., No. 5, pp. 115-133.

Newell, A. (1980). *Physical Symbol Systems*. Cognitive Science, 4, pp. 135-183.

Nilsson, N. J. (1982). *Principles of Artificial Intelligence*. Springer Verlag.

Nilsson, N. J. (1998). *Artificial Intelligence: A New Synthesis*, Morgan Kaufmann Publishers.

Rumelhart, D. E. (1986). *Parallel Distributed Processing*, MIT Press.

Russell, S. J. and Norvig, P. (1995). *Artificial Intelligence: A Modern Approach*, Pearson Education, Inc., as Prentice Hall, Inc, and Tsinghua University Press.

Shannon, C. E. (1948). *A Mathematical Theory of Communication*, BSTJ, Vol. 27, pp. 379-423, pp. 632-656.

Simon, H. A. (1981). *The Science of the Artificial*, 2nd edn., MIT Press.

Turing, A. M. (1950). *Computing Machinery and Intelligence*, Mind, No. 59, pp. 433-460.

Wiener, N. (1961). *Cybernetics*, 2nd edn., The MIT Press and John Wiley & Sons.

Zadeh, L. A. (1965). *Fuzzy Sets Theory*, Info. & Contr., 8, pp. 338-353.

Zhong, Y. X. (1988). *Principles of Information Science*, Beijing: BUPT Press.

Zhong, Y. X. (2000). *A Framework of Knowledge Theory*, J. Chin. Eng. Sci. pp. 50-64.

Zhong, Y. X. (2007). *Principles of Cog-netics in Machine*, Beijing: Science Press.

Zhong, Y. X. (2013). *Information Conversion, An Integrated Theory for Information, Knowledge, and Intelligence*, Sci. Bull., Vol. 58, No. 14, p.1300-1306.

Zhong, Y. X. (2014). *Advanced Theory of Artificial Intelligence*, Beijing: Science Press.

Chapter 6

Topoi of Systems: On the Onto-Epistemic Foundations of Matter and Information

Rainer E. Zimmermann

Lehrgebiet Philosophie, FK 13 SG, Hochschule (UAS)
Dachauer Str. 100a, D – 80636 Muenchen, Germany
Clare Hall, Cambridge, UK
pd00108@mail.lrz-muenchen.de

Before dealing with the problem of philosophical foundation, it is necessary to clarify the definition of the concepts involved. In the case of systems, matter, and information, this has not yet been achieved in a sufficiently satisfactory manner. As it turns out, the adequate language for such an enterprise would be that of mathematics. This adds a lot of precision and consistency to the chosen objective. But until now, this has been done only in very rare cases. In 2012, I have pointed to the most important aspects of such an approach in a joint paper with José M. Díaz Nafría published in two parts in the journal "Information".[1] In this present paper here, the results of this earlier work are collected in order to discuss the underlying problems of definition and foundation derived there from. I will show that it is *topos theory* that is the adequate mathematical instrument to deal with the theory of systems. On the other hand, it is the philosophical reflexion of topos theory that opens the path

---

[1]*Information* **2012**, *3*(3), 472-503; doi:10.3390/info3030472 and: *Information* **2013**, *4*(2), 240-261; doi:10.3390/info4020240.

towards concrete details concerning the foundation of the prime concepts involved which are matter (energy-mass) and information (entropy-structure), respectively. As it turns out, within their conceptualization, one cannot be separated from the other, and the approach to both is a generically interdisciplinary enterprise. With respect to the concept of information in particular, this present paper follows the line of argument as discussed in Helmut Klemm's review paper of 2003.[2] But note that here, different from earlier approaches, the discussion is unified with a view to *both matter and information* in the first place, so that information science for itself is showing up as a *part of the project* rather than the whole project. The idea is that the concept of information cannot be actually unified without unifying matter and information at the same time.

1. Introduction

When we discussed the recently introduced new approach to a consistent definition of systems (Zimmermann, 2015, 27) at the is4is conference in June 2015 at the TU Vienna, following up the debate initiated with our former papers (Zimmermann, Díaz Nafría, 2012–2014), it became apparent immediately that some of the constitutional parts of this definition would have to be re-considered closely. Recall this definition: "We call *system* a network of interacting agents producing a space with a well-defined boundary that is open in the sense of thermodynamics." Note that in particular, the concept of *agents* is crucial here: By directly referring to game theory, a system gains thus the connotation of intrinsic activity. Merely mapping systems (such as networks of paths or streets, airport connections and so forth) and also systems based on passive agents (that are acting as part of a software within a given computer programme) are excluded from this definition, because the vertices of the graphs visualizing these networks do not represent agents in the strict sense. In order to express an agent's activity, we referred to the earlier

---

[2]Uwe Klemm: Ein grosses Elend. http://www.informatik.uni-leipzig.de/~graebe/Texte/Intern/Klemm-03.pdf (04.03.2016).

definition provided by Stuart Kauffman (2000): "Autonomous agents are self-reproducing systems which can at least perform one thermodynamic work cycle." (Cf. Zimmermann, 2015, 37.) In fact, this definition is somewhat more involved, because in its original and long version it is re-formulated as follows: "Agents are self-reproducing, auto-catalytic systems which achieve a new kind of closure in a given space of catalytic and work tasks propagating work out of non-equilibrium states and playing natural games according to the constraints of their environment." (Ibid.) There are a number of important aspects to this definition:

First of all, *agents are visualized as systems themselves*. They can actually be quantized in the physical sense of minimal, fundamental agents (systems) which constitute all what there is in observable terms. This is the reason for rooting the concept of agent within the depth structure of the (observable) world itself — which is the fundamental level of space-time. Hence, conceptually, *fundamental agents are loops in the sense of loop quantum gravity*. Six of them co-operate (in the sense of game theory) in order to constitute one hexagonal cell of the spin network which underlies the structural web of configurational space. All the other agents on various evolutionary levels can be visualized then as a superposition of fundamental agents. The evolution of superpositions is governed by what Kauffman calls 4th *Law of Thermodynamics* which essentially says that systems maximize the investigation and subsequent settlement of the adjacent possible. This actually defines a principal direction of increasing systemic complexity. (Note that this approach is not reductionist at all, but instead, it is *emergent*. As we will see later, the "stuff" always remains the same (energy-mass, entropy-structure), but it is *complexity* that steers the level of organization.)

On the other hand, *the agent's activity is expressed in terms of physical work*. Obviously, in order to perform work tasks, energy is needed. In the case of the aforementioned loops, their energy (and entropy as to that) is related to the energy of the result of their interaction which is a hexagonal section of the spin network. At the same time, this is the energy that provides the capacity for being able to perform a work task, while the entropy relates to the information that accompanies this capacity with rules of organization. (Cf. Albertini, d'Alessandro, 2005,

Zimmermann 2013.) As is well-known, energy can show up as potential energy or as actualized energy related to motion.[3] Usually, by tradition, the various types of energy are included in the corresponding Lagrangian (or Hamiltonian). Although it is necessary to generalize them for the purposes of quantum physics, we can intuitively express the main characteristics of dynamics and thermo-dynamics in terms of the Lagrangian formalism, i.e. utilizing the principle of least action which can be visualized as producing a result that is expressed in turn by the Euler-Lagrange equations.

In other words, what we do assume from the outset is already quite a lot after all: We assume the universal validity of dynamics and thermodynamics. The former determines the mutual forces acting on systems with respect to a fixed scaling in the appropriate state space. The latter deals with the various balances of energy and entropy. And visualized this way, it is the physical universe which shows up as maximal system (both in microscopic, quantum, and macroscopic, classical, terms, respectively). Consequently, all the constituents of the above definition are mainly based on a suitable foundation of given theories. At the same time, we realize that therefore, the concept of system is not a property of nature, but (by being a concept) a *methodological instrument of human reflexion*, a mapping technique (unless we would think of concepts created by human reflexion as products of nature as well, because we would think of *human beings as products of nature* — but for our purposes here, we will stay with the concept of *internal observer* instead).

In this present paper we will deal mainly with both a mathematical and philosophical conceptualization of these "first elements" that we have chosen as a suitable starting point for our discussion. Hence, we will relate mathematical categories and topoi to what we have introduced above. But before doing so, we have to go back to the fundamental level in order to clarify what we can say about *structures*.

---

[3] In fact, we think of motion here in general as "change of state".

2. Fundamental Concepts in Systems

For our purposes a most interesting paper is that of Louis Kauffman presented in a volume of collected essays honouring the work of Roger Penrose (Kauffman 1998): The idea is to show that what we call *binor identity* of spin networks is essentially the same as the skein identity of the bracket polynomial and the trace identity of the quantum group corresponding to SL(2, C), respectively. The starting point for showing this is a definition of space that is common in topology and deals mainly with purely combinatorial objects such as networks or graphs. Kauffman who is also a specialist on knot theory, straightforwardly, draws a line of connection to this particular field. In principle, this also serves as another connection to categories. Kauffman says: "In formalising these notions one naturally finds that the switch of viewpoints from diagrams, to algebra, to corresponding geometry, to evaluations of contracted tensors all constitute functors among the different categories represented by these concepts. The network appears as a locus for the application of a medley of functors. The network replaces the old concept of space. That space is one of the possible targets of the many functors that extract information from the network. In this way space, time, and the idea of place and coordinate fade away to be replaced by networks and processes that unfold into both the spaces and the evaluations (partition functions, amplitudes) that elucidate the geometry and topology associated with them." (1998, 278)

In epistemic terms, Kauffman's argument can be essentially broken down into two parts: *The first one* is dealing with a generic connection between the bracket state model and the original Jones polynomial. *The second one* is dealing with showing that the trace identity of SL(2, C) is essentially a matrix-algebraic expression of the binor identity such that one can find another relationship between SL(2, C) itself on the one hand, and the bracket polynomial, on the other. As to the relevance of the group SL(2, C), especially with respect to quantum computation, I refer to Zimmermann (2001, 11) for further details, where I have been discussing ideas put forward by John Baez and Dan Christensen (2000).

The first result starts from earlier insight provided by Kauffman as early as in 1985: It is possible to present a model for the original Jones polynomial as. a partition function defined in terms of combinatorial states of the link diagram. This polynomial actually provides an important invariant of classical knots and links that can distinguish them from their mirror images. Kauffman refers to this partition function as the *bracket state model* of the Jones polynomial. The point is that this model is a generalization of the binor calculus given by Roger Penrose already in 1971 (cf. Kauffman, 1998, 278).

When recalling a number of details, we can understand these results roughly as follows: According to Reidemeister (1932/1974) two links are *ambient isotopic* iff the diagrams for each can be transformed into one another by a number of combinatorial moves. Two such links are said to be ambient isotopic, if there is a continuous family of embeddings connecting one to the other. The essential idea of Reidemeister's is to deal with the problem whether it is possible to deform two closed strings continuously into a congruent form. If for instance, an open string is *knotted* (very much in the everyday sense of the word) and its open ends are united, then the resulting form cannot be *de-formed* into a circle. (Cf. Reidemeister, 1) Hence, we recognize immediately the close connection of this problem to loops. In other words: If $r_i(t) = (x_i(t), y_i(t), z_i(t))$ ($i = 1$, 2; $0 \leq t \leq 2\pi$) are two curves in parameter representation and Cartesian co-ordinates that can be mapped continuously onto the circle $x = \cos t$, $y = \sin t$, then these curves are said to be *deformable*, if there is a family of curves $r(t, \tau)$ ($0 \leq \tau \leq 1$) with $r(t, 0) = r_1(t)$, $r(t, 1) = r_2(t)$ which can be mapped uniquely onto the above-mentioned circle. Two such curves are said to be equivalent, if there is an appropriate mapping of the Euclidean space onto itself under which they remain invariant. (Ibid.) As it turns out, when trying to classify possible knots of this type, the problem of knots is nothing else than the common problem of *isotopies of curves*. Recall that isotopies are special *homotopies* which refer to the possibility of deforming one form into another by means of a continuous function. (Reidemeister, 2) Polygons that can be transformed into one another by a chain of deformations are usually called isotopic, whilst a class of isotopic polygons is called a *knot*. A knot which is isotopic to a triangle is said to be a circle. A polygon which is not isotopic to a triangle is said to be *knotted* (Reidemeister, 4). Note that, different from this, the concept of *ambient isotopy* refers to a continuous deformation of some "ambient" space, usually a manifold, such that one knot can be deformed into another one, if, while doing so, it is not broken. Hence, if M and N are suitable manifolds, and g and h are embeddings of N into M, then a continuous map $F: M \times [0, 1] \to M$ is said to be an ambient isotopy, if $F(0)$ is the identity map, and each map F(t) from M to itself is a homeomorphism, and in particular, $F(1) \circ g = h$.[4] Because this implies that orientation is preserved by ambient isotopies, one can show that in general, two knots that are mirror images of each other are not equivalent.

On the one hand, as Reidemeister (Ibid., 13) has already shown, arbitrary knots can also be deformed into braids. Hence, we have a straightforward relationship to braid groups of Artin and other types. On the other hand, it is the possible matrix representation of knots that opens the path towards *group motions* (Reidemeister, 28). This is what we find at the roots of the famous Reidemeister moves mentioned above: Three of them suffice as a criterion for the ambient isotopy of knots. In particular, it is the second and third Reidemeister move that turns out to be useful in the determination of what is called a *framed link* which is basically a link equipped with a vector field. (Kauffman, 279) It is here where the bracket polynomial comes into play: At a given crossing in a knot diagram, we find four local regions. Two of them are called a pair, if they meet only at the vertex. According to Kauffman's terminology, we call one pair the A-pair, and the other the B-pair, respectively. If we join local regions of one or the other pair, we call this a *smoothing* (with the label A or B attached to it). We refrain here from repeating the diagrams emerging from the coupling rules of the smoothing. (Cf. Kauffman, 280.) But important for us is the characteristic relationship of the brackets representing the smoothing obtained and their visualization

---

[4]This result can be generalized to a *differentiable* manifold, if the homeomorphism is replaced by a suitable diffeomorphism.

in terms of a *state summation*: The states involved are the results of the available versions of smoothings performed. According to their type, smoothings contribute a vertex weight to the state sum. The norm of a state S then is defined by the number of Jordan curves in S. The bracket can be expressed then by $\langle K \rangle = \sum \langle K | S \rangle \, d^{|S|-1}$. Here the sum is to be understood as being obtained over all states S of the diagram K, and the composite expression in brackets is the product of the vertex weights. (It is not a coincidence that the brackets remind us of Dirac's formalism for quantum physics!) The factor d is the contribution of the Jordan curves. As it turns out, this bracket polynomial is not invariant under Reidemeister moves, but it can be specialized so as to fulfil the requirements of regular isotopy in terms of the second and third Reidemeister move. (Kauffman, 281) It can be shown then that a normalized version of this polynomial is equal to the original Jones polynomial. (Ibid., Theorem 3.2) It can also be shown in a straightforward manner that *topological invariance* is the key concept towards demonstrating that spin networks in the sense of Penrose show actually up as special cases of the bracket state model for the Jones polynomial. (Kauffman, 282)

Recall that the important point in the approach of Penrose is the idea that for sufficiently large and well-behaved spin networks, the properties of three-dimensional space begin to emerge spontaneously from the network structure such that the latter serves as a purely combinatorial background for the emergence of space and time. (Kauffman, 284; Penrose 1971) Hence, the idea of superposition is already inherent in this approach. Note however that strictly spoken, emergence is not really taking place in absolute terms, but that instead, the human modelling of the underlying foundations is such that the resulting theory works *as if* emergence would happen. This aspect relates to the provisional "ontologization" of epistemic concepts which is common for physics, but which does not suffice for a philosophical conceptualization.

The reason why we have looked up Kauffman's results in some detail is that this approach provides us some illustrative notion of *structure* in the world. As I have shown at another occasion (Zimmermann, 2007a), this point contributes two different types of insight: *One is a unifying framework important for strictly interdisciplinary approaches in the sciences.* This is mainly because the structural formalism employed here opens the path towards a multitude of applications in physics, biology, and computer science. For these fields this has caused a strong tendency to actually converge systematically as well as methodologically. It is thus possible e.g. to derive the organizational structure of the DNA directly from knot theory and its physical interpretations (even by means of quantum gravity) without performing a necessary diversion into chemistry and biology proper. (Kauffman, 1993, 1995, 2005, Kauffman, Magarshak, 1995, see also Baez, Muniain, 1994, Boi, 2005)

The other one is of cognitive nature: As it turns out, the underlying formalism — understood as a representation technique — is not just a successful model language, but is also based primarily on the fundamental layout of human cognition itself. Hence, within the modelling procedure, the choice of terminology and symbolism may appear to be arbitrary, but in fact, they are not. Instead, they reflect the implicit structure of human cognition which is itself the outcome of those phenomena that are actually topical in these research projects. For all practical purposes in physics (or biology), this intrinsic self-reference of research can be neglected, if dealing with concrete problems. But when conceptualizing the research process itself, they have to be taken into account quite explicitly.

They have also to be taken into account in the social domain. This is mainly because here is the place where cognition interferes directly with the results of (scientific) observation, on the same order of magnitude. A prominent example for this is illustrated by the more recent approach of Michael Leyton's within the field of architecture: What Leyton essentially does is to give a theory of dynamical shape construction. (Leyton, 2001) Different from classical geometry (in the sense of Klein's programme) which assumes that there are forms in nature that can be perceived and mapped, Leyton proposes a kind of cognitive dynamics which is based on a permanent process of scanning the environment: Human beings actually construct shapes derived from a cognitive inventory of elementary forms rather than perceiving forms that are readily available in the environment (cf. for details on urban social space: Zimmermann, Soci, Colacchio, 2001, Zimmermann, 2002, Zimmermann, Soci, 2004). Leyton's approach is also a good example for what we can understand as "superposition" of structures in the world.

In fact, the observable macroscopic forms achieved in architecture (e.g.) can be visualized at the same time as a *stored memory* of all the processes that originally caused and thus produced the observed form. In this sense is "structure" a complementary entity to "entropy": If one could re-construct the *morphogenesis* of the form achieved, one would gain plenty of information about its process of becoming. Hence, when Leyton discusses forms as memory, then this is very much on the same line of argument as the one chosen for knot theory in the sense of Kauffman, because a knotted structure can also be visualized as a memory of the genetic history of the knotting which has caused this very structure in the first place! (Cf. Zimmermann, 2015, 85–87, 148–150.) This aspect opens an interesting alley towards a review of the second law of thermodynamics and its consequences (cf. Duncan, Semura, 2004.)

On the one hand, all of this serves as a possible instrument to approach a unified view not only of physics and biology, but also of information theory and logic. For the first two, energy-mass (on the macroscopic level as classical "stuff", on the microscopic level as molecular software which is at the same time hardware, as in the case of the DNA) is primary, though not separable from entropy-structure, whilst for the latter two, entropy-structure is primary, though equally inseparable from energy-mass. The kind of structural *knot logic* involved here and presented by Louis Kauffman under the topical influence of Spencer-Brown, opens the route towards understanding the generically self-referent character of the world such that evolution is often nothing else than *self-recursion* of systems. (Kauffman refers here to Heinz von Foerster who could show that each recursive process possesses a fixed point, a result that is important for understanding the nature of observed objects) (Kauffman, 2011, 2015, Kauffman, Varela, 1980). On the other hand, this also serves as conceptualizing a unified view of ontology and epistemology in the sense of Sandkuehler (1990): As far as we know, until now it is only humans that model the world according to the results of their reflexion. Hence, all these concepts such as energy-mass or entropy-structure have been developed as products of this same reflexive theorizing. It is unlikely that the world is really as we describe it. For all practical purposes, this situation is acceptable provided the applications find a consistent ground on which they can unfold. But in philosophical terms, this is not quite sufficient, because the relationship between *the world as it is really* and *the world as we cognitively perceive it actually* can only be grasped by means of a sound ontology *cum* epistemology. The idea of Sandkuehler is to notice that *the human mode of being is in the processing of human epistemology*. And this is chiefly a refined system of mapping techniques. In other words: It is the processing of knowledge that characterizes this mode of being (= ontological state). In principle, this can be visualized as a materialistic version of Spinozist thought.

Hence, when asking for the most fundamental entities constituting what is observable in the world, we find that we actually deal with two attributes of the world (as we can call them): *energy-mass* on the one hand, and *entropy-structure* on the other. The former is telling us what capacity is available in order to create structures (order), the latter is telling us how this can be actually done. One determines the available "stuff" of the world, the other determines its "form" (or: organization). But note an important conceptual point here: These two attributes is what constitutes *the world as we perceive it* in cognitive terms. Obviously, they will not suffice to describe *the world as it really is*, because human cognition is (necessarily) incomplete, because sensory perception is so. In other words: We are indeed back to Spinoza's conception (cf. Zimmermann, 2000, 2014). Spinoza differed between *reality* and *modality*: the former visualized as the world as it really is, the latter as that part of the world which is accessible to human beings due to their two attributes that fall under their mode of being. Spinoza called them "matter" and "mind" at the time. But he assumed that in principle, there would be an infinity of possible attributes that express reality. Then two such attributes out of an infinity is not very much after all.

The question is raised very often why it should be necessary at all to deal with this ontological difference, because it is not relevant (or at least, it does not appear to be relevant) for most applications. However, the answer is that this is not quite true as I have shown at other occasions (cf. Zimmermann, 2007b, 2013, 2014a.) The point is that if we visualize *ethics* as the inventory of acting adequately with respect to the conditions of environmental nature, and if it turns out that we perceive nature (including ourselves) due to a cognitive process of construction which is the result of evolutionary structures that are produced by this same nature, then obviously, adequacy depends heavily on our manner of approaching the conceptualization of nature. And this begins with the foundations rather than with specific applications.

3. The Significance of Topoi

Recall the definition of mathematical categories: A *category* C is a class of *objects* ob(C) and a class of *morphisms* mor(C) such that each morphism has a unique source and target object, respectively. Also, for every three objects a, b, c there is a binary operation of the form mor(a, b) × mor(b, c) → mor(a, c) called *composition* such that associativity and left and right identity laws are valid. Different from set theory, categories provide thus a kind of intrinsic dynamics for structures: The morphisms take care of the internal motions and actions characterizing a given category by basically describing the possible interactions among objects.

In principle, one would then visualize a *topos* as a category with a specialized logic structure. In fact, in order to be more precise, we can turn this argument the other way round somewhat by stating that it is the category which turns out as a special case of a topos. This is mainly because usually, the latter is associated with an intuitionistic logic based on a Heyting algebra, whilst the former is based on classical logic with a Boolean algebra instead.[5] We can see then that categories or topoi reproduce the onto-epistemic aspects we have discussed above.

---

[5]Probably, one of the inventors of topos theory, William Lawvere, would not really agree to this viewpoint. But for our purposes it is useful to keep the formulation introduced here. (Cf. Lawvere, Rosebrugh, 2003).

In more recent work, Neuman and Nave (2008) demonstrate the relevance of (mathematical) categories and topoi for cognitively generated concept formation giving concrete examples from child development. Insofar they follow the essential line of argument as given by the late Piaget (1992). For more details see also Macnamara and Reyes (1994). The basic idea is to represent the concept construction by means of push-out and pull-back diagrams known from category theory: Take A, B, C as individual cases of some concept D* which is represented by the sign D playing in turn the role of denotating the respective cases as to their associated name. Then the *push-out* is defined by a diagram of the following form:

$$
\begin{array}{ccc}
D^* & & \nwarrow \\
& \nwarrow \; D & \leftarrow B \\
& \nwarrow \; \uparrow & \uparrow \\
& \nwarrow \; C & \leftarrow A
\end{array}
$$

where upward pointing arrows indicate mappings to D*. In this sense, A is the *domain* of B and C which are in turn the *co-domains* of A. The mappings A → B und A → C are similarity indicators (identifyers) for the cases according to which case A can be consistently classified in order to associate it to a suitable underlying concept. Hence, this relation is a sort of equivalence relation. On the other hand, the mappings B → D and C → D associate the cases with names (they denote them). Then the *push-out* is given by the mapping u: D → D* which associates names with their appropriate concept such that the square diagram as part of the complete diagram commutes with u and the accompanying mappings of the upper left-hand cone. (The *pullback* then is the dual diagram which can be generated by simply reversing all directions of arrows.) The important point is that *only both diagrams together* can mediate case A with the concept D* in question such that it can be properly understood. In other words: The *pushout* refers to the conceptual reconstruction according to the *bottom up method*, while the *pullback* refers instead to the conceptual reconstruction according to the *top down method*.

If we utilize the main example given by Neuman and Nave, we see immediately how to apply push-out and pull-back diagrams in practise: Choose the name *Dog* and the associated concept *Dog**. Take as individual cases $C = Chihuahua$, $B = Great Dane$, $A = German Sheperd$. Test then A according to whether it can consistently fall as individual case under the name *Dog*. Obviously, the idea is to look for a similarity criterion in the first place: If A can be shown to be sufficiently similar to B and C, then it falls under D and is thus mediated with the concept D*. The flow of information goes from A to B and C. If both push-out and pull-back exist, we can formulate the result of a deductive algorithm: *If* case B is similar to case A *and if* case C is similar to A, *then* B is similar to C. We notice that the macro-level (of concepts) and the micro-level (of cases) of reflexion determine each other in a mutual and circular manner. (Hence, the syntactic as well as semantic dynamics of language reproduces the dynamics of self-organizing systems.) Note that propositions of the type: *if* $x \cup if$ y, *then* z can be identified with lines of a computer program. In other words: The representation chosen here illustrates the close relationship between categories and the processing of information (computation).

In fact, Neuman and Nave can show that this dual method of cognition determines the concept formation of humans while in the rest of the animal kingdom the usual method of association and diagonalization turns out to be comparatively uneconomical, because the number of possibilities of conceptual mediations does not only increase exponentially and complexity thus becomes difficult to handle very quickly, but the whole system becomes also very insensitive with respect to a possible change of actual contexts. And more than that: The human way can be additionally extended by means of *metaphorization* such that polysemy and degeneration add to strategic flexibility. Deduction is then replaced by *abductive inference*.

Neuman and Nave give the example of calling a child's aunt A "dog" in metaphorical terms. Then the original diagram takes now the form:

$$D^{**} \quad \nwarrow$$
$$\nwarrow D \leftarrow B$$
$$\nwarrow \quad \uparrow \quad \uparrow$$
$$\nwarrow C \leftarrow A$$

where aunt A is being compared with (similar) aunts B and C. However, as the context is shifted now, metaphorization is a mapping of the type $D^* \rightarrow D^{**}$ such that commutation properties stay preserved. This is equally true, if in a more complex case the name D (Dog) is replaced by D' (Hot Dog). Then the diagram must be changed, if applying to dogs in general:

$$D^{**} \qquad \searrow$$
$$\searrow D' \rightarrow B$$
$$\searrow \quad \downarrow \quad \downarrow$$
$$\searrow C \rightarrow A \; .$$

Now A means "Dachshound" e.g., and C "Chihuahua". But B is now "sausage". Hence, if D' is Hot Dog, then D^* is "sausage*". And instead of utilizing similarity mappings as identifyers ("is like" and "is a" as above), a negation shows up now (is not like) in the diagram, if looking particularly at the mapping $D \rightarrow C$. And note the reversal of the arrows directions. Hence, the diagrams represent constraints which act onto the possible interpretations of signs. (And the process of concept formation can thus create dynamical ontologies which are context-depending.) Hence, we have a close relationship between semiosis by means of cognition and communication on the one hand, and logic on the other. (Cf. Baez, Stay, 2008) We can generalize now this promising approach by demonstrating in which sense push-out and pull-back diagrams as introduced by Neuman and Nave into the semiological discussion of concept formation make it possible to define a *topos*. (Cf. Goldblatt

1984,[6] Saunders MacLane, Ieke Moerdijk, 1992; Johnstone, 2002-2003; Zimmermann, Hofkirchner, 2009.) Among other, equivalent definitions, for us important here is the definition which asserts that *a topos is a category with terminal object and pull-backs, with initial object and push-outs, with exponentials, and with a sub-object classifyer.* Note that the first two conditions are clearly demonstrated using the diagrams introduced earlier. Case A of the respective name is an initial object of a category in the first version of the diagrams and a terminal object in the second version.

So what we are talking about here is *a category of denotators* whose objects are the names of type D and whose morphisms are the identifyers (of two types: by denotating of the form "is a" and by metaphorizing of the form "is like"). The various names of individual cases are subobjects of the category. Mappings of the type D $\rightarrow$ D* and D* $\rightarrow$ D**, respectively, are functors between categories. (Hence, we differ between the category of denotators and the category of concepts. And we differ between contexts such that the respective category of concepts is different from the one originally associated with the denotators. The first type of functor represents *deduction* (or *induction* as to that) while the second type represents *creative abduction*.)

A *sub-object classifyer* is essentially a generalized set of truth values Ω such that the diagram of the form

$$
\begin{array}{ccc}
D & & \searrow \\
& \searrow A & \rightarrow C \\
& \searrow \quad \downarrow & \downarrow \\
& \searrow 1 & \rightarrow \Omega
\end{array}
$$

is a pullback. This time D is the denotator (name), A and C are two individual cases, and the mapping 1 $\rightarrow \Omega$ is a monic "true". (A *monic* is the categorial equivalent of a monomorphism which is an injective

---

[6]In this present chapter, I am following Goldblatt's convention when utilizing *topoi* as plural for *topos*. This has not only etymological reasons, it also serves to focus the attention onto the twofold connotation of the word in the sciences of nature and in the humane sciences, respectively.

homomorphism.) The mapping C $\rightarrow$ Ω is called *characteristic arrow*. We can visualize what the subobject classifyer is actually doing by thinking of selecting those arrows which "come through" to the "truth" because they imply mutually compatible interpretations of names. (This also clarifies the meaning of the sub-objects themselves: Basically, a sub-object of a C-object in a category C is thus a monic C-arrow with co-domain in the target object. This is so because the domain of a monic is isomorphic to a subset of the co-domain. And this also introduces *exponentials* which are simply all morphisms from a domain to a co-domain of an object.) Hence, we call the category of denotators utilized in the manner shown above *Neuman-Nave topos* (NN topos). In the following we will have a look at the interpretational consequences of this topos.

The important point is now that a topos turns out to be a Lindenbaum-Tarski algebra for a logical theory whose models are the points of a space. (Vickers, 2004) In other words, we can identify an appropriate space with a logical theory such that its points are the models of this theory, its open sets the propositional formulae, the sheaves the predicate formulae, and the continuous maps the transformations of models. At this point logic connects with model theory: Essentially, a Lindenbaum-Tarski algebra A of a logical theory T consists of the equivalence classes of propositions p of the theory under the relation $\cong$ defined by p $\cong$ q when p and q are logically equivalent in T. That is, in T proposition q can be deduced from p and vice-versa. Operations in A are inherited from those available in T, typically conjunction and disjunction. When negation is also present, then A is Boolean, provided the logic is classical. Conversely, for every Boolean algebra A, there is a theory T of classical propositional logic such that the Lindenbaum-Tarski algebra of T is isomorphic to A. In the case of intuitionistic logic, the Lindenbaum-Tarski algebras are Heyting algebras. (Hence, we deal here with an algebra of logical propositions in which logically equivalent formulations of the same proposition are not differentiated.)

We recognize immediately that it is model theory which relates representation with interpretation. (And this is what the diagrams discussed above are all about.) In other words: Model theory is the mathematical discipline that checks semantic elements of structures by means of syntactic elements in a given language. The latter can have logical as well as non-logical symbols and grammatical rules, but in principle, it is always the explication of a logical theory. Is L such a language, and M some set, then M becomes an L-structure by means of the interpretation of each of the non-logical symbols in L. Each proposition which is formulated according to the rules gains some *meaning* in M. Hence, representation entails interpretation and vice-versa.

It is not the proper place here to enter deeply into the discussion of model theory. (Cf. Hodges, 1997.) But what we can already notice is the relevance of the spatial approach to topoi: We recall from philosophical epistemology that essentially, a *theory* is a set of propositions which satisfy certain rules. If we visualize the theory as an abstract space, then the points of this space are subsets of propositions. Hence, generalized (abstract) spaces (not only within the field of mathematics) are nothing but sets of propositions or subsets of languages. Obviously, the languages serve the purpose of drafting out a picture of the world so as to orient oneself within its complex network of social and non-social interactions.

This aspect is directly projected onto a plane representing an abstract space of reflexive operations in the case of what we call *glass bead game*. (Zimmermann, 2005; Zimmermann, Wiedemann, 2010, 2012) The projection takes place here on a two-dimensional plane which is represented in terms of vertices and edges of a network, where the vertices are points which represent propositions and the edges are logical connectives of these propositions. In principle, this is a graphical representation which maps nicely what the topos concept means when referring to its spatial aspect. The glass bead game consists of sequences of points being consistently connected by appropriate edges such that the resulting path within the network of propositions is the picture of a research process which mirrors the model building common in the sciences. (The idea is taken indeed from the well-known novel of Hermann Hesse's.) Hence, the glass bead game essentially maps a section of social space (namely its scientific section laid down in scientific scripture). And by doing so, it illustrates that this space is intrinsically dynamical, because it is actually constituted by the processing of the sequences of propositions according to given rules. In other words: We deal here with the processing of information (including its organization and interpretation). This conception is well compatible with Lorenzer's theory of "language games" stressing the importance of predicators for the explicit training of social interactions in daily life.

One aspect is still missing which is the concrete *multi-perspectivity* of social space. This is in fact dealt with in detail in the work of Mazzola (2002) in order to take the various perspectives into account which determine the modes of interpretation of given works of music. But this aspect is equally important for social spaces in general. And as it turns out, it can also be included in the terminology of topos theory. This can be shown in terms of what is called "Yoneda lemma":

For an arbitrary pre-sheaf P in C there is a bijection between natural transformations $y(C) \rightarrow P$ and elements of the set $P(C)$ of the form:

$$\theta : \text{Hom}_{\mathfrak{S}} (y(C), P) \rightarrow^{\approx} P(C).$$

Here $\mathfrak{S}$ is the category of all pre-sheaves of C, where C is a fixed small category and C^{opp} is its opposite. The objects of $\mathfrak{S}$ are the functors $C^{opp} \rightarrow$ Sets, and the arrows (morphisms) are all natural transformations between them. Each object c of C gives rise to a pre-sheaf $y(c)$ on C defined on an object D of C by $y(C)(D) := \text{Hom}_{\mathfrak{S}} (D, C)$ and on a morphism $\alpha : D' \rightarrow D$ by $y(C)(\alpha) : \text{Hom}_{\mathfrak{S}} (D, C) \rightarrow \text{Hom}_{\mathfrak{S}} (D', C)$. Pre-sheaves of this form are called *representable*, and in this case y is called an *Yoneda embedding* which is a special case of the lemma quoted above.

For Mazzola, what the Yoneda lemma clarifies, is that it serves as a foundation of multi-perspectivity among local interpretations: In music, let R and S be appropriate vector spaces, and let K in R and L in S be two local compositions. The relations then between the two compositions can be expressed as a morphism $K \rightarrow L$. Essentially, this morphism defines a perspective under which L can be seen. (In fact, we can construct similar pushout and pullback diagrams as shown in the case of the NN topos.) The Yoneda lemma certifies then that the system of all L-perspectives determines the isomorphism class of L. In other words: The morphisms can be visualized as essentially hermeneutic instruments in order to classify and understand local compositions. It is quite straightforward then to generalize this aspect to more "unspecialized" cases as instances of social space. The important point is that most of the time we do not talk here about a space *as it is actually observed*, but instead about a space *as it could be observed*. In other words: The number of possible interpretations is larger than the number of actual interpretations. (Remember that in common social space collections of these interpretations form the practical "world-view".) Hence, not only does space show up as social space in the first place, and not only does social space show up as a space whose points are propositions of logical theories, but moreover social space shows up as well as a *virtual space*. Strictly speaking then, social space is a *special case* of virtual space, and not vice-versa, because the latter's "virtuality" refers to the field of possibilities rather than to the field of actualities which can be empirically observed.

What we see now is that traditionally, there have been already many connections between the human techniques of spatial representation (what has been called *anthropological graphism* elsewhere) (Zimmermann, 2004) and the mapping of processes in terms of logical formulae. The approach of Fontana (1992) (what he calls *algorithmic chemistry = alchemy*) is one example, very much on the line of the Santa Fe school on self-organized criticality. We have also seen that this kind of discussion visualizes processes in the general sense as percolation phenomena (Stauffer, Aharony, 1994), and what is being percolated is information then. And we have seen that it is topos theory that provides an appropriate language in order to deal with these aspects of spatial representation. More than that: A topos can be essentially interpreted as the algebraic expression of the fact that spaces utilized in human cognition are basically constituted by propositions of logical theories. On the other hand, the procedures of deduction and induction as well as creative abduction, available to human logic, can be rephrased in terms of algorithmic procedures. Hence, they are both accessible by means of programmes as they are utilized in computation, and by means of game theory, because on a fundamental level of reflexion games are essentially algorithmic procedures whose strategies are given by its rules. (Houston, 2003) What we realize then is that all of this relates nicely with the approaches of the Kassel and Salzburg schools as described at earlier occasions. (Cf. the volumes of collected essays presenting the results of the INTAS co-operation project "Human Systems in Transition" with the universities of Vienna, Kassel, Kyiv, and the Academy of Sciences, Moscow led by Wolfgang Hofkirchner, and in particular Zimmermann, Budanov, 2005.)

References

Albertini, F., D. d'Allessandro (2005): Model Identification for Spin Networks. Lin. Alg. Appl. 394, 237-256.

Baez, John C., Javier P. Muniain (1994): Gauge Fields, Knots, and Gravity. World Scientific, Singapore.

Baez, John C., Dan Christensen (2000): Spin Foams and Gauge Theories. http://jdc.math. uwo.ca/spin-foams/baez-mail.

Baez, John C., Mike Stay (2008): Physics, Topology, Logic and Computation: A Rosetta Stone. From the Baez web page: http://math.ucr.edu/home/baez/.

Boi, Luciano (2005): Topological Knot Models in Physics and Biology. In Geometries of Nature, Living Systems, and Human Cognition. World Scientific, Singapore, 203-278.

Díaz Nafría, José María, Rainer E. Zimmermann (2013): Emergence and Evolution of Meaning: The GDI Revisiting Programme. Part II: The Regressive Perspective: Bottom-Up. Information, 4, 240-261. (doi:10.3390/info4020240)

Duncan, Todd I., Jack S. Semura (2004): The Deep Physics Behind the Second Law: Information and Energy as Independent Forms of Bookkeeping. Entropy 6, 21-29.

Fontana, Walter (1992): Algorithmic Chemistry. In C. G. Langton (ed.), Artificial Life II, Addison-Wesley, Reading, 159-210.

Goldblatt, Robert (1984): Topoi. The Categorial Analysis of Logic. North-Holland, London.

Henriques, Gil (1992): Morphisms and Transformations in the Construction of Invariants. In Jean Piaget *et al.*, op. cit., 183-206 (ch. 13).

Hodges, Wilfrid (1997): A Shorter Model Theory. Cambridge University Press.

Houston, Robin (2003): Categories of Games. Master thesis, University of Manchester.

Johnstone, Peter T. (2002/2003): Sketches of an Elephant: A Topos Theory Compendium. 2 Vols. Oxford Science Publications.

Kauffman, Louis H. (1987): Self-reference and Recursive Forms. J. Soc. Biol. Struct. 10, 53-72.

Kauffman, Louis H. (1993): Knots and Physics. World Scientific, Singapore.

Kauffman, Louis H. (1995): Knot Logic. In: Knots and Applications. World Scientific, Singapore, 1-110.

Kauffman, Louis H. (1996): Virtual Logic. Systems Res. 13 (3), 293-310.

Kauffman, Louis H. (1998): Spin Networks and Topology. In: S.A. Huggett *et al.* (eds.), The Geometric Universe, Science, Geometry, and the Work of Roger Penrose. Oxford University Press, 277-289.

Kauffman, Louis H. (2005): Knots. In: Luciano Boi (ed.), Geometries of Nature, Living Systems, and Human Cognition. World Scientific, Singapore, 131-202.

Kauffman, Louis H. (2011): Eigenforms and Quantum Physics. (Dedicated to Heinz von Foerster on his 100th birthday, Conference University of Vienna). www.arxiv.org/pdf/1109.1892

Kauffman, Louis H. (2015): Knot Logic — Logical Connèction and Topological Connection. www.arxiv.org/pdf/1508.06028.

Kauffman, Louis H., Francisco J. Varela (1980) : Form Dynamics. J. Soc. Biol. Struct. 3, 171-206.

Kauffman, Louis H., Yuri B. Magarshak (1995) : Vassiliev Knot Invariants and the Structure of RNA Folding. In: Louis H. Kauffman (ed.), Knots and Applications. World Scientific, Singapore, 343-394.

Kauffman, Stuart A. (2000): Investigations. Oxford University Press.

Lawvere, F. William, Robert Rosebrugh (2003): Sets for Mathematics. Cambridge University Press.

Leyton, Michael (2001): A Generative Theory of Shape. Springer, Berlin, Heidelberg, New York.

MacLane, Saunders, Ieke Moerdijk (1992): Sheaves in Geometry and Logic: A First Introduction to Topos Theory. Springer, London.

Macnamara, John, Gonzalo E. Reyes (1994): The Logical Foundations of Cognition. Oxford University Press.

Mazzola, Guerino (2002): Topos of Music. Geometric Logic of Concepts, Theory, and Performance. Birkhaeuser, Basel, Boston, Berlin.

Neuman, Yair, Ophir Nave (2008): A Mathematical Theory of Sign-Mediated Concept Formation. Appl. Math. Comp. 201 (1), 72-81.

Penrose, Roger (1971): Angular Momentum: An Approach to Combinatorial Space-Time. In: Ted Bastin (ed.), Quantum Theory and Beyond. Cambridge University Press, 151-180.

Piaget, Jean *et al.* (1992): Morphisms and Categories. Comparing and Transforming. Terence Brown (ed.), Earlbaum, Hillsdale (N.J.). Gil Henriques (1992): Morphisms and Transformations in the Construction of Invariants. In: Jean Piaget *et al.*, op. cit., 183-206 (ch. 13).

Reidemeister, Kurt (1932): Knotentheorie. Reprint Edition, Springer, Berlin, Heidelberg, New York, 1974.

Sandkuehler, Hans Jörg (1990): Onto-Epistemologie. In: Europaeische Enzyklopaedie zu Philosophie und Wissenschaften [European Encyclopedia of Philosophy and the Sciences], Meiner, Hamburg, vol. 3, 608-615.

Stauffer, Dietrich, Amnon Aharony (1994): Introduction to Percolation Theory. Taylor & Francis, London, 2nd ed.

Vickers, Steven (2004): Locales and Toposes as Spaces (preprint, Birmingham).

Zimmermann, Rainer E. (2000): Loops and Knots as Topoi of Substance. Spinoza Revisited. http://arxiv.org/ftp/gr-qc/papers/0004/0004077.pdf

Zimmermann, Rainer E. (2001): Recent Conceptual Consequences of Loop Quantum Gravity. Part 1: Foundational Aspects. http://arxiv.org/ftp/physics/papers/0107/0107061.pdf

Zimmermann, Rainer E. (2002): Decentralization as Organizing Principle of Emergent Urban Structures. www.arxiv.org/pdf/cond-mat/0203012 (Reprinted in: Rainer E. Zimmermann (ed.), Aktuelle Bloch-Studien 2010-2012, Shaker, Aachen, 2012, 325-357.)

Zimmermann, Rainer E. (2004): Graphismus & Repraesentation. Zu einer poetischen Logik von Raum und Zeit. Magenta, München.

Zimmermann, Rainer E. (2005): The Modeling of Nature as a Glass Bead Game. In: Eeva Martikainen (ed.), Conference Human Approaches to the Universe. An Interdisciplinary Perspective. Helsinki, Agricola Society, 43-65.

Zimmermann, Rainer E. (2007a): Topological Aspects of Biosemiotics. (Contribution to: Gathering in Biosemiotics 6, July 2006, Salzburg) tripleC [Alte Folge], special issue, 5(2), 49-63.

Zimmermann, Rainer E. (2007b): On the Modality of the World. Space and Time in Spinoza. In: F. Linhard, P. Eisenhardt (eds.), Notions of Space and Time, Early Modern Concepts and Fundamental Theories, Zeitsprünge, Klostermann, Frankfurt a. M., II (2007), Heft 1/2, 217-242.

Zimmermann, Rainer E. (2013): Energy and Information in Systems. (emcsr2012 Vienna, Symp. A: Physical and Metaphysical Aspects of Systems after Morin) Systems 1 (1), 69-78.

Zimmermann, Rainer E. (2014a): Ethics from Systems as Metaphysical Reconstruction. (emcsr2014, Vienna) In: Special issue "Ethics from Systems", Systema 2 (3), 4-9.

Zimmermann, Rainer E. (2014b): Nothingness as Ground and Nothing but Ground. xenomoi, Berlin.

Zimmermann, Rainer E. (2015): Metaphysics of Emergence. Part 1: On the Foundations of Systems. xenomoi, Berlin.

Zimmermann, Rainer E., Anna Soci, Giorgio Colacchio (2001): Reconstructing Bologna. The City as an Emergent Computational System. A Study in the Complexity of Urban Structures. Part 1: The Basic Idea & Fundamental Concepts. www.arxiv.org/pdf/nlin.AO/0109025 (Reprinted in: Rainer E. Zimmermann (ed.), Aktuelle Bloch-Studien 2010-2012, Shaker, Aachen, 2012, 261-324.)

Zimmermann, Rainer E., Anna Soci (2004): The Emergence of Bologna and its Future Consequences. Decentralization as Cohesion Catalyst in Guild-Dominated Urban Networks. www.arxiv.org/pdf/cond-mat/0411509 (Reprinted in: Rainer E. Zimmermann (ed.), Aktuelle Bloch-Studien 2010-2012, Shaker, Aachen, 2012, 358-399.)

Zimmermann, Rainer E., V. Budanov (eds.) (2005): Towards Otherland. Languages of Science and Languages Beyond. Kassel University Press.

Zimmermann, Rainer E., Wolfgang Hofkirchner (2009): The Topos of Virtuality. Part I: From the Neuman-Nave Topos to the Explication of Conceptual Social Space, tripleC [Alte Folge], 7(1), 74-87.

Zimmermann, Rainer E., Simon M. Wiedemann (2010): Reconstructing the Glass Bead Game. On the Philosophy of Information. 3rd ICTs & Society Meeting, Barcelona, 2010, tripleC [Alte Folge], 8(2), 136-138.

Zimmermann, Rainer E., Simon M. Wiedemann (2012): Kreativitaet & Form (The Glass Bead Game) Springer-Vieweg, Berlin, Heidelberg.

Zimmermann, Rainer E., José María Díaz Nafría (2012): Emergence and Evolution of Meaning: The GDI Revisiting Programme. Part I: The Progressive Perspective: Top-Down. Information 3, 472-503. (doi: 10.3390/info3030472)

Zimmermann, Rainer E., José María Díaz Nafría (2014): The Systemic Perspective as a Paradigm for Unified Approaches in the Sciences. (Panel I, wcsa2012 conference: Vienna). In: Giulia Mancini, Mariarosalba Angrisani (eds.), Mapping Systemic Knowledge, Lambert Academic, Saarbrücken, 14-34.

Part II

Philosophy of Information

Chapter 7

Transdisciplinarity Seen Through Information, Communication, Computation, (Inter-)Action and Cognition

Gordana Dodig-Crnkovic[a], Daniel Kade[b], Markus Wallmyr[b], Tobias Holstein[b] and Alexander Almér[c]

[a]*Chalmers University of Technology and University of Gothenburg, Sweden*
[b]*Mälardalen University, Sweden*
[c]*University of Gothenburg, Sweden*

Similar to oil that acted as a basic raw material and key driving force of industrial society, information acts as a raw material and principal mover of knowledge society in the knowledge production, propagation and application. New developments in information processing and information communication technologies allow increasingly complex and accurate descriptions, representations and models, which are often multi-parameter, multiperspective, multi-level and multidimensional. This leads to the necessity of collaborative work between different domains with corresponding specialist competences, sciences and research traditions. We present several major transdisciplinary unification projects for information and knowledge, which proceed on the descriptive, logical and the level of generative mechanisms. Parallel process of boundary crossing and transdisciplinary activity is going on in the applied domains. Technological artifacts are becoming increasingly complex and their design is strongly user-centered, which brings in not only the function and various technological qualities but also other aspects including esthetic, user experience, ethics and sustainability with social and environmental dimensions. When integrating knowledge from a variety of fields, with contributions from different groups of stakeholders, numerous challenges are met in establishing common view and common course of action. In this context, information is our environment, and informational ecology determines both epistemology and spaces for action. We present some insights into the current state of the art of transdisciplinary theory and practice of information studies and informatics. We depict different facets of transdisciplinarity as we see it from our different research fields that include information studies, computability, human-computer interaction, multi-operating-systems environments and philosophy.

Keywords: Information; communication; computation; interaction; cognition.

1. Introduction

There is no human today who would possess all knowledge of even one single classical research discipline. In the case of physics, Wikipedia, Outline of Physics, lists 30 different branches of which many have several important sub-branches. The exact number can of course be disputed, but it is evident that they are far too many for an individual researcher to know in depth. As the amount of knowledge constantly grows, and the process of forgetting and loosing previous knowledge nearly gets completely extinct, but on the contrary old sources get digitalized and made available, amount of information and knowledge dramatically increases and specialization, branching and division into new sub-disciplines continues. On the other hand a process in the opposite direction of synthesis and increased connectivity is becoming more and more prominent as well. Based on information communication technologies, humanity is becoming networked through variety of interactions and exchanges constantly going on — from information and knowledge, to money and things, objects, goods, commodities. Communication and exchanges create global society with its global and complex problems — from climate change, pollution, question of resources and other environmental issues that threaten sustainable development, to complex social topics of mass migrations, long-term urban planning and healthcare dealing with epidemics prevention or understanding of diseases on multiple levels of organisation, from molecular to organismic level — to name but a few topics. Complex global problems are calling for systemic, both broad and deep understanding. Also the developments of new technologies, such as internet of everything, digitalization of society, autonomous vehicles, industrial and social robotics, intelligent cities, homes, and infrastructures ... all may be expected to radically change our civilization, and presuppose decision making and problem solving based on knowledge from many traditionally disparate disciplines that range from natural and technical sciences to humanities and arts. They necessitate a team work which is real-life problem oriented and has high direct societal value that necessitates inclusion of variety of stakeholders — such as governmental, industrial and general public actors. As a response to the demand of complex systems understanding, anticipation of behavior, and control, new synthetic knowledge is constantly developed by fusion and cross-pollination of existing knowledge. Klein in The Oxford Handbook of Interdisciplinarity (Frodeman *et al.* 2010), differentiates between 'endogenous interdisciplinarity' with focus on the internal theory building between existing academic disciplines (which might be identified as 'interdisciplinarity proper', in contrast to 'endogenous interdisciplinarity' driven by real-life problems knowledge integration and could be identified with transdisciplinarity. Interdisciplinarity in that context presents a tool for transdisciplinarity, which on top of deep interdisciplinary collaboration between academic research fields adds the factor of real-life relevance and stakeholder involvement.

2. Transdisciplinarity vs. Multidisciplinarity vs. Interdisciplinarity

"So many people today—and even professional scientists—seem to me like someone who has seen thousands of trees but has never seen a forest. A knowledge of the historical and philosophical background gives that kind of independence from prejudices of his generation from which most scientists are suffering. This independence created by philosophical insight is—in my opinion—the mark of distinction between a mere artisan or specialist and a real seeker after truth."

A. Einstein to R. A. Thornton, unpublished letter dated Dec. 7, 1944; in Einstein Archive, Hebrew University, Jerusalem, as quoted in Cooper *et al.* (2007).

Before we start, we briefly introduce some definitions of terms we are going to use. As our focus will be on transdisciplinarity, we just briefly outline the difference between transdisciplinarity, interdisciplinarity and multidisciplinarity.

2.1. *Monodisciplinary research*

In our approach we adopt the view of discipline as a part or a subsystem of a bigger architecture of the knowledge production. According to Choi and Pak (2008), "A discipline is held together by a shared epistemology. (...) The proposed conceptual framework of the knowledge universe consists of several knowledge subsystems, each containing a number of disciplines." Unlike Choi and Pak, we do not see knowledge production in the first place as a hierarchy (even though there is a hierarchy of levels of scale or granularity of domains), but as a network of networks of interrelated disciplinary fields (Dodig-Crnkovic 2016). A discipline corresponds to an academic field of research and education that typically has its own journals and academic departments. Disciplinary research is termed Mode-1 (Nowotny *et al.* 2001), while Mode-2 stands for the production of knowledge through interdisciplinary and transdisciplinary research close to a context of application.

Multidisciplinary research — working with several disciplines — implies that researchers from different disciplines work together on a common problem, but from their own disciplinary perspectives. According to the Klein taxonomy, the main characteristics are juxtaposing, sequencing and coordinating of knowledge (Klein 2010).

Interdisciplinary research — working between several disciplines, used to denote the setting where researchers collaborate transferring knowledge from one discipline to another. According to the Klein taxonomy, the main characteristics are integrating, interacting, linking, focusing and blending.

Transdisciplinary research — From the meaning of the Latin word trans, Nicolescu derives the definition of transdisciplinarity as that knowledge production which is at the same time between, across and beyond all disciplines (Nicolescu 2014). Transdisciplinarity is a research approach that enables addressing societal problems through collaboration between research disciplines as well as extra-scientific actors. It enables mutual learning among and across disciplines as well a between science and society. The main cognitive challenge of the research process is integration which is based on reflexive attitude both oriented towards different actors in the research process and their mutual relations, and towards the research project as a whole in its context (Jahn *et al.* 2012) The main difference to interdisciplinarity, apart from the degree of interaction, is the involvement of extra-scientific stakeholders in transdisciplinary research (Frodeman *et al.* 2010; Hadorn *et al.* 2008). In the course of the research process, boundaries between disciplines dissolve through integrated perspectives, knowledge and approaches from different scientific disciplines and other external sources interfuse, (Flinterman *et al.* 2001). Transdisciplinarity is often applied to address the real world complex problems through context-specific negotiation of knowledge that emerges from collaboration. (Thompson Klein 1996) Research fields include environmental-, sustainability-, gender-, urban-, cultural-, and peace and conflict-, future-, public health- and information studies, policy sciences, criminology, gerontology, cognitive sciences, information sciences, materials science, artificial intelligence, human-computer interaction, interaction design, ICTs and society studies, etc. From the organizational point of view, "Transdisciplinary research is, in practice, team science. In a transdisciplinary research endeavor, scientists contribute their unique expertise but work entirely outside their own discipline. They strive to understand the complexities of the whole project, rather than one part of it. Transdisciplinary research allows investigators to transcend their own disciplines to inform one another's work, capture complexity, and create new intellectual spaces." (Güvenen 2015) Involvement of stakeholders providing the context for the solution of real-world problems is central for transdisciplinary research. Distinctive characteristics of transdisciplinary research, according to Klein taxonomy are transcending, transgressing and transforming (Klein 2010).

Finally, It is important to realize that disciplinary, multidisciplinary, interdisciplinary and transdisciplinary research present different forms that complement and presuppose each other and by no means exclude or replace. There is still however a lot of uncertainty and confusion about the meaning of each form of knowledge production and their mutual relationships. With regard to ontological status of transdisciplinary research, Brenner argues "transdisciplinarity should not be seen as yet another discipline but as an aid to legitimizing and insuring a minimum scientific rigor in creative new approaches to on-going issues." (Brenner and Raffl 2011) To this day, interdisciplinarity and transdisciplinarity is hardly seen at universities, and their slow introduction happens indirectly through courses addressing e.g. sustainability. However, there is a strong need of introducing this knowledge broadly and making it part of curricula so that the next generation of researchers get prepared for work in all types of constellations — from mono-disciplinary to transdisciplinary research, being "vaccinated" against disciplinary chauvinism. The aim of our article is to contribute to better understanding of the existing knowledge production practice and theory based on research connecting information communication, computation, (inter-)action and cognition.

3. Diversity of Sciences, Humanities and Arts

Sciences as we know them today are historically new phenomenon. Since the dawn of western civilization with Aristotle in the ancient Greece and to the 19th century all study of the natural world was known as natural philosophy. Newton, Lord Kelvin, Spinoza, Goethe, Hegel and Schelling were natural philosophers. With the development of specific natural sciences like astronomy, physics, chemistry, biology etc. natural philosophy faded into near nonexistence. Other two branches of traditional philosophy, metaphysics and moral philosophy, continued to this day to study fundamental nature of reality, knowledge, reason, mind, language and values. They contributed and were integrated into the development of humanities and arts and help us get a broader understanding of human conditions. The development of early sciences proceeded by replacing the question "why" (is something)? i.e. the question of telos, or the purpose, goal of something, with the question "how" (is something possible)? or in what way exactly it happens – that is still the focus of modern sciences. Especially the question "why?" as related to Aristotle's final cause was strictly exorcised from modern science, such as Galilean and Newtonian physics, based on classical (linear, exact) logic.

However, in last decades it has become apparent that Aristotle's teleological processes could be described and scientifically modeled with help of memory-based agency such as in living organisms. All living organisms must actively "work" on their own survival — without appropriate environment, food and water an organism cannot exist. That makes them sensitive to the environment where they anticipate future possibilities: they avoid dangers and choose favorable circumstances. Organisms anticipate probabilistically, based on memory of previous experiences. From the contemporary perspective, Aristotle's final cause is nothing mystical, as it is the result of living beings survival strategies — it is not based on an exact knowledge of the future, but on the probabilistic expectation and anticipation. Among living organisms, humans have developed the most sophisticated strategies of anticipation based on learning that is both individual and collective/cultural.

Kant argues in his three Critiques (the Critique of Pure Reason, the Critique of Practical Reason, and the Critique of the Power of Judgment) that all human understanding which shapes our experience is teleological, i.e. goal oriented. He introduces judgment as a basis of decision and action and a way to unify the theoretical and practical perspective (Hanna 2014). Typically we know something because we find it relevant, important and interesting, and useful for acting in the world. All of it is based on values and judgment: what we find good and worthy of our time and efforts. Knowledge and values are inextricably connected (Tuana 2015).

With current prominence of problem-based research, development of increasingly complex technology and taking into account variety of stakeholders involved — the necessity for a broader understanding by each of participants in such projects is becoming central. We again need to acquire a broader view in which sciences, humanities, arts and other human activities form networks of networks of tightly interrelated parts, as we are becoming aware of the complexity of the natural and cultural worlds and ready to approach it (Bardzell and Bardzell 2015).

Natural sciences (primarily physics with its fields of mechanics, thermodynamics and electromagnetism) were the basis for the development of technology that has led to the modern industrial era. Mechanistic ideal of physics have permeated other fields and its strict division of labor appeared for centuries as natural necessity. Even bigger was the division between natural sciences and humanities and arts. Almost sixty years ago, Snow famously addressed the gap between natural sciences and humanities in his book The Two Cultures (Snow 1959). A manifestation of a deep schism, in the 1990s science wars raged between scientific realists and postmodernists, epitomized by Sokal affair (Sokal and Bricmont 1997). The starting point was Sokal's hoax article "Transgressing the Boundaries: Towards a Transformative Hermeneutics of Quantum Gravity" which was caricaturing the relationships between postmodernism of humanities and realism of natural sciences. As an attempt to bridge the gap, biologist Wilson wrote a book Consilience: The Unity of Knowledge, trying to reconciliate "the two cultures" in the academic debate (Wilson 1998). Wilson's proposed solution was "the third culture", which would foster deeper under-standing between humanities and natural sciences. Interestingly, the German term Wissenschaft includes both natural and social sciences as well as the humanities, unlike the English concept of "science" that makes the distinction between sciences and humanities. In terms of education, there is a "third way" where liberal arts education can include languages, literature, art history, philosophy, psychology, history, mathematics, and sciences such as biological and social sciences.

However, Snow's model of knowledge production might have worked for a few individuals, but culture is a mass phenomenon and calls for public involvement. Thus the third culture instead started to emerge as a result of technological development, ICT-revolution and digitalization of society in virtually all its segments. (Kelly 1998; Brockman 1996) Computational devices made it possible to visualize, simulate, communicate and discuss ideas that were before completely inaccessible to the broader audience.

The key for the new knowledge production capable of bridging variety of gaps was in the dialog, collaboration, and crowdsourcing. Such examples are "polymath" online crowd-based mathematical problem solving, and Wikipedia, which shows that crowdsourcing style of public knowledge production can work remarkably well. Maybe the most radical novelty of transdisciplinary research is involving ordinary non-scientific people in the co-production of knowledge together with scientists. It is good to remember, as Nicolescu (Nicolescu 2011) reminds us that given more than 8000 disciplines we can be experts in one but remain equally ignorant as any other common person in all the other thousands of disciplines. Typical real-life problems are complex, often "wicked", and demand expertize in variety of research fields as well as knowledge by acquaintance, experiential knowledge and involvement and engagement in their solution. Examples of such wicked problems are global warming, public health issues or mass migrations. It is necessary to understand kinds of knowledge and skills necessary in addressing of such problems and the process of collaboration and common knowledge production.

Today we have many gaps, big and small between different disciplines. In this article we will argue that the question is not only how to understand the world but also how to make decisions and how to act. So in what follows we will also indicate the connection between understanding and acting in our different research projects that built on transdisciplinarity. To start with, we present various projects of unification and synthetic approaches to information and knowledge, which differ in their goals and preferences, focus and applicability.

4. Unity Through Diversity of Information Processes and Knowledge Production. Transdisciplinary Integration Projects

The traditional linear notion of knowledge pictured as a tree that grows only in one direction, from the root to the branches, is today replaced by images of fractal structure, as Klein pointed out in (Klein 2004) or an organic growing rhizome such as in Deleuze and Guattari (2005). More than anything else, we would say, knowledge production today is associated with network of networks that unites fractals with organically growing structures (Barabasi 2007; Dodig-Crnkovic and Giovagnoli 2013). Importantly, digital space enables non-linear dialog where information flows in all directions and distributed learning happens in all nodes. Not only so that the central node (such as university or research institute) emits knowledge to the crowds, but crowds more and more actively contribute in knowledge production — as a source of data, opinions, values, preferences and all sorts of other knowledge that might be useful for both problem identification, solution and new knowledge generation.

At present we meet variety of notions of information that focus on one segment, dimension or level of reality, most often without exactly positioning itself in relation to the other existing approaches, frameworks or definitions. In those cases where such presentation is given, it has a form of argument why one's own approach is better (for the chosen purpose) than the others. No attempt is made to pragmatically examine under which circumstances some other approaches, frameworks or definitions would be more appropriate. Thus many unification attempts have been done on different grounds in search for the universal idea of information that would suit all its many appearances and applications.

4.1.   *Burgin's Unified General Theory of Information (GTI)*

If we want to understand the process of unification of knowledge, the first step is the unification of information. In his book Theory of Information: Fundamentality, Diversity and Unification (Burgin 2010), Burgin both presents the current state of art in the information studies

(Burgin 2010) addressing the most important theories of information such as dynamic, pragmatic, algorithmic, statistical and semantics, as well as presenting his own proposal for the general theory of information (GTI). Burgin's unification is based on a parametric definition of information that uses "infological system" type (infological as information ontological) as a parameter that distinguishes between kinds of information, such as chemical, biological, genetic, cognitive, personal and social, and in that way constructs the general concept of "information". Burgin's general theory of information is a system of principles and there are two groups of such principles: ontological (defines information that exists: in nature, in living world including human mind, in societies, even in computing machinery with their "virtual reality", and axiological principles that explain evaluation and measurement of information. GTI explicates the relationships between data, information, and knowledge within common framework. With respect to its goals and values Burgin's GTI is a pragmatic and encyclopedic work that aims at logical organisation of information and knowledge with focus on their unity in reality.

4.2. *Hofkirchner's Unified Theory of Information (UTI)*

In a different project for unification of information Hofkirchner characterizes efforts at unification into unity of methods, unity of reality and unity of practice (Hofkirchner 1999).

Starting from the observation that information presents a conceptual building block as fundamental as matter/energy, Hofkirchner argues for the necessity of unified theory of information, UTI conceived as a transdisciplinary evolutionary framework.

> "UTI may thus be regarded as a specific proposal of what theoretical foundations of a new science of information could look like, and tries to connect complex systems thinking to systems philosophy and extend it to the field of information studies (Hofkirchner 2010)."

Constitution of sense in this framework is envisaged as three-level architecture of self-organization: cognition, communication and cooperation levels. Different definitions of information correspond to different domains of applicability, and "none of the various existing information concepts/theories should take its perspective absolute but, in a way, complementary to the other perspectives. "Nice illustration is given by Riegler: "Suppose that we take a piece of chalk and write on the blackboard "A = A." We may now point at it and ask, "What is this?" Most likely we will get one of the following answers. (a) White lines on a black background; (b) An arrangement of molecules of chalk; (c) Three signs; (d) The law of identity" (Riegler 2005). According to Hofkirchner, information depends on how we see the object-subject relation. In "hard" sciences, information is objective, while in "soft" sciences it is subjective. UTI is an integrative framework that aims at bridging the gap. It offers the solution to the Capurro's Trilemma which assumes that the solution to the unification of the concept of information either goes via synonymy, analogy or equivocation (Capurro *et al.* 1997). The UTI solution is the fourth option — synthetic or integrative approach. (Hofkirchner 2009) This unification does not result in a monolithic body of knowledge but seeks unity through diversity (systemic integrativism). UTI adopts Praxio-Onto-Epistemology: methods of systems philosophy, philosophy of information, social philosophy, philosophy of technology and applying of system methods, evolutionary systems theory and Science of information methods. With respect to its goals and values Hofkirchner's UTI is interested in connecting information with cognition, communication and cooperation in a systemic framework.

4.3.   *Brier's Cybersemiotics*

Unlike Burgin and Hofkirchner who have information in the focus, Brier is in the first place addressing knowledge, and he declares in his book Cybersemiotics: why information is not enough! that information (understood in Shannon's formulation) lacks meaning that is fundamental for living organisms. (Brier 2008) Cybersemiotic is thus used as a "new foundation for transdisciplinary theory of information, cognition, meaningful communication and the interaction between nature and culture". (Brier 2013) According to Brier, phenomenological and hermeneutical approaches are necessary in order to build a theory of signification and interpretative meaning, so he questions the possibility of phenomenological computation, such as proposed by the adherents of info-computation and computing nature (Brier 2014). According to Brier, the bridge from physical information to phenomenology requires metaphysical framework and goes through the following five organizational levels: 1. The quantum physical (information) level with entangled causation. 2. The classical physical (information) level with efficient causation based on energy and force. 3. The chemical informational level with formal causation by pattern fitting. 4. The biological semiotic level with non-conscious final causation (where meaning occurs) and 5. The social-linguistic level of self-consciousness, with conscious goal-oriented final causation. Brier argues that integration of these levels made by evolutionary theory through emergent properties is not sufficient, as it lacks a "theory of lived meaning". Cybersemiotics that is offered as a solution for bridging the gap is based on Peirce's semiotic philosophy combined with a Luhmann's cybernetic and systemic view (Brier 2003). Regarding goals and values, Briers approach is much more interested in individual subjective information with roots in phenomenological and hermeneutical tradition.

4.4. *Integration through qualitative complexity: ecology and cognitive processes*

One more important example of a transdisciplinary unification project is done in the domain of qualitative complexity as described by Smith and Jenks in their book Qualitative Complexity: Ecology, Cognitive Processes and the Re-emergence of Structures in Post-Humanist Social Theory (Smith and Jenks 2006). Their book can be seen as a direct answer to The Two Cultures (Snow 1959) with its call for unity of knowledge. Smith and Jenks show the way to move beyond the classical irreconcilable dichotomies (with classical logic of excluded middle) that leave intractable gaps between nature and culture, structure and agency as well as between human and technology. They show how connections can be made between 'humanist paradigm' with its emphasis on human traditional notion of "true knowledge" understood as absolute certainty, and empirically observed oscillations between regularity and contingency, order and disorder in the world. Their unification relies on the insight that humans as well as social systems are special cases of a variety of forms of complex systems. As other complex systems, they are best studied by cross-disciplinary and trans-disciplinary methods. It is a long way ahead before we reach unification, and work out all the details of how complex systems produce culture from nature and agency from structure and back. Smith and Jenks present complexity theory based on conceptual tools from thermodynamics, biology and cybernetics, and explore the emergent and probabilistic aspects of self-organizing phenomena, such as human bodies, ant colonies or markets. 'We are at the beginning [...] of a multi-dimensional reunification' (Smith and Jenks 2006) (p. 276). Complexity theory as an explanatory framework supports a non-linear and interactive concept of causality, where small causes can lead to large emergent outcomes. An available energy 'informs' every entity from the non-living to cells, from humans to technological assemblages (p. 243). Complexity provides a very productive framework for exploring dynamic interactions of components interacting in emergent ways in social, natural and technological phenomena described by self-organisation starting with 'a common ontology of matter and information' (p. 95). This approach has a goal to bridge the gap between "two cultures" and build a new "third culture" that connects the two.

4.5. *Info-computational synthesis through dynamic networking*

While Smith and Jenks approach has its focus on the bridging the gap between the social and the natural, there is an even bigger project that aims at bridging the gap all the way from the microcosm to macrocosm and back, through all immediate emergent phenomena. It aims at generating knowledge in a variety of domains starting with the most fundamental principles of physics and producing more and more complex. We find such a grand project in Wolfram's New Kind of Science (Wolfram 2002) and trace its idea back to 1676 Leibniz quest for Characteristica Universalis, (Leibniz 1966) a universal language that would define the basis for all knowledge.

Leibniz idea of universal language was related to a Calculus Ratiocinator as a method for generation of true statements via logical calculation that is derivation from common premises, with a plan for a universal encyclopedia that would contain all human knowledge. Leibniz's idea further developed within Hilbert's program of formalization of mathematics, logic and parts of physics. Especially through the development of computing machinery used for processing, storage and communication of information, Leibniz's dream of common language of reasoning started to take concrete and practical forms.

One step further, we can imagine that not only rational reasoning that can be articulated as some sort of language and further on expressed computationally, but the whole of human cognition, including emotions and entirety of embodied human behavior as well can be seen as computational in nature (von Haugwitz *et al*. 2015; Dodig-Crnkovic and Stuart 2007; Dodig-Crnkovic and Müller 2011; Dodig-Crnkovic and Burgin 2011; Dodig-Crnkovic 2006). In that case computation is not only logical symbol manipulation but also includes variety of physical, chemical and biological processes going on in human body and its mind (Burgin and Dodig-Crnkovic 2015). Human logical reasoning with symbol manipulation is just a small subset of all natural processes that are going on in humans and that can be described and understood as natural computation, (Ehresmann 2014). Generalizing from Leibniz's project of Characteristica Universalis, we can see not only humans, but also all natural and cultural phenomena, indeed, the whole of our reality as manifestations of a variety of computational phenomena. That view is called computationalism, natural computation or computing nature, (Zenil 2012; Dodig-Crnkovic and Giovagnoli 2013).

Info-computation is a constructive theoretical framework that connects information as a structure and computation as information processing, developed in Dodig-Crnkovic (2006, 2009, 2011). It synthesizes two approaches: informational structural realism (Sayre 1976) (Wheeler 1990; Floridi 2003; Burgin 2010) in which the world/reality is a complex fabric of informational structures, and natural computationalism (Zuse 1970; Fredkin 1992; Wolfram 2002; Chaitin 2007), which argues that the universe is a computational network of networks. Computation is thereby understood in its most general form as natural dynamics, from computational processes in quantum physics, to self-organizing, self-sustaining phenomena such as living organisms and eco-systems. In short, it is continuation and generalization of the same Leibnizian tradition that aimed at common understanding of human behavior, now not only logical reasoning, but its entirety, including human biological, cognitive and social behaviors. Providing mechanisms based on natural computation, from physics, via chemistry to emergent biology and cognition, the info-computational framework enables understanding of mechanisms of science on both object level and meta-levels (that is understanding of understanding). Object level in a sense of describing different phenomena within sciences such as physics, chemistry, biology, neuroscience, etc. as manifestations of the same sort of info-computational structures and processes. Meta levels represent understanding of working mechanisms of cognition and knowledge generation as computation in the info-computational conceptual space.

The proposed unification of sciences in knowledge production diversity goes thus via common language and computational apparatus, and info-computationalism (Dodig-Crnkovic 2010) provides both, in the spirit of Leibniz. Besides classical scientific modeling approaches, it offers additional explorative devices such as simulation, virtual reality and generative models, which Wolfram named "a new kind of science". Emerging info-computational tools such as internet of things and internet of everything offer new means of understanding of the role of human embodiment and embeddedness for production of knowledge through interaction with the physical environment. Info-computing is a method with a capacity of providing a perspective connecting presently disparate fields into a new unified framework comprising natural phenomena from elementary particles to cognitive agents, ecological and social systems, from rational and emotive cognition to (inter)acting in the world. Of special interest is the role of embodied exploratory activity in relation to the virtual and simulated in human-computer interaction (von Haugwitz and Dodig-Crnkovic 2015).

5. Transdisciplinary Work in Technological Applications of Information and Computation

All the above-mentioned approaches (GTI, UTI, Cybersemiotics, qualitative complexity and info-computationalism) to the topic of transdisciplinary knowledge unification are theoretical in nature. Even though all emphasize in one way or the other the importance of pragmatics, agency, embodiment and embeddedness, they do so on the level of description. Info-computational approaches open however up for a computational language application that directly can connect to physical world through computing systems controlled by programming languages and other info-computational structures and processes. Thus the bridge between the code and the execution, the language and action, the description and practice is made.

The practical involvement with the physical reality meets open contexts of individual and particular, through interaction. Thus design and construction of the physical devices requires transdisciplinarity, which gets implemented and tested, evaluated and reinforced through the research process. We present three examples of transdisciplinary research projects where not only gaps between academic knowledge domains are bridged, but even gaps between theoretical and practical knowledge with its aspects of usability, esthetics and other properties of embodiment and embeddedness.

5.1. *Transdisciplinarity as a tool for interdisciplinary teams in research and applications in HCI: Experiences from creating a head-mounted display*

As a consequence of increasingly complex products and services, and increasingly human-centric, stakeholders-aware understanding of technological artifacts, interdisciplinary teams have become a common trend within research and technology related to engineering companies. Companies have discovered that there is an added value in bringing together in the design of their products knowledge from variety of professions and areas. In particular, the driving force in this trend was the shift in how consumers and society think about products. Products do not only need to be functional but also look and feel good, be sustainable from environmental, social, and economical point of view, ethically produced and used. For these reasons, researchers look into how collaborations between different specializations in research and industry can improve their competences to tackle these issues. We will specifically focus on the relationship between interaction design researchers and engineers.

Combining knowledge from different professions to collaboratively solve a common problem or to develop products is necessary when products and solutions need to be developed that are supposed to be innovative and user friendly. In such circumstances interdisciplinary teams are needed that could collaborate to achieve a better outcome by combining their knowledge. However, this new kind of collaboration is not easy to achieve. Only distributing work and accommodating discussions does not allow for an effective interdisciplinary or transdisciplinary team. It has been shown that interdisciplinarity or transdisciplinarity must be learned and governed (Gray 2008; Younglove-Webb *et al.* 1999; Young 2000). The leader of an interdisciplinary or transdisciplinary team needs to moderate problems with team members, make decisions and suggest methods to achieve common goals. In research it has been noticed that there are challenges when building and steering a successful transdisciplinary team, so leaders with the skills to manage collaboratively may make the difference between success and failure (Gray 2008).

When looking at projects run in industry that are interdisciplinary or transdisciplinary, the practical differences in terminologies seem to converge as it gets harder to distinguish at what point a team was or is interdisciplinary or transdisciplinary. The difference might even get smaller when one team member has transdisciplinary knowledge and uses methods to generate knowledge in a transdisciplinary way.

A challenge for interdisciplinary teams can, as we experienced in our project (Kade 2014; Kade *et al.* 2015) already start with the task description and its terminology, or even terminologies in general. Other researchers framed this by saying that "working on ill-structured problems or problems with multiple weak dimensions requires more demanding information activities" (Palmer 2006). In our example, a product designer, an engineer and a computer scientist collaborated on creating a head-mounted display (HMD) as a new research prototype. The task was to create a modern HMD with a modern, neat user-friendly design that might be developed into a commercial product.

The task description was rather vague and led to issues that needed to be overcome when the interdisciplinary team started to work together. The engineer directly thought about the latest and greatest hardware to provide up-to-date features. "Modern", "neat" and "design" were interpreted in terms of hardware design and what technical features the HMD should have. The computer scientist was considering the latest software, its structures and how components could communicate in a smooth way. At the same time the designer was wondering what the words "modern", user-friendly and "neat" could mean in terms of a visual design. Some discussions to clarify what should be done did not solve this issue; only more questions on what would be needed arose. After a long first meeting between the three participants, only the computer scientist and the engineer came to a better understanding of what would be needed to build the HMD, as their technical understanding was closer to each other in terms of technical problem solving.

This is only one example showing that when working in an interdisciplinary team, a common language and understanding of the task or problem at hand is of importance. Others already stated, "in transdisciplinary projects, misunderstanding and disagreement are much more likely" (Gray 2008, p.125). Therefore, they need to be resolved or avoided through good team management and work structures. Even the communication between interdisciplinary or transdisciplinary team members would benefit from a common language and understanding.

Therefore, it is important to use adequate terms and descriptions in such a work setup. In our example it would have been better, to give each of the team members a separate task description in the language they are familiar with. For the engineer and the computer scientist, a requirement list and a description of demanded hardware and software components and features with technical terms would have allowed them to understand the starting point and what work was required from their side. The product designer would have been more driven, when the terms "modern" and "neat" would have been enriched with some more details such as "slim", "simplistic" design with an "organic" and "head-band like" form, allowing for an "ergonomic" and "comfortable fit". However, sometimes this level of detail is negotiated between team members without mediation of a leader who would impose decisions in a top-down manner.

Besides questions of language, and communication in general, an interdisciplinary team needs to be lead and governed well to be effective. This means that an effective interdisciplinary team needs a skilled manager with a good understanding not only of the different fields, members of the team belong to, but also of the dynamics, ways of working and resources in the team.

A question in our concrete research project (Kade *et al.* 2015) was: who should lead the team with the task of creating a new head-mounted display? The designer, the engineer or the computer scientist, or maybe a forth person, trained in project management? It might be any of the above. Apart from the task of managing the project and establishing work and communication flows; issues, misinterpretations and misunderstandings resulting from the interdisciplinary setup of the team must be avoided, identified and solved early on. Nonetheless, it is not self-evident if a project management of an interdisciplinary team should rely on the manager's personality and managing skills or if it needs to be transdisciplinarity skills of a manager who coordinates an interdisciplinary team.

We pose the question if it would for example help to have engineers that understand the work processes and language of a product designer. In our example, this would have improved the situation, as the communication problems or misunderstandings could have been avoided. Managing skills and a suitable personality are certainly of importance to lead a successful interdisciplinary team but the leaders of such teams need to go beyond their field of expertise and should have an understanding of the involved professions, their work terms and ways of working. A good coordination of the work and interactions between the different fields is needed to lead interdisciplinary teams. At the present stage, it is rare that researchers acquire basic competences in interdisciplinary or transdisciplinary research, and new thinking in research education is necessary to remedy this deficiency, as the future of research is in collaboration across disciplinary field borders. Our hope is that next generations of researchers, educated in transdisciplinary thinking will be better prepared to listen and learn and look critically at their own disciplinary knowledge in different contexts and in relation to other fields and disciplines.

When leading interdisciplinary teams, or teams in general, a well-managed distribution of work is a key factor of success of an efficient team. In our specific project, we were interested in the question where do designers stop their work and where do engineers take over. In general, the answer to this question might depend on the setup of the team and the work description. When developing artifacts or devices, the looks might be more important for a user than the functional features and sometimes it might be the other way round. This means that designers might be brought in first to shape the looks and the engineers later on to integrate the technology. On the other hand, it might even be the other way round where engineers work out the technical details and designers shape the looks afterwards.

An ideal situation would be, especially in a multi-, inter- or transdisciplinary team, when all involved members would participate in the design and development process from the beginning to the end. This would shape a collaborative atmosphere where designers and engineers could bring in their full potential. Others mentioned that designers should be constrained to limit unwanted innovation or creativity (Culverhouse 1995) This might be true when time is limited, but doesn't follow the general way of working as a designer, in which creativity and innovation is generally wanted and supported. In a transdisciplinary work it is important to guide and steer innovation in the right way and frame the work of designers so that designers know where creativity or rather innovative solutions are needed and where simpler or existing solutions might be better to use.

To provide such guidance, again, a well-managed team leadership is needed. This involves that structures in a team are given to support a close cooperation between designers and engineers. Methods like rapid prototyping or agile work methods that are getting more and more common to both engineers and designers present a large potential in facilitating collaborations in interdisciplinary teams.

As the question on how to support and nourish the teamwork is of utmost importance, when looking at interdisciplinary or transdisciplinary teams, it is important to have a well-defined work structure with procedures that allow for interwoven problem solving collaboration. This means to involve multiple or all team members to discuss issues and to decide solutions and features. At the same time, it is important to not underestimate the talents of individual team members. Therefore, individual tasks and rolls must be clearly defined and distributed according to the knowledge and skills in the team.

When looking back at our project, in which designers and engineers worked together to create a head-mounted projection display (HMDP), the situation got even more complicated when other stakeholders were involved. For our example, actors were selected as users for the HMDP to support and rehearse their performance. This meant that designers and engineers needed to work with actors who are artists and have a very different way of working and thinking compared to designers and engineers. This new composition of project members allowed for new possibilities. Generally, new views, ways of thinking and expert knowledge from a targeted profession of the designed artifact is beneficial to integrate into a team and to use as a source of knowledge.

Actors as potential users of a designed artifact are of course of central importance in a user-centric design. To understand the needs of actors and how to design and develop for their specific work environment, without spending large amounts of time for background research and gaining such knowledge was essential. Actors involved in an interdisciplinary team, could not only provide user experiences with the HMPD but also expert knowledge and valuable ideas and anticipated solutions in a collaborative design and development process.

Having an interdisciplinary team has its benefits in diversity of knowledge and ideas but needs interwoven structures and connections in order to facilitate understanding and efficient work among team members. Both universities and industry have begun looking for T-shaped engineers conceived by David Guest in 1991 as "a variation on Renaissance Man" with both deep and broad competences (Guest 1991) and researchers (IFM 2008; Leonard-Barton 1995; Palmer 1990) but it seems to be an early stage when it comes to exploring transdisciplinarity as a way to handle interdisciplinary teams successfully. We see transdisciplinarity as an interesting way of solving interdisciplinary problems but see that trained personal and researchers need to be found that can lead such interdisciplinary teams. We have mentioned before that transdisciplinarity teams are not new and have their challenges, such as disagreeing on methodologies that should be used to research or work on a certain topics. Nonetheless, we also see a large potential in interdisciplinary teams consisting in T-shaped researchers and engineers that are led by skilled transdisciplinary leaders.

5.2. *Transdisciplinary research for automotive multi-operating system environments*

As practical exploitation of information is rapidly pervading all spheres of society including technology, more and more of control processes are delegated to information processing devices (computers) and control applied in automotive industry started to transform from classical mechanics-based to information and computation based control. Over the past 30 years cars have changed from purely electro-mechanical vehicles to increasingly complex computerized systems through introduction of more complex features. This is not only driven by the necessity to provide innovations that improve sale rates, but also driven by customer demands and advances in technology. In 2014 new features were up to 70% software related (Bosch 2014). Those can be categorized into different domains: driver assistance (e.g. distance checking, lane assist), comfort (e.g. entertainment, navigation, communication) and safety related features (e.g. ASP, ESP).

Car manufacturers use over 100 years of experience and knowledge from mechanical and electrical engineering and about 30 years of experience in embedded software. Thirty years ago software was rarely used in cars and the first electronic control units (ECU) were independently used for dedicated basic tasks (Broy *et al*. 2007). Today, a basic car architecture includes up to 100 ECUs (Ebert and Jones 2009), which are interconnected through a sophisticated communication infrastructure. Finally, an interface to the driver, the human-machine-interface (HMI), provides access to up to 700 functions of a car (e.g. (BMW 2014)). The overall development of cars is multi-disciplinary and transdisciplinary. Many teams work on different types of problems and contribute to the subsystems- as well as overall product/functions of a car. Introducing new technologies constantly increases the amount of disciplines in this process. Thus (Winner 2013) states, that "today systems are virtually impossible to develop within one engineering discipline" and relates to a manifold of necessary disciplines.

This is reflected in the internal organisation of car manufacturers, where all departments are created and separated based on their own discipline: mechanical engineering, electronics, ergonomics, etc. Software engineering is most often a subdivision of electronics. Departments produce modules, which are integrated in a common car platform (Pötsch 2011). Additionally, complex tasks (e.g. subsystems or specialized components) are often outsourced and commissioned to suppliers. Departments and suppliers rely on the concept of modularity, i.e. the exchange of strict sets of requirements and interface descriptions. However, modular development requires contextual knowledge to interconnected parts. Contrary to earlier expectations of complexity outsourcing, (Cabigiosu *et al.* 2013) states that "modular design does not substitute for high-power interorganizational coordination mechanisms". This supports the current change, especially in research and development departments, towards interdisciplinary and transdisciplinary departments, such as e.g. concept development, which consists of transdisciplinary teams from the fields of design, ergonomics and psychology.

Guidelines for user-centred development of a Driver Assistance System (DAS) (König 2016) state, that "a proven development strategy is to use an interdisciplinary team (human engineering team)". It further describes that the members of this team "must at the very least include engineers and psychologists". But, why are psychologists supposed to be part of the team? In order to understand the answer, the interconnection of the DAS component to other components has to be known. The DAS is connected to the HMI, which is used by the driver. "Physiology and traffic psychology is necessary in order to take into account the demands and the behaviour of drivers" (König 2016). This knowledge contributes to the behaviour and functionality of the DAS.

There is a shift from multidisciplinary to interdisciplinary to transdisciplinary research and development. The more interconnections exist, the more knowledge is necessary to solve particular problems. Automotive components are highly interconnected with other components, systems and services and it is inevitable to understand all of their implications. However, working in multi- or inter-disciplinary teams may cause developers to automatically gain enough knowledge to call the development trans-disciplinary — depending on the level of integration. The gap between inter-disciplinary and trans-disciplinary collaboration is very narrow.

Taking an illustrative application example from the automotive industry, where software developers have to implement prototypes of a new digital instrument cluster (such as digital speed/ rpm gauges as seen in e.g. (Audi 2014, 2016)). This software will be part of the HMI used in a real test-car in order to conduct user studies and to prove or disprove certain factors of the instrument cluster. In order to implement this particular piece of software, a developer has to understand the technical parts of a problem, e.g. how to obtain the speed information from the cars bus system, how to implement safety critical software on a certain platform and how to use a graphical processing unit (GPU) and related frameworks to implement the graphical part of the application. The actual concepts, related story boards and designs are usually created by designers, psychologists and/or ergonomists. However, to implement those in software, the developer must be able to understand the material. For example, how to convert/transform graphical artefacts or certain file formats into a usable piece of code in software. If special user interactions, such as gestures, are required, the developer also has to implement algorithms to detect those gestures. Thus in this specific example software developer has to collaborate with hardware developers, embedded software developers, designers and ergonomists and synthesize information/knowledge from variety of knowledge domains such as computer science, design and ergonomics in a transdisciplinary manner. Mono-disciplinarity in this context provides only the starting ground from which a collaborative project develops.

In our research about automotive multi operating system (Multi-OS) environments every researcher works in a different interdisciplinary field, which depends on the component or layer they are working on. Automotive Multi-OS environments compose multiple heterogeneous electronic control units (ECUs) to single ECUs in order to reduce the amount of hardware, wiring and weight in a car, consequently lowering production costs. This is possible through new technology, which provides powerful hardware and features for hardware/software virtualization. It allows multiple operating systems (OS) to be executed concurrently on a single hardware platform, i.e. an ECU. However, a composition of multiple ECUs or devices is a difficult task and causes problems and challenges on different categorized layers. Lower layers constrain higher layers, while higher layer depend on lower layers (Holstein *et al.* 2015).

A change of hardware in the lowest layer might cause the user-interface (UI) to be unusable. A concrete example is the change of touch screen size and resolution. A bigger screen size might be difficult to use while driving (Rümelin and Butz 2013) and a higher resolution might texts to be displayed too small and thus difficult to read (Stevens *et al.* 2002). Both changes might have a negative effect on user-experience, which is part of the UI layer. Automotive environments have strong requirements regarding safety- and security-related software. Therefore, interconnections between certain components might be restricted or limited. In case of Multi-OS environments an OS is confined to its own hardware resources and only certain interconnections between the different OSs are allowed (Holstein and Wietzke 2015). A lower layer is responsible for the security/safety mechanisms and the transfer of data from one OS to another. An OS may have access to internet services or app stores. This means there is a risk of malicious third party software or faulty software, which in case of an error would only affect a single OS.

In the previous example transdisciplinary knowledge has been used in development. The latter example of our research shows a more profound usage of trans-disciplinarity. Here, trans-disciplinarity will help to understand the implications of inter-connections between different parts of a complex system: How do changes in certain layers affect the overall software architecture? How do restrictions and constraints in lower layers affect the development of user interfaces? Is the separation of operating systems through virtualization leading to a more secure architecture, besides the fact, that a homogeneous user interface requires the previously separated parts to be interconnected? In certain projects a transdisciplinary approach might be essential to the outcome and success of the project.

5.3. *Applied Interaction Design Research — a transdisciplinary practice: Examples from the information-intense industrial machinery*

Designing products concerns applying technology in a form that brings usefulness and value to the user. As software takes an increasing portion of the product development, the more advanced products can be made while still providing a good experience to the user. In this section we will exemplify how transdisciplinary teamwork enhance research in product development, using examples from industry and the connection between industry and academia, arguing that it is even more beneficial the more we enter the infosphere.

Design of interactive digital systems concerns forming an interaction between human users and the artefacts used by them. Design in this perspective is so much more than visual form and esthetics, though they are important components. Design thinking refers to cognitive activities used when designing symbolic and visual communication, material objects, activities and organized services, and complex systems or environments for living, working, playing, and learning (Buchanan 1992).

Kapor defines design in the Software Design Manifesto: "What is design? It's where you stand with a foot in two worlds — the world of technology and the world of people and humans purposes — and you try to bring the two together." (Kapor 1991). The above definition indicates that practicing interaction design is a field involving the application of knowledge, from domains outside of its own field. It acquires input from areas such as human behavior and psychology, from art as well as more traditional design fields, such as architecture and typography. To be able to design for the tasks performed, there must also be knowledge about the application area where the task is performed, the technology to apply and the surrounding eco-system.

5.3.1. *Researching creation of products for the infosphere generation*

Since the above definitions where made, the impact of interaction design has increased a lot in the intercommunication between humans and the digital domain, such as the buzz and commercial success factor identified with "user experience" (Kuutti 2009). As software based systems are getting increasingly complex, the availability of computing power, sensors and actuators made software a much more integrated part of many products and systems, thus providing more and more of the functionality and value. In the automotive space, up to 70% of all innovation in products is currently software related (Bosch 2014). Even though not all of this innovation is related to interaction design, the way the user interacts, both in a sense of receiving information and being able to control the device, can be imperative for the user experience and safe operation of the device. The designer needs to understand how the technology works in combination with the user. This evolution of software systems impacting our life will likely continue, for example with the Internet of Things, where innovations move even further into the era of information generation and information processing and creating what (Floridi *et al.* 2010; Floridi 2010) call "infosphere" that is informational environment corresponding to "biosphere".

Creating systems and products that collect, make use of information and provides a applicable and comprehensible result requires an interdisciplinary approach between natural sciences, social and human sciences and systems theory (Hofkirchner 2013). Such as, that the processes and the real world need to be understood in order to synthesize them into models of computation (Wallmyr 2015). Furthermore it involves the integration from information architectures and means of communication, to technical engineering and functional aspects of getting the different pieces of the system working together. In this, the interaction designer's role is to make sense of these systems and applications to the user. It is important that designers understand the application, technology and theory in order to successfully apply the generalized methods and principles of user interaction. The interaction designer needs to possess T-shaped competence (Guest 1991; Boehm and Mobasser 2015) which means deep knowledge of at least one field and working knowledge of the current problem domains that makes it possible to bridge different research fields and approach technical issues when building utility for the user. Through understanding of different fields a common ground is found that facilitates improved collaboration and result. As Lindell argues, the interplay between interaction design and software engineering is problematic as these two activities have different epistemology. But treating information and code as a material can bring the two traditional disciplines into a combined craftsmanship (Lindell 2014).

Building custom solutions from scratch is many times not a viable option; instead development is done as integration of sub-parts with necessary adaption. Industrial products need to sustain the sometimes harsh environment, be sturdy to withstand years of tough usage, integrate with the way of working, and comply with market standards for e.g. emission and resistance. The final product might then be in production for ten years, with a subsequent lifetime of decades where service and replacement part is needed. Combining these criteria make it nearly impossible use parts from standard of-the-shelf or consumer market and in many cases the single industry domain cannot handle the investment and development themselves. Such an example is the forestry-harvesting sector, where new types of interfaces, using head-up-displays, have the potential to increase harvesting efficiency. However, their market alone is too small to support developing of the technology (Löfgren *et al.* 2007). Investments are thus distributed, as products are done in layers of existing components, software and technology. They must be generic enough so that several markets can use the same product.

To successfully select the right parts and build the right product for many markets needs a team that incorporate and exchange knowledge from several areas, not only technical but also on different market needs. Product realization project often requires a mix of different disciplines, such as mechanical designers, electric engineers, software developers, purchasers, production representatives, prototype builders etc. these teams are often lead by one or several roles, such as project managers, product managers or scrum masters. This creates multidisciplinary teams where different professions work together to build a product.

5.3.2. *An industrial example of transdisciplinary research into infosphere construction*

The question is: Is it necessary to have transdisciplinary teams in order to build next generation products? Perhaps, as working only interdisciplinary the project is constrained by the different professions focusing on their respective problems and solutions. This can lead to increased integration work, more late adjustments and a final outcome that does not reflect the bigger picture. In the case of a company developing hardware and software for industrial machinery it would mean clear disadvantages.

We have studied a company, that was going from a sub-supplier role to creating products of their own design, which in this specific case was a display computer. The company had several years of experience in building custom hardware and software. However, in retrospective it became evident that when building our own product we over focused on our in-house disciplines, our key knowledge that was normally the key contribution in customer projects. Functionality was added because it was technically possible, like TV, radio, modem and GPS. However, the market was either not interested or mature enough to appreciate it, thus leading to an overly complicated and expensive unit. One factor was that the development was not working interdisciplinary between electrical engineering, purchasing and software. Electric components were for example selected that did not have proper driver support, for the chosen operating system. Leading to massive efforts in integration of software and hardware. Another example was the industrial design that only covered mechanic design. The interaction with the display became much more of an office computer experience than what users in industrial machinery where normally accustomed to.

To continue the product development case, following display generations showed higher levels of interdisciplinary work. Such examples where electronic design and software design decisions made much more transdisciplinary, resulting in better component choices and easier integration. Also, a better understanding of customer needs lead to a hardware-software integration layer in software, making it possible for customers to move between different product families with minimal adaptation of their added application software. Simultaneously, the new industrial designer could incorporate both mechanical and software design, leading to a much more coherent experience for the end user. Other disciplines involved were production providing knowledge and experience on efficient production and service.

The above case illustrates how a higher degree of involvement and interaction between disciplines during product design and realization can result in a more integrated, thought-out and purposely facetted product. This is however not the only purpose of the illustration. The other argument is that transdisciplinarity is something that evolves continuously (Dorothy Leonard-Barton 1995) as the knowledge transfers between disciplines and individuals within the project. One of enablers of this process is continuous design review where different team members not only review the current solution, but also exchange knowledge on the factors in technology, usage, cost etc. that contribute to the solution made. As a result, experienced teams that have more interaction with other professions, become more transdisciplinary integrating tighter with other disciplines, understanding their vocabulary, limitations and possibilities. At a managerial level transfer can also be facilitated to share information and create new contacts, for example through information exchange events or relocation of personnel. As an example we can mention Canon that relocates its research and development center every six month (Harryson 1997).

As mentioned, many industries that were earlier more focused towards mechanization and automation are now progressing into the infosphere. More understanding is needed how to efficiently use all this information to benefit users in their respective domains. One factor is to avoid information overload, in automotive system to the level of awareness needed in vehicle interaction solutions, such as for visual perception given in Wördenweber *et al.* (2007, p. 48) that explains how vision constructs reality for an observer. Apart from perception and awareness, another aspect is making the information accessible to the user in an understandable and attractive manner. An example of an industrial application sector of interest is agriculture. Here information technology provides a vital piece when addressing how to efficiently and sustainably to produce food to a growing population. However a farmer or a machine operator is by profession neither a computer professional nor an information analyst. Thus, the move into more information based production systems centered on software engineers' preferences might be associated with obstacles. Sørensen *et al.* (2010) mention that even though the use of computers and internet have improved acquiring of external information as well as management and processing of internal information, "the acquisition and analysis of information still proves a demanding task". The availability of data does not warrant the understanding or usefulness of the data to the user (Chinthammit *et al.* 2014).

Supporting the transformation into information driven applications thus calls for more transdisciplinary development that will provide connection among variety of technologies and between technology and the user, society and environment. To connect to the prior case, we are coming closer to what can efficiently be interacted with using normal displays. Future development, for example see-through interfaces that augment reality and interfaces that use more-than-human visual perception to exchange information. This development has to include competences in information architecture and information design, data communication not only with local system but also cloud communication as well as haptic interaction with the user. In addition even deeper knowledge of industry domain is necessary to build the information system and computation models that provide more automation as well the right information to the user.

5.4. *Bridges between academia and industry — education and the industrial PhD*

Another aspect of transdisciplinarity is the connection between research and industry where one of many methods transdisciplinary bridges between academia and industry is built by industrial PhD students. Giving a dual direction transfer where the industrial researcher brings real-world research questions from industrial settings into academia, while simultaneously bringing information and results from the research community into industry. This ongoing exchange builds information exchange contact points as well as basic understanding of different fields, through persons that can bridge different disciplines and domains of knowledge production.

Industrial projects are to a large extent limited by a fixed description of requirements and defined task to realize, within given resource limits, such as initial time estimation. Thus these projects cannot in the same way as research elaborate on different ways to address problems and solutions. Instead the industrial PhD can bring findings and results from academia into the industrial projects, building on the research findings and adding the needed parts to design and develop or improve an industrial product.

On the other side of the bridge, the research side, it is instead encouraged to seek new and novel solutions. As researchers we are encouraged to publish our results, making information and findings from our work available to the wider research community. Going to conferences and otherwise seeking information for our own research, give inspiration and input when observing results from other application domains, thus sharing and receiving information.

Interaction design research has though been criticized for counteracting its own purpose, with the argument that design science should not be about a science of design but rather a science for design. Instead of being bound by past research it should instead be free to critically examine and question results of scientific research, with the aim of envisioning the future (Krippendorff 2007). Simultaneously design research has been questioned for not valuing application of the science to a specific field as a research result and valid contribution (Chilana *et al.* 2015), thus perhaps limiting the possibilities for interaction design researchers to endeavor into interdisciplinary research. It can be argued that in order to foster interdisciplinary research and improved collaboration, possibilities should be offered that would enable such efforts and results to be published. At present, transdisciplinary research still meets difficulty to find its proper place in academia, that is traditionally organized by disciplines, and publications are by far and large purely disciplinary with a confined view of what constitutes a good contribution. The trend of subdivision of classical disciplines into ever more narrow sub-disciplines should be counteracted by the synthetic approaches of transdisciplinarity that bring cohesion into the otherwise completely disconnected islands of knowledge. As scientists we work often with understanding of the world and how we can improve it. As such, a fitting conclusion is to refer back to Krippendorff: "Design concerns what could work in the future, a future that is more interesting than what we know today."

6. Conclusions

One of the central issues of transdisciplinary knowledge production is communication of information and knowledge across the disciplinary and cultural borders. How do we interpret the same object (boundary object) from the perspective of different disciplines, expressed in their domain languages?

How can our research which ranges from interdisciplinarity to transdisciplinarity contribute both to the existing knowledge as well as further development of practice and theory connecting information, communication, computation, (inter-)action and cognition? Let us examine how some of the characteristics of transdisciplinarity reflect in our research.

6.1. *Reflexivity*

Reflexivity relates both to the inner relationships between knowledge domains as well as the self-reflection over the proposed problem solution and its meaning for the stakeholders. It implies asking both the questions why and how, that makes relation to value systems and ethical deliberation important. The bottom line of every decision-making is the value system (which affects how we see our goals) and the sense of (feeling and understanding of) the current state of the world, that is understanding of where we are and where we want to go.

6.2. *Epistemic and value-basis transparency*

Ethical and epistemic conceptualizations are closely coupled. (Tuana 2015) Epistemic transparency in the research project requires insight in one owns assumptions and knowledge-related choices. Visibility of value grounds, decision-making transparency and analysis are central to the success of a transdisciplinary project. Coupled ethical-epistemic analysis has helped in the past projects identify new and refined research topics, and informed modeling for multi-objective, robust decision-making. (Singh *et al.* 2015) One of important attitudes in knowledge generation over several epistemic domains is attentiveness and respect for both knowledge and ignorance granted for all stakeholders.

Uncertainties and inadequate knowledge play should be identified and carefully tackled.

6.3. *Addressing the complex architecture of the knowledge space*

Understanding of the complex architecture of the multi-level and multi-dimensional knowledge space is a part of reflexive relation to knowledge production. The roles of various stakeholders must be well understood and benevolent mutual communication based on shared goals secured. For example, in medicine, addressing problem of disease requires understanding processes from molecular to cellular and level of organs, the whole organisms and their environment, including psycho-social factors thus knowledge in such a transdisciplinary project is a result of a synthesis and derivation of knowledge from all those classical academic domains in conjunction with its "users" medical institutions, societal groups, etc. In the case of our HCI field- designers, developers, users and other stakeholders are involved in the process of knowledge production.

6.4. *Syntactic vs. semantics vs. pragmatic aspects of knowledge*

As research operates on different levels of knowledge production, all three layers of semiotics are involved: syntactic — often coding of a computer program, semantics — design of programs and other artifacts for specific purposes and pragmatics — study of the behavior of the artifact (design) in practice — use-case studies.

6.5. *Integration process*

Important part of the transdisciplinary process is integration, which presents ontological and epistemological as well as organizational challenges. Riegler (Riegler 2005) mentions the following types of problems met in transdisciplinary integration process: (P1) unfamiliarity among different disciplines with a mutual information deficit; (P2) different terminology — different use of the same terms; (P3) different aims of scientific work — prediction vs explanation; (P4) hard sciences vs. soft sciences; (P5) Basic research vs. applied science and (P6) Individual vs. group research. Riegler addresses this topic from the point of view of constructivist approach which is interested in how exactly different contributions can be integrated in a common framework. He emphasizes the importance of the common worldview, the minimum shared commitment that makes it possible to relate different positions, and identify differences and similarities, granularity level of knowledge and other characteristics. Experiences from our projects indicate as well that commitment must be shared in order for a project to succeed.

6.6. *Embodiment and embeddedness of information, computation, cognition, communication*

One important aspect of research that has an ambition to have relevance for the real life is embodiment and embeddedness, which brings the element of sensualizing. Instead of abstract ideas of solutions, applied research deals with embodied problems that bring sensory qualities to the technological solutions and makes esthetic aspects of design necessary to address. Here we meet decisions made based on function (including its ethical aspects) vs. esthetics and experiential dimensions. Human — computer interaction (HCI) design does not only describe or contemplate possible futures — it builds concrete artefacts that set material constraints on our possible futures. At this stage ICT have applications even in arts and artistic production (Busch 2009).

6.7. *Questions we want answers*

Info-computational approaches today are in the center of our contemporary knowledge production. Both in literal sense of ICT used to communicate information and compute knowledge as well as in a sense of models based on information and computation. Answers fundamental questions: What is reality? What is life? Why do things happen? What is intelligence, mind, and understanding? What will happen next? Why does anything even exist? — are given in terms of infocomputation, providing new and more understandable answers than ever before. Ordinary people can nowadays "see" what atoms do, how quarks behave, how galaxies collide, how universe evolves since the big bang or what possible consequences of global warming might be — all of it via visualizations of computer simulation results. In not so distant future we will have similar possibilities to see alternative consequences of our possible political, economic and other choices. It will bring whole new possibilities for democratic decision-making. As humans we are interested not only in how things are, but we also want to know what we can expect, what is possible and what are the consequences. The promise of new theories, discoveries, inventions and developments will be possible to study in ever increasing detail and in much more systematic and multifaceted, multidimensional way. We want to know why and we want to act based on deep understanding that takes into account not only logic, but the totality of human experience.

6.8. *The underlying logic of change*

Most often logic is taken as tacit part of the theory construction, frameworks for reasoning and action. However, it should be noticed that logic is a research field on its own and a fast developing too. Nicolescu addressed the question of logic especially with regard to the axiom of excluded middle, (Nicolescu 2010) which states that nothing can be at the same time A and non A. This axiom reflects the interest of Aristotle and ancient Greeks in general an interest that is still predominant to this day in structures that persist, and not in the process of change. Transdisciplinarity on the other hand is centered on change. It means that the dynamics of process, when a structure is partly in the current and partly in the next state, is vital, where the middle is necessary included, if the process is continuous. Differences in logics imply differences in what can be expressed and argued for and how. One interesting approach in the context of transdisciplinary research is Brenner's Logic in reality (Brenner 2008) especially applied to the dynamics of information. (Brenner 2012)

Mathematician Chaitin-Chatelin argues in her book Qualitative computing that the Aristotle's classical logic is too limited to capture the dynamics of nonlinear computation. As the necessary tool for addressing the nonlinear dynamics she proposes the organic logic. This logic will be the core of the "Mathematics for Life" yet to be developed (Chaitin-Chatelin 2012). Yet another logical development was Zadeh's fuzzy logic where the "excluded middle" was replaced with a spectrum of possibilities. Even though classical logic is widely used and considered adequate, for better understanding of the process of knowledge production, integration and synthesis, logics that put their focus on dynamical process and nonlinearity are of great interest.

6.9.   *Addressing the issue of learning in transdisciplinary research projects*

The aim of research is traditionally not only to solve concrete problems, but also to contribute to the learning, that is to the shared knowledge of the community of practice (research community, knowledge building community, culture). However, being often focused on specific and real-life problems, transdisciplinary research faces the problem of comparative analysis of the research findings of different groups with different approaches, different stakeholders, values and preferences. Should transdisciplinary research be seen as an alternative to free deliberation such as commonly used in political, social or business decision-making, based on common sense and personal experience of stakeholders? Or can it be used to contribute to the development of classical research fields by informing them about the real world context in which abstract frameworks and academic discourses can be placed in? This two-way learning process can be obtained through individuals who belong both to research in the Mode 1 and the Mode 2 (Gibbons *et al.* 1994), such as industrial PhD students as we described. The interdisciplinary and transdisciplinary knowledge production is new in the university world with its long and persistent traditions, and the best way to contribute to better understanding of the applicability and the role of different modes of knowledge production is to educate future generations of researchers and citizens not only in disciplinary research methods but also in interdisciplinary and transdisciplinary research.

References

Audi, 2016. Audi virtual dashboard. *online*.

Audi, 2014. Dialoge — Das Audi-Technologiemagazin.

Barabasi, A.-L., 2007. The Architecture of Complexity. *IEEE Control Systems Magazine*, 27(4), pp. 33–42.

Bardzell, J. & Bardzell, S., 2015. Humanistic HCI. In *Synthesis Lectures on Human-Centered Informatics Synthesis*, San Rafael, California: Morgan & Claypool Publishers.

BMW, 2014. BMW Technology Guide: iDrive.

Boehm, B. & Mobasser, K.S., 2015. System Thinking: Educating T-Shaped Software Engineers. In *IEEE 28th Conference on Software Engineering Education and Training*, pp. 13–16.

Bosch, J., 2014. Continuous Software Engineering: An Introduction. *Continuous Software Engineering*. pp. 3–13.

Brenner, J., 2008. *Logic in reality*,

Brenner, J., 2012. The Logical Dynamics of Information; Deacon's "Incomplete Nature." *Information*, 3, pp. 676–714.

Brenner, J. & Raffl, C., 2011. Introduction to the Special Issue ICTs and Society — A New Transdiscipline? What Kind of Academic Field do We Need to Meet the Challenges of the Information Age? *tripleC*, 9(2), pp. 593–597.

Brier, S., 2013. Cybersemiotics: A New Foundation for Transdisciplinary Theory of Information, Cognition, Meaningful Communication and the Interaction Between Nature and Culture. *Integral Review*, 9(2), pp. 220–262.

Brier, S., 2008. *Cybersemiotics: Why Information is Not Enough!* Toronto: University of Toronto Press.

Brier, S., 2003. Information Seen as Part of the Development of Living Intelligence: The Five-leveled Cybersemiotic Framework for FIS. *Entropy*, 5(2), pp. 88–99.

Brier, S., 2014. Phenomenological Computation? *Constructivist Foundations*, 9(2), pp. 234–235.

Brockman, J., 1996. The Third Culture: Beyond the Scientific Revolution. *American Journal of Physics*, 64(3), p. 348.

Broy, M. *et al.*, 2007. Engineering Automotive Software. *Proceedings of the IEEE*, 95(2), pp. 356–373.

Buchanan, R., 1992. Wicked Problems in Design Thinking. *Design Issues*, 8(2), pp. 5–21.

Burgin, M., 2010. *Theory of Information: Fundamentality, Diversity and Unification*, Singapore: World Scientific Pub Co.

Burgin, M. & Dodig-Crnkovic, G., 2015. A Taxonomy of Computation and Information Architecture. In M. Galster, ed., *Proceedings of the 2015 European Conference on Software Architecture Workshops (ECSAW '15)*, New York: ACM Press.

Busch, K., 2009. Artistic Research and the Poetics of Knowledge. *Art & Research*, 2(2).

Cabigiosu, A., Zirpoli, F. & Camuffo, A., 2013. Modularity, Interfaces Definition and the Integration of External Sources of Innovation in the Automotive Industry. *Research Policy*, 42(3), pp. 662–675.

Capurro, R., Fleissner, P. & Hofkirchner, W., 1997. Is a Unified Theory of Information Feasible? *World Futures*, 49(3–4), pp. 409–427.

Chaitin, G., 2007. Epistemology as Information Theory: From Leibniz to Ω. In G. Dodig Crnkovic, ed. *Computation, Information, Cognition — The Nexus and The Liminal*. Newcastle UK: Cambridge Scholars Pub., pp. 2–17.

Chaitin-Chatelin, F., 2012. *Qualitative Computing: A Computational Journey into Nonlinearity*, Singapore: World Scientific Publishing Company.

Chilana, P.K., Ko, A.J. & Wobbrock, J., 2015. From User-Centered to Adoption-Centered Design. In *Proceedings of the 33rd Annual ACM Conference on Human Factors in Computing Systems — CHI '15*. New York, New York, USA: ACM Press, pp. 1749–1758.

Chinthammit, W., Duh, H.B.-L. & Rekimoto, J., 2014. HCI in Food Product Innovation. In *Proceedings of the Extended Abstracts of the 32nd Annual ACM Conference on Human Factors in Computing Systems — CHI EA '14*, pp. 1111–1114.

Choi, B.C.K. & Pak, A.W.P., 2008. Multidisciplinarity, Interdisciplinarity, and Transdisciplinarity in Health Research, Services, Education and Policy: 3. Discipline, Inter-discipline Distance, and Selection of Discipline. *Clinical & Investigative Medicine.*, 31(1), pp. E41–E48.

Cooper, S.B., Löwe, B. & Sorbi, A. eds., 2007. *New Computational Paradigms. Changing Conceptions of What is Computable. Springer Mathematics of Computing series, XIII.*, Berlin: Springer.

Culverhouse, P.F., 1995. Constraining Designers and Their CAD Tools. *Design Studies*, 16(1), pp. 81–101.

Deleuze, G. & Guattari, F., 2005. *A Thousand Plateaus: Capitalism and Schizophrenia*, Minneapolis: University of Minnesota Press.

Dodig-Crnkovic, G., 2010. Biological Information and Natural Computation. In J. Vallverdú, ed. Hershey PA, *Information Science Reference*, pp. 1–27.

Dodig-Crnkovic, G., 2009. *Information and Computation Nets. Investigations into Info-computational World*, Saarbrucken: Vdm Verlag.

Dodig-Crnkovic, G., 2006. *Investigations into Information Semantics and Ethics of Computing*, Västerås, Sweden: Mälardalen University Press.

Dodig-Crnkovic, G., 2011. Significance of Models of Computation, from Turing Model to Natural Computation. *Minds and Machines*, 21(2), pp. 301–322.

Dodig-Crnkovic, G., 2016. The Architecture of Mind as a Network of Networks of Natural Computational Processes. *Philosophies*, 1(1), pp.111–125.

Dodig-Crnkovic, G. & Burgin, M., 2011. *Information and Computation*, Singapore: World Scientific.

Dodig-Crnkovic, G. & Giovagnoli, R. eds., 2013. *Computing Nature*, Berlin Heidelberg: Springer.

Dodig-Crnkovic, G. & Müller, V., 2011. A Dialogue Concerning Two World Systems: Info-Computational vs. Mechanistic. In G. Dodig Crnkovic & M. Burgin, eds. *Information and Computation*. Singapore: World Scientific Pub Co Inc, pp. 149–184.

Dodig-Crnkovic, G. & Stuart, S.A.J., 2007. *Computation, Information, Cognition: The Nexus and the Liminal*, Newcastle, UK: Cambridge Scholars Pub.

Dorothy Leonard-Barton, 1995. *Wellsprings of Knowledge: Building and Sustaining the Sources of Innovation*, Harvard Business School Press.

Ebert, C. & Jones, C., 2009. Embedded Software Facts, Figures, and Future. *Computer*, 42(4), pp. 42–52.

Ehresmann, A.C., 2014. A Mathematical Model for Info-computationalism. *Constructivist Foundations*, 9(2), pp. 235–237.

Flinterman, J.F. *et al.*, 2001. Transdisciplinarity: The New Challenge for Biomedical Research. *Bulletin of Science, Technology & Society*, 21(4), pp. 253–266.

Floridi, L., 2010. *Information: A Very Short Introduction*, Oxford: Oxford University Press.

Floridi, L., 2003. Informational realism. In J. Weckert & Y. Al-Saggaf, eds. *Selected Papers from Conference on Computers and Philosophy — Volume 37 (CRPIT '03)*. CRPIT '03. Darlinghurst, Australia, Australia: Australian Computer Society, Inc., pp. 7–12.

Floridi, L., Durante, M. & Ward, T., 2010. A Look into the Future Impact of ICT on Our Live. *Journal of Business*, pp. 17–19.

Fredkin, E., 1992. Finite Nature. In *XXVIIth Rencotre de Moriond*.

Frodeman, R., Klein, J.T. & Mitcham, C. eds., 2010. *The Oxford Handbook of Interdisciplinarity*, Oxford, UK: Oxford University Press.

Gibbons, M. *et al.*, 1994. *The New Production of Knowledge*: *The Dynamics of Science and Research in Contemporary Societies*. London: Sage.

Gray, B., 2008. Enhancing Transdisciplinary Research Through Collaborative Leadership. *American Journal of Preventive Medicine*, 35(2), pp. 124–132.

Guest, D., 1991. The Hunt is on for the Renaissance Man of computing. *The Independent*, p. 09.17.

Güvenen, O., 2015. Transdisciplinary Science Methodology. *European Scientific Journal*, 3.

Hadorn, G.H. *et al.*, 2008. *Handbook of Transdisciplinary Research*. Bern, Switzerland: Springer.

Hanna, R., 2014. Kant's Theory of Judgment. *The Stanford Encyclopedia of Philosophy* (*Summer 2014 Edition*).

Harryson, S.J., 1997. How Canon and Sony Drive Product Innovation Through Networking and Application-Focused R&D. *Journal of Product Innovation Management*, 14(4), pp. 288–295.

von Haugwitz, R. & Dodig-Crnkovic, G., 2015. Probabilistic Computation and Emotion as Self-regulation. In *ECSA 2015 ASDS Workshop*. In *Proceedings of the 2015 European Conference on Software Architecture Workshops (ECSAW '15)*. New York, NY, USA.: ACM.

von Haugwitz, R., Dodig-Crnkovic, G. & Almér, A., 2015. Computational Account of Emotion, an Oxymoron? In *IS4IS Summit Vienna 2015, Vienna University of Technology (online)*. Available at: http://sciforum.net/conference/isis-summit-vienna-2015/track-triangular.

Hofkirchner, W., 2009. How to Achieve a Unified Theory of Information. *tripleC*, 7(2), pp. 357–368. Available at: http://triple-c.at/index.php/tripleC/article/view/114/138.

Hofkirchner, W., 2013. Transdisciplinarity-by-Complexity-Thinking. Lecture 15–17 May.

Hofkirchner, W., 2010. *Twenty Questions about a Unified Theory of Information: A Short Exploration into Information from a Complex Systems View*, Litchfield Park AZ: Emergent Publications.

Hofkirchner, W., 1999. Ways of Thinking and the Unification of Science. In *Proceedings of the 43rd Annual Conference of ISSS* (*The International Society for the Systems Sciences*). pp. 1–9. Available at: https://igw.tuwien.ac.at/igw/menschen/hofkirchner/papers/InfoScience/Unification_Science/9945.pdf.

Holstein, T. *et al.*, 2015. Current Challenges in Compositing Heterogeneous User Interfaces for Automotive Purposes. In M. Kurosu, ed. *Human-Computer Interaction: Interaction Technologies*. Springer International Publishing.

Holstein, T. & Wietzke, J., 2015. Contradiction of Separation Through Virtualization and Inter Virtual Machine Communication in Automotive Scenarios. In *Proceedings of the 2015 European Conference on Software Architecture Workshops*. ECSAW '15. New York, NY, USA: ACM, pp. 4:1–4:5.

IFM, 2008. IfM and IBM. Succeeding through Service Innovation: A Service Perspective for Education, Research, Business and Government. Cambridge, UK.

Cambridge Institute for Manufacturing. Available at: http://www. ifm.eng.cam.ac. uk/ssme/.

Jahn, T., Bergmann, M. & Keil, F., 2012. Transdisciplinarity: Between Mainstreaming and Marginalization. *Ecological Economics*, 79, pp.1–10.

Kade, D. *et al.*, 2015. Head-Mounted Mixed Reality Projection Display for Games Production and Entertainment. *Personal and Ubiquitous Computing*, 19(3), pp. 509–521.

Kade, D., 2014. *Towards Immersive Motion Capture Acting — Design, Exploration and Development of an Augmented System Solution.* Licentiate Thesis. Mälardalen University Press.

Kapor, M., 1991. A Software Design Manifesto. *Dr. Dobb's Journal*, 16(1), pp. 62–67.

Kelly, K., 1998. The Third Culture. *Science*, 279(5353), pp. 992–993.

Klein, J.T., 2010. A Taxonomy of Interdisciplinarity. In R. Frodeman, J. Thompson Klein, & C. Mitcham, eds. *The Oxford Handbook of Interdisciplinarity,* Oxford: Oxford University Press, pp. 15–30.

Klein, J.T., 2004. Interdisciplinarity and Complexity: An Evolving Relationship. *E:CO Emergence: Complexity and Organization*, 6(1–2), pp. 2–10.

König, W., 2016. Guidelines for User-Centered Development of DAS. In H. Winner *et al.*, eds. *Handbook of Driver Assistance Systems.* Springer International Publishing, pp. 781–796.

Krippendorff, K., 2007. Design Research, An Oxymoron? In *Design Research Now: Essays and Selected Projects.* Zürich: Birkhäuser Verlag, pp. 67–80.

Kuutti, K., 2009. HCI and design: Uncomfortable Bedfellows? In *(Re)searching the Digital Bauhaus.* Springer London, pp. 43–59.

Leibniz, G.W., 1966. *Zur allgemeinen Charakteristik. Hauptschriften zur Grundlegung der Philosophie. Philosophische Werke Band 1.*, Hamburg: Felix Meiner.

Leonard-Barton, D., 1995. *Wellsprings of Knowledge: Building and Sustaining the Sources of Innovation*, Harvard Business School Press.

Lindell, R., 2014. Crafting interaction: The Epistemology of Modern Programming. *Personal and Ubiquitous Computing*, 18, pp. 613–624.

Löfgren, B., Tinggård Dillekås, H. & Järrendal, D., 2007. Head-up Display kan ge lägre arbets-belastning och högre produktion. *Resultat från SkogForsk*, 16, p. 4.

Nicolescu, B., 2010. Methodology of Transdisciplinarity — Levels of Reality , Logic of the Included. *Transdisciplinary Journal of Engineering and Science*, 1(1), pp. 19–38.

Nicolescu, B., 2014. Methodology of Transdisciplinarity. *World Futures*, 70(3), p. 186.

Nicolescu, B., 2011. The Need for Transdisciplinarity in Higher Education. Keynote talk at the International Higher Education Congress "New Trends and Issues", Istanbul, Turkey, May 27–29, 2011.

Nowotny, H., Scott, P. & Gibbons, M., 2001. *Re-Thinking Science: Knowledge and the Public in an Age of Uncertainty*, London: Polity Press with Blackwell Publishers.

Palmer, C., 1990. Hybrids' — A Critical Force in the Application of Information Technology in the Nineties. *Journal of Information Technology*, 5, pp. 232–235.

Palmer, C.L., 2006. Weak Information Work and "Doable" Problems in Interdisciplinary Science. In *Proceedings of the American Society for Information Science and Technology* 43.1. pp. 1–16.

Pötsch, 2011. H. D. Volkswagen – Driving Forward. Frankfurt: [s.n.], *Deutsche Bank German and Austrian Corporate Conference 2011.*

Riegler, A., 2005. Inclusive Worldviews: Interdisciplinary Research from a Radical Constructivist Perspective. In D. Aerts, B. D'Hooghe, & N. Note, eds. *Worldviews, Science and Us: Redemarcating Knowledge and Its Social and Ethical Implications.* Singapore: World Scientific.

Rümelin, S. & Butz, A., 2013. How to Make Large Touch Screens Usable While Driving. In *Proceedings of the 5th International Conference on Automotive User Interfaces and Interactive Vehicular Applications*. AutomotiveUI '13. New York, NY, USA: ACM, pp. 48–55.

Sayre, K.M., 1976. *Cybernetics and the Philosophy of Mind*, London: Routledge & Kegan Paul.

Singh, R., Reed, P.M. & Keller, K., 2015. Many-Objective Robust Decision Making for Managing an Ecosystem with a Deeply Uncertain Threshold Response. *Ecology and Society*, 20(3).

Smith, J. & Jenks, C., 2006. *Qualitative Complexity: Ecology, Cognitive Processes and the Re-emergence of Structures in Post-Humanist Social Theory*, London and New York: Routledge.

Snow, C.P., 1959. *The Two Cultures*, London: Cambridge University Press.

Sokal, A. & Bricmont, J., 1997. *Intellectual Impostures: Postmodern Philosopher's Abuse of Science*, London: Profile Books.

Sørensen, C.G. *et al.*, 2010. Conceptual Model of a Future Farm Management Information System. *Computers and Electronics in Agriculture*, 72(1), pp. 37–47.

Stevens, A., Quimby, A., Board, A., Kersloot, T. & Burns, P. (2002). *Design Guidelines for Safety of In-vehicle Information Systems*. Project report PA3721/01. Crowthorne, UK: Transport Research Laboratory.

Thompson Klein, J., 1996. *Crossing Boundaries: Knowledge, Disciplinarities, and Interdisciplinarities*, Charlottesville: University of Virginia Press.

Tuana, N., 2015. Coupled Ethical-Epistemic Analysis in Teaching Ethics. *Communication of ACM*, 58(12), pp. 27–29.

Wallmyr, M., 2015. Understanding the User in Self-Managing Systems. In *Proceedings of the 2015 European Conference on Software Architecture Workshops*.

Wheeler, J.A., 1990. Information, Physics, Quantum: The Search for Links. In W. Zurek, ed. *Complexity, Entropy, and the Physics of Information*, Redwood City: Addison-Wesley.

Wilson, E.O., 1998. Consilience: The Unity of Knowledge. *Issues in Science and Technology*, 15(1), p. 90.

Winner, H., 2013. Challenges of Automotive Systems Engineering for Industry and Academia. In M. Maurer & H. Winner, eds. *Automotive Systems Engineering.* Springer Berlin Heidelberg, pp. 3–15.

Wolfram, S., 2002. *A New Kind of Science*, Wolfram Media.

Wördenweber, B., Wallaschek, J., Boyce, P. & Hoffman, D.D., 2007. *Automotive Lighting and Human Vision*, Berlin Heidelberg: Springer.

Young, K., 2000. What Makes Transdisciplinarity Succeed or Fail? Second Report. In S. Ma & D. J. Rapport, eds. *Transdisciplinarity: Recreating Integrated Knowledge.* Oxford, UK: EOLSS Publishers Ltd.

Younglove-Webb, J. *et al.*, 1999. The Dynamics of Multidisciplinary Research Teams in Academia. *Rev. Higher Educ.*, 22, pp. 425–440.

Zenil, H., (ed.) 2012. *A Computable Universe. Understanding Computation & Exploring Nature As Computation,* Singapore: World Scientific Publishing Company/Imperial College Press.

Zuse, K., 1970. *Calculating Space. Translation of "Rechnender Raum,"* MIT Technical Translation.

Chapter 8

A Unified Science-Philosophy of Information in the Quest for Transdisciplinarity

Wu Kun[*,‡] and Joseph E. Brenner[†,§]

*International Center for the Philosophy of Information
Xi'an Jiaotong University Xi'an 710048, China
†International Center for Transdisicplinary Research, Paris
c/o Chemin du Collège 1, 1865 Les Diablerets, Switzerland
‡WuKun@mail.xjtu. edu.cn
§joe. brenner@bluewin.ch

This book series, intended to describe the role of *Information Science in the Quest for Transdisciplinarity*, makes two major metatheoretical assumptions:

- Transdisciplinarity is a not fully established domain of knowledge whose importance justifies making a quest to augment it.
- Given the convergence in progress between the Science and Philosophy of Information, both can make a contribution to this quest.

For this chapter, we draw on new research by Wu establishing the contours of a potential Unified Science-Philosophy of Information (USPI) and by Brenner on information and the foundations of Transdisciplinarity. Wu states that the underlying interaction of Information Science and Information Philosophy now appears as a convergence toward a potential USPI. We follow the Nicolescu concept of Transdisciplinarity as what lies in, between and beyond disciplines, but feel it requires an amplified, informational ontology which an eventual USPI could provide. We see the combination of these two lines of thought as a trend which could give a new unity and comprehensive form to knowledge. This is exactly the objective stated for Transdisciplinarity itself by Nicolescu in his 1996 *Manifesto*. In the framework of a Unified Science-Philosophy of Information, which would include Transdisciplinarity, philosophy, science and technology may develop in an interactive, more humanistic manner.

Keywords: Convergence; information; logic; knowledge; philosophy; science; transdisciplinarity; unity.

1. INTRODUCTION

1.1 Authors' Background

The reader's comprehension of this chapter will be made easier by a brief introduction of its Authors. The collaboration of the Authors began at the 4th International Conference on the Foundations of Information Science in Beijing in August, 2010. With the publication at that Conference of the first compendium in English of the work of Wu, *A Basic Theory of the Philosophy of Information* (below, BTPI [Wu, 2010]), Wu and Brenner found that it supported and was supported by the non-standard, non-propositional logic of processes proposed by Brenner, Logic in Reality (LIR; [Brenner, 2008]) based on the work of the Franco-Romanian thinker Stéphane Lupasco (1900-1988). The collaboration has resulted to date in joint papers published in the journals *Logic and Logical Philosophy* [Wu and Brenner, 2013 and 2014] and *Foundations of Science* [Wu and Brenner, 2015]. As the Director of the International Center for the Philosophy of Information at his Xi'An Jiaotong University in Xi'An, China, Wu sponsored the 1st and 2nd Conferences on the Philosophy of Information, (in Xi'An, 2013 and in Vienna, 2015) in the organization of which both Authors participated. Further cooperation is in progress in the framework of the International Society for Information Studies (IS4IS), Technical University of Vienna, Austria.

1.2 The Crossroads in Knowledge. Rationale for this Chapter

The Vienna 2015 Summit Conference on Information had the title "The Information Society at the Crossroads" and its specific objective was indicated by its subtitle: "Response and Responsibility of the Information

Sciences". A paper by Brenner [Brenner, 2015] described the *three* crossroads the society can be said to be at, namely socio-political, transdisciplinary and metaphysical, each with positive and negative branches in relation to the common good.

This chapter is based on the hypothesis that it is not only the Information Sciences as such which must be practiced responsibly, but all sciences and systems of thought, logics, philosophies, and ethics; all are users of limited resources. As has been repeated innumerable times, there are two major uses to which knowledge is put: understanding the world to live in harmony with it and other beings and controlling the world for primarily selfish ends. This antagonism in goals is reflected in the form and content of theories and systems for describing, organizing and codifying knowledge: science, philosophy and logic. As the paradigmatic example, standard truth-functional logic, even in its multivalent, fuzzy, deontic and modal forms, is based on absolute separation of premises and conclusions and by implication justifies absolute separations between subject and object, men and women, self and other in the real world.

Such separation is necessary in basic physical and biological science for purposes of analysis, but it becomes far less applicable to the understanding of living beings, characterized by complex interactions, synthetic, cognitive and social. Morally acceptable scientific and philosophical disciplines, therefore, should be ones which have purged themselves of residual binary doctrines that operate against, finally, the implementation of a common economic and social good.

Since the latter part of the 19th Century, it has been the major advances made in science that have driven debates in philosophy. From quantum physics, speculations have come on the ultimate nature of reality; from biology on the differences between living and non-living systems and from computer science on the operation of human consciousness and thinking. After a series of scientific 'revolutions', of which the most recent is the 'information revolution [Floridi, 2014], under the influence of an 'informational turn', we are in the midst of a 'philosophical revolution'. The latter will be discussed in more detail elsewhere [Wu and Brenner, forthcoming].

It would perhaps be too much to say that philosophy is driving debates in science. Scientific experimentation has its own dynamics and historical evolution. However, we argue that scientists and science can benefit by inclusion of the principles and logic of the philosophy of information in the understanding of the sciences, in particular those of man and society. If better understanding of the principles of existence is necessary for people to make choices for the common good (and the philosophy and science of information provide some of that), we feel that there is an ethical rationale for our research. For further discussion of the ethical dimension in information, the reader is referred to the extensive work of Rafael Capurro [Capurro, 2008]. We will focus here on the impact of a Unified Science-Philosophy of Information (USPI) on the complex integral of the various disciplines in interaction that has been designated as Transdisciplinarity.

1.3 Information Science and Philosophy and Transdisciplinarity

From the same origin in 20th Century physics, two different, important systems of thinking about knowledge have emerged in parallel in the last 25 years: 1) Information Science and Philosophy and 2) Transdisciplinarity respectively. The transdisciplinary character of informational processes has been discussed to only a limited extent, but both systems offer methods for insuring that scientific and philosophical approaches are not biased toward anti-social objectives through unrecognized binary assumptions and a disciplinary division of knowledge. Recently, the semiotic theories proposed by Peirce as offering a comprehensive approach to knowledge have been linked to Transdisciplinarity. A critique of Peirce is thus necessary for complete-ness and is included in this chapter.

For the purposes of this paper, we define the following stages in the evolution of the complex process and concept of information that followed the explosive development of the Information and Communications Technologies (ICTs). The ICTs will not be discussed here as such:

- The definition of a field of Information *Science*
- The concept of a Unified *Theory* of Information

- The establishment of a *Philosophy* of Information; the current Informational Turn
- The convergence of the Science and Philosophy of Information toward a *Unified* Science or Science-Philosophy of Information

Research and development in *all* of these areas, especially in the last, is on-going, and it clearly neither possible nor desirable to draw sharp boundaries between them. To establish a basis for a discussion of their relation to Transdisciplinarity, let us make some initial brief characterizations of key features of first three of these domains of knowledge. The last will be the subject of Section 5.

Transdisciplinarity, with or without semiotics, remains a metaphilosophical doctrine whose foundation in and relation to science is not always apparent. The formulation of both Information Science and Transdisciplinarity here is an attempt to bring out the potential synergy between them. The quest for Transdisciplinarity, given the unique characteristics of information processes, the role of Information Science in that quest should be seen as a part of the overall development of knowledge. We propose that a Unified Science-Philosophy of Information (USPI), which would include in particular the concept of the convergence of Information Science and Information Philosophy, together with Transdisciplinarity, provides a robust framework for that development.

1.4 Outline of Chapter

In the next Section 2, we review briefly the major, on-going developments in the field of information, its science and its philosophy. We next (Section 3) introduce the subject of transdisciplinarity (TD) as a developing body of knowledge and method. We describe the major variants of transdisciplinarity and establish one of them as the target of this inquiry. In Section 4 we examine the relation between information, transdisciplinarity and semiotics. We include a critique of semiotics which, as Cybersemiotics, has been proposed as a basis for the unification of knowledge in an informational paradigm. In Section 5 we discuss the current informational turn and the consequent convergence of the Science and the Philosophy of Information toward a USPI. We suggest the link between our preferred form of TD in the context of the additions to the concept and practice of Transdisciplinarity which a USPI could make.

2. THE ARRIVAL OF INFORMATION SCIENCE AND PHILOSOPHY

2.1 Information Science

Since the first proposal of the term 'information science' in 1963 as covering a wide variety of disciplines, the existence and content of *an* Information Science has been the subject of extensive and largely inconclusive debate. The nucleus of Foundations of Information Science initiative, established in 1994 by Marijuan and Conrad and the Conferences to which it led, was another 'quest'. At stated by Marijuan for the 2002 FIS Conference[a], a "quest for a unifying approach capable of introducing a new conceptual order into the contemporary mosaic of disparaging, often reductionist acceptations of the term information." A unifying approach but not a unitary meaning, rather understanding information as an "intellectual adventure of developing a 'vertical' science connecting, so to speak, the different scales of informational processes, similar to that of physics itself, which from a pre-Galilean particularized single term evolved towards a vertical science connecting the previously separated 'celestial', 'sub-lunar' and 'terrestrial' physical occurrences."

However, bringing order into the wide variety of disciplines considered informational remained a problem. The 2002 FIS Conference did result in a degree of convergence among different scientific perspectives, but there was and is still an absence of an integrative vision, particularly in the area of biological information, defined as the multilevel networking of causality instances in living beings. Marijuan

---

[a]P. C. Marijuán, Foundations of Information Science: Selected papers from FIS 2002, *Entropy*, 5, 214-219 (2003).

and his colleagues have made progress toward this goal in a new, non-reductionist way, reported at the 2013 FIS Conference in Xi'An, China [Marijuan, 2013].

2.2 Unified and General Theories of Information

The need for some framework that would encompass and systematize the multitude of disciplines and approaches to information was felt early in both China and the West. In this chapter, we will not attempt to distinguish between unified and general theories of information that have been proposed. Differences in perspective, for example mathematical or philosophical, will be readily apparent to the attentive reader.

The first proposal of a General Theory of Information (GTI) in the West was made by Mark Burgin [Burgin, 2003]. In his recent book [Burgin, 2010], Burgin has presented an extremely complete approach to a GTI based on a thorough analysis of information processes in nature, technology and society. In particular, Burgin gives an extensive treatment of how information is modeled by mathematical structures. The subtitle of Burgin's book, *Fundamentality, Diversity and Unification* clearly indicates the sense of 'general' and the advantages of retaining and using a multi-functional approach to information.

Burgin's GTI treats information from a pragmatic, dynamic perspective, involving changes of structure or behavior of the receiver and sender as well. Information is also characterized by a system of ontological principles such as his General Transformation Principle. This describes the essence of *information* in a broad sense as the potential (capacity) of material and abstract things to cause changes in (transform) other things. Burgin also captures the qualitative character of information in the statement that information involves a transformation of one communication of an information association into another communication of the same association" using some realistic information measure. It is interesting to compare this notion of the essence of information with the approach Wu Kun made independently in China (see below, Section 2.3.2).

The basic rationale for moving from an information science or information sciences to a Unified Theory of Information (UTI), and the problems associated with this move, have been explicitly addressed by Wolfgang Hofkirchner, first in a 2009 paper [Hofkirchner, 2009]. Continuing this movement, from a basis which also includes philosophy and sociology, Wolfgang Hofkirchner has further developed an integrated transdisciplinary approach towards a UTI. His latest book, entitled *Emergent Information. A Unified Theory of Information Framework* [Hofkirchner, 2013] begins with an extensive synthesis of essential prior work. The informational-scientific framework which Hofkirchner has developed for the discussion of the operation of information and information processes in the society represents a significant advance over both simplistic semiotic and strictly computational approaches. An important entry point to comprehension of Hofkirchner's thesis is his insistence, as in the work of Capurro, on a concept of information-as-process. As Hofkirchner writes, a UTI should be *logical* as well as historical, explaining not only the historical appearance (emergence) of new information processes and structures but how these processes and structures are logically linked [Hofkirchner, 2013a]. Brenner has added separately [Brenner, 2010] the additional concept of *how* an identity-diversity is structured dynamically in his Logic in Reality as a "structuring" or "structuration", terms used by both Lupasco and Giddens (in relation to society) to emphasize its process aspects.

This rationale, as such, is in the domain of philosophy or metaphilosophy and the goal of a UTI carries a number of hidden implications. Hofkirchner has avoided the reduction of a UTI to a monolithic identity through his concept of the union of identity-diversity necessary to characterize information.

Recent developments relevant to the problematic of unity have been well summarized by Jordi Cat in his article on the Unity of Science in the *Stanford Encyclopedia of Philosophy* [Cat, 2014]. These can be read as avoiding any principle of 'unity for the sake of unity". Cat notes several positive, anti-reductionist trends in the philosophy of science, for example in moving from dependence on concepts primarily from physics. One is struck in fact by the *diversity* of sense which can be given to the definition of unity! These range from the possible single nature of the underlying 'stuff' of the universe, to the unification of the disciplines within science and with regard to these whether on is dealing with concepts or terms or the higher-level entity of theory and whether the relations are ones of reduction, explanation or logical inference. Cat suggests that the concept of unity can have value at the practical level in science, to justify approaches and goals, and in philosophy to help choose what philosophical questions to pursue and what target areas to explore. The Unity of Science could suggest what science is to be referenced by philosophy as authoritative. He touches upon our point in the first paragraph by suggesting that "unities and unifications help us meet cognitive and practical demands upon our life ..., contribute to our self-image and be seen as a source of aesthetic value, providing a grip on our intellectual imagination."

Our approach extends this view: the value of the Unity of Science, self-referentially, is itself a unity of a sort that neglects, intentionally or not, the value of diversity. We believe it is necessary to do so explicitly. Informational processes, in our theory and logic, are composites of unities and diversities.

2.3 Philosophy of Information. Preliminary Remarks

The development of the field of the Philosophy of Information in the last 20-30 years, led by Wu Kun in China and Luciano Floridi in the West has provided a new framework for the study of the properties and behavior of information, its conceptual nature, basic principles and relevant sciences, including computer science and information technology.

This chapter is based on an ontology and epistemology of information and information processes proposed over a period of 30 years by Wu Kun [Wu, 2010]. The first part of the theory proposes the fundamental origin of information in a new segmentation of reality (the existential field) and defines the ontological essence, classification and quality of information analyzed in terms of different grades or levels. The second part of Wu's theory is an informational epistemology that sees the origin of the properties of information in the relationships existing due to the differences between things. This concept was developed by Wu [Wu, 1989] independently of earlier work of Donald

MacKay and Gregory Bateson [Leydesdorff, 2014]. It can be usefully compared with the latter's well-known dictum that information is "a difference that makes a difference". It includes a noegenesis of the doctrine of informational intermediaries, that is, informational structures or linkages that mediate between the cognitive subject and the informational structure and properties of the cognitive object.

Further progress in an informational picture of cognition also requires understanding of the dynamic logic of information processes, in particular their movement between actuality and virtuality or potentiality. A non-standard logic that can accept the essential dynamic contradictions in the nature of information has been developed by Brenner [Brenner, 2008)] based on the philosophical logic of Stéphane Lupasco [Lupasco, 1987]. We summarize here and in Section 5 the major philosophical conceptions in Wu's theory. Details in English are provided in an article in *Information* [Wu, 2012]. Major topics are:

2.3.1 *The Segmentation of the Existential Field*

In the philosophy of information proposed by Wu, all existence (the world, nature) can be put into three categories of objective reality, objective unreality and subjective unreality. The scope of objective existence is thus broader than objective reality. The material category does not include the entire mental "world". There is a field of "objective unreality" between the material and mental to which traditional science and philosophy have not paid adequate attention, even in a physicalist interpretation (Smith, 2004).

The existential field can be divided into objective and subjective, but also it can be divided into real and unreal. Because only objective reality is real, the categories of the real and the material both possess the features of and are fully consistent with connotation and extension. The reflection in consciousness of an existential object outside consciousness is a replication and knowledge of this object in consciousness. Therefore, in the final analysis, subjective existence is an indirectly existing reflection of direct existence. Direct existence is a domain that we place in the usual material category, but indirect existence can be related to the concept of "information" in modern science.

2.3.2 *The Essence of Information*

In the discussion of the issue of the essence of information, it is, accordingly, impossible to proceed either by simple analogy with pragmatic scientific explanations, or by using traditional philosophical categories. Wu argues rather that the issue of the essence of information requires a two-fold philosophical critique: on one side is the critique of the philosophy of science, involving the elimination of the limitations of scientific interpretations of information that result in narrow views, enabling philosophy to grasp information in a way that goes beyond the classical scientific approach. On the other side, his critique is of philosophy itself. The intention of this latter critique is to overcome the limitations of the framework of traditional philosophy and its theoretical interpretation of the essence of information, thereby making a philosophical grasp of information into a double critique that goes beyond the approach of old systems of philosophy and traditional forms of analysis, including but not limited to phenomenology.

According to Wu, in the mode in which it exists, and despite its constitution by energy, information is not a direct material existential form; information develops its own existence in the performance, external expression of movement, appearances and the meaning of its characteristics. Information is the form of the indirect existence of the (ontological) features of things.

Among Western philosophers of science, John Collier has put together a very complete set of defining concepts around the phenomenon of information as a causal process [Collier, 2012]. He approaches the properties of information from the formal-mathematical side and his critique of Shannon, as well as of some current computational views of information rejoins ours.

2.4 The Philosophy of Information as a Metaphilosophy. Informational Thinking

As previously outlined, [Wu, 2010] Wu's informational philosophy points toward a scientific theory of information processes as part of a global change in science and philosophy. In other terms, by seeing the relations between the changes in values that take place in human informational activities and the forms of society, a more profound understanding of information is possible that could be a contribution to overall progress and sustainable development of human civilization. This metaphilosophical view of information[b] "is not directed toward the codification of *a* Metaphilosophy of Information as yet another static discipline or body of knowledge". It rather proposes an attitude toward an adequate Philosophy of Information as encompassing a critical component of all disciplines, beyond the scientific content specific to them, in a way similar to Transdisciplinarity. In Wu's approach, metaphilosophy is not something 'more abstract' than philosophy; it must be able to deal with the essential aspects of all disciplines and their theories. As it exemplifies the suggested dynamics of Logic in Reality, it resembles real physical processes, and provides insight into the real interactions in the real world that are our ultimate concern.

The Metaphilosophy of Information requires attention to the informational aspects of complex processes as a methodological necessity, in a process that Wu called Informational Thinking. Informational Thinking *(IT)*, as conceived of by Wu, refers to a way of grasping and describing the essential characteristics and attributes of things by reference to the structure and dynamics of the information involved in their evolution, from their historical origins to future possibilities and probabilities. The phenomenology of Wu, unlike that of Husserl, does not have to be "naturalized" [Wu, 2010a], that is, brought into the domain of natural science. It is already there.[c] Wu discloses directly the mechanisms of the processes involved in an individual's understanding at the level of the integrated object and subject, with internal and external interactions providing the necessary multi-level objective and subjective mediation. We see here echoes of the deeper

---

[b]J. E. Brenner, Wu Kun and the Metaphilosophy of Information, *International Journal* "Information Theories and Applications", 18(2), pp. 103-128, 2011.

[c]J. Petitot *et al.* (eds.). *Naturalizing Phenomenology. Issues in Contemporary Phenomenology and Cognitive Science.* Stanford University Press, Stanford, 1999.

concepts of process and reality of Whitehead: "The first Category of Explanation is that the actual world is a process, and that the process is the becoming of actual entities, or actual occasions, the first Category of Existence. Two descriptions are required for an actual entity, one which is analytical of its potentiality for 'objectification' in the becoming of other actual entities and another which is analytical of the process which constitutes its own becoming."

We will look further later at the principles, philosophical, logical and scientific underlying our concepts of Information Science and Philosophy. Let us now address the object of our quest — Transdisciplinarity — in the next section.

3. TRANSDISCIPLINARITY: SUBJECT OR OBJECT?

3.1 The Hermeneutic Sequence

The explosion of knowledge has stimulated research into non-reductionist, non-classificatory schemes for organizing scientific and philosophical disciplines that can make evident some form of functional interrelationships. The emergence of the field of Transdisciplinarity is one response to this need. Another has been the concepts of a unified theory and/or science of information, based on the consideration that information is ubiquitous in nature and knowledge. In this chapter, we will explore to what extent these conceptions lead to workable syntheses that provide additional tools for understanding.

To address the specific objective of this Series — the Quest for Transdisciplinarity through Information Science — we must first point out that the practice of Transdisciplinarity itself is a 'quest', a quest for both new knowledge and the application of that knowledge for the common good. Transdisciplinarity, especially in the acceptation of Basarab Nicolescu [Nicolescu, 2002], includes a logic, an epistemology and a methodology which are used, to a greater or lesser extent, in applications of *it*. It is thus not appropriate to discuss here the growing number applications of Transdisciplinarity and Transdisciplinary approaches to science and society *per se*. Similarly, we cannot discuss the role of Information Science in them since, as in any human activity today, it is ubiquitous and massive.

The questions we address here are therefore in the following more limited domains:

- Where do the content and characteristics of Information Science and of a potential Unified Science of Information suggest new functional content for Transdisciplinarity that could enhance its effectiveness?
- Where have existing applications of Transdisciplinary methods failed or been limited by either 1) the absence of such content or 2) inclusion of doctrines that operate against the desired goals which an informational approach might correct?

Our next task is therefore to summarize the general understanding of the terms Transdisciplinarity and Transdisciplinary on the on hand and Science, Information Science and Unified Information Science on the other.

3.2 The Forms of Transdisciplinarity

The title of this Book Series, *Information Science and the Quest for Transdisciplinarity (TD)*, implies that TD is a not fully established domain of knowledge whose importance justifies making a quest to augment it. In fact, as we will see, two major theories of TD already exist which we will label TD1 and TD2. The objective of any 'quest' for TD can only be either 1) to establish which might be preferred and why; or 2) what is missing in either or both of them to which new knowledge, in particular coming from the domain of information, might make a contribution to improving.

The TD1 form will not be discussed further here. The discussions and applications taking place in and around it constitute, in fact, 90% of the published information available under the term 'transdisciplinarity'. We note only that TD1 is both a property of knowledge and a product of study (transdisciplinary knowledge production). Organizational networks devoted to transdisciplinary research and publication such as *td-net* in Switzerland, The*ATLAS*[d] and *INIT*[e] provide centralized sources of information and opportunities for exchange of ideas about TD, correlating scientific capabilities with human individual and social needs.

We will also not discuss the interface between interdisciplinarity, especially as obtaining between pairs of disciplines, and TD which is in any case, in our view, ill-defined for TD1. (For a recent discussion of interdisciplinary scholarship see the *Undisciplining Knowledge* of Harvey Graff [Graff, 2015].)

3.3 Transdisciplinarity in the Nicolescu Acceptation

The general approach of TD2, which has led to some very important applications in the social and educational fields, is based on the work of Basarab Nicolescu. Its key concept is that Transdisciplinarity is something 'more' that lies across, between and beyond disciplines. Since the publication in 2002 by Nicolescu of his *Manifesto of Transdisciplinarity* [Nicolescu, 2002] and in 2008 of his compendium *Transdisciplinarity — Theory and Practice* [Nicolescu, 2008], applications of transdisciplinarity in both areas have greatly increased. In the acceptation of Basarab Nicolescu [Nicolescu, 2011], the three 'pillars' of transdisciplinarity are complexity, levels of reality and the logic of the included middle or third. This logic is based on the non-truth-functional, non-linguistic extension of logic to real process systems originally proposed by Lupasco [Lupasco, 1987] and up-dated by Brenner and made available to English-language readers as Logic in Reality (LIR) [Brenner, 2008].

Perhaps a simple way of characterizing Transdisciplinary and Informational Thinking is that they require one, additional iteration which amounts to 'thinking about thinking'. Other expressions of the same thing are 'having a certain distance' from a problem, 'depth', and

---

[d]The Academy of Transdisciplinary Learning and Advanced Studies, Texas Tech University, Lubbock, TX.

[e]International Network for Interdisciplinarity and Transdisciplinarity, Swiss Academy of Arts and Sciences, Berne

others. All involve the further input of energy, for example, to manage two perspectives, say, Western and Chinese, not simultaneously, but alternately. Lupasco saw the logic of energy in operation in all such complex phenomena including theories and scientific judgments. These are always revisable and incomplete, since they never can be absolutely definitively separated from the opposing, contradictory judgment (or experience, or law) on which its existence depends. We repeat again that reference to the law of gravity or other simple physical laws (Stokes law), which do not involve opposites as such, does not constitute a counterargument. These laws are based on aspects of the universe and the consequent properties of matter that lie outside the domain of thermodynamic change to which everything human belongs. Thinking about thinking is a paradigm example of a process to which the Logic in Reality does apply. As a corollary, it is not necessary to worry about an infinite regress (thinking about thinking about thinking) since in Reality the process stops as no new information, in both sense, is added or emerges.

The difficulty of capturing the complex concept of transdisciplinarity in a single definition is well-recognized. Nicolescu summarized in [Nicolescu, 2011] the thinking behind three major forms of transdisciplinarity: theoretical transdisciplinarity, phenomenological transdisciplinarity, and experimental transdisciplinarity. He gives examples of each which will not be repeated here. The three forms of transdisciplinarity are by no means totally separated or independent but overlap and inform one another.

In the most general way, one may say that the practice of Transdisciplinarity consists in application of the theory and methodology of transdisciplinarity to 1) the understanding of the relations between specific disciplines; 2) the solving of specific practical problems and 3) the understanding of the relation of transdisciplinarity to structured human thought, philosophy, logic and epistemology. In this chapter, we will focus on the third area, in particular regarding the emerging science and philosophy of information as conceptual structures directed at similar objectives.

We feel the third form of Transdisciplinarity is best thought of in terms of levels, one referring to specific disciplines and what lies beyond them and a higher level referring to the 'meta-science-philosophy' resulting from the internal integration of concepts from science and philosophy (see Section 5.4 Convergence). We may thus already discern a relation between our theory and the metaphysics of Transdisciplinarity and changes in philosophy analyzed recently by Eric Weislogel [Weislogel, 2014]. In Weislogel's radically new vision philosophy becomes *praxis*: we know by changing and change by knowing. As in our approach, one goes from discourse, 'disciplined' philosophy/ metaphysics but without the sciences to an 'undisciplined' philosophy/ metaphysics that can serve as a transdisciplinary metascience, wisdom in the best sense of the word. Weislogel concludes that metaphysics pursues the 'more' that Transdisciplinarity demands and hence is allied with it. We claim the same 'alliance' for the metaphilosophy of information.

3.4 Logic in Reality; Logic of Transdisciplinarity

In previous work, both Nicolescu and Brenner have discussed the Logic of Transdisciplinarity, one of its 'pillars'. They have showed its origin in the logic of the included third of Stéphane Lupasco. This logic has now been presented in relation to information in several recent, readily available documents [Brenner, 2011] and will not be reviewed here. We simply emphasize the point here, critical for the discussion of information and the future of transdisciplinarity, that the approaches of Nicolescu and Brenner are similar in that they include the emergence of new states through the principle of dynamic opposition, the dialectic and interactive relation between the dual elements of all real processes. The difference is that Nicolescu looks 'upward' toward the transcendental aspects of existence, using the Lupasco logic to cover the relations between what he states as ontological but we consider primarily epistemological Subjects and Objects, designated as Transdisciplinary, at higher levels of cognitive reality. LIR focuses on the explication of the evolution of complex real systems, their ontological subjects and objects in a more standard physical but non-reductionist sense, and the information processes directly associated with them. This point, involving different views of 'ontology' is critical for the discussion of Transdisciplinarity in relation to Information Science and will be addressed again in Section 4 below on semiotics. (The latter view of Transdisciplinarity and its relation to a logic is similar to the discussion by Roderick Lawrence in his paper "Transgression of Disciplinary Frontiers" [Lawrence, 2008].)

We further propose that LIR and its associated ontology, as a metatheoretical scheme that can deal with scientific theories and their data, and with inter-theoretical relations, where those relationships involve some kind of real, structural or structuring interactions. Theories are today more generally viewed as classes of models, rather than classes of statements or propositions (the 'non-statement' view), and the model-theoretical or structuralist standpoint is more easily accommodated by the dynamic structuralist aspects of LIR, those that are derived from the dynamic structure of energy.

Like any good empirical theory that makes an appropriate representation of a field of experience, by this definition, LIR offers a structural model of at least part of reality. Its Principle of Dynamic Opposition holds between some pairs of theories where the degree of interaction is adequate. This is the case for Information Science, in its most recent form as a Unified Science-Philosophy of Information (USPI) and Transdisciplinarity, and LIR thus relates directly to *their* relation.

3.5 Further Philosophical Issues

3.5.1 *Paradigm Change*

The questions of whether change, progress or 'revolution' in science exist and if so in what they consist are among the most difficult in philosophy and the philosophy of science. The observations of change in stances, paradigms or conceptual frameworks and their relation to new empirical information may be more related to styles of thought that to any absolute provable 'truths' or simplistic taxonomic classifications. One of us (Wu) can claim the authority for this report which reflects his experience and observations of the 'scene' in China for over thirty years. The other logical 'pillar' of this study can be seen in operation in the 'experimental' domain of the intertheoretic relation. Accordingly, the change to a new theory can preserve structural properties allowing a certain ontological continuity accompanying a conceptual revolution[f]. This ontological *synthesis* is a dialectical picture of growth and progress in science that reconciles essential continuity with discontinuous appearance in the history of science, a process that, again, is a logical one in LIR.

3.5.2 *Consistency and Continuity*

We may ask, for example "is science fully consistent?" If it is, it does not correspond to reality. If it is not, it is both consistent and inconsistent. Consistent simple processes can be handled by standard truth-functional, bi-valent, or multivalent and modal logics. Inconsistent complex processes require a non-propositional dynamic logic of change whose elements are non-standard probabilities. Paraconsistent logics are still propositional and are only partly applicable [Brenner, 2008]. Accordingly, if a philosophical or scientific theory includes a requirement of absolute consistency, we may question not the validity of the theory but its ability to describe reality. There is thus a close relation between consistency and continuity.

3.5.3 *Transdisciplinary Attitude (TA) and Method (TM)*

In our 'quest' for Transdisciplinarity (TD), we want to exclude references to work involving any actual or implied reification of the term. Transdisciplinarity should be above all a process, an open system of relations and linkages between disciplines in relation to and as applied to human needs and situations, not to be tied down by any immutable excluding definition. We agree completely with Nicolescu in his reference [Nicolescu, 2002] to a transdisciplinary *attitude* (TA), one that combines the characteristics of rigor in thinking, openness to new ideas and the unknown and tolerance of opposing or countervailing views.

Nicolescu takes this a step further by ascribing a functional role to the TA at the base of all disciplines, that is, a part of the attitude

---

[f] T. Y. Cao, *Conceptual Developments of 20th Century Field Theories*, Cambridge University Press, Cambridge, UK, 1997.

among their practitioners that gives the disciplines their meaning and structure. We quote here from Article 4 of the Charter of Transdisciplinarity promulgated at the 1st World Congress of Transdisciplinarity held in Arrabida, Spain in 1994: "The keystone of Transdisciplinarity is the semantic and practical unification of the meanings that traverse and lie beyond different disciplines. It presupposes an open-minded rationality by re-examining the concepts of definition and objectivity. An excess of formalism, rigidity of definitions and a claim to total objectivity (WK/JEB: as it is usually understood), entailing the exclusion of the subject, can only have a life-negating effect."

Note that the redefinition of objectivity is a core concept in the approach of Wu [Wu, 2012] to the nature and function of information as a component of the existential field. As regards a Transdisciplinary Method (TM), we note the general statements by Nicolescu that are consistent with a Transdisciplinary Attitude, what Nicolescu calls his 'Methodology of Transdisciplinary Research. For Nicolescu, Transdisciplinary Methodology involves the taking into account, "to a greater or lesser extent", of the three pillars of Transdisciplinarity noted above. Further, this TM is different from the methodology of modern science and the classical science of being, reflecting a co-evolution of the human being and the world.

At this point, we note two possible interpretations of Transdisciplinary Research: research *in* or *with* Transdisciplinarity. Both are acceptable, but we prefer to focus on the use of the TM outside Transdisciplinarity. For this, we therefore emphasize here a neglected concept of Lupasco [Lupasco, 1979], namely, *dialectomethodology* (*dialectométhodologie*), which brings the above back into a relation to science. Lupasco saw the origin of dialectics itself in the contradictorial properties of systems evolving according to the logic of the included middle, and coined the corresponding terms of Dialectogenesis and Dialectology. Studying these implies what Lupasco described as a Dialectomethodology of knowledge: "... in the presence of every element or event, of every system and every structure, as of every system of systems and structure of structures, one must extract their internal dialectics and seek the contradictory antagonistic dialectics of every antagonistic and contradictory element or event, of every system and every structure, of every system of systems and structure of structures. It is this method of cognitive investigation of phenomena, whatever they may be, that I call the *Dialectomethodology* of knowledge."[g]

Let us now make a first discussion of Transdisciplinarity and information together in order to relate Information Science to the quest for Transdisciplinarity in Section 5 below.

4. TRANSDISCIPLINARITY AND INFORMATION

The link between Transdisciplinarity in the acceptation of Nicolescu and information was established in two papers by Brenner in the on-line *Transdisciplinary Journal of Engineering & Science*. Both refer to the basic theories of Wu Kun [Brenner, 2011a and 2015a]. Reference to the Nicolescu position has also been made by Brier in his objective statement[h] for the Transdisciplinarity Track at the Vienna 2015 Information Summit and in detail in [Brier, 2013], and in the concept of Transdisciplinarity as presented also by Nicolescu at that Summit and elsewhere. A discussion of information in relation to TD has also been made by Marilena Lunca in an article entitled "Transdisciplinary Potentials of Information" in the Nicolescu compendium, *Transdisciplinarity; Theory and Practice* [Lunca, 2008].

Another statement of a relation between information and Transdisciplinarity was made by Hofkirchner and his colleagues in 2007 [Hofkirchner, 2007]: the study of the complex field of the Information and Communications Technologies (ICTs) is best regarded as a trans-disciplinary entity or transdiscipline. One can distinguish between the science of information and information technology, and a science of an information society. This is an essential aspect of the capacity of an Information Science to play a role in the ethical development of the ITCs toward a Globally Sustainable Information Society.

Hofkirchner's approach [Hofkirchner, 2009] to a Unified Theory of Information (UTI) is to eliminate the absolute and in our view

[g]S. Lupasco, *L'univers psychique,* Denoel-Gonthier, 1979.
[h]"How to get to a truly transdisciplinary information science"

artificial separation between critical concepts of information in favor of a dialectical relationship similar to the ancient intuition of 'unity-in-diversity'. Specifically, his "UTI seeks a concrete-universal concept of information rather than an abstract one". Hofkirchner considers information as a 'superconcept', which includes a group of overlapping concepts such as message, signal, *etc.* as they apply to communication, cognition and cooperation between human and non-human systems. Hofkirchner asks how matter and idea, mind, information, *etc.* can be grasped as complements and with them information as a thing (a structure, a flow) or as a human construction. Hofkirchner gives a dialectical answer to the implied division between subject and object, eliminating the need for mind and with it information to be of a different 'materiality' than 'non-emergent' states of matter. In our view, these characteristics of a superconcept, beyond any specific discipline, as well as its application to human problems, make it *ipso facto* transdisciplinary. More recently, in his *Emergent Information*, whose subtitle is a *Unified Theory of Information Framework* [Hofkirchner, 2013], Hofkirchner states that the interdependence of the subdomains of Information Science requires a transdisciplinary method that goes beyond the border of the individual disciplines. This formulation is close to that of Transdisciplinarity by Nicolescu.

4.1 What is missing in the Quest for Transdisciplinarity?

Despite this promising start, as was seen by the Editors of this Book Series, Transdisciplinarity, as a doctrine, has not, in any case not yet, achieved a definitive form and is still undergoing transformation. As suggested above, one way in which this is occurring is *via* the increased actual application of the concept by researchers (cf. the *Handbook of Transdisciplinary Research* [Hirsch, 2008]). Another is that of followers of TD2 who are exploring TD in relation to ethics and the humanities. However, there is frequently no reference to Transdisciplinarity as such. 'Transdisciplinary' often becomes a place-holder for what is little more than the use of a multiplicity of disciplines. There are in fact two critiques of current conceptions of information and transdisciplinarity that in our view need to be discussed: one refers to the Nicolescu view of

Transdisciplinarity (TD2) outlined above and the other to the semiotic approach of Sören Brier and his associates.

4.2 Ontology or Epistemology

We propose that although Transdisciplinarity should and does have many facets, any version of it should not substitute ontology and science with epistemology at its foundations. We recall that the Nicolescu concept of Transdisciplinarity includes the Logic of the Included Third of Lupasco as one of its pillars, and that this logic is explicitly grounded in the structure and dynamics of the universe.

Thus the statement by Nicolescu himself [2002] that "in the depths of every discipline is found the abyss that links the transdisciplinary Subject and Object" can be interpreted only within the framework of the *epistemic* picture which Nicolescu paints of the structure of knowledge. In contrast, the original Lupasco conception of the dynamic interaction between the Knower, Knowing and the Known as processes can be related, through their necessary physical properties, to the ontological view of information defended in this chapter. Our position is that the quest for Transdisciplinarity cannot be said to have ended. There is something still missing in it that prevents it from becoming more useful as a doctrine for knowledge That 'something' is a proper ontology which an eventual Unified Science of Information can provide.

We thus agree with Nicolescu's conception of "a *new objectivity* arising from contemporary science, an objectivity that is no longer linked only to an object but to a complex subject/object interaction. In this way, one would be able to speak about the subjective objectivity of science and the objective subjectivity of tradition. Our potential, our opportunity, is that we can make the two poles of a contradiction coexist in ourselves simultaneously." This corresponds to the formula of Wu of the philosophization of science and the scientification of philosophy. However, we can also take this statement as an example of one that can be amplified by applying the Lupascian methodology to the term simultaneous. In the LIR picture of space-time, simultaneity and succession are *also* dialectically, contradictorially connected, and this amplification can be visualized as information-as-process.

From this Transdisciplinary Methodology, however, Nicolescu [2011] takes a different path than we toward a Transdisciplinary Hermeneutics. His 'approach to Reality' defines three types of meaning: 1) horizontal, with interconnections at a single level of Reality, essentially, Multidisciplinarity; 2) vertical, interconnections involving several levels of Reality, as in poetry, art and quantum physics; 3) meaning of meaning, interconnections involving all of Reality, including the Transdisciplinary Subject, Object and Hidden Third. The search for the latter is stated to be the ultimate *object* of transdisciplinary research. While we agree that the meaning of meaning is at a higher cognitive and ontological level, we are concerned in this chapter only with its immanent aspects, without any implied epistemic-ontological cut implied by the above hermeneutics. The discussion that follows will be based on this position.

A key concept in the Nicolescu concept of TD is that no level of reality is privileged over the others as in a simplistic hierarchy. But for us, the essential aspect based on the Lupasco logic is that there is always a real, physical dialectics in which 'internal' and 'external', for complex, especially living systems cannot be separated absolutely. This has been shown by Ulanowicz among others [Ulanowicz, 2009]. Thus, Nicolescu's transdisciplinarity does include the Lupasco logic, but only as a cognitive process system whose properties and development must follow the Principle of Dynamic Opposition.

4.3 Semiotics, Cybersemiotics and Transdisciplinarity

No serious discussion of Transdisciplinarity in relation to information can be made today without reference to the recent extensive work by Sören Brier on information and semiotics [Brier, 2014]. From a theoretical standpoint, the fundamental properties of information might be expected to be closely related to those of signs. Semiotics, the study of signs as categorizing linguistic entities and processes in the representation of meaning, has a position intermediate between the philosophy and science of information. It therefore has a role to play as a system of classification which complements the knowledge of the universe that we gain from scientific facts about it. Semiotics is particularly valuable as a doctrine in the deconstruction of some naïve, positivist conceptions of science. However, as we will see, opposite our theory which has largely eliminated these conceptions by other means, the semiotic approach begins to look anti-scientific, reducing the value of its legitimate insights.

The subtitle of Brier's major book [Brier, 2008], *Cybersemiotics* is *Why information is not enough.* Why not? One answer is that information, while foundational, may only be a methodological pointer toward the presence in the world of complex dynamic cognitive phenomena, especially, knowledge (or knowing), human intelligence and semiotics, signs working to produce meaning in human and other living systems.

Brier argues for a transdisciplinary framework where signs, meaning and interpretation are the foundational concepts within which informational concepts have to function, and that C. S. Peirce's doctrine of semiosis is the basis for such a new paradigmatic transdisciplinary framework. Cybersemiotics, further, proposes a new transdisciplinary framework integrating Peirce' triadic semiotics with a cybernetic view of information on the basis of an ontology of emptiness. The proposed framework offers an integrative multi- and transdisciplinary approach, which uses *meaning* as the overarching principle for grasping the complex area of cybernetic information science for nature and machines *AND* the semiotics of the cognition, communication, and culture of all living systems. "My theory and philosophy of science is that in a total naturalism the four basic approaches to understanding provided by the exact natural sciences, the life sciences, the phenomenological-hermeneutic humanities and the discursive view of sociology: cognition, communication, meaning and consciousness are all equally fundamental but need to be united in a transdisciplinary theory of information, semiotics, embodied consciousness and intersubjective communication. Transdisciplinarity demands the development of such a new and broader framework, which will therefore offend all those researchers who prefer to stay within the received view of their own knowledge or paradigm. To choose Peirce means to accept most of his triadic pragmaticist and realist view of science and his semiotic theory of cognition and communication."

Standard semiotic theory is particularly concerned with explicating higher-order concepts such as meaning, sign use, representation, language, intersubjectivity, *etc.*, along with their interrelations. The standard Peircean definition of semiosis is that of a process of meaning making, of construing a material entity or phenomenon as a sign. In this acceptation, Semiotics is thus a theory of representation — it is things standing for other things, clearly to be distinguished from physical systems, which are termed "Dynamical Objects". Peircean semiotics thus also provides an overview of knowledge from physical sciences to the complexities of human cognition and language.

The original rationale for the Peircean extension of semiotics, developed totally independently from the comprehensive system of Lupasco, was to provide an alternative to the only available reductionist paradigms of 19th Century physics, while maintaining faith in their mathematics. Cybersemiotics integrates third person knowledge from the exact sciences and the life sciences with first person knowledge described as the qualities of feeling in humanities and second person intersubjective knowledge of the communicative interactions, partly linguistic, on which the social and cultural aspects of reality are based.

4.4 Ontology or Epistemology, Again

The semiotic view presented by Brier is grounded explicitly in Peirce's view that the underlying principle of the universe is one of randomness and chance, sometime referred to a 'pure spontaneity'. Human reasoning then 'discovers' the world by taking this picture, plus a requirement for mathematical truth and codifying it in terms of an epistemological partitioning of existence into three categories or classifications indicated above. Signs are stated to be different from energy and not equivalent to information as such, but nevertheless to carry information and be causally effective, *e.g.*, by causing cognitive reactions. Brier's somewhat illogical argument is that since science *had* not found an explanation of the origin of consciousness, self-awareness and emotion, science *cannot* do so. Only a phenomenology with *its* origin in human experience and behavior can. Our position is simply that this disjunction with science, which implies a non-physical origin for the causal effectiveness of signs, is neither necessary nor desirable.

Our critique of the above doctrine is not that semiotics exists as a domain that refers to certain epistemic aspects of knowledge, but that in the Brier acceptation it is arbitrarily grounded and hence lacks explanatory power for, in particular, utility in the ethical domain. A critique can be made of each of Peirce's choices despite our agreement with his obvious starting point of the inability of 'science' of he gave the most limited possible conception to explain the emergence of meaning.

In a Section in Brier, 2013 entitled "The Ontological Basis of Cybersemiotics", Brier writes that a Peircean biosemiotics may contribute to a new transdisciplinary framework for the understanding of knowledge, consciousness, meaning and communication. But to do this, new elements have to be integrated to unite the functionalistic approaches to information and communication coming from cybernetics and computer science with the semantic pragmatic approaches coming from the linguistic turn and semiotics. Concepts of closure, self-organization, and differentiation of biological, psychological, and social systems developed in second-order cybernetics and autopoiesis theory need to be integrated into theories of embodiment and Peircean biosemiotics. Hofkirchner explicitly supports the views of Brier in another recent paper regarding the central role of Peirce's ontology [Hofkirchner, 2014]. We basically agree with the humanistic objectives behind the above approaches. However, we feel that this approach can be amplified and corrected by looking more closely at the dynamic properties of information itself.

Some further criticisms of Peircean Semiotics have been made in the recent concept of Cognitive Semiotics developed by Jordan Zlatev and others [Zlatev, 2012]. Semiotic theory is particularly concerned with explicating higher-order concepts such as *meaning, sign use, representation, language, intersubjectivity*, etc., along with their interrelations. Bringing in empirical research as in Cognitive Semiotics can both contribute to their explication and, at the same time, produce new insights. Cognitive Semiotics is thus less directly dependent on any particular semiotic theory such as that of Peirce, and suggests that other kinds of Semiotics may also offer useful perspectives.

Brier states [2013] that "only Peirce's phenomenologically and pure mathematically based categories in combination with his tychism, synechism, agapism and pragmaticism combined into a semiotics seem to be the best philosophy so far" to arrive at a "triadic pragmaticist and realist view of science and his semiotic theory of cognition and communication". "There seems to be no logical way from an objective concept of information to a triadic pragmaticist semiotics, which has the ethics, aesthetics and phenomenological philosophical basis that makes it compatible with human conscious and linguistic thinking processes." If we do not want to take this path to a 'triadic pragmaticist semiotics', we are at liberty to find other ways to go from an objective concept of information to human conscious and linguistic thinking processes, including ethics and esthetics.

Finally, the relevance of transdisciplinarity in the resulting largely epistemic sense, with reference to the foundations of Peircean semiotics depends on whether one considers Peirce's work as sufficiently encompassing of science. As Brenner has discussed elsewhere, there is no consensus on this issue. In addition to the problems of its foundations, the way the categories of Peircean semiotics (Firstness, Secondness and Thirdness) are usually presented as being all-encompassing but having their origin in human thought poses a problem of self-reference. Either the categories include themselves, and reasoning based on them is tautological, or they do not and then they are not complete. This is in fact a weakness of any theory based only on epistemic considerations and allows its conclusions to be questioned.

In the approach of Logic in Reality, any incompleteness of Peircean theory, *pace* its proponents, would not be a weakness but a self-evident aspect of any theory, realist or anti-realist, with an ontological purport. Unfortunately, this argument tends to be rejected by Peirceans, since it would open other aspects of their position to scientific and philosophical critique. We have found no 'non-Peircean' concept of semiosis, other than Zlatev's mentioned above, that has been discussed in connection with information.

To conclude this Section, we would like to emphasize our interest in the on-going debate and discussion of different ontological and epistemological approaches to the relation between semiotics and information. We present our most recent views as our contribution to this discussion. Thus, we can only regret the truncated version of Wu's in-depth approach to information given in a very recent paper by Liqian Zhou and Brier [Zhou and Brier, 2015] who write: "Actually, we think that Wu's philosophy of information is not a philosophy about information in the traditional meaning. He just borrows the term information to refer to the area he found in the field of existence." The authors embrace Peircean semiotics rather than Wu's metaphysics (better, metaphilosophy) because they claim it lacks a basis for meaning and significance without which "we cannot distinguish information from other physical processes".

We can only refer the authors to the first comprehensive document on Wu's work published in English, namely his Basic Theory of the Philosophy of Information, made available at the 4th International Conference on the Philosophy of Information held in Beijing in 2010 [Wu, 2010]. In this compendium of Wu's prior publications in Chinese, to which Zhou refers, the subject of meaning is discussed in some fifteen passages, related to self-organization and feedback in phenomena, and otherwise given a rigorous foundation. If anything we would accept a critique that the Wu philosophy of information is not about information in the traditional sense, since that sense is actually an extremely limited, reductionist one which our joint theory essentially deconstructs. Readers who may be interested in the details of Wu's critique of the article by Zhou and Brier are directed to Appendix I, Some Problems of Semiotic Information Theory.

Let us accordingly return to the quest for Transdisciplinarity using the most appropriate recent insights of our joint scientific and logical concept of information grounded in reality.

5. TOWARD A UNIFIED SCIENCE-PHILOSOPHY OF INFORMATION

The results of the most recent work of Wu Kun and his associates in the area of the science and philosophy were presented at the Vienna summit and are being published under the following two headings:

- The Development of Philosophy and Its Fundamental Informational Turn
- The Interaction and Convergence of the Philosophy and Science of Information

The philosophical approach of Wu Kun to the definition of Information Science represents a new and major shift in its positioning as a part of knowledge. In addition, in last 3-4 years as noted, Wu's basic philosophy has been supported and augmented by incorporation of the principles of Brenner's Logic in Reality (LIR). The implications of this approach for the current quest for Transdisciplinarity are thus being explored here for the first time, despite the prior involvement of LIR with some versions of TD, as we will see. The question then arises, however, of the relationship between Wu's Philosophy of Information and science and the Philosophy of Science in general. Skeptics will express concern over a lack of scientific rigor, and semioticians will miss their preferred grounding of complex cognitive processes in pheno-menology. We hope this chapter will improve the quality of future dialogue in these areas.

Before proceeding with the presentation of Wu's new theory, we would like to make two statements regarding confirmation and metatheory

5.1 Confirmation

We would like to anticipate and if possible defuse potential objections to the thesis outlined here on the grounds of lack of experimental, let us say statistical, evidence for its confirmation. Depth of experimental evidence is certainly desirable, but agreement is in any case still lacking on the nature of explanation in science and its relation to such evidence [Crupi, 2015]. The literature on confirmation, *e.g.*, Bayesian confirmation theories, is primarily a recapitulation of primitive examples based at most on standard inductive logic. In the social sciences and philosophy, especially if one is trying to define trends, convergence and turns, the discussion is inevitably vague. However, if one takes seriously the fact that contradictory positions have been taken and defended by their proponents as 'true' on all critical issues, there must be some scientific and/or logical reason for this.

A degree of 'quasi-confirmation' of observations of trends, *etc.* then, can be ascribed to our approach if it is *open* to criticism and debate, a key tenet of Transdisciplinarity. To the extent that the logic of (our) transdisciplinarity has a basis in science, it confirms a degree of order on the discussion process, since it includes a concept of the inevitability of opposing positions, defended by thinkers with opposite mental structures. LIR is thus in one sense a scientific theory and, to the extent that its physical postulates or underpinnings can be disproved, it could meet Popper's criterion of falsifiability. There are problems with the Popper approach, but the idea is still useful in many cases.

In another sense, LIR is a metatheory that proposes analyzing the extent to which other theories adequately represent the non-separable properties of real phenomena. In this regard, LIR suggests a new criterion of falsehood. Any theory whose argument depends on the absolute independence of the entities or interpretations under discussion may be biased in favor of one other, resulting in errors or omissions. For itself, LIR avoids this trap because it *assumes* the existence of a counter-theory with which it is necessarily in a dialectical relationship. Reality, for LIR, includes the existence both of LIR and an anti-LIR and their conjunction. The basis of our approach in the doctrine of Logic in Reality is thus clear: we do not require that any observed trend or turn be complete, exclusive, non-contradictory or unidirectional. The discussion of turns and convergence in the next two Sections should be read with that in mind.

5.2 Metatheory

Wu has characterized his Philosophy of Information as a Metaphilosophy, and this chapter, which deals with Information Science and the Quest for TD should be considered as a metatheoretical or metascientific study, since it discusses the ways in which theories are constituted and operate in the evolving informational world. We may say for example that Wu has constructed an informational model of knowledge which includes as its proper parts the Informational Sciences and their data. Regarding this, Brenner has shown that in the Logic in Reality framework, a science does not have to be separated conceptually from its substrate (although they obviously are physically). Further, the process carried out by Wu in reasoning about and with his informational model can be discussed using the language of Model-Based Reasoning (MBR) [Magnani and Nersessian, 2002]. Briefly, the more a model is dialectic and abductive, the greater the level of confidence it can enjoy.

The questions of whether change, progress or 'revolution' in science exist and if so in what they consist are among the most difficult in philosophy and the philosophy of science. The observations of change in stances, paradigms or conceptual frameworks and their relation to new empirical information may be more related to styles of thought that to any absolute provable 'truths' or simplistic taxonomic classifications. One of us (Wu) can claim the authority for this report which reflects his experience and observations of the 'scene' in China for over thirty years. The other logical 'pillar' of this study can be seen in operation in the 'experimental' domain of the intertheoretic relation. Accordingly, the change to a new theory can preserve structural properties allowing a certain ontological continuity accompanying a conceptual revolution [Cao, 1997]. This ontological *synthesis* is a dialectical picture of growth and progress in science that reconciles essential continuity with discontinuous appearance in the history of science, a process that, again, is a logical one in the logic in and of reality (LIR).

5.3 The Development of Philosophy and Its Fundamental Informational Turn

Information is an entity or process, or set of entities and processes, that is unique in both science and philosophy. It requires acceptance as a concept that cannot be defined as an identity, but only as a dynamic interactive dualism of matter-energy (ontological properties) and meaning (epistemological properties). Cognitive processes, as well as their corresponding analyses and theories, instantiate similar dualities, of which the prime example is that of self and other. Information has both physical and apparently non-physical components, both a real dynamic and algorithmic descriptions. Thus, the properties of information common to both science and philosophy can be used to reconcile the physical, scientific properties of information with its epistemological, philosophical characteristics as a carrier of meaning. *Both* a physics (science) and mutually consistent philosophy of information are required and that both the philosophy and science of information must inform one another.

As we have seen earlier in the initial discussion of the Wu theory in Section 2, we are dealing with a major change in the content of philosophy that is qualitative not quantitative. The quantitative impact of computer science and information technology as such on knowledge is unquestionable and requires no further comment here. It is the basis of both the 'informational revolution' that has been described by Floridi. His proposal of an 'informational ontology' correctly critiques the limited, computational concept of a digital ontology. However, as Wu has pointed out, Floridi has not addressed the core problem of the nature of information and the impact of the philosophy of information on philosophy in general. The suggestion by Capurro [Capurro, 2006] that 'Digital Ontology' should refer to the value of the existence of digital phenomena as such as "being" rather than only a metaphysical value of their "Being-of-being" is closer to our position. That Digital Ontology in this sense is today's pervading "casting" of being is of more significance than that digital ontology pervades, also, as metaphysics, society as a whole including scientific methods and philosophical reflection.

For Wu, traditional philosophy insists on the duality of matter and Sprit, considering that all things and phenomena in the world can be categorized into two major areas, namely the material and the Spiritual. This is an article of faith of traditional philosophy he has summarized as: existence = matter + Spirit. Such a segmentation of the field of existence is the most basic ontological principle in traditional philosophy. From this ontological derives materialism or idealism depending on the interpretation between of the relation between matter and Spirit.

There are two major meanings of the term "spirit": that of an 'objective' existing spirit which refers to God or an Absolute idea and a personal spirit of human beings, corresponding to the terms "mind" or "consciousness" in Western thought. As Wu points out, in modern Chinese philosophical terminology, the term "spirit" can be used in both those situations. Chinese and Western materialists do not accept the existence of an objective spirit as defined. The so-called objective spirit, which does not exist in the real objective world, is only a creation of personal spirit. It is, however, unnecessary to distinguish the two concepts of spirit in Chinese, and my use of the terms spirit and spiritual in this chapter is exclusively in the personal sense. They have been capitalized to insure that this usage is kept in mind by the reader. Spirit has not been translated as 'mind' in order to mark that the concept remains open to alternative meanings.

Western philosophy has defined turns major 'turns' in its development, namely from ontology to epistemology and then to linguistics. One can add a phenomenological turn and theories of existence, and philosophies of value and practice as also constituting major turns. However, there are no natural, general criteria provided for these so-called turns; their only claim to be called turns of philosophy refers to the changes in the main corresponding groups of philosophical problems.

For us, innovation in philosophy does not simply lie in classifications in groups of problems and their related disciplines, but in a new discourse on the domains, ideas, and contents of its inherent basic theory of existence. Up till now, philosophical theories, all the interpretative theories of schools of philosophy are grounded in a concept of the field of existence that is heavily dependent o prior understanding of general existence field and of the relation of human and object. These theories focus mainly on the relationships between matter and Spirit, subject and object as discussed above. The differences between various philosophical theories and schools of philosophy lie in the rejection or suspension of some aspects of these two kinds of relations, or more or less emphasis on the leading role of one opposite aspect vs. the other in the two kinds of relations. Some more extreme theories give a status of absolute supremacy to some factors or modes of the Spirit or object, thus even more absolute, partial and simplistic characterizations [Wu, 2013].

For us, philosophical ontology is a hierarchical paradigm. The method of segmentation of the realm of existence (extant domain) is the highest paradigm. The interpretation of the relationship between the different fields of existence is a secondary paradigm because only after determining the different fields can we study the relationship among them. If the general paradigm of traditional philosophy, "existence = matter + Spirit" is its highest paradigm, then traditional materialism and idealism are not the highest paradigms of traditional philosophy, but secondary theoretical paradigms. If the segmentation mode of the field of existence field does not change but involves just a different interpretation of the relationship of matter and Spirit, then it cannot constitute a fundamental philosophical revolution. This is why the bases of a fundamental revolution in the development of human philosophy, in its true sense have never so far been realized. In contrast to the previous philosophical turns, because the informational turn, which incorporates (or is incorporating as we see it) a re-segmentation of the field of existence at the highest philosophical, paradigmatic level, has a fundamental significance for knowledge. It is from this philosophical position, 'Informational Stance' [Wu and Brenner, 2014] that we can establish the relation to Transdisciplinarity or at least the metaphilosophical aspects of Transdisciplinarity 2 (see above).

5.4 Information and a Transdisciplinary Hermeneutics

John van Breda uses the Nicolescu concept of Transdisciplinarity in an approach to a Transdisciplinary Hermeneutics [Van Breda, 2008] inspired by a vision of the world in which our knowledge-systems have become unified, where the intellectual and institutional space and framework for complex thinking and learning have been created by an ongoing and truly transdisciplinary dialogue. Like our approach to information, it is based on the Lupasco logic of the included middle that is at the heart of this form of Transdisciplinarity. Van Breda's key strategy is the replacement of the overly simplistic doctrines of idealism, positivism and deconstructionism with Transdisciplinarity as a new way of representing the complex unity of the subject — object relation. The finality of the Transdisciplinary Hermeneutics which could result is the understanding not only of the complexity of our multi-leveled relationship to the world, but the use of such understanding for the purposes of building the scientific mind capable of engaging with a complex world and finding long-term, sustainable solutions.

We fully agree with and support this approach. The 'Informational Hermeneutics' of our Unified Science-Philosophy of Information is consistent with that of van Breda but adds an informational dimension. The resulting difference with the Nicolescu-van Breda conception is that we do not believe that the definition of *transdisciplinary* Subjects and Objects is necessary to model the complexity of the subject-object interaction. We also see "the impossibility of transcendental or 'directly' accessible knowledge" but on the basis of the characteristics of information and information processes alone.

5.5 Consilience

Wilson [Wilson, 1998] re-introduced the term "consilience" to describe the unification of disciplines by cause-and-effect explanations (epigenetic rules). The current interdisciplinary discourse is seen as an instantiation of Whewell's 19th Century original Consilience of Inductions, "by which science can not only progress but can achieve a type of '*unity*' in the face of complexity and postmodernism." Wilson uses the term of "the convergence of the great branches of learning" in this connection (see next Section). But as Nicolescu says in regard to Transdisciplinarity, the unity of knowledge should not be taken to imply a new, closed ideology. The unity of science and the unity of knowledge are objectives to be achieved in specific respects for the common good, inspired by a vision that knowledge should be at the service of humanity as a whole.

5.6 The Interaction and Convergence of the Philosophy and Science of Information: End of the Quest?

The distinguishing feature of a Unified Science of Information, as it has been formulated by Wu, is thus its explicit reference to the current convergence [Wu, 2015a] of the Information Science and a Philosophy of Information, defined as a metaphilosophy. This convergence is obviously not intended to imply an 'end' to philosophy or its conflation with science. Philosophy will continue to explore issues that arise, in particular, in relation to language and knowledge in their aspects as unique cognitive products of the human condition, with a substantial abstract content. But the question of the relation of that condition to the rest of the world logically requires retaining the scientific properties of that world to insure the validity of the comparison.

As we have seen, there is a set of new and unique relationships that are developing between the classical disciplines of science and philosophy as a consequence of new understandings of the science and philosophy of information. The overall movement is that of a philosophization of science and a scientification of philosophy leading to their convergence. However, in this paper and elsewhere, we use the term Unified Science of Information. This is not strictly accurate, as our convergent theory includes the Philosophy of Information as a proper part, without conflation. We therefore propose, despite its awkwardness, the term Unified Science-Philosophy of Information (USPI) as the best possible description of the field of our endeavor. In fact, it is the terms of a USPI that are most relevant to our 'quest for transdisciplinarity'. The major objective of the quest was to find ways of reinforcing Transdisciplinarity as a doctrine having the finality of a Unity of Knowledge. As a metaphilosophy, Transdisciplinarity had already implied a form of unification of science and philosophy. It is to this that the Philosophy of Information, also as a metaphilosophy brings an additional informational dimension.

We think we have partially achieved this objective by providing an informational framework for Transdisciplinarity within what we call a Unified Science-Philosophy of Information (USPI). This emerging USPI and Transdisciplinarity (TD) in at least one acceptation are highly complex metaphilosophical systems for organizing and discussing knowledge, lying at the interface between science and philosophy. In this paper, we show how both systems have been constituted historically, based in different ways on the progress in physics made in the early 20th Century. Among the key components of the USPI, we have looked in particular at the development of a Philosophy of Information, both in China and the West. Its incorporation of the existential properties of information leads to the convergence in progress of science and philosophy in general and ultimately to a USPI. Among the key components of Transdisciplinarity is the non-aletheic, non-linguistic logic of processes which we call Logic in Reality (LIR) that can handle the contradictions and inconsistencies of the real, informational world. It is an integral part of our USPI. We have presented a major critique of Peircean theory applied to information in the acceptation of Brier based on what we consider an inadequate grounding in the non-reductionist view of science, philosophy and logic that is now possible.

We thus believe we are witnessing the emergence of a new system of science, a metascience in a complex, dynamic reciprocity with philosophy that amounts to a paradigmatic revolution in thought. But much work remains to be done to make the tools offered by both a Unified Science-Philosophy of Information and Transdisciplinarity capable of being used constructively and routinely.

APPENDIX I: SOME PROBLEMS OF SEMIOTIC INFORMATION THEORY

In regard to the criticism from Liqian Zhou and Brier in [Zhou and Brier, 2015], mentioned in Section 4 above, Wu wrote [Wu, 2015b] that the authors emphasized that "an appropriate information theory framework should be an interdisciplinary framework covering objective laws, subjective meanings and inter-subjective norms, which is very correct in my view. However, without admitting the existentiality of objective information how is it possible to cover objective laws? In my information philosophy, information ontology, information epistemology, information practice theory and information axiology are syncretic and unified, exactly as in the grand information theory system that Zhou and Brier stressed in their article. Such Philosophy of Information can not only embody the unique properties and characteristics of information, but also contain the explanation for the uniformity of objective information, subjective information and social information. Such a PI can not only unify the grammar (form) of information, semantics (meaning) of information and pragmatics (value) of information, but also give semiotic information a proper derivation and status." "In my Philosophy of Information, semantic information is only one kind of form of information that is invented by human beings, and its essence is that through regulation methods human beings use information patterns to indicate other information patterns. Thus, the situation can be illustrated by the fact that different symbols can be used to indicate the same object, or the same symbol can be used to indicate different objects. The viewpoint presented in Zhou and Brier's article proposing to use a semantic Philosophy of Information as all of the Philosophy of Information is too narrow. Actually, semantic Information Philosophy is by no means the highest level of Information Philosophy; it does not have the quality of a *general* Information Philosophy, and the general properties of information exceed the parochial vision of semantic Information Philosophy. It is Information Philosophy that contains and governs semantic Information Philosophy and not the contrary.. Such a relationship also applies to the connection between other research approaches to the Philosophy of Information philosophy and what I have proposed elsewhere in Chinese, to which at least one of the above authors has had access. The other research approaches of information philosophy include the computational approach, information ethics approach, information phenomenology approach, communication information approach, information cognition approach and so on."

In another paper [Wu, 2011], Wu also pointed out the limitations of semantic information as generally defined. He wrote: "the encoding scheme of human thinking and the knowledge information obtained by thought is really not only semantic information. According to contemporary scientific theory, the subjective knowledge acquired by humans can be categorized into two types: one of them is the "classificatory knowledge" which can be encoded by symbols; the other one is "silent (non-linguistic) knowledge" which is difficult to encode by symbols. The former usually presents itself as information that is easy to express and directly communicate, while the latter presents itself as first-person experience and spiritual/mental informational activities that are not easily encoded by symbols. Therefore, as important as the symbolic coding approach of human consciousness is, still it is not a complete, overall coding approach of human consciousness. The information of non-linguistic knowledge, subconscious activities and so on may be encoded by hidden non-symbolic forms, such as emotion and affectivity, or even more specific physiological material forms.

Semantic information coding can not be independently processed in at the level of consciousness but is necessarily accompanied by the corresponding information encoding activities of material forms at the physiological level. For this reason, people can ascertain part of the content of human thinking processes by studying physiological mechanisms (electrical and chemical activities) of the human brain. These studies can be used to define principles of brain input (and output) based on computer and virtual reality technology for exploring human perception and cognition. Accordingly, even in the domain of human consciousness, semantic information cannot be considered as constituting the whole of human world and setting absolute bounds on it. Compared to the general concept of the world symbolizing being as a whole, the semantic symbol's place in the world is only as a local microcosm."

References

Brenner, J. E. (2008). *Logic in Reality*, Springer, Dordrecht.

Brenner J.E. (2010). The Logic of Ethical Information, In *Knowledge, Technology, Policy,* H. Demir (Ed.), 23(1-2), pp. 109-133.

Brenner, J.E. (2011). Information in Reality: Logic and Metaphysics, *triple-C*, 9(2), pp. 332-341.

Brenner, J. E. (2011a). Systems and Information: A Transdisciplinary Study. *Transdisciplinary Journal of Engineering & Science*, 4, pp. 1-20.

Brenner, J. E. (2015). Three Aspects of Information Science in Reality: Symmetry, Semiotics and Society, *Information*, 6, pp. 750-772.

Brenner, J. E. (2015a). Information and the Future of Transdisciplinarity. *Transdisciplinary Journal of Engineering & Science*, 6, pp. 86-100.

Brier, S. (2008). *Cybersemiotics: Why Information is not Enough,* University of Toronto Press, Toronto, Canada.

Brier, S. (2013). Cybersemiotics: A New Foundation for Transdisciplinary Theory of Information, Cognition, Meaningful Communication and the Interaction Between Nature and Culture, *Integral Review*, 9(2).

Brier, S. (2014). The Riddle of the Sphinx Answered: On How C. S. Peirce's Transdisciplinary Semiotic Philosophy of Knowing Links Science,

Spirituality and Knowing. In *One Hundred Years after Charles S. Peirce (1839-1914)*, C. Tandy (ed.). Ria University Press: Ann Arbor, MI, p. 114.

Burgin, M. (2003). Information Theory: A Multifaceted Model of Information, *Entropy*, 5, pp. 146-160. Burgin, M. (2010). *Theory of Information: Fundamentality, Diversity and Unification*; World Scientific, Singapore.

Cao, T. Y. (1997). *Conceptual Developments of 20th Century Field Theories.* Cambridge, UK, Cambridge University Press.

Capurro, R. (2006). Towards an Ontological Foundation of Information Ethics, *Ethics and Information Technology*, 8 (4), pp. 175-186. http://www. capurro.de/oxford.html. Accessed March 2015.

Capurro R. (2008). Information Technology as an Ethical Challenge, *ACM Ubiquity*, http://ubiquity.acm.org, pp. 9–22.

Cat, J. (2014). The Unity of Science, *The Stanford Encyclopedia of Philosophy* (Winter 2014 Edition), Edward N. Zalta (ed.), http://plato.stanford.edu/ archives/win2014/entries/scientific-unity/.

Collier, J. (2012). Information, Causation and Computation, In: *Information and Computation: Essays on Scientific and Philosophical Understanding of Information and Computation*, (eds. Dodig-Crnkovic, G. and Burgin, M.), World Scientific, Singapore.

Crupi, V. (2015). Confirmation, *The Stanford Encyclopedia of Philosophy* (Fall 2015 Edition), Edward N. Zalta (ed.), http://plato.stanford.edu/archives/ fall 2015/entries/confirmation/.

Floridi, L. (2014). *The Fourth Revolution. How the Infosphere is Reshaping Human Reality*, Oxford University Press, Oxford, U.K.

Graff, H. J. (2015). *Undisciplining Knowledge,* Johns Hopkins University Press, Baltimore.

Hirsch Hadorn, G. *et al.* (eds). (2008). *Handbook of Transdisciplinary Research,* Dordrecht, Springer.

Hofkirchner, W., Fuchs, C., Raffl, C., Schafranek, M., Sandoval, M., & Bichler, R. (2007). ICTs and Society: The Salzburg Approach. *University of Salzburg   Research Paper No. 3, December*. Salzburg: ICT&S Center.

Hofkirchner, W. (2009). How to Achieve a Unified Theory of Information, *triple-C*, 7(2), pp. 357-358.

Hofkirchner, W. (2013). *Emergent Information: A Unified Theory of Information Framework,* World Scientific, Singapore.

Hofkirchner, W. (2013a) Emergent Information. When a Difference Makes a Difference. *triple-C* 11(1), pp. 6-12.

Hofkirchner, W. (2014) The Commons from a Critical Social Systems Perspective, *Recerca, Revista di Pensamenti Analisi*, 14, pp. 73-91.

Lawrence R.J. (2008) Transgresser les Frontières Disciplinaires. In: *Le Défi de l'Inter- et Transdisciplinarité*, F. Darbellay, T. Paulsen (eds.), Presses Polytechniques et Universitaires Romandes, Lausanne, pp. 223-238.

Leydesdorff, L. (2014). Information, Meaning and Intellectual Organization in Networks of Inter-Human Communication, http://arxiv.org/ftp/arxiv/papers/1406/1406.5688.pdf.

Lunca, M. (2008). Transdisciplinary Potential of Information. In Nicolescu, B. (ed.)., *Transdisciplinarity; Theory and Practice*, Hampton Press, Cresskill,   NJ, 201-211.

Lupasco S. (1979). L'Univers Psychique. Paris: Denoel-Gonthier.

Lupasco S. (1987). *Le principe d'antagonisme et la logique de l'énergie*, Éditions du Rocher, Paris. (Originally published in Paris: Éditions Hermann,   1951).

Magnani, L. and Nersessian, N. J. (eds), (2002). *Model-Based Reasoning*, Kluwer Academic/Plenum Publishers, Dordrecht, 2002.

Marijuán, P. C. (2003). Foundations of Information Science: Selected papers from FIS 2002, *Entropy*, 5, pp. 214-219.

Marijuan, P.C. (2013) The Uprising of the Informational: A New Way of Thinking in Information Science. Presented at 1st International Conference in   China on the Philosophy of Information, Xi'an, China, 18 October 2013.

Nicolescu, B. (2002). *Manifesto of Transdisciplinarity*, State University of New York Press, Albany, NY.

Nicolescu, B., (ed.). (2008). *Transdisciplinarity; Theory and Practice*, Hampton Press, Cresskill, NJ.

Nicolescu, B. (2011). Methodology of Transdisciplinarity-Levels of Reality, Logic of the Included Middle and Complexity, In: *Transdisciplinarity: Bridging Natural Science, Social Science, Humanities & Engineering*, A. Ertas (ed.), http://www.theatlas.org/atlas-books.pdf, pp. 22-45.

Ulanowicz, R. E. (2009). Increasing Entropy: Heat Death or Perpetual Harmonies? *Int. of Design & Nature and Ecodynamics*, 4 (2), pp. 83-96.

Van Breda, J. (2008). Overcoming the Disciplinary Divide; Towards the Possibility of a Transdisciplinary Hermeneutics. In: *Exploring Sustainability Science – A Southern Africa Perspective* (Burns, M and Weaver, A., eds.), Sun Press, Stellenbosch, South Africa, pp. 1-46.

Weislogel, E. L. (2014) On the Relationship of Metaphysics to Transdisciplinarity. In *Transdisciplinary Education, Philosophy and Applications* (eds.) B. Nicolescu and A. Ertas. C online The Atlas Publishing, 2014.

Wilson E. O. (1998). *Consilience: The Unity of Knowledge.* A. A. Knopf, New York.

Wu, K. (1989). Cognition: Informational Constructional Activity in Multi-intermediaries. *J. Changsha Univ. Sci. Technol. (Soc. Sci.)*, 3, pp. 17–22. (In Chinese)

Wu, K. (2010). *The Basic Theory of the Philosophy of Information.* 4th International Conference on the Foundations of Information Science, August, 2010. Beijing.

Wu, K. (2011). The Fundamental Turn of Philosophy and Basic Philosophical Issues, *Hebei Academic Journal*, 4, pp. 11-21. (In Chinese)

Wu, K. (2012). The Essence, Classification and Quality of the Different Grades of Information, *Information,* 3, pp. 403-419.

Wu, K. 2013. The Development of Philosophy and its Fundamental Turn. Presented at the 1st International Conference in China on the Philosophy of Information, Xi'an, China, 18 October 2013. (Originally published in *Journal of Humanity* 5, pp. 1-6.)

Wu, K. (2015) The Development of Philosophy and Its Fundamental Informational Turn, *Information* 6, pp. 693-703.

Wu, K. (2015a). The Interaction and Convergence of the Philosophy and Science of Information. Presented at the 2nd International Conference on the Philosophy of Information, Vienna, Austria, 6 June 2015.

Wu, K. (2015b) The Unique Flavor and Extraordinary Character of Information Philosophy, *Philosophical Analysis*,1, pp. 43-52 (In Chinese).

Wu, K. and Brenner, J. E. (2013). The Informational Stance: Philosophy and Logic. Part I: The Basic Theories. *Logic and Logical Philosophy*, 22, pp. 1–41.

Wu, K. and Brenner, J. E. (2014). The Informational Stance: Philosophy and Logic. Part II From Physics to Society. *Logic and Logical Philosophy*, 23, pp. 81–108.

Wu, K. and Brenner, J. E. (2015). An Informational Ontology and Epistemology of Cognition. *Found. Science*, 20, pp. 249-279.

Zlatev, J. (2012). Cognitive Semiotics: An Emerging Field for the Transdisciplinary Study of Meaning, *The Public Journal of Semiotics* IV(1), October 2012, pp. 2-23.

Zhou, L. and Brier, S. 2015. The Metaphysics of Chinese Information Philosophy: A Critical Analysis of Wu Kun's Philosophy of Information. *Cybernetics and Human Knowing*, 22(1), pp. 35-56.

Chapter 9

Natural Information and Spiritual Information as an Outcome of the Transdisciplinary Methodology

Basarab Nicolescu

International Centre for Transdisciplinary Research (CIRET), Paris, France
19 Villa Curial, 75019 Paris, France
basarab.nicolescu@gmail.com

When two people try to communicate there is inevitably confrontation: representation against representation, subconscious against subconscious. As this confrontation is subconscious, it often degenerates into conflict. A new model of civilization is necessary, the keystone being the dialogue between human beings, nations, cultures and religions for the survival of humanity. In forming a new model of civilization the methodology of transdisciplinarity is crucial. In this context, it is important to distinguish between natural information and spiritual information.

Keywords: Methodology of transdisciplinarity; levels of reality; included middle; hidden third; natural information; spiritual information.

1. Introduction

Can we really dialogue?
The word "dialogue" appeared in fact at the foundation of modernity, but it referred only to nature.[1]

---

[1]Galilei Galilei. 1962. *Dialogue Concerning the Two Chief World Systems, Ptolemaic and Copernican,* trans. Stillman Drake, foreword by Albert Einstein. Berkeley: University of California Press. The first edition appeared in 1632, year which could be considered as the birth date of modernity.

Each person has his/her prejudices, his/her convictions, his/her subconscious representations. When two people try to communicate there is inevitably a confrontation: representation against representation, subconscious against subconscious. As this confrontation is subconscious, it often degenerates into conflict.

Language is the vehicle of these subconscious representations. We use the same words, but their meaning can be radically different. We are manipulated by our own representations. The dialogue is strictly impossible in the absence of a methodology of dialogue. We can only monologue. It is impossible to be at the place of the other.

The same considerations apply in the case of nations, cultures, religions and spiritualities: interest against interest, representation against representation, dogma against dogma, hidden spiritual assumptions against hidden spiritual assumptions.

This situation is aggravated by the large number of languages (more than 6000), which display each its own systems of representations and values. A completely accurate translation from one language to another is impossible.

This is also aggravated by the contemporary immense means of destruction and the continuing destruction of the environment. The inevitable conflicts could lead, for the first time in the history of mankind, at the disappearance of the human species.

A new model of civilization is necessary, the keystone is the dialogue between human beings, nations, cultures and religions for the survival of humanity.

We have therefore to face a number of important questions:
- What is the methodology of dialogue?
- The suspension, during the dialogue, of our prejudices to arrive at a "fusion of horizons"[2] is it necessary?
- The abandonment of the binary logic and the adoption of non-classical logic is it necessary?

---

[2]Hans-Georg Gadamer. 1960. *Gesammelte Werke, Hermeneutik I. Wahreit und Methode.* Tübingen: J. C. B. Mohr.

- Can we dialogue without first identifying the levels of reality involved in the dialogue?

- How can we take complexity into account?

- Are the transcultural and the transreligious crucially important for a methodology of dialogue of cultures, of religions, and of spiritualities?

- The dialogue between cultures is it a social and/or a political gamble?

- Is the danger of the dissolution of cultures in the context of globalization real?

- Are there big cultures, small cultures and falling cultures?

- Peoples of the world are they prepared for a real dialogue of cultures?

- What is the role of the spiritual dimension in this dialogue?

We can answer all these questions by adopting the methodology of transdisciplinarity.

I proposed in 1985[3] the inclusion in the word "transdisciplinarity", introduced by Jean Piaget[4] in 1972, of the meaning "beyond disciplines" and I developed this idea over the years in my articles and books and also in different official international documents. Many other researchers over the world contributed to this development of transdisciplinarity. A key-date in this development is 1994, when the Charter of Transdisciplinarity was adopted by the participants at the First World Congress of Transdisciplinarity (Convento da Arrábida, Portugal)[5].

The crucial point here is the status of the Subject.

---

[3]Basarab Nicolescu. 1985. *Nous, la particule et le monde*. Paris: Le Mail.

[4]Jean Piaget. 1972. « L'épistémologie des relations interdisciplinaires ». In *L'interdisciplinarité — Problèmes d'enseignement et de recherche*, edited by L. Apostel, G. Berger, A. Briggs and G. Michaud, 131-144. Paris : Centre pour la Recherche et l'Innovation dans l'Enseignement, Organisation de Coopération et de développement économique.

[5]"The Charter of Transdisciplinarity" (in French, Spanish, English, Portuguese, Turkish, Arab, Italian, Russian, and Romanian). 1994. Paris: CIRET. Accessed on December 30, 2015. http://ciret-transdisciplinarity.org/index.php

"Beyond disciplines" precisely signifies the Subject, more precisely the Subject-Object interaction. The transcendence, inherent in transdisciplinarity, is the transcendence of the Subject.

The meaning "beyond disciplines" leads us to an immense space of new knowledge. The main outcome was the formulation of the methodology of transdisciplinarity. It allows us also to clearly distinguish between multidisciplinarity, interdisciplinarity, and transdisciplinarity.

2. Multidisciplinarity, Interdisciplinarity, and Transdisciplinarity

Multidisciplinarity concerns itself with studying a research topic in not just one discipline only, but in several at the same time. Any topic in question will ultimately be enriched by incorporating the perspectives of several disciplines. Multidisciplinarity brings a plus to the discipline in question, but this "plus" is always in the exclusive service of the home discipline. In other words, the multidisciplinary approach overflows disciplinary boundaries while its goal remains limited to the framework of disciplinary research.

Interdisciplinarity has a different goal than multidisciplinarity. It concerns the transfer of methods from one discipline to another. Like multidisciplinarity, interdisciplinarity overflows the disciplines, but its goal still remains within the framework of disciplinary research. Interdisciplinarity has even the capacity of generating new disciplines, like quantum cosmology and chaos theory.

Transdisciplinarity concerns that which is at once *between* the disciplines, *across* the different disciplines, and *beyond* all discipline. Its goal is the understanding of the present world, of which one of the imperatives is the unity of knowledge.

As one can see, there is no opposition between disciplinarity (including multidisciplinarity and interdisciplinarity) and transdisciplinarity, but a fertile complementarity. In fact, there is no transdisciplinarity without disciplinarity.

3. Methodology of Transdisciplinarity

A remarkable achievement of transdisciplinarity in present times is, of course, the formulation of the methodology of transdisciplinarity, accepted and applied by an important number of researchers in many countries of the world.

The axiomatic character of the methodology of transdisciplinarity is an important aspect. This means that he have to limit the number of axioms to a *minimum* number. Any axiom which can be derived from the already postulated ones, have to be rejected.

After many years of research, I have arrived at the following three axioms of the methodology of transdisciplinarity[6]:

i. *The ontological axiom*: There are, in Nature and in our knowledge of Nature, different levels of Reality of the Object and, correspondingly, different levels of Reality of the Subject.

ii. The logical axiom: The passage from one level of Reality to another is insured by the logic of the included middle.

iii. *The epistemological axiom*: The structure of the totality of levels of Reality is a complex structure: every level is what it is because all the levels exist at the same time.

The above three axioms give a precise and rigorous *definition of transdisciplinarity*.

Let me now describe the essentials of these three transdisciplinary axioms.

4. The Ontological Axiom: Levels of Reality

The key concept of the transdisciplinary approach to Nature and knowledge is the concept of *levels of Reality*.

Here the meaning we give to the word "Reality" is pragmatic and ontological at the same time.

---

[6]Basarab Nicolescu. 2002. *Manifesto of Transdisciplinarity*, trans. Karen-Claire Voss. New York: State University of New York (SUNY) Press. The first edition appeared in French in 1996.

By "Reality" we intend first of all to designate that which *resists* our experiences, representations, descriptions, images, or even mathematical formulations.

In so far as Nature participates in the being of the world, one has to assign also an ontological dimension to the concept of Reality. Reality is not merely a social construction, the consensus of a collectivity, or some inter-subjective agreement. It also has a trans-subjective dimension: for example, experimental data can ruin the most beautiful scientific theory.

Of course, one has to distinguish the words "Real" and "Reality". *Real* designates that which *is*, while *Reality* is connected to resistance in our human experience. The "Real" is, by definition, veiled forever, while "Reality" is accessible to our knowledge.

By "level of Reality", I designate a set of systems which are invariant under certain general laws (in the case of natural systems) and under certaingeneral rules and norms (in the case of social systems). That is to say that two levels of Reality are different if, while passing from one to the other, there is a break in the applicable laws, rules or norms and a break in fundamental concepts (like, for example, causality). Therefore there is a *discontinuity* in the structure of levels of Reality.

A new *Principle of Relativity*emerges from the coexistence between complex plurality and open unity in our approach: *no level of Reality constitutes a privileged place from which one is able to understand all the other levels of Reality.* A level of Reality is what it is because all the other levels exist at the same time. This Principle of Relativity is what originates a new perspective on religion, spirituality, politics, art, education, history, and society. And when our perspective on the world changes, the world changes.

In other words, the transdisciplinary approach is not hierarchical. There is no fundamental level. But its absence does not mean an anarchical dynamics, but a coherent one, of all levels of Reality, already discovered or which will be discovered in the future.

Every level is characterized by its *incompleteness*: the laws governing this level are just a part of the totality of laws governing all levels. And even the totality of laws does not exhaust the entire Reality: we have also to consider the Subject and its interaction with the Object.

The zone between two different levels and beyond all levels is a zone of non-resistance to our experiences, representations, descriptions, images, and mathematical formulations. Quite simply, the transparence of this zone is due to the limitations of our bodies and of our sense organs — limitations which apply regardless of what measuring tools are used to extend these sense organs. We therefore have to conclude that the topological distance between levels is finite. However this finite distance does not mean a finite knowledge. Take, as an image, a segment of a straight line – it contains an infinite number of points. In a similar manner, a finite topological distance could contain an infinite number of levels of Reality. We have work to do till the end of times.

The unity of levels of Reality and its complementary zone of non-resistance constitutes what we call the transdisciplinary Object.

Inspired by the phenomenology of Edmund Husserl,[7] I assert that the different levels of Reality of the Object are accessible to our knowledge thanks to the different levels of Reality of the Subject which are potentially present in our being.

As in the case of levels of Reality of the Object, the coherence of levels of Reality of the Subject presupposes a zone of non-resistance. The unity of levels Reality of the Subject and this complementary zone of non-resistance constitutes what we call the *transdisciplinary Subject*.

The two zones of non-resistance of transdisciplinary Object and Subject must be identical for the transdisciplinary Subject to communicate with the transdisciplinary Object. A flow of spiritual

---

[7]Edmund Husserl. 1966. *Méditationscartésiennes*. Paris : Vrin. Translated from the German by G. Peiffer and E. Levinas.

information that coherently cuts across different levels of Reality of the Subject must correspond to the flow of naturalinformation coherently cutting across different levels of Reality of the Object. The two flows are interrelated because they share the same zone of non-resistance.

We need to define what we call "spiritual". We call "spiritual" a level of functioning of the human being which cannot be reduced to the physical level. This assertion is, of course, in contradiction with the reductionist ideology.

The scientific meaning of the word *reduction* is the following: A is reduced to B, B to C, C to D etc. until reaching what is considered to be the most fundamental level. Indeed, human thinking aims for the same process of reduction. Reduction is, in many ways, a natural process of thinking and there is nothing wrong with that. The only question concerns the understanding of what is at the end of the reduction chain: is this chain circular? If not, how can we justify the concept of the *end* of a chain?

With regard to *scientific reductionism*, things are very different. This designates the explanation of spiritual processes in terms of mental processes, which, in turn, are explained in terms of biological processes, which, in turn, are explained in terms of physical processes. In other words, a scientist who complies with the life of his/her community reduces spirituality to materiality. But this is, in fact, an ideological claim and not a scientific claim.

Philosophical reductionism reverses the chain: it reduces materiality to spirituality.

The two types of reductionism belong to what might be called *mono-reductionism*.

Some philosophers adopt a dualistic approach: they consider that materiality and spirituality are fundamentally distinct. The dualistic approach is a version of philosophical reductionism: it corresponds to what we may call *multi-reductionism*. We can even identify a different version in New Age literature: that of *inter-reductionism*: certain properties of material nature are attributed to spiritual entities or, conversely, certain properties of spiritual nature are attributed to material objects.

Anti-reductionism, the approach that is opposed to reductionism, is expressed through *holism* (meaning that the whole is more than the sum of its parts and determines the properties of its parts) and through *emergentism* (which means that new structures, behaviors and properties are generated by relatively simple interactions that give rise, in turn, to increasing levels of complexity). Holism and emergentism have their own difficulties: they must explain where *novelty* comes from, without providing *ad hoc* arguments.

The concept of *levels of reality* is crucial in order to reconcile reduction, which is so necessary to the scientific approach, with anti-reductionism, which is so necessary to the study of complex systems. The transdisciplinary theory of levels of Reality is, in some aspects, a multi-reductionist theory, *via* the existence of multiple, discontinuous levels of Reality. However, it is also a non-reductionist theory, *via* the Hidden Third, which restores the continuous interconnectedness of Reality. The reductionism/non-reductionism opposition is, in fact, a result of binary thinking, based upon the excluded middle logic. The transdisciplinary theory of levels of Reality allows us to define, in such a way, a new view on Reality, which can be called *trans-reductionism.*[8]

The transdisciplinary notion of levels of Reality is incompatible with reduction of the spiritual level to the psychical level, of the psychical level to the biological level, and of the biological level to the physical level. Still these four levels are united through the Hidden Third.

Knowledge is neither exterior nor interior: it is simultaneously exterior and interior. The studies of the universe and of the human being sustain one another.

---

[8]Basarab Nicolescu, "The Idea of Levels of Reality and its Relevance for Non-Reduction and Personhood," *Transdisciplinarity in Science and Religion,* 4 (2008): 11-26.

The zone of non-resistance plays the role of a *third* between the Subject and the Object, an Interaction term, which allows the unification of the transdisciplinary Subject and the transdisciplinary Object while preserving their difference. In the following I will call this Interaction term the Hidden Third.

Our ternary partition {Subject, Object, Hidden Third} is, of course, different from the binary partition{Subject vs. Object} of classical realism.

The transdisciplinary Object and its levels of Reality, the transdisciplinary Subject and its levels of Reality and the Hidden Third define the transdisciplinary approach of Reality. Based on this ternary structure of Reality, we can deduce several ternaries of *epistemological levels* which are extremely useful in the analysis of concrete situations:

Levels of organization – Levels of structuring – Levels of integration

Levels of confusion – Levels of language – Levels of interpretation

Physical levels – Biological levels – Psychical levels

Levels of ignorance – Levels of intelligence – Levels of contemplation

Levels of objectivity – Levels of subjectivity – Levels of complexity

Levels of knowledge – Levels of understanding – Levels of being

Levels of materiality – Levels of spirituality – Levels of non-duality

5. The Logical Axiom: The Included Middle

The incompleteness of the general laws governing a given level of Reality signifies that, at a given moment of time, one necessarily discovers contradictions in the theory describing the respective level: one has to assert A and non-A at the same time.

However, our habits of mind, scientific or not, are still governed by the classical logic, which does not tolerate contradictions. The classical logic is founded on three axioms:

1. *The axiom of identity*: A is A.

2. *The axiom of non-contradiction:* A is not non-A.

3. *The axiom of the excluded middle*: There exists no third term T ("T" from "third") which is at the same time A and non-A.

History will credit Stéphane Lupasco (1900-1988)with having shown that the logic of the included middle is a true logic, mathematically formalized, multivalent (with three values: A, non-A, and T) and non-contradictory.[9]

In fact, the logic of the included middle is the very heart of quantum mechanics: it allows us to understand the basic principle of the superposition of "yes" and "no" quantum states.

Our understanding of the axiom of the included middle — there exists a third term T which is at the same time A and non-A — is completely clarified once the notion of "levels of Reality", not existing in the works of Lupasco, is introduced.

In order to obtain a clear image of the meaning of the included middle, let us represent the three terms of the new logic — A, non-A, and T — and the dynamics associated with them by a triangle in which one of the vertices is situated at one level of Reality and the two other vertices at another level of Reality. The included middle is in fact an *included third*. If one remains at a single level of Reality, all manifestation appears as a struggle between two contradictory elements. The third dynamic, that of the T-state, is exercised at another level of Reality, where that which appears to be disunited is in fact united, and that which appears contradictory is perceived as non-contradictory.

It is the projection of the T-state onto the same single level of Reality which produces the appearance of mutually exclusive, antagonistic pairs (A and non-A). A single level of Reality can only create antagonistic oppositions.

---

[9]Stéphane Lupasco. 1951. *Le principe d'antagonisme et la logique de l'énergie - Prolégomènes à une science de la contradiction.* Paris: Hermann & Cie.

The action of the logic of the included middle on the different levels of Reality induces an open structure of the unity of levels of Reality. This structure has considerable consequences for the theory of knowledge because it implies the impossibility of a self-enclosed complete theory. *Knowledge is forever open.*

6. The Epistemological Axiom: The Universal Interdependence

There are several theories of complexity.

In the context of our discussion, what is important to be understood is that the existing theories of complexity do include neither the notion of levels of Reality nor the notion of zones of non-resistance.[10] It is therefore useful to distinguish between the *horizontal complexity*, which refers to a single level of reality and *vertical complexity*, which refers to several levels of Reality.

From a transdisciplinary point of view, complexity is a modern form of the very ancient principle of universal interdependence.

7. Trans-Reality and the Hidden Third

In the transdisciplinary approach, the Subject and the Object are immersed in the Hidden Third.

The transdisciplinary Subject and its levels, the transdisciplinary Object and its levels, and the Hidden Third define the transdisciplinary Reality or *trans-Reality* (see Figure 1).

---

[10]Paul Cilliers and Basarab Nicolescu. 2012. "Complexity and Transdisciplinarity — Discontinuity, Levels of Reality and the Hidden Third". *Futures* 44 (8): 711–718.

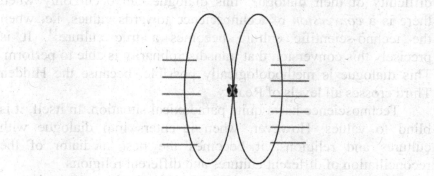

Fig. 1. Trans-reality.

The Hidden Third, in its relationship with the levels of Reality, is fundamental for the understanding of *unus mundus* described by cosmodernity. Reality is simultaneously a single and a multiple One. If one remains confined to the Hidden Third, then the unity is undifferentiated, symmetric, situated in the *non-time*. If one remains confined to the levels of Reality, there are only differences, asymmetries, located in time. To simultaneously consider the levels of reality and the Hidden Third introduces a breaking in the symmetry of *unus mundus*. In fact, *the levels of Reality are generated precisely by this breaking of symmetry introduced by time.*

In the transdisciplinary approach, the Hidden Third appears as the source of knowledge but, in its turn, needs the Subject in order to know the world: the Subject, the Object and the Hidden Third are inter-related.

Cultures and religions are not concerned, as academic disciplines are, with fragments of levels of Reality only: they simultaneously involve one or several levels of Reality of the Object, one or several levels of Reality of theSubject *and* the non-resistance zone of the Hidden Third.

Technoscience is entirely situated in the zone of the Object, while cultures and religions cross all three terms: the Object, the Subject and the Hidden Third. This asymmetry demonstrates the difficulty of their dialogue: this dialogue can occur only when there is a *conversion* of technoscience towards values, i.e. when the techno-scientific culture becomes a true culture[11]. It is precisely this conversion that transdisciplinarity is able to perform. This dialogue is methodologically possible, because the Hidden Third crosses all levels of Reality.

Technoscience has a quite paradoxical situation. In itself, it is blind to values. However, when it enters into dialogue with cultures and religions, it becomes the best mediator of the reconciliation of different cultures and different religions.

Homo religiosus existed from the beginnings of the human species, at the moment when the human being tried to understand the meaning of our life. The *sacred* is our natural realm. We tried to capture the unseen from his/her observation of the visible world. Our language is that of the imaginary, trying to penetrate higher levels of Reality — parables, symbols, myths, legends, revelation.

Homo economicus is a creation of modernity. We believe only in what is seen, observed, measured. The *profane* is our natural realm. Our language is that of just one level of Reality, accessible through the analytic mind — hard and soft sciences, technology, theories and ideologies, mathematics, informatics.

The only way to avoid the dead end of homo religiosus *vs.* homo economicus debate is to adopt *transdisciplinary hermeneutics.*[12] Transdisciplinary hermeneutics is a natural outcome of transdisciplinary methodology.

Transdisciplinary hermeneutics is able to identify the common germ of *homo religiosus* and of *homo economicus,* which can be called *homo sui transcendentalis*.

---

[11]Basarab Nicolescu. 2004. "Toward a Methodological Foundation of the Dialogue Between the Technoscientific and Spiritual Cultures". In *Differentiation and Integration of Worldviews*, edited by Liubava Moreva, 139-152. Sankt Petersburg: Eidos.

[12]Basarab Nicolescu. 2007. "Transdisciplinarity as Methodological Framework for Going beyond the Science and Religion Debate". *Transdisciplinarity in Science and Religion* 2: 35-60.

Transdisciplinary hermeneutics avoids the trap of trying to formulate a super-science or a super-religion. Unity of knowledge can be only an open, complex and plural unity.

The human person appears as an interface between the Hidden Third and the world. The erasing of the Hidden Third in knowledge signifies a one-dimensional human being, reduced to its cells, neurons, quarks and elementary particles.

A unified theory of levels of Reality is crucial in building sustainable development and sustainable futures. The considerations made until now in these matters are based upon reductionist and binary thinking: everything is reduced to society, economy and environment. The individual level of Reality, the spiritual level of Reality and the cosmic level of Reality are completely ignored. Sustainable futures, so necessary for our survival, can only be based on a unified theory of levels of Reality.

8. Transdisciplinary Ethics and the Anthropocene

The consequences on ethics of such a vision of Reality are crucial in the context of *Anthropocene,* of the existence of the danger, for the first time of history, of the annihilation of the entire human species.[13] As Clive Hamilton writes in his book *Requiem for a Species*, it is difficult to accept the idea that human beings can change the composition of the atmosphere of the earth to a point of destroying their own civilization and also the human species. One can predict the elevation of the sea level by several meters during this century and the total dissolution of the Arctic ice in one or two decades. One can even predict that the ice of the entire planet will disappear in several centuries, leading to elevation of sea level of around 70 meters. From my point of view, in agreement with Clive Hamilton, it is not the technology which will save our species but a radical change of our vision of Reality. Reality is

---

[13]Clive Hamilton. 2010. *Requiem for a Species — Why We Resist the Truth about Climate Change*. London: Earthscan.

One. For a sustainable future, we have to consider simultaneously all levels of Reality and also the Hidden Third.

We are part of the ordered movement of Reality. Our freedom consists in entering into the movement or perturbing it. We canrespond to the movement or impose our will of power and domination. Our responsibility is to build sustainable futures in agreement with the overall movement of Reality.

We are witnessing a new era — *cosmodernity* — founded on a new vision of the contemporary interaction between science, culture, spirituality, religion, and society.

Cosmodernity means essentially that all entity in the universe is defined by its relation to the other entities. The human being, in turn, is related as a person to the Great Other, the Hidden Third. The old idea of cosmos, in which we are active participants, is resurrected.[14]

Reality is plastic. Reality is not something outside or inside us: it is simultaneously outside and inside. We are part of this Reality that changes due to our thoughts, feelings and actions. This means that we are fully responsible for what Reality is. The world moves, lives and offers itself to our knowledge thanks to some ordered structures of something that is, though, continually changing. Reality is therefore rational, but its rationality is multiple, structured on levels.

The levels of Reality correspond to the *levels of understanding*, in a fusion of knowledge and being. All levels of Reality are interwoven. The world is at the same time knowable and unknowable.

The Hidden Third between Subject and Object denies any rationalization. Therefore, Reality is also *trans-rational*. The Hidden Third conditions not only the flow of the interconnected natural and spiritualinformation between Subject and Object, but also the flow of spiritual information between the different levels

---

[14]Basarab Nicolescu. 2014. *From Modernity to Cosmodernity – Science, Culture, and Spirituality*. New York: State University of New York (SUNY) Press.

of reality of the Subject and the flow of natural information between the different levels of reality of the Object. The discontinuity between the different levels is compensated by the *continuity and unification of information* held by the Hidden Third. Source of Reality, the Hidden Third feeds itself from this Reality, in a cosmic breath which includes us and the universe.

The irreducible mystery of the world coexists with the wonders discovered by reason. The unknown enters every pore of the known, but without the known, the unknown would be a hollow word. Every human being on this Earth recognizes his/her face in any other human being, independent of his/her particular religious or philosophical beliefs, and all humanity recognizes itself in the infinite Otherness.

A new spirituality, free of dogmas, is already potentially present on our planet. There are exemplary signs and arguments for its birth, from quantum physics till theater, literature and art.[15] We are at the threshold of a true New Renaissance, which asks for a new, cosmodern consciousness.

References

"The Charter of Transdisciplinarity" (in French, Spanish, English, Portuguese, Turkish, Arab, Italian, Russian, and Romanian). 1994. Paris: CIRET. Accessed on December 30, 2015. http://ciret-transdisciplinarity.org/index.php

Cilliers, Paul, and Basarab Nicolescu. 2012. "Complexity and Transdisciplinarity — Discontinuity, Levels of Reality and the Hidden Third". *Futures* 44 (8): 711–718.

Gadamer, Hans-Georg. 1960. *Gesammelte Werke, Hermeneutik I. Wahreit und Methode.* Tübingen: J. C. B. Mohr.

Galilei, Galileo. 1962. *Dialogue Concerning the Two Chief World Systems, Ptolemaic and Copernican,* trans. Stillman Drake, foreword by Albert Einstein. Berkeley: University of California Press.

Hamilton, Clive. 2010. *Requiem for a Species — Why We Resist the Truth about Climate Change.* London: Earthscan.

---

[15]Nicolescu 2014.

Husserl, Edmund. 1966. *Méditations Cartésiennes*. Paris : Vrin. Translated from the German by G. Peiffer and E. Levinas.

Lupasco, Stéphane. 1951. *Le principe d'antagonisme et la logique de l'énergie - Prolégomènes à une science de la contradiction*. Paris: Hermann & Cie.

Nicolescu, Basarab. 1985. *Nous, la particule et le monde*. Paris: Le Mail.

Nicolescu, Basarab. 2002. *Manifesto of Transdisciplinarity*, trans. Karen-Claire Voss. New York: State University of New York (SUNY) Press.

Nicolescu, Basarab. 2004. "Toward a Methodological Foundation of the Dialogue Between the Technoscientificand Spiritual Cultures". In *Differentiation and Integration of Worldviews*, edited by Liubava Moreva, 139-152. Sankt Petersburg: Eidos.

Nicolescu, Basarab. 2007. "Transdisciplinarity as Methodological Framework for Going beyond the Science and Religion Debate". *Transdisciplinarity in Science and Religion* 2: 35-60.

Nicolescu, Basarab. 2014. *From Modernity to Cosmodernity — Science, Culture, and Spirituality*. New York: State University of New York (SUNY) Press.

Piaget, Jean. 1972. « L'épistémologie des relations interdisciplinaires ». In *L'interdisciplinarité — Problèmes d'enseignement et de recherche*, edited by L. Apostel, G. Berger, A. Briggs and G. Michaud, 131-144. Paris : Centre pour la Recherche et l'Innovation dans l'Enseignement, Organisation de Coopération et de développement économique.

Chapter 10

A New Perspective on the Existence and Non-existence

Tianqi Wu

Xi'an Jiaotong University Humanities and Social Sciences College,
Xi'an 710049, China
wnkun@mail.xjtu.edu.cn

The existence is one of the ultimate concepts in the studies of western philosophy. Almost all well-known philosophers in history had their own understandings of this concept. As a new philosophical form in new era, the philosophy of information states that philosophy of information and information science should develop together. The existence in philosophy needs to be redefined. The segmentation of existential field should be the first step to tackle with the issue of existence and non-existence. In the view of the philosophy of information, there are four levels of the existence: A. objective direct existence, B. objective indirect existence, C. subjective for-itself existence and D. subjective regenerated existence. The existential levels of a certain thing cover four levels in part or in its totality. Consequently, the non-existence, as the opposite concept of the existence, has also changed. The existence and non-existence can be transformed into each other, with five properties in the process, those are: continuity, developmental feature, contingency, retrospective feature and predictability.

Keywords: Existence; non-existence; philosophy of information; level; transform.

As the existence is one of the ultimate concepts in the studies of western philosophy, information ontology proposed by Wu Kun begins with the segmentation of the existential field. The development of information science and philosophy of information (PI) present the new view of the composition of existential field and the complexity of human beings' ways of understanding. This new classification and interpretation of the existence has fundamentally changed the scope and connotation of the existence, and subsequently altered that of the non-existence.

1. SEGMENTATION OF THE EXISTENTIAL FIELD IN THE PHILOSOPHY OF INFORMATION

The philosophy of information (PI) highlights the question of existence from basic philosophical issues, seeks the relationship between mind and matter, and determines the scope of existence to explain and understand the world in light of information. [Wu Kun, 2011] The philosophy of information considers that science and philosophy are in common development and progress by mutually mapping, internal integrating as each other's reference and reflection. Scientific discoveries are bound to arouse reflection in philosophy, while new ideas and approaches in philosophy can also be reflected in science. If necessary, philosophy can also provide insight to new ways of scientific research and be examined by science at the same time. The re-discovery of information in science domain offers the third basic property of the world, the information, different from the matter and energy. With this new view, the philosophy of information interprets and understands, in a brand new way, the composition of existence and human being's way of understanding by applying the complexity theory, so as to break the monotony of subject-object dualism to explain the world as before.

Western philosophers and scientists have made effort for the unity of philosophy and science. Dainis Zeps proposed to interpret the concept of time and space of idealistic philosophy in light of contemporary physics. Firstly, he states several reasons that the studies of philosophy and science should not be separated:

1) *The mind and the objective world is the same or, at least, by no way can be separated one from another;*
2) *Space and time, actually being constructs of mind, are more psychological notions than physical or, at least, by no discernable way can be classified as distinctly belonging to one or another;*

3) *We see only with the mind, visional seeing being for scientific inquire far too deceiving, i.e. visional seeing in no way may be used as instrument for scientific inquire;*
   and
4) *Universe globally is alive even if life forms eventually may as if originate from "nonalive" matter if considered immoderately locally.* [Dainis Zeps, 2010]

Generally speaking, though with the expansion and development of the world domain and level that scientific research can reach, the known world is still a small part of the real universe. Science needs the philosophy to provide more diversified insights and assumptions, and philosophical assumptions, in turn, need empirical practice of science and technology to prove them and put them into use; thus, the two complement each other.

The information in PI, different from its narrow definition in applied science, is a generalized concept of unreality as the opposite of reality. We can illustrate this by the following example.

You may say that it is the same "person" of one man and the image on his selfie, but clearly it's not true. The former one is a true person, whereas the latter one is only an image similar to his figure, the outcome of optical effect. The photo simply mimics the same optical image for our naked eyes. The man is a reality, while the photo is only an image on the film and cannot be equated to the man himself. The content and characteristics of an object's reflection are clearly not the equivalent to itself, or to the reflection itself. The content of photo is objective, and such content delivered by the photo is a new existential field, that is objective unreality.

According to description of PI proposed by Wu Kun, *objective unreality is the general term of the content of reaction (similar to reflection) among objects. In objective world, the universal exiting "traces" to reflect and construct all the relations among objects are the given coding structure to store the content of various kinds of relations. In this particular sense, we point out that the existing way of objective unreality is entirely different from that of objective reality representing the material world.* [Wu Kun, 2005] But we shouldn't simply regard information as reaction or reflection. Wu, in his work "Philosophy of Information", emphasized for many times that object itself expects no pre-existing recipient. [Wu Kun, 2013]

The segmentation of existential world in PI is as below (Figure 1).

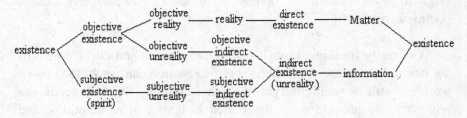

Figure 1. Segmentation diagram of the existential field (1986, Wu Kun) [Wu Kun, 2005].

If objective reality is the term for existence of material world, then the corresponding term of indirect existence can refer to the existence of information world. Based on this, a new outlook on existence is established that the world is unified on the basis of material with dual existence of material and information (direct existence and indirect existence).

2. THE LEVELS OF EXISTENCE

According to the new segmentation of existential field, existence can be, in a simple way, classified into three levels: direct existence, objective indirect existence and subjective existence. From the perspective that the essence of subjective existence is subjective information, subjective existence can be further divided into two categories, for-itself information (grasped by subject) and regenerated information (created by subject), or subjective for-itself existence and subjective regenerated existence respectively. Therefore, we can summarize as four levels of existence:

A. Objective direct existence (ODE),

B. Objective indirect existence (OIE),

C. Subjective for-itself existence (SFE), and

D. Subjective regenerated existence (SRE).

A complete object, with subjective involvement, should have these four existential levels. Thereinafter goes the discussion of their meanings. ODE and OIE are the basic existing forms of general things. Without subjective involvement of intelligent beings, they are the only two forms in the world, which could not be known or understood in any way. Nature moves and develops in accordance with its own rules and its very nature. If we admit the eternal existence of the world itself, we must admit that both the objective matter and information are the eternal existing forms of the world; they mutually formulate and transform, complement each other, eternally move and change its specific shape at any time. Nature evolves with the outcome of the formation of life, and then to the intelligent beings.

As intelligent beings, human beings firstly take a look on Nature, and then go to know, understand and change Nature. New existential form comes into being in the mind of human beings on behalf of all intelligent beings, and that is the subjective existence. Subjective existence presents with two levels, SFE and SRE. *The content of SFE is for-itself information, a primary existence of the subjective indirect existence, and also the informational state of in-itself information directly grasp by subject.* [Wu Kun, 2005] It is, in effect, a reflective information of the biological nervous system, and a nerve reflection of the organism to the eternal movement and changes of objective existence. This specific form of reflection select, change and reconstruct information with the processing of biological structures and certain cognition approaches as intermediary; but the information in this level, to its essence, doesn't experience any intentional involvement of subject. It is only the existence grasped by biological subject's sensation and consciousness. The outside world we studied as materialists is corresponding to the objective existence, but doesn't equate to; because phenomena and experience based on our sensation are for-self information within the scope of SFE field. We deduce the ODE by our feelings of for-itself existence in the process where OIE acts as intermediary. The intermediary can only provide us with one or some levels of objective existence in altered specific form. These levels could only be parts of the objective existence rather than the whole. In other words, different existential levels can only share the same state instead of the same structure. That is why these existential levels shouldn't be mixed up.

The last existential level is SRE, of which the content is the regenerated information. In PI, *regenerated information is defined as the higher level of subjective indirect existence, the subject's creative processing of information, and its basic forms are concept-phenomenon information and symbol information. The former one is new images created by human minds, while the latter is the information-representing code created by human minds.* [Wu Kun, 2005] This classification is based on the two innovative ways of thinking of human beings, namely the thinking in terms of image and abstract thinking. This existential level is unique to higher intelligent beings. It is the outcome of processing and reconstructing sensible information by intelligence and wisdom, and a special existential form created by human minds.

Let's take an apple for example. The apple on the desk is an objective reality; this is the objective direct existence of the apple. By radiation or reflection of various particles and wave field, the apple displays its difference on the mode of its special field distribution, or reflects itself in certain outside objects, like the water or mirror; and this is the demonstration of the apple's objective information, i.e. its OIE. When these particles and wave field carrying the apple's difference interact with our sensory organs, our mind, by certain operation of the nervous system, creates the corresponding information, such as its size, shape, color, smell, hardness and temperature. We can transform these subjective information to long-term or short-term memory by internal process; and the subjective display and memory of the apple is the subjective for-itself information, namely the SFE. Then, we can build up a general abstract mode of apple via internal processing of all apples in our memories, such as comparing, classifying and comprehensive thinking; and thus our minds create concept-phenomenon information. We can also use a symbol to represent this concept-image of SRE, such as Pingguo in Chinese pinyin, or apple in English alphabets; we can draw a picture of an apple, carve it into a sculpture and etc. All these words, pictures and sculptures are the apple's symbol information.

The concept-image information and symbol information is created by the subject, that is to say, its subjective regenerated existence.

From the above example, there are four existential levels of an apple. The apple of ODE: it is the basic existential level, on which the other three levels are based; the apple of OIE: it has characteristics of multiple layers and displays its own statue; the apple of SFE: it is the objective indirect existence grasped by subject, the window of intelligent beings to understand the world, and the basic raw materials of the creation of SRE; and the apple of SRE: it is the information state of subjective creativity, and processed subjective for-itself existence in the mind.

3. EXISTENCE AND NON-EXISTENCE

Since PI has determined the paradigm of existence which compromises of two parts, material and information (including mind), a new issue comes into being, that is how to define the non-existence as the opposite to existence.

Parmenides firstly put forward the concept of existence. He stated that existence is timeless, uniform, necessary and unchanging and essentially denied the possible existence of a void, which he identified it with nothing. And he also went to prove opposite characteristics of existence and non-existence repeatedly. He believed that non-existence is inconceivable, so cannot be put into words. In fact, his definition of non-existence is not the absolute nothingness. He considered all reflection/images in minds and description by words didn't exist; only the real world behind the images is true existence. So in this sense, Parmenides' existence meant the existing objects, things outside the mind. [Dunhua Zhao, 2001]The opposition of mind/spirit against existence, the long-time traditional thought of western philosophy, has born great influence on western philosophy as followed.

In eastern philosophy, such as Taoism, the concepts of "Tao" and "Wu" don't mean absolutely nothing either. Laozi illustrated the relation of Tao and Wu that Tao is beyond description, and easily confused as nothing; its shape is shapeless; its appearance is that of nothing; we cannot see it, hear it or touch it; and we cannot track it down.

[Wang Bi, 2001] Although he talked a lot about how Tao is difficult to understand, he never denied its existence. He confirmed Tao as an independent but inclusive existence, the highest level of existence, which could be determined and proven. It is the mankind who can't recognize the Tao, but it is also the mankind that can define and prove the Tao. In the book of Tao Te Ching, Laozi regarded these very people as sages, who could bring their understanding and experience of the Tao into daily life to guide human being's cognition and behaviors. [Wang Bi, 2001]

Furthermore, Buddhist's "emptiness" doesn't mean absolutely nothing either. Theravada Buddhism put forward that man is composed of skandhas (five aggregates): forms, feelings, perceptions, impulses and consciousness, so does the world. The essence of both human and the world is emptiness. It is derived from the opposite to various changes in the world, avoid of the false images of secular understandings, and manifests that everything is empty. This notion is a perception of the changes and complexity of the world in a passive way. After the introduction of Buddhism to China, it borrow ideas from Taoism to explain the emptiness, and then give dialectical and assimilated explanation among the opposite concepts, such as form and the void, etc. This is the Middle Way or Central Path often mentioned in Buddhism which advocates form does not differ from the void, and the void does not differ from the form; form is the void, and the void is form. This thought about emptiness denies movement and change; however, the eternal movement and change are actually the essence of the world.

Hegel's thought about existence and non-existence was originated from Parmenides, Taoism and Buddhism. However, in order to provide the basis for his notion of pure being, Hegel came up with the concept of pure being and pure non-being. Pure being is inconceivable. [Hegel, 2001]Pure non-being is similar to the being. Then he unified these two concepts and "the truth of being and non-being come in to inter-beings. [Hegel, 2001]His very act of combing two concepts contributed nothing but the proposition itself. And obviously, the aforementioned concepts related to existence and non-existence are not the pure being or non-being.

The pure being should include all the entities in the whole world, and non-existence should be absolute emptiness. Parmenides once mentioned that non-existence was inconceivable and also was beyond description. However, at the time when he brought about the word of non-existence, he was able to offer a clear definition, that is nothing or void. So, at least, non-existence as a notion can be understood and expressed. The definition exists. As it is the non existence, so all should share no differences and contain no content. But it can be known, and even be classified, but there is nothing under the classification. The definition of non-existence and the classification belong to the existential field of information.

This is actually a common case. For example, the word "apple" belongs to the category of information; it sums up the characteristics of material apple. There are also many examples of definitions with no content, like mythological character Zeus. Many actors play this role but Zeus maintains a concept in informational level with no respective material entity. In other words, the ODE and OIE of these very definitions, if any, belong to the field of non existence (of course this is from an atheist view), like examples of moon man, ether, perpetual motion machine and so on.

In mathematics, the issue of non-existence is the issue of zero and empty set. M.S. El Naschie mentioned in his work that Menger-Urysohn empty set theory is extended from the empty set. [M.S. El Naschie, 2004] Zero contains nothing and at the same time belongs to the category of infinity; and it is its non-content that makes it truly infinite. In my paper "Some thinking on the concept of 'infinity' of Anaximander", I have conducted the comparative study of the "infinity" concept of Anaximander and non-existence.

As mentioned in Naschie's another paper, he extended the empty set dim $d_{nu} = -1$ to the completely empty set dim $d_{MU} = -\infty$. [M.S. El Naschie, 2009] This extension is an mathematical attempt to build a bridge between zero and infinity. Mathematical zero is probably the closest concept to non-existence, and everything except zero is existent. The content of empty set is zero, so all the empty sets belong to non-existence. But as the word of non-existence, words like "zero", "empty set", "Wu" themselves, indicating their existential field, belong to the existence.

In the "Being and Nothingness" of Sartre, he described the embedding of nothingness in the being is like a worm inside an apple. [M.S. El Naschie, 2011] There were a lot of discussion of nothingness or non-existence embedded issue, as mentioned in "Being and Almost Nothingness" of Kris Mc Daniel, such as continuity, integrity of being and the "hole" in the being, all these problems indicate the mutual relation between existence and non-existence. [Kris Mc Daniel, 2010] If compare the non-existence to an embedded hole in an apple, we shall compare existence to a floating island in the ocean of the non-existence, changing its position and form at any time with the surrounding of endless sea. So, the author prefers the description that the non-existence surrounds existence, instead of considering non-existence is embedded in existence (Figures 2 and 3).

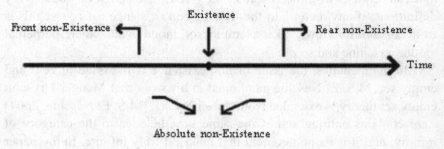

Figure 2. Diagram of existence and non-existence.

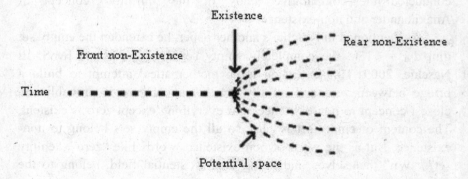

Figure 3. Diagram of existence and non-existence.

As shown in Figure 2, existence is a moving node in time axis, and the past route and route to go through all belong to non-existence, as well as all the other space outside the time axis. This figure is drawn in order to better describe the position of absolute non-existence, and to present a clear relationship among time, pre non-existence, post non-existence and absolute non-existence. In fact, the post non-existence doesn't need to follow one certain way, so that a more accurate illustration is shown as Figure 3. The post non-existence should be in an unfolded space with various possibilities, indicating all the chances existence may develop as time passing by. The space outside all the possibilities of post non-existence should belong to the absolute non-existence.

In the sense of time, past time and future time all fall into the category of non-existence, so does the existence; existence of the past and future belong to the non-existence, which are indicated with dot lines in time axis. The true existence is the very spot on the time axis, and it changes along the axis. So we can see that existence changes endlessly along with time and there is no eternal existence.

The past time and existence are pre non-existence, which include all possibilities of evolvement in the past. But several levels of past substantial existence may retain behind, and they may be decided by several properties along the transformation. For the transformation between pre non-existence and existence, it mainly refers to the continuity and retrospective feature, which will be covered in next chapter.

There exists multi-route possible space in the evolving process of existence. This idea, firstly proposed by self-organization theory, is about possible space, random selection and emergence in the process of self-organization. There also concerns the transformation of existence and non-existence. Existence evolves to the present, and all possible options afterwards, whether the existence choose or not, pertain to the non-existence. Once the selection made, all the other possibilities fall into the category of pre non-existence.

The last category is absolute non-existence, which means the absolute impossibility on the time axis.

Existence is depended on the time, and issues related to time are both the study object of science and philosophy. However, because time bears distinctive characteristic of process and uncertainties, which is contrary to the certainty and uniqueness which human pursue continuously. Then, what is this uniqueness that we have always pursued? Is it the nature of human existence or just our wishful thinking? Jan Baars mentioned that because of the zealous urge for certainties, human has only paid attention to the two points, birth and death, instead of the whole process of life, growing and aging, which is actually the most important part. That is the reason why there are so little studies about aging and senior group [Jan Baars, 2010]. Actually, the existence comes forth with the flow of time, which means the process of existence coming into being is the most vital thing. Heidegger also stated that knowing birth and death, it seems like one person's whole life, but all events of birth and death just help us to think about every day of the present, that is "now" [Ruth Irwin, 2010].

4. SEVERAL PROPERTIES OF THE TRANSFORMATION OF EXISTENCE AND NON-EXISTENCE

During the process of transformation, there are five properties worth our attention; they are continuity, developmental feature, contingency, retrospective feature and predictability.

1. Continuity: The continuity is the foundational feature of existence so that existence can maintain a steady characteristics and structure in a relatively stable state for certain length in the time stream. But the time length of continuity varies in a traumatic way, from picosecond (10^{-12} seconds) of a b quark (propelled by particle accelerator) before decay to over billions of years of stars' lifespan. No matter the time length, the lifespan of every existent is only certain period of time for it to stay comparatively stable. As there is a lifespan, there is the change; actually existence always changes with time. Every true existence is the present moment. But it doesn't mean that existent changes with every second, because though existents only exist for the present, it changes but stays relatively stable existing pattern in certain period of time due to the continuity. We can say the I in the past am myself, the I in the future am also myself, but only I at present is the real and true existence, different from the same me at any time, whereas the past or future me only a continuous part of the present me. I cannot become the past me, or to catch the future me in advance, only the present me is the most real one, the true existence itself. This way of description reminds me of Heidegger's notion of Dasein, that "*Dasein is unfold its exist at living.*" [Heidegger, 2010]

2. Developmental feature: The developmental feature of existence is decided by the movement and evolution law of the whole world, and it is the basis of the retrospective feature and predictability. Continuity decides that every existent has the position on the timeline; but as existent is always restricted by its lifespan, ultimately, it will go to annihilation (or change into other existent). Mass quality and energy transform from one existent to another existent or to quality-energy form, restricted by the external environment or the internal structure. The second law of thermodynamics describes the development of object with environment in a synchronized way. According to one standard version of big bang theory, if the density in the universe we inhabit were equal to the critical density, the expansion would slow down and stop because the pull of the gravity, but the gravity is not strong enough to cause collapse again, so the universe stay in the heat death state, where all particles are evenly distributed of all existents and information. Alternatively, if the mass density of the universe were greater than the critical density, the universe would reach a maximum size, and begin to collapse again, then to black holes in the end, even to the singularity; all existence and information are dead and there would be no independent existents or information. It is the absolute non-existence, or the emptiness, according to Hawking's theory. But what is it in singularity? This expects no person to answer. Some theories deem that cosmos wouldn't reach the true singularity, because in certain extreme state before singularity, the cosmos will explode again and begin to expand. In this way, the universe is a circular cosmos, where substance and information will be in movement and transformation eternally, no absolute ending or annihilation. If true, it will fit the scenario of eternal material proposed by materialism, which at the same time, denies the creation of the God.

It is the developmental feature that determines the state and evolving of existents. According to cosmological laws and principles, existents progress in a relatively stable way along with time. But the developmental feature is not absolutely necessary or mechanical; all evolving development enjoys certain level of freedom, and the freedom is the contingency.

3. Contingency: Contingency coexists with developmental feature. The manifestation of freedom in the process of development refers to the possible space of post non-existence as shown in Figure 3. Thus, contingency could become possibility, and it doesn't follow the evolving rules of the universe, rather, it is the fluctuation in the process. Self-organization theory puts that the direction of development has sensitive dependence on initial conditions, that is to say, a very small change of initial conditions would create a significantly different outcome. It is initially found on the data of weather model in computer, so is named as butterfly effect.[a] Contingency brings about randomness, which could be affected by outside environment or the free perturbation inside, namely the external randomness and inherent randomness. Because all existents in the universe are open and interactive systems, there are no absolutely isolated existents. The experiments conducted in lab are under ideal conditions without any disturbance, so lots of experiments with inevitable outcome are not reliable under natural circumstance. Nevertheless, contingency is restricted by evolving laws. Even though existence has many options to develop, all its choices remain in the space of possibilities; there is no way to develop in the field of non-existence. In the end, all existence will choose among all possibilities, and develop

---

[a] Edward Lorenz coined this term, named after the shape of attracters in his weather model on computer. The point is that a small change in parameter inputting to computer program can result in large differences. The metaphorical example comes into being that minor perturbation such as the flapping of the wings of a distant butterfly several weeks could influenced the weather of another place.

into next level along the time axis. That makes the predictability mentioned after more uncertain.

4. Retrospective feature: Because of the continuity and developmental feature, the existence has the retrospective feature, which is shown in the way of information. As we can retrospect the development of existents, the evolving laws of the universe can be summarized and understood. Passing time is the history of existents, and parts of its existence remains in the structure and process of present existence in the form of information, this is the OIE with ODE as its carrier. That is also why PI considers all objects are both substance and information, the unified form of subjective existence and objective existence. Cognitive subject could take part of the whole information of the past and record/recognize them as history, summarize the rules and theories. Once extracted, analyzed and summarized by human minds, the existence levels of SFE and SRE come into being. Cognitive subject's memory is recorded from history, and actually, major parts of human being's memory belong to SFE and SRE, and lots of ODE and OIE turn into pre non-existence. When we read a man's autobiography, his life story looks vivid and seemingly true, but those are only the subjective regenerated existence in our mind. Our understanding of him is only a small fraction of the true himself, even we couldn't call it ODE or OIE; it's just a figure we created for ourselves. The existence of the author had become the pre non-existence; we couldn't conceive him merely from parts of his thoughts. Non-existence is beyond speaking. When you made an example, the example itself is an existent, but only a regenerated thought, not even the object you are mean to describe. How are you able to talk about the objects of non-existence?

5. Predictability: All individual with subjective consciousness could make prediction based on the present existence by applying his/her intelligence and life experience before the transformation of existence and non-existence. But as mentioned before, because of the contingency, prediction could be inaccurate. And most often, it can only predict general scope; this is true especially in the case of complicated issues. It is impossible to make any prediction by the chaos model with so many variables. The simplest example of prediction is the falling of an apple; even many animals have this ability, which doesn't require complex theory and most of it are the summary of life experience and cause-effect principle. We can also have many complex examples, like weather forecast, which is basically just guessing nowadays. Since cognitive subjects have subjective initiatives, because they are able to make certain prediction of the transformation of existence, thus they can change the world according to natural laws and physics principles. The human society is build on the basis of such subjective initiatives, and there is no way that humanized nature could come into existence without the natural evolution of intelligent beings. Human existences have changed the direction of development of many existents and make many post non-existence become existence, like farm land, tools, road and house, etc.

References

Wu Kun. (2011). Fundamental questions of philosophy with the fundamental shift of philosophy, *Hebei Academic Journal* 4, pp. 11-21 (in Chinese).

Dainis Zeps. (2010). Cognitum hypothesis & cognitum consciousness: how time and space conception of idealistic philosophy is supported by contemporary physics, *Journal of Consciousness Exploration & Research*, 1, pp. 5-15

Wu Kun. (2005). *The Philosophy of Information, Theory, System and Method*, Beijing: the Commercial Press (in Chinese).

Wu Kun. (2013). Segmentation in the field of existence and the significance of the "new philosophy revolution" of the philosophy of information, *The Journal of Humanities*, 5, pp. 1-6 (in Chinese).

Dunhua Zhao. (2001). *New Modern Western Philosophy*, Beijing: Peking University Press (in Chinese).

Wang Bi. (2011). *The Note of Lao tze*, Beijing: Zhong Hua Press (in Chinese).

Hegel. (2009). *Logic (Volume 1)*, Translation by Yang Yizhi, Beijing: The Commercial Press (in Chinese).

M.S. El Naschie. (2004). A review of E-infinity theory and the mass spectrum of high energy particle physics, *Chaos, Solitons & Fractals*, 19, pp. 209-236.

M.S. El Naschie. (2009). The theory of Cantorian spacetime and high energy particle physics (an informal review), *Chaos, Solitons & Fractals*, 41, pp. 2635-2646.

M.S. El Naschie. (2011). On the philosophy of existence and nothingness in fundamental physics, *Chaos, Solitons & Fractals*, 1, pp. 4-5.

Kris Mc Daniel. (2010). Existence and almost nothingness, *NOUS*, 44(4), pp. 628-649.

Jan Baars. (2010). *Philosophy of Aging, Time, and Finitude. A Guide to Humanistic Studies in Aging: What Does it Mean to Grow Old?* Baltimore: Johns Hopkins University Press, pp. 105-120.

Ruth Irwin. (2010). Climate change and Heidegger's philosophy of science, *Essays in Philosophy*, 11, pp. 16-30.

Heidegger. (2006). *Being and Time*. Translation by Cen Jiaying, Beijing: Sanlian Bookstore Press (in Chinese).

Part III

Applications of Information

Chapter 11

Information and the Evolution
of Human Communication

Manuel Bohn

Department of Developmental and Comparative Psychology
Max Planck Institute for Evolutionary Anthropology
Deutscher Platz 6, 04103 Leipzig, Germany
manuel_bohn@eva.mpg.de

Animals communicate by exchanging signals that contain information. The type and amount of information contained in a signal is restricted and shaped by long lasting evolutionary processes. In the course of human evolution, the emergence of a special set of cognitive abilities and social motivations changed the way in which information is transmitted by a given signal. First, the interpretation of a signal depends on whether it is used with the intention to provide information. Second, humans expect signals to be cooperatively intended and therefore expect them to provide relevant and useful information. Finally, the signal is interpreted in the light of the facts and beliefs that are shared between the interlocutors. In this chapter I will argue that these changes enabled humans to flexibly create and understand signals in unprecedented ways. This in turn changed the way that information was transmitted across individuals and generations.

Keywords: Communication; evolution; social cognition; cooperation.

1. Animal Communication

All animals that interact socially with one another communicate with one another. Very broadly speaking, communication could be defined as the exchange of information via signals. The signal itself is some physical or chemical entity that is emitted by the sender and detected by the receiver. The information carried by the signal is determined by what the signal indicates about a certain state of affairs to the receiver (Dretske, 1988). For example, if a honeybee communicates to her hive mates the location of food by dancing, the specifics of how she moves her body indicate to the other bees where the food is located and how far it is away (Gould and Gould, 1988). A central question is, of course, how this signal comes to bear this information. A short but nevertheless meaningful answer is that natural selection shaped the behavior of bees so that signalers would dance in the direction of the food source when returning to the hive and receivers would search in the indicated direction after seeing another bee dancing. Bees that behaved like this were evolutionary more successful and therefore the behavior spread.

This description of communication contains no assumptions about the psychological implementation of the relevant variables within the interacting individuals. Is the signal produced intentionally? Does the sender intend to provide information to the receiver? Is the receiver expecting any kind of information from the sender? While these questions might be intriguing from a philosophical point of view, the answers to them are not relevant for the exchange of information. The information provided by the signal is the same whether it is produced in a reflexive or intentional way. Why? Because the information is a property of the signal itself. Receivers can directly perceive the information when they observe the signaler dancing and no further inference is required. Therefore, whether the signaler dances with or without the intention to inform does not change the information provided for the receiver. In a similar way, whether the signaler expects the receiver to provide information or not does not change the information in the signal. This pattern applies not only to bees but also to most other forms of communication in the animal kingdom like the roaring of deer, barking of dogs or singing of birds (Scott-Phillips, 2015).

2. Human Communication

Human communication is quite different. The information contained in a signal (a word, a gesture, a letter, etc.) is not just a property of the signal itself; it is a function of the psychological states within the individuals who engage in the interaction. Take for example a simple pointing gesture. The physical properties of the signal involve an outstretched index finger pointing in a certain direction. First of all, if this signal is produced unintentionally, as for example when you see that I press my index fingers against my temples while concentrating, it provides no information at all. Furthermore, if the signal is produced without the intention to inform someone else, it also fails to transmit information.

This would be the case when you see how I intentionally hit the return key on my keyboard. Next, the signal might be intended to transmit information but fail to do so if the receiver does not recognize that the sender intends to communicate something with it. If you see me standing in front of a poster with my index finger touching a part of it you will probably think that I use my finger to focus my attention not that I'm trying to inform you about something. What is missing in this case is that I produce the signal with the intention that you recognize that I produced this signal in order to inform you. One intention has to be embedded within another. Consider the same situation in front of the poster but this time I openly look at you while pointing at the poster. Now, if you recognize that I produce the signal *for you* and not someone else, we have actually entered a meaningful communicative interaction (Grice, 1989, Sperber and Wilson, 2001, Tomasello, 2008, Clark, 1996, Scott-Phillips, 2015). However this is still not enough to specify the information that is transmitted by the signal. It is unclear whether the point is directed at the color of the poster, a specific word on it or the fact that there is a poster at all (Wittgenstein, 1953). To specify the intended information, let's say the fact that there is a poster at all, you have to remember that we were searching for that poster all morning and furthermore you have to expect that the fact that I remember this is the reason that I point at the poster. Thus, the information of the signal is specified by our shared common ground, that is the facts and beliefs about the world that we know we share (Clark, 1996). Importantly, and this is to come back to the last one of the questions posed above, you have to expect me to provide you with information that is relevant to you (Sperber and Wilson, 2001). As we have seen, my gesture is utterly underdetermined and it requires considerable inference on your side to recover the intended information. In order to limit the range of possible inferences, receivers expect that senders choose their signals so that they are easily interpretable. This requires both of us to enter the exchange with a fundamentally cooperative attitude towards one another (Grice, 1989, Tomasello, 2008). I signal in a way that I think is easy for you to understand within our common ground and you expect my signal to be designed that way.

The psychological structure described here is not a peculiarity of pointing gestures but it applies to all forms of human communication including language (Clark, 1996). Cases in point are deictic expressions like "this" and "there". The object or state of affairs that is indicated with such an expression depends on who issues them to whom under which circumstances. Nouns such as "dog" or "house" seem to be more constraint in what they can be used to indicate. However, what is indicated with them still requires a considerable amount of inference. The physical object that is indicated by "book" in "Can you give me the book back?" depends on who is talking to whom. Two people can refer to completely different objects even if they utter the same sentence in the same context. For example, in a library person A returns a copy of *The Man Without Qualities* and B returns a copy of *Don Quixote*. Now, depending on who returns to the counter and asks to have the book back, the librarian will interpret it as referring to a different physical entity. The previous interaction between the librarian and that person was about a specific book and "the book" could therefore only be the one that is now part of their common ground.

So, to sum up, human communication involves three components that change the way information is transmitted from the sender to the receiver. First, the production of the signal has to be under intentional control of the sender. Second, the signal has to be produced openly with the intention to provide information and it has to be recognized as intended that way. That is, senders use signals to change the mental states of receivers and receivers' mental states change because they recognize that the corresponding mental states of the senders. Human communication therefore requires a sophisticated insight into the mental live of others. Third, the signal has to be cooperatively intended and embedded in the common ground shared by the sender and the receiver.

3. Information in Human Communication

Now we can look at how this form of communication changed the way information is transmitted from the sender to the receiver.

In contrast with most forms of animal communication as described above, the information that is transmitted is not a property of the signal itself. This increases the range and flexibility of human communication tremendously as it allows humans to use one and the same signal to communicate about a myriad of things. Signals can be re-used. Take again a pointing gesture. In a situation in which you are packing your things together to go to work, I can point to your wallet to inform you about the fact that you forgot to put it in your bag. In a different situation in which you are looking for your subway ticket, the same pointing gesture to the wallet can inform you about the fact that I think that the ticket is in your wallet.

We can also use the same signals to communicate about things we have never communicated about before. I could, for example, use the same pointing gesture to point to an unfamiliar plant to ask whether you know anything about it. Applying existing signals to novel circumstances poses a nearly impossible challenge to animal communication systems. For example, a bee could not use the direction that is encoded in a certain dance to inform her hive mates about a source of danger in that direction. This is because the signal itself includes the information that food is located in that direction. It evolved in the context of food acquisition and this is the only context it can be used in. The directionality of the signal cannot be separated from the referent. Bees evolved in a way that they can directly perceive the information. As a result, the transmission of information does not require any inference and cognition but at the same time it is limited to a single context.

Under the right circumstances a signal indicating the direction of danger might well evolve in a bee colony. However, it would take many generations to do so and the new signal would be restricted in its range of application in the same way as the signal informing about a food source. The same constraints do not apply to human communication. Humans can flexibly create novel communicative signals on the spot. For example, I want to inform you about your wallet which is lying on the table behind a vase. In a first attempt, I point to the table. When you look at me in a puzzled way because you don't see it there (the vase is covering it), I can elaborate my signal by moving my index finger around an imaginary vase in front of me thereby iconically depicting the way you have to look to find your wallet. You will understand the signal even though you have never seen it before. This is possible because you expect me to provide you with relevant information given the momentary focus of attention within our shared common ground.

Based on these processes, humans are able to create a potentially unlimited number of signals. Thereby we can transmit any kind of information one could possibly imagine. In contrast, the number of signals that make up the communication system of a given species tend to be rather small compared to humans (Fitch, 2010). Every new signal has to evolve over a long period of time. Furthermore, the kind of information that is transmitted is mostly restricted to evolutionary important topics such as locating food, spotting predators or finding a mate. These topics are directly linked to an individual's fitness and provide the necessary selective pressure for new signals to evolve (Tomasello and Call, 1997).

4. Evolutionary Origins

However, the flexibility of human communication comes at a price. The cognitive processes that enable communication in humans involve intentional control over the production of communicative signals, the representation of others' mental states (intentions, knowledge, beliefs) and the detailed tracking of shared experiences. Furthermore, these cognitive components have to be supplemented by a motivation to behave helpful and cooperative towards others. These abilities and motivations are not widespread in the animal kingdom and, to a large extend, only emerged in the course of human evolution fairly recently (Tomasello, 2014). In order for new cognitive abilities or motivations to evolve they have to solve an adaptive problem. That is, they have to be necessary for survival and not just something nice to have. If survival would be possible without them, individuals who do not posses these abilities would do better because they would not have to pay the additional costs associated with them. It is therefore necessary to specify how the human way of life crucially depends on the presence of the abilities and motivations described above.

A starting point for this analysis should not be us humans but our closest living ancestors, the great apes. The last common ancestor of humans, chimpanzees and bonobos lived only six million years ago. As a result, we should see a large number of similarities between the species, not only in terms of morphology but also in terms of the psychological architecture. After all, the bulk of our evolutionary history is identical. By specifying to what extend our ape cousins also possess the abilities and motivations that are the bedrock of human communication we can further narrow down which aspects of it are uniquely human. For example, if we would find that chimpanzees already possess intentional control over their communicative signaling, the last common ancestor of humans and chimpanzees most likely did so, too. Thus, this ability would have already been present when humans turned onto their unique evolutionary path. In the following sections I will provide a short overview of the cognitive and motivational foundations of great ape communication.

4.1. *Intentional communication in great apes*

There is ample evidence that great apes are intentional communicators. However, the intentional production of their communicative signals is primarily restricted to their gestural signaling. Most of their vocal signals, such as alarm calls or food grunts, are produced in a rather reflexive way as a consequence of emotional arousal (Wheeler and Fischer, 2012, Tomasello, 2008). In contrast, all great ape species, and also some monkey species, use gestures to communicate in an intentional way (Call and Tomasello, 2007, Woodruff and Premack, 1979). This is evident in the fact that they adjust their gesturing to the extent that they reach their communicative goal with it. They persist or elaborate their gesture when their interlocutor does not react in the way that they want him to. For example, in one study, captive chimpanzees were presented with two food options, one of high value and the other of a lower value. Naturally they started gesturing towards the high value food. When the experimenter handed over the requested food, gesturing stopped. However, when the experimenter handed over the low value food instead, chimpanzees not only persisted with but also elaborated their gesturing (Leavens *et al.*, 2005). The same pattern of persistence and elaboration is regularly observed among conspecifics both in captivity and the wild (Hobaiter and Byrne, 2011, Pika *et al.*, 2005, Roberts *et al.*, 2013). Thus, it seems that the intentional production of communicative signals is not unique to humans.

4.2. *Representing other's psychological states in great apes*

Research on great apes' ability to represent others' mental states has a long tradition within comparative psychology (Premack and Woodruff, 1978). Within the last 40 years a considerable number of studies have been conducted in order to specify to what extend great apes understand that others have mental states. Even though the field is far from reaching a definitive conclusion on how to best interpret the available data, there is now a solid body of evidence that suggests that great apes have some insight into the mental life of others (Call and Tomasello, 2008, Hare *et al.*, 2001, Karg *et al.*, 2015, but see Heyes, 2015, Penn and Povinelli, 2007). For example, in a competitive feeding situation subordinate chimpanzees prefer to approach food items that a dominant individual does not know about (Hare *et al.*, 2001). Furthermore, chimpanzees interpreted a human's action differently depending on whether it was performed intentionally and accidentally (Call *et al.*, 2004, Call and Tomasello, 1998). In communicative interactions, great apes adjust their signaling to the attentional state of the receiver. When the receiver is looking away, they either move into her line of sight or use tactile gestures instead (Call and Tomasello, 2007, Liebal *et al.*, 2004). Interestingly, this shows that apes not only use their communicative signals intentionally, but that they also act with the intention that a specific individual recognizes their signal. This could be a sign of the embedding of one intention within another, which I described in section 2 (Moore, 2015).

Nevertheless, great apes seem to be limited in their ability to represent other's mental states. So far, no study has shown that apes understand that others have beliefs (Krachun *et al.*, 2009, Call and Tomasello, 1999, Kaminski *et al.*, 2008). Attributing beliefs to others requires a deeper understanding of their mental live compared to attributing perceptions or knowledge. Ascribing knowledge to you entails that I evaluate a certain state of affairs in the world with regard to whether you also know about it or not. If this state of affairs changes or if I focus on something else, my knowledge about your knowledge is lost. I don't ascribe to you a mental live of your own that is independent of my own in that its content depends on *your* experiences. Ascribing beliefs entails that I think that even when the state of affairs or my own knowledge changes, your knowledge still persists in your mental life until you receive some information that changes it. That is, I understand that your knowledge might be false and that your knowledge might be altered by new information. The latter part is especially important for our analysis of human communication. The target of my communicative act is the alteration of your mental state. In the above example, when I stand in front of the poster and openly point for you, I do so because I know that you lack this information and that by pointing it out for you I can change your knowledge state. Taken together, great apes understand that others have a mental live but they might be limited in their under-standing of how this mental life can be influenced by their own communicative acts.

4.3. *Common ground in great ape communication*

The notion of common ground in human communication has two important aspects. On the one hand, it requires the detailed tracking of what is experienced with whom. This is a prerequisite to assess what information the interlocutor already has and what additional information needs to be included in the signal. On the other hand, it requires that the both interlocutors know that this background information is shared between them. Only if it is mutually assumed that both interlocutors have certain information the intended information can be accurately inferred (Sperber and Wilson, 2001, Clark, 1996). The possible inferences would be limitless otherwise.

Neither of these aspects has been extensively studied in great apes. A notable exception is a recent study that investigated whether great apes adjust their communicative acts to what they have previously experienced with a human (Bohn *et al.*, 2015, 2016). The results suggest that apes adjust their communication to different aspects of the previous interactions such as what the human knows or what she is able to do.

However, they did not integrate these aspects with one another. Whether or not apes represent certain information as shared with someone else has, to my knowledge, not been investigated so far.

To assess the importance of common ground in ape communication despite the lack of experimental evidence, we can look at how apes communicate with one another. Here we see that, among conspecifics, apes mostly use naturally meaningful embodied signals that lack the ambiguity of human signals (Moore, 2013, Tomasello, 2008). Thus, even though it is unclear whether apes are cognitively capable to form common ground with an interlocutor their daily communicative interactions seem not to depend on it.

4.4. *Motivational underpinnings of great ape communication*

In section 2, I argued that in order for human communication to work, both interlocutors have to enter the interaction with a cooperative attitude. A cooperative attitude in this context entails that we both expect one another to provide information that is relevant. Importantly, the information must be relevant within our shared common ground not only to myself. As a consequence, humans use communication not just to request or order things, but also to inform others about things they did not know (Tomasello, 2008).

Communication among apes seems to rest on a different motivational foundation. First of all, apes' communicative acts are almost exclusively imperative (Rivas, 2005, Tomasello, 2008). That is, they use communication to get others to do things. This pattern is illustrated by a study in which apes could inform a human experimenter about the location of a tool that was needed to operate an apparatus (Bullinger *et al.*, 2011). In one condition, the apparatus provided food for the ape. In the other condition it provided food for the human. Apes readily informed the human about the tool when the food was dispensed to them, however, they refrained to do so when the human benefited from obtaining the tool. Furthermore, apes have problems to flexibly use the information that others provide them with. When a human uses a cooperative gesture (e.g. pointing or pantomiming) to inform them about the location of food, apes often struggle to use this information

(Bohn *et al.*, 2016, Herrmann and Tomasello, 2006). This finding is somehow puzzling because apes themselves use pointing to indicate things they want. Furthermore, they even visually follow the direction of the gesture but then fail to use the information provided by it (MacLean and Hare, 2015). A reason for this could be that they do not expect others to communicate cooperatively (Hare and Tomasello, 2004, Tomasello, 2008). Another study looked at whether apes would use communication to coordinate their decisions in a collaborative game in which both participants would benefit from doing so (Duguid *et al.*, 2014). The finding was that, if at all, apes did not inform their partner about what they were planning to do, but only ever communicated with her after they already made their decision. This post-decision communication served to summon the partner to do the same as they did. Thus, apes and human communication seem to be motivated in a different way.

5. Evolution of Uniquely Human Communication

As we have seen in the last section, some important aspects of human communication are also present in great apes. They are therefore most likely evolutionary ancient and were already possessed by the last common ancestor of apes and humans. However, there are also some important differences between apes and humans. As humans, we are exceptionally motivated and cognitively equipped to engage with the mental live of others. Importantly, we do so not only from an observer's point of view, merely tracking what others do and therefore know and believe, but we create a shared mental live with them and design our communicative acts so that they can easily infer our underlying mental states. This requires cognitive abilities for sharing mental states as well as a fundamentally cooperative attitude towards one another (Tomasello, 2014, Tomasello *et al.*, 2005). Therefore, the unique aspects of human communication most likely evolved in an environment in which cooperation among individuals was necessary for survival (Tomasello, 2014). A hypothetical and simplified example would be an environment in which our only food source are tubers that grow under stones that are too heavy for one of us to lift alone. Only if we work together in a coordinated way will we be successful. In this scenario, whether or not I get food depends entirely on whether we manage to cooperate (Tomasello *et al.*, 2012). As a consequence, our chances to survive and reproduce depend on our motivational and cognitive abilities that allow us to successfully cooperate.

First we can look at the motivational consequences of obligate cooperation. If my success depends on your success, it is in my best interest to ensure your success. This allows me to enter our interaction with a fundamentally cooperative attitude towards you without a fear of being exploited. After all, you depend on me the same way as I depend on you and if you try to cheat the whole activity fails and both of us go empty handed. This also enables my cooperative attitude towards you while communicating. Informing you results in a direct benefit to me as it increases the likelihood of success of our cooperative activity. In a similar way, the open advertisement of my mental states is also beneficial under these circumstances as it makes my behavior more predictable to you. The better you can predict what I'm about to do, the better you can adjust your behavior to it. In a competitive environment, a propensity to inform others combined with an open advertisement of my mental states would easily be exploited. As we have seen above, assuming a cooperative partner greatly reduces the potential interpretations of a given signal. If communicative acts would not be used to honestly inform others but to deceive them, these inferential boundaries would no longer apply. For example, if I point to a hole in the ground to inform you about food that is hidden there, our common ground (we are looking for food) determines the information of the signal. In an environment in which communication is used to deceive I would not only be better off to ignore your signal, furthermore, I could not extract any information about the world from it. Just taking the opposite of what the cooperative interpretation of your signal would be would not work because this opposite interpretation would not be specific. If you tell me something is black, I could not infer from it that it is in fact white because the opposite of black is simply non-black. It could be green or yellow or any other color except black. Communication in such an environment would simply be a waste of time and energy.

Second, our need to cooperate has consequences for the way that I represent your mental life. In order to determine which information is relevant for you, I cannot rely on my own perspective on the world. The experiences I make might be different from the ones you make and what is new information differs between us. It is therefore not enough for me to know that you have mental states about certain things in the world, that is, whether or not you perceive something or know about something. My understanding about your mental live would be limited to the part of the world that I'm currently engaged with. To provide you with information that is relevant to you, I have to understand that your perspective might be different from mine (Tomasello and Moll, 2013). As a consequence, my understanding of your mental states is not bound to how I see things but to how you see them. Whatever I experience since you last saw something does not change how *you* think about it. I have to understand that the information you have about the world might not be valid anymore but that it nevertheless persists in your mental life. This allows me to provide you with a relevant update. In a similar way, if I don't understand that your mental life is independent and different from my mental life, I will not assume that you could know more than me and that you could provide me with relevant information. I have to understand that my own information might be false as well. The need to successfully cooperate creates a need to accurately represent your mental life and to view my own mental life as potentially false.

Finally, obligate cooperation is also a fertile ground for common ground. Our activity requires us to coordinate our behavior and that makes it important for both of us to know what information the other one already has and which she lacks. Providing the right information at the right time is absolutely crucial for success. We can further assume that the same kind of information is relevant to us in this situation because we engage in the same cooperative activity with the same goal. This is the basis for representing information not just as known by the respective other but also as shared between us.

Taken together, the psychological processes that enable the flexibility of human communication evolved in order to facilitate cooperation among individuals. This is reflected in the fundamentally cooperative nature of human communication. Once in place, these processes allowed humans to spontaneously create a potentially unlimited number of novel signals that were conventionalized and eventually became a symbolic language (Tomasello, 2008). Conventional linguistic symbols single out a specific aspect of an experiential situation (the same person may be construed as a friend, a women, a mother, etc.) (Tomasello and Rakoczy, 2003). This facilitates communication between individuals who interact less and therefore do not share the necessary common ground to specify this aspect otherwise. This again had profound effects on how humans transmitted information across individuals and generations and enabled news ways of cooperation (Tomasello, 1999, Tomasello, 2014).

6. Conclusion

The way that humans use signals to transmit information among each other is fundamentally different from the way that most animal species do it. Animal signals evolve over long periods of time and can only be used to transmit a very limited amount of information. Humans can flexibly create novel signals and are therefore in no way restricted in what they can communicate about. The foundation of this uniquely human ability is a set of psychological processes that motivate and enable humans to create a shared mental live. These processes evolved in humans to enable them to cope with an environment that required individuals to cooperate in order to survive. Human communication and sociality are inextricably linked.

Acknowledgments

I thank Gregor Stöber for his helpful comments on an earlier version of this paper.

References

BOHN, M., CALL, J. & TOMASELLO, M. 2015. Communication about absent entities in great apes and human infants. *Cognition,* 145, 63-72.

BOHN, M., CALL, J. & TOMASELLO, M. 2016. Comprehension of iconic gestures by chimpanzees and human children. *Journal of Experimental Child Psychology,* 142, 1-17.

BOHN, M., CALL, J. & TOMASELLO, M. 2016. The role of past interactions in great apes' communication about absent entities. *Journal of Comparative Psychology,* 130, 351-357.

BULLINGER, A. F., ZIMMERMANN, F., KAMINSKI, J. & TOMASELLO, M. 2011. Different social motives in the gestural communication of chimpanzees and human children. *Developmental Science,* 14, 58-68.

CALL, J., HARE, B., CARPENTER, M. & TOMASELLO, M. 2004. 'Unwilling' versus 'unable': Chimpanzees' understanding of human intentional action. *Developmental Science,* 7, 488-498.

CALL, J. & TOMASELLO, M. 1998. Distinguishing intentional from accidental actions in orangutans (*Pongo pygmaeus*), chimpanzees (*Pan troglodytes*), and human children (Homo sapiens). *Journal of Comparative Psychology,* 112, 192-206.

CALL, J. & TOMASELLO, M. 1999. A nonverbal false belief task: The performance of children and great apes. *Child Development,* 70, 381-395.

CALL, J. & TOMASELLO, M. 2007. *The Gestural Communication of Apes and Monkeys,* New York, Lawrence Erlbaum Associates.

CALL, J. & TOMASELLO, M. 2008. Does the chimpanzee have a theory of mind? 30 years later. *Trends in Cognitive Sciences,* 12, 187-192.

CLARK, H. H. 1996. *Using Language,* Cambridge, Cambridge University Press.

DRETSKE, F. I. 1988. *Explaining Behavior: Reasons in a World of Causes,* Cambridge, MA, MIT Press.

DUGUID, S., WYMAN, E., BULLINGER, A. F., HERFURTH-MAJSTOROVIC, K. & TOMASELLO, M. 2014. Coordination strategies of chimpanzees and human children in a Stag Hunt game. *Proceedings of the Royal Society B — Biological Sciences,* 281.

FITCH, W. T. 2010. *The Evolution of Language,* Cambridge, MA, Cambridge University Press.

GOULD, J. L. & GOULD, C. G. 1988. *The Honey Bee,* New York, Scientific American Library.

GRICE, H. P. 1989. *Studies in the Way of Words,* Cambridge, MA, Harvard University Press.

HARE, B., CALL, J. & TOMASELLO, M. 2001. Do chimpanzees know what conspecifics know? *Animal Behaviour,* 61, 139–151.

HARE, B. & TOMASELLO, M. 2004. Chimpanzees are more skilful in competitive than in cooperative cognitive tasks. *Animal Behaviour*, 68, 571-581.

HERRMANN, E. & TOMASELLO, M. 2006. Apes' and children's understanding of cooperative and competitive motives in a communicative situation. *Developmental Science*, 9, 518-529.

HEYES, C. 2015. Animal mindreading: What's the problem? *Psychonomic Bulletin & Review*, 22, 313-327.

HOBAITER, C. & BYRNE, R. W. 2011. The gestural repertoire of the wild chimpanzee. *Animal Cognition*, 14, 745-767.

KAMINSKI, J., CALL, J. & TOMASELLO, M. 2008. Chimpanzees know what others know, but not what they believe. *Cognition*, 109, 224-34.

KARG, K., SCHMELZ, M., CALL, J. & TOMASELLO, M. 2015. The goggles experiment: Can chimpanzees use self-experience to infer what a competitor can see? *Animal Behaviour*, 105, 211-221.

KRACHUN, C., CARPENTER, M., CALL, J. & TOMASELLO, M. 2009. A competitive nonverbal false belief task for children and apes. *Developmental Science*, 12, 521-535.

LEAVENS, D. A., RUSSELL, J. L. & HOPKINS, W. D. 2005. Intentionality as measured in the persistence and elaboration of communication by chimpanzees (*Pan troglodytes*). *Child Development*, 76, 291-306.

LIEBAL, K., CALL, J., TOMASELLO, M. & PIKA, S. 2004. To move or not to move: How apes adjust to the attentional state of others. *Interaction Studies*, 5, 199-219.

MACLEAN, E. L. & HARE, B. 2015. Bonobos and chimpanzees exploit helpful but not prohibitive gestures. *Behaviour*, 152, 493-520.

MOORE, R. 2013. Evidence and interpretation in great ape gestural communication. *Humana Mente*, 24, 27-51.

MOORE, R. 2015. Meaning and ostension in great ape gestural communication. *Animal Cognition*, 19, 223-231.

PENN, D. C. & POVINELLI, D. J. 2007. On the lack of evidence that non-human animals possess anything remotely resembling a 'theory of mind'. *Philosophical Transactions of the Royal Society B-Biological Sciences*, 362, 731-744.

PIKA, S., LIEBAL, K., CALL, J. & TOMASELLO, M. 2005. The gestural communication of apes. *Gesture*, 5, 41-56.

PREMACK, D. & WOODRUFF, G. 1978. Does the chimpanzee have a theory of mind. *Behavioral and Brain Sciences*, 1, 515-526.

RIVAS, E. 2005. Recent use of signs by chimpanzees (*Pan troglodytes*) in interactions with humans. *Journal of Comparative Psychology*, 119, 404-417.

ROBERTS, A. I., VICK, S. J. & BUCHANAN-SMITH, H. M. 2013. Communicative intentions in wild chimpanzees: Persistence and elaboration in gestural signalling. *Animal Cognition*, 16, 187-196.

SCOTT-PHILLIPS, T. C. 2015. *Speaking our Minds: Why Human Communication is Different, and How Language Evolved to Make it Special*, New York, NY, Palgrave Macmillan.

SPERBER, D. & WILSON, D. 2001. *Relevance: Communication and cognition*, Cambridge, MA, Blackwell Publishers.

TOMASELLO, M. 1999. *The Cultural Origins of Human Cognition*, Cambridge, MA, Harvard University Press.

TOMASELLO, M. 2008. *Origins of Human Communication*, Cambridge, MA, MIT Press.

TOMASELLO, M. 2014. *A Natural History of Human Thinking*, Cambridge, MA, Harvard University Press.

TOMASELLO, M. & CALL, J. 1997. *Primate Cognition*, New York, NY, Oxford University Press.

TOMASELLO, M., CARPENTER, M., CALL, J., BEHNE, T. & MOLL, H. 2005. Understanding and sharing intentions: The origins of cultural cognition. *Behavioral and Brain Sciences*, 28, 675-691.

TOMASELLO, M., MELIS, A. P., TENNIE, C., WYMAN, E. & HERRMANN, E. 2012. Two key steps in the evolution of human cooperation: The interdependence hypothesis. *Current Anthropology*, 53, 673-692.

TOMASELLO, M. & MOLL, H. 2013. Why don't apes understand false beliefs? *Navigating the Social World: What Infants, Children, and Other Species Can Teach Us*, New York, NY: Oxford University Press; US.

TOMASELLO, M. & RAKOCZY, H. 2003. What makes human cognition unique? From individual to shared to collective intentionality. *Mind & Language*, 18, 121-147.

WHEELER, B. C. & FISCHER, J. 2012. Functionally referential signals: A promising paradigm whose time has passed. *Evolutionary Anthropology*, 21, 195-205.

WITTGENSTEIN, L. 1953. *Philosophical Investigations,* Oxford, B. Blackwell.
WOODRUFF, G. & PREMACK, D. 1979. Intentional communication in the chimpanzee — development of deception. *Cognition,* 7, 333-362.

Chapter 12

Information Processing and Fechner's Problem as a Choice of Arithmetic

Marek Czachor

Katedra Fizyki Teoretycznej i Informatyki Kwantowej
Politechnika Gdańska, 80-952 Gdańsk, Poland
Centrum Leo Apostel (CLEA)
Vrije Universiteit Brussel, 1050 Brussels, Belgium
mczachor@pg.gda.pl

Fechner's law and its modern generalizations can be regarded as manifestations of alternative forms of arithmetic, coexisting at stimulus and sensation levels. The world of sensations may be thus described by a generalization of the standard mathematical calculus.

1. Introduction

Human beings operate like information processing devices. Since the influential book by Fechner on 'elements of psychophysics' (Fechner, 1860) it is known that relations between external stimuli and internal sensations occurring in our brains can be modeled mathematically. The models can be tested experimentally in analogy to, or even by means of physical measurements. Hence the term 'psychophysics', coined by Fechner.

Fechner himself was a physicist but psychophysics in general does not attract attention of modern pure physicists. A notable exception seems the work of Norwich (Norwich, 1993) on information-theoretic foundations of the laws of perception. The fact that formally psychophysics may share some elements with pure physics was intuitively felt by psychologists already in 1930s (Stevens, 1935), who understood that psychological experiments are essentially as operational as quantum measurements (Busch, Grabowski & Lahti, 1995), while 'inner psychophysics' of Fechner is as beyond scientific reach as putative hidden variables in quantum mechanics, or interiors of black holes in general relativity. In this sense the degree of objectivity and repeatibility of results of psychophysical measurements are similar to what one encounters in fundamental physics.

For a pure theoretical physicist the field of psychophysics may be, however, interesting also for other reasons. The goal of the present paper is to look at psychophysics as a non-trivial, theoretical and experimental example of a natural science where a non-Diophantine arithmetic (Burgin, 1997, 2010) plays a prominent role.

Non-Diophantine arithmetic is determined by a function f and its inverse f^{-1} (or, more generally, by two independent functions f and g). The role of f is similar to that played in psychophysics by the 'Fechner function' (Luce & Edwards, 1958). As shown recently (Czachor, 2016), one can reformulate the laws of physics in terms of a non-Diophantine arithmetic and its corresponding non-Diophantine calculus. The formalism found applications in fractal theory (Aerts, Czachor & Kuna, 2016), but what is still missing is the law that determines the form of f.

In this respect, non-Diophantine physics is in a similar situation as psychophysics. We need f, but we also need a fundamental law that determines it. This is why all approaches to psychophysics which try to understand the fundamental and general laws that govern f are so intriguing.

On the other hand, one may hope that an abstract theoretical-physics insight into the meaning of f may lead to some new ideas for experimental psychology. Anyway, this is how psychophysics started on 22 October 1850...

2.   Non-Diophantine Arithmetic and Calculus

Assume the set X is equipped with generalized arithmetic operations (addition $\oplus$, subtraction $\ominus$, multiplication $\odot$, division $\oslash$), defined by (Czachor, 2016)

$$x \oplus y = f^{-1}\big(f(x) + f(y)\big), \tag{1}$$
$$x \ominus y = f^{-1}\big(f(x) - f(y)\big), \tag{2}$$
$$x \odot y = f^{-1}\big(f(x)f(y)\big), \tag{3}$$
$$x \oslash y = f^{-1}\big(f(x)/f(y)\big), \tag{4}$$

where $x, y \in X$, and $f : \mathbb{R} \supset X \rightarrow Y \subset \mathbb{R}$ is a bijection. The set Y is equipped with the 'standard' arithmetic of real numbers: $\pm$, $\cdot$, and $/$.

Neutral elements of addition and multiplication in X are defined by

$$0' = f^{-1}(0), \tag{5}$$
$$1' = f^{-1}(1), \tag{6}$$

since then $0' \oplus x = x$, $1' \odot x = x$, $x \oslash x = 1'$ (for $x \neq 0'$) and $x \ominus x = 0'$ (for any $x \in X$).

One verifies the standard properties: (1) associativity $(x \oplus y) \oplus z = x \oplus (y \oplus z)$, $(x \odot y) \odot z = x \odot (y \odot z)$, (2) commutativity $x \oplus y = y \oplus x$, $x \odot y = y \odot x$, (3) distributivity $(x \oplus y) \odot z = (x \odot z) \oplus (y \odot z)$. This is an example of a non-Diophantine arithmetic in the sense of Burgin (Burgin, 1997, 2010).

The well known Weber–Fechner problem (Baird & Noma, 1978) now can be reformulated as follows: Find a generalized arithmetic such that $(x + kx) \ominus x$ is independent of x. In other words, we have to find f solving

$$(x + kx) \ominus x = f^{-1}\big(f(x + kx) - f(x)\big) = \delta x, \tag{7}$$

with x-independent δx. Acting with f on both sides of (7) we get

$$f(x + kx) - f(x) = f(\delta x) \tag{8}$$

which is the standard psychophysical Abel problem (Luce & Edwards, 1958) for f, with constant Weber fraction $\Delta x / x = k$. The solution is $f(x) = a \ln x + b$, $f^{-1}(x) = e^{(x-b)/a}$, and thus $0' = f^{-1}(0) = e^{-b/a}$, $1' = f^{-1}(1) = e^{(1-b)/a}$. Clearly, $0' \neq 0$ and $1' \neq 1$. This type of difference occurs in physics in the approach of Benioff (Benioff, 2011, 2015) where $f(x) = px$, $p \neq 0$, and $0' = 0$ but $1' = 1/p$.

Let us try to understand the logical structure of (7). We have two real numbers, x and $x' = x + kx$, and we have two ways of subtracting them. $x' \ominus x$ clearly corresponds to the sensation continuum, while $x' - x$ is the 'usual' way of subtracting employed at the stimulus side. From the arithmetic perspective one expects that not only subtraction, but also addition, multiplication and division are perceived in some 'Fechnerian way'. In principle, any form of change can be perceived in a non-Diophantine way.

The idea, when explored in its full generality, leads from non-Diophantine arithmetic to non-Diophantine calculus (Czachor, 2016). In particular, a derivative of a function $A : X \to X$, is naturally defined by

$$\frac{d'A(x)}{d'x} = \lim_{h \to 0'} \big(A(x \oplus h) \ominus A(x)\big) \oslash h. \tag{9}$$

The derivative should not be confused with the 'usual' one, defined for functions $B : Y \to Y$,

$$\frac{dB(y)}{dy} = \lim_{h \to 0} \left(B(y + h) - B(y)\right)/h. \tag{10}$$

An integral is defined in a way that guarantees the two fundamental laws of calculus,

$$\frac{d'}{d'x} \int_a^x A(x') \odot d'x' = A(x), \tag{11}$$

$$\int_a^b \frac{d'A(x')}{d'x'} \odot d'x' = A(b) \ominus A(a). \tag{12}$$

With any $A : X \to X$ one can associate the conjugate map $B = f \circ A \circ f^{-1}$, $B : Y \to Y$. Then (9)–(12) imply

$$\frac{d'A(x)}{d'x} = f^{-1}\left(\frac{dB\big(f(x)\big)}{df(x)}\right), \tag{13}$$

$$\int_a^b A(x) \odot d'x = f^{-1}\left(\int_{f(a)}^{f(b)} B(y) dy\right), \tag{14}$$

as one can directly verify from definitions.

In order to appreciate the difference between $d'/d'x$ and d/dx take $f(x) = x^3$ and let $\sin_f x = f^{-1}\big(\sin f(x)\big) = \sqrt[3]{\sin(x^3)}$. Then

$$\frac{d \sin_f x}{dx} = \frac{x^2 \cos(x^3)}{\sin^{\frac{2}{3}}(x^3)}, \tag{15}$$

whereas

$$\frac{d' \sin_f x}{d'x} = \sqrt[3]{\cos(x^3)} = \cos_f x. \tag{16}$$

The non-Diophantine derivative is easier to compute: One only replaces sin by cos in (16), and neither f nor f^{-1} get differentiated. This is why we do not need any continuity or differentiability assumption about f. In fact, f can be as weird as the Cantor function (Czachor, 2016; Aerts, Czachor & Kuna, 2016). The property may be useful since in the psychophysical theory of numbers (Baird & Noma, 1975; Noma & Baird, 1975; Weissmann, Hollingsworth & Baird, 1975; Baird, 1975a,b) the corresponding psychophysical functions have discontinuous first derivatives, and in principle can be discontinuous themselves.

Moreover, even the simple case of a power function $f(x) = x^q$, $q \neq 1$, leads to non-differentiability at 0 of either f or f^{-1}. Yet, the result (16) shows that this is not a difficulty since neither f nor f^{-1} are differentiated in the course of computing $d'/d'x$. The power function is an important alternative to Fechner's logarithm (Stevens, 1975), similarly to the unification of logarithm and power, derived by Norwich (Norwich, 1993). In the present proof-of-principle analysis we restrict the examples to Fechnerian f.

3. Non-Diophantine Fechnerian Arithmetic Operations

Let us now find the explicit forms of non-Diophantine arithmetic operations corresponding to the Fechnerian case.

3.1. Addition

$$x \oplus y = f^{-1}\big(f(x) + f(y)\big) \tag{17}$$
$$= e^{(f(x)+f(y)-b)/a} \tag{18}$$
$$= e^{(a\ln x+b+a\ln y+b-b)/a} \tag{19}$$
$$= e^{\ln x+b/a+\ln y} \tag{20}$$
$$= xye^{b/a} = xy/0'. \tag{21}$$

In particular,

$$x \oplus 0' = x0'e^{b/a} = xe^{-b/a}e^{b/a} = x. \tag{22}$$

3.2. Subtraction

Subtraction is the only non-Diophantine arithmetic operation that implicitly occurs in the psychophysics literature.

$$x \ominus y = f^{-1}\big(f(x) - f(y)\big) \tag{23}$$
$$= e^{(f(x)-f(y)-b)/a} \tag{24}$$
$$= e^{(a\ln x+b-a\ln y-b-b)/a} \tag{25}$$
$$= e^{\ln x-\ln y-b/a} \tag{26}$$
$$= e^{-b/a}x/y = 0'x/y. \tag{27}$$

In particular,

$$x \ominus x = e^{-b/a}x/x = e^{-b/a} = 0', \tag{28}$$
$$(x + kx) \ominus x = e^{-b/a}(x + kx)/x = e^{-b/a}(1 + k). \tag{29}$$

Assuming that for a single just noticable difference one should find $(x + kx) \ominus x = 1'$ one arrives at

$$e^{-b/a}(1 + k) = 1' = e^{(1-b)/a}, \tag{30}$$

and thus $1 + k = e^{1/a}$, $a = 1/\ln(1 + k)$. This leads to the known form of solution of Abel's equation for the Fechner problem (Luce & Edwards, 1958),

$$f(x) = \frac{\ln x}{\ln(1 + k)} + b, \tag{31}$$

where b is an arbitrary constant.

A negative of x is

$$\ominus x = 0' \ominus x \tag{32}$$

$$= e^{-b/a}0'/x = e^{-2b/a}/x. \tag{33}$$

Let us cross-check,

$$\ominus x \oplus x = (\ominus x)xe^{b/a} \tag{34}$$

$$= (e^{-2b/a}/x)xe^{b/a} \tag{35}$$

$$= e^{-b/a} = 0'. \tag{36}$$

Note that although $x > 0$ in $f(x) = a \ln x + b$, one nevertheless has a well defined negative number $\ominus x = e^{-2b/a}/x$, which is... positive. The apparent paradox disappears if one realizes that we speak of two different types of negativity, defined with respect to two different choices of arithmetic.

3.3. Multiplication

$$x \odot y = f^{-1}\big(f(x)f(y)\big) \tag{37}$$

$$= e^{(f(x)f(y)-b)/a} \tag{38}$$

$$= e^{((a \ln x+b)(a \ln y+b)-b)/a} \tag{39}$$

$$= e^{(a^2 \ln x \ln y+ab \ln x+ab \ln y+b^2-b)/a} \tag{40}$$

$$= e^{a \ln x \ln y+b \ln x+b \ln y+b^2/a-b/a} \tag{41}$$

$$= x^{a \ln y}x^b y^b e^{b(b-1)/a}. \tag{42}$$

In particular

$$x \odot 1' = x^{a \ln e^{(1-b)/a}} x^b e^{b(1-b)/a} e^{b(b-1)/a} \tag{43}$$

$$= x^{a(1-b)/a}x^b = x, \tag{44}$$

$$x \odot 0' = x^{a \ln e^{-b/a}} x^b e^{b(-b)/a} e^{b(b-1)/a} \tag{45}$$

$$= x^{-b}x^b e^{-b/a} = e^{-b/a} = 0'. \tag{46}$$

3.4. Division

$$x \oslash y = f^{-1}\big(f(x)/f(y)\big) \tag{47}$$

$$= e^{(f(x)/f(y)-b)/a} \tag{48}$$

$$= e^{((a\ln x+b)/(a\ln y+b)-b)/a} \tag{49}$$

$$= e^{(\ln x+b/a)/(a\ln y+b)-b/a} \tag{50}$$

$$= e^{\ln x/(a\ln y+b)}e^{(b/a)/(a\ln y+b)}e^{-b/a}. \tag{51}$$

In particular,

$$x \oslash x = e^{(1-b)/a} = 1'. \tag{52}$$

3.5. Multiplication as a repeated addition

Everybody knows that $1 + 1 = 2$, or $2 + 2 = 4$. In non-Diophantine arithmetic these rules hold as well, but in a subtle form. First of all, let us define $n' = f^{-1}(n)$, $n \in \mathbb{N}$. Now,

$$n' \oplus m' = f^{-1}\big(f(n') + f(m')\big) \tag{53}$$

$$= f^{-1}(n + m) = (n + m)' \tag{54}$$

$$n' \odot m' = f^{-1}\big(f(n')f(m')\big) \tag{55}$$

$$= f^{-1}(nm) = (nm)'. \tag{56}$$

Similarly,

$$n' \odot m' = f^{-1}(nm) \tag{57}$$

$$= f^{-1}\big(\underbrace{m + \cdots + m}_{n \text{ times}}\big) \tag{58}$$

$$= f^{-1}\big(\underbrace{f(m') + \cdots + f(m')}_{n \text{ times}}\big) \tag{59}$$

$$= \underbrace{m' \oplus \cdots \oplus m'}_{n \text{ times}}. \tag{60}$$

So, $1' \oplus 1' = 2'$, $2' \oplus 2' = 4' = 2' \odot 2'$. This is how it looks at the internal sensation space. At the stimulus level the calculation looks somewhat different,

$$1' \oplus 1' = e^{(1-b)/a} \oplus e^{(1-b)/a} = e^{(1-b)/a}e^{(1-b)/a}e^{b/a} = e^{(2-b)/a} = 2', \tag{61}$$

$$2' \oplus 2' = e^{(2-b)/a} \oplus e^{(2-b)/a} = e^{(2-b)/a}e^{(2-b)/a}e^{b/a} = e^{(4-b)/a} = 4'. \tag{62}$$

Multiplication is more involved,

$$2' \odot 2' = e^{(2-b)/a} \odot e^{(2-b)/a} \tag{63}$$

$$= e^{a\ln e^{(2-b)/a}\,\ln e^{(2-b)/a}+b\ln e^{(2-b)/a}+b\ln e^{(2-b)/a}+b^2/a-b/a} \tag{64}$$

$$= e^{(4-b)/a} = 4'. \tag{65}$$

4. Non-Diophantine Fechnerian Exponential Function

Let us now switch from non-Diophantine arithmetic to calculus.

An important example is provided by the exponential function which, by definition, solves the following problem

$$\frac{d'A(x)}{d'x} = A(x), \tag{66}$$

$$A(0') = 1'. \tag{67}$$

The unique solution is $A(x) = f^{-1}\left(e^{f(x)}\right) = \exp_f x$ (Czachor, 2016), and thus

$$A(x) = e^{(e^{a\ln x + b} - b)/a} \tag{68}$$

$$= e^{(e^b e^{\ln x^a} - b)/a} \tag{69}$$

$$= e^{e^b x^a/a} e^{-b/a}. \tag{70}$$

Let us check the initial condition:

$$A(0') = A(e^{-b/a}) = e^{(e^b (e^{-b/a})^a - b)/a} = e^{(1-b)/a} = 1'. \tag{71}$$

It is an instructive exercise to compute the derivative directly from definition:

$$\frac{d'A(x)}{d'x} = \lim_{h \to 0'} (A(x \oplus h) \ominus A(x)) \oslash h \tag{72}$$

$$= \lim_{h \to 0'} (e^{e^b (x \oplus h)^a/a} e^{-b/a} \ominus e^{e^b x^a/a} e^{-b/a}) \oslash h \tag{73}$$

$$= \lim_{h \to e^{-b/a}} (e^{e^b (xhe^{b/a})^a/a} e^{-b/a} \ominus e^{e^b x^a/a} e^{-b/a}) \oslash h \tag{74}$$

$$= \lim_{h \to e^{-b/a}} \left(e^{-b/a} \frac{e^{e^b (xhe^{b/a})^a/a} e^{-b/a}}{e^{e^b x^a/a} e^{-b/a}} \right) \oslash h \tag{75}$$

$$= \lim_{h \to e^{-b/a}} e^{(\ln e^{-b/a} + x^a h^a e^{2b}/a - e^b x^a/a + b/a)/(a \ln h + b) - b/a} \tag{76}$$

$$= \lim_{h \to e^{-b/a}} e^{(-b/a + x^a h^a e^{2b}/a - e^b x^a/a + b/a)/(a \ln h + b) - b/a} \tag{77}$$

$$= \lim_{h \to e^{-b/a}} e^{(x^a h^a e^{2b}/a - e^b x^a/a)/(a \ln h + b) - b/a} \tag{78}$$

$$= \lim_{c \to b} e^{(x^a (e^{-c/a})^a e^{2b}/a - e^b x^a/a)/(a \ln e^{-c/a} + b) - b/a} \tag{79}$$

$$= \lim_{c \to b} e^{\frac{e^{b-c}-1}{b-c} e^b x^a/a - b/a} \tag{80}$$

$$= e^{e^b x^a/a - b/a} = A(x), \tag{81}$$

which was to be proved.

One further finds that

$$\exp_f(x \oplus y) = \exp_f x \odot \exp_f y. \tag{82}$$

The inverse function

$$\ln_f x = f^{-1}\big(\ln f(x)\big) \tag{83}$$
$$= e^{(\ln f(x) - b)/a} \tag{84}$$
$$= e^{-b/a} f(x) \tag{85}$$
$$= e^{-b/a}(a \ln x + b) \tag{86}$$

satisfies

$$\ln_f(x \odot y) = \ln_f x \oplus \ln_f y. \tag{87}$$

5.   Final Remarks

The fact that the Abel-equation approach to psychophysics may be regarded as an example of non-Diophantine arithmetic is quite evident. The formula for explicit Fechnerian subtraction,

$$x \ominus y = e^{-b/a} x/y, \tag{88}$$

shows that a ratio at the stimulus level is directly proportional to a difference in the sensation space. $x \ominus y$ is a natural measure of 'subjective dissimilarity', and it satisfies the law of additivity,

$$(x \ominus y) \oplus (y \ominus z) = x \ominus z, \tag{89}$$

as required in more modern approaches to the Fechner problem (Dzhafarov & Colonius, 2011). One may also wonder if we have here any obvious counterpart of a just noticeable difference. $0'$ is a candidate since it is non-zero at the stimulus level, but it marks the threshold of 'non-zero change' in the sensation space.

Much more interesting is the issue if experimental psychologists can make sense of the remaining arithmetic operations, and if the corresponding calculus can find experimental applications. I hope the paper will trigger some research in these directions. From the point of view of theoretical physics the ultimate goal is to find a general law that determines the form of arithmetic. Psychophysical insights might be very helpful here.

References

Aerts, D., Czachor, M. and Kuna, M. (2016). Crystallization of space: Space-time fractals from fractal arithmetic, Chaos, Solitons and Fractals, 83, 201-211; arXiv:1506.00487 [gr-qc].

Baird, J.C. and Noma, E. (1975). Psychophysical study of numbers (I): Generation of numerical responses, Psychological Research, 37, 281-297.

Baird, J.C. (1975). Psychophysical study of numbers (IV): Generalized preferred state theory, Psychological Research, 38, 175-187.

Baird, J.C. (1975). Psychophysical study of numbers (V): Preferred state theory of matching functions, Psychological Research, 38, 188-207.

Baird, J.C. (1997). Sensation and Judgement: Complementarity Theory of Psychophysics, Lawrence Erlbaum Associates, Mahwah.

Baird, J.C. and Noma, E. (1978). Fundamentals of Scaling and Psychophysics, Wiley, New York.

Benioff, P. (2011). New gauge field from extension of space time parallel transport of vector spaces to the underlying number systems, International Journal of Theoretical Physics, 50, 1887-1907.

Benioff, P. (2015). Fiber bundle description of number scaling in gauge theory and geometry, Quantum Studies: Mathematics and Foundations 2, 289-313.

Burgin, M. (1997). Non-Diophantine Arithmetics, Ukrainian Academy of Information Sciences, Kiev (in Russian).

Burgin, M. (2010). Introduction to projective arithmetics, arXiv:1010.3287 [math.GM].

Busch, P., Grabowski, M. and Lahti, P.J. (1995). Operational Quantum Physics, Springer, Berlin.

Czachor, M. (2016). Relativity of arithmetic as a fundamental symmetry of physics, Quantum Studies: Mathematics and Foundations 3, 123-133.

Dzhafarov, E.N. and Colonius, H. (2011). The Fechnerian idea, American Journal of Psychology, 124, 127-140.

Fechner, G.T. (1860). Elemente der Psychophysik, Breitkopf und Hartel, Leipzig.

Luce, R.D. and Edwards, W. (1958). The derivation of subjective scales from just noticable differences, Psychological Review, 65, 222-237.

Marks, L.E.. (1974). Sensory Processes: The New Psychophysics, Academic Press, London.

Noma, E. and Baird, J.C. (1975). Psychophysical study of numbers (II): Theoretical models of number generation, Psychological Research, 38, 81-95.

Norwich, K.H. (1993). Information, Sensation, and Perception, Academic Press, San Diego.

Stevens, S.S. (1935). The operational definition of psychological concepts, Psychological Review, 42, 517-527.

Stevens, S.S. (1975). Psychophyscis: Introduction to its Perceptual, Neuronal, and Social Prospects, Wiley, New York.

Weissmann, S.M., Hollingsworth, S.R. and Baird, J.C. (1975). Psychophysical study of numbers (III): Methodological applications, Psychological Research, 38, 97-115.

Chapter 13

A Few Questions Related to Information and Symmetries in Physics

György Darvas

Symmetrion, 29 Eötvös St., Budapest, H-1067, Hungary
symmetry@symmetry.hu

Information exchange between inanimate objects (like individual physical particles, or systems) involve special approaches, due to the peculiarity that conscious information emitters/recipients are excluded. This paper aims at answering a part of questions arising by these approaches. One can put the question, whether can we speak about physical information when there is no live percipient to accept, evaluate and use it? Can one speak about physical information (e.g., signal exchange) between inanimate physical objects? (Cf., e.g., Feynman diagrams.) If so, what is the nature of that information? Is (physical) information a passive phenomenon, or its existence presumes activity? What does, e.g., a signal represent if it is not perceived and used at another end, and where is that end when one can say: that signal was lost without perception or use? I try to illustrate my personal answers with a few examples quoted from the history of 20th century physics. My answers to the questions are not intended to be enunciations and to provide final solutions, rather they serve as arguments and indicate that nothing is closed, the discussion is open.

1. Introduction

There are two kinds of interpretation of physical interaction between two physical objects, first of all fermions. 1: Activity is an antropomorph phenomenon. 2: There is inanimate activity, i.e., there exists reception of information between physical agents and their reaction to it. I argue for the latter concept, i.e., for activity is not an antropomorph phenomenon. There is inanimate activity, that means, reception of information between physical agents and their reaction to it.

First, I investigate interaction between two (electric) charges in light of the history of its study. Electromagnetic interaction between two charges is a coincidence of two types of interaction: (a) Coulomb type, whose source is the *scalar* part of the Hamiltonian (*H*), and (b) Lorentz type, whose source is the *vector* part of *H*. At the end of the twenties, early thirties, there were elaborated two types of theories of the interaction between electric charges. The first type of theories considered in primary approximation *interaction between the scalar parts,* and in the second approximation the *effect of the vector potentials,* as perturbation. The second type of the theories considered in primary approximation the *action of the Lorentz force,* and in the second approximation the *effect of the Coulomb force,* as perturbation. Dirac [1928], Breit [1929, 1932], Heisenberg, and the first paper by Fermi supported the first type, Møller [1931] and a later paper by Fermi, did the second type. Bethe, in a common paper with Fermi [1932] showed the equivalence between the two approaches. However, Bethe realised that the roles of the two interacting particles in the scattering matrix derived in the paper by C. Møller [1931] were asymmetric. He considered that this contradicts to the paradigm, accepted by all others that time, that the roles of two interacting particles must be equivalent (i.e., interchangeable, thus symmetric). Therefore, he artificially symmetrised Møller's scattering matrix in their common paper with Fermi. Although this approach did not hold even that time (cf., the Pauli exclusion principle), this mistaken step was not questioned until the early two-thousands, probably due to the high authority of the two authors (both Nobel laureates later). Today, we put the coin for Møller. The roles of two interacting particles should be asymmetric. When they interact, they form a system, and must obey the Pauli principle.

2. Discussion

There arises a question that physicists put rarely: how do the charges, ready to interact, get information from each other, more precisely, whether the partner is ready for interaction? (That is., it is in an opposite state, at least in respect of one of its physical properties, like spin.) In other words: how do they get information from (the state of) each other?

My argumentation involves that answering the related questions needs to re-evaluate a few widely accepted paradigms, like the equivalence of interacting particles. In philosophical sense, equivalence does not mean identity. Equivalence reduces to certain properties, whose cluster is defined in each concrete case, while the same particles may differ in one (or more) other property(ies).

As another example, e.g., the 'classical' (20th century) relativity theories demanded that all physical laws were invariant under the Lorentz transformation. Lorentz invariance of physical laws was in fact a symmetry principle (conservation of the form of the laws during reference frame change). This invariance proved to hold for many other physical theories, so later this symmetry principle was extended to other physical laws as well.

The Lorentz invariant relativity theory included a further consequence: there is no distinct (odd) reference frame in nature. In other words, all reference frames are equivalent. Aren't they? Based on Noether's theorems [1918], one can show that conservation laws hold in all reference frames. However, the quantity of the conserved property (e.g., mass, charge, etc.) may vary in the different reference frames. For example, the amount of mass of matter in a closed system depends on the velocity of the observer relative to that system where the mass is to be measured. One can always find a reference frame from which the amount of the measured mass is minimal. This fact contradicts to the absence of a distinct (odd) reference frame. And there are more. Thus, there is natural to ask: is there any invariance that compensates this lost equivalence of all reference frames?

It presents itself that these invariances or their violation depend on the relative *velocity* of the observed and the observer systems. It is the role of the Lorentz transformation to handle this velocity dependence. We will see that invariance under the Lorentz transformation works properly when it has to manage the form of the physical laws when there is changed only the velocity [Wigner, 1967]. Insufficiency arises when other concerned physical properties change along with velocity. (This was the case with the Dirac equation that was formally Lorentz-invariant but Dirac himself noticed in the introduction to his paper [Dirac, 1928] that his theory was only an approximation. Now we would say, it was semi-classical.) What did the original Dirac equation miss? It did not take into consideration the change of the masses and charge densities with the increase of the velocity [cf., Darvas, 2013].

At the end of the chapter we will conclude that Lorentz invariance is a necessary, but not a sufficient condition of physical laws. We conclude that along with the development of physics, at least at extreme high energies, there is' no more enough to demand invariance under the Lorentz transformation. At extended conditions, one should demand the invariance under a combination of the Lorentz invariance and an additional invariance. That additional invariance must take into account the velocity dependence of the masses and charge densities as well. We must notice that the gravitational and the inertial masses, the Coulomb and the Lorentz type electric charges, etc., behave in different way under a velocity boost. Therefore, if their values were equal at rest or at not too extreme velocities, this is not the case at higher velocities (energies). At those circumstances we must make a distinction between them. This means, there will appear two kinds of field-charges in the transformation matrices that will not transform in the same way like in the case when only one type of the given field-charge was present. Fortunately, there is an invariance [Darvas, 2011] that can transform them into each other. In short, we demand invariance under (all applicable) transformations.

Let us concentrate now on, what would be that other transformation, and what would be an acceptable combined transformation.

The conclusion in the previous paragraphs involves also that when two charges (let they be either gravitational, electric, or other field-charges) interact, they make a distinction between each other. A system, composed of the interacting two field-charges, follows the Pauli principle. That means, the two interacting field-charges must be in different quantum states. In order to get in interaction, they must have information about the quantum state of the other. We investigate now, how contemporary physics handles this problem.

When two fermion particles interact, they must exchange information about the states of each other. For this reason, one of them emits a boson, and the other absorbs it. The spin of the emitted boson transmits the information about the spin of the emitting fermion. The spin of the mediating boson represents itself physical information. If the recipient fermion is in an opposite spin state than the emitting one, it absorbs the boson, and the interaction has taken place. Otherwise not.

When an emitted boson does not meet a partner fermion which were able to absorb it, does this mean that the boson did not convey information, *or* it conveyed, only that information has *not* been *used*? The answer is that the latter holds.

Let us illustrate the information exchange between two electrons on Feynman diagrams (subscript indices mark spin) (Figure 1).

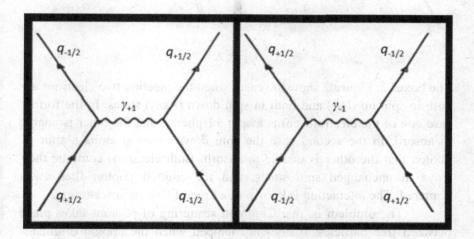

Figure 1.

In the left box, a spin up (+1/2) electron emits a spin +1 photon, and the spin down (−1/2) electron absorbs it. The emitting electron lost spin 1 and the absorbing one received spin 1. Then, the former continues its way as a spin down electron, and the latter as a spin up electron.

In the right box, a spin down electron emits a spin −1 photon, and the spin up electron absorbs it. The emitting electron gained spin 1 and the absorbing one lost spin 1. Then, the former continues its way as a spin up electron, and the latter a spin down electron.

What could happen, when the meeting electrons are not in opposite spin states (i.e., they are not ready to interact with each other)?

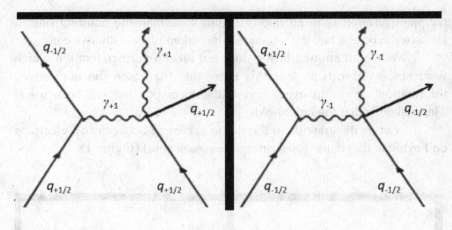

Figure 2.

The boxes in Figure 2 show the cases when the meeting two electrons are both in spin up (left) and both in spin down (right) states. In the former case one of the electrons emits a spin +1 photon that the other is unable to absorb. In the second case the spin down electron emits a spin −1 photon that the other is unable to absorb. Both electrons continue their ways in unchanged spin states, and the emitted photon flies away scattered. The interaction is known as a kind of Compton scattering.

The problem is, that Compton scattering of photons takes place between free particles. It does not happen when the photon originates from electrons that are both in bound states. (For example, imagine, what would happen if identical spin state electrons, placed in different shells around an atom, continuously emit Compton photons towards each other: the atom would continuously lose energy.) How do they know to refuse the overture of the other? In other words, what way get they informed about how to behave in their given situation?

Free particles interact in different way than *bound* ones. Free particles are actors in an open system, bound particles in a closed one. What distinguishes, if any, (closed and open) systems, in the aspects of *information* and of *symmetries*? What is the role of information in this delimination? Is (physical) information a passive phenomenon, or its existence presumes activity? If the latter holds, how wide can we extend the meaning of activity to be still accepted for generating information?

As regards *information*, we should assume, there is something other transmitter beside the Standard Model boson (here photon) that mediates this information [Darvas, 2009, 2011]. We assume something still hidden.

As regards *symmetry*, we must make a choice: we maintain our trust either in the paradigm of the equivalent roles of the interacting particles, or in the Pauli principle. I vote for the latter. And yet, certain symmetries play principal role in physical interactions. If there is another, still hidden, boson that transmits information, similar to its elder brothers, it must be subject of certain symmetry as well [Darvas, 2009, 2011].

What are the roles of different appearances of *symmetries* in taking a stand in the mentioned questions? What kinds of symmetry (e.g., reflexivity, circulation, thermodynamic temporal asymmetry, gauge invariant phenomena, scale invariance, Lorentz invariance, etc., or their absence) may play role in making decision in the listed problems?

As mentioned above, the Lorentz invariance is a candidate to be investigated closer. Since the principle of invariance under the Lorentz transformation proved to hold in several physical theories, it was extended from the Special Theory of Relativity (STR) to other, then to all physical theories. The physical laws should be the same in all reference frames. At the same time, it was known from the beginning that there appear distinct (odd) reference frames in the universe. Thus, the absolute role of the Lorentz invariance was questionable. The two Noether theorems [1918] tell us that the amount of physical quantities is conserved in all reference frames. However, this amount varies according to the chosen reference frame. Is there a reference frame in which this amount is extreme? Of course, there must exist such reference frame in which it is minimal.

Since the absolute role of the Lorentz invariance can be questioned, is there any invariance that compensates this lost equivalence of all reference frames?

In searching the answer to this question, the role of activity of inanimate objects enters the scene. Inanimate objects should react when they perceive information received from another object, e.g., to evaluate the source of a (gravitational or inertial) force, or make distinction between Coulomb charges and the Lorentz-type (current) charges, and so on ..., in short, make distinction between effects of the *scalar* and *vector* parts of H [Darvas, 2012a, 2012b, 2013a, 2014]. What are the most important differences between the two parts of a Hamiltonian? The source of the former is scalar, characterised by one parameter, and it depends on space-time co-ordinates; the source of the latter is a 3-vector, characterised by three parameters and depends directly on velocity (and only indirectly on space-time co-ordinates).

At relatively low energies, there is no difference between the amount of these field-charges, but there should be something hidden behind, at least at high relative velocities (energies). This difference may become observable over energies that appear at high velocities when the mass difference between the interacting two fermions becomes significant (e.g., the mass of a particle doubles over cca. $0.85c$ and increases ten times at $0.995c$, twenty two times at $0.999c$, and so on exponentially). The sources of the scalar and vector parts of H seem similar at lower energies. Their difference shows itself over that range. The sources of the scalar and the vector fields of a given physical interaction (at least numerically) coincide at lower energies. For preciseness, however, we must distinct them. E.g., the source of the scalar part of gravitational field is the gravitational mass, the source of the vector part of the gravitational field is the inertial mass, and so on. Similar brothers of the field charges appear in the electromagnetic interaction (Coulomb- and Lorentz-type charges), and so on. We call these brothers *Isotopic Field-Charges* (IFC). They are sources of fields that appear in the scalar and vector (potential and kinetic, marked V and T) parts of the system's Hamiltonian [Darvas, 2011].

What is more interesting, these pairs are subject of a common gauge invariance. The most important properties of the IFC-s are the following:
- they are subject to a group transformation — similar to that of the spin;
- they can exchange their roles (switch into each other);
- they do this by the exchange of a gauge boson (additional to the graviton and the photon, respectively);

- we call these additional particles *delta bosons* (dions). [Darvas, 2013b]

The boson exchange between the isotopic field charges is demonstrated in Figure 3.

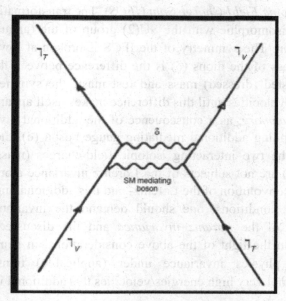

Figure 3. The letter ך (dalet) denotes a general IFC (independent of the concrete interaction field), the indices V and T refer to the potential (scalar) and the kinetic (vector) parts of the Hamiltonian respectively, SM is the abbreviation of the Standard Model of physics, and δ denotes the dions.

Since the IFC-s are subject of a group transformation, and this transforms them into each other, they are subjects of a symmetry group [Darvas 2017]. This symmetry is broken at lower energies. However it appears at high energies. At those high energies, the difference between the IFC partners becomes apparent. This difference between the field charges destroys the invariance under the Lorentz transformation. (One can easily check this, for in the formula of the Lorentz transformation there appear unique charges in each matrix element, but if one inserts different charges in the individual matrix elements, the invariance of the multiplication of the matrix loses.) The lost invariance can be restored by a symmetry group transformation that transforms the IFC pairs into each other. [Darvas, 2014]

Under that transformation, the IFC-s behave similar to the spin. Therefore their property that changes its value under their transformation is called *Isotopic Field-Charge Spin* (*IFCS*). The transformation group of the IFCS is isomorphic with the SU(2) group of the (angular- and the isotopic-) spin. The symmetry of the IFCS is broken at lower energies. Since the mass of the dions (δ) is the difference between the particle's Lorentz boosted (dressed) mass and rest mass, the symmetry remains hidden up to velocities until this difference makes itself apparent.

In summary: as a consequence of the additional invariance and the corresponding additional mediating gauge boson (δ), the respective systems of the two interacting isotopic field-charges (masses, electric charges, etc.) are not subjects of the Lorentz invariance alone. They are subject of a convolution of the Lorentz- and this additional invariance. At extended conditions, one should demand the invariance under a combination of the *Lorentz invariance* and the discussed *additional invariance*. In the light of the above considerations, in general we can demand in physics invariance under (applicable) transformations. However, at not very high energies/velocities this additional invariance is broken.

Applying this strongly relativistic approach to the Dirac equation (what is most accepted to describe quantum electrodynamics in a partially relativistic way), this combined (Lorentz $\otimes$ IFCS) that means $(SO^+(3,1) \otimes SU(2))$ invariance of an extended form of the Dirac equation allows to reinterpret our earlier imagination on the invariances of physical equations. As we noticed at the beginning of this chapter, there was a long lasting paradigm in physics that equations of the physical interactions must be subject of invariance under the Lorentz-transformation, and this is not only a necessary, but also a sufficient condition. Now, we see this can no more be maintained. In fact, no physical principle stated that Lorentz-invariance was a sufficient condition demanded for the physical equations. There are other invariances that may appear together and combined with Lorentz's. The invariance described algebraically in [Darvas 2017 and introduced analytically in Darvas 2009, 2011] is interpreted in the presence of a kinetic gauge field. The Lorentz-invariance is a combined symmetry in itself. The $SO^+(3,1)$ group of the proper Lorentz-transformation can be characterised by six independent subgroups. These six independent subgroups can be separated to and characterised by three $[4 \times 4]$ rotation matrices $[R(\varphi)]$ in the space-time, and three $[4 \times 4]$ velocity boosts $[\Lambda(\dot{x})]$ into a given direction in the configuration space $(= R \otimes \Lambda)$. Since the IFCS invariance $[\Delta(\dot{x})]$ is interpreted also in a kinetic field, it seems reasonable to apply the $R \otimes (\Lambda \otimes \Delta)$ transformation. This requires certain intendment change in the approach to the world-picture.

$R(\varphi)$, $\Lambda(\dot{x}_v)$ and $\Delta(\dot{x}_v)$ are universal invariance groups, i.e., they concern all fundamental interactions. Nevertheless, the *isotopic field-charge spin*'s SU(2) symmetry is broken at lower energies. At the same time, these invariances are extended by a specific invariance group, characteristic to the given interaction; e.g., in case of electromagnetic interaction by U(1), in case of electroweak interaction by U(1) ⊗ SU(2), and in case of strong interaction by SU(3).

3. Conclusions

The information that we missed on the example of a system composed of two coinciding spin bound electrons when we discussed the absence of Compton scattering is assumed to be transmitted by dions. However, dions are still hypothetical particles that are responsible for some hidden information in the interaction between fermions.

Two interacting charges *make a system*.

They *exchange information*.

They *obey each other's state* and *follow the Pauli principle*: they must be in different quantum states.

According to the two-boson exchange model: even in free-state 'systems' the states — in which they differ — should be characterised by *two properties;* one of which should be the recently introduced property (IFCS).

The state of this two-particle system must be characterised also by the recently proposed property. I.e., each of the particles must be in one of the two stable positions of the isotopic field-charge that are rotated into each other *by* an SU(2)-like symmetry group *in* the *isotopic field-charge field*. The isotopic field-charge field is a gauge field. These two stable positions are called, by an analogically given name, the *isotopic field-charge spin* (IFCS, not identical either with the *angular momentum spin* or the *isotopic spin*). Consequently, the IFCS is a conserved property.

When two field-charges interact, they must be in the *opposite IFCS states*. In the Møller-model (at least in the unperturbed state) they still do not have information about each other's angular spin. The *information* that they exchange about each other is about this state: they check whether the partner is in the opposite IFCS state. Otherwise they were 'not allowed' to interact (Pauli's exclusion principle). The *information exchange* takes place by the exchange of a δ boson (called also dion) between them, in addition to the exchange of the traditional mediating bosons (like graviton, photon, weak charged and neutral bosons, or gluons).

That *delta* (δ) *boson* switches the *emitting charge* from *inertial* to *potential* state, and the *absorbing charge* from *potential* to *inertial* state.

The asymmetry of the interacting charges has been explained. It was subject of *information exchange* between the interacting particle partners. In order to meet the Pauli principle, physical objects should exchange information about the (opposite) states of each other before getting into active interaction.

The explanation led to the loss of an invariance property. However, this loss has been restored
- by introducing an additional physical property (isotopic field-charge spin),
- by proving its conservation, and
- completing the Lorentz invariance with the respective invariance attributed to the shown conservation.

This additional invariance embodied by the associated intermediate bosons convey also *information* between the interacting fermions.

In short, we considered the asymmetry between charges to interact. It is subject of information exchange between the interacting particle partners. In order to obey the Pauli principle, physical objects should exchange information about the (opposite) states of each other before getting into active interaction. The explanation led to the loss of an invariance property. However, this loss could have been restored by having introduced a new physical property, by having proven its conservation, and by having completed the Lorentz invariance with the respective invariance attributed to the proven conservation. For this purpose, we applied meta-physical approach, using "meta-" in Aristotelian sense, i.e., beyond formal physics. The latter summary explains the transdisciplinary character of the paper.

References

Bethe, H., Fermi, E. (1932) Über die Wechselwirkung von zwei elektronen, *Zeitschrift für Physik*, 77, 5-6, 296-306.

Breit, G. (1932) *Phys. Rev.*, 34, 553, (1929); and Breit, G.: *Physics Review*, 39. 616.

Darvas, G. (2009) Conserved Noether currents, Utiyama's theory of invariant variation, and velocity dependence in local gauge invariance, *Concepts of Physics*, VI (1), 3-16.

Darvas, G. (2011) The isotopic field charge spin assumption, *International Journal of Theoretical Physics*, 50(10), 2961-2991. DOI: 10.1007/s10773-011-0796-9.

Darvas G. (2012a) Isotopic Field charge spin conservation in general relativity theory, pp. 53-65, in: (eds.): M.C. Duffy, V.O. Gladyshev, A.N. Morozov, P. Rowlands *Physical Interpretations of Relativity Theory, Proceedings of the International Scientific Meeting PIRT-2011*, Moscow, 4-7 July, Moscow, Liverpool, Sunderland: Bauman Moscow State Technical University, 347 p.

Darvas, G. (2012b) GTR and the isotopic field charge spin assumption, *Hypercomplex Numbers in Geometry and Physics*, 1 (17), 9, 50-59.

Darvas, G. (2013a) The isotopic field-charge assumption applied to the electromagnetic interaction, *International Journal of Theoretical Physics*, 52, 11, 3853-3869.

Darvas, G. (2013b) A symmetric adventure beyond the Standard Model — Isotopic field-charge spin conservation in the electromagnetic interaction, *Symmetry: Culture and Science*, 24(1-4), 17-40.

Darvas, G. (2014) Electromagnetic interaction in the presence of isotopic field-charges and a kinetic field, *International Journal of Theoretical Physics*, 53, 1, 39-51.

Darvas, G, (2017) The algebra of state transformations in strongly relativistic interactions.

Dirac, P.A.M. (1928) The quantum gravity of the electron, *Proceedings of the Royal Society A: Mathematical, Physical and Engineering Sciences* 117 (778), 610-624, doi:10.1098/rspa.1928.0023.

Møller, C. (1931) Über den Stoß zweier Teilchen unter Berücksichtigung der Retardation der Kräfte, *Zeitschrift für Physik*, 70, 11-12, 786-795.

Noether, E. A. (1918) Invariante variations probleme, *Nachrichten von der Königlichen Gesellschaft der Wissenschaften zu Göttingen: Mathematisch-physikalische Klasse*, 235-257.

Wigner, E.P. (1967) Events, laws of nature and invariance principles, pp. 38-50, in: Wigner, *Symmetries and Reflections*, Bloomington: Indiana University Press.

Chapter 14

The "Sociotype" Approach to Social Structures and Individual Communication: An Informational Exploration of Human Sociality

R. del Moral[*], J. Navarro and P. C. Marijuán[†]

Bioinformation and Systems Biology Group
Aragon Health Sciences Institute (IACS)
Aragon Health Research Institute (IIS Aragon)
CIBA Building, Avda. San Juan Bosco 13, 50009, Zaragoza, Spain
[*]*rdelmoral.iacs@aragon.es*
[†]*pcmarijuan.iacs@aragon.es*

The present work discusses the pertinence of a "sociotype" construct, both theoretically and empirically oriented, based on the conceptual chain genotype-phenotype-sociotype. It suggests the existence of an evolutionary preference in humans for some determined averages of social structure and communicative relationships. Although human individuals become highly adaptive and resilient concerning the implementation of their sociality, a core pattern, or "sociotype" might be delineated for their social structures and relationships. Anthropologically, this construct dovetails with recent developments in origins of language, social networks, and the "Social Brain Hypothesis." From several points of view, properly framing the sociotype construct and submitting it to empirical testing could be a timely enterprise. In our times, dramatic changes are occurring in the social relationships of entire communities. Economic globalization, new communication technologies, and the demographic transition towards elderly populations are configuring a new panorama of social intercourse, paradoxically characterized by an increasing level of

387

isolation. Such perceived isolation and feelings of loneliness become an unrewarding condition for individuals, an unwanted state, and also a risk factor for mental health. An empirical search throughout the sociotype lens could provide useful orientations for these problems — a pilot study on the social relationships of young people is herein included.

Keywords: Sociotype; social brain hypothesis; bonding relationships; loneliness; mental health.

1. Introduction

Sociality is an essential trait of the human species — as Aristotle wrote in *The Politics* "man is by nature a political animal" [Fowler and Schreiber, 2008]. Indeed the crucial novelties of our evolutionary and historical past revolve around essential aspects of sociality — e.g. origins of language, emotional communication, group behavior, morals and ethics, religious and legal codes, political institutions, knowledge systems, and so on [Diamond, 1998]. So fluid and culturally diverse are the emerging structures of human sociality that, apparently, they defy any precise classification or quantitative specification. Traditionally, a number of schools of thought have followed culturally-oriented approaches to this 'open ended' phenomenon of human sociality [Derridá, 1976; Lévi-Strauss, 1981], while some others have emphasized views closer to biological determinism [Lorenz, 1965; Wilson, 1977]. It is the old conflict between the biological and the political disciplinary points of view, the "nature" versus "nurture" unfortunate dichotomy. Rather unluckily, scientific discussions have also been compounded by the many fields of study involved — anthropological, communicational, neurobiological, ethological, psychological, social, political, philosophical, economical network science, etc. So, instances of convergence have been scarce. More recently, however, some anthropological and social science approaches have achieved an interesting degree of convergence about fundamentals of human sociality [Chapais 2008, 2011; Sennet, 2012]. Hypothesis such as the "social brain" have also contributed to advance a new bond-centered approach on the evolutionary emergence of human sociality.

The presence of a series of significant regularities in the size and structures of social groups, notwithstanding their remarkable variability, suggests the plausibility of a "deep structure" of social bonding for the human species [Chapais, 2011; Hill *et al.*, 2011]. There seems to be an average of social networking, with very ample upper and lower limits, concerning the number and types of bonding relationships that an individual is able to maintain meaningfully [Dunbar, 2004; Dunbar and Shultz, 2007; Fowler and Schreiber, 2008; Hill *et al.*, 2011]. The finding of networking regularities such as the famous "Dunbar's number" (150-200 individual acquaintances) would make a lot of evolutionary and anthropological sense.

1.1. *The social brain hypothesis*

The social brain hypothesis has posited that, in primate societies, selection has favored larger brains and more complex cognitive capabilities as a mean to cope with the challenges of social life [Silk, 2007]. In primate societies, a tight correlation has been observed between the size of social groups and the neocortex relative proportion (roughly, "brain size") (see Figure 1). Actually, the idea of relating brain size with the demands of communication in social life was already hinted by C. Darwin in "The Descent of Man" [1871]. More than a century later, J. Allman and others reconsidered the idea and framed it as a social hypothesis [Allman, 1999]. Also known as the *Machiavellian intelligence hypothesis*, it was more rigorously formulated by R. Dunbar [1996, 2004] and extended into other mental and biomedical fields [Baron-Cohen *et al.*, 1999; Badcok and Crespi 2008]. Although the hypothesis has been criticized from several grounds [Balter, 2012], and it is unclear whether it can be extended to the generality of mammalian societies, it has gained momentum regarding the evolutionary explanation of the 'natural' groups and structures formed in human societies. In the present work, the social brain views have been taken as one of the main references to structurally develop the sociotype hypothesis.

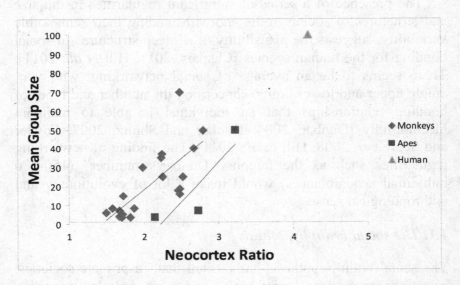

Figure 1. Representation of the mean social-group size in monkeys and apes (ordinates) versus the relative neocortex volume (abscises); in human species both data are disproportionably high. In the figure, diamonds represent monkeys, squares represent apes, and the triangle represents humans. Modified from [Marijuán and Navarro, 2010].

1.2. *Further relational and mental health aspects*

Nevertheless, the main argument of this chapter will depart from the social brain hypothesis in two important respects. First, the emphasis will be put, not just in the size structures of social groups, but mostly in the communication practices that underlie the formation and maintenance of the individual's bonding networks — so, the relational, linguistic activities. In itself, every interpersonal bond is but a "shared memory", consisting in specialized neural *engrams* that encode a variable number of *ad hoc* behavioral episodes between the individuals, positively or negatively finalized [Collins and Marijuán, 1997]. Thus, being far more than collections of mere recognition events, bonds are ensconced upon synaptic memories that occupy an important quota of cortical space, presumably with each bond's occupancy depending on its specific contents and 'strength'. That these bond engrams rely on vast cortical spaces would be in accordance with the relevant multi-area activations produced by social interactions and social evaluations, as observed in different neuroimaging studies [Greene, 2001; Iacoboni 2004; Cacciopo and Patrick, 2008]. Subsequently, the overall cortical conformation and capacity of our species, vastly enlarged regarding other Anthropoidea, would greatly influence the really high number of bonds that, comparatively, human individuals can meaningfully sustain. However, like many other brain/mind phenomena, exactly how bonds are made, maintained, differentiated, eroded, finalized, restored, etc. is not sufficiently understood yet — although in all probability it is a species-specific phenomenon.

In many respects, language appears as the essential tool for bond-making in human societies, although not the only one [Dunbar, 1996; Benzon, 2001; Tomasello, 2008; Desalles, 2007; Marijuán and Navarro, 2010]. The way emotions impinge in social communication and upon language itself represents another distinctive factor of utmost importance [Scherer, 2003; Fiske, 2011]. Also, distinguishing several classes of bonds (related to their strength and to their positive or negative valence) would be important in order to assess their respective relevance within the relational sociotype of the individual. It can be said that bonds claim for their actualization, and linguistic practices claim for their regular realization. Thereafter, the daily conversation/ communication budget of each individual has to be apportioned among the different bonding classes of his/her sociotype so that the talking exercise becomes sufficiently rewarding — providing enough grooming — taking into account the existing diversity of possible encounters and communication channels. Analyzing the different conversation-time distributions could lead to very interesting comparatives: by age, gender, status, professions, cultures, communication channels, etc.

Another important aspect in which the present work departs from the social brain hypothesis concerns its empirical, or better, pragmatic orientation. Herein the emphasis will be put on elaborating a construct finally oriented towards mental-health problems, roughly exploring the potential application of the sociotype as an indicator capable of gauging the whole relational networks of the person and how much daily conversation/communication he/she is engaged in a regular basis, so that the corresponding communicational needs are sufficiently covered or not. The contents exchanged are not of much importance. Seemingly, rather than the exchange of functional information, it is trivial conversation, gossiping about social acquaintances which represents the human equivalent of primate *grooming* [Dunbar, 1996; Desalles, 2009].

In what extent could human language be a 'virtual' equivalent to physical grooming? It has been claimed that a variety of grooming practices (touching, scratching, tickling, chase playing, wrestling, massaging, etc.) are essential to restore the inter-individual bonds in primate groups and societies [Dunbar, 1996, 2004]. The molecular cocktail involved in these grooming relationships activates the reward system in both parties, groomer and groomee, with effects in stress quenching, immune boosting, and learning consolidation, thus contributing to reinforce synaptic bond memories erased in the behavioral "noise" of these societies. Therefore, human 'languaging' would have been evolutionarily co-opted as a virtual system for social grooming, subsequently stimulating in our "social brain" the production of neuropeptides and neurohormones that relieve stress and boost immune system and nervous system [Dunbar, 2004; Nelson and Geher, 2007; Shutt *et al.*, 2007]. The repercussions in daily life cannot be overstated:

talking becomes one of the preferred and most affordable types of mental stimulation. Counting with an appropriate network of relationships with people to talk with becomes a necessity for the wellbeing and mental health of individuals. Having access to and participating in amusing conversations becomes an essential ingredient of our social, psychological, and physical wellbeing feelings.

Notwithstanding a number of recent studies on social networks, technologically oriented, that have tracked vast amounts of interpersonal exchanges [Pentland, 2014], the metrics of the relational structures necessary for mental health and wellbeing have not been properly addressed yet. Hopefully, the progressive delineation of a sociotype concept, pragmatically oriented, and susceptible of both theoretical and empirical demarcation, could contribute to a better understanding of the structures and dynamics of human sociality, and even provide some practical help when sociality itself is in crisis, as seem to be happening with the current "epidemics of loneliness" affecting large population tracts [Oldenburg, 1999; Stivers, 2004; Hawkley and Cacioppo, 2010; Yang and Victor, 2011]. From a biomedical perspective, in spite of the pervasive loneliness and lack of meaningful relationships in contemporary societies, there is a dearth of adequate indicators gauging conversational activities of the individual. Actually, none of the existing questionnaires on the topic (e.g. UCLA loneliness scale, SNI, Duke, SELSA, MOS, SSB, etc.) have addressed the basic, face to face relational phenomena centered by the sociotype.

1.3. *Loneliness and its psychobiological consequences*

In our times the absence of social bonds has become a common experience: over 80% of children and 40% of those over 65 report feeling alone from time to time. Loneliness levels gradually decline in the middle years of adulthood and increase with age, reaching the maximum around age 70 [Weeks, 1994; Oldenburg, 1999; Pinquart and Sorensen, 2001; Berguno *et al.*, 2004; Cacioppo and Cacioppo, 2014]. As numerous studies have shown, there is an association between social isolation, primarily perceived isolation, and poor physical and mental health, which cannot be explained away using different health behaviors. Social isolation decreases life years of social species, from *Drosophila* [Ruan & Wu, 2008] to *Homo sapiens* [House *et al.,* 1988]. The lack of social bonds has deleterious effects on health through its effect on the brain, the hypothalamic-pituitary-adrenal (HPA), vascular processes, blood pressure, gene transcription, inflammatory, immune, and sleep quality [Cacioppo and Hawkley, 2009]. Research indicates that perceived social isolation (i.e., loneliness) is a risk factor, and may contribute to poorer cognitive performance, greater cognitive impairment and poorer executive function and an increased negativity and depressive cognition that accentuate sensitivity to social threats [Berkman, 2009]. In fact, loneliness is associated not only with poor physical health; it also includes psychiatric conditions such as schizophrenia and persona-lity disorders, suicidal thoughts, depression and Alzheimer [Berk-man, 2009; Wilson *et al.,* 2007; Cacioppo and Hawkley, 2009].

1.4. *A growing social problem*

In today's societies there is a significant change in the way social relationships are maintained. The intrusion of new information and communication technologies (ICTs), notwithstanding many other positive effects, would have contributed to the important social disintegration that is occurring also for other reasons — work instability, economic crisis, marginalization of minorities, urban sprawl, migration, etc. In our times, relational networks are apparently larger and faster, but more transient and devoid of personal contact, so that individuals are at greater risk of social isolation, particularly the elderly. The diminished relationships and bonding structures of "social capital" penalize the development of daily life and decrease individuals' wellbeing [Putnam, 2000]. The evidence in fast-developing countries is that economic growth and technological development spurred by the 'information revolution' have gone hand-in-hand with an increase in mental and behavioral disorders, family disintegration, social exclusion, and lower social trust [Bok, 2010; Huppert, 2010]. It's supposed we are living in a society "technologically civilized", where the ubiquitous presence of Media and ICTs has dramatically altered life styles. But it is unclear the effect that such ICT pervasiveness and overuse are having in our social relationships and quality of life. In what extent could computers, cell phones, and TVs replace our need of face-to-face relationships? Are they facilitators, or surrogates and false substitutes, or both? [Easterbrook, 2003; Stivers, 2004; Roberts, 2014].

In 1950, 4 million Americans lived alone, making up 9% of households; the census data from 2011 show that nearly 33 million Americans are living alone, making up 28% of American households: three hundred per cent increase. The same process is taking place in different countries, for example in Sweden the percentage of households "single" reaches 47%, Britain 34%, 31% in Japan, 29% in Italy and 25% in Russia. Living alone, paradoxically, could symbolize our social need to reconnect [Klinenberg, 2012]. Similarly, mental disorders such as schizophrenia, depression, epilepsy, dementia, alcoholism and other substances abuse constitute 13% of the global disease burden, a percentage that surpasses cardiovascular diseases and cancer [Collins *et al.*, 2011]. European studies estimate that in the period of one year, 165 million people (38% of the population) will develop a mental illness [Wittchen *et al.*, 2011].

In Spain, according to the Time Use Survey (INE, 2010), people spend less and less time to interact physically and face to face. Between 2003 and 2010 participation in social life and fun activities decreased, while the time spent with computers (social networks, information retrieval, computer games) substantially increased, from 17.3% of population in 2003 to 30% in 2011. Socializing and fun activities were performed by 57% of the population, while seven years earlier (2003) these activities were performed by 64.4%. In recent years there has been a significant transfer of social life and collective fun activities to individualized activities such as computer games, Internet, TV watching. In this regard, it is significant that in Spain and in other countries, suicide rates have increased dramatically in the last three decades.

In the US Census, 1985, the average number of confidants was three; in the 2004 census the average was 2, but the most common figure was *zero* confidants for almost 25% [Cacciopo and Patrick, 2008]. The phenomenon is similar in most Western countries.

In spite of the pervasive epidemics of loneliness and lack of meaningful relationships in contemporary societies, there is a dearth of adequate indicators gauging the social networking and relational activities of the individual. What daily average does he/she talk? With whom? Which channel: face-to-face, by phone, via Internet? How often does he/she socialize? Does he/she exercise alone? This type of questions has to be properly addressed and integrated with the measurement of the social networks around the individual, and further correlated with wellbeing and mental health questionnaires. That's what the sociotype hypothesis aims— and also what a few of the most recent enquiries are beginning to ask for [Pearson, 2015; Servick, 2015].

2. The Sociotype Hypothesis

The term sociotype has already appeared in the literature, though very scantly. In psychology, it has been put into use by a Jungian oriented school, "socionics", meaning the specific profile attributed to some well-recognized professions: lawyer, policemen, firefighter, etc. [Jung, 1971]. In the biomedical area, Berry [2011] has recently proposed the sociotype as an integrative term covering internal and external factors for the management of chronic disease, imply the integration of bio-psycho-sociology with systems biology. Also, some of the present authors have already utilized the term within the triad genotype-phenotype-sociotype, implying the social-evolutionary meaning herein proposed [Marijuán, 2006, 2009; del Moral and Navarro, 2012].

The sociotype construct is an attempt to cover the social interactions (bonding structures and communication relationships) that are adaptively demanded by the 'social brain' of each individual. In the same way that there is scientific consensus on the validity of the genotype and phenotype constructs for the human species, notwithstanding their respective degrees of variability, a metrics could also be developed applying to the relative constancy of the social environment to which the individuals of our species are evolutionarily adapted. The average brain stimulation coming from relational interactions in that social environment, as we have argued, together with further substitutes and surrogates culturally elaborated, would constitute a mental necessity for the individual's well being. Thus, the interest of appropriately gauging the bonding structures and communication relationships by means of a questionnaire, or a series of questionnaires, including also the influence of factors related to age, gender, personality, affluence, profession, culture, etc. This sociotype construct could provide relevant help for psychological counseling and early psychiatric intervention.

2.1. *Fundamental hypotheses*

More concretely, developing the sociotype construct would imply addressing and putting into test the following fundamental hypotheses:

1. There exists in human beings a characteristic way to conform the structure and dynamics of social bonds, that probably can be related to the functionality of the main cortical brain structures.
2. It is possible to develop a questionnaire to assess and measure the sociotype's main dimensions, and to validate it in the general population (quite probably in subpopulations segmented by age).
3. The sociotype can be a useful indicator of mental health and physical health in the population, becoming an adjuvant tool for psychiatric diagnosis and risk assessment of mental illness.

Thereafter, the following objectives have been addressed.

2.2. *Central objective*

The central goal is establishing a new indicator, based on a standard questionnaire, to collect essential data on the structure of the individual's social bonds, as well as their dynamic update (conversation), and correlate it with other indicators of mental health.

2.3. *Secondary objectives*

1. Develop a questionnaire that can measure and validate the sociotype concept in the Spanish population.
2. Generalize the sociotype concept and its associated indicators as a general means of social and psychological study.
3. Framing the sociotype as an indicator of mental and general health in the various segments of the population (youth, adults, seniors, and elderly).
4. Demonstrate its use as adjuvant tool for the psychiatric diagnosis and social isolation risk in patients with depression and other mentally disturbing pathologies.

2.4. *Pilot study*

In order to address both the structural and dynamic aspects of the sociotype construct, a pilot study has been undertaken analyzing the social networks around adolescents. Subsequently, a sociotype questionnaire has been developed, initially tailored for the adolescent population. In this preliminary study we have selected a young population due to the high prevalence and intensity of the feelings of loneliness, actually higher in adolescence and transition to adulthood (16-25 years) than in any other group except the elderly (>80 years) [Pinquart and Sorensen, 2003]. The study in older people has been discarded precisely because most research in loneliness has already been done in older population [Cacioppo and Hawkley, 2009]. A total of 165 students were interviewed with the preliminary version of the "Sociotype Test" developed by the Bioinformation Group and the Research on Mental Health in Primary Care Group Mental Health Group of IACS. A group of 95 students was recruited from last two courses of High School (16-18 years old), and another group of 70 students was recruited from the first courses of university (19-20 years old).

3. Methodology

3.1. *Design*

It is an exploratory, observational, cross-sectional study.

3.2. *Study population*

In this study we had applied a "convenience sampling" [Cohen *et al.*, 2003], where the subjects were students who came from two education centers which we had access. The total sample of students was 165. There were two samples, *Sample_1* was recruited from last two courses of High School, its sample size was $n = 95$ (38.3% men and 61.7% women) and the age average 17.81 (SD = 4.24). *Sample_2* was composed by students from the first course of University, its sample size was n = 70 (80% women and 20% men) and the average age was 19.37 (SD = 2.44).

All the individuals were Spanish and none suffered any mental illness that prevented the realization of the task, so they were able to understand and complete the questionnaire. Inclusion criteria were as follows: age 17-25 years, good mastery of Spanish language. Exclusion criteria were: to suffer from severe mental disorder, any clinical o psychological illness that prevented the realization of the test.

Sample_1 was interviewed with the "Sociotype Test" in order to explore both structural and dynamic aspects of social networking, and Sample_2 was also interviewed with the GHQ-28

(General Health Questionnaire), addressed to relate the social networks with mental health and psychological well-being.

The Ethical Committee of Aragón had previously surveyed the Questionnaire and the Methodology of the Study, as part of the Project FIS PI12/01480.

3.3. *Sociotype questionnaire*

This preliminary sociotype questionnaire was developed by the Bioinformation and Systems Biology Group and the Research on Mental Health in Primary Care Group of the Aragon Health Sciences Institute. Based on the opinion of experts from different fields of knowledge (e.g., sociology, anthropology, psychiatry/psychology, neuroscience) a set of 6-8 dominions to assess the concept were developed. Using qualitative methods (in-depth interviews, discussion groups, etc.), healthy people and patients with psychiatric and physical disorders were approached to identify about 50 key questions to assess those dominions. Finally, factorial analysis was used to identify the definitive items included in the questionnaire following the usual methods to develop new questionnaires [Montero-Marín and García-Campayo, 2010].

This preliminary version of the Sociotype Questionnaire was made up of 20 items. It included basic socio-demographic questions (age, gender, educational level, family status...), and also questions related to the way relationships are kept (time talking face-to-face, telephone, social networks or other channels). They were requested for the four different layers of social relationships considered (nuclear family, close friends, relatives & parenthood, social acquaintances). The auto-evaluation of sociability, as well as the self-satisfaction level was asked too; and also changes in personal state. The questionnaire showed adequate psychometric properties that will be described in an independent paper.

3.4. GHQ-28 questionnaire

The General Health Questionaire-28 is a screening tool to detect emotional distress and the risk of developing psychiatric disorders. Through factor analysis, the GHQ-28 considers four subscales: somatic symptoms, anxiety/insomnia, social dysfunction and severe depression.

The scoring method (CGHQ) takes into account the chronicity of psychiatric symptoms. It is superior to the conventional scoring method in yielding a wider range of scores, a more normal distribution and a well validated measure of neurotic illness. We used the validated Spanish version of the questionnaire [Lobo *et al.*, 1986].

3.5. Statistical analysis

Frequency distributions of the qualitative variables were calculated in each category (gender, pets…). Quantitative variables (time talking, number of contacts…) were tested for normal distribution by means of Kolmogorov-Smirnov test, and indicators of central tendency (mean, trimmed mean or median) and dispersion (standard deviation or percentiles) were elaborated. Correlation between social variables and psychological risk factors were performed by means of contrast hypothesis, comparing proportions of qualitative variables (chi-square, Fisher exact test) or by comparison of means of quantitative variables (Student's t, ANOVA). When the distribution wasn't adjusted to normalcy, the U Mann Whitney or Kruskal Wallis tests were used. The analysis was executed by means of the SPSS 15.0 for Windows. A significance level (alpha) of 5% was used to consider statistical significance.

4. Results

Structural and relational data were obtained. In the former, four levels of relationships were distinguished (arguably, three levels could have been better, as will be discussed in the next section). The results may be seen just in Table 1.

Table 1. Number of people in the different layers of social relationships

	Mean	SD
Nuclear Family	5.05	1.24
Close Friends	6.02	3.23
Relatives&Parenthood	13.03	10.21
Social Acquaintances	77.06	92.85

About the relational data, they have been presented in minutes per week, for an easy calculation, and they are aggregated for the whole population (see Table 2). They are also compared by gender (Table 3), in that case including equivalence in hours per day.

Table 2. Conversation time (min/weekly)

	Mean	SD
Family Face-to-Face	464.40	394.17
Family Phone	41.52	62.65
Couple Face-to-Face	495.19	342.39
Couple Phone	96.59	95.01
Friends Face-to-Face	492.33	380.50
Friend Phone	69.36	80.58
Acquaintances Face-to-Face	127.10	149.57
Acquaintance Phone	19.89	34.48

Table 3. Time spent in conversation, by gender. 5% Trimmed mean

	Minutes per Week		Hours per Day	
	Women	Men	Women	Men
Family Face-to-Face	473.89	421.11	1.13	1.00
Family Phone	58.98	31.85	0.14	0.08
Couple Face-to-Face	542.64	272.22	1.29	0.65
Couple Phone	101.34	35	0.24	0.08
Friends Face-to-Face	518.06	593.33	1.23	1.41
Friends Phone	108.06	29.44	0.26	0.07
Acquaintances Face-to-Face	131.81	131.11	0.31	0.31
Acquaintance Phone	15.83	12.96	0.04	0.03

The statistical analysis of the relationship between the most relevant variables in the Sociotype Questionnaire and the General Health Questionaire-28 is shown in Table 4. The data are corresponded to the four psychiatric subscales, and quite many of them show statistical significance.

Table 4. Relationhips between the subscales psychiatrics and the variables of interest. Medians (Interquartile Range) are shown for the quantitative variables; Frequency (Percentage) for the qualitative variable. *indicates statistical significance ($p<0.05$)

	Somatic Symptoms		Anxiety & Insomnia		Social Dysfunction		Severe Depression	
	Not Probably	Probably	Not probably	Probably	Not probably	Probably	Not probably	Probably
Gender (women)	33 (80.5%)	23 (79.3%)	21 (77.8%)	35 (81.4%)	54 (83.1%)*	2 (40%)*	50 (80.6%)	6 (75%)
Almost 3 people you can trust when facing a problem	39 (95.1%)*	23 (79.3%)*	26 (96.3%)	36 (83.7%)	59 (90.8%)*	3 (60%)*	57 (91.9%)*	5 (62.5%)*

(Continued)

Table 4. (*Continued*)

People get in touch– weekly	53 (90)	39 (27)	45 (64)*	41 (34)*	42 (40)	19 (36)	44 (42.5)	38 (32.5)
Time talking – min/week	2760 (3555)	1620 (4270)	2880 (4620)	2280 (4020)	2430 (3965)	1320 (3200)	2385 (3927.5)	1890 (4627.5)
Tapas/Café – weekly	1 (2)	0 (2)	2 (3)*	0 (2)*	1 (2)	0 (2)	1 (2)	0 (3.25)
Go for a walk accompanied– weekly	3 (4)	2 (4)	4 (4.25)*	2 (4)*	3 (3)*	0 (1.5)*	2.5 (3)	0.5 (3.5)
Sociability Level	75 (12.5)	80 (13.5)	75 (15)	80 (10)	80 (10)*	63 (45)*	80 (10)*	55 (39.5)*
Satisfaction Personal Relationship	80 (20)*	70 (25)*	80 (20)	80 (20)	80 (15)	80 (43.5)	80 (15)	73.5 (60)

5. Discussion and Comments

To the authors' information, this is the first attempt to identify and measure a construct related with the way that human beings develop and maintain their structure of relational bonds. Neither the emerging structures nor the dynamic relationships have been studied in their mutual interaction yet. As mentioned in the Introduction, the very important changes in the patterns of socialization within the "information societies" demand more sophisticate conceptual apparatuses to better tackle the inherent problems. Although in this discussion we have to refer to preliminary results obtained from a very limited survey, the topics which surface are of general interest and confirm the potential of the sociotype construct.

A number of observations can be made about the social structure depicted in Table 1. Overall, the whole data indicate a pattern of superimposed social structures with a consistent number of 100 members among young people (mean age = 17.81,

SD = 4.24). Certainly this value is not much close to Dunbar's, but probably it is different due to the fact that the structural pattern at this age is not totally established. Actually the standard deviation for social acquaintances is even higher than the mean itself. A significant number of students responded with pretty low figures, while other referred to several hundreds. So to speak, at this age an independent sociotype is in the making, and for some adolescents that is an unwanted task, while for others an unbridled social excitation reigns. Correlating the type of structural values obtained with personality traits would be quite interesting –to be done in a near future. Besides, the number of layers or levels to distinguish is also an interesting aspect. In some societies, the 'extended family' layer makes little sense, while in others it becomes the fundamental strata (power of clans).

In view of the obtained results in Table 2 we confirm the average of 3-4 h of daily conversation time referred in the literature (Dunbar, 2004). We find gender as a fundamental factor (Table 3): women spend 1 hour per day more than men in communication (4.64h women vs. 3.63h men). Obviously these data should be studied in more detail and with larger samples. Although the conversation time is not strictly correlated with any subscale, there is an evidence of higher probability of developing a psychiatric disorder when the talking time is too low. As we have already argued, conversational 'grooming' would be essential to our social, psychological and physical well-being.

Attending to the influence of social networks on mental health (see Table 4), we find very interesting correlations: *Severe Depression* is directly correlated with the number of people you can trust when facing a problem, as well as with the sociability level; the same parameters correlate to *Social Dysfunction*, plus gender and going for a walk accompanied, and gender; *Anxiety and Insomnia* also correlates with the number of people you get in touch weekly, going for a walk accompanied, and going out for 'tapas' or café weekly; *Somatic Symptoms* and the self-satisfaction with your personal relationships. These results emphasize that loneliness may be a risk factor by interfering with some forms of psychosocial distress. In this questionnaire the concept of loneliness is considered as a separate entity from social isolation and depression, so these measures of relationships include the distress that an individual may subjectively feel.

As a further step, theoretical network approaches could be applied to the present data. What is the equivalent in terms of structural sociotype of the gain and loss of bonds in the different categories? How the sociotype evolves with age? How resilient is this structure regarding changes in the social environment, e.g., migrations? How do contemporary technological-communication changes affect its dynamics? In what extent could computers, cell phones, and Internet exchanges accelerate our bonding relationships? May all those ICTs gadgets replace our need of face-to-face contact? In what extent is continuous "accessibility" irrespective of the interpersonal environment a disturbing circumstance?

This Pilot Study has shown an intriguing panorama of correlations to be explored carefully, hinting at comparative studies on age and cultural differences. It also conduces to highly debated topics on mental health and psychiatry, such as the therapeutic influence of changing life styles [Walsh, 2011], which have to be urgently addressed by mental health professionals for fostering individual and social well-being, and for preserving and optimizing cognitive function. The social support concept and the so-called "buffering hypothesis" may also be considered under the sociotype angle [Qureshi *et al.*, 2013].

The main limitations of the study are the following: First, the questionnaire used to assess the sociotype is preliminary and should be subject to more thorough validation—but the preliminary results suggest that the construct *exists* and can be measured. Second, sample size is relatively small and not representative of the general population. Future studies with larger populations and including both healthy people and patients with psychiatric and physical disorders are warranted. Third, the concept of sociotype should be related not only with psychological variables but also with more biological variables such as genetic/epigenetic parameters, neuroimage and immuno-neuro-endocrine explorations, and physiological variables as well, in order to confirm the validity of the construct and the proposed alignment *genotype-phenotype-sociotype*.

In any case, the present work is but an exploratory attempt, and further research on the sociotype topic is under way in a national mental health project (Spanish FIS Project, Carlos III Health Institute).

6. Evolutionary Coda

From the evolutionary point of view, the present "epidemics of loneliness" is nonsense, an arbitrary imposition stemming from both socio-cultural and techno-economic automatisms that are scarcely understood in their self-generating complexity. Much of the burden on health systems, particularly in mental health, derives from social disintegration — the lack of a community in which people can talk and feel connected to each other. It has been proved that people with the most extensive social networks and the highest levels of social engagement have the lowest rates of physical and cognitive decline. But it is very difficult investigating levels of social engagement, and even more measuring them. In some occasions, coining a new scientific concept helps to advance more useful ideas and social policies. The sociotype hypothesis and the preliminary questionnaire herein presented may somehow contribute.

Sources of support

This pilot study is related to the Project FIS PI12/01480, which is carried out by a grant from the Carlos III Health Institute (Spanish Ministry of Economy and Innovation).

Acknowledgements

This study has been funded by project PI12/01480 (Instituto de Salud Carlos III) and by FEDER funds: "Una manera de hacer Europa".

Conflict of interest statement

None declared.

References

Allman, J. (1999). *Evolving Brains*. New York: Scientific American Library.

Badcock, C. and Crespi, B. (2008). Battle of the sexes may set the brain. *Nature*, 454(7208), pp. 1054-1055.

Balter, M. (2012). Why are our brains so big? *Science*, 338(6103), pp. 33-34.

Baron-Cohen, S., Ring, H., Wheelwright, S., Bullmore, E., Brammer, M., Simmons, A. and Williams, S. (1999). Social intelligence in the normal and autistic brain: an fMRI study. *European Journal of Neuroscience*, 11(6), pp. 1891-1898.

Benzon, W. (2001). *Beethoven's Anvil*. New York: Basic Books.

Berguno, G., Leroux P., McAinsh K., and Shaikh S. (2004). Children's experience of loneliness at school and its relation to bullying and the quality of teacher interventions. *Qualitative Report*, 9, pp. 483-499.

Berkman, L. (2009). Social epidemiology: Social determinants of health in the United States: Are we losing ground? *Annual Review of Public Health*, 30(1), pp. 27-41.

Berry, E. (2011). The role of the sociotype in managing chronic disease: Integrating bio-psycho-sociology with systems biology. *Medical Hypotheses*, 77(4), pp. 610-613.

Bok, D. (2010). *The Politics of Happiness*. Princeton, NJ: Princeton University Press.

Cacioppo, J. and Hawkley, L. (2009). Perceived social isolation and cognition. *Trends in Cognitive Sciences*, 13(10), pp. 447-454.

Cacioppo, J. and Patrick, W. (2008). *Loneliness*. New York: W.W. Norton & Co.

Cacioppo, J. and Cacioppo, S. (2014). Social relationships and health: the toxic effects of perceived social isolation. *Social and Personality Psychology Compass*, 8(2), pp. 58-72.

Chapais, B. (2008). *Primeval kinship*. Cambridge, Mass.: Harvard University Press.

Chapais, B. (2011). The deep social structure of humankind. *Science*, 331(6022), pp. 1276-1277.

Cohen, L., Manion, L. and Morrison, K. (2003). *Research Methods in Education*. London: Routledge Falmer.

Collins, K. and Marijuán, P. (1997). *El cerebro Dual*. Barcelona: Hacer.

Collins, P., Patel, V., Joestl, S., March, D., Insel, T., Daar, A., Bordin, I., Costello, E., Durkin, M., Fairburn, C., Glass, R., Hall, W., Huang, Y., Hyman, S., Jamison, K., Kaaya, S., Kapur, S., Kleinman, A., Ogunniyi, A., Otero-Ojeda, A., Poo, M., Ravindranath, V., Sahakian, B., Saxena, S., Singer, P., Stein, D., Anderson, W., Dhansay, M., Ewart, W., Phillips, A., Shurin, S. and Walport, M. (2011). Grand challenges in global mental health. *Nature*, 475(7354), pp. 27-30.

Darwin, C.R. (1871). *The Descent of Man, and Selection in Relation to Sex*. London: John Murray.

Derrida, J. (1976). *Of Grammatology*. Baltimore: Johns Hopkins University Press.

Dessalles, J. (2007). *Why We Talk*. Oxford: Oxford University Press.

del Moral, R. and Navarro, J. (2012). *AAAS Annual Meeting 2012. The 'Sociotype': A New Conceptual Construct on the Structure and Dynamics of Human Social Networks*. Vancouver, Canada. (http://aaas.confex.com/aaas/2012/webprogram/Paper7882.html)

Diamond, J. (1998). *Guns, Germs, and Steel*. New York: W.W. Norton & Co.

Dunbar, R. (1996). *Grooming, Gossip, and the Evolution of Language*. Cambridge, Mass.: Harvard University Press.

Dunbar, R. (2003). Psychology: Evolution of the social brain. *Science*, 302(5648), pp. 1160-1161.

Dunbar, R. (2004). *The Human Story*. London: Faber and Faber.

Dunbar, R.I.M., Shultz S. (2007). Evolution in the social brain, *Science,* 317, pp. 1344-1347.

Easterbrook, G. (2003). *The Progress Paradox*. New York: Random House.

Fiske, S. (2011). *Envy Up, Scorn Down*. New York: Russell Sage Foundation.

Fowler, J. and Schreiber, D. (2008). Biology, politics, and the emerging science of human nature. *Science*, 322(5903), pp.912-914.

Greene, J. (2001). An fMRI investigation of emotional engagement in moral judgment. *Science*, 293(5537), pp. 2105-2108.

Hawkley, L. and Cacioppo, J. (2010). Loneliness matters: A theoretical and empirical review of consequences and mechanisms. *Annals of Behavioral Medicine*, 40(2), pp. 218-227.

Hill, K., Walker, R., Bozicevic, M., Eder, J., Headland, T., Hewlett, B., Hurtado, A., Marlowe, F., Wiessner, P. and Wood, B. (2011). Co-residence Patterns in hunter-gatherer societies show unique human social structure. *Science*, 331(6022), pp. 1286-1289.

House, J.S., Landis K.R., and Umberson D. (1988). Social relationships and health. *Science*, 29; 241(4865), pp. 540-545.

Huppert, F. (2010). Happiness breeds prosperity. *Nature*, 464(7293), pp. 1275-1276.

Iacoboni, M., Lieberman, M., Knowlton, B., Molnar-Szakacs, I., Moritz, M., Throop, C. and Fiske, A. (2004). Watching social interactions produces dorsomedial prefrontal and medial parietal BOLD fMRI signal increases compared to a resting baseline. *NeuroImage*, 21(3), pp. 1167-1173.

Jung, C., Read, H., Fordham, M. and Adler, G. (1971). *The Collected Works of C.G. Jung*. New York: Pantheon Books.

Klinenberg, E. (2012). *Going Solo*. New York: Penguin Press.

Lévi-Strauss, C. (1981). *The Naked Man*. New York: Harper & Row.

Lobo, A., Pérez-Echeverría, M. and Artal, J. (1986). Validity of the scaled version of the General Health Questionnaire (GHQ-28) in a Spanish population. *Psychological Medicine*, 16(01), pp. 135-140.

Lorenz, K. (1965). *Evolution and Modification of Behaviour*. University of Chicago Press.

Marijuán, P.C. (2006). *Foundations on Information Science: FIS Discussion Archives*. "On information ethics". (https://webmail.unizar.es/pipermail/fis/2006-March/001309.html)

Marijuán, P.C. and Navarro J. (2010). The bonds of laughter: A multidisciplinary inquiry into the information processes of human laughter. arXiv: 1010.5602v1 [q-bio.NC].

Marijuán, P.C. (2009). The role of information networks in the evolution of social complexity. Banquete_nodes and networks. Ed. Seacex/Turner. Madrid, España.

Montero-Marín, J. and García-Campayo, J. (2010). A newer and broader definition of burnout: Validation of the "Burnout Clinical Subtype Questionnaire (BCSQ-36)". *BMC Public Health*, 10(1), p. 302.

Nelson, H. and Geher, G. (2007). Mutual grooming in human dyadic relationships: An ethological perspective. *Current Psychology*, 26(2), pp. 121-140.

Oldenburg, R. (1999). *The Great Good Place*. New York: Marlowe.

Pearson, H. (2015). The lab that knows where your time really goes. *Nature*, 526(7574), pp. 492-496.

Pentland, A. (2014). *Social Physics*. New York: The Penguin Press.

Pinquart, M. and Sorensen, S. (2001). Influences on loneliness in older adults: A meta-analysis. *Basic and Applied Social Psychology*, 23(4), pp.245-266.

Pinquart, M. and Sörensen, S. (2003). Risk factor for loneliness in adulthood and old age — A meta-analysis. In S.P. Shohov (Ed.). *Advances in Psychology Research*, Vol. 19: 111-143. Hauppauge, NY: Nova Science Publishers.

Putnam, R. (2000). *Bowling Alone*. New York: Simon & Schuster.

Qureshi, A., Collazos, F., Sobradiel, N., Eiroa-Orosa, F., Febrel, M., Revollo-Escudero, H., Andrés, E., del Mar Ramos, M., Roca, M., Casas, M., Serrano-Blanco, A., Escobar, J. and García-Campayo, J. (2013). Epidemiology of psychiatric morbidity among migrants compared to native born population in Spain: a controlled study. *General Hospital Psychiatry*, 35(1), pp. 93-99.

Roberts, P. (2014). *The Impulse Society*. New York: Bloomsbury.

Ruan, H. and Wu, C. (2008). Social interaction-mediated lifespan extension of Drosophila Cu/Zn superoxide dismutase mutants. *Proceedings of the National Academy of Sciences USA*, 105(21), pp. 7506-7510.

Scherer, K. (2003). Vocal communication of emotion: A review of research paradigms. *Speech Communication*, 40, pp. 227-256.

Sennett, R. (2012). *Together*. New Haven, CT: Yale University Press.

Servick, K. (2015). Proposed study would closely track 10,000 New Yorkers. *Science*, 350(6260), pp. 493-494.

Shutt, K., MacLarnon, A., Heistermann, M. and Semple, S. (2007). Grooming in Barbary macaques: better to give than to receive? *Biology Letters*, 3(3), pp. 231-233.

Silk, J. (2007). Social components of fitness in primate groups. *Science*, 317(5843), pp. 1347-1351.

Stivers, R. (2004). *Shades of Loneliness*. Lanham, MD: Rowman & Littlefield.

Tomasello, M. (2008). *Origins of Human Communication*. Cambridge, MA, MIT Press.

Walsh, R. (2011). Lifestyle and mental health. *American Psychologist*, 66(7), pp. 579-592.

Weeks, D. (1994). A review of loneliness concepts, with particular reference to old age. *Int. J. Geriat. Psychiatry*, 9(5), pp. 345-355.

Wilson, E. (1977). *Sociobiology, the New Synthesis*. Cambridge, Mass.: The Belknap Press.

Wilson, R., Krueger, K., Arnold, S., Schneider, J., Kelly, J., Barnes, L., Tang, Y. and Bennett, D. (2007). Loneliness and risk of Alzheimer disease. *Arch Gen Psychiatry*, 64(2), p. 234.

Wittchen, H., Jacobi, F., Rehm, J., Gustavsson, A., Svensson, M., Jönsson, B., Olesen, J., Allgulander, C., Alonso, J., Faravelli, C., Fratiglioni, L., Jennum, P., Lieb, R., Maercker, A., van Os, J., Preisig, M., Salvador-Carulla, L., Simon, R. and Steinhausen, H. (2011). The size and burden of mental disorders and other disorders of the brain in Europe 2010. *European Neuropsychopharmacology*, 21(9), pp. 655-679.

Yang, K. and Victor, C. (2011). Age and loneliness in 25 European nations. *Ageing and Society*, 31(08), pp. 1368-1388.

Chapter 15

Information Outliers and Their Detection

A. Duraj* and P. S. Szczepaniak

Lodz University of Technology
Institute of Information Technology
ul. Wolczanska 215, 90-924 Lodz, Poland
*agnieszka.duraj@p.lodz.pl

This chapter deals with the problem of outlier detection a data mining technique with a range of potential applications across many disciplines. In particular, it concentrates on the detection of outlier information in numeric and textual records. A brief survey of the literature concerning outlier detection methods, including those using linguistic summaries, is followed by an overview of outlier detection methods applied to numeric attributes. The techniques for the analysis of textual records are also discussed, with a particular focus on the n-gram and generalized n-gram methods. Then, the concept of linguistic summaries is explained in some detail and applied to the process of outlier detection to enable a simultaneous analysis of both textual and numeric records. The proposed solution is illustrated with examples.

Keywords: Outlier information; outlier detection in numeric data; outlier information in textual records.

1. Introduction

Every cognitive process associated with information processing seeks to improve the efficiency of deductive reasoning aimed at reaching a particular decision. An important task in the field of data mining is to provide methods to facilitate the process of data analysis aimed at identifying the crucial pieces of information in large datasets.

Outlier detection is an area of research which has developed substantially in the last decade. It has grown to become a prominent data-mining technique with a diversity of vital, real-life applications. It may be applied to various data domains, including medical, sociological and economic records, as well as technical ones (related to the diagnostics of devices). Thus, outlier detection is an area of study that crosses many disciplinary boundaries. It is a broad field of vital practical importance, with a number of potential benefits for the society, since it allows one to gain a better insight into a given phenomenon, the conditions governing a given population, boundary conditions etc.

As opposed to many other fields of scientific research, which often aim at finding a general pattern or seek for regularities while analysing a given phenomenon, outlier detection aims at identifying elements of a dominating or unusual character. The field of outlier detection offers a significant potential for transdisciplinary research. The detection and analysis of outliers in two seemingly diverse areas of study may provide surprising results. The overlap of outliers found in two superficially different areas under examination may indicate that there exists a common ground between them. Not only is it worth detecting outliers, but it is also interesting to examine why they occur. However, it is clear that in order to explain the reasons for the occurrence of outliers, one needs to first possess the ability to detect them. This, in turn, requires developing techniques of different types, dedicated to various data domains. The present paper endeavours to explore the problem of outlier detection in numeric and textual records.

There is no single, universally applicable definition of an outlier. The formulation of such a definition depends largely on a particular area of application. The detected object which is assumed to be an outlier can change the entire context of the analyzed data, or change the decision.

The most popular definitions of outliers are the ones proposed by Hawkins [13], Aggarwal and Yu [1], Aggrawal [3] and Barnet and Lewis [5] as well as by Knorr and Ng [26].

- Hawkins [13] writes: "An outlier is an observation which deviates so much from the other observations as to arouse suspicions that it was generated by a different mechanism".
- Aggarwal and Yu [1] define outliers as noise points lying outside the set which defines the clusters, or, alternatively, outliers can be defined as points lying outside the set of clusters but are separated from the noise.
- Aggrawal [3]: "An outlier is an observation which deviates so much from the other observations as to arouse suspicions that it was generated by a different mechanism."

- Barnett and Lewis [5] write: an observation (or subset of observations) which appears to be inconsistent with the remainder of that set of data.
- Knorr and Ng [26]: "A point p in a data set is an outlier with respect to the parameters k and λ, if no more than k points in the data set are at a distance λ or less from p".

In the literature, a large variety of methods have been proposed to detect outliers. Those methods can be divided into two groups. The first group comprises a variety of approaches which, regardless of the intended application, are algorithmically very similar, but differ in the understanding of the concept of an outlier. The other group encompasses a range of methods which differ in the algorithmic approach, but employ the same definition of the outlier (see e.g. [29]).

2. Related Works

Many disciplines including KDD-applications (KDD stands for Knowledge Discovery and Data-Mining) require means of detecting rare instances, called outliers. The methods of detecting outliers presented in the literature are based on statistical methods and machine learning. Barnett and Lewis [5], Rousseeuw and Leroy [38] focus on finding and analyzing outliers using a wide family of statistical methods. It is also possible to divide the methods into those based on: distance [27,38], density [18] and clusters [14]. An example of a cluster-based approach is the method proposed by Yu and Zhang[48]. It is based on a wavelet transform, which detects outliers by removing clusters from the original dataset.

The existing outlier detection methods apply various assumptions and modeling techniques. Barnett and Lewis [5] and Aggrawal [1,3] focused on the most common problems associated with outlier detection.

It is also worth mentioning the works of Knorr and Ng [26], who standardized statistical distribution-based approaches and introduced the concept of distance-based-outlier (DB-outlier for short) [27,28]. Those works influenced the development of many spatially oriented approaches to outlier detection, for example, the works by Ramaswamy *et al.* [37], in which the authors measured the distance to the k-nearest neighbors and ranked the objects according to their distances from the kth NN; Pei *et al.* [36] in which approximation was based on reference points and Orair *et al.* [35] which approximated algorithms for mining DB-outliers. See also: [4,6,8,39].

The Local outlier factor (LOF) [7], Connectivity-based Outlier Factor (COF) [18] and Density Based Spatial Clustering of Applications with Noise (DBSCAN)[11] algorithms are also popular.

The detection and interpretation of outliers can be applied to a variety of fields, e.g. medicine, where detecting outliers such as unusual, abnormal values may indicate disease; geophysics, where abnormal values may indicate a mineral deposit or an erroneous measurement result; or structural integrity testing, where abnormal values, may indicate faults in a given structure (see, e.g.,[3, 29, 39]).

Techniques based on statistical methods or data mining algorithms were used to detect outliers considered inappropriate behaviors in online auctions [9], or to detect the procedure known as shill bidding [41, 42]. Statistical methods, Markov's models Xu and Cheng [44] and Bayesian inference [12] are also in use. There are also other approaches to detecting outliers, which employ time series, or in stream data in categorical or ordinal data, or in uncertain data. For example, see [3].

A specific problem is the formulation of outlier in linguistic data (many records, rich textual database or full textual documents). The first work to consider the textual type of outlier was probably [2]. Recently, a novel and useful method of detection of possible outliers in textual records has been proposed in [10]. This approach uses interpretations having roots in the fuzzy sets theory and in its core. It is based on Yager's concept of linguistic summarization [45].

3.　Detection of Outliers in Numeric Data

As indicated in the introduction to this study, outlier detection is a vital task applicable to a variety of domains. A considerable amount of research has been conducted within the field of outlier detection in numerical data. For example, see the works, which concern such areas as statistical methods [13], algorithms based on distance [19, 37, 40], or algorithms based on density [18].

Statistical Methods

In the traditional methods based on statistics the detection of outliers for numerical data begins with defining "correct" (normal) values of the characteristics $x_1, x_2, \ldots, x_n$. Then, the standard deviation σ is also calculated and a threshold is assumed. The value of the characteristics of x is defined as an outlier (outlying data) if, for a predefined threshold and the designated interval $[E - k0 \cdot \sigma, E + k0 \cdot \sigma]$, the value of x does not belong to this interval. Here E is usually determined as the arithmetic mean of these normal values ($E = \frac{x_1 + x_2 + \cdots + x_n}{n}$), and $k0 > 1$ is some pre-selected value (in the literature most frequently: $k0 = 2, 3$, or 6).

Outliers, also referred to as deviations, or outlying data, can be detected in numerical data using statistical methods, e.g. linear regression. In the case of detecting the outliers by using linear regression an observation which has a very large absolute value of the so-called standardized residual is tested.

In this case, the concept of residual is important, because their analysis provides more precise results than, for example, observation of points on the scatter plot. Let us assume that the value $y_i - \widetilde{y}_i = y_i - (b_0 \cdot x_i + b_1)$ is the value of residual e_i for i-th observation. Therefore, e_i is the difference between the actual value of the dependent variable and the predicted value. The standard error for such a residual is: $SE_i = s \cdot \sqrt{(1 - h_i)}$ where s is the average deviation of the actual values from the predicted values, and h_i is the influence of ith observation on the regression equation. The h_i is calculated as follows $h_i = \frac{1}{n} \frac{(x_i - \overline{x})^2}{\sum_{i=1}^{n}(x_i - \overline{x})^2}$, where $\overline{x}$ denotes arithmetic mean of x_i, $i = 1, 2, \ldots, n$. The values $\frac{1}{n}$ and $\sum_{i=1}^{n}(x_i - \overline{x})^2$ can be treated as fixed and they determine the value of the lever for the i-th observation. With the increase in the difference between the actual value and the mean value of the variable x, the value of lever for the given observation increases. In practice the values of the lever are in the range $[0, 1]$, and therefore if the value is greater than $4/n$ it indicates abnormality of the analyzed observation, because it has a high value of the lever. In order to identify outliers the so-called studentized residual r_i is used, due to the fact that residual values may be different for successive values of x_i. The residual values are studentized in the case when they have the same scale and are defined as follows:

$$r_i = \frac{e_i}{SE_i} = \frac{y_i - \widetilde{y}_i}{s \cdot \sqrt{1 - h_i}}. \tag{15.1}$$

Analyzing the remaining values using studentized residual allows detection of actually outlying points, while omitting those that only seem outlying after analyzing residuals e_i, and in fact are not. If the remainder is positive, the actual value of the variable y is greater than the value calculated by the regression equation for a given value of x. In the case of negative remainder, the actual value of the variable y is smaller than the predicted value. From a practical point of view, an observation (point) is considered outlying if its studentized residual values are outside the range $[-2, 2]$.

In the case when in the analyzed set there is an outlying observation (a point), but it has a small value e_i, the analysis of studentized residuals will not qualify it as outlier, although in reality it is an outlying observation. Therefore, one should use the so-called modified studentized residuals d_i that examine the difference between the actual value Y_i, and its predicted value for the ith observation omitted in the analysis. Modified residual d_i is defined by the following formula: $d_i = Y_i - \widetilde{Y}_{i_i}$ where $\widetilde{Y}_{i_i}$ is the predicted value of dependent variable for the set of all the observations except the ith observation. The value of the modified studentized residual is defined by the formula (15.2), where SE_{d_i} is the standard error of the modified residual.

$$t_i = \frac{d_i}{SE_{d_i}}. \tag{15.2}$$

While detecting outliers using linear regression, what is important are the observations that take very high or very low (and therefore untypical) value of the covariate x for a typical value of the dependent variable y. We then called them high leverage point observations. Influential observations are also important, namely such observations whose presence in the dataset affects the linear regression coefficient by changing its slope. Not every outlying observation or high leverage point is an influential observation. Usually, an influential point combines the features of a high leverage point and a high residual value, so although it will not be recognized as either of them, it will still be an influential point. The influence of the ith observation h_i is defined as the difference between the actual value of the variable x_i and the predicted value $\widetilde{x}_i$. The higher the square of the difference, the bigger the influence. For the model, in which the total number of predictors and dependent variables is v there is the equality $\sum_{i=1}^{n} h_i = v$, as well as $1 \leqslant h_i \leqslant \frac{1}{n}$. In view of this equality, it should be noted that for the impact of the value h_i to be typical, it should not be greater than v/n. In the case where for the i-th observation h_i has a value of above $2v/n$ it can be considered as potentially influential. In many works, the detection of outliers using regression is treated as a preliminary analysis of the data. For example, see [15–17, 38, 43].

Local Outlier Factor Algorithm

Local Outlier Factor Algorithm (LOF) introduces the concept of the so-called local outlier, which refers to an object in the analyzed dataset which is significantly different from most other objects — its local neighbors. LOF detects outliers based on the determined factor, thanks to which each object is assigned a degree of uniqueness. Only the local neighborhood of an object is taken into account. This algorithm assigns each object in a multidimensional dataset the LOF factor and defines the points with the highest value as outliers.

It is assumed that the object whose LOF factor is approximately 1 ($LOF \in (0.8; 1.2)$) belongs to a designated group of objects (belongs to the cluster). Objects whose LOF factor changes abruptly in relation to its local neighbors (a sudden increase or decrease in the values can be observed) are called local objects (points) — the local outliers detected in the dataset. The so-called rank of uniqueness, allocated to each object by the LOF factor, is dependent on how much the object is isolated in relation to its surrounding neighbors. The local factor outlier is defined by formula (15.3).

Def. 15.1. Local Outlier Factor

$$LOF_{M_{int}} = \frac{\sum_{o \in N} \frac{LGO_{M_{int}}(o)}{LGO_{M_{int}}(x)}}{\mid N_{M_{int}(x)} \mid}, \tag{15.3}$$

where LGO is the local density of object p defined by (15.4) and $N_{M_{int}}(x)$ is the proximity of the object p.

Def. 15.2. Local Density of Object p
Local density of the object p is defined as the inverse of the average distance achieved, given as initial conditions, in the MinPts coefficient of the nearest neighbor of p, while obr — $d_M(x, o)$ denotes the achievable distance of the object p from the object o.

$$LGO_M(x) = \frac{\mid N_{M_{int}}(x) \mid}{\sum_{o \in N}^{max} obr - d_M(x, o)}. \tag{15.4}$$

If in the dataset there are points p which overlap (or if there are the smallest objects $MinPts$, different from p) then the sum of all the derived distances equals 0. The LOF factor is the average ratio of local density achieved for the object p and its q nearest neighbors defined in the coefficient $MinPts$. This coefficient, therefore, determines the degree of uniqueness of the object p. The higher it is, the greater the probability that point p is an outlier.

In the case when the objects are located in the center of the cluster, LOF is approximately equal to 1 and the objects are not treated as outliers. This is a core property of the LOF factor. If the nearest neighborhood $MinPts$ of the object p belong to different clusters with different density, we observe changes in LOF (an increase or a decrease) for the object p.

Connectivity-Based Outlier Factor Algorithm

The Connectivity-Based Outlier Factor Algorithm, called COF (Connectivity Outlier Factor) for short, is based on the distance between objects, while also taking into account the density of the objects in the set. This is a modification of the LOF algorithm described above.

The following situations may occur in a dataset under examination. Firstly, it is possible to detect a cluster of low density, which means that the number of points in the vicinity of the objects is relatively small. Secondly, it is possible to detect an isolated cluster, which in turn means that the neighboring objects to point p are located within its surrounding at a distance equal to the radius r. This isolation may be a cluster of low density but this is not the rule. Low density of an outlier results from the deviation of the given object from (the samples of) the cluster of high density, whereas isolation of an outlier results from the deviation of the object from the samples located in its vicinity.

The main idea of the COF algorithm is to determine the so-called COF isolation coefficient(factor) for each object from the dataset. This factor determines how much the object is isolated from the whole set. The analysis of the value of COF factor divides the data into the set of proper objects and the set of outliers.

Let G be a set of objects. Let the set $\{p_1, p_2, , p_r\} \in G$ for each $i \in [1, r-1]$ the p_{i+1} element is the nearest neighbor to the set $\{p_1, p_2, \ldots, p_i\}$ in $\{p_1, p_2, \ldots, p_r\}$. Let the set $\{p_1, p_2, \ldots, p_r\}$ be the shortest path from p_1 to G indicating the order in which the nearest objects are presented. Let every sequence $\{e_1, e_2, \ldots, e_{r-1}\}$, for which for all and $i \in [1, r-1]$ element of the sequence $e_i = (o_i, p_{i+1})$,where $o_i \in \{p_1, p_2, \ldots, p_i\}$ and $d(e_i) = d(o_i, p_{i+1}) = d(\{p_1, p_2, \ldots p_i\}, \{p_{i+1}, p_{i+2}, \ldots, p_r\})$ be called the trace of the shortest path. Each e_i is called the edge, and the sequence $\{d(e_1, e_2, \ldots, e_{r-1})\}$ is called the cost description $\{e_1, e_2, \ldots, e_{r-1}\}$. Then $SCP_G(p_1)$ is defined as (15.5) is called the average distance of connection from p_1 to $G - \{p_1\}$ or the average cost of connection from p_1 to $G - \{p_1\}$.

$$SCP_G(p_1) = \sum_{i=1}^{r-1} \frac{2(r-i)}{r(r-1)} d(e_i). \tag{15.5}$$

Def. 15.3. The isolating factor COF

Let $p \in P$, $k \in N$. The isolating factor COF for p regarding its k — neighborhood N_k is the proximity factor of the following form (15.6):

$$COF_k(p) = \frac{|N_k(p)| \cdot SCP_{N_k(p)}(p)}{\sum_{o \in N_k(p)} SCP_{N_k}}. \tag{15.6}$$

Connectivity-Based Outlier Factor Algorithm COF, according to the above definitions, requires three input parameters: the number of objects of the nearest neighborhood, isolation threshold Pr, and a set of data for instance $D = p_1, p_2, \ldots, p_n$. In the first step, the algorithm determines the COF factor for each object p taking into account its k — nearest neighborhood, or $COF_k(p)$. Next, the selection of outliers takes place. The object p is regarded as an outlier if the value of the designated factor COFk(p) for this object is greater than the isolation threshold Pr, in other words, $COF_k(p) > Pr$. In many studies, objects with values of COF greater than 1 are likely to be classified as outliers, while objects for which the value of COF is close to 1 belong to the pattern. But it is not clear, therefore, we should also define how the COF values for objects considered to be outliers differ from the highest value of COF. Therefore, let us introduce the definition of the indicator of uniqueness.

Def. 15.4. The indicator of uniqueness
Let O be a set of k objects. Let $COF(o)$ be an isolating factor for the object $o \in O$ and $COF_{max} = max\{COF(o_1), COF(o_2), \ldots, COF(o_k)\}$. The object is called an outlier when its isolating factor $COF(o)$ fulfills the following condition (15.7):

$$COF(o) > COF_{max} - \frac{COF_{max} - 1}{WW}, \qquad (15.7)$$

while WW is called the indicator of uniqueness, $WW \notin 0$.

Using the indicator of uniqueness WW sets the ratio between the proximity of the object to the detected outlier and the difference between $COF(o)$ and the value of 1. The following two cases may be noted here:

- The lower the indicator of uniqueness WW is, the more objects can be indicated as outliers by the COF algorithm.
- For the indicator of uniqueness equal to 1 ($WW = 1$), the outliers will be those objects whose isolating factor is greater than 1 ($COF > 1$).

The advantage of the COF algorithm is that it is able to detect outliers from the data of different densities as well as outliers that are close to areas with low density, due to which it may be difficult to detect them using other algorithms (especially those based only on the density).

Density-Based Spatial Clustering of Applications with Noise
Density-Based Spatial Clustering of Applications with Noise (DBSCAN)

belongs to a group of methods based on the concept of density of a set of objects. It is assumed that all dense collections of objects which are separated by regions of low density are clusters. DBSCAN allows locating clusters of any shape. It identifies clusters in large datasets, considering the local distribution of its elements. Classification for core objects (belonging to the cluster) and border objects is based on two parameters, namely the maximum neighborhood radius (Eps) and a minimum number of points in Eps-neighborhood ($MinPts$).

Def. 15.5. The density cluster

The cluster is called a density cluster if it is the largest in terms of density achievable by the collection of density-connected objects. An object that does not belong to any cluster is an outlier.

A cluster can be formed from one of the basic points and always has the same shape. Let p be the starting point in cluster C at a certain minimum distance (Eps) and the minimum number of points at that distance ($MinPts$). If the cluster O is density-reachable from the point p for the same $MinPts$ and Eps, the cluster C corresponds to the designated cluster O.

In order to find a cluster, the Density Based Spatial Clustering algorithm begins to search from any point p and finds all points density-reachable from p, taking into consideration the assumed values of Eps and $MinPts$. If p is a point designated as the starting point, this procedure results in a cluster, depending on the Eps and $MinPts$. If p is a border point, and the next points are not density-reachable from the point p, the DBSCAN checks another point in the database. $MinPts$ is defined as the core point if in the adjacent neighborhood of the point there are at least $MinPts$ objects. DBSCAN checks Eps-neighborhood for each of the objects and defines a new cluster in the case where the neighborhood of the point n contains at least $MinPts$ objects and adds all Eps-neighbors of the point n to this cluster. The algorithm is repeated for the next core points which were incorporated into the new cluster and then for the other points. In a situation where one core point is included in another cluster, there is a merger of clusters.

In this algorithm, outliers are the points which are not assigned to any cluster. Undoubtedly, the advantage of DBSCAN is the ability to detect clusters (areas) of irregular shapes. However, the difficulty lies in the proper selection of input parameters.

4. Outlier Information in Textual Records

Outlier information can also be contained in textual documents. Of course, the problem of outlier detection in textual records may be analyzed at many levels. However, it seems natural to approach this problem from the point of view of semantics. There is still a wide scope for research in this field. The problem at hand has been recognized by Aggrawal [2], who mentioned using outlier analysis for the detection of anomalies, such as first story detection in a text stream.

According to Aggrawal, latent semantic indexing significantly enhances the representation of textual data, which often contain synonymy and polysemy. The issue of detecting the first story in a stream of documents, as observed for example in a newswire service, provides the focal point of studies on detecting outliers in a textual data. Usually, the first story is detected as a non-temporal case, which, in the context of temporal data, is a novelty. Aggrawal [2] explains the problem of first story detection by means of proximity-based and probabilistic models. He briefly describes the vector-space based TF-IDF (time frequency — inverse document frequency) representation, often used for text processing. Aggrawal also applies the cosine function to vector-space representations in order to measure the similarity between two normalized document frequency vectors x and y. The are a variety of similarity measures described in the literature. Most of them refer to the similarities between the values of the attributes (by means of various normalization techniques), or similarity in context. However, to the best of our knowledge, there are no measures which refer to outliers in textual data.

Outlier detection can be seen as a way of ensuring that the summary of a database, in this case — a text or text-numeric database, is complete. Sometimes what the user needs is a synthetic and easily interpretable description of the contents of the database, i.e its short description in a natural or semi-natural language — in other words — a summary.

Summary is the process of extracting important information from a source in order to create its shorter, more concise form, and thus make it more useful for the user and for a given task [31]. Different types of summaries can be employed to provide the user with a timely access to, and digest of, information cataloged in a comprehensive database. In light of the above, outlier detection can be regarded as a vital element contributing to the creation of a complete picture of the database.

As in the case of numerical data, the comparison of textual data also requires an appropriate tool. There are many ways to compare strings and text, which, if correctly applied, can be useful in creating summaries and identifying outliers. Due to the limited length of this paper, we will concentrate exclusively on the generalized n-gram method.

Comparison of textual records

Frequently, when comparing and analyzing texts, one counts occurrence of certain substrings in the compared words (textual records). In the generalized n-gram method used here see [32–34], one calculates (15.8):

$$\mu_{RS}(s_1, s_2) = \frac{2}{N^2 + N} \sum_{i=1}^{N(s_1)} \sum_{j=1}^{N(s_1)-i+1} h(i,j), \qquad (15.8)$$

which can be interpreted as the relation of similarity between two words (strings), where s_1, s_2 are words from the set S, RS is the fuzzy relationship of the membership function $\mu_{RS} : S \times S \longrightarrow [0,1]$, $h(i,j) = 1$ if the i-element substring of characters appearing in the word s_1 and beginning at the jth position in the word s_1 occurs at least once in the word s_2; $h(i,j) = 0$ if the i-element substring of characters appearing in the word s_1 and beginning at the jth position in the word s_1 does not occur in the word s_2; $N(s_1), N(s_2)$ — the number of characters in the words s_1 and s_2 respectively; $N = max\{N(s_1), N(s_2)\}$.

Note, that the result of the similarity between two words depends on the order of words compared. The above concept can be interpreted in terms of fuzzy set and fuzzy relations introduced by Zadeh in [47].

In a natural way, the similarity of sentences can be defined as follows:

$$RZ = \{(< z_1, z_2 >, \mu_{RZ}(z_1, z_2)) : z_1, z_2 \epsilon Z\}, \qquad (15.9)$$

where $\mu_{RZ} : Z \times Z \longrightarrow [0,1]$ can be interpreted as a membership function and it is defined as (15.10):

$$\mu_{RZ}(z_1, z_2) = \frac{1}{N} \sum_{i=1}^{N(z_1)} \max_{j\epsilon 1,...,N(z_2)} \mu_{RW}(w_i, w_j), \qquad (15.10)$$

where s_i is the ith word in sentence z_1, s_j is the jth word in the sentence z_2, and g is the membership function defined by the formula (15.10). Note that this formula opens the possibility of comparison of text pieces longer than just one sentence.

Example 1

Let us take two words $s_1 = OUTLIER$ and $s_2 = OUTLAW$. Let us compare these words with fuzzy relation of RS. Then $N(s_1) = 7, N(s_2) = 6$, so $N = max\{N(s_1), N(s_2)\} = 7$. According to the formula (15.8) one obtains:

$$\mu_{RS}(s_1, s_2) = \frac{2}{7^2 + 7} \sum_{i=1}^{7} \sum_{j=1}^{7-i+1} h(i,j) = \frac{2(4+3+2+1)}{56} = \frac{20}{56} = 0.3571$$

because there are:

- four single substrings (O, U, T, L)
- three double substrings (OU, UT, TL)
- two triple substrings (OUT UTL)
- one four-element substring (OUTL).

Example 2

Let $z_1 = $ "GOOD VISIBILITY ON THE ROAD" be the reference sentence and $z_2 = $ "GOOD VISIBILITY" be the second sentence compared to the base sentence z_1. Here $N(z_1) = 5$, $N(z_2) = 2$, $N = max\{N(z_1), N(z_2)\} = 5$. Using the formula (15.10) one obtains.

$\mu_{RZ}(z_1, z_2) = \frac{1}{5} \sum_{i=1}^{4} max_{j \in 1,2,3,4} g(s_1, s_2)$
$= \frac{1}{5} max\{\mu_{RS}(Good, Good), \mu_{RS}(Good, Visibility)\}$
$+ max\{\mu_{RS}(Visibility, Visibility), \mu_{RS}(Visibility, Good)\}$
$+ max\{\mu_{RS}(on, Visibility), \mu_{RS}(on, good)\}$
$+ max\{\mu_{RS}(the, good)), \mu_{RS}(the, Visibility)\}$
$+ max\{\mu_{RS}(raod, good), \mu_{RS}(road, visibility)\} = 0.4.$

Note that the greater the difference in the length of word pair s_1, s_2, the smaller the degree of their similarity i.e. the greater the difference between them. The more common letters there are in the strings s_1, s_2, the more similar the strings are. An analogous observation holds for the comparison of sentences.

5. Detection of Outlier Information in Numeric and Textual Records Using Linguistic Summaries

The approach to generating linguistic summaries employed in the present paper uses Yagers proposal [45,46] to construct such a sentence in a natural language that describes the quantity of the set of objects charactarized by properties included in the query. This approach was later elaborated by Kacprzyk, Yager and Zadrozny [20] and Kacprzyk and Yager [21]. The very fact that it involves quantity description suggests that the method may be useful for detection of rare objects, facts or statements, which can be regarded as outliers. The method of detecting outliers using linguistic summaries developed by the authors of this chapter allows the simultaneous analysis of textual and numerical records.

According to Yager, a linguistic summary of data is in the form of ordered four elements: $\langle Q, P, S, T \rangle$ where:

Q — is a linguistic quantifier, or quantity in agreement, which is a fuzzy determination of amount. Quantifier Q determines how many records in the analyzed database fulfill the required condition - has the characteristic S.

P — subject of summary, it means the actual objects stored in the records in the database

S — the summarizer, the feature by which the database is scanned

T — the degree of truth, it determines the extent to which the result of the summary, expressed in a natural language, is true.

The linguistic summary of a database is given by Def. 15.6:

Def. 15.6. *The linguistic summary is on the form:*
Q P are (have) S [T]
or, in an extended version
Q of objects being P are S (have property S)
[and correctness of this is of degree T].

Example 3
If we ask:
How many young patient in hospital are in good condition.
The resulting summary could be:
Few young patient are in good condition [0.40].
Many young patient are in good condition [0.10].
Almost all young patient are in good condition [0.03].
Degree of membership [0.40], [0.1], [0.03] confirms the truth of our inquiry.

The definition of an outlier in linguistic summaries for numerical and textual data
As stated in the introduction, an outlier is a single element or a very small group of objects, that compared to the other objects in the database, are distinguished by the values of the analyzed feature. Therefore, considering

the definition of outliers given by Hawkins and the definition of a linguistic summary formulated above (Def. 15.6), an outlier in the sense of linguistic summaries can be defined. The method of generating linguistic summaries can be used to detect exceptions, which constitutes an original contribution of the authors. A factor, which determines whether there are outliers in the database, is the defined set of linguistic variables Q and the determined degree of truth T. The procedure itself is the same as for Yager's linguistic summaries. Consequently, the proper definition of an outlier is as follows.

Def. 15.7. **Outlier**
*If for any subject P being R and having property S, the amount determination Q is **small** and T is **big** the P is considered **to be abnormal**. The "**smallness**" of Q and "**big value**" (or "**satisfactory grade**") of confidence T need to be defined (by the user or the system designer).*

Outlier detection using linguistic summaries
The procedure begins with defining a set of linguistic values $X = \{Q_1, Q_2, \ldots, Q_n\}$ and establishing the "big value" of the degree of truth T_b. Then, the value of r is calculated by the formula (15.11). According to the procedure of generating a linguistic summary proposed by Kacprzyk and Zadrozny [22–25], r is determined for a summary of many attributes. In our case, one attribute is textual while the other one is numeric. Then, the average membership of objects r from the set Y limited by the feature S to the set of objects with complex feature R is defined as (15.11):

$$r = \frac{\sum_{i=1}^{n}(\mu_R(x_i) \cdot \mu_S(x_i))}{\sum_{i=1}^{n} \mu_R(x_i)}. \tag{15.11}$$

We continue to generate the summary for the designated r by setting the value of the degree of truth as (15.12):

$$T = \mu_Q(r). \tag{15.12}$$

The most essential stage of the detection of outliers is the verification of the value T_b by comparison with the obtained value of T of the generated summary. If, for the "smallness" of the Q value, we obtain T belonging to T_b, then the outliers are found to be present in the database under examination.

The algorithm involves the following steps:

(1) Definition of the set of linguistic variables $Q = \{$ "*very few*", "*few*", "*many*", "*almost all*"$\}$. The smallness of $Q_{smallness} = $ "*very few*".

(2) Setting a big value of $T_b = n$, where $n \in [0,1]$.

(3) Entering a query to a database relating to the numerical attribute and textual attribute, for example.

Query 1: How many P being R are S?

Query 2: Are there QP being R which are S?

(4) Determining the membership functions for the feature S of the text attribute for all the records $\mu_S(x_i)$.

(5) Introducing the base statement and compare it with sentences in each record.

(6) Defining similarity function of the base statement for each sentence as a textual attribute $\mu_R(x_i)$.

(7) Calculating r according to the formula (15.11).

(8) Determining the degree of truth T by the formula (15.12).

(9) Results of generation of linguistic summary::

For Query 1:

Q_1 P being R are $S[T]$

Q_2 P being R are $S[T]$

$\vdots$

Q_N P being R are $S[T]$

For Query 2:

Q_1 P being R are $S[T]$

(10) Verifying the obtained T with T_b for the value $Q_{smallness}$.

(10a) If for $Q_{smallness}$ the value of $T \geq T_b$ outliers are detected.

(10b) If for $Q_{smallness}$ the value of $T < T_b$, outliers are not detected.

6. Examples of Outliers Detection

The search for outliers was carried out in a set of 599 records. The database contained information on the factors of heart attack. According to the definition, a myocardial infarction diagnosis is based on clinical events and laboratory examination. Myocardial infarction is a condition in which, together with clinical symptoms of ischemia (chest pain, shortness of breath, nausea, diaphoresis, etc.) there is evidence of necrosis of the cells. The high risk group includes men aged over 40 who suffer from abdominal obesity and hypertension.

In the analyzed database, the factors taken into account to assess the patient's risk of a heart attack were, among others, age, systolic blood pressure, diastolic blood pressure, cholesterol, body mass index, number of

Table 15.1. The decisive attribute defining the degree of risk of myocardial infarction.

No	Degree of high risk of myocardial infarction
1	High risk of myocardial infarction.
2	Patients at high risk of myocardial infarction.
3	High degree of infarct risk.
4	A patient with a high infraction risk degree
5	Low risk of myocardial infarction.
6	Medium degree of risk of myocardial infarction.
7	High degree of risk of myocardial infarction.

cigarettes smoked. The decisive attribute defining the risk degree of developing myocardial infarction by a given patient was a text attribute. Table 15.1 shows examples of the value of the attribute "risk of myocardial infarction". Special attention was paid to ensuring that the base did not contain any empty values in the records, which is important for the detection of outliers.

The first stage of the research concerned the detection of outliers for numeric attributes. For both the DBSCAN algorithm and the COF algorithm used for research, the initial values were determined experimentally. For DBSCAN the best results, that is the detection of 21 outliers, were obtained for the values of $Eps = 15$, the number of elements = 3. An increase or a decrease in Eps resulted in a significant deterioration of detection of outliers. For $Eps > 15$ all the outliers were qualified as valid data.

The results obtained by the COF algorithm show that the change of threshold value $Pr = \{90, \ldots, 99\}$ to a value greater than 95 with the number of nearest-neighbor $k = \{3, 5\}$ does not alter the number of detected outliers i.e. it does not affect the accuracy of the search. COF algorithm correctly found 21 outliers at the $k = 3$ and $Pr = 95$. The results are shown in Table 15.2.

Table 15.2. Outliers detected with the DBSCAN and COF algorithms.

DBSCAN			COF		
Eps	The number of elements	The number of detected outliers	The accuracy of threshold	The number of nearest neighbors	The number of outliers detected
15	3	21	95	3	21
20	3	0	97	3	21
5	5	6	90	5	7
10	5	14	93	5	12
15	5	19	95	5	19
20	5	0	97	5	19

The performance time of both algorithms, DBSCAN and COF, was comparable. Analyzing the detection of outliers for numerical attributes we gain knowledge about the number of outliers in the analyzed set. We are also able to identify the record which contains an outlying feature. However, we must carefully examine the attributes of the detected record in order to identify the feature which makes it unique.

In the method proposed by the authors of this chapter, the number of outliers is expressed not as a numeric value (e.g. 5 outliers, 15 outliers or 21 outliers) but in the form of sentences in a natural language. The generated linguistic summary may indicate that there are outliers in the analyzed set, but it does not identify the records where the outliers are contained. Undoubtedly, the advantage of using linguistic summaries in the detection of outliers is that when analyzing the query it is known which attributes are considered. Additionally, the presented solution enables the analysis of outliers both in text and numerical data simultaneously.

Detection of outliers using linguistic summaries

Let us, therefore, detect outliers using linguistic summaries. Let us consider both numerical and text attributes. According to the procedure of detecting outliers in linguistic summaries, let us determine the initial parameters. Let us define a set of linguistic values as $X = \{$ *"very few"*, *"few"*, *"many"*, *"almost all"*$\}$. The graphical interpretation of linguistic values is shown in Fig. 15.1. Let the value of "smallness" be $Q_{smallness} =$ *"very few"* and let the "big value" of T_b be 0.70. Let us consider the following query:

Query 1) How many young patients are at high risk for infarct.

The age is a number attribute, whereas the risk is a text attribute. The succeeding text records are compared against the base sentence: "High risk of myocardial infarction" using the membership function of similarity (15.9, 15.10). Table 15.3 shows the similarity scores obtained for a number of selected records.

In the present query, we are looking for young patients. Therefore, let us define the membership functions of young people in the form of (15.13).

$$y_{youngpatient}(x) = \begin{cases} 0 & x < 24, \\ \frac{x-24}{3} & 24 \le x < 27, \\ 1 & 27 \le x < 30, \\ \frac{34-x}{4} & 30 \le x < 34, \\ 0 & x \ge 34. \end{cases} \qquad (15.13)$$

We proceed to determine the linguistic degree of truth of the generated

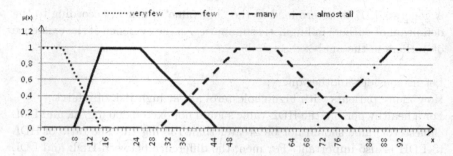

Fig. 15.1.   Graphical interpretation of linguistic variable X.

Table 15.3.   The similarity scores between the selected sentences and the base sentence.

	Determination of the risk of myocardial infarction	Similarity of the two sentences
1	High risk of myocardial infarction.	0.6577
2	Patients at high risk of myocardial infarction.	0.7157
3	High degree of infarct risk.	0.4793
4	A patient with a high infraction risk degree	0.0219
5	Low risk of myocardial infarction.	0.5387
6	Medium degree of risk of myocardial infarction.	0.5395
7	High degree of risk of myocardial infarction.	0.6654

linguistic summary. On the basis of formula (15.11) we determine the value of r as (15.14) and generated T (15.12).

$$r = \frac{\sum_{i=1}^{n} [\mu_{youngpatient}(x_i) \cdot \mu_{similarity}(z_i)]}{\sum_{i=1}^{n} \mu_{youngpatient}(x_i)}. \qquad (15.14)$$

We receive a generated linguistic summary in the form:
Few young patients are at high risk of myocardial infarction; $T[0.72]$.
Many young patients are at high risk of myocardial infarction; $T[0.36]$.
Almost all young patients are at high risk of myocardial infarction; $T[0.07]$.

The analysis of the detection of an outlier:
The determined smallness value of $Q_{smallness}$ of the set of linguistic variables was *"very few"*. Therefore, we check whether the determined degree of truth is greater than or equal to the predetermined big value T_b for $Q_{smallness}$. In the generated linguistic summary, the degree of truth was $T = 0.72$ for the $Q_{smallness} = $ *"very few"* and thus the value of $T > T_b$ (T

is generated, T_b is determined as the "big value"), which, according to the definition of outliers in linguistic summaries, is the evidence of the existence of outliers in the analyzed set.

Let us consider another query:
How many patients with high cholesterol are at high risk of infarct.
For a healthy person, the HDL value should not exceed 200 mg/dl, and LDL cholesterol value should not be greater than 135 mg/dl. The ratio of HDL to LDH is also important. For men, the difference between HDL and LDL should be between 30 and 70 mg/dl, while for women this difference should be in the range of 40-80 mg/dl. Therefore, the three following standards were defined as: $HDL - LDH < 30$ below normal; $30 < HDL - LDH < 80$ normal; $HDL - LDH > 80$ above normal.

For each standard a fuzzy set was prepared. The graphic interpretation of the normal cholesterol level is shown in Fig. 15.2. Initial conditions of the procedure of detecting outliers in linguistic summaries are the same as in the example given above, $Q_{smallness} =$ "very few", $T_b > 0.7$. Analogously to query 1, we proceed to determine the linguistic degree of truth of the generated linguistic summary. We determine the value of r (15.15) and generated T by (15.12).

$$r = \frac{\sum_{i=1}^{n} [\mu_{HDL}(x_i) \cdot \mu_{similarity}(z_i)]}{\sum_{i=1}^{n} \mu_{HDL}(x_i)}. \tag{15.15}$$

We receive a generated linguistic summary in the form for query 2:
Few patients with high cholesterol are at high risk for heart attack; $T[0.21]$.
Many patients with high cholesterol are at high risk for heart attack; $T[0.85]$.
Almost all patients with high cholesterol are at high risk for heart attack; $T[0.35]$.

In this case, therefore, the outliers have not been detected because for the $Q_{smallness} =$ "very few", the value $T < 0.7$.

7. Summary

The aim of this study was to present a practical solution to the problem of outlier detection in a dataset of numeric, or both numeric and linguistic character. First, the selected outlier detection algorithms for numeric data were presented and evaluated. The advantages and disadvantages of each

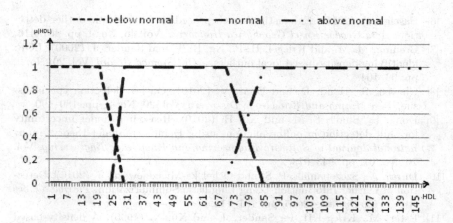

Fig. 15.2. Graphical interpretation of the normal cholesterol level.

proposal were pointed out. It may be concluded that the DBSCAN and COF algorithms detect outliers in numerical data quickly and accurately. However, the choice of initial parameters for those algorithms is a complicated task. Moreover, they cannot directly be used for the analysis of textual data. Thus, a non-standard approach to the detection of outliers using linguistic summaries has been proposed. As shown by the results, a non-trivial use of linguistic summaries opens up new possibilities for the detection of outliers in databases containing both numeric and textual data. A major advantage of the proposed method is the simplified choice of input parameters. The results obtained in the form of sentences in a natural language are clear, understandable and user friendly.

References

[1] Aggarwal, Ch. C. and Yu, P. S. (2001), Outlier detection for high dimensional data, *ACM Sigmod Record*, Vol. 30, No. 2, pp. 37–46.

[2] Aggarwal, Ch. C. (2013), *Outlier Detection in Categorical, Text and Mixed Attribute Data, Outlier Analysis*, Springer, pp. 199–223.

[3] Aggarwal, Ch. C. (2013), *Outlier Analysis*, Springer Science & Business Media.

[4] Angiulli, F., and Pizzuti, C. (2002), *Fast Outlier Detection in High Dimensional Spaces, PKDD*, Vol. 2, pp. 15–26.

[5] Barnett, V. and Lewis, T. (1994), *Outliers in Statistical Data*, Wiley, New York, Vol. 3.

[6] Baselga, S. (2011), Exhaustive search procedure for multiple outlier detection, *Acta Geodaetica et Geophysica Hungarica*, Vol. 46, No. 4, pp. 401–416.

[7] Breunig, M. M. and Kriegel, H.-P., Ng, R. T. and Sander, J. (2000), LOF: identifying density-based local outliers, *ACM Sigmod Record*, Vol. 29, No. 2, pp. 93–104.

[8] Chawla, S., Hand, D. and Dhar, V. (2010), Outlier detection special issue, *Data Mining and Knowledge Discovery*, Vol. 20, No. 2, pp. 189–190.

[9] Dong, F., Shatz, S. M. and Xu, H. (2010), Reasoning under uncertainty for shill detection in online auctions using Dempster–Shafer theory, *International Journal of Software Engineering and Knowledge Engineering*, Vol. 20, No. 07, pp. 943–973.

[10] Duraj, A., Szczepaniak, P. S. and Ochelska-Mierzejewska, J. (2016), Detection of Outlier Information Using Linguistic Summarization, *Flexible Query Answering Systems 2015*, pp. 101–113.

[11] Ester, M., Kriegel H. P., Sander, J. and Xu, X. (1996), A density-based algorithm for discovering clusters in large spatial databases with noise, *Kdd*, Vol. 96, No. 34, pp. 226-231.

[12] Goel, A., Xu, H. and Shatz, S. M. (2010), A multi-state bayesian network for shill verification in online auctions, *SEKE*, pp. 279–285.

[13] Hawkins, D. M. (1980), *Identification of Outliers*, Springer, Vol. 11.

[14] He, Z., Xu, X. and Deng, S. (2003), Discovering cluster-based local outliers, *Pattern Recognition Letters*, Vol. 24, No. 9, pp. 1641–1650.

[15] Hekimoglu, S., Erenoglu, R. C. and Kalina, J. (2009), Outlier detection by means of robust regression estimators for use in engineering science, *Journal of Zhejiang University Science A*, Vol. 10, No. 6, pp. 909–921.

[16] Hodge, V. J. and Austin, J. (2004), A survey of outlier detection methodologies, *Artificial Intelligence Review*, Springer, Vol. 22, No. 2, pp. 85–126.

[17] Hoeting, J., Raftery, A. E. and Madigan, D. (1996), A method for simultaneous variable selection and outlier identification in linear regression, *Computational Statistics & Data Analysis*, Vol. 22, No. 3, pp. 351–270.

[18] Jin, W., Tung, A. K. H. and Han, J. (2001), Mining top-n local outliers in large databases, *Proceedings of the seventh ACM SIGKDD International Conference on Knowledge Discovery and Data Mining*, ACM, pp. 293–298.

[19] John, G. H. (1995), Robust decision trees: removing outliers from databases, *KDD*. pp. 174–179.

[20] Kacprzyk, J., Yager, R. R. and Zadrożny, S. (2000), A fuzzy logic based approach to linguistic summaries of databases, *International Journal of Applied Mathematics and Computer Science*, Vol. 10, No. 4, pp. 813–834.

[21] Kacprzyk, J. and Yager, R. R. (2001), Linguistic summaries of data using fuzzy logic, *International Journal of General System*, Vol. 30, No. 2, pp. 133–154.

[22] Kacprzyk, J., Wilbik, A. and Zadrożny, S. (2008), Linguistic summarization of time series using a fuzzy quantifier driven aggregation, *Fuzzy Sets and Systems*, Vol. 159, No. 12, pp. 1485–1499.

[23] Kacprzyk, J., Wilbik, A. and Zadrożny, S. (2010), An approach to the linguistic summarization of time series using a fuzzy quantifier driven aggregation, *International Journal of Intelligent Systems*, Vol. 25, No. 5, pp. 411–439.

[24] Kacprzyk, J. and Zadrożny, S. (2010), Computing with words is an implementable paradigm: fuzzy queries, linguistic data summaries, and natural-language generation, *IEEE Transactions on Fuzzy Systems*, Vol. 18, No. 3, pp. 461–472.

[25] Kacprzyk, J. and Zadrożny, S. (2012), Bipolar queries: some inspirations from intention and preference modeling, *Combining Experimentation and Theory*, pp. 191–208.

[26] Knorr, E. M. and Ng, R. T. (1997), A unified notion of outliers: properties and computation, *KDD*, pp. 219–222.

[27] Knorr, E. M. and Ng, R. T. and Tucakov, V. (2000), Distance-based outliers: algorithms and applications, *The VLDB Journal* Vol. 8, No. 3-4, pp. 237–253.

[28] Knox, E. M. and Ng, R. T. (1998), Algorithms for mining distancebased outliers in large datasets, *Proceedings of the International Conference on Very Large Data Bases*, pp. 392–403.

[29] Kreinovich, V., Longpré, L., Patangay, P., Ferson, S. and Ginzburg, L. (2005), Outlier detection under interval uncertainty: algorithmic solvability and computational complexity, *Reliable Computing*, Vol. 11, No. 1, pp. 59–76.

[30] Kriegel, H.-P., Kröger, P., Schubert, E. and Zimek, A. (2009), LoOP: local outlier probabilities, *Proceedings of the 18th ACM Conference on Information and Knowledge Management*, ACM, pp. 1649–1652.

[31] Mani, I. and Maybury, M. T. (1999), *Advances in Automatic Text Summarization*, MIT Press, Vol. 293.

[32] Niewiadomski, A. and Szczepaniak, P. S. (2006), News generating based on interval type-2 linguistic summaries of databases, *Proceedings of IPMU 2006 conference*, pp. 1324–1331.

[33] Niewiadomski, A. (2008), A type-2 fuzzy approach to linguistic summarization of data, *IEEE Transactions on Fuzzy Systems*, Vol. 16, No. 1, pp. 198–212.

[34] Niewiadomski, A. (2008), *Methods for the Linguistic Summarization of Data: Aplications of Fuzzy Sets and Their Extensions*, Akademicka Oficyna Wydawnicza" Exit.

[35] Orair, G. H. and Teixeira, C. HC. and Meira Jr., Wagner Y. and Wang, Y. and Parthasarathy, S. (2010), Distance-based outlier detection: consolidation and renewed bearing, *Proceedings of the VLDB Endowment*, VLDB Endowment, Vol. 3, No. 1–2, pp. 1469–1480.

[36] Pei, Y., Zaiane, O. R. and Gao, Y. (2006), An efficient reference-based approach to outlier detection in large datasets, *2006. ICDM'06. Sixth International Conference on Data Mining*, IEEE, pp. 478–487.

[37] Ramaswamy, S., Rastogi, R. and Shim, K. (200), Efficient algorithms for mining outliers from large data sets, *ACM Sigmod Record*, Vol. 29, No 2, pp. 427–438.

[38] Rousseeuw, P. J. and Leroy, A. M. (2005), *Robust Regression and Outlier Detection*, John Wiley & Sons, Vol. 589.

[39] Schubert, E., Zimek, A. and Kriegel, H.-P.(2014), Local outlier detection reconsidered: a generalized view on locality with applications to spatial, video, and network outlier detection, *Data Mining and Knowledge Discovery*, Springer, Vol. 28, No. 1, pp. 190–237.

[40] Tang, J., Chen, Z., Wai-chee Fu, A. and Cheung, D. (2001), *A robust detection scheme for large data sets, 6th Pacific-Asia Conference on Knowledge Discovery and Data Mining*.

[41] Trevathan, J. and Read, W. (2009), *Detecting shill bidding in online English auctions, Handbook of research on social and organizational liabilities in information security, Information Science Reference*, pp. 446–470.

[42] Wang, J.-Ch. and Chiu, CQ.(2005), Detecting online auction inflated-reputation behaviors using social network analysis, *Proceedings of North American Association for Computational Social and Organizational Science*, pp. 26–28.

[43] Wisnowski, J. W., Montgomery, D. C. and Simpson, J. R. (2001), A comparative analysis of multiple outlier detection procedures in the linear regression model, *Computational Statistics & Data Analysis*, Vol. 36, No. 3, pp. 351–382.

[44] Xu, H. and Cheng, Y.-T,(2007), Model checking bidding behaviors in Internet concurrent auctions, *International Journal of Computer Systems Science & Engineering*, Vol. 22, No. 4, pp. 179–191.

[45] Yager R. R. (1982), A new approach to the summarization of data, *Information Sciences*, Elsevier, Vol. 28, No. 1, pp. 69–86.

[46] Yager, R. R. (1995), Linguistic summaries as a tool for databases discovery, *Workshop on Fuzzy Databases System and Information Retrieval*, Springer.

[47] Zadeh, L. A. (1965), *Information and Control*, World Scientific, Vol. 8, No. 3, pp. 338–353.

[48] Zhang, K. and Hutter, M. and Jin, H. (2009), A new local distance-based outlier detection approach for scattered real-world data, *Advances in Knowledge Discovery and Data Mining*, pp. 813–822.

Chapter 16

A Physicist's Perspective on How One Converts Observation into Information

Robert W. Johnson*

Alphawave Research,
Jonesboro, GA 30238, USA
robjohnson@alphawaveresearch.com

A fundamental question in science is how investigators are to convert their observations of the universe into information about the universe. That question is answered best using the language of probability theory. Using that language, what one expects to observe in any situation is given by the expectation value of the observable function with weight conditioned on the information one has accumulated. Before any observations have been reported, one must set the stage by defining the geometry of the parametric manifold. Because the observable must be expressed as a function to be evaluated mathematically, all models for the universe necessarily are parametric, even those which claim to be parameter free. As a concrete example of the process, a detailed study is made here of the simple problem of assigning a binary type to objects as they cross some specified line in space. The stage is set using the transformation group approach to establish the prior state of knowledge, and how one establishes the reliability of one's predictive power is expressed. When the probabilistic nature of observation is respected, one realizes that even perfect knowledge of the likelihood of an event's occurrence cannot yield perfect predictions of its occurrence, because the action of observation amounts to the selection of one particular universe out of the many which are possible.

1. Introduction

The premise of the scientific method is that observation of what the universe does yields information about how the universe works. The most fundamental observation that can be made is the occurrence of an event, which

---
*Current address: Department of Physics, Kennesaw State University, 1100 South Marietta Pkwy., MD # 9041, Marietta, GA 30060, USA.

immediately introduces the set of natural numbers to the discussion that count how many events occur within some specified region of space-time. That we have a universe at all implies the existence of a parametric manifold describing its geometry. The reason why the scientific method works is because the properties of the universe it hopes to describe are mathematical, a position argued strongly by Tegmark[1] recently. From the perspective of this physicist, what the success of quantum theory teaches us is that the action of observation is by nature probabilistic. Any particular record of observations is just one out of the many which are possible.

That the laws of physics apply equally to energy and information has recently been demonstrated[2] by the construction of an apparatus that implements Maxwell's demon using a photonic gas. In that experiment, the acquisition of information is accompanied by a measurable transfer of energy. In other words, there is no free lunch; in order to gain information about how the universe works, we have to work for it. When the cost of observation is high, one hopes to make the most out of every datum. How one does that over the years has been called many things, including but not limited to data analysis, predictive statistics, the art of the deal, or quite simply, physics.

A common problem that appears in many guises is how to predict the type of some unidentified particle knowing only its location, given a list of locations for where such particles of identified type have been found. One example of such a problem is the prediction of whether a passerby crossing some particular line in space is male or female based upon knowledge of where on the line previous passersby of known gender have crossed. The problem is predicated on the assumption that measurements of location are inexpensive compared to measurements of classification, so that after an initial training set of data has been evaluated some algorithm can then be used to predict the classification based only upon a given location with some degree of certainty that can be determined.

A specific case of this problem has recently been addressed using the method of kth nearest neighbor classification by Hall, *et al.*[3] In that paper, an optimal choice of k is evaluated empirically from the data, allowing for a nonparametric estimate of the desired probability. Another approach commonly employed for problems of this type is kernel density estimation.[4-6] In this chapter, we will examine how a parametric model is integrated over the parameter manifold with respect to the evidence measure to yield a prediction which depends only upon the given location. The transformation group aspect of the algorithm refers to the use of uninformative priors for the parameters, which nonetheless may be non-uniform for some particular choice of coordinate mapping of the parameter manifold. An analysis similar in spirit to this one has been presented by Poitevineau *et al.*[7]

The process of inductive reasoning is best described using the language of conditional probability theory.[8-10] Let us quickly review the notation and nomenclature that will be used in this chapter. The formal statement of the expression for the probability of A given conditions B can be written as

$$p(A \mid B) \equiv p_B^A, \tag{1}$$

where A and B can have arbitrary dimensionality; for example, A could be a vector of measurements, and B could include both the vector of parameters associated with some model as well as any other conditioning statements such as the model index. The sum and product rules of probability theory yield the expressions for marginalization and Bayes' theorem,

$$p^A = \int_{\{B\}} p^{A,B} \, dB, \tag{2}$$

$$p_A^B p^A = p_B^A \, p^B, \tag{3}$$

where marginalization follows from the requirement of unit normalization, and Bayes' theorem follows from requiring logical consistency of the joint density $p^{A,B} = p^{B,A}$. Certain names have come to be associated with the various factors above, but as Sivia[10] points out, what one calls a probability is irrelevant, as the distinction between p_B^A and p_C^A is carried explicitly by the differences in the conditioning statements. Nonetheless, the terms "likelihood" and "prior" are useful for describing how new data updates one's state of knowledge. Instead of the term "posterior" for the estimate of the parameter probability we will use "evidence", and the chance of measuring the data based on no other knowledge will not be named as it is not necessary for the normalization of the evidence measure nor for the evaluation of the relative evidence for competing models.

2.   Definition of the Model

For consistency of comparison, we will follow as closely as possible the notation used by Hall, *et al.*[3] The population of particles decomposes into two classifications, denoted type X and type Y, and the location for each particle type is assumed to follow an independent normal distribution in the spatial dimension z. The measured locations of the particles identified as type X can be expressed as the vector $\mathbf{X} \equiv X_j$ for integer $j \in [1, J]$, and similarly $\mathbf{Y} \equiv Y_k$ for $k \in [1, K]$, such that $N = J + K$ gives the total number of classified particles. The location measurements for type X are assumed to be drawn from the normal distribution $p_{\tilde{f},\tilde{f}}^{X_j} \equiv f(X_j)$, where

$$f(z) = (2\pi \tilde{f}^2)^{-1/2} \exp^{-1/2}[(\bar{f} - z)/\tilde{f}]^2, \tag{4}$$

and similarly for $p_{\tilde{g},\tilde{g}}^{Y_k} \equiv g(Y_k)$, using notation $\exp^{\alpha}(\beta) \equiv e^{\alpha\beta}$ with an economy of brackets when possible. One may alternately interpret that equation to mean that the standard deviation of the location measurement process is equal to $\tilde{f}$ (or $\tilde{g}$). The relative likelihood of a particle being a Y rather than an X is denoted by the parameter m, such that the absolute likelihood of being an X is $p_m^X = (1 + m)^{-1}$. The parametric model, then, for the probability that some new, unclassified datum is of type X knowing only its location z is

$$p_{z,m,\bar{f},\bar{g},\tilde{f},\tilde{g}}^{X \text{ at } z} = [1 + m\,\zeta(z)]^{-1}, \tag{5}$$

where $\zeta(z) \equiv g(z)/f(z)$, and by normalization $p_{z,m,\bar{f},\bar{g},\tilde{f},\tilde{g}}^{Y \text{ at } z} = 1 - p_{z,m,\bar{f},\bar{g},\tilde{f},\tilde{g}}^{X \text{ at } z}$. The desired quantity, however, is the estimate of that likelihood given the data $p_{z,N,J,K,\mathbf{X},\mathbf{Y}}^{X \text{ at } z}$. Inductive reasoning is used to relate these quantities of interest.

For brevity of notation, any knowledge that can be derived from the conditioning statements explicitly present will be suppressed, *e.g.* $p_{z,N,J,K,\mathbf{X},\mathbf{Y}}^{X \text{ at } z} = p_{z,\mathbf{X},\mathbf{Y}}^{X \text{ at } z}$. Let us also collect the coordinates of the parameter manifold into the contravariant position vector $\mathbf{r} \equiv (m, \bar{f}, \bar{g}, \tilde{f}, \tilde{g})$, such that $\nabla \equiv \partial/\partial \mathbf{r}$ is a covariant vector. By marginalization, the desired quantity can be written as the expectation value of the observable as a function of the parameters weighted by the evidence measure integrated over the entire parameter manifold, formally expressed as

$$p_{z,\mathbf{X},\mathbf{Y}}^{X \text{ at } z} = \int_{\{\mathbf{r}\}} p_{z,\mathbf{X},\mathbf{Y}}^{X \text{ at } z,\mathbf{r}}\,d\mathbf{r} \tag{6a}$$

$$= \int_{\{\mathbf{r}\}} p_{z,\mathbf{r}}^{X \text{ at } z} p_{\mathbf{X},\mathbf{Y}}^{\mathbf{r}}\,d\mathbf{r} \equiv \langle p_{z,\mathbf{r}}^{X \text{ at } z} \rangle_{\mathbf{r} \mid \mathbf{X},\mathbf{Y}}, \tag{6b}$$

where the conditioning on N is implicit. This evaluation of the desired quantity is robust against alternate choices of the coordinate mapping for the parameter manifold, whereas an estimate based on its value at the location of the parameter mode is not.

The evidence measure decomposes into a product of factors according to what knowledge is required for their determination $p_{\mathbf{X},\mathbf{Y}}^{\mathbf{r}} \propto p_{J,K}^m p_{\mathbf{X}}^{\bar{f},\tilde{f}} p_{\mathbf{Y}}^{\bar{g},\tilde{g}}$, which themselves factor into products of likelihoods and priors. For example, the evidence density for m is $p_{J,K}^m \propto p_m^{J,K} p^m$, and similarly for the remaining factors. Addressing first the likelihood factors, the chance of observing K out of N particles of type Y given m is

$$p_m^{J,K} = m^K/(1+m)^{J+K} = m^K(1+m)^{-N}, \tag{7}$$

whereas the chance of observing locations $\mathbf{X}$ given values for $\bar{f}$ and $\tilde{f}$ is

$$p_{\bar{f},\tilde{f}}^{\mathbf{X}} = \prod_{z \in \mathbf{X}} f(z) = (2\pi\tilde{f}^2)^{-J/2} \exp^{-1/2} \sum_{z \in \mathbf{X}} [(\bar{f} - z)/\tilde{f}]^2, \tag{8}$$

and similarly $p_{\bar{g},\tilde{g}}^{\mathbf{Y}} = \prod_{z \in \mathbf{Y}} g(z)$. The likelihood of the data at manifold position $\mathbf{r}$ is then given by their product $p_{\mathbf{r}}^{\mathbf{X},\mathbf{Y}} = p_m^{J,K} p_{\bar{f},\tilde{f}}^{\mathbf{X}} p_{\bar{g},\tilde{g}}^{\mathbf{Y}}$.

Next let us look at the prior factors $p^{\mathbf{r}} = p^m p^{\bar{f},\tilde{f}} p^{\bar{g},\tilde{g}}$. The transformation group approach to selecting an uninformative prior is based on the principle of indifference as represented by the requirement of consistency under various transformations of the parameter or data coordinate mappings. Dose[11] gives an excellent description of the process. According to Jaynes,[12] the prior suggested by Jeffreys for the parameters of a Gaussian distribution results from satisfaction of the functional equation for transformations in location and scale, thus $p^{\bar{f},\tilde{f},\bar{g},\tilde{g}} \propto (\tilde{f}\tilde{g})^{-1}$. In that paper, he argues that the same functional form $p^n \propto n^{-1}$ is appropriate for the rate parameter of a Poisson process, which will be called n. In the presentation by Hall, *et al.*,[3] the arrival of the particles at the axis of measurement is assumed to follow the Poisson distribution with parameters μ and ν for types X and Y respectively, thus the total number of particles expected in one unit of time is $n = \mu + \nu$. Writing $m = \nu/\mu$, the determinant of the Jacobian is $\det \mathbf{J} = n/(1+m)^2$, leading to the transformation of the prior $p^{n,m} = p^{\mu,\nu} \det \mathbf{J}$, whereby

$$p^m \propto n^2(1+m)^{-2}\mu^{-1}\nu^{-1} = m^{-1}, \tag{9}$$

which states that m is just as likely to be between 0.1 and 1 as it is to be between 1 and 10 before any observations are recorded. The prior measure for the parameter manifold is thus $p^{\mathbf{r}} \propto (m\tilde{f}\tilde{g})^{-1}$, where the constant of proportionality is determined by the limits of consideration. In particular, finite limits for m must be symmetric in scale about unity so that the prior expectation of finding a particle of type X,

$$\langle p_m^X \rangle_{m\,|\,m_\infty} \equiv \frac{\int_{1/m_\infty}^{m_\infty} m^{-1}(1+m)^{-1}dm}{\int_{1/m_\infty}^{m_\infty} m^{-1}dm}, \tag{10}$$

remains unbiased (equal to 1/2) and so that $\langle m \rangle_{m\,|\,m_\infty} = \langle m^{-1} \rangle_{m\,|\,m_\infty}$.

3. Comparison to Simpler Models

If the parameters $\bar{f}$, $\bar{g}$, $\tilde{f}$, and $\tilde{g}$ for the Gaussian distributions are known in advance, then only m need be estimated from the data. Using the notation $q_\beta^\alpha \equiv -\log p_\beta^\alpha$, the "parameter info" (information content of the evidence density) is

$$q_{J,K}^m = q_m^{J,K} + q^m + C = N\log(1+m) - (K-1)\log m + C, \qquad (11)$$

where C is the logarithm of the normalizing constant, equal to $\log\beta(J,K)$ when $m_\infty = \infty$. Its mode may be found from the equation for a vanishing gradient

$$0 = \partial_m q_{J,K}^m = m^{-1}(1+m)^{-1}[1 - K + m(J+1)], \qquad (12)$$

whose solution $m_0 = (K-1)/(J+1)$ may be negative when $K = 0$, in which case the mode is at the lower limit of consideration; if one inverts the identity of X and Y, one finds that the evidence for the inverted m has its mode at the position given by the analytic formula. In the limit of $m \in [0,\infty]$, the expectation that some new particle is of type X is $\langle p_m^X \rangle_{m\,|\,J,K} = (1 + K/J)^{-1}$, the expectation value for m is $\langle m \rangle_{m\,|\,J,K} = K/(J-1)$, and that for m^{-1} is $\langle m^{-1} \rangle_{m\,|\,J,K} = J/(K-1)$. When the new particle's location z also is known, one may evaluate $\langle p_{z,\zeta,m}^{X\,\text{at}\,z} \rangle_{m\,|\,J,K}$ as the prediction for its type being X; when both J and K are large, that value is approximately given by simply using the expectation for m in the model for $p_{z,\zeta,m}^{X\,\text{at}\,z}$, i.e. $\langle p_{z,\zeta,m}^{X\,\text{at}\,z} \rangle_{m\,|\,J,K} \approx p_{z,\zeta,\langle m \rangle_{m\,|\,J,K}}^{X\,\text{at}\,z}$ for $J, K \gg 1$. In Figure 1, we compare the value of $\langle p_{z,\zeta,m}^{X\,\text{at}\,z} \rangle_{m\,|\,J,K}$ to $p_{z,\zeta,\langle m \rangle_{m\,|\,J,K}}^{X\,\text{at}\,z}$ as a function of $\zeta(z)$ for various values of J and K.

Let us next consider the case where only the deviations $\tilde{f}$ and $\tilde{g}$ are known in advance, so that now $\bar{f}$ and $\bar{g}$ must also be estimated from the data. For convenience, let us further suppose that $\tilde{f} = \tilde{g} = 1$, setting the unit for the locations z. The values of the parameters used to generate the data will be denoted m_Ω, $\bar{f}_\Omega$, and $\bar{g}_\Omega$, where the subscript Ω indicates conditioning on the sum of all knowledge, i.e. they are the "true" values unknown to mere mortals. According to the model, the actual chance of finding an X at some z is given by $p_{z,\Omega}^{X\,\text{at}\,z} = [1 + m_\Omega\zeta_\Omega(z)]^{-1}$, thus the estimation of that quantity, as well as its reliability, from the data at hand is the desired goal of the statistical analysis. The manifold position $\mathbf{r}_\Omega$ of course is not allowed to be part of that process, as its knowledge preclude the need to collect any data for its estimation.

Retaining only m, $\bar{f}$, and $\bar{g}$ in $\mathbf{r}$, the evidence density is

$$p_{\mathbf{X},\mathbf{Y}}^{\mathbf{r}} \propto p_m^{J,K} p_{\bar{f}}^{\mathbf{X}} p_{\bar{g}}^{\mathbf{Y}} p^{m,\bar{f},\bar{g}}, \qquad (13)$$

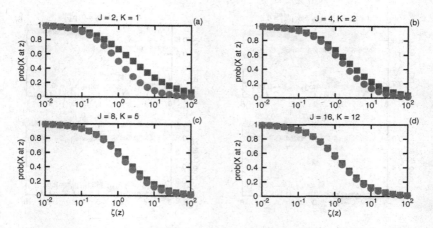

Fig. 1. Comparison of prob(X at z) as a function of $\zeta(z)$ estimated from the expectation value $\langle p_{z,\zeta,m}^{X\,\text{at}\,z} \rangle_{m\,|\,J,K}$ shown as $\square$ to its approximation $p_{z,\zeta,\langle m \rangle_m\,|\,J,K}^{X\,\text{at}\,z}$ shown as $\bigcirc$ for J and K as indicated above each panel.

where the prior is normalized to unit volume, thus the parameter info is

$$q_{\mathbf{X},\mathbf{Y}}^{\mathbf{r}} = q_m^{J,K} + q^m + q_{\bar{f}}^{\mathbf{X}} + q_{\bar{g}}^{\mathbf{Y}} + C, \tag{14}$$

and the value of C is chosen according to the task at hand. For taking expectation values, one convenient choice is that which normalizes the peak of the evidence to unity $C_0 = -q_0$, whereas for hypothesis testing (model selection) C must equal the logarithm of the normalizing constant for the prior, and the remaining terms must retain any constants found in the likelihood, unless they happen to cancel out of the relative evidence ratio. Here, $C_{\mathbf{r}} = \log(2\log m_\infty) + 2\log\Delta_z$ when $m \in [m_\infty^{-1}, m_\infty]$ and $\bar{f}, \bar{g} \in [-\Delta_z/2, \Delta_z/2]$. The expression

$$q_{\bar{f}}^{\mathbf{X}} + q_{\bar{g}}^{\mathbf{Y}} = \frac{N}{2}\log(2\pi) + \frac{1}{2}\sum_{z\in\mathbf{X}}(\bar{f}-z)^2 + \frac{1}{2}\sum_{z\in\mathbf{Y}}(\bar{g}-z)^2 \tag{15}$$

gives the additional likelihood info coming from the location measurements, and its mode is easily found to be at $\bar{f}_0 = \langle X_j \rangle_j$ and $\bar{g}_0 = \langle Y_k \rangle_k$.

Because the preferred locations $\bar{f}$ and $\bar{g}$ are themselves estimated, one must ask whether the data would be more efficiently represented by a single Gaussian, which we will call $h(z)$ with mean $\bar{h}$. The relevant factors in the relative evidence ratio are those which do not depend on m, and the problem reduces to the well-known example of whether the difference in means between two populations is statistically significant. The answer is

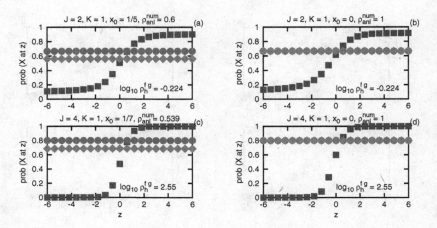

Fig. 2. Comparison of the numerical estimate for $\langle p_m^X \rangle_{m\,|\,J,K}$ displayed as $\Diamond$ to that for $\langle p_{z,\mathbf{r}}^{X\,\mathrm{at}\,z} \rangle_{\mathbf{r}\,|\,\mathbf{X},\mathbf{Y}}$ displayed as $\square$ using limits of integration given by $\Delta_z = 12$ and x_0 as indicated above each panel, with the analytic value for $\langle p_m^X \rangle_{m\,|\,J,K}$ displayed as $\bigcirc$.

given by the ratio of the expectation values for the likelihood of each model,

$$\rho_h^{fg} \equiv \frac{\langle p_{\bar{f},\bar{g}}^{\mathbf{X},\mathbf{Y}} \rangle_{\bar{f},\bar{g}}}{\langle p_{\bar{h}}^{\mathbf{X},\mathbf{Y}} \rangle_{\bar{h}}} = \frac{\int_{-\Delta_z/2}^{\Delta_z/2} \int_{-\Delta_z/2}^{\Delta_z/2} p_{\bar{f},\bar{g}}^{\mathbf{X},\mathbf{Y}} p^{\bar{f},\bar{g}}\, d\bar{f} d\bar{g}}{\int_{-\Delta_z/2}^{\Delta_z/2} p_{\bar{h}}^{\mathbf{X},\mathbf{Y}} p^{\bar{h}}\, d\bar{h}} \tag{16a}$$

$$\approx \frac{p_{\bar{f}_0}^{\mathbf{X}} p_{\bar{g}_0}^{\mathbf{Y}}}{p_{\bar{h}_0}^{\mathbf{X},\mathbf{Y}}} \left(\frac{2\pi N}{\Delta_z^2 J K} \right)^{1/2}, \tag{16b}$$

where the first factor is the ratio of peak likelihoods (when the prior is uniform), the second (Occam) factor is the ratio of the filling fractions for each model, and the approximation results from taking infinite bounds in the integrals. The filling fraction for a model is a number between 0 and 1 which indicates how much the evidence fills the parameter manifold with respect to the prior measure. If the relative evidence ratio is well below unity $\rho_h^{fg} \ll 1$, then probability theory is telling one to neglect the z dependence and simply use m as the basis for any prediction regarding the type of some unidentified particle. If either J or K equals 0, attention to factors reveals that $\rho_h^{fg} = 1$ in that case, as the evidence density is uniform along the irrelevant parameter.

Using finite limits for numerical integration can have an impact on the result. Recalling that conditioning on N has been implied throughout, let us compare the estimate of $\langle p_m^X \rangle_{m\,|\,J,K}$ to $\langle p_{z,\mathbf{r}}^{X\,\mathrm{at}\,z} \rangle_{\mathbf{r}\,|\,\mathbf{X},\mathbf{Y}}$ for the two cases of $m_\infty = N + 1$ and $m_\infty = \infty$. The former represents a prior state of knowledge in which one is certain to observe particles of both types eventually, even though particles of only one type have been observed so far. The numerical integration is more easily accomplished upon a change of variables $x = (1 + m)^{-1}$ such that

$$\int_{1/m_\infty}^{m_\infty} m^{K-1}(1 + m)^{-J-K}\, dm = \int_{x_0}^{1-x_0} x^{J-1}(1 - x)^{K-1}\, dx \quad (17a)$$

$$\leq \beta(J, K), \quad (17b)$$

with equality in the limit $x_0 \to 0$. One way to assess the reliability of one's estimate is to inspect the ratio of the numerically integrated evidence volume to that derived analytically for the infinite manifold, identified as $\rho_{\text{anl}}^{\text{num}}$. Figure 2 shows the comparison of the estimated operators for values of $N = 3$ and $N = 5$ using $\bar{f}_\Omega = 1$ and $\bar{g}_\Omega = -1$, as well as the analytic expression for $\langle p_m^X \rangle_{m \mid J,K}$ when $m_\infty = \infty$. With only a few measurements, the numerical estimate for $\langle p_{z,\mathbf{r}}^{X\,\text{at}\,z} \rangle_{\mathbf{r} \mid \mathbf{X},\mathbf{Y}}$ approaches the analytic value for $\langle p_m^X \rangle_{m \mid J,K}$ only when m_∞ is very large. After more measurements have accumulated, the limits on m have less impact; however, if the mode in m is close to the numerical limit, the estimate may still be inaccurate.

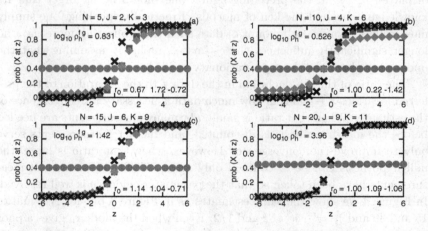

Fig. 3.   Comparison of the analytic value for $\langle p_m^X \rangle_{m \mid J,K}$ displayed as $\bigcirc$ to the numerical estimate for $\langle p_{z,\mathbf{r}}^{X\,\text{at}\,z} \rangle_{\mathbf{r} \mid \mathbf{X},\mathbf{Y}}$ displayed as $\square$ for values of N as indicated above each panel, with their weighted mean $p_{z,\rho}^{X\,\text{at}\,z}$ displayed as $\Diamond$ and the underlying distribution $p_{z,\Omega}^{X\,\text{at}\,z}$ displayed as $\times$. Also shown are the values for the parameter mode $\mathbf{r}_0$.

To collect the estimates from the two possible models into a single prediction, one simply averages them with weights given by their relative evidence,

$$p_{z,\rho}^{X\,\text{at}\,z} \equiv [\rho_h^{fg}\langle p_{z,\mathbf{r}}^{X\,\text{at}\,z}\rangle_{\mathbf{r}\,|\,\mathbf{X},\mathbf{Y}} + \langle p_m^X\rangle_{m\,|\,J,K}](\rho_h^{fg}+1)^{-1}. \qquad (18)$$

As evidence accumulates in favor of the fg model, their average quickly approaches the estimate from just that model, as seen in Figure 3. Using values of $m_\Omega = 1$, $\bar{f}_\Omega = -\bar{g}_\Omega = 1$ and integration limits of $\Delta_z = 12$ and $x_0 = 0$, it takes only a few tens of measurements before the evidence for the null hypothesis (the h model) is negligible. As the number of measurements in the training data grows, the estimate $p_{z,\rho}^{X\,\text{at}\,z}$ converges to the underlying Ω distribution for the chance of finding an X at z.

So far we have said nothing about the rate of convergence of the estimate $\langle p_{z,\mathbf{r}}^{X\,\text{at}\,z}\rangle_{\mathbf{r}\,|\,\mathbf{X},\mathbf{Y}}$ as a function of the number of measurements N. Partly that is because we have summarized our inference about $p_{z,\mathbf{X},\mathbf{Y}}^{X\,\text{at}\,z}$ into a single number, the expectation value of the observable $p_{z,\mathbf{r}}^{X\,\text{at}\,z}$, and to answer the question of convergence requires keeping track of two numbers for the inference, representing for example its central location and its width. That procedure will be addressed later in this article. While we have blithely displayed $p_{z,\Omega}^{X\,\text{at}\,z}$ in the preceding figure, one should never forget that its knowledge is beyond the ken of mortals. Practically speaking, one simply must collect a sufficient amount of data such that collecting more data no longer significantly influences the estimate, implicitly assuming that the underlying physical process is stationary in time.

The ratio of the the deviation in the data $\tilde{f}$ to the separation of the preferred locations $\bar{f} - \bar{g}$ affects how much data is necessary for convergence of the estimate. When that ratio is small, not many measurements are needed before the null hypothesis is discounted, and further measurements serve only to improve the convergence. However, when that ratio is large, the null hypothesis can be discounted only after a sufficient number of measurements have been taken so that the parameter evidence is well resolved. In Figure 4 we show the same estimates as in Figure 3 but for N equal to 15 and 30 and $\tilde{f}_\Omega = -\bar{g}_\Omega$ of 2 and 1/2. Even when the mode $\mathbf{r}_0$ gives a poor reckoning of the underlying process, the expectation value $\langle p_{z,\mathbf{r}}^{X\,\text{at}\,z}\rangle_{\mathbf{r}\,|\,\mathbf{X},\mathbf{Y}}$ is fairly accurate when $\rho_h^{fg} \gg 1$. To make from ρ_h^{fg} a number comparable to the P (or Q) value of frequentist methods, one would state that the null hypothesis (h model) is discounted at the level of $P = 1/(\rho_h^{fg}+1)$.

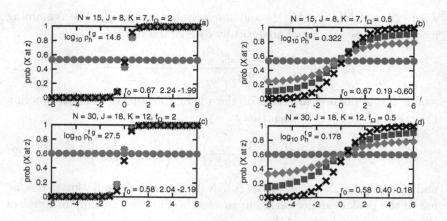

Fig. 4. Comparison of the analytic value for $\langle p_m^X \rangle_{m \mid J,K}$ displayed as $\bigcirc$ to the numerical estimate for $\langle p_{z,\mathbf{r}}^{X \text{ at } z} \rangle_{\mathbf{r} \mid \mathbf{X},\mathbf{Y}}$ displayed as $\square$ for values of N and $\bar{f}_\Omega = -\bar{g}_\Omega$ as indicated above each panel, with their weighted mean $p_{z,\rho}^{X \text{ at } z}$ displayed as $\Diamond$ and the underlying distribution $p_{z,\Omega}^{X \text{ at } z}$ displayed as $\times$. Also shown are the values for the parameter mode $\mathbf{r}_0$.

4.   Integration Over Unknown Deviation

Let us now consider the more realistic situation where the deviations of the location distributions are not known in advance. For convenience, let us assign them all the domain of $\sigma \in [\sigma_0, \sigma_\infty]$ with prior $p^\sigma \propto \sigma^{-1}$. The normalization constant is $\Delta_{\log \sigma} \equiv \log \sigma_\infty - \log \sigma_0$, which equals infinity if either $\sigma_\infty = \infty$ or $\sigma_0 = 0$. The first task is to evaluate the relative evidence of the models,

$$
\rho_h^{fg} = \frac{\int_{-\Delta_z/2}^{\Delta_z/2} \int_{-\Delta_z/2}^{\Delta_z/2} \int_{\sigma_0}^{\sigma_\infty} \int_{\sigma_0}^{\sigma_\infty} \tilde{f}^{-J-1} \tilde{g}^{-K-1} \exp^{-1/2}(\chi_f^2 + \chi_g^2) \, d\tilde{f} d\tilde{g} d\bar{f} d\bar{g}}{\Delta_z \Delta_{\log \sigma} \int_{-\Delta_z/2}^{\Delta_z/2} \int_{\sigma_0}^{\sigma_\infty} \tilde{h}^{-N-1} \exp^{-1/2}(\chi_h^2) \, d\tilde{h} d\bar{h}},
$$

(19)

where $\chi_f^2 \equiv \sum_{z \in \mathbf{X}} [(\bar{f} - z)/\tilde{f}]^2$ and similarly for χ_g^2 and χ_h^2, which can be approximated as before by taking the Gaussian integrals over infinite limits yet retaining the finite normalization to yield

$$
\rho_h^{fg} \approx \left(\frac{2\pi N}{\Delta_z^2 JK} \right)^{1/2} \frac{\int_{\sigma_0}^{\sigma_\infty} \int_{\sigma_0}^{\sigma_\infty} \tilde{f}^{-J} \tilde{g}^{-K} \exp^{-1/2}(\xi_f^2/\tilde{f}^2 + \xi_g^2/\tilde{g}^2) \, d\tilde{f} d\tilde{g}}{\Delta_{\log \sigma} \int_{\sigma_0}^{\sigma_\infty} \tilde{h}^{-N} \exp^{-1/2}(\xi_h^2/\tilde{h}^2) \, d\tilde{h}},
$$

(20)

where $\xi_f^2 \equiv J(\langle X_j^2 \rangle_j - \langle X_j \rangle_j^2)$ and similarly for ξ_g^2 and ξ_h^2. The remaining integrals can be evaluated analytically to give the result

$$\rho_h^{fg} \approx \left(\frac{\pi N}{JK} \right)^{1/2} \frac{\xi_h^{N-1} \Delta_\Gamma(\xi_f) \Delta_\Gamma(\xi_g)}{2\Delta_z \Delta_{\log \sigma} \xi_f^{J-1} \xi_g^{K-1} \Delta_\Gamma(\xi_h)}, \tag{21}$$

where Δ_Γ is defined in terms of the upper incomplete gamma function $\Gamma(a, z) \equiv \int_z^\infty t^{a-1} e^{-t} dt$, such that

$$\Delta_\Gamma(\xi_f) \equiv \Gamma\left(\frac{J-1}{2}, \frac{\xi_f^2}{2\sigma_\infty^2} \right) - \Gamma\left(\frac{J-1}{2}, \frac{\xi_f^2}{2\sigma_0^2} \right), \tag{22}$$

and similarly for $\Delta_\Gamma(\xi_g)$ and $\Delta_\Gamma(\xi_h)$. Note that this formulation makes no use of the peak evidence ratio but instead is expressed entirely in terms of the data and the limits of the prior.

To recover the peak evidence ratio (and thus the Occam factor), one needs to evaluate the model evidence densities at their mode positions. The parameter info for the **X** data is now

$$q_{\mathbf{X}}^{\bar{f}, \tilde{f}} = (J+1) \log \tilde{f} + (2\tilde{f}^2)^{-1} \sum_{z \in \mathbf{X}} (\bar{f} - z)^2 + C, \tag{23}$$

whose gradient is given by

$$\nabla q_{\mathbf{X}}^{\bar{f}, \tilde{f}} = \tilde{f}^{-3} \left[\begin{array}{c} \tilde{f} \sum_{z \in \mathbf{X}} (\bar{f} - z) \\ (J+1)\tilde{f}^2 - \sum_{z \in \mathbf{X}} (\bar{f} - z)^2 \end{array} \right], \tag{24}$$

which vanishes at the mode $\nabla q_{\mathbf{X}}^{\bar{f}_0, \tilde{f}_0} = 0$. As before, the mode in $\bar{f}$ is at the mean of the locations $\bar{f}_0 = \langle X_j \rangle_j$, and the mode in $\tilde{f}$ can be written as $\tilde{f}_0 = (J+1)^{-1/2} \xi_f$. The position of the mode for the remaining Gaussian parameters is found similarly.

Let us briefly discuss the limits of integration hence the normalization of the prior. If the prior is not to be based upon the current crop of measurements, where does the information for the limits come from? The practical answer is that the limits are determined by the nature of the measurement apparatus. Any set of measurements collected within a finite span of time necessarily are limited by the range and resolution of the device used for their collection, for example measurements of the voltage of a circuit collected by a common voltmeter. As long as no measurement "pegs the needle" one can safely use limits based on the range of the device; those that do can be addressed through an appropriately modified contribution to the likelihood beyond the scope of this article. Similarly, the resolution of the device (or the width of the particle) sets a lower limit on what can be said about any measured deviations in the population locations. For the evaluation of the evidence ratio ρ_h^{fg} as well as $\rho_{\text{anl}}^{\text{num}}$, we will set the limits for the deviations as $\sigma_\infty = \Delta_z$ and $\sigma_0 = 10^{-4}\Delta_z$, with $\Delta_z = 12$ and $x_0 = 0$ as above.

The evaluation of the expectation value of the observable $\langle p_{z,\mathbf{r}}^{X\,\text{at}\,z}\rangle_{\mathbf{r}\,|\,\mathbf{X},\mathbf{Y}}$ proceeds as before, only now the integration is over a 5 dimensional parameter manifold. As *Numerical Recipes*[13] states, "Integrals of functions of several variables, over regions with dimension greater than one, are *not easy*." For problems of Bayesian inference, the majority of the contribution to the integral comes from a region localized around the peak of the evidence density when sufficient data exists that the limits of the prior are irrelevant. Luckily, for this problem the evidence mode is unique and analytic, so that one may select limits for the numerical integration much tighter than those given by the prior while still encompassing 99.9% of the normalized evidence density. The evaluation is performed using an adaptive grid algorithm[14,15] over a small region of the manifold centered on the position of the optimal parameter values.

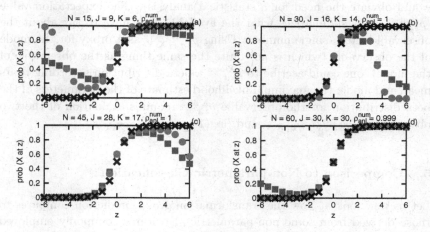

Fig. 5. Comparison of the expectation value $\langle p_{z,\mathbf{r}}^{X\,\text{at}\,z}\rangle_{\mathbf{r}\,|\,\mathbf{X},\mathbf{Y}}$ displayed as $\square$ to the estimate from the parameter mode $p_{z,\mathbf{r}_0\,|\,\mathbf{X},\mathbf{Y}}^{X\,\text{at}\,z}$ displayed as $\bigcirc$ for $N = 50$ as well as the underlying distribution $p_{z,\Omega}^{X\,\text{at}\,z}$ displayed as $\times$ with parameter values as given in Table 1.

In Figure 5 we compare the expectation of the observable $\langle p_{z,\mathbf{r}}^{X\,\text{at}\,z}\rangle_{\mathbf{r}\,|\,\mathbf{X},\mathbf{Y}}$ to that given by evaluating the observable using the parameter mode $p_{z,\mathbf{r}_0\,|\,\mathbf{X},\mathbf{Y}}^{X\,\text{at}\,z}$, with the results given in Table 1. As the number of measurements increases, those estimates draw closer, according to the narrowing of

Table 1.   Parameters corresponding to Figure 5.

panel	$\log_{10}\rho_h^{fg}$ J	N K	m_Ω m_0	$\bar{f}_\Omega$ f_0	$\bar{g}_\Omega$ g_0	$\tilde{f}_\Omega$ $\tilde{f}_0$	$\tilde{g}_\Omega$ $\tilde{g}_0$
a	-0.397 9	15 6	1 0.5	1 0.634	-1 -0.84	1 0.994	1 0.715
b	3.1 16	30 14	1 0.765	1 0.87	-1 -1.05	1 0.654	1 1.19
c	3.45 28	45 17	1 0.552	1 1.15	-1 -0.85	1 0.953	1 1.38
d	4.77 30	60 30	1 0.935	1 0.9	-1 -0.879	1 1.08	1 0.936

the peak in the evidence density. The estimate from the expectation value is "more conservative" than that from the mode, in that it is closer to the estimate $\langle p_m^X \rangle_{m\,|\,\mathbf{X},\mathbf{Y}}$ (not shown). While the estimate from the mode more closely resembles the underlying distribution $p_{z,\Omega}^{X\,\text{at}\,z}$ when there is sufficient data, in a real world situation we are not privy to that knowledge (which would obviate the need for a statistical analysis). The expectation value $\langle p_{z,\mathbf{r}}^{X\,\text{at}\,z} \rangle_{\mathbf{r}\,|\,\mathbf{X},\mathbf{Y}}$ summarizes what the available data have to say about the observable into a single number. Using $p_{z,\mathbf{r}_0}^{X\,\text{at}\,z}|_{\mathbf{X},\mathbf{Y}}$ as a proxy for the mode of the observable (which is not quite the same thing as the observable of the mode), one could ascribe to $p_{z,\mathbf{r}}^{X\,\text{at}\,z}$ a beta distribution according to its mean and mode; the maximum likelihood estimate of the parameters of the beta distribution for the observable $p_{z,\mathbf{r}}^{X\,\text{at}\,z}$ requires evaluation of the two observables $\langle \log p_{z,\mathbf{r}}^{X\,\text{at}\,z} \rangle_{\mathbf{r}\,|\,\mathbf{X},\mathbf{Y}}$ and $\langle \log(1 - p_{z,\mathbf{r}}^{X\,\text{at}\,z}) \rangle_{\mathbf{r}\,|\,\mathbf{X},\mathbf{Y}}$.

5. Comparison to Non-parametric Classification

Let us now look at how the transformation group prediction compares to those derived from some non-parametric algorithms commonly employed for this type of problem. For this section we will use the same data for each method generated using parameter values $m_\Omega = 1$, $\bar{f}_\Omega = -\bar{g}_\Omega = 2$, and $\tilde{f}_\Omega = \tilde{g}_\Omega = 2$ for various N. We will consider both a nearest neighbor classification scheme which produces its estimate from a subset of the data "close" to the desired location as well as a classification scheme based upon a kernel density estimate of the identified particle distributions. The transformation group estimates from these sets of data are shown in Figure 6 with parameter modes in Table 2.

Table 2. Parameters corresponding to Figure 6.

panel	$\log_{10} \rho_h^{fg}$ J	N K	m_Ω m_0	$\bar{f}_\Omega$ f_0	$\bar{g}_\Omega$ g_0	$\tilde{f}_\Omega$ $\tilde{f}_0$	$\tilde{g}_\Omega$ $\tilde{g}_0$
a	3.09 15	24 9	1 0.5	2 2.02	-2 -2.58	2 2.05	2 1.22
b	7.82 28	48 20	1 0.655	2 2.3	-2 -1.99	2 1.98	2 1.27
c	6.77 34	72 38	1 1.06	2 1.58	-2 -1.62	2 1.92	2 1.64
d	15.8 49	96 47	1 0.92	2 2.08	-2 -2.52	2 1.76	2 2.11

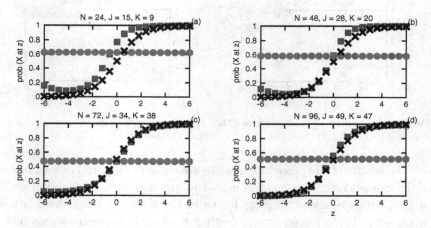

Fig. 6. Comparison of the expectation value $\langle p_{z,\mathbf{r}}^{X\,\text{at}\,z} \rangle_{\mathbf{r}\,|\,\mathbf{X},\mathbf{Y}}$ displayed as $\square$ to $\langle p_m^X \rangle_{m\,|\,\mathbf{X},\mathbf{Y}}$ displayed as $\bigcirc$ for various N as well as the underlying distribution $p_{z,\Omega}^{X\,\text{at}\,z}$ displayed as $\times$ with parameter values as given in Table 2.

Starting with nearest neighbor classification, its prediction for the type of some new particle,

$$p_{z,\kappa,\mathbf{X},\mathbf{Y}}^{X\,\text{at}\,z} \equiv \kappa_X / (\kappa_X + \kappa_Y), \tag{25}$$

is conditioned on the number of neighbors $\kappa = \kappa_X + \kappa_Y$ chosen to be influential, denoted here as $\kappa \equiv \rho_\kappa N$ for $0 < \rho_\kappa \leq 1$ such that κ is an integer. The selection of κ is arbitrary, but Hall, *et al.*[3] describe a method for choosing its value based upon bootstrap estimates from the data. Here, however, we are interested in the case where there is so little data that bootstrap estimates are unlikely to be reliable. Consequently, we will consider the set of ratios $\rho_\kappa \in [1/8, 1/4, 1/2, 1]$. Another distinction is that they assign a type of X or Y to the new particle at z according to whether $p_{z,\kappa,\mathbf{X},\mathbf{Y}}^{X \text{ at } z}$ is greater or less than $1/2$, such that the region boundaries form a decision surface in one dimension, rather than retaining the expression of the chance of finding an X at z as a probability.

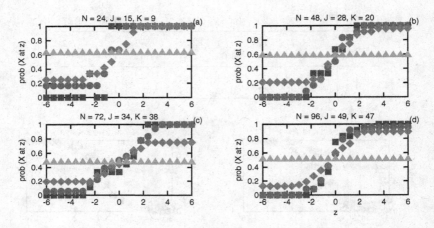

Fig. 7. Comparison of the nearest neighbor estimates $p_{z,\kappa,\mathbf{X},\mathbf{Y}}^{X \text{ at } z}$ for various κ given by $\kappa/N \in [1/8, 1/4, 1/2, 1]$ shown as $\square$, $\bigcirc$, $\Diamond$, and $\triangle$ respectively.

The results of the preceding method are shown in Figure 7. One feature of the nearest neighbors method is that its prediction is quantized in units of $1/\kappa$, which can lead to large jumps in the estimate when there is not much data. These jumps yield an estimate which is not smooth as a function of z, even as the number of measurements approaches 100. By basing its prediction on the rank of the distances from the data to the desired location, this method throws away information pertinent to the analysis. Consequently, its prediction is a coarsely grained representation of the underlying distribution, even for moderately large sets of data. If one were to implement a decision surface as in Hall, *et al.*,[3] one would have a prediction that oscillates wildly between 0 and 1 in the region where the particle types significantly overlap.

Alternately, we can consider a classification scheme based upon a kernel density estimate[4–6] of the particle distributions by type. Its prediction $p_{z,\lambda,\mathbf{X},\mathbf{Y}}^{X \text{ at } z}$ is conditioned on the bandwidth parameter λ for the kernel resolution. The kernel basis chosen is that given by the Gaussian distributions $\delta_\lambda(z) \equiv \exp^{-1/2}(z^2/\lambda^2)$, with peaks normalized to unity for convenience later. The kernel density estimate for the distribution of type X is equal to the sum of the kernel basis functions centered on the datum locations $f_{\lambda,\mathbf{X}}(z) \equiv \sum_j \delta_\lambda(z - X_j)$, and similarly for $g_{\lambda,\mathbf{Y}}(z)$. The classification prediction is then determined from the ratio

$$p^{X \text{ at } z}_{z,\lambda,\mathbf{X},\mathbf{Y}} \equiv f_{\lambda,\mathbf{X}}(z)/[f_{\lambda,\mathbf{X}}(z) + g_{\lambda,\mathbf{Y}}(z)], \qquad (26)$$

conditioned on the value of the bandwidth parameter.

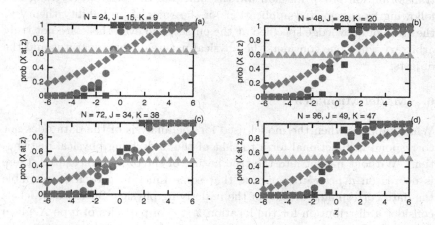

Fig. 8.   Comparison of the kernel density estimate predictions $p^{X \text{ at } z}_{z,\lambda,\mathbf{X},\mathbf{Y}}$ for various λ given by $\lambda \in [1/4, 1, 4, \infty]$ shown as $\square$, $\bigcirc$, $\lozenge$, and $\triangle$ respectively.

The results for the preceding method, using values of $\lambda \in [1/4, 1, 4, \infty]$, are shown in Figure 8. Again, large jumps are apparent in the estimate when the kernel width is much smaller than what we know the particle deviations to be, but the values are continuous rather than being quantized. The effect of the kernel basis is that of a smoothing filter which spreads the information from each datum over a range of nearby locations according to λ. In essence, with this method one is convoluting the data with some point spread function to produce an estimate of the observable at all locations z based on the discrete list of measured locations for classified particles.

The term "non-parametric" is actually a bit of a misnomer, as the evaluation of either method requires specification of a parameter representing the bandwidth of the resolution filter. While the bandwidth in z for the kernel density prediction is constant for a given λ, for a given κ that for the nearest neighbor prediction is not, based as it is on the rank of the distances in z rather than their values. In the limit of infinite bandwidth, such that the z dependence disappears, both models give a prediction equal to that of the Bayesian estimate $\langle p_m^X \rangle_{m \mid \mathbf{X},\mathbf{Y}} = J/(J+K)$, as indicated by $\triangle$ in the figures — the reason for the peak normalization of the kernel basis is so the kernel density estimates equal J or K for all z in this limit. The selection of the optimal value of the bandwidth parameter requires definition of some metric for its merit, introducing yet another source of subjectivity into the methodology. In contrast, the only arbitrary elements of the transformation group method are the limits of the prior, everything else following from repeated applications of the rules of probability theory to the state of knowledge specified at the outset, and even those are not truly arbitrary when one considers the physical nature of the apparatus and the objects.

6. Model Mismatch

What happens when the model used for the analysis of the data does not correspond in functional form to that of the underlying physical distribution? Without insight into the true nature of the objects measured, there is no reason *a priori* to suppose that some function chosen to resemble the data corresponds to that of the underlying physics. Specifically, let us consider a distribution for the location $z < \bar{\phi}$ of particles of type X given by

$$f_\Omega(z_f \mid \tilde{\phi}) = z_f^{\tilde{\phi}-1} e^{-z_f/\tilde{\phi}} / \tilde{\phi}^{\tilde{\phi}} \Gamma(\tilde{\phi}), \tag{27}$$

where $z_f \equiv \bar{\phi} - z$, and similarly for $g_\Omega(z_g \mid \tilde{\gamma})$ using $z_g \equiv z - \bar{\gamma}$, which one may recognize as a gamma distribution with a mean of $\tilde{\phi}^2$ and a variance of $\tilde{\phi}^3$ reflected in z and offset by $\bar{\phi}$. In panels (a) and (b) of Figure 9 are histograms of the locations of X and Y particles drawn from such a distribution with $m_\Omega = 1$, $\tilde{\phi}_\Omega = \tilde{\gamma}_\Omega = 1.5$, and $\bar{\phi}_\Omega = -\bar{\gamma}_\Omega = 4$.

Using the model of the preceding section, we get the estimates for the observable $\langle p_{z,\mathbf{r}}^{X \text{ at } z} \rangle_{\mathbf{r} \mid \mathbf{X},\mathbf{Y}}$ and $p_{z,\mathrm{ro} \mid \mathbf{X},\mathbf{Y}}^{X \text{ at } z}$ shown in panel (c) of Figure 9. While the observable resembles the physical distribution in the region of overlap between the particle types the model is not designed to handle the case of finite boundaries in the location distribution. For the unidentified particles found outside that region, this model will almost always make the wrong prediction. One's suspicion might be aroused by noticing that the only measurements in the extreme regions are in contradiction to the model's estimate. Of course, simply looking at the histograms reveals that the symmetric Gaussian model is not going to be the best fitting distribution for the identified particle locations.

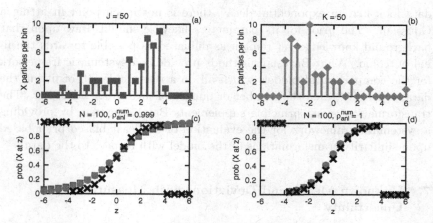

Fig. 9. Histograms of location for type X in (a) and Y in (b) with a bin width of 0.5 for a set of 100 particles which yield the predictions $\langle p_{z,\mathbf{r}}^{X \text{ at } z}\rangle_{\mathbf{r}\,|\,\mathbf{X},\mathbf{Y}}$ displayed as $\square$ and $p_{z,\mathbf{r}_0\,|\,\mathbf{X},\mathbf{Y}}^{X \text{ at } z}$ displayed as $\bigcirc$ using the Gaussian distribution in (c) and the gamma distribution in (d) as well as the underlying distribution $p_{z,\Omega}^{X \text{ at } z}$ displayed as $\times$.

Suppose now that somehow we gain knowledge of the functional form for $f_\Omega(z)$ and $g_\Omega(z)$, for example by learning that the particles are racquetballs hit out of a tunnel such that X balls are bounced off the right wall and Y balls are bounced off the left, with the measurements for the z locations taken some distance away from the outlet of the tunnel. The parameters $\tilde\phi_\Omega$ and $\bar\gamma_\Omega$ are assumed to be known from the geometry of the apparatus, with the parameters $\mathbf{r} = (m, \tilde\phi, \tilde\gamma)$ to be determined. The new parameter evidence is $p_{\tilde\phi,\mathbf{X}}^{\tilde\phi} \propto \tilde\phi^{-1}\prod_{z\in\mathbf{X}} f(z_f)$ when the prior $p^{\tilde\phi} \propto \tilde\phi^{-1}$ is used, and similarly for $\tilde\gamma$. To remain finite as $z_f \to 0$, one requires $\tilde\phi \geq 1$, and the mode value $\tilde\phi_0$ is easily found numerically, yielding the mode estimate $p_{z,\mathbf{r}_0}^{X \text{ at } z}$, as shown in panel (d) of Figure 9. An upper limit of $\tilde\phi \leq 4$ is consistent with the measurements, and the expectation of the observable $\langle p_{z,\mathbf{r}}^{X \text{ at } z}\rangle_{\mathbf{r}\,|\,\mathbf{X},\mathbf{Y}}$ can be evaluated, also shown in panel (d). Having the correct physical model, even if its parameters are undetermined, is certainly an asset when attempting to use measurements to make predictions.

The point of this section is to emphasize how important one's knowledge of the situation is to the determination of one's results. The model one selects should be based upon as much information as is available. When no single model presents itself as being physically correct, one must consider the alternatives, most often after having looked at the data—if the data look like an exponential decay, there is not much point in fitting a Gaussian. The prior for its parameters likewise should draw upon that background knowledge yet remain as unbiased as possible towards the final outcome. What Bayesian methods provide is a systematic framework for the comparison of models which all do a reasonable job of fitting the data, especially when the number or quality of measurements is low. The transformation group principle supplements Bayes' theorem by providing a systematic framework for the evaluation of the least biased prior based upon similarity transformations of the model with respect to the data.

7. Unknown Means and Deviations with Measurement Uncertainty

Returning to the use of the Gaussian model for the particle locations, let us now suppose the even more realistic situation where the location measurements are themselves subject to Gaussian deviation σ, presumed to be known from calibration of the measurement device, which for convenience will be set equal to the unit for z such that $\sigma \equiv 1$. The particle locations are supposed to be drawn from independent distributions as before, whose parameters are to be determined. The model selection ratio can be written in terms of the relative model likelihoods as

$$\rho_h^{fg} \equiv \frac{\langle p_{\bar{f},\tilde{f}}^{\mathbf{X}} \rangle_{\bar{f},\tilde{f}} \langle p_{\bar{g},\tilde{g}}^{\mathbf{Y}} \rangle_{\bar{g},\tilde{g}}}{\langle p_{\bar{h},\tilde{h}}^{\mathbf{X},\mathbf{Y}} \rangle_{\bar{h},\tilde{h}}} = \frac{\rho_f \rho_g}{\Delta_z \Delta_{\log \sigma} \rho_h}, \tag{28}$$

with the prior limits notated as before. Focusing on the model for type X, each datum likelihood must now be expressed as an integral over all possible values of X_j according to the resolution of the apparatus,

$$p_{\sigma,\bar{f},\tilde{f}}^{X_j} = \int_{-\infty}^{\infty} f(z_j) p_{\sigma,X_j}^{z_j} \, dz_j \tag{29a}$$

$$= \int_{-\infty}^{\infty} (2\pi \tilde{f})^{-1} \exp^{-1/2} \{[(\bar{f}-z_j)/\tilde{f}]^2 + (X_j - z_j)^2\} \, dz_j \tag{29b}$$

$$= [2\pi(1+\tilde{f}^2)]^{-1/2} \exp^{-1/2}[(\bar{f}-X_j)^2/(1+\tilde{f}^2)]. \tag{29c}$$

The parameter evidence is now given by

$$p_{\sigma,\mathbf{X}}^{\bar{f},\tilde{f}} \propto \tilde{f}^{-1}[2\pi(1+\tilde{f}^2)]^{-J/2} \exp^{-J/2}[(\bar{f}^2 - 2\bar{f}\langle X_j \rangle_j + \langle X_j^2 \rangle_j)/(1+\tilde{f}^2)], \tag{30}$$

retaining explicitly the normalization of the likelihood but not the prior. The integral over $\bar{f}$ proceeds as before,

$$p_{\sigma,\mathbf{X}}^{\tilde{f}} = \int_{-\infty}^{\infty} p_{\sigma,\mathbf{X}}^{\bar{f},\tilde{f}} \, d\bar{f} \tag{31a}$$

$$\propto \tilde{f}^{-1}[2\pi(1+\tilde{f}^2)]^{(1-J)/2} J^{-1/2} \exp^{-1/2}[\xi_f^2/(1+\tilde{f}^2)], \tag{31b}$$

yielding the marginal evidence for $\tilde{f}$. Under a change of variable $\tilde{\sigma}^2 = 1+\tilde{f}^2$ such that $\tilde{f}^{-1}d\tilde{f} = \tilde{\sigma}(\tilde{\sigma}^2 - 1)^{-1}d\tilde{\sigma}$, the marginal evidence for $\tilde{f}$ can be rewritten as

$$p_{\sigma,\mathbf{X}}^{\tilde{\sigma}} \propto (2\pi)^{(1-J)/2} J^{-1/2}(1-\tilde{\sigma}^{-2})^{-1}\tilde{\sigma}^{-J} \exp^{-1/2}(\xi_f^2/\tilde{\sigma}^2), \tag{32}$$

thus the remaining integral over $\tilde{\sigma}$ can be written as an infinite series,

$$\rho_f \approx (2\pi)^{(1-J)/2}(8J)^{-1/2} \sum_{\alpha=0}^{\infty} 2^{(J+2\alpha)/2} \xi_f^{1-J-2\alpha} \Delta_\Gamma(\alpha, \xi_f), \tag{33}$$

where the approximation results from finite Δ_z and Δ_Γ now depends on α as well as the limits of integration $\tilde{\sigma}_{0,\infty} = (1 + \sigma_{0,\infty}^2)^{1/2}$,

$$\Delta_\Gamma(\alpha, \xi_f) \equiv \Gamma\left(\frac{J+2\alpha-1}{2}, \frac{\xi_f^2}{2\tilde{\sigma}_\infty^2}\right) - \Gamma\left(\frac{J+2\alpha-1}{2}, \frac{\xi_f^2}{2\tilde{\sigma}_0^2}\right). \tag{34}$$

The relative likelihoods ρ_g and ρ_h are evaluated similarly.

The gradient of the parameter info,

$$\nabla q_{\sigma,\mathbf{X}}^{\bar{f},\tilde{f}} = \left[\begin{array}{c} J(1+\tilde{f}^2)^{-1}(\bar{f} - \langle X_j \rangle_j) \\ \tilde{f}^{-1} + J(1+\tilde{f}^2)^{-1}\tilde{f}[1 - (1+\tilde{f}^2)^{-1}(\bar{f}^2 - 2\bar{f}\langle X_j \rangle_j + \langle X_j^2 \rangle_j)] \end{array} \right], \tag{35}$$

yields the same mode for the central location $\bar{f}_0 = \langle X_j \rangle_j$. When that value is substituted into the expression for $\partial_{\tilde{f}} q_{\sigma,\mathbf{X}}^{\bar{f},\tilde{f}}$, the equation for the mode of the deviation becomes

$$0 = (J+1)\tilde{f}_0^4 + (J+2-\xi)\tilde{f}_0^2 + 1, \tag{36}$$

whose root minimizes its contribution to the parameter info,

$$\tilde{f}_0 = \min_{\tilde{f}}[\log \tilde{f} + \log(1+\tilde{f}^2)^{J/2} + \xi_f^2/2(1+\tilde{f}^2)]. \tag{37}$$

The remaining modes $\tilde{g}_0$ and $\tilde{h}_0$ are found similarly.

The uncertainty in the measurement apparatus must also be taken into account when evaluating the observable. Given some measured location z for an unidentified particle, what we know is that its actual value z_Ω is distributed around z with deviation σ. Consequently, the integration is now over not only the 5-dimensional parameter manifold but also over all possible values of z_Ω,

$$p_{z,\sigma,\mathbf{X},\mathbf{Y}}^{X \text{ at } z} = \int_{-\Delta_z/2}^{\Delta_z/2} p_{z_\Omega,\sigma,\mathbf{X},\mathbf{Y}}^{X \text{ at } z_\Omega} p_{z,\sigma}^{z_\Omega} dz_\Omega \qquad (38a)$$

$$= \int_{-\Delta_z/2}^{\Delta_z/2} \int_{\mathbf{r}} p_{z_\Omega,\mathbf{r}}^{X \text{ at } z_\Omega} p_{\sigma,\mathbf{X},\mathbf{Y}}^{\mathbf{r}} p_{z,\sigma}^{z_\Omega} \, d\mathbf{r} dz_\Omega, \qquad (38b)$$

which is evaluated numerically as before. The restricted limits of integration are found for the independent submanifolds such that the net integration measure is approximately normalized, $\rho_{\text{anl}}^{\text{num}} \approx 1$.

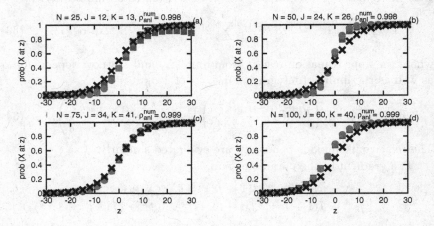

Fig. 10. Comparison of the expectation value $\langle p_{z,\sigma,\mathbf{r}}^{X \text{ at } z} \rangle_{\mathbf{r} \mid \sigma,\mathbf{X},\mathbf{Y}}$ displayed as □ to the estimate from the parameter mode $p_{z,\sigma,\mathbf{r}_0 \mid \sigma,\mathbf{X},\mathbf{Y}}^{X \text{ at } z}$ displayed as ○ as well as the underlying distribution $p_{z,\sigma,\Omega}^{X \text{ at } z}$ displayed as × with parameter values as given in Table 3.

In Figure 10, we show the results of such an integration for N particles as indicated above each panel generated using parameters found in Table 3 with $\Delta_z = 60$. We can see that, despite the additional dimension of integration, the results are quite similar to what we had before. That should be no surprise, as the normal distribution has the feature that its mean and mode are at the same value. If during the calibration procedure a resolution (point spread) function other than Gaussian is determined for the apparatus, it should of course be used instead.

Table 3. Parameters corresponding to Figure 10.

panel	$\log_{10}\rho_h^{fg}$ J	N K	m_Ω m_0	$\bar{f}_\Omega$ f_0	$\bar{g}_\Omega$ g_0	$\tilde{f}_\Omega$ $\tilde{f}_0$	$\tilde{g}_\Omega$ $\tilde{g}_0$
a	1.99	25	1	10	-10	10	10
	12	13	0.923	10.7	-7.41	7.38	9.25
b	11.1	50	1	10	-10	10	10
	24	26	1	11.3	-14.1	7.56	8.02
c	8.98	75	1	10	-10	10	10
	34	41	1.14	8.98	-9.45	8.64	9.08
d	14.9	100	1	10	-10	10	10
	60	40	0.639	9.59	-12.5	9.55	9.52

8. Reliability of the Estimate

So far we have danced around the topic of determining the reliability of the estimate strictly from the measurements at hand. In all the previous figures we have displayed the underlying physical distribution as a means of establishing that the method does indeed approach the "true" value as the number of measurements increases. However, in the real world, that knowledge is beyond our ken; we must make do with what the data have to say for themselves. That information is encoded in the evidence density for the model parameters given the measurements and the resolution of the apparatus.

When sufficient data exist that the significant evidence is restricted to some tiny region around a mode $\mathbf{r}_0$ that barely moves as more data is collected, then we may as well call the prediction from the mode our single best estimate of the underlying distribution, $p_{z,\sigma,\mathbf{r}_0}^{X\,\mathrm{at}\,z} \approx p_{z,\sigma,\Omega}^{X\,\mathrm{at}\,z}$. In that case, the chance of making the correct prediction $P \in \{X,Y\}$ for some new datum $O \in \{X,Y\}$ is given by a simple truth table. Using the notation $x_\Omega \equiv p_{z,\sigma,\Omega}^{X\,\mathrm{at}\,z}$, we have

$$p(O = P\,|\,z,\sigma,\mathbf{r}_0) \approx \mathrm{Tr}\begin{bmatrix} x_\Omega^2 & x_\Omega(1-x_\Omega) \\ x_\Omega(1-x_\Omega) & (1-x_\Omega)^2 \end{bmatrix} = x_\Omega^2 + (1-x_\Omega)^2, \quad (39)$$

which indicates that even knowledge of the physical distribution does not guarantee a certain prediction for the particle type of the new datum; to be absolutely certain of the new particle's type for any location, one must measure its classification. The error rate is greatest at the location where the particles appear with equal likelihood, as the chance of a successful prediction there is $1/2$. When the mode of the model parameters is extremely well determined by the data, the error rate lies between 0 and 50% according to the value of $p_{z,\sigma,\mathbf{r}_0}^{X \text{ at } z}$.

While the prediction from the mode is the most likely contribution, the prediction from the mean of the observable is what encodes our best inference about its value into a single number. If we want to know more about the observable, we have to do more work. As mentioned earlier, to describe the distribution around the expected value of the observable at some location, we need an additional parameter for its width and some function for its shape. The natural distribution for unit normalized positive quantities is the beta distribution $p_{a,b}^x = x^{a-1}(1-x)^{b-1}/\beta(a,b)$ that we have encountered in various guises already. Here, the problem is to determine its parameters a_z and b_z given empirical knowledge of the distribution of $x_z \equiv p_{z,\sigma,\mathbf{X},\mathbf{Y}}^{X \text{ at } z}$.

One can easily show that the maximum likelihood estimate of the parameters is given by the solution of the system of equations

$$\Lambda_1(a_z) - \Lambda_1(a_z + b_z) = \langle \log x_z \rangle, \qquad (40)$$

$$\Lambda_1(b_z) - \Lambda_1(a_z + b_z) = \langle \log(1 - x_z) \rangle, \qquad (41)$$

using the notation $\Lambda_k(r) \equiv (\partial_r)^k \log \Gamma(r)$ for the polygamma functions with integer order k and real argument r, which selects the parameters for the beta distribution whose values of $\langle \log x_z \rangle$ and $\langle \log(1 - x_z) \rangle$ equal those estimated from the empirical measurements. We set aside (for this article) the question of whether a non-uniform prior $p^{a,b}$ should be incorporated here on the grounds that a lot of effort will be put into converging the integrals such that the prior should have little effect.

The task now is to evaluate those expectation values conditioned on the given set of data. Instead of a single observable at each displayed location, there are now two to calculate, the first given by

$$\langle \log x_z \rangle = -\int_{-\Delta_z/2}^{\Delta_z/2} \int_{\mathbf{r}} \log[1 + m\zeta(z_\Omega)] p_{\sigma,\mathbf{X},\mathbf{Y}}^{\mathbf{r}} p_{z,\sigma}^{z_\Omega} \, d\mathbf{r} dz_\Omega, \qquad (42)$$

and the second given by

$$\langle \log(1 - x_z) \rangle = \langle \log x_z \rangle + \int_{-\Delta_z/2}^{\Delta_z/2} \int_{\mathbf{r}} \log[m\zeta(z_\Omega)] p_{\sigma,\mathbf{X},\mathbf{Y}}^{\mathbf{r}} p_{z,\sigma}^{z_\Omega} d\mathbf{r} dz_\Omega. \qquad (43)$$

From those two estimates one finds the corresponding a_z and b_z according to Equations (40) and (41) above. The integral over z_Ω in the second term can be expressed analytically when taken over infinite limits,

$$\int_{-\infty}^{\infty} \log[m\zeta(z_\Omega)] p_{z,\sigma}^{z_\Omega} dz_\Omega = \log\left(\frac{m\tilde{f}}{\tilde{g}}\right) + \frac{(z - \bar{f})^2 + 1}{2\tilde{f}^2} - \frac{(z - \bar{g})^2 + 1}{2\tilde{g}^2}, \qquad (44)$$

Table 4.   Parameters corresponding to Figure 11.

panel	$\log_{10}\rho_h^{fg}$ J	N K	m_Ω m_0	$\bar{f}_\Omega$ f_0	$\bar{g}_\Omega$ g_0	$\tilde{f}_\Omega$ $\tilde{f}_0$	$\tilde{g}_\Omega$ $\tilde{g}_0$
a	2.72	20	1	10	−10	10	10
	8	12	1.22	10.5	−13.6	6.24	9.52
b	3.7	40	1	10	−10	10	10
	19	21	1	10.9	−6.62	9.95	7.73
c	8.6	60	1	10	−10	10	10
	35	25	0.667	9.21	−11.6	8.85	8.41
d	11.5	80	1	10	−10	10	10
	42	38	0.86	10.6	−12.3	10.2	9.86

thereby reducing the amount of effort required for its evaluation. Having found a_z and b_z, the mean of the observable x_z may be determined according to $\langle x_z \rangle = a_z/(a_z + b_z)$, and its mode is given by $x_{z,0} = (a_z - 1)/(a_z + b_z - 2)$ when $a_z, b_z \geq 1$ else may be found at 0 or 1.

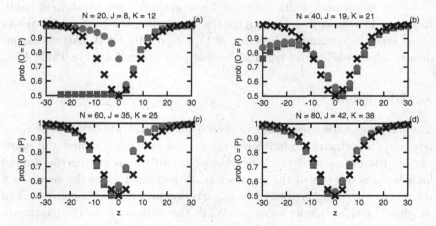

Fig. 11.   Comparison of the empirical success rates given by Equation (45a) displayed as □ and by Equation (46a) displayed as ○ to the optimal success rate displayed as × with parameter values given in Table 4.

When using the empirical distribution to make predictions, the chance of a successful prediction is itself given by an expectation value. The closest thing we have to knowledge of x_Ω is what we know about the distribution of x_z. If one uses $\langle x_z \rangle$ as the basis of prediction, by comparing it to a uniformly drawn random deviate u, then the chance of a successful prediction is given by

$$\langle p(O = P \mid z, \sigma, \langle x_z \rangle) \rangle = \langle x_z \langle x_z \rangle \rangle + \langle (1 - x_z)\langle 1 - x_z \rangle \rangle \qquad (45\text{a})$$

$$= \langle x_z \rangle^2 + (1 - \langle x_z \rangle)^2 = \frac{a_z^2 + b_z^2}{(a_z + b_z)^2}, \qquad (45\text{b})$$

which amounts to inserting the expectation value of x_z into the expression for the optimal success rate, Equation (39). We can, however, do better than that. If we compare u instead to a value x drawn from the distribution $p_{a,b}^x$ at z, the chance of a successful prediction is then given by

$$\langle p(O = P \mid z, \sigma, a_z, b_z) \rangle = \langle x_z^2 + (1 - x_z)^2 \rangle = \langle x_z^2 \rangle + \langle (1 - x_z)^2 \rangle \quad (46\text{a})$$

$$= \frac{a_z^2 + b_z^2 + a_z + b_z}{(a_z + b_z)(a_z + b_z + 1)}, \qquad (46\text{b})$$

which is greater than or equal to the success rate based on $\langle x_z \rangle$ for all $a_z, b_z > 0$. As promised, the Bayesian methodology has delivered an estimate of the observable used for predicting the type of unclassified particles as well as an estimate of its error rate based entirely upon the data at hand. In Figure 11 we compare the empirical success rates of Equations (45a) and (46a) with the optimal success rate of Equation (39), for N particles as indicated above each panel generated using parameters found in Table 4.

9.   Discussion

The purpose of the preceding exercises is to demonstrate how Bayes' theorem and the principle of indifference are used to extract meaningful information from a set of data. When the observable representing the desired knowledge is not one of the parameters of the model, then the single best inference of its value is given by its expectation over the parameter manifold weighted by the evidence measure. While the estimate from the parameter mode is the single most likely contribution, it is the mean of the observable which takes into account how much evidence there is in the data for other possibilities. When the transformation group principle is used to find the invariant measure for the parameter manifold, the results of a Bayesian analysis are the least biased possible, as each datum updates the evidence density according to its contribution to the available information which starts with the statement of the geometric properties of the model with respect to the data.

One feature of Bayesian data analysis as expressed in the language of conditional probabilities is that it forces one to specify the state of background knowledge upon which any estimate is based. Whenever real data are discussed, such statements necessarily include remarks on the nature of the measurement apparatus. That apparatus can be in the form of either a physical device such as a voltmeter or an abstract device such as a survey. While the parameter z has been given the interpretation of a spatial coordinate, it represents any observable that can be expressed in terms of a location-type parameter with uniform measure over an arbitrarily large domain. That parameter can of course be generalized to a data vector of any dimensionality according to the complexity of the situation at hand.

When one is not certain that the background knowledge includes specification of the physically correct functional form for the constituent distributions, there is a formal procedure for comparing the relative likelihood of competing models. That comparison is expressed not by the ratio of the peak likelihoods given by each model's parameter mode but rather by the ratio of the expected likelihoods given by the integral of the evidence over each model's parameter manifold. The distinction is important, as it is the latter which takes into account the principle of efficiency through the Occam factor. The most useful form of the parameter evidence density is that which drops the normalization of the prior yet retains any constant factors in the likelihood, as its integral appears as both the relative likelihood of the model and the normalization constant for taking expectation values of observables. Care must be taken when dropping constants from an evaluation (whether numerical or analytic), as it is easy to make a mistake regarding the appropriate normalization for the given task.

When not all of the prior normalization factors cancel out of the model comparison ratio, then they must be accounted for explicitly. Quite often the transformation group prior will yield an infinite normalization when allowed to extend over an infinite domain, which is no less a problem for a maximum likelihood analysis that assigns any and all parameters a uniform prior. In that case, one is forced to consider more fully the nature of the apparatus as well as of the objects to be measured in order to determine sensible boundaries for one's prior state of knowledge. One generally hopes that finite boundaries do not truncate significantly the evidence density, but there can be times when physical constraints (such as positivity) dictate that what would otherwise be the mode lies outside the allowable parameter domain.

The process of inductive reasoning, through which one expresses one's degree of belief in the value of some observable, is not restricted to the simple distributions considered here but extends naturally to much more complicated situations. By going through the development of the methodology for increasingly less restrictive states of prior knowledge, we hope that readers have gained some insight into how to apply the method to problems they encounter. While almost everyone is comfortable with the process of finding the parameter mode, and most with taking expectation values according to the evidence density, the process of model selection often seems mysterious until one realizes that the relevant factors are just the relative expected likelihoods and any leftover prior normalizations.

10.   Conclusion

In this article, we have explored the transformation group approach to the problem of predicting the type of some unclassified particle given its location and a list of locations for particles of identified classification. The process of inductive reasoning is used to relate these quantities of interest, which incorporates both Bayes' theorem and the principle of indifference to produce the least biased estimate from the data at hand. The expectation value of the observable is compared to that derived from the parameter mode, and they converge on the underlying distribution when sufficient data exists and the model function is known to be physically correct. When competing models must be compared, the procedure of evaluating the evidence ratio in terms of the relative likelihoods and prior normalizations has been explicitly determined.

The prediction from the Bayesian method is found to be superior to those from non-parametric algorithms, such as nearest neighbor or kernel density estimation, especially when not much data exists for analysis. The reason is because conditional probability theory makes full use of all the available information rather than discarding the contribution from some datum on the grounds that it is far away from the desired location or smearing that information out according to some linear operator. The essential difference between inductive and deductive methods is that the former inverts the model to predict the data whereas the latter inverts the data to predict the model — see Ref. 16 for an explicit example regarding sums of exponential functions and Ref. 17 as regards the Fourier transform. Having invested in the presumably expensive classification of the particles in the training set, it makes sense that one should choose the most reliable method for analyzing that data. It is only those of us who generate data cheaply that worry about the expense of computing an integral.

A major advantage of the Bayesian method is that it is extensible. As new effects are brought into play, their parameters are included in the analysis in a straightforward manner. The language of conditional probability theory is sufficiently general that it can handle whatever state of background knowledge one specifies, including those which admit that competing models are available as well as those which admit that the measurements are themselves subject to error. "Reasoning in the face of uncertainty" is an apt description of inferential logic and is a problem often faced in the imperfect real world. The use of Bayes' theorem requires one to specify the conditions upon which any and all probabilities are based, which seems like a lot of work at the outset but leads to a robust analysis upon completion. It also recognizes the difference between the most likely value of some observable and its expected value, which is important to consider when not many measurements are available. By working through the tasks of model selection, parameter estimation, and observable prediction explicitly for the case of these simple distributions, we hope the reader has learned how to apply the transformation group method to more complicated cases of data analysis.

References

1. M. Tegmark, *Our Mathematical Universe*. Random House (2014). URL https://books.google.com/books?id=y6kRmwEACAAJ.
2. M. D. Vidrighin, O. Dahlsten, M. Barbieri, M. S. Kim, V. Vedral, and I. A. Walmsley, Photonic Maxwell's Demon, *Physics Review Letters* **116**, 050401 (Feb, 2016). doi: 10.1103/PhysRevLett.116.050401. URL http://link.aps.org/doi/10.1103/PhysRevLett.116.050401.
3. P. Hall, B. U. Park, and R. J. Samworth, Choice of neighbor order in nearest-neighbor classification, *Annals of Statistics.* **36**(5), 2135–2152 (2008). doi: 10.1214/07-AOS537. URL http://dx.doi.org/10.1214/07-AOS537.
4. M. Eberts and I. Steinwart, Optimal regression rates for SVMs using Gaussian kernels, *Electronic Journal of Statistics* **7**, 1–42 (2013).
5. J. Kim and C. D. Scott, Robust kernel density estimation, *Journal of Machine Learning Research* **13**, 2529–2565 (Sep, 2012).
6. G. R. Terrell and D. W. Scott, Variable kernel density estimation., *Annals of Statistics* **20**(3), 1236–1265 (1992). doi: 10.1214/aos/1176348768. URL http://dx.doi.org/10.1214/aos/1176348768.
7. J. Poitevineau and B. Lecoutre, Implementing Bayesian predictive procedures: The K-prime and K-square distributions, *Computational Statistics*

and Data Analysis **54**(3), 724–731 (2010). ISSN 0167-9473. doi: 10.1016/j. csda.2008.11.004. URL http://dx.doi.org/10.1016/j.csda.2008.11.004.

8. G. L. Bretthorst, *Bayesian Spectrum Analysis and Parameter Estimation*. Springer-Verlag, Berlin, Germany (1988).

9. R. Durrett, *The Essentials of Probability*. Duxbury Press, A Division of Wadsworth, Inc., Belmont, CA (1994).

10. D. S. Sivia, *Data Analysis: A Bayesian Tutorial*. Oxford Science Publications, Oxford University Press, Oxford, UK (July, 1996). ISBN 0198518897.

11. V. Dose, Hyperplane priors, *AIP Conference Proceedings*. **659**(1), 350–360 (2003). doi: 10.1063/1.1570552. URL http://dx.doi.org/10.1063/1. 1570552.

12. E. T. Jaynes, Prior probabilities, *IEEE Transactions On Systems Science and Cybernetics*. **4**(3), 227–241 (1968). doi: 10.1109/TSSC.1968.300117. URL http://dx.doi.org/10.1109/TSSC.1968.300117.

13. W. Press, S. Teukolsky, W. Vetterling, and B. Flannery, *Numerical Recipes in C*, 2nd edn. Cambridge University Press, Cambridge, England (1992).

14. J. Berntsen, T. O. Espelid, and A. Genz, An adaptive algorithm for the approximate calculation of multiple integrals, *ACM Transactions in Mathematical Software* **17**(4), 437–451 (Dec., 1991). ISSN 0098-3500. doi: 10.1145/ 210232.210233. URL http://doi.acm.org/10.1145/210232.210233.

15. A. Genz and A. Malik, Remarks on algorithm 006: An adaptive algorithm for numerical integration over an N-dimensional rectangular region, *Journal of Computational and Applied Mathematics* **6**(4), 295–302 (1980). ISSN 0377-0427. doi: 10.1016/0771-050X(80)90039-X. URL http://dx.doi.org/ 10.1016/0771-050X(80)90039-X.

16. R. W. Johnson, Fitting a sum of exponentials to lattice correlation functions using a non-uniform prior, *The European Physical Journal C — Particles and Fields* **70**, 233–241 (2010). ISSN 1434-6044. doi: 10.1140/epjc/s10052-010-1438-8. URL http://dx.doi.org/10.1140/epjc/ s10052-010-1438-8.

17. R. W. Johnson, MaxEnt power spectrum estimation using the Fourier transform for irregularly sampled data applied to a record of stellar luminosity, *Astrophysics and Space Science* **338**, 35–48 (2012). ISSN 0004-640X. doi: 10.1007/s10509-011-0922-4. URL http://dx.doi.org/10.1007/ s10509-011-0922-4.

Chapter 17

The Concept of Systemic-Resonance Bioinformatics: Resonances and the Quest for Transdisciplinarity

Sergey V. Petoukhov and Elena S. Petukhova

Mechanical Engineering Research Institute, Russian Academy of Sciences
Laboratory of Biomechanical Systems, Moscow, Russia
spetoukhov@gmail.com

The article is devoted to an important role of the concept of resonances not only in classical and quantum mechanics but also in genetics and biological communication. Matrix representations of oscillators with many degrees of freedom are used to model some phenomena of Mendelian genetics and to analyze structures of genetic-molecular alphabets. To explain phenomena of segregation in these molecular alphabets, the existence of dominant and recessive resonances in nitrogenous bases of DNA and RNA are postulated by analogy with dominant and recessive alleles in Mendelian genetics. Relations of genetic alphabets with modulo-2 addition, dyadic groups of binary numbers and matrices of dyadic shifts are shown. A connection of structures of genetic alphabets with known formalisms of noise-immunity coding (Rademacher and Walsh functions, Hadamard matrices) are discussed taking into account noise-immunity properties of genetic encoding.

Keywords: Genetic code; resonance; dominant; recessive; Mendelian genetics; symmetry.

1. Introduction

From an information standpoint, biological organisms are informational essences. They receive genetic information from their ancestors and transmit it to descendants. Science has discovered that all organisms are identical to each other by their basic molecular-genetic structures. Due to this revolutionary discovery, a great unification of all biological

467

organisms has happened in science. A new understanding of life itself has appeared: *"life is a partnership between genes and mathematics"* [Stewart, 1999]. The question about principles and mathematical bases of genetic informatics became one of the main challenges in mathematical natural sciences today.

It is well known that people use oral speech and singing for a communication due to an inherited ability to tune into resonances and to use resonances as carriers of information. Our voice apparatus is the appropriate oscillatory system with many degrees of freedom. But according to the classics of structural linguistics, our language did not come out of nowhere, but it is a superstructure over the oldest language - the genetic language [Jakobson, 1987, 1999; Petoukhov and He, 2010, Chapter 12]. This is one of reasons to study genetic informatics, including genetic alphabets, from the standpoint of mathematics of resonances.

Moreover any living organism is a huge chorus of coordinated oscillatory processes (mechanical, electrical, piezoelectrical, biochemical, *etc*.), which are connected with their genetic inheritance along chains of generations. Since ancient times, chronomedicine believes that all diseases are the result of disturbances in the ordered set of oscillatory processes. From a formal point of view, a living organism is an oscillatory system with a great number of degrees of freedom. Theory of oscillations uses mathematics of matrices to study resonant characteristics of oscillatory systems with many degrees of freedom (see, for example, [Gladwell, 2004]). We use matrices to study genetic phenomena.

Genetic molecules DNA and RNA exist on principles of quantum mechanics, but they encode structures of living macroorganisms, which are subjects of classical mechanics. By this reason, mathematics of genetic systems should be appropriate to quantum mechanics and classic mechanics simultaneously. Mathematics of resonances of oscillatory systems is appropriate for quantum mechanics and classic mechanics since such mathematics uses in both cases the same property of matrices to express resonances.

The concept of resonances plays fundamental and interdisciplinary role in science. Quantum mechanics has begun in 1900 due to works by M. Planck, who has analyzed a great set of resonant oscillators inside the cavity and in the result has received his famous law of electromagnetic radiation emitted by a black body in thermal equilibrium. One can say that Planck has represented the matter as a set of vibrating oscillators and set the task to study the equilibrium established in the result of the exchange of energy between the oscillators and radiation.

Later, after more than 50 years of successful development of quantum mechanics, E. Schrodinger emphasised the basic meaning of resonances: *"The one thing which one has to accept and which is the inalienable consequence of the wave-equation as it is used in every problem, under the most various forms, is this: that the interaction between two microscopic physical systems is controlled by a peculiar law of resonance»* [Schrodinger, 1952, p. 115]. In considering an exact balance in nature between bundles of energy, lost by one system and gained by another, he noted: *«I maintain that it can in all cases be understood as a resonance phenomenon»* [ibid, p. 114]. He wrote in his resonance concept of quantum interactions, that chemical reactions, including photochemical reactions, can be explained on the base of resonances.

His book [Schrodinger, 1944] said that the chromosome is an aperiodic crystal since its atoms are connected each other by forces of the same nature that atoms in crystals. But vibrations and resonances play a very important role in physics of crystals. One can hope that a resonance approach can usefully serve also in genetics.

L. Pauling used ideas of resonances in quantum mechanical systems in his theory of resonance in structural chemistry. His book [Pauling, 1940] about this theory is the most quoted among scientific books of the 20th century. The theory was developed to explain the formation of hybrid bonds in molecules. The actual molecule, as Pauling proposed, is a sort of hybrid, a structure that resonates between the two alternative extremes; and whenever there is a resonance between the two forms, the structure is stabilized. His theory uses the fundamental principle of a minimal energy because — in resonant combining of parts into a single unit — each of members of the ensemble requires less energy for performing own work than when working individually.

In classic mechanics, the concept of resonances has also wide theoretical and engineering applications due to vibrational phenomena of a resonant synchronization of oscillatory processes, vibrational separation and structuring of multiphase systems, vibro-transportation of substances, vibro-transmission of energy within systems, *etc.* [Blekhman, 2000; Ganiev *et al.*, 2015]. Our results give a basis for wider use of these phenomena in modeling biological phenomena.

2. Background

Matrices possess a wonderful property to express resonances, which sometimes is called as their main quality. Physical resonance phenomenon in classical mechanics is familiar to everyone. The expression y = A*S models the transmission of a signal S via an acoustic system A, represented by a relevant matrix A. If an input signal is a resonant tone, then the output signal will repeat it with a precision up to a scale factor y = λ*S by analogy with a situation when a musical string sounds in unison with the neighboring vibrating string. In the case of a matrix A, its number of resonant tones S_i corresponds to its size. They are called its eigenvectors, and the scale factors λ_i with them are called its eigenvalues or, briefly, spectrum A. Frequencies $\omega_i = \lambda_i^{0.5}$ [Gladwell, 2004, p. 61] are defined as natural frequencies or resonance frequencies of the system, and the corresponding eigenvectors are defined as its own forms of oscillations (or simply, natural oscillations).

　　　This article uses the tensor product of matrices, which is denoted by $\otimes$ and is widely applied in mathematics, physics, informatics, control theory, *etc.* It is applied for algorithmic generation of higher dimensional spaces on the basis of spaces with smaller dimensions (reminding a growth of degrees of freedom in the ensemble of cells of growing organism in the result of their division). In quantum physics, in considering the quantum system consisting of two subsystems, its state space is constructed in the form of the tensor product of state spaces of the subsystems. Quantum physics uses Hermitian matrices (or self-adjoint matrices) with complex entries and real eigenvalues. The tensor product of two Hermitian matrices gives a new Hermitian matrix.

Correspondingly, the tensor product of matrices is used in our researches of genetic systems represented in matrix forms (Petoukhov, 2016).

By definition, the tensor product of two square matrices V and W of the orders m and n respectively is the matrix $Q = V \otimes W = \|v_{ij}*W\|$ with the order m*n [Bellman, 1960]. The tensor product has the property of inheritance of mosaic structure of the original matrix under its tensor exponentiation. This property connects the tensor product of matrices with fractals [Gazale, 1999, Chapter X].

The tensor product of matrices is also endowed with the property of "inheritance" of their eigenvalues: if the original matrix V and W have the eigenvalues λ_i and μ_j respectively, then in their tensor product $Q = V \otimes W$ all eigenvalues are equal to $\lambda_i*\mu_j$ (figuratively speaking, λ_i and μ_j are inherited in this tensor way).

3. The Analogy Between Punnett Squares and Tables of the Tensor Inheritance of Eigenvalues of Matrices

Features of the tensor inheritance of eigenvalues of the original matrices (or "parental" matrices) in the result of their tensor product can be conveniently represented in the form of "tables of inheritance". The top row of Fig. 1 shows the example of two simplest cases, conventionally referred to as monohybrid and dihybrid cases of a tensor hybridization of vibrosystems. In the first case, the tensor product of two (2*2)-matrices V and W, which have the same set of eigenvalues H and h, gives the (4*4)-matrix $Q = V \otimes W$ with its 4 eigenvalues H*H, H*h, H*h, h*h. In the second case, the tensor product of (4*4)-matrices, having the same set of eigenvalues HB, Hb, hB, hb, gives (16*16)-matrix with 16 eigenvalues, represented in the tabular form.

One can see that the internal content of the table of inheritance in the dihybrid case (Fig. 1 top) is equal to [HH, Hh; Hh, hh]⊗[BB, Bb; Bb, bb]; in other words, the spectrum of the dihybrid vibrosystem is equal to the tensor product of spectra of two monohybrid vibrosystems. Similar tables of inheritance for *n*-hybrid cases ($n = 3,4,\ldots$) of the tensor hybridization of vibrosystems can be constructed by analogy.

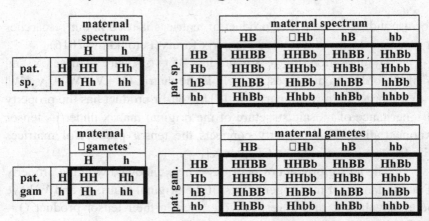

Fig. 1. Comparison of Punnett squares and tables of inheritance of eigenvalues of matrices under the tensor product. Top row: examples of tables of inheritance of eigenvalues under the tensor product in cases of (2*2)-matrices (left) and (4*4)-matrices (cases of monohybrid and dihybrid hybridizations). Bottom row: examples of Punnett squares for monohybrid and dihybrid crosses of organisms under the laws of Mendel. «Pat. sp.» and «pat. gam.» mean «paternal spectrum» and «paternal gametes».

The author notes that these tables of the tensor inheritance for spectra of vibrosystems are identical to Punnett squares for poly-hybrid crosses of organisms (Fig. 1, bottom). In genetics from 1906 year, Punnett squares represent Mendel's laws of inheritance of traits under poly-hybrid crosses. Only in Punnett squares, instead of eigenvalues of matrices and their combinations, exist similar combinations of dominant and recessive alleles of genes from parent reproductive cells — gametes. By tradition, dominant alleles of genes are represented by uppercase letters and recessive alleles — by lowercase letters.

This formal analogy — between Punnett squares of combinations of alleles and tables of tensor inheritance of eigenvalues of matrices of oscillators - generates the following idea:
— alleles of genes and their combinations can be interpreted as eigenvalues of (2^n*2^n)-matrices from tensor families of matrices of oscillatory systems. For genetic systems, this model approach focuses an attention on the possible importance of a particular class of mutually

related resonance frequencies from tensor families of matrices, which play the role of biological "matrix archetypes".

In this modeling approach, each allele of a gene, which has a polyatomic structure, is characterized by a single number: an eigenvalue of a matrix of an oscillatory system with a corresponding number of degrees of freedom. It resembles the phenomenon, known in vibrational mechanics since the time of C. Huygens, of self-synchronization of a plurality of pendulums mounted on a common movable platform: the self-synchronization provides that all the pendulums begin to oscillate with a single common frequency, although initially each of them could have its own natural frequency of oscillation.

The author has put forward and argued the hypothesis that genetic alphabets are based on systems of resonances [Petoukhov, 2016]. Now we describe new results of studying genetic systems from this standpoint.

3. Segregations Inside Genetic Alphabets and the Mendel's Law of Segregation

Genetics has arisen from the Mendel's discovery of mathematical regularities in phenomena of inheritance of traits in poly-hybrid crosses of organisms. Mendelian genetics explained these phenomenological regularities, which are observed at the level of the whole organisms, on the base of the idea about dominant and recessive alleles of genes from parent reproductive cells — gametes. By analogy with the Mendelian theory, we introduce below a notion of dominant and recessive resonances of genetic molecules to explain some phenomenological regularities of genetic alphabets, which are based in DNA on nitrogenous bases — adenine A, cytosine C, guanine G and thymine T (uracil U in RNA). In particular we will analyze the known phenomenon of segregation of the set of 64 triplets into two equal sub-sets on the basis of strong and weak roots, i.e., the first two positions in triplets [Rumer, 1968]: a) 32 triplets with strong roots, i.e., with 8 "strong" doublets AC, CC, CG, CT, GC, GG, GT, TC; b) 32 triplets with weak roots, i.e., with 8 "weak" doublets AA, AG, AT, GA, TA, TT, TG. Code meanings of triplets with strong roots do not depend on the letters on their third positions; code meanings of triplets with weak roots depend on their third letter (see details in Petoukhov, [2016]).

Science does not know why the basic alphabet of DNA consists of the four polyatomic letters A, C, G, T of very simple structures. But it is known that the set of these four structures is not quite heterogeneous, but it carries on itself the symmetric system of binary-oppositional traits. The system of such traits divides the genetic four-letter alphabet into various three pairs of letters, which are equivalent from a viewpoint of one of these molecular traits or its absence (Fig. 2): 1) C = T & A = G (according to the binary-oppositional traits: "pyrimidine" or "purine"; 2) A = C & G = T (according to the traits: amino or keto); 3) C = G & A = T (according to the traits: three or two hydrogen bonds are materialized in these complementary pairs, that is strong or weak bonds) [Gumbel *et al.*, 2015; Petoukhov, 2008; Stambuk, 1999]. Below we use traditional denotations of these traits: purine — R, pyrimidine — Y, amino — M, keto — K, strong hydrogen bonds — S, weak hydrogen bonds — W.

TRAITS	G	A	□C	T(U)
1) purine (R), pyrimidine (Y)	R	R	Y	Y
2) amino □M, keto (K)	K	M	M	K
3) strong hydrogen bonds (S), weak hydrogen bonds (W)	S	W	S	W

Figure 2. The division of the four-letter alphabet of DNA (RNA) into three binary sub-alphabets in accordance with three binary-oppositional traits, which are interpreted as resonances with their symbols R, Y, M, K, S and W.

Each of traits of nitrogenous bases A, C, G, T(U) in Fig. 2 can be interpreted as connected with its own resonance characteristics. For example, it is obvious that purines may have resonances that differ from the resonances of pyrimidines due to differences in the structure of the purine and pyrimidine molecules. In this light, each of mentioned pairs of binary-oppositional traits can be treated as a pair of oppositional resonance characteristics (Petoukhov, 2016).

The genetic code lies in the bases of living matter. But what kinds of laws lay in the base of the genetic code itself? Attempts of answering on this question have led the author to the idea about special biological rules («laws») of segregation of molecular-genetic alphabets. These rules are formally similar to the Mendelian law of segregation, which acts at levels of whole organisms, but they act at molecular levels and, from the standpoint of our modeling approach, they are related with resonances of dominant and recessive types in bases A, C, G, T(U) and in their combinations in DNA and RNA. In this Section, we give an explanation of the structure of the natural phenomenon of segregation of the set of 16 doublets into two equal sub-sets, the first of which contains 8 strong doublets and the second one contains 8 weak doublets.

Our model approach considers nitrogenous bases C, G, A, T(U) as carriers of pairs of resonant traits since we postulate that the resonant frequencies and the corresponding oscillatory energies are key factors for encoding. One can see from Fig. 2 that for an unambiguous assignment of each of the nitrogenous bases it is enough to take into account two of its three traits. We will characterize each nitrogenous base in terms of its resonances taken from the oppositional pairs of resonances "M or K" and «Y or R». In quantum mechanics, two resonance frequencies of an oscillator with two degrees of freedom lie on the main diagonal of the diagonal $(2*2)$-matrix, which characterizes the oscillator. We will use such matrix representation. For example, adenine A is the single nitrogenous base with the pair of resonance traits M and R, therefore, in such bi-resonance representation, one can write adenine A = [M, 0; 0, R] (for brevity, we will denote this matrix by the symbol MR). Accordingly, for other nitrogenous bases their bi-resonance representations are the following: cytosine C = [M, 0; 0 Y] (or briefly MY), guanine G = [K, 0; 0, R] (or KR), thymine T = [K, 0; 0 Y] (or KY). These diagonal $(2*2)$-matrices characterize quantum mechanical state spaces of all of these objects A, C, G, T.

Corresponding state spaces of doublets and triplets are constructed by means of the tensor product of state spaces of their nitrogenous bases, which are subsystems of doublet and triplets. For example, the state space of the doublet CA is characterized by the diagonal matrix $(4*4)$: [M, 0; 0 Y] $\otimes$ [M, 0; 0, R] = [MM, 0, 0, 0; 0, MR, 0, 0; 0, 0, YM, 0; 0, 0, 0, YR] and state space of the doublet AC, which has the inverse order of the same letters, is characterized by another diagonal matrix $(4*4)$: [M, 0; 0, R] $\otimes$ [M, 0; 0, Y] = [MM, 0, 0,

0; 0, MY, 0, 0; 0, 0, RM, 0; 0, 0, 0, RY]. The tensor product is non-commutative operation. By this reason, the difference of these two matrices is not equal to zero. When recording sequences of nitrogenous bases in their bi-resonance representations, we will separate two-letter symbols of adjacent nitrogenous bases by means of vertical dash: for example the doublet CA will be denoted as MY|MR.

CC	CA	AC	AA
MY|MY	MY|MR	MR|MY	MR|MR
CT	CG	AT	AG
MY|KY	MY|KR	MR|KY	MR|KR
TC	TA	GC	GA
KY|MY	KY|MR	KR|MY	KR|MR
TT	TG	GT	GG
KY|KY	KY|KR	KR|KY	KR|KR

		Maternal gametes	
		H	h
Paternal	h	HH	hh
gametes	H	HH	Hh

Fig. 3. The segregation of the set of 16 doublets into subsets of 8 strong doublets (black color) and 8 weak doublets (white color); under each doublet, bi-resonance traits of its two letters are shown. On the right: the Punnet square for monohybrid crosses of organisms; combinations of alleles H and h, which contain at least one dominant allele H, are marked by black color.

Each of two families of 4 doublets with their first letter from the complementary pair C and G contains of 3 strong doublets and 1 weak doublet (Fig. 3, left). In contrary, each of two other families of 4 doublets with their first letter from another complementary pair A and T contains of 1 strong doublet and 3 weak doublets. But the same ratio 3:1 is realized in the Mendel's law of segregation of traits of whole organisms in the case of monohybrid crosses of organisms, whose gametes contain one dominant allele of a corresponding gene and one recessive allele of the same gene (here we mean the situation of complete dominance, when the effect of the dominant allele completely masks the effect of the recessive allele). This case of crosses of organisms is traditionally shown by means of the Punnet square with the same mosaic ratio 3:1 (Fig. 3).

Based on this analogy — between segregations of traits in the case of molecular doublets and in the case of whole organisms under the law of Mendel —, the author puts forward the following hypothesis:
— The principle of dominant and recessive factors plays its genetic key role in segregation phenomena not only at the level of whole organisms but also at the level of ensembles of genetic molecules; the mentioned resonances of genetic molecules play roles of dominant and recessive factors in laws of segregation of traits in molecular-genetic ensembles.

This hypothesis allows explaining some features of segregations inside genetic alphabets. In addition it allows thinking that Mendel's laws, which are true at supra-chromosome levels, did not come out of nowhere, but they have precursors in form of phenomena of segregation at sub-chromosomal levels. In this case, some analogies of phenomena of segregations in populations of whole organisms (for example, the division into male and female organisms with their sexual interrelations) can exist in the world of biological molecules, including proteins (Petoukhov, 2004). It could lead to new points of view about existence of appropriate oppositional groups of proteins and about similar interrelations among them, etc. It seems to be logical that regularities of the world of macro-organisms reproduce regularities of the bio-molecular world for genetic encoding and a survival of organisms in the chain of generations. We show now one of examples of positive applications of this hypothesis.

In Mendelian genetics, those dominant and recessive factors, which are responsible for segregation at the level of organisms, are called "alleles". In our approach — for a terminological unity — those dominant and recessive factors, which are responsible for segregation at the level of molecular-genetic alphabets, will be called "pro-alleles". We suppose that mentioned molecular resonances of nitrogenous bases play the role of such «pro-alleles». Let us show how the idea of dominant and recessive resonances of nitrogenous bases (Fig. 2) explains the segregation of strong and weak doublets inside the mentioned four families of doublets, presented in Fig. 3. It is obvious that inside each of families of 4 doublets in tabular quadrants (Fig. 3), the second letter in each doublet defines a strong or weak character of the doublet.

Initially one can look at two families of doublets with the first letter C or G in them (they will be called as the C-family and the G-family of doublets). Each of these families contains 3 strong doublets (CC, CT, CG and GC, GT, GG correspondingly) and 1 weak doublet (CA and GA) (Fig. 3, left). In both mentioned doublets CA and GA, their second letter — adenine A — is the carrier of two resonance pro-alleles M and R. By analogy with combinations of dominant and recessive alleles in the case of monohybrid crosses of organisms in Mendelian genetics (Fig. 3, right), one should conclude that — in the C-family and G-family of doublets — the resonances M and R are recessive pro-alleles in the second letters of all the doublets. Correspondingly, two oppositional resonances K and Y play the role of dominant pro-alleles in the second letters of all the doublets. By analogy with the Mendelian scheme of complete dominance, we assume for these families, that any pair of resonance pro-alleles, which contains at least one of dominant pro-alleles K and Y, defines the dominant character of the second letter of a doublet and, by this reason, the dominant character of the doublet as a whole. In each of the C-family and G-family, 3 mentioned doublets contain these dominant resonances K and Y in their second letters (CC, CT, CG and GC, GT, GG) and only 1 doublet does not contain them in its second letter (CA and GA, which are weak doublets).

Now let us turn to other two families of doublets with the first letter A or T in them (the A-family and the T-family of doublets). Each of these families has the opposite ratio of quantities of strong and weak doublets (Fig. 3): 3 weak doublets (AA, AT, AG and TA, TT, TG correspondingly) and 1 strong doublet (AC and TC). In both named doublets AC and TC, their second letter — cytosine C — is the carrier of two pro-alleles M and Y, which should be interpreted as recessive pro-alleles. Then two opposite resonances K and R play the role of dominant pro-alleles in the second letters of all doublets of these families. By analogy with the Mendelian scheme of complete dominance, one can again assume that any pair of resonance pro-alleles, which contains at least one of dominant pro-alleles K and R, defines the dominant character of the appropriate second letter of a doublet. In each of the A-family and

T-family, 3 named doublets contain these dominant resonances K and R in their second letters (AA, AT, AG and TA, TT, TG correspondingly) and only 1 doublet does not contain them in its second letter (AC and TC).

    It should be specially noted that resonances Y and R correspondingly play the oppositional roles of dominant and recessive pro-alleles in the C-family and G-family of doublets, but in the A-family and T-family, they play the inverse roles of recessive and dominant pro-alleles. But in Mendelian genetics it is well known that dominant and recessive characteristics are not absolute features, but they are relative: the same trait is dominant or recessive depending on the biological environment of its manifestation. For example, a trait of baldness is dominant at men and recessive at women. Therefore, to explain the phenomenon of the reverse segregation concerning strong and weak doublets in these families of doublets, it is sufficient to take by analogy the following. The C-family and G-family of doublets are conditionally "male" families, in which the resonance Y of the second letter of each doublet is one of dominant pro-alleles and the resonance R is one of recessive pro-alleles for the considered phenomenon. In contrast, the A-family and T-family of doublets are conditionally "female" families, in which the same resonances Y and R are correspondingly the recessive and dominant pro-alleles of the second letter of each doublet. In other words, the first letter of each doublet defines, what kind of resonances Y or R in the second letter of the doublet will be dominant or recessive. Our modeling approach has shown that members of the molecular alphabet of 16 doublets are resonance hybrid entities, which are similar to hybrids in Mendelian genetics of organisms.

Modern science explains Mendel's laws on the base of division of pairs of homological chromosomes. Mendel's laws do not be spread to levels below the level of chromosomes. Correspondingly, the rules of segregation of the molecular alphabet of 16 doublets, which are described in our article, have an independent character in relation to Mendel's laws since they cannot be deduced from them [Petoukhov, 2004].

4. Dyadic Groups of Binary-Oppositional Resonances, Genetic Alphabets and Hypercomplex Numbers

This Section shows various aspects of logic connections of genetic alphabets with modulo-2 addition and dyadic groups of binary numbers. Modulo-2 addition is utilized broadly in computer technology and the theory of discrete signal processing as the fundamental operation for binary variables. By definition, the modulo-2 addition of two numbers, written in binary notation, is made in a bitwise manner in accordance with the following rules: $0 \oplus 0 = 0, 0 \oplus 1 = 1 \oplus 0 = 1, 1 \oplus 1 = 0$ ($\oplus$ is the symbol for modulo-2 addition). By means of modulo-2 addition, binary n-bit numbers form so called dyadic groups, including 2^n members. For example, the set of binary 2-bit numbers 00, 01, 10, 11 forms a dyadic group, in which modulo-2 addition serves as the group operation [Harmuth, 1989]. The distance in this symmetry group is known as the Hamming distance. Below we show that the structural organization of genetic systems is related to logic of modulo-2 addition.

The work [Petoukhov, 2016] noted that the binary-oppositional structure of resonance characteristics of members of the genetic alphabet A, C, G, T(U) (Fig. 2) can be connected with binary numbers for using logic of their dyadic groups in operating genetic binary computers on the base of resonances inside organisms. Correspondingly, each of the pairs of binary-oppositional resonances "R or Y", "M or K", "S or W" of this alphabet (Fig. 2) can correspond to its own binary units: $Y = 0$ and $R = 1$; $M = 0$ and $K = 1$; $S = 0$ and $W = 1$.

The theory of discrete signal processing uses so called (2^n*2^n) matrices of dyadic shifts, in each of which three dyadic groups of binary n-bit numbers are employed for binary numerations of its rows, columns and cells [Ahmed, Rao, 1975]. Figure 4 shows the simplest examples of such (2^n*2^n) matrices, where $n = 1, 2$, for two dyadic groups: 0, 1 and 00, 01, 10, 11. Numeration of any matrix cell is given by modulo-2 addition of numerations of its row and column. Let us use these classical numeric matrices of dyadic shifts to represent the specificity of genetic alphabets, members of which are carriers of the binary-oppositional resonance characteristics.

For matrices of genetic alphabets in Fig. 4, one can denote binary numerations of columns by means of the first pair Y = 0 and R = 1 and binary numerations of rows — by means of the second pair M = 0 and K = 1. In this case, we get a coordinate grid, in which each cell contains those nitrogenous bases A, C, G or T, which are carriers of resonances depicted in symbolic numerations of the row and the column of the cell. For example, inside these resonant coordinates, the intersection of resonances M and R from numerations of rows and columns always defines inside appropriate cells adenine A, which is the carrier of this pair of resonances M and R (Fig. 2). In addition, one can see from the (2 ∗ 2)-matrix in Fig. 4 that inside cells, each of nitrogenous bases has its own binary representation: C = G = 0, A = T = 1. From this standpoint, each of doublets inside its cell is represented by a corresponding binary combination: for example, the doublet AG is read as binary number 10, which coincides with the binary numeration of its cell in (4 ∗ 4)-matrix in Fig. 4. One can check that such binary readings of all doublets inside their cells in Fig. 4 coincide with binary numerations of their cells in classical matrices of dyadic shifts. The (4 ∗ 4)-matrices of doublets in Figs. 3 and 4 are identical.

	Y(0)	R(1)
M(0)	MY	MR
	C (0)	A (1)
K(1)	KY	KR
	T (1)	G (0)

	YY (00)	YR (01)	RY (10)	RR (11)
MM	MY|MY	MY|MR	MR|MY	MR|MR
(00)	CC (00)	CA (01)	AC (10)	AA (11)
MK	MY|KY	MY|KR	MR|KY	MR|KR
(01)	CT (01)	CG (00)	AT (11)	AG (10)
KM	KY|MY	KY|MR	KR|MY	KR|MR
(10)	TC (10)	TA (11)	GC (00)	GA (01)
KK	KY|KY	KY|KR	KR|KY	KR|KR
(11)	TT□(11)	TG (10)	GT (01)	GG (00)

Figure 4. Matrices of dyadic-group representations of resonance traits for genetic alphabets of 4 monoplets and 16 doublets. Numerations of rows and columns use binary-oppositional resonances (Fig. 2) with the conformity M = 0, K = 1, Y = 0, R = 1. Strong doublets are marked by black color.

The distribution of strong and weak doublets inside the alphabet of 16 doublets far from random. In the dyadic-shift matrix of 16 doublets in Fig. 4, one can denote each of strong doublets (black color) by number +1 and each of weak doublets by opposite number −1. In the result, a numeric matrix P arises (Fig. 5), each rows of which coincides with one of Rademacher functions known in theory of discrete signal processing. The dyadic-shift decomposition of this matrix P shows that P is the sum of four sparse matrices: $P = P_0 + P_1 + P_2 + P_3$ (Fig. 5). This set of 4 matrices P_0, P_1, P_2, P_3 is unexpectedly closed relative to multiplication: the product of any two matrices from this set gives a matrix from the same set. This property is expressed by the multiplication table coinciding with the multiplication table of hypercomplex numbers known from 1849 year as split-quaternions by J. Cockle (https://en.wiki pedia.org/wiki/Split-quaternion) (Fig. 5, below). In particular split-quaternions are used in the Poincaré disk model of hyperbolic geometry (Lobachevskian geometry) for the theory of special relativity particularly Minkowski spacetime.

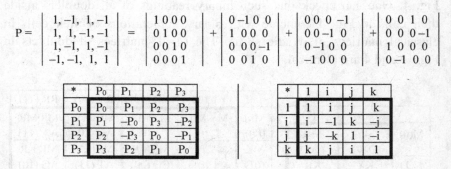

Fig. 5. The dyadic-shift decomposition of the matrix $P = P_0 + P_1 + P_2 + P_3$, where P_0 is the identity matrix. Bottom: the multiplication table of the sparse matrices P_0, P_1, P_2, P_3 is identical to the multiplication table of split-quaternions (https://en.wikipedia.org/wiki/Split-quaternion).

So, the numeric matrix P, which was received from the genetic matrix based on the idea about dominant and recessive resonances in 16 doublets, represents the split-quaternion with unit coordinates: $P = 1 + I + j + k$, where i, j, k are basis elements of split-quaternions. This unexpected result testifies that the logic of organization of molecular-genetic systems — in relation to strong and weak doublets — is connected with the multiplication table of split-quaternions.

The alphabet of bases A, C, G, T(U) is divided into two sub-alphabets in the ratio 3:1 in accordance with another phenomenological genetic feature. Thymine T has a unique status and differs from other three letters A, C and G: 1) only thymine T is replaced by another molecule U (uracil) in transferring from DNA to RNA; 2) only thymine T hasn't the functionally important amino group NH_2. This binary opposition can be expressed as: $A = C = G = +1$, $T = -1$. All letters of each of doublets can be replaced to these numbers for numeric representation of the doublet as the product of these numbers. In the result, the dyadic-shift matrix of 16 doublets (Fig. 4) gets its numeric representation in a form of the Hadamard matrix $H = [1, 1, 1, 1; -1, 1, -1, 1; -1, -1, 1, 1; 1, -1, -1, 1]$, rows of which coincide with a complete orthogonal system of Walsh functions for 4-dimensional space.

Hadamard matrices and their Walsh functions are one of main tools in informatics of noise-immunity coding and in digital signal processing. On the basis of Hadamard matrices, noise-immunity coding of information is used on the spacecrafts "Mariner" and "Voyager" for transmission to Earth photos of Mars, Jupiter, Saturn, Uranus and Neptune. Hadamard matrices are used in quantum computers ("Hadamard gates") and in quantum mechanics in the form of unitary operators, *etc.* [Ahmed, Rao, 1975; Seberry *et al.*, 2005]. Dyadic-shift decompositions of some Hadamard matrices show their connections with systems of hypercomlex numbers (see for example [Petoukhov, 2008a, 2008b, 2010]). Hadamard matrices play basic role in the sequency analysis [Harmuth, 1970, 1977, 1989], which is one of important types of spectral analysis in communication technologies and which has found extensive applications in electronics, acoustics, optics, and so forth. Genetic coding systems provide phenomena of noise-immunity of genetic information, and our results has revealed that genetic systems are phenomenologically connected with Hadamard matrices. (By analogy with the alphabet of 16 doublets, one can show that phenomenology of the alphabet of 64 triplets is connected with Hadamard $(8 * 8)$-matrices).

5. Some Concluding Remarks

The concept of resonances is important for information studies and the quest for transdisciplinarity, reflected in books [Burgin, 2010; Hofkirchner, 2013] since it is one of the main concepts in modern science in the whole. This concept serves as a bridge among many scientific fields for their mutual enrichment.

An organism during its life on genetic basis should solve algorithmic problems of two types: 1) informational, providing coordinated energy processes; 2) energetic, providing information processes. Systems of resonances can be used as a common basis of such "two-faced" algorithms since resonances are associated both with oscillatory energy and with informatics of communications among objects. In biology there are many interesting works concerning resonances and vibrations. For example, one can note the followings.

L. Pauling (1940) has created the theory of resonance in structural chemistry to explain the formation of hybrid bonds in molecules. The real molecule, as Pauling proposed, is a sort of hybrid, a structure that resonates between the two alternative extremes; and whenever there is a resonance between the two forms, the structure is stabilized. His theory uses the fundamental principle of a minimal energy because — in resonant combining of parts into a single unit — each of members of the ensemble requires less energy for performing own work than when working individually. Pauling supposed that living organisms are chemical in nature, and resonances in their molecules should be very essential for biological phenomena.

Ji [2012, 2015] postulates an analogy between enzymic catalysis and blackbody radiation, which was modeled by Planck due to his idea about huge number of resonances. He has noted that some important biological phenomena are described by histograms, which are analogical to histograms of blackbody radiations. This author has proposed a generalization of the Planck equation for modeling many biological phenomena, having long-tailed histograms. By analogy with the principle of quantization of energy in quantum mechanics, Ji postulates a quantization of free energy levels in enzymes. He also proposes an original theory of molecular machines with using Franck-Condon mechanisms concerning vibronic transitions, which are simultaneous changes in electronic and vibrational energy levels of a molecule.

Genetic encoding provides innate algorithms of animal motions. For example, newborn turtles and crocodiles, when they hatched from their eggs, crawl due to quite coordinated movements ahead to water without any training from anybody; centipedes crawl by means of coordinated movements of a great number of their legs on the basis of inherited algorithms of control. In these motions, a great number of muscle elements works in a coordinated manner and with economy of energy. We study such problems of dependence of inherited structures and processes from the genetic code by means of the concept of systemic-resonance genetics.

In our opinion, an organism can be seen as a musical synthesizer with multiple settings of inherited resonant modes [Darvas *et al.*, 2012; Petoukhov, 2015]. Music is a game with acoustic resonances, to which people are remarkably predisposed. Throughout tens of thousands of years, people create musical instruments, adjusting them to specific systems of resonances. Over the centuries, people have learned to combine individual instruments and singers into orchestras and choirs as coordinated oscillating systems with an increased number of degrees of freedom. Gottfried Leibniz declared that music is arithmetic of soul, which computes without being aware of it. Taking into account that music is represented by systems of resonances, one can reformulate this declaration: systems of resonances are the arithmetic of soul, which computes without being aware of it.

In the frame of the concept of systemic-resonance genetics, the author has proposed the bases of "genetic" music on Fibonacci-stages scales [Petoukhov, 2008; Darvas *et al.*, 2012]. This new direction of musical culture is been developing now in the Moscow P.I. Tchaikovsky Conservatory. This Conservatory has represented the first concert of genetic music on 4 June 2015 in Vienna in the frame of the International conference «IS4IS Summit Vienna 2015». Video of fragments of this concert with some explanations is located at website http://youtu.be/ gagKLDuO9z8.

References

Ahmed, N. and Rao, K. (1975). *Orthogonal Transforms for Digital Signal Processing*, Springer-Verlag Inc., USA.

Bellman, R. (1960). *Introduction to Matrix Analysis*, MacGraw-Hill Book Company, USA.

Blekhman, I.I. (2000). *Vibrational Mechanics*, World Scientific, Singapore.

Burgin, M. (2010). *Theory of Information: Fundamentality, Diversity and Unification*, World Scientific, Singapore.

Darvas G., Koblyakov A., Petoukhov S., Stepanyan, I. (2012). Symmetries in molecular-genetic systems and musical harmony, *Symmetry: Culture and Science*, 23, No. 3-4, pp. 343-375.

Ganiev, R.F., Ganiev, S.R., Kasilov, V.P., Pustovgar, A.P. (2015). *Wave Technology in Mechanical Engineering*, Scrivener Publishing LLC, Massachusetts.

Gazale, M.J. (1999). *Gnomon. From Pharaohs to Fractals*, Princeton Univ. Press, USA.

Gladwell, G.M.L. (2004). *Inverse Problems in Vibration*, Kluwer Academic Publishers, London.

Gumbel M., Fimmel, E., Danielli, A., Strüngmann L., 2015. On models of the genetic code generated by binary dichotomic algorithms, *BioSystems*, 128, pp. 9-18.

Harmuth, H.F. (1970). *Transmission of Information by Orthogonal Functions*, Springer, Berlin.

Harmuth, H.F. (1977). *Sequency Theory: Foundations and Applications*, Academic Press, USA.

Harmuth, H.F. (1989). *Information Theory Applied to Space-Time Physics*, The Catholic University of America, USA.

Hofkirchner, W. (2013). *Emergent Information: A Unified Theory of Information framework*, Vol. 3, World Scientific Series in Information Studies.

Jakobson, R. (1987). *Language in Literature*, MIT Press, Cambridge.

Jakobson, R. (1999). *Texts, Documents, Studies*, RGGU, Moscow (in Russian).

Ji, S. (2012). *Molecular Theory of the Living Cell: Concepts, Molecular Mechanisms, and Biomedical Applications*, Springer, New York.

Ji, S. (2015). Planckian distributions in molecular machines, living cells, and brains: The wave-particle duality in biomedical sciences, *Proc. Intern. Conf. Biology and Biomedical Engineering*. Vienna, March 15-17, pp. 115-137.

Pauling, L. 1940. *The Nature of the Chemical Bond and the Structure of Molecules and Crystals*, 2nd edn. Oxford University Press, London.

Petoukhov, S.V. (2004). Symmetries in Biology. Supplement of the book: Shubnikov A.V., Koptsik V.A. *Symmetry in Science and Art*, 3d edn. Institute of Computer Studies, Moscow, pp. 489-546. (in Russian, http://petoukhov.com/petoukhov-shubnikov-kopcik.pdf).

Petoukhov, S. V. (2008a). *Matrix Genetics, Algebras of the Genetic Code, Noise Immunity*, Regular and Chaos Dynamics, Moscow (in Russian, http://petoukhov. com/ matrix-genetics-petoukhov-2008.pdf).

Petoukhov, S.V. (2008b). Matrix genetics, part 4: cyclic changes of the genetic 8-dimensional Yin-Yang algebras and the algebraic models of physiological cycles. Preprint, http://arxiv.org/abs/0809.2714.

Petoukhov, S.V. (2010). The degeneracy of the genetic code and Hadamard matrices. Preprint, http://arxiv.org/abs/0802.3366.

Petoukhov, S.V. (2011). Matrix genetics and algebraic properties of the multi-level system of genetic alphabets, *Neuroquantology,* 9, No. 4, p. 60-81.

Petoukhov, S.V. (2014). Matrix genetics: algebra of projection operators, cyclic groups and inherited ensembles of biological cycles, *Proc. 2nd Intern. Conf. Theoretical Approaches to BioInformation Systems*, pp. 189-204, www.tabis2013.ipb.ac.rs/ tabis2013.pdf.

Petoukhov, S.V. (2015). Music and the modeling approach to genetic systems of biological resonances, *Intern. Conf. IS4IS Summit Vienna 2015*, http://sciforum. net/conference/70/paper/2812.

Petoukhov, S.V. (2016). The system-resonance approach in modeling genetic structures, *Biosystems*, 139, pp. 1-11, http://petoukhov.com/PETOUKHOV_ARTICLE_IN_ BIOSYSTEMS.pdf.

Petoukhov, S.V., He M., 2010. *Symmetrical Analysis Techniques for Genetic Systems and Bioinformatics: Advanced Patterns and Applications*, IGI Global, USA.

Rumer, Yu.B. (1968). Codon systematization in the genetic code. *Doklady Akademii Nauk SSSR,* 183, No. (1), 225-226.

Schrödinger, E. (1944). *What is Life?* Cambridge University Press.

Schrödinger, E. (1952). Are there quantum jumps? Part I, *The British Journal for the Philosophy of Science*, Vol. 3, No. 10, pp. 109-123.

Seberry, J., Wysocki, B.J., Wysocki, T.A. (2005). On some applications of Hadamard Matrices, *Metrica*, 62, pp. 221-239.

Stambuk, N. (1999). Circular coding properties of gene and protein sequences, *Croatia Chemica Acta*, 72, No. 4, pp. 999-1008.

Stewart, I. (1999). *Life's Other Secret: The New Mathematics of the Living World*, Penguin, New York.

Chapter 18

Information Society and Apartheid in the Context of Evolutionary Economics: Perspectives from Information Theory

Rodrick Wallace* and Mindy Thompson Fullilove

New York State Psychiatric Institute
Columbia University, USA
* Wallace@nyspi.columbia.edu, rodrick.wallace@gmail.com

The current forms of American Apartheid express longstanding and persistent dynamics of segregation and serial forced displacement that have successfully adapted to challenge over several centuries. Segregation confines non-white people to closely specified areas while serial forced displacement moves them repeatedly from one place to another. Both inhibit or destroy the nondisjunctive 'weak' ties that unify a community across its inherent or imposed divisions. Absent these social ties, it is almost impossible to carry out normal daily life, let alone advance the civil rights struggle. How are such ties to be reconstructed? While community-building is an inherent human activity, and significant mobilizations of any kind will begin to reknit social cohesion, the policies of serial forced displacement are so powerful that it impossible to do the work of rebuilding ties without simultaneously fighting for community stability. Thus, for many Americans, the Future Information Society, in the absence of suppression of the evolving institutions that instantiate racism, will simply resemble the past. Driving the self-perpetuating and highly adaptive modalities of American Apartheid to extinction remains today as urgent a calling as was the Abolitionist enterprise of previous centuries.

Keywords: Apartheid; historical trajectory; evolutionary economics; institutional evolution; racism; segregation; serial forced displacement; USA.

1. Introduction

Shannon's communication theory enables construction of a set of necessary conditions statistical models that can be applied to evolutionary economics. Using these, we reexamine the dynamic structure of racism in the United States, taking up again the conundrum studied more than seventy years ago in the famous application of heterodox economic theory to the problem by Gunnar Myrdal. It is clear that, in the future information society, the institutional structures surrounding segregation and serial forced displacement will continue to adapt to political, social, and technological challenge, requiring constant regulation for their mitigation, or a fundamental reorganization of society for their elimination.

Indeed, the cultural traditions of racism in the United States have undergone repeated policy-driven adaptations in response to persistent and recurring opposition since the Founding Fathers defined a slave as '3/5 of a man' for representation purposes. Combining Fanon's theory of colonialism with recent advances in coevolution and control theories, we adapt the perspective of evolutionary economics to explore mechanisms behind the unstable system the American martyr Malcolm X characterized as 'The names have changed, but the game's the same'.

In particular, viewing American Apartheid as a coevolutionary Red Queen between competing cultural traditions, much as workgroups within an institution can vie for status and resources, we generalize the Data Rate Theorem that relates control and information theories to understand what level of 'control information' is needed to end the cycle of instability. It becomes clear that passing and enforcing 'Civil Rights Laws' is problematic in the absence of strong nondisjunctive social linkages across a polity. This suggests the need for renewal of the nonviolent direct action perspectives and strategies of the Civil Rights Movement, made far more difficult by the effective riposte of serial forced displacement against concentrations of minority economic and social empowerment in the United States (Fullilove and Wallace 2011).

The tools we use require some introductory comment. An emerging body of work, summarized by Aldrich *et al.* (2008), describes how Darwinian principles cover the evolution of social or economic entities. Although there are important differences between biological and cultural domains and the selection processes that affect them, and the particular mechanisms of variation, inheritance, and selection differ in important ways, yet the overarching general principles remain. Aldrich *et al.* argue that we must regard institutions as cohesive entities having some capacity for the retention and replication of problem solutions, and that innovation is about the creation of new variations, while selection is about how these are tested in the real world. An essential strain in their argument is a paradigm of program-based behavior that requires an explanation of emergence through both natural selection and individual development, in the context of Eldredge's and Gould's 'punctuated equilibria' (Gould, 2002).

Hodgson and Knudsen (2010) describe how evolutionary theory as such provides no single model or axiomatic system. Instead, it is a metatheoretical framework that stimulates further inquiry and provides a repository for contingent auxiliary theories and models and that the construction of a comprehensive evolutionary-theoretical system capable of generating powerful predictive models to rival established alternatives in the social sciences is some way off. As with the application of evolutionary principles to biology, the first and principal achievement is to build a conceptual engine capable of guiding specific inquiry into detailed causal mechanisms. The secondary process — of showing how these principles operated in specific contexts — required a century of detailed empirical and experimental study before Darwinian theory triumphed in the 1940s.

Here, we apply very recently developed necessary conditions statistical models of evolutionary process to parse the historical trajectory of American Apartheid, seeking deeper insight into the strengths and weaknesses of its appalling dynamics. Although there are no medical magic bullets against embedded racism, there appear to be 'magic strategies' that can, if relentlessly pursued, suppress its most pathological phenotypes.

Similar ideas can be explored without invoking mathematical models. Pouncy (2002), for example, writes that

> Institutional theory [which often embodies evolutionary perspectives]... provides an analysis of the continuation of racism despite evidence of its invalidity as a biological construct and its disfavor as a societal institution. Institutional theory argues that racism, like any institution that does not serve to maximize opportunity, must be supported by a strongly inculcated system of mythology in order to prevent that institution from becoming subject to a market related process that may result in its change or destruction... The myth [of racism] retains vitality because it continues to be an effective way to allocate benefits and burdens between the powerful and the disempowered.

A similar approach was taken by Gunnar Myrdal in his classic 1944 empirical study *An American Dilemma: The Negro Problem and Modern Democracy*. Myrdal concluded that economic analysis can only become complete when embedded in the wider social context. As Elsner *et al.* (2015) put it,

> [Myrdal] found that only the analysis of the whole institutional setup of a socioeconomy, the rules, conventions, customs, mores, folkways, norms and belief systems could explain major socioeconomic problems, such as lasting racism in the USA. Economic and social factors and variables turned out to be in an evolutionary interaction and typically mutually reinforcing to push a system on a cumulative path with some lock-in at the end... [In contrast with the negative feedback formalisms of conventional economic theory] positive feedback and cumulative causation was the crucial mechanism in large parts of the system's motions...

From our viewpoint, however, such cultural structures can have a life of their own, becoming self-replicating institutions — 'firms' in the sense of evolutionary economics. Some are parasites that evolve around policies designed to suppress them. The resulting 'Red Queen' coevolutionary dynamics, as those who study agricultural and other pest infestations can testify, may be very difficult to remedy.

2. The Coevolutionary Trap

Racism is deeply embedded in the bones of the United States: to reiterate, the nation's founding Constitution directs that a slave is to be counted as '3/5 of a man' in apportioning representation to the national government. The subsequent historical trajectory is a rollercoaster of reform and retrenchment.

Indeed, the expression of racism is highly dynamic: it has shifted markedly over time. In the 1600s, 'chattel slavery' was established in the English colonies in the Americas. This slavery was distinct from slavery in earlier historic periods and civilizations in being defined as ownership of one human being by another, a condition that lasted a lifetime and was transmitted to the slaves descendants. This absolute degradation of human life because of the condition of servitude was, as described above, engraved in the foundation stones of the nation. Slaves revolted from the beginning, using active and passive means, joined in their efforts by abolitionists. One advertisement for the abolitionist movement was a 'slave token', a medal that showed a black woman kneeling in prayer, and read, 'Am I not a woman and a sister?' See Figure 1.

Figure 1.   19th century Abolitionist slave token. AM I NOT A WOMAN & A SISTER, 1838.

As the movement to abolish slavery gained power, it was possible for fugitive slaves to follow with relative ease the well-worn paths of the Underground Railroad.

To maintain their hold on their slaves the Southern plantation owners seceded from the Union in 1861. The Civil War lasted for four years. The South lost, the nation was reunited and Reconstruction was implemented, a remarkable experiment in bringing the bondsmen and women into full citizenship. This period was marked by gains in electoral representation, education, and land ownership. The disenfranchised southern oligarchy sought to regain their control, succeeding in the making a deal for the removal of federal troops in 1877. The efforts to disenfranchise poor blacks, and return them to pseudo-slavery were eventually effective in instituting the Jim Crow system. Poor whites, including industrial workers, intermittently allied with Blacks to fight for common interests, but racism was repeatedly used to break up these alliances.

The Jim Crow era, which is formally dated to 1890, the year the state of Louisiana adopted a law providing for 'equal but separate accommodations for the white and colored races' on the streetcar system. This was later upheld by the Supreme Court's 1896 decision in Plessy v. Ferguson. 'Separate but equal'laws and practices proliferated, encompassing schools, hospitals, playgrounds and residential areas. The 'long civil rights movement' began in 1905 with the formation of the Niagara Movement by Dr. W.E.B. Du Bois and others. Dr. Du Bois set the tone and content in his speech to the first meeting of the movement, when he said, 'We will not be satisfied to take one jot or tittle less than our full manhood rights. We claim for ourselves every single right that belongs to a freeborn American, political, civil and social; and until we get these rights we will never cease to protest and assail the ears of America'.

Victories in the integration of baseball (1946), the armed forces (1948), schools (1954), transportation (1955), hospitals (1965) and voting rights (1965) dismantled much of the machinery of Jim Crow, and fulfilled many parts of the demand for equal rights. At the same time, federal, state and local policies had built a system of residential segregation that had been firmly linked to the banking system. In 1949, as the Civil Rights movement gained momentum, the federal program of urban renewal began to systematically dismantle black neighborhoods in the name of 'progress'. Urban renewal was followed by a series of similar policies — all promoted as 'progress' — that have caused upheaval and displacement for Black communities. These have included deindustrialization, planned shrinkage, mass incarceration and gentrification. These policies solidified the inequity in the distribution of public goods, shifting the weight of system of inequality from the earlier formulation of not-a-person to a new formulation of not-a-competent-person. This emerging form of racism justifies a detachment from the problems of the oppressed, who evidently have equal rights and therefore fail because of their own incompetence. This has been accompanied by a marked shift from overt racism to implicit bias.

During the 2015 protests following the murder of 25-year-old Freddie Gray while in police custody, contrasting perceptions of the problems of Baltimore were reported by the press. A black woman, living in West

Baltimore, was aware of the neglect from the which the area had suffered, while a white woman living in a nearby neighborhood, reported that the '[riots] are not our reality'.

Alisha Snead (Shane 2015):

> This is the land time forgot. They want to act like the CVS [which was burned] is the Taj Mahal. They have dilapidated buildings everywhere. They have never invested in the people. In fact, it's divested. They take every red cent they can from poor black people and put it in the Inner Harbor [redevelopment project].

Ashley Fowler (Blinder 2015):

> [The riots] are not our reality. They're not what we're living right now. We live in, not to be racist, white America... [The police] kept us safe... I knew I was going to be O.K. because I knew they weren't going to let anyone come and loot our properties of our businesses or burn our cars.

As the Kerner Report put the matter after the 1965 riots (NACDD 1968),

> Our nation is moving toward two societies, one black, one white — separate and unequal... What white Americans have never fully understood — but what the Negro can never forget — is that white society is deeply implicated in the ghetto. White institutions created it, white institutions maintain it, and white society condones it.

This relentless back-and-forth seems likely to persist well into the 21st Century, when 'White' US citizens become simply another minority in a nation that has been repeatedly rescued and enriched by the influx of highly motivated foreign-born populations, although Native American peoples may not agree.

American Apartheid, as it has evolved over the centuries, thus represents an adaptive, self-replicating cultural tradition that has been repeatedly challenged by other cultural traditions and economic realities. The slave system of the South had to spread endlessly via a kind slash-and-burn economic dynamic, while never really being able to match the developing industrial capacities of the (less slave-dependent) North. The matter has been well-studied since the time of Karl Marx (Marx and Engels 1937). The classic work of Massey and Denton (1998) examines the current status in finer detail.

But, in the face of each successive challenge, American Apartheid has adapted and retransmitted its adapted structure, and this coevolutionary morass is the central focus of our study.

2.1. The colonial enterprise

The French-trained psychiatrist Frantz Fanon represents colonial systems like American Apartheid as instantiating the Manichean Heresy. That is, the colonial system is a unitary structure, but arbitrarily segmented into Good and Evil. He writes (Fanon 1966)

> The colonial world is a world divided into compartments... The zone where the natives live is not complementary to the zone inhabited by the settlers. The two zones are opposed, but not in the service of a higher unity. Obedient to the rules of pure Aristotelian logic, they both follow the principle of reciprocal exclusivity. No conciliation is possible, for of the two terms, one is superfluous... This world is divided into compartments, this world cut in two is inhabited by two different species... In the colonies the economic substructure is also a superstructure... At times this Manicheism goes to its logical conclusion and dehumanizes the native, or to speak plainly it turns him into an animal...
>
> A world divided into compartments, a motionless Manicheistic world, a world of statues: the statue of the general who carried out the conquest... a world which is sure of itself, which crushes with its stones the backs flayed by whips: this is the colonial world. The native is being hemmed in; apartheid is simply one form of the division into compartments of the colonial world...

Regarding the dynamics of opposition, Fanon writes

> We have said that the colonial context is characterized by the dichotomy which it imposes upon the whole people. Decolonization unifies that people by the radical decision to remove from it its heterogeneity...

Similarly, the American civil rights martyr Rev. Martin Luther King Jr. writes, regarding the strategic practice of Agape, or disinterested love, that (King 1958)

> [Agape]... springs from the need of the other person — his need for belonging to the best in the human family... Since the white man's personality is greatly distorted by segregation, and his soul is greatly scarred, he needs the love of the Negro. The Negro must love the white man, because the white man needs his love to remove his tensions, insecurities, and fears... Agape is not a weak, passive love. It is love in action. It is insistence on community when one seeks to break it. Agape is a willingness to sacrifice in the interest of mutuality...

> In the final analysis, agape means a recognition of the fact
> that all life is interrelated. All humanity is involved in a single
> process. . . Injustice anywhere is a threat to justice everywhere.

It is something of the inherent tension between Manichaenism and Agape, in the context of the American historical trajectory, that we will explore here, using, among other tools, newly-developed formal methods from evolutionary theory (R. Wallace and R.G. Wallace 1998, 1999, 2008; Wallace *et al.* 2003; R. Wallace and D. Wallace 2008, 2009, 2011; R. Wallace 2009, 2010, 2011a–c, 2012a, b, 2013a–c, 2015).

2.2. The evolutionary perspective

Humans, like many other higher animals (Jablonka and Lamb 1995), are enmeshed within a number of intersecting heritability mechanisms: genetic, chemical-epigenetic, cultural, and environmental (we change an environment that subsequently imposes its own rules). Perhaps the most unique, however, is culture (Durham 1991). The cultural psychologists, in fact make clear that a 'human' without a learned culture is not a complete animal, but is an entity deprived of its full developmental potential (Heine 2001). As the evolutionary anthropologist Robert Boyd put it, "Culture is as much a part of human biology as the enamel on our teeth" (e.g., Richerson and Boyd 2006).

Culture, genetic heritage, and the 'rules' imposed by environment and history, each involve a self-replicating information source that interacts with others via mechanisms of crosstalk (Wallace 2012a). What is of particular interest here is that, like the 'firm' studied by the institutional ecologists who live in business schools (Hodgson and Knudsen 2010; Wallace and Fullilove 2008; Wallace 2015), an individual culture is composed of a number of different subsystems that self-replicate and contend or cooperate within a larger embedding historical dynamic. Selection pressures on each varying and self-replicating subcomponent of a culture — pressures from without or from within — result in evolutionary and coevolutionary dynamics.

So far, the cultural subcomponent of American racism has not become extinct, but simply dodged whatever the latest bullet may be, much like a cancer that evolves around the repeated challenges presented by a medical oncology team (Wallace *et al.* 2003). Indeed, the cancer model may prove to be a useful, if limited, analogy.

Similar arguments can be made regarding both cognitive processes and embedding environments (Wallace 2012 a, b). Here, we aver that cultural

trajectories involve self-replicating subcomponents that can be characterized as information sources, and that these interact under competitive and
cooperative conditions constituting selection pressures that result in complex, ongoing, cultural dynamics.

The perspective is not unique. As William James put it (James 1880
p. 441),

> A remarkable parallel, which to my mind has never been
> noticed, obtains between the facts of social evolution and the
> mental growth of the race, on the one hand, and of zoological
> evolution, as expounded by Mr. Darwin, on the other.

Classic evolutionary process is seen as involving repeated splitting of
historical trajectory. Figure 2, from Charles Darwin's notebooks, provides
the basic example. We are particularly interested in how two interacting,
self-reproducing cultural entities can become each other's primary evolutionary selection pressures, a coevolutionary process.

It is important to reiterate that social evolution, unlike biological evolutionary or coevolutionary process, involves considerable institutional cognition. That is, we join together in social structures
that — collectively — identify options and choose among them. Such
choice is inherently a reduction in uncertainty that directly implies the
existence of an information source, one that interacts with purely cultural
heritage mechanisms, although the formal expression of cognition as 'language' can be somewhat complex (Wallace 2012a, 2013b).

The interaction of cognition with cultural tradition is particularly expressed in trajectories of public policy, for example the serial forced displacement of minority communities in the United States (Fullilove and
Wallace 2011).

2.3. Strength of weak ties

A first approximation to the dynamics of American Apartheid through the
intersection of cultural heritage and cognitive public policy can be most
easily expressed in terms of Granovetter's 'strength of weak ties' argument
(Granovetter 1973). 'Strong' ties, taking Granovetter's perspective, dis-
jointly partition a population into equivalence classes. These might be divisions according to age or income cohort, ethnicity, socially-defined 'race',
religious or sexual preference, gender, political party, occupational affilia-
tion, country of origin, sports team preference, and so on. 'Weak' ties are
connections across a community that do not produce equivalence class di-

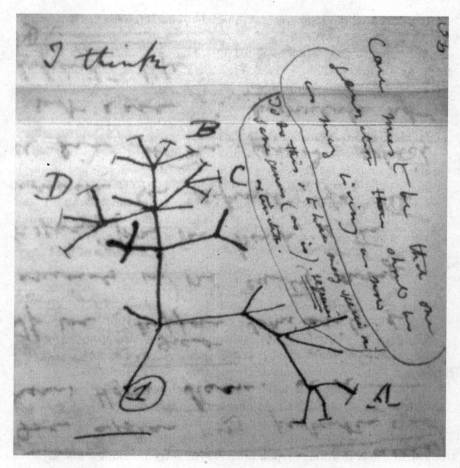

Figure 2. From the notebooks of Charles Darwin, the repeated bifurcation of historical trajectory. Social systems may see such multiple cascades of outcome, or may experience the effect in terms of a single developmental path, with the pruning of 'less fit' branches by deliberate public or other policy.

visions. Weak ties permit transmission of information and resources across an entire community, thus strengthening it.

As has been argued at great length elsewhere (e.g., Feynman 2000; Wallace 2012a, b), information is a form of free energy, and this permits imposition of methods abducted from statistical mechanics to the dynamics of evolutionary process, producing the punctuated equilibrium of Eldredge and Gould (1972) (Gould 2002) as a series of phase transitions. The simplest model is via a 'temperature' index that characterizes the strength of weak ties across a polity.

We view the interaction of cultural heritage and public policy in terms of a set of information sources $X_1, \ldots, X_m$ having a joint uncertainty $H[X_1, \ldots, X_m]$ defined in terms of the probability of joint 'statements' $z = (z_1, z_2, \ldots, z_n, \ldots); z_i = \{x_i^1, \ldots, x_i^m\}$. Each x_i^j represents the output of information source X_j at 'time' i. The details are standard (Cover and Thomas 2006; Khinchin 1957).

Assume a division across a polity by equivalence classes defined by strong ties and indexed by α, and let T represent the average strength of nondisjunctive weak ties across that polity. Let H_α be the Shannon uncertainty defined by the intersection of policy, community cognition, and cultural tradition within subdivision α. The argument-by-abduction from statistical physics is that a pseudoprobability can be defined by the relation

$$P[H_\alpha] = \frac{\exp[-H_\alpha/kT]}{\sum_\alpha \exp[-H_\alpha/kT]}, \tag{1}$$

where κ is an appropriate scaling factor.

Divisions by equivalence classes define groupoid symmetries, by standard methods. Groupoids are generalizations of the group symmetry concept, and the simplest such is a disjoint union of groups, so that a 'product' is only locally defined (Brown 1987; Weinstein 1996).

Landau's fundamental insight regarding phase transitions in physical systems was that certain critical phenomena take place in the context of a significant alteration in symmetry, with one phase being far more symmetric than the other (Landau and Lifshitz 2007; Pettini 2007). A symmetry is lost in the transition — spontaneous symmetry breaking. The greatest possible set of symmetries in a physical system is that of the Hamiltonian describing its energy states. Usually states accessible at lower temperatures will lack the symmetries available at higher temperatures, so that the lower temperature phase is less symmetric: the randomization of higher temperatures ensures that higher symmetry/energy states will then be accessible to the system. The shift between symmetries is highly punctuated in the temperature index.

A possible free energy function for invocation of Landau's spontaneous symmetry breaking in a mixed cultural/institutional evolutionary context is then a 'groupoid free energy' F defined by

$$\exp[-F/\kappa T] \equiv \sum_\alpha \exp[-H_\alpha/\kappa T]. \tag{2}$$

Then, using the free energy-analog F, we can apply Landau's spontaneous symmetry breaking arguments to the groupoid associated with the set of cultural/policy/community cognition information sources. Increasing the strength of weak ties permits higher symmetries across the entire community, allowing higher functioning of institutional cognition in the face of patterns of challenge or affordance. Conversely, a decline in weak ties can trigger a sudden fragmentation that politically and economically emasculates a targeted community as described in Fullilove and Wallace (2011).

2.4. Red Queen coevolution

A second approach extends and expands this result using an analog to the empirical nonequilibrium thermodynamics of Onsager (de Groot and Mazur 1984). The essence of the perspective is that an entropy analog can be defined using F of equation (2) via a Legendre transform in a set of n independent variates Q^i as (Pettini 2007)

$$S = F - \sum_i Q^i \partial F / \partial Q^i. \tag{3}$$

One central point is that, under stochastic circumstances involving 'noise' processes B^j, the time dynamics of the independent variates can be written, to first order, as a set of empirical stochastic differential equations (Protter 1990) in the gradients of the entropy-analog, i.e., in terms of $\partial S / \partial Q_i$ (de Groot and Mazur 1984), although there are no 'reciprocity relations' since information processes are locally irreversible. What emerges in evolutionary process is the set (Wallace 2015)

$$dQ_t^j = \sum_i [L_{i,j}(t, \ldots \partial S/\partial Q^j \ldots)dt + \sigma_{i,j}(t, \ldots \partial S/\partial Q^j \ldots)dB_t^i]$$

$$\equiv L_j(t, Q^1, \ldots, Q^n)dt + \sum_i \sigma_{i,j}(t, Q^1, \ldots, Q^n)dB_t^i, \tag{4}$$

where t represents time, the second expression collects terms, and the 'noise' processes B^j have characteristic quadratic variations (Protter 1990). The formalism is standard, if somewhat involved, and follows the nonequilibrium thermodynamics formalism of Onsager (de Groot and Mazur 1984).

Two points: First, setting the expectation of equation (4) equal to zero and solving for nonequilibrium steady conditions (i.e., $< dQ_t^i >= 0$) gives attractor states, since the noise terms preclude unstable solutions. Second, what is converged to may be a limit cycle or a pseudorandom 'strange attractor' in which the system seems to chase its tail endlessly within a bounded region, the trap of Van Valen's (1973) classic 'Red Queen' coevolutionary dynamic between predator and prey where each is the principal selection pressure for the other, and each must continually evolve to escape extinction.

Programming of such coevolutionary 'machines' — in a large sense — is not well understood. See Wallace (2009b) for discussion and references. Nonetheless, some work has been done, via new linkages uncovered between control and information theories.

2.5.   A control theory framework

The Data Rate Theorem (DRT) states that there is a minimum rate of feedback control information necessary to control an inherently unstable system. More explicitly, the DRT, a generalization of the classic Bode Integral Theorem for linear control systems, describes the stability of feedback control under data rate constraints (Nair *et al.*, 2007). Given a noise-free data link between a discrete linear plant and its controller, unstable modes can be stabilized only if the feedback data rate $\mathcal{H}$ is greater than the rate of 'topological information' generated by the unstable system. For the simplest incarnation, if the linear matrix equation of the 'plant', in a large sense, is of the form $x_{t+1} = \mathbf{A}x_t + \ldots$, where x_t is the n-dimensional state vector at time t, then the necessary condition for stabilizability is that

$$\mathcal{H} > \log[|det \, \mathbf{A}^u|] \tag{5}$$

where *det* is the determinant and $\mathbf{A}^u$ is the decoupled unstable component of $\mathbf{A}$, i.e., the part having eigenvalues ≥ 1. The determinant represents a generalized volume. Thus there is a critical positive data rate below which there does not exist any quantization and control scheme able to stabilize an unstable system (Nair *et al.*, 2007).

The DRT, and its variations, relate control theory to information theory and are as fundamental as the Shannon Coding and Source Coding Theorems, and the Rate Distortion Theorem for understanding complex cognitive machines and biological phenomena (Cover and Thomas, 2006).

It is possible to extend the DRT to the less constrained models of equation (4) that are more likely to represent complicated social interactions (Wallace and Fullilove 2014), and this will be done below, but for our immediate purposes the essential point is that the inherently unstable cycling Red Queen of American Apartheid is an out-of-control feedback loop between conflicting cultural traditions that can be stabilized by imposition of draconian regulations, by the systematic dispersal of the power structures whose policies create that instability, or by an extension of 'weak ties' sufficient to effectively integrate the US polity, triggering a permanent transition to a stable and more humane mode.

2.6.   Implications

Evolutionary processes, driving social as well as purely 'biological' phenomena, are not confined to gradual changes. Dynamics of 'punctuated equilibrium' emerge in which an evolutionary system appears quasi stable for a comparatively long period, but is then subject to relatively rapid periods of development and selection (Eldredge and Gould 1972; Gould 2002). In contrast to such 'simple' biological process, for social systems, institutional cognition plays a central role in determining both selection pressures and rates-of-change, a matter that is the primary focus of the emerging discipline of evolutionary economics (Hodgson 1993; Hodgson and Knudsen, 2010; Wallace and Fullilove 2008; Wallace 2013c, 2015).

One essential feature of the models above — as in evolutionary economics (e.g., Wallace 2015 Ch. 7) — is that decline in the richness of inclusive real-time social communication as indexed by the strength of weak ties measure T, or in the ability of that communication to influence response, as indexed by κ, can lead to punctuated decline in the complexity of cognitive and cultural process within the institutional entity of interest, or, conversely, to its enrichment if both are increasing.

As described, this permits a Landau-analog phase transition analysis in which the quality of nondisjunctive social contact serves to raise or lower the possible richness of a community's cognitive response to patterns of challenge or opportunity. If κT is relatively large — a rich and varied pattern of social contact within and across the community of interest — then there are many possible cognitive responses. If, however, constraints of history or policy limit the magnitude of κT, then behavior collapses in a highly punctuated manner to a kind of ground state in which only limited responses are possible, represented by a pathologically simplified cognitive structure. The latest set of policing-related riots in US minority communities subjected to serial forced displacement comes to mind (Badger 2015).

As Fanon (1966) put it in a somewhat different context,

> The native is a being hemmed in... The first thing which the
> native learns is to stay in his place, and not to go beyond cer-

> tain limits. This is why the dreams of the native are always
> of muscular prowess; his dreams are of action and of aggres-
> sion... The colonized man will first manifest this aggressiveness
> which has been deposited in his bones against his own people.
> This is the period when the niggers beat each other up, and the
> police and magistrates do not know which way to turn.

An antidote to such systematic poisoning, within the US context, sur-
faced during the Civil Rights Movement through adaptation by the Black
Church and others of the nonviolent direct action methods pioneered by
the Indian decolonization movement: King's active Agape, which triggered
the formation of weak ties across progressive elements. This resulted in
considerable national policy change — the various 'Civil Rights Laws' of
the time.

The 'Red Queen' model then becomes relevant. Subsequent policy
contributing to a continuation of the serial forced displacement of minority communities successfully dispersed or disempowered minority religious
and political organizations, making disciplined responses to ongoing patterns of oppression and disenfranchisement difficult indeed (Fullilove and
Wallace 2011; Badger 2015). The initiatives included 'planned shrinkage'
and 'gentrification' in New York City, and regional 'voluntary' resegrega-
tion by suburbanization around Detroit, St. Louis, and elsewhere. Poste
and Riposte. 'The names have changed, but the game's the same', and
the Red Queen predator/prey dynamic between Manicheanism and Agape
continues.

To escape such a trap, we cannot simply recognize that it exists, but
must achieve a deep understanding of both its nature and its vulnerabilities
in order to design effective counterstrategies (Wallace 2009b; Wallace and
Fullilove 2014).

Fullilove and Wallace (2011) examine the policy-driven serial forced displacement that repeatedly targets concentrations of social and economic
capital of African American communities. Since the 1930's, this process
has operated under different labels: Redlining and urban renewal (Fullilove
2013), planned shrinkage (Wallace and Wallace 1998), Hope VI, and 'gentrification'. Massey and Denton (1993) have documented the serial reseg-
regation of forcibly-displaced populations of color over much of the same
period.

As Wallace *et al.* (1996) argue, rapidly displaced communities can become trapped in a race-to-the bottom social ratchet where messages of individual efficacy become encoded in acts of violence to overcome the noise

imposed by social disintegration, acts that further destabilize the nondisjunctive weak ties that bind together a functioning polity and thus accelerate social disintegration and the consequent loss of both socioeconomic and political capital.

It is in the context of such policy-driven social fragmentation that current calls are made by the power structures of American Apartheid to remove African American families from their 'toxic' environments (Editorial Board 2015). It is interesting to note that the Editorial Board of the New York Times, which is now calling for another Move to Opportunity program, has also repeatedly called for reductions in the fire extinguishment services needed to maintain urban densities of poor populations in New York City, reductions that are deeply implicated in the persistence of current social burdens afflicting those populations (Wallace and Wallace 1998).

Adaptation of an evolutionary economics model of the firm (Wallace 2015, Ch. 7), which we do not pursue here, emphasizes that the rate of community displacement appears to be an extremely powerful independent factor that can become synergistic with the degree of forced displacement — of ethnic cleansing — to break a community into disjoint fragments unable to act collectively at a rate sufficient to meet changing patterns of threat and affordance.

What, then, is the opposite of disintegration? What is community integration? The larger body of work of which our exploration is a part stems from Alexander Leighton's postulate that community integration is the foundation of mental health and the obvious corollary is that community integration is the foundation of all health. Leighton, in the theoretical foundation for his Stirling County study, meticulously traced the links between personality and society, using observations in diverse settings, such as in the Navajo Nation, Japanese internment camps, and post-World War II Europe (Leighton, 1959). He concluded that human society is composed of self-integrating social units that might be arranged on a continuum. Theoretically anchoring the fully-integrated end was the 'model', in which the members were collectively responsible for the good of all, while anchoring the disintegrated end was the 'collection', disconnected individuals, each responsible for and to only him/herself. The integrated model community would, Leighton postulated have lower rates of mental illness than would the collection. His study provided substantial support for this proposal.

Integration and disintegration are not permanent features of communities, but characteristics that arise from the process of self-integration in constant struggle against the forces of disintegration. Among the latter Leighton included: recent history of disaster, ill health, extensive poverty, secularization, migration, and rapid social change (p. 327). A model community, exposed to one or more of those pressures, might be transformed into a collection, characterized by: high frequency of broken homes, few and weak associations, fear and weak leaders; few patterns of recreation; high frequency of hostility; high frequency of crime and delinquency; and weak and fragmented network of communication (pp. 318–319).

It is this observation — that model communities can be transformed by negative events and processes — that is so pressing in understanding the social history of American neighborhoods that have evidenced social collapse. Studies by Watkins (2000) and Simms (2008) have documented social transformation along the lines predicted by Leighton. Watkins demonstrated the link to policy in her study of the decline of Harlem, and documented the harms of urban renewal, deindustrialization, planned shrinkage, and other policies between 1950 and 1990. Gentrification has caused additional upheaval after 1990.

A stage-state picture of social disintegration hypothesized that communities that have suffered from a series of negative events would exhibit collapse after each (Fullilove, 2000). In the absence of adequate mitigation, this meant that the collapse was a steady downhill progress from integration towards disintegration. With each collapse there is a shift in the social organization and the behavioral languages that are useful in that state. All of these policies push community down a disastrous spiral, away from the model and toward the collection.

The names of the imposed policies do indeed change, but the basic game is always the same (Figure 3).

3.   Extending Control Theory

The second section examined the coevolutionary Red Queen of US racism that, from slavery to Jim Crow, redlining, urban renewal, planned shrinkage, and mass incarceration, has competed with more humane aspects of the country's culture, from Abolition through the Civil Rights Movement, to the current 'Black Lives Matter' initiatives (King 1958; Badger 2015). That section introduced ideas centering on evolutionary and coevolutionary processes in the context of the dynamics of institutional cognition associated with the various underlying sociocultural traditions and their self-replicating and intertwining historical trajectories, much in the spirit of

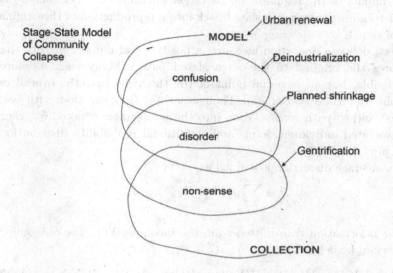

Figure 3. State-stage picture of community disintegration under repeated policy assaults. The ultimate degree of fragmentation, according to our formal analysis, will be inversely determined by the rate of repeated insult.

current evolutionary economics theories of the firm (Wallace 2015).

Here, taking the somewhat different approach of Wallace and Fullilove (2014), we focus on breaking the 'game' of American Apartheid via a rate distortion perspective on system control. To do this we must introduce some mathematical formalism. While the results suggest a prime role for public policy in maintaining or eliminating the American Apartheid, underlying patterns of Granovetter's (1973) nondisjunctive 'weak ties' remain critical determinants of system dynamics.

3.1. The Rate Distortion Theorem

It is clear that many regulatory problems within the domain of the Data Rate Theorem are also inherently rate distortion problems, in a formal sense, and this enables a deeper understanding of coevolutionary process.

The implementation of a complex cognitive structure, say a sequence of control orders generated by some regulatory information source Y, having output $y^n = y_1, y_2, \ldots$ is 'digitized' in terms of the observed behavior of the regulated system, say the sequence $b^n = b_1, b_2, \ldots$. The b_i are thus the actual impact of the regulator on its target environment. Let each b^n be then deterministically retranslated back into a reproduction of the original control signal, $b^n \rightarrow \hat{y}^n = \hat{y}_1, \hat{y}_2, \ldots$.

Next, define a distortion measure, a positive real number $d(y, \hat{y})$, that compares the original to the retranslated path. Many such measures are possible, but an essential point of the theory is that the overall results are the same (Cover and Thomas 2006). Suppose that with each path y^n and b^n-path retranslation into the y-language, denoted $\hat{y}^n$, there are associated individual, joint, and conditional probability distributions $p(y^n), p(\hat{y}^n), p(y^n|\hat{y}^n)$.

The average distortion is defined as

$$D \equiv \sum_{y^n} p(y^n) d(y^n, \hat{y}^n) \geq 0. \tag{6}$$

The information transmitted from the incoming Y to the outgoing $\hat{Y}$ process can be defined as

$$I(Y, \hat{Y}) \equiv H(Y) - H(Y|\hat{Y}) = H(Y) + H(\hat{Y}) - H(Y, \hat{Y}). \tag{7}$$

If there is no uncertainty in Y, given the retranslation $\hat{Y}$, then no information is lost, and the regulated system is perfectly under control. In general, this will not be true.

Recall that the Shannon uncertainties all have the form $-\sum_j P_j \log(P_j)$, where the P_k constitute a probability distribution (Cover and Thomas 2006).

The rate distortion function (RDF) $R(D)$ for a source Y with a distortion measure $d(y, \hat{y})$ is defined as

$$R(D) = \min_{p(y|\hat{y}); \sum_{(y, \hat{y})} p(y)p(y|\hat{y})d(y, \hat{y}) \leq D} I(Y, \hat{Y}). \tag{8}$$

Cover and Thomas (2006) provide more detail.

The minimization is over all conditional distributions $p(y|\hat{y})$ for which the joint distribution $p(y, \hat{y}) = p(y)p(y|\hat{y})$ satisfies the average distortion constraint (i.e., average distortion $\leq D$).

The Rate Distortion Theorem states that $R(D)$ is the minimum necessary rate of information transmission — essentially minimum channel capacity — that ensures the transmission does not exceed average distortion D (Cover and Thomas 2006). The rate distortion function has been calculated for a number of systems, using Lagrange multiplier methods.

Cover and Thomas (2006) show that $R(D)$ is necessarily a decreasing convex function of D, that is, always a reverse J-shaped curve. This is a critical observation, since convexity is an exceptionally powerful mathematical condition (Ellis 1985; Rockafellar 1970).

Recall the classic relation between information source uncertainty and channel capacity. First, $H[\mathbf{X}] \leq C$, where H is the uncertainty of the source X and C the channel capacity. Recall also that C is defined according to the relation $C \equiv \max_{P(X)} I(X|Y)$, where $P(X)$ is the probability distribution of the message chosen so as to maximize the rate of information transmission along a channel Y (Cover and Thomas 2006).

For a Gaussian channel between regulator and target systems having added white noise of zero mean and variance σ^2, a Lagrange multiplier method shows the RDF under the squared distortion measure is

$$R(D) = \frac{1}{2} \log[\sigma^2/D].$$ (9)

We are interested in regulatory systems subject to internal system noise, in addition to that inherent to the channel itself.

A heuristic approach is fairly simple. Following the Data Rate Theorem argument, given a rate of control information, say $\mathcal{H}$, a system might be expected have a large number of replications of a regulatory substructure, either in parallel or sequentially.

For an average distortion D, the channel capacity, a free energy measure, must be at least $R(D)$, a convex function.

Using a standard Gibbs model, one can write, for the average of R and some unknown monotonic increasing function $F(\mathcal{H})$, the approximate relation

$$\langle R \rangle = \frac{\int_0^\infty R \exp[-R/F(\mathcal{H})]dR}{\int_0^\infty \exp[-R/F(\mathcal{H})]dR} = F(\mathcal{H}).$$ (10)

What is the form of $\mathcal{H} = F^{-1}(\langle R \rangle)$, the rate of control information needed to stabilize the system according to the Data Rate Theorem? One suspects, in first order, a linear expression, using the first two terms of a Taylor series expansion, i.e., $\mathcal{H} \approx \kappa_1 \langle R \rangle + \kappa_2$.

Jensen's inequality for a convex function, here

$$R(\langle D \rangle) \leq \langle R(D) \rangle$$

suggests:

$$\mathcal{H} \geq \kappa_1 R(<D>) + \kappa_2,$$ (11)

where κ_1, at least, is quite large as the result of entropic loss, in a general sense. The next section introduces methods that can be applied under less restricted conditions and to more complicated structures.

As the Black-Scholes calculation of the Mathematical Appendix shows, a more precise, if still approximate, exactly solvable model gives the first-order result that

$$\mathcal{H} = \kappa_1 R + \kappa_2. \tag{12}$$

Thus the needed rate of control information will, for this model, grow linearly with the channel capacity needed to ensure the average distortion between regulatory intent and regulatory effect is D. The constant κ_1 may, however, be very large indeed, as a consequence of 'entropic' losses in the translation of policy to practice. This suggests that onset of social disintegration or of active, organized resistance by the cognitive forces behind Apartheid, can result in severe demands on regulatory efforts. That is, regulation can rapidly become prohibitively difficult with increase in κ_1 for this model, suggesting the necessity of serious penalties for regulatory violations.

3.2.   Coevolution again

Extending the rate distortion perspective on control theory involves addressing a coevolutionary set of stochastic differential equations constituting the feedback loop

$$dR_t = f_1(t, R, \mathcal{H})dt + g_1(t, R, \mathcal{H})dW_t,$$
$$d\mathcal{H}_t = f_2(t, R, \mathcal{H})dt + g_2(t, R, \mathcal{H})dW_t, \tag{13}$$

where dW_t represents white noise.

Several features emerge from invoking such a coevolutionary approach (Champagnat *et al.*, 2006):

1. Setting the expectation of equations (13) equal to zero and solving for stationary points gives attractor states since the noise terms preclude unstable equilibria.
2. Such a system may — again — converge to limit cycle or pseudorandom 'strange attractor' behaviors in which the system seems to chase its tail endlessly within a limited venue — the Red Queen pathology often characterized by a particular kind of instability in the variance in demand for control information, a matter we will explore in detail below for Gaussian channels.

3. The noise terms in equation (13) may not be white, allowing for more subtle behaviors determined by the quadratic variation in the extended version of the Ito chain rule. Indeed, changing the spectrum of noise 'color' may be a signaling modality that carries information.

4. The complete space of quasi-stable modes to which the system can converge — the set of fixed points or strange attractors of the expectation of equation (13) — may itself have a topology allowing definition of 'open sets' within it. These must have the properties (i) that the union of open sets is itself an open set, (ii) the finite intersection of open sets is open, and (iii) the complete space and the zero set are both open.

5. This topological space may have characteristic internal dynamics that are to be mapped onto the structure, providing a kind of change-of-variables that may give a simplified description of the system, much as spherical coordinates can be useful in addressing problems with spherical symmetry.

6. Setting the time-average expectation of equation (13) to zero defines an index theorem in the sense of Atiyah and Singer (1963) and Hazewinkel, (2002), relating analytic results to an underlying topological structure. This instantiates relations between 'conserved' quantities — the quasi-stable non-equilibrium steady states of basins of attraction in parameter space — and underlying topological form. The inherent symmetries, however, are typically those of groupoids defined by equivalence classes of paths rather than by groups (Glazebrook and Wallace 2009). This suggests the associated 'conserved quantities' will be represented as distinct sets of quasi-stable modes, as described in Figures 1 and 2 of Wallace (2010), leading to the next point.

7. Nonequilibrium stationary sets of the system's coevolutionary dynamics are subject to 'ecosystem resilience' transitions between them when driven by increasing noise or by forcing functions of policy that can themselves often be described as the output of information sources, a central matter we will explore below.

8. Different quasi-stable points of this system will have widely different levels of associated regulatory information cost $\mathcal{H}$.

3.3. Stability

The rate distortion function places limits on information source uncertainty. Thus average distortion measures D can drive information system dynamics as well as $R(D)$, via the convexity relation. That is, the rate distortion function itself has a homological relation to free energy density, in the sense of Feynman (2000), and one can apply arguments from Onsager's nonequilibrium thermodynamics using D as a driving parameter (de Groot and Mazur 1984).

Defining a 'Rate Distortion entropy' for an ordinary Gaussian channel under white noise as the Legendre transform

$$S_R = R(D) - D dR(D)/dD = 1/2 \log[\sigma^2/D] + 1/2 \qquad (14)$$

the simplest possible nonequilibrium Onsager equation (de Groot and Mazur 1984) is just

$$dD/dt = -\mu dS_R/dD = \mu/2D, \qquad (15)$$

where t is the time and μ is a diffusion coefficient. By inspection,

$$D(t) = \sqrt{\mu t}. \qquad (16)$$

This is the classic solution to the diffusion equation, a 'correspondence reduction' serving as a base to argue upward in both scale and complexity.

Management and regulation do not involve the diffusive drift of average distortion. On the contrary, following the arguments above, massive rates of control signal information $\mathcal{H}$ are consumed in regulatory activities at and across various scales and levels of organization. Let $G(\mathcal{H})$ represent a monotonic increasing function of the rate of control information consumption $\mathcal{H}$. Then a plausible generalization of equation (15), in the presence of an internal regulatory noise in addition to the channel noise defined by σ^2, is

$$dD_t = \left(\frac{\mu}{2D_t} - G(\mathcal{H}) \right) dt + \frac{\beta^2}{2} D_t dW_t. \qquad (17)$$

This has the nonequilibirum steady state solution, when the expectation of dD_t is zero, of

$$D_{nss} = \frac{\mu}{2G(\mathcal{H})} \qquad (18)$$

representing the (often massive) control signal information needed to limit distortion between the intent and effect of regulation: $\mathcal{H}$ can be expected to increase very sharply with rise in G.

Using the Ito chain rule on equation (17), one can calculate the variance in the distortion as $E(D_t^2) - (E(D_t))^2$.

Letting $Y_t = D_t^2$ and applying the Ito relation (Protter 1990),

$$dY_t = \left[2\sqrt{Y_t}\left(\frac{\mu}{2\sqrt{Y_t}} - G(\mathcal{H})\right) + \frac{\beta^4}{4}Y_t \right] dt + \beta^2 Y_t dW_t, \qquad (19)$$

where $(\beta^4/4)Y_t$ is the Ito correction to the time term of the stochastic differential equation.

Some elementary algebra shows that no real number solution for the expectation of $Y_t = D_t^2$ can exist unless

$$G(\mathcal{H}) \geq \frac{\beta^2}{2}\sqrt{\mu} \qquad (20)$$

roughly analogous to standard results on the moment stability of stochastic differential equations (e.g., Khasminskii 2012). Complex solutions usually imply cycling behavior — in our context, the Red Queen.

But more can be done, as follows.

From equations (12) and (18),

$$G(\mathcal{H}) = \frac{\mu}{2\sigma^2}\exp[2(\mathcal{H}-\kappa_2)/\kappa_1] \geq \frac{\beta^2}{2}\sqrt{\mu}. \qquad (21)$$

Solving for $\mathcal{H}$ gives the necessary condition

$$\mathcal{H} \geq \frac{\kappa_1}{2}\log[\frac{\beta^2\sigma^2}{\sqrt{\mu}}] + \kappa_2 \qquad (22)$$

for there to be a real second moment in D. κ_1 is, again, expected to be very large indeed.

Given the context of this analysis, failure to provide adequate rates of control signal information $\mathcal{H}$ sets off a regulatory stability catastrophe. The corollary, of course, is that state policies deliberately increasing β or σ, or reducing μ, would be expected to overwhelm internal controls, triggering cyclic Red Queen recurrence or other instability.

Variants of the model are possible. The next plausible iterative solution to the Black-Scholes model, as shown in the Mathematical Appendix, is

$$\mathcal{H}_{nss} = \frac{2C}{b^2}\log[R] + \kappa_1 R + \kappa_2 \qquad (23)$$

with $C > 0$.

Clearly, there are two particular modes of central interest: $\kappa_1 = 0$, which grows only as $\log[R]$, and $\kappa_1 > 0$, which grows linearly with R, possibly at a very great rate.

If $\kappa_1 = 0$, this is proportional to C, a much less demanding relation than equation (22).

If, within a society, public policy and changing cultural mores drive $\kappa_1 \to 0$, control of the expressions of racism becomes far easier, and the impacts of external perturbations can be lessened.

3.4.   Implications

We have adapted the formal tools of Wallace and Fullilove (2014) to the problem of stabilizing a very general coevolutionary Red Queen in the presence of noise, without assuming a restrictive 'linear plant' model. Equations (22-23) suggest that controlling a recurrent dynamic in the presence of system perturbations, if a society is structured so that $\kappa_1 > 0$, can be a very difficult matter, requiring draconian levels of imposed regulation under pathological conditions. That is, both passing 'Civil Rights Laws' and making them work are problematic if the Manichean tendencies of cultural trajectory are exacerbated by contemporary stresses. Excesses of Western cultural atomism — exemplified by Margaret Thatcher's famous assertion that *There is no 'Society'* — are at war with the networks of nondisjunctive weak ties needed to pass civil rights laws and make them work in practice. Cultural entities for which $\kappa_1 = 0$, in this model, will be easier to control.

The nonequilibrium quasi-stable modes of coevolutionary systems are subject to sudden shifts and excursions constrained by asymptotic limit theorems similar to those of information theory. More particularly, Champagnat *et al.* (2006) argue that shifts between the quasi-equilibria of a coevolutionary system as characterized by equation (13) can be analyzed using the large deviations formalism. To paraphrase them, the dynamics of drift away from trajectories predicted by the canonical equation can be investigated by considering the asymptotic of the probability of 'rare events' for the sample paths of the diffusion. These events are the diffusion paths drifting far away from the direct solutions of the canonical equation. The probability of such rare events is governed by a large deviation principle, driven by a 'rate function' $\mathcal{I}$ defined in terms of the parameters of the diffusion.

This perspective can be used to study asymptotic behavior of the diffusion process when there are multiple attractive singularities, here, multiple quasi-equilibria in a Red Queen coevolutionary dynamic. As argued by Champagnat *et al.*, the most likely path followed by the diffusion when exiting a basin of attraction is the one minimizing the rate function $\mathcal{I}$ over possible trajectories.

The central fact of large deviations theory is that the rate function $\mathcal{I}$ can be given a canonical form

$$\mathcal{I} = -\sum_j P_j \log(P_j) \tag{24}$$

for a probability distribution in the P_k (Dembo and Zeitouni 1998).

Equation (13) is now seen as subject to large deviations that represent output of an externally-imposed information source L_D with source uncertainty $\mathcal{I}$. This imposition drives system parameters that can trigger punctuated shifts between quasi-stable topological modes of the system of interacting cultural submodules determining the Red Queen of American Apartheid. Sufficiently strong imposed control — renewal of the Civil Rights Movement — can, it seems, drive the system to a persistent and relatively benign stable mode without cycling, ending the 'game'.

Absent, however, such renewal, and in particular rebirth of the unifying strategies of King (1958) and others of similar mind, it seems unlikely that much progress can be made in stabilizing the coevolutionary rollercoaster of American Apartheid, with its recurrent patterns of degradation that violate the most basic tenets of our religious traditions.

4. Summary

Two interrelated problems have produced the current form of American Apartheid: segregation and serial forced displacement. While segregation operates to confine non-white people to certain specified areas (Massey and Denton 1998), serial forced displacement moves non-white people from one place to another (Fullilove and Wallace 2011). Both of these mechanisms inhibit or destroy nondisjunctive weak ties. Without weak ties that unify a community across its inherent or imposed divisions, it is impossible to carry out the civil rights struggle. The question, then, is how are such ties to be rebuilt? This, it turns out, is not fundamentally difficult, as community-building is an inherent activity of human beings, and mobilizations of any kind will begin to reknit society. Projects that range from repairing housing, creating community gardens, teaching needed skills, or promoting exercise have all been shown to contribute to the creation of social cohesion (Fullilove 1998).

Because people of color live in neighborhoods that have been denied resources for maintenance, their homes, public buildings and public spaces are often in tatters. The reknitting of weak ties also depends on creating stabilizing the habitat so that it is fit for human life. This requires both resources and involvement of people in the repair of their neighborhood (Fullilove, Green, and Fullilove 1999).

But what has been observed repeatedly over the past two decades is that the policies of serial forced displacement are so powerful that it impossible to do the work of rebuilding ties without simultaneously fighting for community stability. Therefore, it is essential to fight serial forced displacement while building weak ties and restoring the damages to the urban ecosystem. Groups like the University of Orange are pioneering this kind of work, which requires local, national and international coalitions in order to succeed (Fullilove 2013).

For many Americans, the Future Information Society, in the absence of principled intervention to suppress policies instantiating the historical trajectory of racism, will continue to resemble the past. Driving the self-perpetuating and adaptive institutions of American Apartheid into extinction remains today as urgent a calling as was the Abolishinist enterprise of previous centuries.

5.   Mathematical Appendix: Black-Scholes

Although the Black-Scholes formalism for financial options trading (Black and Scholes 1973) fails in practice for fundamental reasons (e.g., Derman and Taleb 2005; Haug and Taleb 2011) — it is an exactly solvable approximate model — the methodology remains a conceptual tool that can be generally applied to regulation, including the management of a destabilized, coevolutionarily cycling Apartheid system.

The central purpose of the approach is to eliminate or mitigate the effects of unpredictability, here represented as an added white noise, the classic random walk of Brownian motion. More sophisticated models are possible, at the expense of further mathematical overhead.

Consider the canonical example of a stock price S, whose dynamics are determined by the stochastic differential equation

$$dS_t = \mu S_t dt + b S_t dW_t, \tag{25}$$

where dW_t/dt is white noise, having a uniform spectral density.

Given a known payoff function $V(S,t)$, one uses the Ito chain rule (Protter 1990) to define another stochastic differential equation, in the usual manner. Now define a 'portfolio function' as the Legendre transform of V;

$$\mathcal{L} = -V + S\partial V/\partial S, \tag{26}$$

Manipulation, using the derived SDE for V, gives the result that

$$\Delta\mathcal{L} = \left(-\partial V/\partial t - \frac{1}{2}b^2 S^2 \partial^2 V/\partial S^2\right)\Delta t \tag{27}$$

which subsumes the noise term into the Ito correction factor in b. Assuming $\Delta\mathcal{L}/\Delta t \propto \mathcal{L}$ and a bit more algebra gives the classic Black-Scholes equation.

The question arises whether a regulator can apply similar hedging strategies to mitigate the effects of noise.

The change in average distortion with time can be seen as representing the dynamics of the disjunction between the intent of a regulator and the actual responses of the regulated system. Let R_t be the RDF of the channel connecting them at time t. The relation can, under conditions of both white noise and volatility, be expressed as

$$dR_t = f(t, R_t)dt + bR_t dW_t. \tag{28}$$

Let $\mathcal{H}(R_t, t)$ represent the necessary rate of control information according to the Data Rate Theorem, that is to be associated with R_t at time t, and expand using the Ito chain rule:

$$dH_t = [\partial\mathcal{H}/\partial t + f(R_t, t)\partial\mathcal{H}/\partial R + \frac{1}{2}b^2 R_t^2 \partial^2\mathcal{H}/\partial R^2]dt$$
$$+[bR_t\partial\mathcal{H}/\partial R]dW_t. \tag{29}$$

Again, define $\mathcal{L}$ as the Legendre transform of the control signal information rate $\mathcal{H}$, a kind of entropy index (e.g., Wallace 2015), having the form

$$\mathcal{L} = -\mathcal{H} + R\partial\mathcal{H}/\partial R. \tag{30}$$

Using the heuristic of replacing dX with ΔX in these expressions, and applying the results of equation (29), produces an exact analog to equation (27):

$$\Delta\mathcal{L} = \left(-\partial\mathcal{H}/\partial t - \frac{1}{2}b^2 R^2 \partial^2\mathcal{H}/\partial R^2\right)\Delta t. \tag{31}$$

As in the Black-Scholes calculation, the terms in f and dW_t cancel out, giving a relation in which the effects of noise are again subsumed in the Ito correction involving b. The approach invokes powerful regularity assumptions that may often be violated. Questions then revolve about model robustness in the face of such violation.

$\mathcal{L}$, as the Legendre transform of the free energy rate measure $\mathcal{H}$, is a kind of entropy index that can be expected to rapidly reach an extremum at nonequilibrium steady state (nss) (e.g., Derrida 2007). There, $\Delta\mathcal{L}/\Delta t = \partial\mathcal{H}/\partial t = 0$, and we obtain the final relation:

$$\frac{1}{2}b^2 R^2 \partial^2\mathcal{H}/\partial R^2 = 0 \tag{32}$$

having the solution of equation(20):

$$\mathcal{H}_{nss} = \kappa_1 R + \kappa_2 \tag{33}$$

in accordance with the heuristic result of equation (19).

More complicated models, depending on the assumed form of $\Delta\mathcal{L}/\Delta t$, are clearly possible. In particular, the models obtained by setting $\Delta\mathcal{L}/\Delta t = C > 0, \propto \mathcal{L}$ are also exactly solvable, if somewhat more complicated. The second model produces classic Black-Scholes result.

As described above, of some considerable interest is the mixed condition $\partial\mathcal{H}/\partial t = 0, \Delta\mathcal{L}/\Delta t = C > 0$ at nonequilibrium steady state. That is, a constant production of an 'entropy' at the rate $\Delta\mathcal{L}/\Delta t = C$, with the control information $\mathcal{H}$ at a fixed peak. Then

$$\mathcal{H}_{nss} = \frac{2C}{b^2}\log[R] + \kappa_1 R + \kappa_2. \tag{34}$$

Two particular modes emerge: for $\kappa_1 = 0$, demand for control information grows only as $\log[R]$, and $\kappa_1 > 0$ which grows linearly in R, possibly with very large κ_1.

References

Aldrich, H., *et al.*, 2008, In defense of generalized Darwinism, Journal of Evolutionary Economics, 18:577-596.

Atlan, H., I. Cohen, 1998, Immune information, self-organization and meaning, International Immunology, 10:711-717.

Atiyah, M., I. Singer, 1963, The index of elliptical operators on compact manifolds, Bulletin of the American Mathematical Society, 69:322-433.

Badger, E., 2015, The long, painful and repetitive history of how Baltimore became Baltimore, Washington Post Wonkblog, April 29, 2015. Available online.

Binney, J., N. Dowrick, A. Fisher, M. Newman, 1986, The Theory of Critical Phenomena, Clarendon Press, New York.

Black, F., M. Scholes, 1973, The pricing of options and corporate liabilities, Journal of Political Economy, 81:637-654.

Blinder, A., 2015, Baltimore residents away from turmoil consider their role, New York Times 5/5/15.

Brown, R., 1987, From groups to groupoids: a brief survey, Bulletin of the London Mathematical Society, 19:113-134.

Champagnat, N., R. Ferriere, S. Meleard, 2006, Unifying evolutionary dynamics: from individual stochastic process to macroscopic models, Theoretical Population Biology, 69:297-321.

Cover, T., J. Thomas, 2006, Elements of Information Theory, Second Edition, Wiley, NY.

de Groot, S., P. Mazur, 1984, Non-equilibrium Thermodynamics, Dover, NY.

Dembo, A., O. Zeitouni, 1998, Large Deviations: Techniques and Applications, Springer, NY.

Derman, E., N. Taleb, 2005, The illusions of dynamic replication, Quantitative Finance, 5:323-326.

Derrida, B., 2007, Nonequilibrium steady states, Journal of Statistical Mechanics: Theory and Experiment, p07023.

Durham, W., 1991, Coevolution: Genes, Culture, and Human Diversity, Stanford University Press, Stanford CA.

Editorial Board, 2015, Housing Apartheid, American Style, New York Times, May 17 Sunday Review Editorial.

Eldredge, N., S. Gould, 1972, Punctuated equilibrium: an alternative to phyletic gradualism. In T. Schopf (ed.), Models in Paleobiology, pp. 82-115, Freeman, Cooper and Co., San Francisco CA.

Ellis, R., 1985, Entropy, Large Deviations, and Statistical Mechanics, Springer, New York.

Elsner, W., T. Heinrich, I. Schwardt, 2015, The Microeconomics of Complex Economies: Evolutionary, Institutional, Neoclassical and Complexity Perspectives, Academic Press, Waltham, MA.

Fanon, F., 1966, The Wretched of the Earth, Grove Press, New York.

Feynman, R., 2000, Lectures on Computation, Westview Press, New York.

Fullilove, M. T., L. Green, R. E. Fullilove, 1999, Building momentum: An ethnographic study of Inner-city redevelopment. American Journal of Public Health, 89:840-844.

Fullilove M.T., and R. Wallace, 2011, Serial Forced Displacement in American Cities 1916-2010, Journal of Urban Health, 88:381-389.

Fullilove, M.T., 1998, Promoting social cohesion to improve health, Journal of the American Medical Women's Association, 53:72-76.

Fullilove, M.T., 2000, AIDS and social context. In A.M.L. Ellen G. Feigal, and R. J. Biggar (Ed.), AIDS-Related Cancers and Their Treatment (pp. 371-385), Decker, New York.

Fullilove, M.T., 2013, Urban Alchemy: Restoring joy to America's sorted-Out Cities, New Village Press, New York.

Glazebrook, J.F., R. Wallace, 2009, Rate distortion manifolds as models spaces for cognitive information, Informatica, 33:309-346.

Gould, S., 2002, The Structure of Evolutionary Theory, Harvard University Press, Cambridge MA.

Granovetter, M., 1973, The strength of weak ties, American Journal of Sociology, 78:1360-1380.

Haug, E., N. Taleb, 2011, Option traders use (very) sophisticated heuristics, never the Black-Scholes–Merton formula, Journal of Economic Behavior and Organization, 77:97-106.

Hazewinkel, M., 2002, Encyclopedia of Mathematics, 'Index Formulas', Springer, New York.

Heine, S., 2001, Self as cultural product: an examination of East Asian and North American selves, Journal of Personality, 69:881-906.

G. Hodgson, 1993, Economics and Evolution: Bringing Life Back into Economics, University of Michigan Press, Ann Arbor, MI.

Hodgson, G., T. Knudsen, 2010, Darwin's Conjecture: The Search for General

Principles of Social and Economic Evolution, University of Chicago Press, Chicago, IL.

Jablonka, E., M. Lamb, 1995, Epigenetic Inheritance and Evolution: The Lamarckian dimension, Oxford University Press, Oxford, UK.

James, W., 1880, Great men, great thoughts, and the environment, Atlantic Monthly 46 (October 1880):441-459.

Khasminskii, R., 2012, Stochastic Stability of Differential Equations, Second Edition, Springer, New York.

Khinchin, A., 1957, Mathematical Foundations of Information Theory, Dover Press, New York.

King, M.L., 1958, Stride Toward Freedom, Harper and Row, New York.

Landau, L., E. Lifshitz, 2007, Statistical Physics Part I, Third Edition, Elsevier, New York.

Leighton, A.H., 1959, My Name is Legion: Foundations for a Theory of Man in Relation to Culture (Vol. I), Basic Books, New York.

Marx, K., F. Engels, 1937, R. Enmale, ed. The Civil War in the United States, International Press, New York.

Massey, D., N. Denton, 1998, American Apartheid: Segregation and the Making of the Underclass, Harvard University Press, Cambridge, MA.

Myrdal, G., 1944, An American Dilemma: The Negro Problem and Modern Democracy, Harper & Bros., NY.

NACDD, 1968, Report of the National Advisory Commission on Civil Disorders, US Government Printing Office.

Nair G., et al., 2007, Feedback control under data rate constraints: an overview, Proceedings of the IEEE, 95:108-137.

Pettini, M., 2007, Geometry and Topology in Hamiltonian Dynamics and Statistical Mechanics, Springer, NY.

Pouncy, C., 2002, Institutional economics and critical race/LatCrit theory: the need for a critical 'raced' economics, Rutgers Law Review 54:841-852.

Protter P., 1990, Stochastic Integration and Differential Equations: A new approach, Springer, NY.

Richerson, P., R. Boyd, 2006, Not by Genes Alone: How Culture Transformed Human Evolution, University of Chicago Press, Chicago IL.

Rockafellar, R., 1970, Convex Analysis, Princeton University Press, Princeton, NJ.

Shane, S., 2015, Baltimore riots are another scar on a city long battered by neglect, New York Times 4/29/15.

Simms, E.M., 2008, Children's lived spaces in the inner city: historical and political aspects of the psychology of place, Humanistic Psyologist, 36:72-89.

Van Valen, L., 1973, A new evolutionary law, Evolutionary Theory 1:1-30.

Wallace, D., R. Wallace, 1998, A Plague on Your Houses. Verso Press, London and New York.

Wallace, D., R. Wallace, 2000, Life and death in upper Manhattan and the Bronx: toward an evolutionary perspective on catastrophic social change, Environment and Planning A, 32:1245-1266.

Wallace, D., R. Wallace, 2011, Consequences of massive housing destruction: the New York city fire epidemic, Building Research and Information, 39:395-411.

Wallace, R.G., R. Wallace, 2009, Evolutionary radiation and the spectrum of consciousness, Consciousness and Cognition, 18:160-167.

Wallace, R., R.G. Wallace, 1998, Information theory, scaling laws and the thermodynamics of evolution, Journal of Theoretical Biology, 192:545.

Wallace, R., M. Fullilove, A. Flisher, 1996, AIDS, violence and behavioral coding: information theory, risk behavior and dynamic process on core-group sociogeographic networks, Social Science and Medicine, 43:339-352.

R. Wallace, R.G. Wallace, 1999, Organizations, Organisms and Interactions: An information theory approach to biocultural evolution, BioSystems, 51:101.

Wallace, R., D. Wallace, J. Ullmann, H. Andrews, 1999, Deindustrialization, inner-city decay, and the hierarchical diffusion of AIDS in the USA: How neoliberal and cold war policies magnified the ecological niche for emerging infections and created a national security crisis, Environment and Planning A, 31:113-.

Wallace, R., R.G. Wallace, D. Wallace, 2003, Toward cultural oncology: The evolutionary information dynamics of cancer, Open Systems and Information Dynamics 10:159-181.

Wallace, R., R.G. Wallace, 2008, On the spectrum of prebiotic chemical systems: an information-theoretic treatment of Eigen's paradox, Origins of Life and Evolution of Biospheres, 38:419-455.

R. Wallace, D. Wallace, 2008, Punctuated equilibrium in statistical models of generalized coevolutionary resilience: how sudden ecosystem transitions can entrain both phenotype expression and Darwinian selection, Transactions on Computational Systems Biology, IX, LNBI 5121, 23-85.

Wallace, R., M. Fullilove, 2008, Collective Consciousness and its Discontents: Institutional Distributed Cognition, Racial Policy and Public Health in the United States, Springer, New York.

Wallace, R., D. Wallace, 2009, Code, context and epigenetic catalysis in gene expression, Transactions on Computational Systems Biology, XI, LNBI 5750:283-334.

Wallace, R., D. Wallace, R.G. Wallace, 2009, Farming Human Pathogens: Ecological Resilience and Evolutionary Process, Springer, New York.

Wallace, R., D. Wallace, 2011, Cultural epigenetics and the heritability of complex diseases, Transactions on Computational Systems Biology XIII, LNBI 6575: 131-170.

Wallace, R., R. Fullilove, 2014, State policy and the political economy of criminal enterprise: mass incarceration and persistent organized hyperviolence in the USA, Structural Change and Economic Dynamics, 31:17-31.

Wallace, R., 1991, Expanding coupled shock fronts of urban decay and criminal behavior: How U.S. cities are becoming hollowed out, Journal of Quantitative Criminology, 7:333-.

Wallace, R., 2002, Adaptation, punctuation, and rate distortion: non-cognitive 'learning plateaus' in evolutionary process, Acta Biotheoretica, 50:101-116.

Wallace, R., 2009a, Metabolic constraints on the eukaryotic transition, Origins of Life and Evolution of Biospheres, 39:165-176.

Wallace, R., 2009b, Programming coevolutionary machines: the emerging conundrum, International Journal of Parallel, Emerging, and Distributed Systems 24:443-453.

Wallace, R., 2010, Expanding the modern synthesis, Comptes Rendus Biologies, 333:701-709.

Wallace, R., 2011a, A formal approach to evolution as self-referential language, BioSystems, 106:36-44.

Wallace, R., 2011b, Forced Displacement of African Americans in New York City and the International Diffusion of Multiple-Drug-Resistant HIV. Chapter 7 in Megacities and Public Health, O. Kahn, G. Pappas (eds.), APHA Press, Washington, DC.

Wallace, R., 2011c, On the evolution of homochirality, Comptes Rendus Biologies, 334:263-268.

Wallace, R., 2012a, Consciousness, crosstalk, and the mereological fallacy: an evolutionary perspective, Physics of Life Reviews, 9:426-453.

Wallace, R., 2012b, Metabolic constraints on the evolution of genetic codes: Did multiple 'preaerobic' ecosystem transitions entrain richer dialects via Serial Endosymbiosis? Transactions on Computational Systems Biology XIV, LNBI 7625:204-232.

Wallace, R. 2013a, A new formal perspective on 'Cambrian explosions', Comptes Rendus Biologies, 337:1-5.

Wallace, R., 2013b, Cognition and biology: perspectives from information theory, Cognitive Processing, 15:1-12.

Wallace, R., 2013c, A new formal approach to evolutionary process in socioeconomic systems, Journal of Evolutionary Economics, 23:1-15.

Wallace, R., 2014, Statistical models of critical phenomena in fuzzy biocognition, BioSystems, 117:54-59.

Wallace, R., 2015, An Ecosystem Approach to Economic Stabilization: Emerging from the Neoliberal Wilderness, Routledge, London.

Watkins, B.X., 2000, Fantasy, Decay, Abandonment, Defeat, and Disease: Community Disintegration in Central Harlem 1960-1990, Columbia University, New York.

Weinstein, A., 1996, Groupoids: unifying internal and external symmetry, Notices of the American Mathematical Association, 43:744-752.

Chapter 19

Artificial and Natural Genetic Information Processing

Guenther Witzany

Telos-Philosophische Praxis
Vogelsangstr. 18c, 5111-Buermoos, Austria
witzany@sbg.at

Conventional methods of genetic engineering and more recent genome editing techniques focus on identifying genetic target sequences for manipulation. This is a result of historical concept of the gene which was also the main assumption of the ENCODE project designed to identify all functional elements in the human genome sequence. However, the theoretical core concept changed dramatically. The old concept of genetic sequences which can be assembled and manipulated like molecular bricks has problems in explaining the natural genome-editing competences of viruses and RNA consortia that are able to insert or delete, combine and recombine genetic sequences more precisely than random-like into cellular host organisms according to adaptational needs or even generate sequences de novo. Increasing knowledge about natural genome editing questions the traditional narrative of mutations (error replications) as essential for generating genetic diversity and genetic content arrangements in biological systems. This may have far-reaching consequences for our understanding of artificial genome editing.

523

Keywords: Genetic code; genetic engineering; natural code editing; RNA consortia; viruses.

1. Introduction

The dominating concepts of molecular biology and genetics in the last half a century, (i) the one gene-one protein hypothesis, (ii) the central dogma of molecular biology (DNA-RNA-protein-anything else), and (iii) the assumption that noncoding DNA is 'junk', are falsified meanwhile [Shapiro, 2009, 2011]. Since the rise of epigenetics the focus on the logic of molecular syntax of genetic sequences has lost its importance, because methylation and histone markings may add multiple meaning functions to identical molecular sequence syntax [Slotkin and Martienssen, 2007; Jirtle, 2009; Barlow, 2011]. Also it is becoming increasingly clear that noncoding RNAs serve as key regulatory elements in all steps and even sub-steps of replication, transcription, translation, recombination, repair and immunity [Mattick, 2009; Witzany, 2009; Cech and Steitz, 2014]. Most interestingly, research on the roles of persistent viruses in host genomes as main drivers of evolutionary processes, their various roles as mobile genetic elements, and their remaining roles as 'defectives' integrated as counterbalanced modules such as, e.g. restriction/modification, insertion/deletion and toxin/antitoxins, shows the abundance of agents competent in terms of arranging genetic content by integrating persistently into host genomes without destroying former coding regions [Villarreal, 2005, 2009; Koonin, 2009, Mruk and Kobayashi, 2014; Curcio and Derbyshire, 2003]. How does this current empirical knowledge fit the old core assumption of molecular biology and genetics and its theoretical concepts of the genetic code? This review will highlight some historical perspectives and compare them with the recent advances in the understanding of natural genome editing.

2. The Detection of the Genetic Code, Artificial Genetic Engineering and Genome Manipulation

Soon after the detection of the molecular syntax of the genetic code and its molecular biological features the idea arose of technically manipulating genetic content arrangements for various goals such as optimisation of the human gene pool, fighting various diseases, knocking out dangerous genes, optimising plant and animal breeding, and developing new techniques such as gene therapy. 'Now, biological research is in a ferment, creating and promising methods of interference with "natural processes" which could destroy or could transform nearly every aspect of human life which we value' [Wolstenholme, 1963]. Finally, the hope is that if the human genome can be deciphered completely then it will be easier to fight the major diseases affecting humans.

At the dawn of artificial genetic engineering mutations were caused, e.g. in plants, with few expected beneficial results at the beginnings that were object to further breedings. In a second step the real history of artificial genetic engineering began, with the manipulation of restriction enzymes, recombination of DNA in bacteria, better sequencing methods, and polymerase chain reaction. Interestingly, at this stage it was the investigation, understanding and use of virus-derived capabilities represented by plasmids and phages which were technically exploited. However, genetic engineering was thought not only to recombine genetic content arrangements within one species but also to apply a transspecies method to develop multiresistant plants, new drugs and even gene therapy. This was the consequence of the realisation that the genetic code is used by all living entities on this planet.

New insights into DNA splicing and the rise of epigenetics made it increasingly clear, however, that the molecular syntax of the genetic storage medium DNA did not really represent what is finally transcribed into RNA and translated into proteins, which means different epigenetic marking of identical genetic sequences could lead to different and in extreme cases opposing protein coding functions [Mattick and Gagen, 2001; Mattick, 2010; Tang *et al.*, 2015, Werner *et al.*, 2015]. Yet it is clear that the epigenetic markings on the genome are of similar importance to the sequence syntax. Epigenetic markings serve as a resource for RNA-mediated regulatory tools and additionally can represent impacts of environmental circumstances that may be heritable or not [Cuzin and Rassoulzadegan, 2010; Shapiro, 2014; Tognini *et al.*, 2015]. The role of epigenetics looks also like a memory tool which does not alter sequence structure but changes its regulation and function in multiple ways according environmentally induced adaptational needs [Mattick, 2010; Bredy *et al.*, 2011; Mercer and Mattick, 2013], and therefore it is also a main cause of diseases if regulatory networks get out of control [Marraffini and Sontheimer, 2010; Spadafora, 2015). Therefore it represents one of many kinds of natural genetic engineering for installing information via proteins and/or RNAs to DNA, i.e. converting the central dogma of molecular biology [Shapiro, 2009, 2011, 2014].

In the realm of artificial genetic engineering gene synthesis arose as a technique of synthetic biology for producing artificial genes in laboratories. In contrast to molecular cloning and polymerase chain reactions gene synthesis does not need pre-existing DNA, but is synthesised as double-stranded DNA without limit in terms of length or sequence content.

A more accessible technique is artificial genome editing, not solely genetic engineering. The assumption is that just as editing a written text in human language involves adding, removing, or replacing words in sentences, in genome editing the genome sequences are changed by adding, replacing, or removing nucleotides [Jasin, 1996; Lyons *et al.*, 2003]. For genome editing gene 'scissors' are used for deleting certain sequence structures/ genes to see what effect the 'knock out' of certain genes has. This goal is reached by site-specific endonucleases that are used as an appropriate tool for selective genome cleavage [Jasin, 1996; de Souza, 2012]. Such endonucleases make it possible to direct gene targeting. The three methods that are currently used are based on zinc finger endonucleases, TALEN- gen 'scissors' and the more recent CRIPRS/Cas9 technique that has been detected as an adaptive immune system in prokaryotes in which small parts of the genome of natural genetic parasites are integrated into the host genome and serve to ward off similar genetic parasites. Artificial genome editing therefore uses identification and manipulation techniques that may have far-reaching and in extreme cases infinite consequences on germ cells of organisms that are manipulated accordingly [Iranzo *et al.*, 2013; Hsu *et al.*, 2013; Lin *et al.*, 2014; O'Connell *et al.*, 2014].

Here it should be said that artificial genome manipulation is confronted with a number of technical problems such as the low quality of oligonucleotides, faults in the syntax of sequences, and damage or problems in terms of nucleotide assembly. Additionally, overlapping regions may cause identity problems with newly synthesised genes and error correction methods could be optimised. Last but not least we have to rethink the possible consequences of manipulation techniques which were first mentioned in the Asilomar conference and are now the subject of current discourse [Berg *et al.*, 1975; Baltimore *et al.*, 2015; Sugarman, 2015] and which act on sequence syntax, not forgetting that natural genomes are the result of long-lasting selection processes in vivo, which means they happened within the context of an abundance of various lifeworlds together with rather different co-consortia, such as symbionts, bacteria and an abundance of viruses and infectious RNAs, all of them absent in in vitro technical set-ups [Villarreal, 2005; Ryan, 2009].

Therefore there is a crucial difference in the theoretical assumptions: is the genome the result of natural editing by competent agents that assemble a genetically conserved background resulting out of a rich evolutionary history of billions of years or is it solely the result of a variety of selection processes within some genetic drift passages of chance mutations in the realm of cell machineries that can be viewed as molecular bricks that can be restructured and rebuilt in a Lego-like fashion? In the first perspective we have a superficial nucleotide sequence grammar which can be epigenetically marked in different ways like a hidden, deep grammar that is not obvious in the superficial grammar. In the second perspective there is only one superficial grammar, and it is visible, measurable and can be computed by algorithm-based procedures. The hidden deep grammar is not the focus here.

Because the consequences of the contradictory perspectives are subject to ethical debates, and the science of ethics is beyond the expertise of natural sciences, this is not further evaluated here.

3. The Old Concept: The Genetic Code in a Quantifiable Sequence Space

In the early 1960s it became increasingly clear that genetic information is stored in a molecular structure of nucleotide sequences termed the genetic code. It resembles all features of natural codes, an alphabet of nucleotides which can be assembled in only one reading direction and read, transcribed (into intermediate RNA) and translated at least into proteins which form organismal bodies, i.e. their parts and metabolism. The rules governing how gene alphabet characters are combined naturally (i.e. the molecular syntax) were identified by Erwin Chargaff (Chargaff rules) who demonstrated the results of his investigations to the young James Watson and Francis Crick. The latter afterwards detected the molecular structure of the double helix and Crick termed it a 'code without commas'. He also observed that information transfer direction is irreversible in the traditional 'central dogma of molcular biology': DNA — RNA — proteins — anything else [Crick, 1970].

At the same time information theory and cybernetic systems theory emerged and the genetic code was immediately interpreted in the light of these two emerging theories by molecular biologists and geneticists. Therefore the natural genetic code was viewed as a molecular structure that can be measured, explained and understood by natural laws, physics, chemistry and information theory [Schrödinger, 1944; Eigen, 1971]. Recently, Sydney Brenner argued that cells and living organisms represent the best examples of Turing and von Neumann machines [Brenner, 2012;

Witzany and Baluska, 2012]. However, the concept of Alan Turing and John von Neumann meanwhile became a 'Touring' machine, i.e. 'touring' through the history of science: no real Turing machine has been seen in reality since all the expected and visionary predicted beneficials of the last 70 years.

The reason why system theory and information theory are preferred in molecular biology and genetics is that there was a far-reaching discourse on building up an exact scientific language in contrast to non-scientific ones (metaphysics, vitalism) which would lead to exact science (natural sciences) in which only such sentences as were formalisable would fulfil the science criteria. Only formalisable sentences could depict material reality, i.e. reality built of physics and chemistry, and every entity of this reality would be formalisable in a mathematical 'Hilbert space' [Hilbert and Bernays, 1934, 1939; Whitehead and Russell, 1910, 1912, 1913] by unique coordinates that could be depicted in mathematical equations in principle. This concept later on was adapted to "biology as sequence space" [Eigen and Biebricher, 1988]. Built on these assumptions, systems theory and information theory were assumed to be the best methods for explaining the genetic information representing self-organised matter, i.e. the molecular structure of the genetic code [Eigen, 1971]. Both became privileged concepts for investigating the genetic code coherently, as shown by the importance of bioinformatics, biolinguistics, systems biology, mathematical biology, synthetic biology, i.e. quantifiable analyses of the features of the genetic code [Witzany, 2010].

4. Discredited Theoretical Assumptions in Molecular Biology

In the 1990s if not before the theoretical core assumptions in molecular biology and genetics changed dramatically. The central dogma of molecular biology that sequential information cannot be transferred from protein to either protein or nucleic acid was disproved in multiple examples [Shapiro, 2009, 2011]. This led to Crick's prediction that the wrong assumption ' ... would shake the whole intellectual basis of molecular biology' [Crick, 1970]. Additionally, the one gene-one protein hypothesis was disproved. One gene can code for several proteins because the epigenetic marking of the gene sequence may cause several transcription and translation patterns. Of equal importance was the disproving of the assumption that gene sequences that do not code for proteins represent former evolutionary stages without any function, remaining as useless 'junk' DNA. However, we know that nearly all of the non-coding DNA is also transcribed into a variety of RNAs that are split up by several co-ordinated steps into small noncoding RNAs such as micro RNAs that fulfil a variety of essential functions in gene regulation [Mattick and Gagen, 2001; Mattick and Makunin, 2006; Mattick *et al.*, 2010].

Unexpectedly, the most powerful development was the comeback of virology. Although it was observed many years ago that '....life may have remained in the virus stage for many millions of years before a suitable assemblage of elementary units was brought together in the first cell' [Haldane, 1929], with the rise of molecular biology the idea re-emerged that viruses represent escaped parasites of cellular organisms that are non-essential parts of the tree of life. That viruses emerged earlier than cellular life was dismissed for decades. Empirical knowledge now indicates that several genomic features of viruses cannot be found in any cellular genome, which indicates an older evolutionary status [Villarreal, 2005; Koonin *et al.*, 2006; Villarreal and Witzany, 2010].

5. Essential Features of Natural Codes

After the aforementioned attempts to generate an exact scientific language to depict material reality by using formalisable equations to represent objective entities within a formalisable 'universe of entities' as proposed by Hilbert, Whitehead and Russell the theory of science discourse turned into pragmatics thanks to late Ludwig Wittgenstein. Wittgenstein demonstrated that the exact science language that he founded early in his famous 'Tractatus logico philosophicus' was a fundamental error [Wittgenstein, 1953; Witzany, 2014a]. In contrast to artificial language constructions such as formalizable scientific languages natural everyday languages are the ultimate source material for investigations into how natural languages arise and function: consortia of competent living agents develop sign systems of various forms by themselves for cooperation and coordination of everyday behaviour, which means natural languages are inherently a kind of social interaction mediated by signs (indices, signals, symbols and behavioural embodiments that can express similar functions). Only once one cannot follow rules. Rule following is inherently a kind of customized social interactions. One biological entity alone could never emerge for the first time, with the consequence that the theoretical assumption of LUCA (last universal common ancestor) in terms of cellular life remains a chimera of false theoretical pre-assumptions [Villarreal and Witzany, 2010].

The semantics of signs, i.e. the meanings of the signs depend on the context in which signs are used by biological interacting groups [Witzany, 2010]. This means the same 'word' or alphabetic sequence can have multiple meanings within different contextual circumstances. The 'word' (or similar syntactic sign assemblies) has a visible superficial grammar, but the range of contextual usages may add several different meanings to the identical word grammar. This represents the deep grammar inherently interconnected with the situational context of the usage of a word that is not visible in the superficial grammar but can be used by living agents according to their different situational needs [Witzany and Baluska, 2012].

Additionally but of similar importance than this result of Wittgenstein, Kurt Gödel demonstrated in his incompleteness theorem that the assumptions Hilbert used to construct a contradiction-free axiomatic system in 'Hilbert space' are impossible in principle, because in natural language-using populations there is an inherent possibility of generating new sentences, new sign sequences that do not result from previous ones and cannot be predicted 'by algorithm-based procedures [Gödel, 1931].

If the genetic code is not the result of replication errors in the self-organisation of matter, but an inherent active biological phenomenon, and additionally an ecosphere habitat for a rich lifeworld of RNA species that not only compete but cooperate, then we now need to focus on the new perspective of the natural genetic code [Mauricio, 2005; Brookfield, 2005; Le Rouzic *et al.*, 2007; Vennera *et al.*, 2009; Witzany, 2015a].

Most importantly, no natural language speaks itself; nor does a natural code code itself. There is an essential precondition for natural languages and codes, i.e. living agents which act as semiotic subjects; this means groups, societies, swarms that share the three levels of (syntactic, pragmatic and semantic) rules of language/code usage with which they organise and coordinate common behaviour. The relationship of living agents with their (historically evolved) real-life situation we term pragmatics [Witzany, 2014b]. Consortia of living agents share pragmatic rules to install sign-mediated interactions. It is important to note that semiotic rules — although quite conservative — may be changed by the user communities according to adaptational needs. This is the crucial difference of semiotic rules that determine sign usage to natural laws that cannot be changed but every entity underlies them in a strict sense [Witzany, 2015b].

In summary, living agents that cooperate and coordinate their behaviour via sign(al)s follow three levels of rules to combine signs correctly to generate more complex sign sequences (syntactic rules), choose behavioural patterns that are appropriate for fostering cooperative behaviour (pragmatic rules) and therefore determine the information content for the designation needs the signs serve (semantic rules).

Last but not least we have to look at how natural code users save energy costs. In natural codes we have a limited number of signs and a limited number of rules with which living agents generate and coordinate behaviour. Because natural language/code tools are limited, the information-bearing sequences may designate several independent and even contradictory contents.. One word may have several different meanings, because living agents cannot invent new 'words' or sign sequences for every new situation or designation. Similar or equal combinations of signs, characters and words which result in sentences can be used as informational tools to transport different meanings. The phrase 'The shooting of the hunters', for example, cannot be understood unequivocally. In the one context this may indicate a common shooting of hunters of non-self targets, in the other it may mark dramatic misbehaviour [Witzany and Baluska, 2012]. The marking of syntactic sequences by marking tools is common practice in natural languages/codes and determines semantic content according to the needs of the pragmatic interacting agents.

To investigate syntactic sequences without knowing something about the real-life behaviour of code-using agents is senseless because syntactic structures do not represent unequivocably semantic meaning. Quantifiable analyses of signs, words or sequences cannot extract meaning. Only in a rather restricted quantifiable sense is this possible through sequence comparison with its known functions. All these features are absent in non-animate nature. If water freezes to ice no living agents or semiotic rules or signs are necessary and present.

6. Natural Genome Editing: What Does it Mean?

The genetic code in systems theory and information theory is not the result of interacting agents but of selection of replication errors (mutations) of biological macromolecules. Because Manfred Eigen assumes that information-bearing codes in macromoleclar systems, as well as in complex phenotypic systems such as human brains, represent self-organising matter, it is less difficult to move from a single macromolecule to a living cell than assume the transition of the single cell to an intelligent human being [Eigen, 1971, 2013]. Information in this sense is a molecular property within a dynamic theory of matter that gets its value through its self-reproductivity. Eigen's conclusion that there is no essential difference between abiotic matter and biotic entities except the emergence of biological information by hypercycles of quasi-species is inevitable. Both depend on natural laws that govern physico-chemical cause and effects. A series of replication errors (muta-tions) of master copies leads to quasi-species, that are mutant distributions of primitive replicating entities. Such dynamic distributions of genomes that share genetic variation, competition and selection generate the fittest types (i.e. master copies) or in the extreme case error thresholds, i.e. excessively high mutation rates/variations, in that information cannot further reproduce in the case of excessive mutational load [Eigen, 1971].

Although the quasi-species concept predominated evolution biology for nearly half a century it is not an appropriate model for coherently explaining more recent empirical data on co-operative consortia of RNA groups and viruses or its "defectives" that co-operate [Villarreal and Witzany, 2013a,b]. The evidence that the evolution, conservation and plasticity of genetic identities are the result of co-operative consortia of RNA stem loops being able to use natural code and edit this code, even with the generation of new sequences opens a new perspective on artificial genome editing as well [Witzany, 2011; Villarreal and Witzany, 2015].

Especially the ability to generate really new sequences (not out of previous ones) allows such groups constantly to infect other nucleic sequence-based agents, whether virus-like or cellular genomes. The generation of such new sequences by co-operating RNA stem loop groups lead to identity groups such as viruses that represent toxic codes and even counteracting antitoxins. Persistently (non-lytic) infected host organisms are the preferred habitat where former competing agent groups are unified in the basic behavioural motif of 'addiction modules' (*Gangen hypothesis*) that can be identified as TA, RM, ID modules; all of the former competing groups are now unified to form stable/ unstable modules that are counter-regulated and also provide immunity against related genetic parasites [Villarreal, 2009, 2011a, 2015]. In this way the result of unifying viruses and their defective parts (quasi-species consortia: qs-c) can explain the evolution, conservation and plasticity of genetic identities more coherently than the previous quasi-species concept [Villarreal and Witzany, 2015].

7. Consequences for Artificial Genome Editing

Natural genome editing means changing nucleotide sequences actively, not to be colonised but to colonise, i.e. a passive chemical process (copying by complementary base pairing) vs. active editing of code (changing the nucleotide order to colonise/ manipulate former sequences). The groups of various counter-balanced ribozymes assemble single competences into a complex competence. It is important to note that previously deleted or fragmented RNA remnants may be re-used and re-integrated into group-building later [Villarreal and Witzany, 2013a, 2015, Villarreal, 2015].

Most importantly, this ensemble-building is context-dependent in terms of the history of the ecosphere: temperature (cold, hot), light (yes, no), water (fluid, icy), ph gradients, density, dry land, and combinations and intermediates may determine which ribozymatic features dominate, which are less dominant, which compete, which preclude each other and which cooperate. In particular, the intermediate stages in most cases cannot be defined in a formalisable way, which was a resulting problem in the above mentioned philosophy of science discourse [Witzany, 2007].

Additionally, the RNA group assemblies represent key features of ecological conditions. To 'survive', rapid changeability and less stability are necessary, because only permanent innovation of sequences guarantees the emergence of better colonisers or, in a cooperative way, the integration of parts of genetic parasites as useful weapons to defeat similar parasites through effective immune functions as represented by the various adaptive immune systems [Villarreal, 2011b; Moelling and Broecker, 2015]. In the light of natural genome editing error replication events (chance mutations) would not optimise but reduce the emergence of beneficial innovations. The other extreme, mutational overload ("error catastrophe") in natural genome editing, means: Too many innovations and sign-sequence generations cannot be shared in a community ecology of the RNA-based genome inhabitants because integration into the group competence within a real life world is too much new information tools. We know that from our experience: New words and terms may be usefull to understand new experiences or observations. The use of too many new terms confuses our competence to build society-based conventions regarding how to use such terms.

Now we have to see whether there are agents that are competent naturally to edit genetic code as sequence syntax and additionally mark the whole complex genome epigenetically. This must be coherent with molecular features, atomic structure, information processing and code editing rules, i.e. syntax, semantics and, most importantly, pragmatics, because the context determines semantics/meaning. So, what are these agents?

8. At the Core of Natural Genetic Novelty: Interacting RNA Consortia

Similarly interesting is this new perspective on the genome because it combines the atomic level and molecular level via nucleic acid sequences into a variety of unique and novel sequence combinations that are not object to algorithm-based procedures. The emergence of new genetic information is not the result of processes being subject to formalisable/mathematical equations, but the inherent feature of single-stranded RNA sequences which fold back and form stem-loop structures in a rather dynamic way, serving as a passive template or catalytically active agent, switching in between in unpredictable ways [Kumar and Joyce, 2003; Smit *et al.*, 2006; Gwiazda *et al.*, 2012; Müller *et al.*, 2012; Müller, 2015]. This is an important strategy for unlimited progression of the interplay between infectious agents, host organisms that conserve this by integrating genetic information of the identity of the infectious agents to ward off related infectious agents, and the generation of new genetic information which again may "overrule" such immune functions [Villarreal, 2009; Villarreal, 2011a,b].

The result is a completely new level of information content that is absent in inanimate nature. In contrast to agglomeration in pure chemical nature we have a finite number of characters of the nucleotide alphabet within an infinite combinatorial space of nucleic acid sequences. On the single-stranded RNA level we can see the formation of loops that fold back to the single strand, to build a double stranded (base-paired) RNA with a single-stranded loop.

In this context the RNA loop can generate an identity which other based/non-base-paired assemblies do not share. Additionally, the RNA stem loop has a part, the non-pairing loop, with a rather "sticky" section and can interact with other RNAs of the same or other RNA groups with similar non-base pairing loops or even single-stranded remants of former RNA agents [Witzany, 2014c]. They can be found by testing other sequences, identifying them as appropriate binding sequences or rejecting them because sequence structure does not fit. This interaction motif can be termed RNA sensing or RNA monitoring action. Here we can find some sort of identification competence where the single RNA stem loop or a group or RNA stem loops represents a kind of biological 'self' which can identify other 'self' or 'non-self' RNA groups to cooperate or reject [Villarreal, 2009a,b, 2011a]. This is the reason why RNA groups may act in an active catalytic way or simply be a passive template for replication. Interestingly, thanks to this inherent double function they may change both functions in a rather non-predictive way. Whereas DNA forms a predictable double helix, RNA comprises single strands that fold up into loops, bulges, pseudo-knots, hammerheads, hairpins and other motifs. These structures flip and twist between different forms in a non-predictive manner.

With the identification of the essential agents of natural genetic engineering and natural genome editing, RNA consortia of various groups, and their inherent ability to build base-pairing parts and non-base pairing but sensing and monitoring loops we have identified the core agents of genetic novelty, i.e. of evolutionary processes. It is important to note that this is not error replication (mutation) but represents real evolutionary history-derived and stored competence to generate new sequence motifs.

Now, after identifying the agents that naturally edit genetic code and are the main source of genetic novelty let us have a look at the core process of genetic novelty. It is not just an error replication event (mutation) as suggested by former theoretical concepts which view this as a process of self-organisation of matter. If this is a process which depends on interactions of RNA groups then it is inherently interwoven with self/non-self interactions, i.e. group building, integration of appropriate beneficial agents into groups or preclusion, deletion of RNAs or RNA groups which do not fit into the pre-existing group [Vaidya *et al.*, 2012]. This means the process of genetic novelty is interwoven into a more complex process of essential group identity, preserving group identity and attack against group identity infection, destruction or damage [Osborn and Boltner, 2002; Huda *et al.*, 2010; Villarreal, 2012]. On the other hand, we then have to look at the various motifs and techniques that are available in RNA groups to prevent infection events such as the generation of a diversity of immunity tools or weapons to attack and destroy invading omnipresent genetic parasites (such as endonucleases) [Villarreal, 2012; Moelling, 2013]. Additionally there must be tools to integrate beneficial group members to build more complex groups. This is the most powerful ligase tool.

More generally, the crucial difference between biological identities and non-biological identities is that the first are based on a biological code by agents that share code-using rules, whereas the latter miss both, i.e. no biological codes or competent code-using agent groups are present.

First, we should look at the more basic process that is loop building within RNA consortia. This happens when within a stem or a loop the base-pairing nucleotides are broken up into a section of non-base-pairing (single-stranded regions of) nucleotides. The results are various. They may reach from plus strand variation to negative strand variation, both influencing all RNA consortia/ group interactions and e.g., in the editosome or in the spliceosome a complete loss of function of the former entire agents [Villarreal and Witzany, 2013a,b; Witzany, 2011]. The ongoing generation of such loops is the natural core competence for producing novelty, for which no immune function exists and which serves as an evolutionary tool to invade or, as a persistent integrated feature in a host, preclude infectious agents.

The various consequences in a group of RNA agents such as the ribosomal subunits, the editosome, the spliceosome and others with multiple RNA stem loops that build a cooperative agent are therefore algorithmically unpredictable, because of the unlimited possibilities of combinations of certain group identities which may result from a single broken stem which then builds a loop. If we look for example at the ribosomal subunits the folding (pragmatics) of the sub-groups determines their functionality, not their sequence syntax [Bokov and Steinberg, 2009; Harish and Caetano-Anolles, 2012; Petrov *et al.*, 2013].

9. Comeback of the Century? Viruses and Virus-Like RNA Agents Interact as Cooperative Groups

Current research results additionally indicate that viruses are the most abundant biological agents on this planet (10 times more abundant than cellular genomes), and only viruses assemble all known features of the genetic code, such as double-stranded or single-stranded RNA or DNA (+ and − stranded) [Forterre and Prangishvili, 2009; Geuking *et al.*, 2009; Rossinck, 2011, 2012; Jalasvuori, 2012; Koonin and Dolja, 2014; Koonin *et al.*, 2015]. In prokaryotes phages are nearly omnipresent and massively determine their host gene word order. Also, the eukaryotic nucleus resembles a variety of large dsDNA virus features. In every mitochondria, endoplasmic reticulum or even plasmids we can find persistent viral parts. The endogenous retroviruses (active and/or defective) play crucial roles in the evolution of higher animals [Canchaya *et al.*, 2004; Briones *et al.*, 2006; Carbonell *et al.*, 2012; Crespi and Nosil, 2013].

We can identify virally derived insertions that remain as defectives such as non-coding RNAs essential in gene regulation as intronic regions that are spliced out during exon assembly.

Some persistent viruses/virus-derived parts which are counter-regulated by opposing or former competing genetic parasites have been identified such as DNA viruses, DNA transposons, RNA viruses, non-retroviral RNA viruses, endo- genous retroviruses, LTRs retrotransposons, non-LTRs (SINEs, LINEs, ALUs), group II introns, group I introns. All of these active parts play essential roles in natural nucleotide recombination techniques such as those used in DNA/RNA structuring and restructuring, amplifying or silencing functions, sub-steps of transcription (post-transcriptional RNA editing, RNA splicing, ribosome assembly), translation, DNA replication, chromatin organisation, epigenetic markings and modifications, DNA repair [Xiong and Eickbush, 1988; Baranowski *et al.*, 2001; Sun *et al.*, 2006; Weiner, 2006; Feschotte, 2008; Perot *et al.*, 2012; Cowley and Oakey, 2013; Swart and Nowacki, 2015, Zimmerly and Semper, 2015]. Perhaps the best examples of persistent life style of viruses are represented by the organisation of the various forms of adaptive and innate immunity systems such as CRISPRs/Cas or the amaizingly complex VDJ immune system [Villarreal, 2009 a,b, 2011b].

All these examples show that the genome is not merely a molecular structure with a storage function but rather an ecosphere habitat with an abundance of RNA-derived settlers that compete for a rather limited resource [Witzany, 2012]. Most interestingly, to get access to this limited resource some cooperative behavioural patterns have been selected whereby formerly competing agents find a way to cooperate, to counter-regulate within the host genome. This new identity co-oparation of former competing genetic parasites also may lead to new identities of host tissues, organs or organisms, really evolutionary novelty. It is possible to imagine how different tissues evolved in quite different species;

this is a coherent event because of an abundance of persistent (non-lytic) viruses which share a tissue specificity not a species specificity [Villarreal, 2005]. In single infection events up to 100 new genes can transfer to a new host. This is not a small step as in error replication events (chance mutations) but an evolutionary non-random drive with far-reaching consequences as documented by e.g. the retroviral infections that lead to the transfer of syncytin genes, which resulted into the evolutionary novelty of placental mammals [Villarreal, 2005; Perot *et al.*, 2012].

Unexpectedly, the controversial theoretical concepts of evolutionary novelty being essential for diversity and its selection processes are no longer the undirected or directed mutation narrative, nor teleological vitalism metaphysics (more recently 'intelligent design'), nor the molecular biological self-organisation of matter (Eigen-Schuster narrative), nor the increasing complexity of a self-emerging property of systems (Kauffman narrative), but natural genetic content organisation by competent microbial/viral agents that cooperate for their survival goals which may coincide with those of their hosts as documented in the variety of endosymbiotic evolutionary processes [Witzany, 2006].

10. Conclusions

The old success story of genetic engineering and the more recent dawn of genome editing faces some technical problems. On the other hand, the current debate on the ethical justification of these techniques of genome manipulation is still open. Of similar importance are the dramatic changes in theoretical pre-assumptions together with recent empirical knowledge about the capabilities of RNA consortia, persistent viruses and other infectious genetic parasites. The old narrative of molecular entities that assemble according to physico-chemical properties of matter dictated by natural laws such as thermodynamics, quantum physics and chemical binding is increasingly enriched by the finding that groups of RNA stem loops generate an abundance of nucleic acid code-based consortial interactions. We find single RNA stem loops with fast-changing identities that build groups such as ribosomal subunits, editosome, spliceosome as active (catalytic) or passive (template-like) agents switching in a non-predictable way. With these behavioural motifs the emergence of biological identity (self/non-self identification competence) occurs. RNA groups are able to act as de novo producers of nucleic acid sequences, identify sequence-specific target sites, coherently integrate such sequences into pre-existing ones (without destruction of former content arrangements), recombine according to adaptational needs and mark sequence sites to vary meaning epigentically or identify sequences to be marked for excision or deletion. In all these processes the genetic identity of the genetic parasite and/or the host genome may vary, with far-reaching consequences in terms of the function, co-operation and coordination of various regulatory networks. Natural genome editing is therefore far from being a random-like process as a result of error replication (mutations). Artificial genome editing will have to integrate the agent-based perspective into its theoretical assumptions as well as the contextual real lifeworlds of these agents to achieve a more realistic and integrative view on the empirical data currently available. The perspective on natural genetic information processing is changing dramatically.

References

Baltimore, D. *et al.* (2015). A prudent path forward for genomic engineering and germline gene modification. *Science* 348, pp. 36-38.

Baranowski, E., Ruiz-Jarabo, C.M and Domingo, E. (2001). Evolution of cell recognition by viruses. *Science* 292, pp. 1102-1105.

Barlow, D.P. (2011). Genomic imprinting: a mammalian epigenetic discovery model. *Annu. Rev. Genet.* 45, pp. 379-403.

Berg, P., Baltimore, D., Brenner, S., Roblin, R.O. and Singer, M.F. (1975). Summary statement of the Asilomar conference on recombinant DNA molecules. *PNAS* 72, pp. 1981-1984.

Bokov, K. and Steinberg, S.V. (2009). A hierarchical model for evolution of 23S ribosomal RNA. *Nature* 457, pp. 977-980.

Bredy, T.W., Lin, Q., Wie, W., Baker Andresen. D. and Mattick, J. (2011). Micro RNA regulation of neural plasticity and memory. *Neurobiol. Learn. Mem.* 96, pp. 89-94.

Brenner, S. (2012). Life's code script. *Nature* 482, p. 461.

Briones, C., de Vicente, A., Molina-París, C. and Domingo, E. (2006). Minority memory genomes can influence the evolution of HIV-1 quasispecies in vivo. *Gene* 384, pp. 129-138.

Brookfield, J.F.Y. (2005). The ecology of the genome. Mobile DNA elements and their hosts. *Nat. Rev. Genet.* 6, pp. 128-136.

Canchay, C., Fournous, G. and Brussow, H. (2004). The impact of prophages on bacterial chromosomes. *Mol. Microbiol.* 53, pp. 9–18.

Carbonell, A., Flores, R. and Gago, S. (2012). *Hammerhead Ribozymes Against Virus and Viroid RNAs*. Eds. Erdmann, V.A. and Barciszewski, J., "From nucleic acids sequences to molecular medicine", Springer, Berlin, Heidelberg, pp. 411–427.

Cech, T.R. and Steitz, J.A. (2014). The noncoding RNA revolution — trashing old rules to forge new ones. *Cell* 157, pp. 77–94.

Cowley, M. and Oakey, R.J. (2013). Transposable elements re-wire and fine-tune the transcriptome. *PLoS Genet.* 9, e1003234.

Crespi, B. and Nosil, P. (2013). Conflictual speciation: species formation via genomic conflict. *Trends Ecol. Evol.* 28, pp. 48–57.

Crick, F. (1970). Central dogma of molecular biology. *Nature* 227, pp. 561-563.

Curcio, M.J. and Derbyshire, K.M. (2003). The outs and ins of transposition: from mu to kangaroo. *Nat. Rev. Mol. Cell Biol.* 4, pp. 856-877.

Cuzin, F. and Rassoulzadegan, M. (2010). Non-Mendelian epigenetic heredity: gametic RNAs as epigenetic regulators and transgenerational signals. *Essays Biochem.* 48, pp. 101-106.

de Souza, N. (2012). Primer: genome editing with engineered nucleases. *Nat. Meth.* 9, p. 27.

Eigen, M. (1971). Selforganization of matter and the evolution of biological macromolecules. *Naturwissenschaften* 58, pp. 465-523.

Eigen, M. (2013). *From Strange Simplicity to Complex Familiarity: A Treatise on Matter, Information, Life and Thought*. Oxford University Press, Oxford, UK.

Eigen, M. and Biebricher, C. K. (1988). *Sequence Space and Quasipecies Distribution*. eds. Domingo, E., Ahlquist, P. and and Holland, J.J. "RNA genetics", vol. 3. CRC Press, Boca Raton, USA, pp. 211-245.

Feschotte, C. (2008). Transposable elements and the evolution of regulatory networks. *Nat. Rev. Genet.* 9, pp. 397-405.

Forterre, P. and Prangishvili, D. (2009). The great billion-year war between ribosome- and capsid-encoding organisms (cells and viruses) as the major source of evolutionary novelties. *Ann. N.Y. Acad. Sci.* 1178, pp. 65-77.

Geuking, M.B. *et al.* (2009). Recombination of retrotransposon and exogenous RNA virus rersults in nonretroviral cDNA integration. *Science* 323, pp. 393-396.

Gödel, K. (1931). Über formal unentscheidbare Sätze der Principia Mathematica und verwandter Systeme. *Monatsh. Math. Phys.* 38, pp. 173-198.

Gwiazda, S., Salomon, K., Appel, B. and Mueller, S. (2012). RNA self-ligation: from oligonucleotides to full length ribozymes. *Biochimie* 94, pp. 1457-1463.

Haldane, J.B.S. (1929). The origin of life. *Rationalist Ann.* 148, pp. 3-10.

Harish, A. and Caetano-Anolles, G. (2012). Ribosomal history reveals origins of modern protein synthesis. *PLoS One* 7, e32776.

Hilbert, D. and Bernays, P. (1934/1939). *Grundlagen der Mathematik*. Vol.1/2. Springer, Berlin/New York.

Hsu, P.D. *et al.* (2013). DNA targeting specificity of RNA-guided Cas9 nucleases. *Nat. Biotech.* 31, pp. 827-832.

Huda, A., Mariño-Ramírez, L. and Jordan, I.K. (2010). Epigenetic histone modifications of human transposable elements: genome defense versus exaptation. *Mob. DNA* 25, p. 2.

Iranzo, J. *et al.* (2013). Evolutionary dynamics of the prokaryotic adaptive immunity system CRISPR-Cas in an explicit ecological context. *J. Bacteriol.* 195, pp. 3834-3844.

Jalasvuori, M. (2012). *Revolutionary Struggle for Existence: Introduction to Four Intriguing Puzzles in Virus Research*, ed. Witzany, G. Viruses: Essential Agents of Life", Springer, Dordrecht, NL, pp. 1-19.

Jasin, M. (1996). Genetic manipulation of genomes with rare-cutting endonucleases. *Trends Genet.* 12, pp. 224-228.

Jirtle, R.L. (2009). Epigenome: the program for human health and disease. *Epigenomics* 1, pp. 13-16.

Koonin, E.V. (2009). On the origin of cells and viruses: primordial virus world scenario. *Ann. N.Y. Acad. Sci.* 1178, pp. 47-64.

Koonin, E.V., Senkevich, T.G. and Dolja, V.V. (2006). The ancient Virus World and evolution of cells. *Biol. Direct.* 1, p. 29.

Koonin, E,V, and Dolja, V.V. (2014). Virus world as an evolutionary network of viruses and capsidless selfish elements. *Microbiol. Mol. Biol. Rev.* 78, pp. 278-303.

Koonin, E., Dolja, V.V. and Krupovic, M. (2015). Origins and evolution of viruses of eukaryotes: The ultimate modularity. *Virology* 479/480, pp. 2-25.

Kumar, R.M. and Joyce, G.F. (2003). A modular, bifunctional RNA that integrates itself into a target RNA. *PNAS* 100, pp. 9738-9743.

Le Rouzic, A., Dupas, S. and Capy, P. (2007). Genome ecosystem and transposable elements species. *Gene* 390, pp. 214-220.

Lin, S., Staahl, B.T., All, R.K. and Doudna, J.A. (2014.) Enhanced homology-directed human genome engineering by controlled timing of CRISPR/Cas9 delivery. *eLife* 3, e04766.

Lyons, A.J. and Robertson, H.D. (2003). Detection of tRNA-like structure through RNase P cleavage of viral internal ribosome entry site RNAs near the AUG start triplet. *J. Biol. Chem.* 278, pp. 26844-26850.

Marraffini, L.A. and Sontheimer, E.J. (2010). Self versus non-self discrimination during CRIPR RNA-directed immunity. *Nature* 463, pp. 568-571.

Mattick, J.S. (2009). The genetic signatures of non-coding RNAs. *PLoS Genet.* 5, e1000459.

Mattick, J.S. (2010). RNA as a substrate for epigenome-environment interactions: RNA guidance of epigenetic processes and the expansion of RNA editing in animals underpins development, phenotypic plasticity, learning and cognition. *Bioessays* 32, pp. 548-552.

Mattick, J.S. and Gagen, M.J. (2001). The evolution of controlled multitasked gene networks: the role of introns and other noncoding RNAs in the development of complex organisms. *Mol. Biol. Evol.* 18, pp. 1611-1630.

Mattick, J.S. and Makunin, I.V. (2006). Non-coding RNA. *Hum. Mol. Genet.* 1, pp. 17-29.

Mattick, J.S., Taft, R.J. and Faulkner, G.J. (2010). A global view of genomic information-moving beyond the gene and the master regulator. *Trends Genet.* 26, pp. 21-28.

Mauricio, R. (2005). Can ecology help genomics: The genome as ecosystem. *Genetica* 123, pp. 205-209.

Mercer, T.R. and Mattick, J.S. (2013). Structure and function of long non- coding RNAs in epigenetic regulation. *Nat. Struct. Mol. Biol.* 20, pp. 300-307.

Moelling, K. (2013). What contemporary viruses tell us about evolution: a personal view. *Arch. Virol.* 158, pp 1833-1848.

Moelling, K. and Broecker, F. (2015). The reverse transcriptase-RNase H: from viruses to antiviral defense. *Ann. N.Y. Acad. Sci.* 1341, pp. 126-135.

Mruk, I. and Kobayashi, I. (2014). To be or not to be: regulation of restriction-modification systems and other toxin–antitoxin systems. *Nucleic Acids Res.* 42, pp. 70-86.

Mueller, S. (2015). Engineering of ribozymes with useful activities in the ancient RNA world. *Ann. N.Y. Acad. Sci.* 1341, pp. 54-60.

Mueller, S., Appel, B., Krellenberg, T., Petkovic, S. (2012). The many faces of the hairpin ribozyme: Structural and functional variants of a small catalytic RNA. *IUBMB. Life* 64, pp. 36-47.

O'Connell, M.A., Oakes, B.J., Sternberg, S.H., East-Seletsky, A., Kaplan, M. and Doudna, J.A. (2014). Programmable RNA recognition and cleavage by CRISPR/Cas9. *Nature* 516, pp. 263-266.

Osborn, A.M. and Boltner, D. (2002). When phage, plasmids, and transposons collide: genomic islands, and conjugative — and mobilizable — transposons as a mosaic continuum. *Plasmid* 8, pp. 2002-2012.

Perot, P., Bolze, P.A. and Mallet, F. (2012). *From viruses to genes: syncytins*, ed. Witzany, G. "Viruses: Essential Agents of Life", Springer, Dordrecht, NL, pp. 325-361.

Petrov, A.S., Bernier, C.R., Hershkovits, E., Xue, Y., Waterbury, C.C. *et al.* (2013). Secondary structure and domain architecture of the 23S and 5S rRNAs. *Nucleic Acids Res.* 41, pp. 7522-7535.

Roossinck, M.J. (2011). The good viruses: viral mutualistic symbioses. *Nat. Rev. Microbiol.* 9, pp. 99-108.

Roossinck, M.J. (2012). *Persistent Plant Viruses: Molecular Hitchhikers or Epigenetic Elements?* ed. Witzany, G. "Viruses: Essential Agents of Life", Springer, Dordrecht, NL, pp. 177-186.

Ryan, F. (2009). *Virolution*. Harper Collins, London, UK.

Schrödinger, E. (1944). *What is Life? The Physical Aspect of the Living Cell*. Cambridge University Press, London, UK.

Shapiro, J.A. (2009). Revisting the central dogma in the 21st century. *Ann. N.Y. Acad. Sci.* 1178, pp. 6-28.

Shapiro, J.A. (2011). *Evolution: A View from the 21st Century*. FT Press, Washington DC, USA.

Shapiro, J.A. (2014). Epigenetic control of mobile DNA as an interface between experience and genome change. *Frontiers Genet.* 5, pp. 1-16.

Slotkin, R.K. and Martienssen, R. (2007). Transposable elements and the epigenetic regulation of the genome. *Nat. Rev. Genet.* 8, pp. 272-285.

Smit, S., Yarus, M. and Knight, R. (2006). Natural selection is not required to explain universal compositional patterns in rRNA secondary structure categories. *RNA* 12, pp. 1-14.

Spadafora, C. (2015). A line-1-encoded reverse transcriptase-dependent regulatory mechanism is active in embryogenesis and tumorigenesis. *Ann. N.Y. Acad. Sci.* 1341, pp. 164-171.

Swart, E.C. and Nowacki, M. (2015). The eukaryotic way to defend and edit genomes by sRNA-targeted DNA deletion. *Ann. N.Y. Acad. Sci.* 1341, pp. 106-114.

Sugarman, J. (2015). Ethics and germline gene editing. *EMBO Rep.* 16, pp. 879-880.

Sun, F.J., Fleurdepine, S., Bousquet-Antonelli, C., Caetano-Anolles, G. and Deragon, J.M. (2006). Common evolutionary trends for SINE RNA structures. *Trends Genet.* 23, pp. 26-33.

Tang, W.W. *et al.* (2015). A unique gene regulatory network resets the human germline epigenome for development. *Cell* 161, pp. 1453-1467.

Tognini, P. *et al.* (2015). Experience-dependent DNA methylation regulates plasticity in the developing visual cortex. *Nat. Neurosci.* 18, pp. 956-958.

Vaidya, N., Manapat, M.L., Chen, I.A., Xulvi-Brunet, R., Hayden, E.J. and Lehman, N. (2012). Spontaneous network formation among cooperative RNA replicators. *Nature* 49, pp. 72-77.

Vennera, S., Feschotte, C. and Biemonta, C. (2009). Transposable elements dynamics: toward a community ecology of the genome. *Trends Genet.* 25, pp. 317-323.

Villarreal, L.P. (2005). *Viruses and the Evolution of Life.* ASM Press, Washington, USA.

Villarreal, L.P. (2009a). *Origin of Group Identity: Viruses, Addiction and Cooperation.* Springer, New York.

Villarreal, L.P. (2009b). The source of self: genetic parasites and the origin of adaptive immunity. *Ann. N.Y. Acad. Sci.* 1178, pp. 194-232.

Villarreal, L.P. (2011a). *Viruses and Host Evolution: Virus-Mediated Self-Identity.* ed. Lopez-Larrea, C. "Self and Non-Self", Landes Bioscience and Springer Science-Business Media, Austin, USA, pp. 185-217.

Villarreal, L.P. (2011b). Viral ancestors of antiviral systems. *Viruses* 3, pp. 1933–1958.

Villarreal, L.P. (2012). *The Addiction Module as a Social Force.* ed. Witzany, G. "Viruses: Essential Agents of Life", Springer, Dordrecht, NL, pp. 107-145.

Villarreal, L.P. (2015). Force for ancient and recent life: viral and stem-loop RNA consortia promote life. *Ann. N.Y. Acad. Sci.* 1341, pp. 25-34.

Villarreal, L.P. and Witzany, G. (2010). Viruses are essential agents within the roots and stem of the tree of life. *J. Theor. Biol.* 262, pp. 698-710.

Villarrreal, L.P. and Witzany, G. (2013a). The DNA habitat and its RNA inhabitants. At the dawn of RNA sociology. *Genom. Ins.* 6, pp. 1-12.

Villarreal, L.P. and Witzany, G. (2013b). Rethinking quasispecies theory: From fittest type to cooperative consortia. *World J. Biol. Chem.* 4, pp. 79-90.

Villarreal, L.P. and Witzany, G. (2015). When competing viruses unify: evolution, conservation, and plasticity of genetic identities. *J. Mol. Evol.* 80, pp. 305-318.

Weiner, A.M. (2006). *SINEs and LINEs: Troublemakers, Saboteurs, Benefactors, Ancestors*. Eds. Gesteland, R.F., Cech, T.R. and Atkins, J.F. "The RNA World", 3rd edn. Cold Spring Harbor Laboratory Press, New York, USA, pp. 507-534.

Werner, A., Piatek, M.J. and Mattick, J.S. (2015). Transpositional shuffling and quality control in male germ cells to enhance evolution of complex organisms. *Ann. N.Y. Acad. Sci.* 1341, pp. 156-163.

Whitehead, A.N. and Russell, B. (1910,1912,1913). *Principia Mathematica*, 3 vols., Cambridge University Press, Cambridge, UK.

Wittgenstein, L. (1953). *Philosophical Investigations*. Basil Blackwell, Oxford, UK.

Witzany, G. (2006). Serial Endosymbiotic Theory (set): the biosemiotic update. *Acta Biotheor.* 54, pp. 103-117.

Witzany, G. (2007). *From Biosphere to Semiosphere to Social Lifeworlds. Biology as an Understanding Social Science*. Ed. Barbieri, M. "Biosemiotic research trends", Nova Science Publishers, New York, USA, pp. 185–213.

Witzany, G. (2009). Noncoding RNAs: Persistent viral agents as modular tools for cellular needs. *Ann. N.Y. Acad. Sci.* 1178, pp. 244-267.

Witzany, G. (2010). *Biocommunication and Natural Genome Editing*. Springer, Dordrecht, NL.

Witzany, G. (2011). The agents of natural genome editing. *J. Mol. Cell Biol.* 3, pp. 181–189.

Witzany, G. (2012). *From Molecular Entities to Competent Agents: Viral Infection-derived Consortia act as Natural Genetic Engineers*, Ed. Witzany, G. "Viruses: Essential agents of life", Springer, Dordrecht, NL, pp 407-419.

Witzany, G. (2014a). *Language and Communication as Universal Requirements for Life*. Ed. Kolb, V. "Astrobiology. An evolutionary approach", CRC Press, Boca Raton, USA, pp. 407-419.

Witzany, G. (2014b). Pragmatic turn in biology: from biological molecules to genetic content operators. *World J. Biol. Chem.* 5, pp. 279-285.

Witzany, G. (2014c). RNA sociology: Group behavioral motifs of RNA consortia. *Life* 4, pp. 800-818.

Witzany, G. (ed.) (2015a). *The DNA Habitats and Their RNA Inhabitants*. John Wiley & Sons, Hanover, USA.

Witzany, G. (2015b). Life is physics and chemistry and communication. *Ann. N.Y. Acad. Sci.* 1341, pp. 1-9.

Witzany, G. and Baluska, F. (2012). Life's code script does not code itself. The machine metaphor for living organisms is outdated. *EMBO Rep.* 13, pp. 1054-1056.

Wolstenholme, G. (ed.) (1963). *Man and his future. A Ciba Foundation Volume*. J. & A. Churchill Ltd. London, UK.

Xiong, Y. and Eickbush, T.H. (1988). Similarity of reverse transcriptase-like sequences of viruses, transposable elements and mitochondrial introns. *Mol. Biol. Evol.* 5, pp. 675-690.

Zimmerly, S. and Semper, C. (2015). Evolution of group II introns. *Mob. DNA* 6, p. 7.